TOM BRUCE

# The Anatomy of Bereavement

# THE ANATOMY OF BEREAVEMENT

Beverley Raphael

Basic Books, Inc., Publishers      New York

Library of Congress Cataloging in Publication Data

Raphael, Beverley.
  The anatomy of bereavement.

  Bibliography: p. 407
  Includes index.
  1. Bereavement—psychological aspects.   I. Title.
BF575.G7R36   1982          155.9′37          83-70760
ISBN 0-465-00289-7 (cloth)
ISBN 0-465-00290-0 (paper)

To Cassie

and goes inside,
or leaves upon a bus,
speaks to you for the last time:
most times you do not know
the lastness of a word upon the air.

Q. B. Willowby, "Last Warmth"

# CONTENTS

Preface                                                                          xi

1. Human Bonds and Death:
   The Background to Bereavement                                                   3

2. The Experience of Bereavement:
   Separation and Mourning                                                        33

3. The Bereaved Child                                                             74

4. The Adolescent's Grief and Mourning                                          139

5. Loss in Adult Life: The Death of a Spouse                                    177

6. Loss in Adult Life: The Death of a Child                                     229

7. The Griefs of Growing Old                                                    283

8. Death and Disaster                                                           320

9. Caring for the Bereaved                                                      352

10. Living with Loss:
    Passion, Compassion, and Defense                                            402

References                                                                       407

Index                                                                            423

# PREFACE

This book has grown out of my work and research with bereaved people over many years. The form and content have developed from my reading and understanding of the work of many of the innovative and valuable contributors to this field. Bereavement is an ubiquitous human experience—painful and inevitable. In this book I try to share the experience of many different bereavements, how they are dealt with, understood, and eventually adapted to in the ongoing framework of human life. The work has derived from the workers who have written in this field, but especially from the people who have experienced and shared their losses and their deaths.

There are many people who have helped me in many ways with the writing of this book. It gives me great pleasure to be able to thank them for their support and assistance over many years.

Firstly, I would like to thank all those bereaved people who have shared their feelings and thoughts and experiences with me over the years. They have greatly influenced my understanding of grief and its processes. They will not recognize themselves directly in the histories in this book for these are a complex amalgam of many, many different losses. But I do hope they will feel represented by what I have written. I especially wish them to know of my warm gratitude.

I would like to thank my professional colleagues who have shared their experience and understanding of bereavement and who have offered constructive criticisms, thoughts, and questions that have all helped shape what appears here. In particular, I am deeply indebted to Dr. John Bowlby who has offered me great support and encouragement of my work, a support offered from outside my own country, which has meant a great deal to me. I am also indebted to the late Professor David Maddison who first persuaded me to become interested in the field of bereavement, whose studies were the beginnings from which my own work grew, and who was a generous mentor and friend until the time of his death.

My close friends and professional colleagues at the Faculty of Medicine, University of Newcastle, New South Wales, Australia, have given me their generous support and encouragement over recent years. In particular I wish to thank Dr. Bruce Singh and Dr. Robert Adler, who helped free my time for the writing of this book as well as provided the intellectual challenges that helped shape it. I would also like to thank especially my friend and secretary, Mrs. Wendy Smith, whose unstinting loyalty and patience resulted in the technical production of the manuscript; and my professional officer, Mrs. Penny Johnston, whose untiring support and organization brought forth references, criticism, bibliographies, proofreading, and the essentials without which the book could never have been completed. My other professional colleagues at the Faculty of Medicine, particularly the professorial staff, were most kind in their support and understanding of my commitment to this volume, and I would like to extend to each one of them also my heartfelt thanks.

Over the years, many workers in the field of bereavement—social workers, psychologists, nurses, doctors, psychiatrists, clergy, and volunteer workers, to name a few—have discussed with me their work and cases, and this too has contributed to my understanding. I would wish to thank each and every one of them, especially my friends and colleagues in the National Association for Loss and Grief (NALAG). A number of colleagues have generously made available to me their unpublished work in the field of bereavement and I am especially indebted to them, particularly Des Tobin, Rosemary Montgomery, and Christine Gapes. Similarly my book has been influenced by those many researchers in this field whose work I have studied and frequently quoted. While these are too numerous to name individually, I would like especially to acknowledge my indebtedness to the work of Colin Murray Parkes, Erna Furman, Elisabeth Kübler-Ross, as well as, of course, the work of Freud, Klein, and many others.

The research of my own studies has been supported by the National Health and Medical Research Council of Australia to which I am most deeply indebted. I also wish to thank the New South Wales Institute of Psychiatry which provided me with a three-year research fellowship during which my original studies of preventive intervention with bereaved widows were carried out. My thanks are also extended to those who have assisted with this research over the years, especially Christine O'Loughlin, Joystna Field, Helen Kvelde, and Joanna Barnes.

I would like to thank my publishers, Basic Books, Inc., and in particular Jane Isay, whose patience and encouragement were instrumental in the writing of this book.

And from the bottom of my heart I would like to thank my family who, with their love and support over many years, have given me the strength to bear the bereavement pain others have shared with me. They have also borne with and encouraged the writing of this book.

Woodville, New South Wales, Australia
November 22, 1982

# The Anatomy of Bereavement

# CHAPTER 1. Human Bonds and Death: The Background to Bereavement

---

"When I met Pete it was as if the whole world changed—as if everything would never be the same again. It was as if I'd been waiting for him . . . waiting for him all of my life."

*Annie, age 22*

"Our baby, our baby, that little growing part of Pete and me . . . our baby is coming. . . . He'd put his ear against my womb and smile secretly. 'I'm sure it's Melissa,' he would say."

*Annie, age 24*

"My days are filled with our life as a family—our children, our friends. . . . Our family is now."

*Annie, age 28*

In human society the loss of one who is dearly loved brings great emotional pain and grief. Some suggest that this pain has significance for the species—that it serves the function of binding the social group, the group essential for survival.

The bonds of human societies take many different forms. There are the intimate, intense, interwoven bonds of the nuclear family. There are the attenuated, yet still powerful bonds of the extended family; bonds of blood, relatedness, shared background, shared experience. There are also the bonds of great friendships—valued, enduring, built upon mutualities of personality and not of blood. There are the complex social bonds of neighborhood and workplace, of acquaintance and community, that go to make the social milieu in which the individual lives. From birth to death, this fabric of family and social relationships will provide the interpersonal context that is the essence of human existence.

Death is also an inevitable part of human experience. The awareness of death grows slowly through childhood, tingeing its latter years with fears and denial, games of magic and ghosts. The specter of personal death is the antithesis of the thrust and joy of adolescence: death seems impossible when all is growth and love; yet in the darkness of death lies mystery and romance as well. Man sets the thought of his own death aside in the years of his young adult life. He makes his family and embarks upon his achievements. Yet death will not be denied: in his middle years he glimpses it again, reminding him that his time is not infinite. In the latter half of his life, its reminders become more constant, more persistent. And, at last he meets it, fearfully or as a friend, his own, his personal death.

Death has other powers as well. It may come when it is neither expected nor wanted. Its time is its own. It is always unknown and unknowable, mystery and uncertainty. It may be peaceful or violent, anticipated or sudden, and it may be accompanied by stigma, shame, pain, or pride. And it has the awesome power to rob one of those one loves—to bring the greatest of human pain, grief. To understand bereavement it is necessary to have a conceptual framework in which to view two key elements: the human relationships that may be lost; the human deaths that may bring these losses.

## Human Bonds

Human bonds take many different forms. There are many ways of conceptualizing them and many different ways to view the key components of such bonds. The most intimate and intense relationships are those that are associated with the greatest grief when they are lost, though less intense relationships may also be a source of grief. Relationships are characterized by many different feeling stages, many different interactional patterns, and many needs that they meet.

Weiss (1974*b*) outlines a series of "provisions" or needs that are normally met in relationships. These include *attachment,* providing a sense of security and place; *social integration and friendship,* providing for shared concerns; *nurturing,* providing a sense of being needed; *reassurance of worth,* attesting to a person's competence; *a sense of reliable alliance,* providing dependable assistance; and *guidance,* so important in stressful situations.

Hinde (1979) attempts to provide a framework that summarizes the scientific understanding of human relationships and their dynamics, providing dimensions wherein they are described. His work has been extremely important in delineating some of the components of relationships in operational terms. Thus, he suggests that to describe a relationship, the content, qualities, and patterning of its component interactions must first be understood. Relationships have both affective and cognitive aspects. They exist over time. The experiences of relationships are stored as symbols that can be manipulated. It is probably his own perception of the relationship that seems most important to the individual, even though it may not always reflect its true characteristics.

Interactions may occur on many levels. They may be verbal or nonverbal. There may be overt communications with metacommunications that are different. Interactions may be intense in their frequency, affect, and duration; or they may be diffuse. Such interactions may also be frustrating or rewarding, depriving or gratifying. Hinde notes two key categories of reciprocity and complementarity. Relationships that are reciprocal have symmetrical, similar patterns of interaction which may occur simultaneously or alternately. Reciprocity tends to characterize relationships between peers, equals, and colleagues. Some marital intimacy may also involve such interactions. Complementarity in relationships involves different but complementary interactions, such as the mother-infant behaviors of that dyad. Some marital relationships may be predominantly complementary in terms of roles where role definition is very clear—for example, the provider and the provided for. This may set the total pattern of the relationship, or it may represent only one facet with other aspects being much more reciprocal. Relationships that are flexible may change their patterns in terms of situation and need. Power and dominance are also important in relationships, as are issues of permissiveness and control.

Relationships may be reinforced by similarity, or the complementarity of difference may be valued. Not only may those who are similar have more opportunities for relationships, but also social pressures and norms as well as attitudinal similarities may reinforce the shared world even further. For others, however, the stimulus of difference may be much more valued and arousing. It may also be that, as people spend more time in interaction, in relating they become more similar. Kreitman et al. (1970) found from their study of sixty married couples that wives of neurotic husbands grew more neurotic than did those in a control population. This fits well with psychodynamic concepts such as those of Dicks (1967) that conceptualize such dyads in terms of mutual interlocking psychopathology.

Out of these many factors some key elements emerge. Relationships

5

are made up of interactions that operate on many different levels. Relationships also occur over time. The past of the relationship experience and other related relationship experiences are stored as symbols, which may be conceptualized as the "inner image" that is held of the relationship at any one time. That image is composed of the present symbols and the many other symbols that can be called from past memory stores. Symbols will be experienced not as affectless memories, but rather in association with the inevitable human feeling and emotion that are attached to them. Such images will influence interactions as well as the individual's perceptions of the relationship and will in turn be influenced by them.

The most intimate of human relationships, those of attachment, require primary consideration. The seminal work of John Bowlby (1969) defines attachment in the human species, building from a variety of sources, including the ethological. He defines clearly the attachment behaviors of the infant to its mother and their vital role in the mother-infant bond. Close human relationships are often spoken of as attachments, and the person with whom an individual is involved in the most important of these relationships is said to be the primary attachment figure. Although there has been some argument against such a broad definition, perhaps it is useful when attempting to define close relationships and differentiate them from the wider group of social relationships. The value of this distinction is shown in a study of the dimensions of relationships conducted by Henderson, Byrne, and Duncan-Jones (1981). Henderson's group developed an instrument that attempts to quantify and qualify human relationships. They devise an interview schedule that clearly differentiates, at least in terms of the individual's perceptions of them, the differences between primary attachments and other social relationships and their relative importance.

MODELS OF PRIMARY BONDS

Because grief and bereavement are so much more clear-cut and intense with the loss of primary attachments, it is worth elaborating further a conceptual model of these attachments to help explain the effects of their loss.

Annie is fifteen. She has straight hair, dark eyes. Her life is full and joyful. Her mother is warm, friendly and rather disarrayed. Her father is strong, caring, but tends to be impatient. Her brothers and sister form part of the rich fabric of family life. Annie likes life. She dates a pleasant young man called Joe. She enjoys school. She is filled with excitement as she feels her womanhood within her—the woman she is to become, the dreams of the husband she will marry, the babies she will bear. Some of these fantasies she shares with her best friend, Mary. Others she nourishes privately, feeding them, watching them grow. Joe is nice: a good friend, a step to adult life, but not her man. She knows she is not ready yet for him. She has so many things to do, so much to be, such a lot of the great world she wishes to sample and explore.

Annie is twenty-two. Her hair is straight, her fine dark eyes, warm and full of life. She enjoys her work as a teacher.

"When I met Pete it was as if the whole world changed—as if everything would never be the same again. It was as if I'd been waiting for him—waiting for him all of my life. It was at a party. He caught my eye—half a smile, that was all. Then later that evening, he came and sat beside me. We started to talk. I felt this thrill, this excitement. I like him. I liked everything about him. I felt so good inside—warm, happy, excited. He was so attractive—strong, caring, good looking. I could feel he liked me, too—we just knew it was something special between us. I felt as though he was like someone I'd known before, but of course, I hadn't.

"We talked for hours. There were so many things we shared, so many thoughts and feelings, so many things we both liked. There were new, exciting things, too—his work, the world he knew.

"Those weeks were magic. We saw one another every moment we could. When we were apart, we missed one another dreadfully. He was in my thoughts all the time. I would see his face—think I heard him, dream I was with him. I was so much in love, I did not know if I could bear it. When he wasn't there, it was as though there was a pain inside me waiting for him, longing for him. And when he came, I felt right and whole. He was like another part of myself. He made me feel complete. When we made love, there were whole new worlds we found in each other. They were really happy times for us both.

"I suppose it could not last in such an intense way. Perhaps no relationship can. I was so disappointed—so hurt that day. How could he feel so differently to me; how could he value something like that? I was sad and cross. I hated him for a minute, for he'd broken my perfection, my ideal. Then he grinned his friendly old grin and it was all right again.

"There were more times like that, but really they weren't much. They were the differences between us, the other sides of the coin. Some things about him really frustrated me. There were things in me that disappointed him too. Sometimes we would have a dreadful row. How could I love this man, I would think. How could I? And for a moment, just a moment, I might hate him again. They were only moments. I suppose he changed a little for me, too, and I knew I changed a little for him. In a way, we grew closer. Perhaps most important of all, we were ourselves—and as time went on I knew, knew in my heart that he loved me and accepted me as I was, and that I, too, loved him in that way as well."

ADULT-TO-ADULT PAIR BONDS

To adult pair bonds, each partner brings an inner image of such relationships and how they should be—a constellation of cognitive symbols with memories and affects attached. It is composed of all the earlier experiences and perceptions that the individual has known. It may include internalizations of his parents' relationship at its various stages and in its positive and negative aspects. There may be internalizations of dyadic components from his own relationship with the opposite-sex parent, and also, but perhaps to a lesser degree, with the same-sex parent. There will be fantasies of dyads from the individual's society and culture. There will be all the earlier dyadic experiences as they have been internalized.

The influence of the quality of previous relationships is evidenced by an interesting study carried out by Uddenberg, Englesson, and Nettelbladt (1979). They found that women's relationships with their opposite-sex partners and their sons, but not their daughters, were related to their perceived relationships with their fathers. It semed that the father-daughter relationship influenced the daughter's way of relating to significant males. This fits closely with psychodynamic theories that would hypothesize the importance of family relationships and oedipal constellations in such adult object choice.

Not only may these factors influence the choice of partner, but similarities in attitude, behavior, and personality may also be important. A study by Hendrick and Brown (1971), using the Maudsley Personality Inventory, shows that in choosing a reliable friend, extroverts tended to choose extroverts while introverts preferred introverts. Similarities may operate through inherited predispositions, the opportunities that people have to meet, and the propinquity that similar involvements may bring. Differences may also attract, perhaps because, as the psychodynamic view might suggest, the individual looks for the absent or denied parts of himself to give him the sense of wholeness, oneness, that the adult pair-bond seems to offer.

Hinde (1979, p. 305) suggests that the stages in the development of a relationship may be progressively influenced by various factors: at first external factors such as the opportunity to meet and discover common interests may be important. Physical attributes may also be very important in the early stage and, what is considered attractive physically will vary with culture, subculture, individual, and historical time. As a relationship develops, complementarity of attitudes and needs becomes more important and may then determine the progress or consolidation of the relationship as it moves toward intimacy and commitment. Needs may change as the relationship progresses. Compatibility of values seems to become more important too as the relationship grows, although this may vary with the type of relationship.

The kind of framework in which a relationship commences and develops may depend on social and cultural factors. Thus, young adults may refer to their relationship as one of "being in love" if their culture or subculture idealizes such romantic love. Certainly the "falling in love," the passionate love of romantic novels, is not universal to all cultures. Some cultures may expect adult pair-bonding to be based on a prearranged pattern, or on good sense, or on exchanges such as those of services or property. The image each partner brings to the relationship will thus be strongly influenced by such social and cultural value systems. Then the inner image brought to an adult pair bond will be more of the role and its values for that culture than the personal characteristics of the potential partner.

Nevertheless, the falling-in-love pattern provides a useful model for considering the processes involved in the formation and consolidation of the adult pair bond. Like the mother's falling-in-love bonding with her infant, the adult pair bond is initially very intense but later settles into a more regular interactional pattern with mutual adjustments of expectations and needs. Like the mother-child relationship, it too goes through phases of development and adaptation.

When the adult (or adolescent) falls in love he brings to this dyadic encounter the complex inner amalgam of memories and feelings, conscious and unconscious, that forms the image of his "ideal" mate. This ideal may consciously represent personally or culturally valued attributes of man or woman, parent, lover, friend. At a deeper level it may represent desired psychodynamic constellations that fit and meld with the unconscious dynamic processes of the individual. In most instances these psychodynamic images are considerably weighted toward gratifying adult needs, even producing further maturation and growth in the individual should he find the partner to fit. There will always be some residues of the more infantile and neurotic parts of the self seeking some complementarity to these in the partner, but this is usually outweighed by the healthy components. For some, of course, it is not. The infantile neurotic parts of the self covertly and unconsciously demand a complementarity and matched pathology in the partner.

The person who is the "object" with whom the man or woman fall in love seems, initially at least, to fit in every way the "subject's" inner image. In the glowing and idealized beginnings of such a relationship there are intense positive feelings, an ebullient joy and passion, as each partner seems to find the fit between the other and his own wish fulfillment. Sexual attraction may initiate or reinforce such feelings. The interactions build. They are intense and gratifying and tend to operate on many interpersonal levels at one time. The inner image becomes enriched by these glowing and positive attributes. The primitive dyadic processes involved in this intense attachment phase are not dissimilar from those of that phase of the mother-infant relationship. There is an intense preoccupation with the face of the beloved. It is touched and cherished. Touch has a magnetic and gratifying quality. Long mutual gazing, filled with intense and personal exploration of each other, is common.

Like the mother-infant relationship this interactional pattern of the adult bond, too must be increasingly adapted to the real qualities and real interactions of the individuals in it. While initially each partner notices only the similarities between them and the degree to which the other person approaches the idealized image, as time progresses, they begin to recognize differences. These differences may be either accepted and incorporated into each partner's image or they may lead to frustration and negative affects. In the latter case, this produces a strand of ambivalence that will become part of the relationship. This ambivalence may trigger links with buried ambivalences in a partner's internalized image, reawakening reverberations of negativity from earlier relationships. These may be significant, leading to an increased expectation of such painful affects in the present relationship. Old repetition-compulsion patterns may thus be set in train.

If the disillusionment with the relationship is great, the relationship may be relinquished: it cannot continue because the realities of each partner make it untenable for the other. Or the disillusionment may be one-sided, leaving the other partner his intense and unrequited love. Sometimes, instead of the relationship breaking down, one partner may try to force the other to behave as the idealized fantasy. This may be temporarily successful if the partner forcing change wields great power over the other. When such behavior meets mutual needs a distorted relationship of false ideal-selves may result. Another possible consequence, so elegantly outlined by Henry Dicks (1967) is that partners may switch to mutual negative projections. In this pattern of relating, each partner starts to interpret characteristic behaviors and interactions of the other from an increasingly negative viewpoint, selecting especially for condemnation those aspects of the other partner that unconsciously represent the aspects of himself he hates and denies.

The bonds in such a relationship may be very strong, yet filled with negative affects of hate and anger. One, or both partners, may not want to give up the other, since he may only feel a sense of completeness when able to condemn such "bad" parts of himself, yet retain them in his partner. Also, as Dicks points out, the unconscious may select a partner with consummate skill; it may chose one who, on the surface, would appear to have all the potential for providing a positive relationship; yet who underneath, as it turns out, is ideally matched to meet more neurotic and ambivalent needs.

Of course a great many adult pair bonds do not have such negative outcomes. Instead, in the phase where idealization is beginning to be relinquished (and perhaps grieved for), the interactions with the real and different aspects of the partner prove rewarding. The emotional investment is then transferred to the real characteristics of the partner and the image modified to include these. They become part of what is valued in the inner representations of that relationship. The negative thread exists in the relationship but is not an overwhelming affective component.

Thus the levels and patterns of ambivalence in adult pair bonds will vary enormously. Negative levels may be high if there are covert neurotic needs and intense neurotic interaction. Or, they may be minimal and very acceptable as part of the differences between two people who find each other fulfilling and gratifying. Ambivalence may be heightened at different stages in the development of the relationship.

The levels of mutual dependence in adult pair bonds are substantial, as each relies on the other to meet certain needs. Usually this is the reciprocal dependence of equals, adult to adult. Sometimes it seems, however, the dependence represents more symbiotic and infantile needs. This latter situation may be transient and part of normal relating and regression, or it may affect the whole tone and life of the relationship, leading to pathology.

Self-disclosure becomes an important component of a relationship as intimacy deepens. It is part of the way in which each partner gets to know the other better. Some of what is revealed through it may be acceptable to the other, while some may not be so. Trust must deepen to allow self-disclosure, yet with disclosure each runs a risk. Even with increasing intimacy there are aspects of the self the individual does not disclose. These may be important to the individual in that they represent areas that are not exposed to the power or influence of others (Kelvin 1977). Kelvin also discusses the enormous power of physical intimacy, comparing, as Hinde (1979, p. 303) notes, "the lovers' exploration of each other's body images" with the exploration of their self-concepts. Each has the potential for positive gains on the one hand and increased vulnerability on the other.

Thus, the adult pair bond grows and develops over time—with mutual exploration, disclosure, acceptance, and adaptation. The relationship is represented by the multiple kinds and levels of interaction that occur over time; by the progressive images and their associated feelings as they are internalized. And, it represents as well, the specific roles that each partner in the dyad fulfills for the other. At any one time, it may reflect the fulfillment or frustration of certain interpersonal needs, including among others, the affectional, emotional, and instrumental.

Another aspect of the adult pair bond, of great importance should the bond dissolve, is the way in which the partners gain meaning and identity in their lives. Thus, a woman may feel that her sense of self is very closely linked to her function as mother to infant, wife to husband. A man may feel that his sense of self is closely linked to his function as father to child, husband to wife. The image each person has of himself may be, to varying degrees, dependent on the other. For example, a person may only feel good if he gains narcissistic supplies from others' interactions with him, or be reassured of his power by the effect of his interactions with another. Thus, the dissolution of such a relationship may involve not only the loss of intimacy and the ritual of interactions including frustrations and rewards, but there may also be, to some degree, a loss of some meaning one partner gave to the other, some loss or change in the sense of self as determined by the other.

Annie is twenty-four. Her hair is straight, gently coiled. Her dark eyes brood with hidden inner mystery.

"Our baby, our baby, that little, growing part of Pete and me—our baby is coming.

"I could tell, I could really tell from the moment we conceived that this time, this time would be our baby. Our baby would be beautiful—fine and intelligent. If it was a boy, he would be strong and good looking—like his father. If it was a girl, she would be beautiful of course. That baby, our baby, was to be all a baby could be, full of good things, beautiful and strong for life.

"My pregnancy was fine. The baby would kick and play. Pete would laugh and tickle me and say 'Let's see if she's still awake—let's have a game with her.' Then he'd put his ear against my womb and smile secretly. 'I'm sure it's Melissa,' he would say. And I would say, 'It's Phillip of course.' Those were the names we had chosen. I was worried sometimes: what if something was wrong with the baby, what if the birth went wrong, or if I wasn't any good as a mother? But that all seemed ridiculous. Sometimes I was afraid that the 'gods' might envy us our happiness and take it away. I didn't really know if we deserved it when there were lots of people in the world so unhappy. Pete would laugh at me and say 'It's ours, old girl.' Then I'd relax and all would be well again.

"At seven months, I gave up work. That was sad for me—I loved the school and the children. For a moment I resented the baby. Perhaps I realized for the first time that my life was going to be different, that I couldn't turn back the clock, that the baby meant a whole new existence for me, for Pete, for us both. We wouldn't have the same freedom we'd had before.

"The birth was good. Pete was there with me as we'd planned. He was so excited you would really think he'd been in labor himself. Well, it was Melissa. She was quite perfect, quite beautiful. For a moment, just a little time, I felt sad, as though I'd lost Phillip, but then I touched her and held her, and she was mine, she was part of me. I'd known her inside me for so long, and now I'd really know her. She was part of me, part of Pete. We were both there together, in her forever.

"I was so tired. I have never been so tired. I didn't know, I never realized how busy one could be with a new baby. Pete wanted me, needed me, yet I seemed to have so little time left over for him. Those weeks were hard—some of the hardest I've ever known. I was so cross and tired. Pete seemed so demanding. Melissa never seemed to settle; she was so alert, so full of smiles and play. Then things seemed to settle. Pete was loving, I felt loving too, and Melissa found her place in our family. I suppose that was it—we became a family—a complicated little family, but a family we were."

THE MOTHER-INFANT RELATIONSHIP

Like the adult pair bond, the mother-infant relationship will also eventually develop further in interactions with the live baby when it is born and as it matures. The mother brings to this relationship, as each person brings to a new relationship, an inner image of relating potential, symbols, or pictures, made up of past experiences of the same or similar relationships. Thus she brings to it internalized memories and experiential traces of her own experiences of being mothered, of the caring relationships of others toward her, of the mothering she has carried out with younger siblings, the dolls of her childhood, and the children of family and friends. Her image of mothering and of the relationship she will have with the baby will also be influenced by social and cultural attitudes and norms of mothering in her society.

The image of the relationship and the baby may represent conscious memories, but also unconscious fantasies that become, as a consequence of need and conflict, linked to mothering and babies. Thus the mother who has experienced deprivation may have constellations of this emotional pain associated with her image of mothering and baby.

She may also have compensatory fantasies of good/perfect mothering and baby associated with the image. If her early deprivation has been in part healed by subsequent caring relationships, her image may incorporate this experience. If she has been further wounded in caring relationships, then the painful images may be reinforced. Thus the image she holds and brings to the conception of the child will be a complex amalgam and condensation of all these past affects and experiences of mother-baby type dyads. These images may also be powerful factors in leading to the beginning of the mother-infant relationship, motivating the conception in some instances (Raphael 1972a). It is likely that very similar images come into play for the father as well.

With the conception of the baby, the image becomes influenced by the beginnings of interaction. The effects of the fetus and pregnancy on the woman's body are associated with the baby-to-be, the unborn child, and they impinge on the image. If these changes are negative, they may reinforce ambivalent aspects of the image; whereas, if they are chiefly positive, the more positive aspects of the attachment to the unborn child may be reinforced and the image enhanced. This early interaction with the real fetus, the real baby-to-be, is quite indirect and may evoke minimal response. Later, as the unborn child grows, this interaction becomes more specific. With movement and then later activity as pregnancy progresses the interactional effects become clearer. The mother and father may touch the abdomen, feel the baby's movements, respond to them. The mother may often talk to this intrauterine companion who is so constantly with her. It has been said that this is a rehearsal for the real parenting to come.

The process of giving birth will be a further emotional experience of gratification and/or pain. The parents' image of the baby takes on the affects and memories of this experience too. Then the real baby arrives. The real interactions commence with the earliest skin contact and movements between mother and baby. They build and become more complex as this "couple" comes to know and understand each other. Communications are verbal and nonverbal: sounds, expressions, body contact, smell, movement, and visual signs. These are the interactional behaviors—the sequences of behavior that build the relationship further. They will have many rewarding, positive qualities, yet also some frustrating, negative ones. These affects and memory experiences will become linked to the new and deepening image that each holds inside to symbolize the relationship.

Hinde (1979) notes, however, that the earliest patterns of infant "interaction" are much more geared to eliciting responses from the mother than to responding to her. Soon the infant does start to respond to her. The patterns of simple movements including finding the nipple, suckling, movements conducive to mother-infant contact, signal movements such as smiling and crying. These responses are elicited initially by a range of situations that become progressively more specific. The infant's smile subsequently becomes elicited by familiar caregivers, especially the mother, and he is likely to focus on his mother's face and later to fixate her eyes. Infants vary in their general activity, in the threshholds at which certain behaviors appear, and in the degree to which experience modifies such behaviors. Most infants learn rapidly and soon show "intentionality and emotional expressivity directed towards persons" (Hinde 1979, p. 309). Hinde suggests that the mother and baby are active in transmitting their understanding to each other after two to three months, and this interaction becomes much more specific and developed when the baby is capable of recognizing the mother toward the latter half of that first year.

Hinde goes on to discuss the mother's ways of interacting in greater detail, noting that many of these are similar to those used with adults, but modified in important ways: with the infant, her manner is usually both exaggerated in space and extended in time. She looks and speaks to the baby, and there are long mutual gazes, which reinforce her relationship with her baby (Stern 1977). However, in the earliest phases, the interactions are very dependent on the mother's sensitivity to both the infant's ability to interact and to its needs to withdraw from stimulus. Episodes of mutual attention and disengagement extend. As the baby grows, its capacities to interact develop, but they still require sensitive responses from the mother. No mother always responds appropriately to the baby. The inevitable frustrations as the baby learns about himself and his mother facilitate a social learning of what relationships are about. Some even suggest that such frustrations are essential for the infant's ego development.

The relationship will grow in its positive and negative meanings for the mother. Where the relationship is chiefly rewarding, the positive loving threads will be the strongest, and love will be the principal emotional tone of the image she holds. Where interactions are chiefly frustrating, higher levels of negative affect will be linked to that image. Where the fit between mother and infant is poor, either because of her mothering difficulties or because of the baby's temperamental differences from her relating capacities (and she lacks the sensitivity to match his needs), then the relationship may become very negative. Cycles of negative interaction may build up even further, perhaps leading to rejection, or even abuse of the baby; or, repression of these feelings may lead to some bonding anomaly such as overprotectiveness, with intrusive control rather than affectionate care. Not only may affects of "badness" be felt by the mother but the "badness" may be projected onto the child.

As the infant matures he develops further interactive capacities. These are verbal and behavioral. He may bite and spit out as well as suck. He may say "No!" and "I hate you," as well as "I love you." He may hit out as well as touch tenderly. He may walk away as well as lift his arms to evoke care. Interaction in the relationship will grow and change. The image the mother holds of the relationship will be further molded by these changes.

Another key theme of the mother-infant relationship is the infant's dependence on the mother (or some similar surrogate mothering person). This dependence is total in the early stages but becomes modified with infant growth and development. The degree to which his dependence is age and state appropriate will be important in the quality of the relationship.

Attempts to measure the relative levels of affection, care, control, and rejection in the mother-child relationship or father-child relationship as perceived by the child have resulted in the development of a Parental Bonding Instrument (Parker 1979). This has proved valuable in defining some dimensions of these bonds.

THE FATHER-INFANT RELATIONSHIP

The father's relationship with the infant has been studied less, but it probably follows many patterns similar to that of the mother. It lacks the biological parameters of the intrauterine experience and the bodily intimacy of breast feeding. Yet when the father is closely involved in the birth of the infant and interaction with it afterward, the bonds may become very close. The same threads of ambivalence are likely to weave their way through this relationship as in the mother-infant dyad. However, the dependent needs will be less clear and direct, since they are not as evidently linked to the baby's survival as they are with the mother. The inner images the father holds and the real interactions will still be the core elements of the relationship.

The bond of a man to his child may be built and reinforced in a number of other ways. His identification with the baby as part of himself, and as an externalization of himself, may be powerful. He may also identify with his wife and her bonding to the baby; and he may consider his bond as a continuation of his line, his greater family, in real and symbolic terms. Where he has been closely involved in the decision to conceive the baby, he may be bonded to it as a creation of his own, an extension of his own ego. The baby is thus *his* baby, and his bond to it may be very strong.

THE INFANT-PARENT RELATIONSHIP

From the infant's point of view he brings to his relationship with his mother some biopsychosocial precursor of relating capacities. His behaviors trigger her bonding to him, and this in turn reinforces certain of his behavioral patterns. The precise point just when he starts to hold an image of his relationship inside him is unclear, but it probably commences toward the end of the first half of the first year (see chapter 3), and earlier potentials or traces may exist before that time. So until then, his relationship is purely of the here and now, composed of the gratification and frustration, the actuality of interaction and the primordial affectual experiences attached to such interaction. These may be positive precursors of the primary affects of pleasure; or negative precursors of the primary affects of "unpleasure" (Engel 1962), anxiety, or depression-withdrawal. Thus the beginning of the ambivalent strands of his relating will commence and develop as the duration of the relationship extends. These infant-parent relationships will ultimately be chiefly gratifying and loving for many infants and unfortunately frustrating and painful for others. As the infant grows he gains more control over his own interactions, and his affects become more differentiated. The balance of positive and negative experience will alter from time to time during his development. All these stages will be progressively incorporated into his increasingly complex inner amalgam of feelings and memories, his image of the relationship. The infant's need to depend on his mother for survival will dominate the earliest years, so this strand will be powerful then, attenuating as he grows older, unless some special dyadic processes reinforce the dependence as a binding force in the relationship beyond the time it is developmentally appropriate. The infant-father relationship, and later the child-father relationship, will follow a similar path.

LOSS IN THE PARENT-INFANT/INFANT-PARENT DYAD

Many dimensions of the parent-infant/infant-parent relationship make it very vulnerable when there is a loss of one partner.

1. The intensity of the relationship and its interactions is of primary importance here, though this intensity will vary from pair to pair, depending on the needs of the dyad. Even though intensity may vary, it is always sufficient to make the effects of loss profound.

2. Because each partner brings to the relationship a certain role he fulfills in relation to the other—such as mother, father, child—and there is complimentarity in these roles, if a member is lost, so is a role and its functions.

3. These relationships meet the needs for nurture and succor as well as others, such as affection, achievement, love, and status. These could all be lost if the relationship were lost.

4. The relationship usually exists in a family context: either a new family just formed or else a larger family into which the relationship brings new parameters. Loss would dramatically alter these.

5. The parent-fetus relationship changes to the parent-infant relationship and then to the parent-child relationship, and that eventually to the parent-adolescent relationship, and finally to the parent-adult child relationship. The intensity of interaction is likely to be greatest in the early stages, progressively lessening. Thus the images each holds will reflect condensation of all the experiences of the early stages of the relationship. Ambivalence may be minimal or extensive throughout this time span and may vary in intensity at different stages. Dependence will lessen through development. Should development be impaired or distorted, these variables may be influenced in different directions, for instance, to prolonged dependence and intensity of interaction to the exclusion of the development of other dyads. These factors will have implications for response to loss.

The parent-infant/infant-parent bonds are of course, the most intimate of bonds. But there are many other close bonds that may be lost. The fabric of family life comprises complex, interlocking, and interweaving patterns of relationships, all of which involve strong bonds. Each of these relationships affects others—the relationship of the mother and the father affects the mother-child relationship just as the father-child and mother-child relationships affect sibling relationships. Within the family system there are many patterns of interaction meeting many different needs. There are also different affect patterns within the family system. These may, for instance, involve strong sanctions within the family about certain bonds, certain interactional levels, and affect expression. For example, a family system may reinforce mother-child relations above those of husband and wife, or may restrict interactional intensity by its subcultural norms so that the adult pair share little intimacy. Or norms may dictate that the acknowledgement or expression of negative affects must be denied. The loss of a particular relationship may have different effects on individuals of one type of family system than on those of a differently structured system that suffers the same loss.

Annie is twenty-eight. Her hair is elegantly plaited up on her head. Her eyes are friendly, mature, and with a certain calm.

"My days are filled with our life as a family—our children, our friends. Pete is the dear and loving man he has always been. There is a security in our marriage, in the ritual of our lives, that I cherish. Sometimes I long for excitement, for newness. But mostly I am so grateful, so very grateful, for all we have. Sure there are times when we have our ups and downs, when I wish for my freedom again, when I get furious with Pete, and he gets furious with me.

"Sometimes there is pain, frustration, sometimes even anger. But they pass. Melissa is a joy to me, full and bubbling, curious—she tells me everything. 'Mummy,' she says, 'You *must*, you *simply must* hear what happened at school today,' or 'You *must*, you *simply must* see this picture I've drawn.' John is little and proud. He follows her like a shadow. He looks at me with his big trusting eyes and puts up his little hand, and there's a whole world of love and warmth between us. He is strong and sturdy like Pete and like my father too. The world of our family life is like an ongoing tide, a river, flowing on, taking us all with it. Sometimes it's the way we want to go, but even if it isn't, we would have to go with it. Sometimes I feel a little sad about my teaching. I was a good teacher and that's been left behind—on the bank somewhere. I guess I'll come back to it someday—maybe. But our family is now. It's Melissa off to school, John and me in our secret world of sand trays and little boys, our magic days. It's the family in the evening, the story by the fire. It's the love and the battles, the disorganization and the impatience, it's the talk and the quiet, the good and the bad. It's the magic I still feel of Pete's strong, hard body beside me, in me, in the bed at night, and the children sleeping quietly in the room next door."

# Death and Deaths

Death has many meanings: the grim reaper; a sleep from which the sleeper does not awake; catastrophe and destruction; nonbeing; transition to another life; the end; the loss of loved ones; the death of self. It is the inevitable part of human experience. The knowledge of its inevitability is incorporated into the psychological structure of each person, and it is accommodated in many different ways. Human society, from its earliest times, has evolved rituals and myths in its attempts to give meaning to death: the mysterious, fearful and unknown (Aries 1974).

Through the ages man has devised many symbolic, primitive, and ritualistic ways to cope with death and bereavement. Many include magical beliefs about the causes of death and the ways one may be protected from it—as if in an attempt to control it and make meaning of it. In a consideration of death in American society, Parsons (1963) described three distinct orientations that he believed were evolving. These were hell-fire, damnation fundamentalism; existential despair; and the "sugary sentimentality" of positive thinking. It is commonly assumed that many contemporary societies are death denying. Others (including Gorer 1959) would suggest that there is a pornography of death—that it is obscene, taboo, yet stimulating and relished. In some ways, Western society has even romanticized death (Schneiderman 1971). These symbols of death in the social system may reflect from and reverberate with similar death symbolizations in the mind of man.

Death is conceptualized in many ways. In early childhood, its nature and finality cannot be easily visualized, yet as the individual grows he comes to understand it as personal and inevitable and associated with the natural cessation of body processes. The individual may understand this for others, but analytic views would suggest that the unconscious mind cannot accept death, and that man cannot contemplate his own death as an absolute cessation of all existence. Freud suggested that the man of prehistoric times survives unchanged in our unconscious. "Our unconscious then, does not believe in its own death; it behaves as if it were immortal" (Freud 1915, p. 259). Freud thought that all interest in immortality was a denial of death. Jung, on the other hand, saw enormous significance in the symbolic idea of immortality, yet he recognized the fear of death, a "fear that envelopes the sleepless one like a smothering blanket" (Jung 1934, p. 405).

That fear or anxiety may be associated with death seems commonly accepted. The nature of such fear of death has been subject to many interpretations. In psychoanalytic theories, it has been seen as a development of the fear of separation or object loss, of castration, of superego abandonment or persecution; in other words, death anxiety has been seen as secondary to other anxieties. An opposite view is that death anxiety is primary, and other anxieties derive from it. It may evolve into or be associated with "the death instinct" in some theories (Storolow 1973). Others see it in object-relations terms as both the fear of individuation and the fear of symbiosis. Death anxiety, in these conceptual frameworks, is a multifaceted phenomenon and is probably, as Storolow suggests, a contributor to personality structure in that the defenses built against it will influence the form of personal psyche and behavior.

But this fear is not a unified single concept. Storolow quotes Murphy: "It is apparent that fear of death is not psychologically homogenous at all, even in a narrowly defined cultural group. It is a very complex thing with conscious, preconscious, and unconscious aspects and all sorts of predetermining cultural, historical, and religious factors" (Storolow 1973, p. 483).

Fear of death may be regarded in many ways: as the fear of pain, of destruction, or of mutilation, for example. It is a fear of the unknown, a fear of the annihilation of self. It may be a fear of the process of dying with loss of function, dependence on others, incapacity to tolerate the pain involved; or it may be a fear of being alone. The fear of death is also associated with fears of loss, the loss of those beloved and essential to the self. These fears may be faced as a person faces death himself. They may be realistic or divorced from the reality of this threat at this time. The fear of death may be evoked in the individual by many factors: by the process of his development making it real to him as his cognitive capacities allow him to incorporate its full meaning; by phases of development which heighten it, such as midlife; by aging and illness which may make the inevitable approach of death obvious; and by crises that lead one to confront it. Fear may be experienced at these times, or defenses may come into play to deal with it, among them, denial, repression, intellectualization, displacement, and projection (see Templer 1970; Nelson and Nelson 1975; Warren and Chopra 1979). Various dimensions of death anxiety have been identified: death avoidance, death fear, death denial, and reluctance to interact with the dying. The reactions associated with death anxiety may have considerable physiological impact, leading to affective responses to symbolic death words and, even more specifically, to blood pressure changes as the individual attempts to avoid ontologic confrontation with death (Thauberger and Cleland 1976).

The extent to which the fear of death influences personality structure and the ways in which it does so remain to be determined. Similarly, (vis-à-vis psychosomatic illness) the physiological effects on the individual of personal confrontation with death and its fears are yet to be understood.

Out of his fear of death man builds many futures for himself. And most of these include some symbolic concepts of immortality. It seems such concepts manifested themselves concretely even in the prehistoric man: the Neanderthal man buried his dead, sometimes with great tenderness and care; with the dead, he buried tools and food for the journey of the soul to the next life and red ochre for the life-giving blood (Montagu 1976). The myth of immortality is almost universal in human cultures and is revealed in the burial ceremonies and mourning rituals that prepare the dead for a journey to another world and that acknowledge the influence of his spirit long after his bodily death. Lifton (1975) notes however, that now symbolic immortality may take on many forms: there is the biological mode, whereby one lives on and in one's sons and daughters and in their children and in their children's children; there is the theological idea of a life after death or a higher plane of existence after death. Or immortality may be sought through the works and creations one leaves behind. Some believe it to exist in eternal nature itself and the oneness of man and spirit with nature, or in a psychic state of "existential transcendence" where time and death disappear. As Pollock (1975) points out, it may even be reflected in concepts of Utopia.

Today man may try to extend his symbols of immortality into "reality" through the technologies of medicine and science. Montagu (1976) points out how the personal belief in immortality may interfere with health-related behaviors. Yet, man may also attempt to defy death by freezing in anticipation of scientific progress when he may be revived for further treatment. Now, intensive care and resuscitative technologies keep alive those who would otherwise be classed as dead. Medical definitions of death have become ensconced in legal declarations because the boundaries of life and death have become less clear. As man seeks more control over death, the uncontrollable, the nature of death and mortality must change: for example, now it is possible to freeze a man's sperm so that he can father a child after he dies. Such developments of science may be far in advance of society's capacity to assimilate their social and legal consequences and even further in advance of the individual's ability for psychic incorporation of such possibilities. One aspect of and response to this may be the current preoccupation with "near-death" experiences (Kellehear 1983).

It is quite clear when one studies the fantasies of death and dying that these remain primitive in the mind of man. They are associated with fear, terror, excitement, and curiosity. Death may seem the fulfillment of sexual, destructive, mutilating, and/or sadistic pleasures when indulged in vicariously and at a distance. The great popularity of dramas of terror, horror, death, destruction, and war amply attest to this.

22

The crowds drawn to the site of massive death in disaster are able to indulge the sadistic, destructive, aggressive aspects of death in their own fantasy, safely and at a distance, as they attempt to gain mastery over death and what it might mean to them. This excitement of death as the fulfillment of aggressive and destructive fantasies is often denied; it is overtly viewed with shame and stigma, although it is a very real part of human experience.

Not only are fantasies of aggression and destruction aroused by and linked to death but there are also fantasies of killing and being killed. Death is seen in terms of causes, as the child sees it with his more primitive conceptual modes. The individual was killed *by* something. He died *of* a certain disease. These explanations represent attempts to gain control of death by cognitive mastery and understanding. They also reflect deeper level fantasies that death must be caused by someone or something and may therefore be prevented or revenged.

The death of a loved one means not only the loss, but also the nearness of personal death, the threat to self. One is close to death and may be touched or contaminated by it. All the personal and internalized meanings of death will be evoked by the death of a loved one. All the personal vulnerabilities associated with death will be aroused by its closeness to the self.

Death means something further too. It means the dead human body. The altered state of death is frightening when first encountered—alien to life. The lack of breath, the stillness, the coldness, the absence of response bring a pain that cuts to the core of personal experience. Professionals who work with death—doctors, nurses, and others—become "used to death." But few forget their first experience of the dead human body, or the passage of life from someone in their presence. Painful as the reality of the dead body may be, it is important that it be incorporated into the death experience of the bereaved. There is a peace in the face of death as well as a finality. Seeing the body provides the opportunity to say farewell to the dead person, and it brings as well a knowledge of one's own real death.

There are many different forms of death, many ways to die, and many small or partial deaths or losses one experiences. Each will have special significance in terms of how it is experienced, its cultural meaning, and its intrapsychic meaning for the individual. Deaths may be sudden or long anticipated. They may be violent, premature, or the natural conclusion of the biological aging process. There are many deaths for many people, but only one death for each individual.

23

ANTICIPATED DEATHS

Deaths that are anticipated usually occur as a consequence of illness or aging, or occasionally as a late sequel to injury. The experience of those bereaved following such deaths is essentially different from that following sudden and unanticipated deaths in that there has been some opportunity to prepare, to come to terms with the closeness of death and the probability of loss. Yet these deaths take many different forms.

The gradual relinquishment of life with the gentle fading of body functions in the very old person is seen as "natural" death. The person dies, often gently, of old age. He may die in his sleep. To die peacefully in this way is seen by most people as the most acceptable form of the unacceptable death. And death may be expected, awaited, and even welcomed by both the dying and the bereaved.

Many anticipated deaths of the elderly do not come so sweetly, but rather as a culmination of ill health and marked body failure. The physical experiences of shortness of breath and diminished capacities may be accompanied by a range of other symptoms. The distress levels may be high even if there is no physical pain. In these cases, death is not viewed as "natural," but rather as the result of disease or some system failure. Thus, even though the death of an older person is anticipated, the bereaved still perceives that he was taken away by heart disease or pneumonia, for example. The quality of the dying is influenced by the effects of the disease on biological processes. This will have effects not only on the dying person, but also on those who will grieve his death. They may suffer empathically; they may shoulder with acceptance or resentment the burdens of his illness; they may find their relationships altered with this person who is now so psychologically different in response to the disease process; and they may grieve and mourn his death even if it does not come.

Such disease processes may also cause "untimely" deaths, when they occur in those who are relatively young. The experience of the impending death for the dying and bereaved will reflect not only the processes outlined above, but also the great sense of being cheated of the life each expected for the future. Those anticipated years of life will be seen as wasted and lost, and both the dying and bereaved will feel cheated of the relationship that was to be, the experiences that would have been shared. The younger the person who dies, the greater will have been the expectation of the future, and thus, the greater will be the loss that is added to the death itself. This is made even more bitter

24

for those who have struggled to reach a point where all they had sought seems about to reach fruition. Death's power to deprive is most painfully experienced.

The common illnesses of life may have a range of meanings in society, and these may become associated with the meaning of a death. Thus, heart disease, for example, is frequent in Western society and may have certain symbolic meanings associated with it. The symptoms, distress, and nature of the disease and terminal illness experience may be governed by expectations built on one's experience of others, especially from one's family, who have died from the same condition. The patterns of care and medical systems may be ritualized and thus become part of the medical mythology of the individual, the family, and the society. These factors will also influence the experience both of the dying one and of the bereaved. The symbolic meanings of the heart as the center of life and emotion may become associated with the death, just as death from stroke or respiratory disorder may have other symbolic meanings. The loss of the personality in brain damage deaths, the loss of "the breath of life" in respiratory deaths all contribute to what each death may mean. Of specific importance though is the nature and times of the deaths of parents. The dying person may dread that death will also do to him what it did to his father or mother as he approaches that age.

Even when death is anticipated and seems timely it may not come at the time it is expected. Even if awaited in the elderly it may be unexpected at a particular time, thus producing shock effects. These shock effects may be even greater in the untimely deaths of the young, thus complicating the adaptation to loss. Of all the anticipated deaths, death from cancer has the most symbolic power. Cancer symbolizes malignancy growing and taking over the body. It symbolizes death and pain. It symbolizes destruction that cannot be stopped. Regardless of the reality that much neoplastic disease is satisfactorily treated, with long survival periods or cure, the popular image of cancer is of death. Attempts to combat this powerful threat with media campaigns that "Cancer is a word, not a sentence" may do little to counteract this deeply entrenched image.

Deaths from cancer may indeed be dreadful. They may be accompanied by a progressive taking over of the body by the disease; the relentless spread of metastases; the failure of therapeutic procedures; the hopelessness conveyed by systems of care; the wasting of the human body to a pale and different shadow of its former self; the loss of function and independence; the subjugation to pain and disease; and the inexorable progress of death. There may be special potency and significance in certain types of cancer: the destruction of the core of the private and feminine self in genital cancer (Raphael and Maddison 1981); the mysterious taking over of the blood by white cell malignancy in leukemia; the destruction of language and face by cancers of the oropharynx; the loss of control and dirtiness of cancers of the bowel; and the choking to death of cancers of the lung. The modes of cancer therapy also have many realities and fantasies associated with them that may influence the experience of the dying and bereaved. The mutilation of massive surgery, the illness associated with some radiotherapy, and the distressing side effects of much chemotherapy are widely known. They will bring their own fears and distresses to the cancer deaths.

There are special feelings of contamination too in association with cancer—as though some of the malign, crablike encroachment of the condition may spread beyond the body of the sufferer to one's own body. This sense of contamination, as well as the helplessness many feel in the face of cancer, may mean that the dying person becomes isolated from others who cannot bear to be with him, who do not know what to say to comfort him. Thus, the dying person may die a social death long before the death of his body.

The person facing death from cancer goes through his own anticipatory grief—the dying patient's grief (Aldrich 1963). Those who are to lose him also suffer this as well as all the implications, real and fantasized, of his cancer death. Fortunately such issues are now widely acknowledged and increasingly well understood owing to the sensitive and pioneering work of Elisabeth Kübler-Ross (1969). Nevertheless, the special meanings of each aspect of the cancer, its treatment, its prognosis, and the death it brings, must be carefully explored and understood for each dying person and each family member who grieves his death in anticipation and then mourns him when he dies (Maddison and Raphael 1970).

Even when the psychological aspects of such deaths are understood and responded to, all concerned must become aware of their impact on the functioning of the family. In financial and human resource terms the processes of caring for the terminally ill person may deplete individuals and the family, so that the painful empathy with the dying person is further complicated by the battle for personal and family survival in the face of his illness (Fisher et al. 1976).

Sometimes, of course, an illness that has been perceived as inevitably fatal may not lead to death. Remission may occur or recovery be facilitated. Modern treatments of childhood leukemia, for example, have led to a much greater uncertainty of prognosis. Both the potentially dying and the potentially bereaved may see themselves in a no-man's-land between life and death, living one day at a time, uncertainly. Hope increases as time progresses and the hold to health and life is maintained. Nevertheless such experiences are highly distressing and may lead to an altered view of life and different patterns of interpersonal relationship that are geared to the fragility of existence.

In all these circumstances of death, where the death is anticipated, the hold to life may fluctuate from time to time. Various phases of response from denial to acceptance of death have been described (see, for example, Kübler-Ross 1969). Yet life is precious even in the face of terrible and painful disease. Both the dying person and the bereaved may hold strongly to hope and to life. That is, of course, their right and prerogative. Those issuing medical care and treatment will also have their various levels of acceptance or denial of death that may or may not intermesh with those of the dying person and his family.

There is however, for a great many of those who succumb to the anticipated death, the very important aspect of saying good-bye (Meares 1981). This may be formal or, more usually, informal, as there is an overt or covert recognition between the dying person and others that his death is near. The farewell represents a setting in place of life and the relationship, a recognition of the departure from both.

Another category of anticipated death is "chronic" death. This is when the dying person has a disease that is inevitably fatal, yet death may be a long way off. Huntington's Chorea is one such condition. The dying and bereaved live long with death. It becomes a part of life. No end is in sight, yet the end will eventually come. This situation may not be dissimilar to the permanently injured person who seems so severely impaired, perhaps through cerebral damage, that his life is a living death. In these circumstances those who are dying and those who will be bereaved may have many problems with the enigma of the future.

There are thus many deaths that may be anticipated, and each will have a certain meaning. The processes of dying will have an effect on the dying person as well as on those who will be bereaved. The relationship between them may be very substantially changed by the processes of the illness and the expectation of the death. There may be greater closeness and intimacy. There may be greater distance and withdrawal. There may be heightened ambivalence, or earlier ambivalences may be resolved for greater love. There may be greater dependence and new complementarities of roles. The death and the bereavement will be different from the death and bereavement of sudden death because their presence is known.

SUDDEN DEATHS

When death occurs with little or no warning, and especially if it occurs in the younger years, then an extra parameter is added. There has been no opportunity for anticipation, for preparation beforehand. The death brings an extra effect of shock over and above the normal. It is at the same time a most potent reminder of human mortality and human impotence, since one cannot know or control the time of the death. The bereaved is confronted by the power of death to kill and deprive and human helplessness in the face of it. The circumstances of sudden death may also be filled with violence: accidents are common causes, or there may be a sudden collapse with desperate attempts at resuscitation. The bereaved may be present at the time of the death and helpless to prevent it. Or, if not present he may be unable to comprehend it as a reality for the loved one who was last seen healthy and alive.

The shock effect of sudden death may be so great as in itself to induce a traumatic stress syndrome in the bereaved (Horowitz 1976). The event of the death in which the bereaved was involved or the circumstances under which news of the death was received may be so stressful as to overwhelm the ego. Ego resources then become taken up with trying to master the helplessness and other flooding affects. Traumatic memories of the event preoccupy and intrude repetitively; temporarily repressed, they intrude again, with all their panic and powerlessness. Dreams and nightmares of the scene and memories of the moment of the death disturb the night. The shock of the death is an overwhelming experience, psychologically complicating any response to it.

When sudden deaths are violent, bereavement may take on other dimensions. Destructive fantasies may develop, and death may become linked to killing and ambivalence. Violent death may occur as the result of an accident, as in road deaths. If others are involved in the accident, the death may become a shared traumatic experience; it may perhaps involve a battle for survival from personal injury or the relief of having survived oneself and yet the guilt that one should feel this way in the face of another's death. Accidental deaths are extremely frequent in many Western societies. Associated with these are cause and effect assumptions as well as legal processes of judgment and blame. Fantasies of vengeance and retribution as well as guilt are common among survivors. Violent deaths involving murder evoke, of course, even more strongly the psychic law of the talion principle. The shock of the death is complicated by hate for the killer, preoccupation with judgment and retribution. The violence of these deaths compounds the trauma and shock effects of sudden death, particularly when killing is involved, and these responses are difficult to resolve. Violent and accidental deaths are all the more shocking, abnormal, and difficult to assimilate when they involve children. These are evocative of the most painful fantasies.

Where death is not instantaneous, extensive technological attempts to save the victim's life may also profoundly affect the dying and those who will be bereaved. Intensive care and resuscitation are vital attempts to prevent untimely deaths and are, of course, frequently successful. When they fail, however, the dying takes on a special aura, for the dying person may seem distanced and dehumanized by the tubes and machines, by the drips and the respirators. These resuscitative attempts are critical of course for both the dying and those who will be bereaved, but their psychological and social relevance must be recognized (Sherizen and Paul 1977) for it is often a constraint upon the individuals and family unit.

Violent death also accompanies war and disaster. The violent deaths of war may be socially sanctioned, and the bereaved are often not directly involved. Wars have special meaning in that a "cause" is fought for, and the responses of the bereaved may reflect their values—positive or negative—of the "cause" for which the person died. Their responses may be especially bitter if they perceive these deaths as having no point, as serving no purpose. Deaths caused by disasters awaken themes of violence. Where there are many deaths together, the massive nature of the shared death is overwhelming. These deaths clearly have no purpose, unless they were altruistic in nature, having occurred in the course of saving others. They are bitterly resented when seen as an "act of God" in natural disaster or an "act of man" in man-made disaster.

The mechanisms whereby sudden deaths are dealt with in the society may also affect responses. The body is often not easily available for the bereaved to view, so that this reality of the acceptance of death, the dead human body, the dead body of a loved one, is not available to aid in acceptance of death's finality. The body may not be found, or it may be mutilated beyond all recognition, or may be anonymous in the field of battle. When the body is available, the bereaved may be "protected," mistakenly, by others from seeing it, or he may himself be inhibited by his own fears of doing so. Thus, this kind of death is harder to reconcile, still mysterious and hidden, and little connected with the absence of the person who was last seen so alive and well.

Legal systems are also more likely to be called into play in violent, sudden, or accidental death than in anticipated ones, and they will bring with them an additional system of psychosocial meaning: blame, guilt, retribution, and punishment. They are useful as well, of course, in stating and reviewing, in documenting and describing the nature of the death and its circumstance.

Suicides are deaths of special significance. Here the person has chosen to die, to desert those who are bereaved. These deaths may be violent, as with hanging, stabbing, or shooting. Or they may be quiet, as with self-poisoning. They leave a legacy of suicide (Cain 1966), of uncertainty, of guilt, of blame, and hostility. They frequently come on the background of ambivalence and hostility, sometimes with a threat or warning that was not heeded. The very circumstances that are chosen, the roles that are left, may then all add to the psychic trauma of the survivors.

Acute or fulminating medical disease or surgical emergency may lead to sudden death. The sudden deaths of the young, or the young-old (aged sixty to seventy-five) from cardiovascular or cerebrovascular lesions or disease fall into these categories. These deaths may be immediate, or they may occur after a few days or weeks. Because there is usually such an intense battle for life, the possibilities of death may be put aside in the fight for survival. Then the suddenness of the death, despite forewarning, still brings great shock, although perhaps not so much as in those deaths that are immediate. These deaths are hardest to accept in the young. Yet because they are a consequence of a disease process, not of killing, not of violence, they are often somehow a little easier to incorporate as part of life. Deaths from fulminating infection may also come into this category, although modern antibiotic therapy has made them a rare part of Western society. All these deaths are seen as a consequence of the failure of the human body in illness, and thus they have less blame attached, unless of course they clearly represent a failure of care, either on the part of the patient or the medical care system.

Mysterious sudden deaths where no cause can be found, especially those of infancy or childhood such as the sudden infant death syndrome, are particularly difficult to conceptualize, and ultimately to accept.

Sudden death may occur away from the home, and even from the hospital. It may occur on a roadside or in a strange place. The person dies alone, or with strangers—painful for him and for those who survive him. It is not surprising that sudden, unexpected, and untimely deaths are associated with greater problems for the bereaved than are anticipated deaths: greater difficulties with acceptance of the loss and adjustment to it; greater difficulties with health and with a return to normalcy (Lehrman 1956; Parkes 1975*b*). Sudden deaths prove to be a risk factor for poor outcome following bereavement (Raphael 1977*b*).

There is one further aspect of sudden death that is important. Whereas the anticipated death may alter the quality of the relationship between the bereaved and the dying person, sudden death may instead cut across the pattern of the relationship, highlighting the images and experience that it entailed at the time it was lost. Sudden death may cut across the ambivalence, the intimacy, the withdrawal and in so doing will throw into relief that particular phase of the bond, the particular meaning it held. Ambivalences that may have been resolved in the ebb and flow of everyday life are held in frozen frame, perhaps with extra guilt and pain. Intimacies that were transient but part of the last experience are treasured with gratitude. The entity of the relationship is of course important. But these special aspects may be thrown into sharp relief by the death.

Some deaths may seem more fitting than others. They may seem to have some purpose, some meaning, to gain some end. Some people may wish to die in the course of duty, or in saving the lives of others, or fighting for a highly valued cause (see chapter 4). Others may wish to die quietly in their sleep, or at an advanced age indulging in the pleasures of youth. Some would see sudden death as the ideal way to die—no knowledge of death coming, little time for fear, no confrontation with one's nonexistence. Yet others would rather have the opportunity to put their affairs in order, to make things right in their world, to say their good-byes. Many may wish for a peaceful death for their loved ones or themselves. Thus, a bereaved person's first question upon a loved one's death may be "Did he suffer?" Death is often equated with suffering and suffering with the worst kind of death.

Religion may provide man with a framework from which to view and come to terms with death. The structure of religious belief and concepts of afterlife or immortality may be important. Religion may provide a ritualized system for dealing with death and loss, or a pattern of pastoral care. Many religions will try to offer comfort and consolation for the suffering of death or some way of giving meaning to it. They may provide, as well, some formal acknowledgment of the end of life, perhaps in confession, absolution, and final rites. However they may differ, they are all concerned with finding ways to deal with death. The faith they offer may be of great assistance to the dying or bereaved or may, in a secularized society, offer little consolation.

Whether or not man sees human, or philosophical, or theological systems as offering answers about death, he must still, inevitably, face the deaths of those he loves, and indeed his own death. We may not die in the way we would wish, nor may our loved ones. Yet die we will.

Pete and Melissa were coming home from the shops. Pete always liked to take Melissa to the supermarket with him. It was a private ritual between them, full of imaginings and love. It was a ritual of her being his girl, of them having their special outing together. They are driving home slowly, chatting excitedly together. A heavy rig, its brakes failing, slews across the road, crushing Pete's car against the cliff. Pete dies instantly, Melissa after two days in intensive care.

Annie is twenty-nine. Her hair hangs limply. Her eyes are lost, bewildered, emptied.

"Pete cannot be dead. Pete could not die—he has always been so alive—so strong, so careful. He could not have let this happen. God could not take him away. He is my life, my world. Melissa cannot die. I will not let her. God would not take them both from me, I know. They are my life, my world. They *cannot* be gone."

# CHAPTER 2. The Experience of Bereavement: Separation and Mourning

"I thought that I would never survive—that John and I could not live through it all. How could we live when they were dead? When our family was torn apart?"

*Annie, age 29*

"It was then, after that—those days, those endless days, those empty nights—that I knew to the core of my being that they were gone."

*Annie, age 29*

"It was like so many things in life—I'd been Pete's wife and Melissa's mother, and John's too, of course. I felt as though I'd been those things forever, and now I wasn't them any more—so who was I?"

*Annie, age 30*

"Now the year has come, and gone since his death ..."

*Annie, age 30*

Bereavement is the reaction to the loss of a close relationship. Sometimes grief is also used to describe this reaction, but in this work grief will be used to refer to the emotional response to loss: the complex amalgam of painful affects including sadness, anger, helplessness, guilt, despair. Mourning will be used here to refer to the psychological mourning processes that occur in bereavement: the processes whereby the bereaved gradually undoes the psychological bonds that bound him to the deceased. The rituals of mourning, such as burial, are discussed separately. The concepts of bereavement discussed here have been developed from the valuable contribution of many workers including Freud, Lindemann, Parkes, and Bowlby whose individual contributions are cited throughout the chapter.

The bereavement reaction may be described as comprising a series of phases, representing some of the processes of adaption to loss. It must be acknowledged, however, that any such phases are not clear-cut or fixed, and that the bereaved may pass backward and forward among them or may indeed become locked in one or another, partially or completely.

## Shock, Numbness, Disbelief

The first response to the news of the death of a loved one is one of shock, numbness, and disbelief. The bereaved person feels a sense of unreality, as though what has been said or what has happened could not possibly be true—as though it could not have been said, as though it must be happening to someone else. The bereaved may feel distanced from the horror and its implications, frozen in time. There is a feeling of being in a dream or a nightmare from which he will awake.

This effect of shock is most pronounced when the death itself is totally unexpected. Yet it also occurs to some degree with the majority of bereaved people when they first hear of a death or realize it has occurred. It may be that the ego virtually closes its boundaries and defenses against the trauma that is perceived as overwhelming and a threat to its survival. These moments or hours of numbness or shutting out give the ego time to mobilize its resources so that the death and the loss may be dealt with gradually, controlling the stimuli so they are more manageable, thus allowing for greater ego control. The bereaved may say: "When they told me, I felt I was far away, as though it was happening to someone else, and I was watching from a distance"; or "I wanted to turn back the clock, to go back to where I was before—my whole world seemed to have been turned upside down"; or "To keep going I had to shut it out so that I could do the things I had to do"; or "It was like a great black hole; I had to go round it at first until I was strong enough to look at it." The words and news of death may be felt as an assault. "It was a terrible blow; I didn't know what had hit me; I couldn't take it in"; or "I felt as if I had been struck—hit across the face"; or "It hit me in the guts—it really winded me"; or "It knocked me out; it was too much to take."

The words of death are also significant. The bereaved wants not to hear them, wants them not to be said, dreads their reality, their harshness. It is as though, by not speaking of it, the death may be reversible, untrue; and that the actual words somehow make it real, perhaps even make it happen. Yet there is at the same time a desperate need to bear and encompass the exact reality of what has happened, as though only this can provide a solid foundation in a shattered world.

This same shock and emotional denial occur when there is the threat of death with the diagnosis of fatal injury or illness. The family members may reflect this when they insist that the patient "must not be told," that "he couldn't take it." Here there is the same wish to hold back, control, and deny what has happened by not speaking of it, the same fantasy that if the words are not said, it may not be real. There is also projection: "He couldn't take it," reflecting the family members' own stunned feelings.

Such denial must, of course, ultimately be relinquished in the face of reality. The anguish of recognition breaks through, perhaps in great cries of intense distress or anger. The factors that facilitate the facing of reality are many: the need for the bereaved to communicate about the death to significant others; the legal processes concerned with the death such as certification; the need to arrange for the disposal of the body; and the presence and words of others who acknowledge the death. Thus in the early days following the death there is a progressive intrusion of the reality of the "absence" of the dead person which leads to a lessening of denial.

Certain factors consolidate reality. If the bereaved has been present at the death, the body and physical changes in the dead person will bring an image, a reality of his altered state. The coldness, the lack of movement and breathing, the absence of facial response, all reinforce the departure of life or spirit from the dead person. This departure of life is a powerful farewell. When the bereaved has not been present at the death, seeing the dead person (identifying the body, or seeing it to say good-bye) may be the turning point at which reality breaks through, or a point to which the bereaved can return in memory to be reminded of the reality that *is* death. All evidence suggests that seeing the body of the dead person is an important part of the adjustment process: it provides an opportunity to see and become familiar with the realities of death; it is an opportunity to see and touch, for the last tenderness, for the last good-bye; perhaps hold the dearly loved one for the last time. Unfortunately many medical and legal systems, as well as well-meaning others may intrude to prevent this from happening or may limit it, thus frustrating its adaptive function for the bereaved. In many instances the bereaved may only be allowed to view the body through a screen, or not be allowed to touch it, or, very often, not be allowed to hold it. There may be no opportunity for a private time with the dead person—a time for reminiscence and regret, sadness and farewell. The experience of seeing and saying good-bye to the dead person as a dead person makes it possible for the bereaved to develop an image of the person as dead, different and altered from the living image. This image may then be held alongside the living image in the processes of separation and mourning.

Seeing the dead person also facilitates a testing out of death related fantasies. Many bereaved in Western society have never previously seen a dead person. Fantasies of the facial appearance and state of death may be far more frightening than the realities, especially as they are often linked to more primitive magical thinking styles of childhood. When there has been prolonged illness and suffering leading to the death, the bereaved may feel a greater sense of relief in seeing the peaceful face of the dead person—"It was so good to see him at peace—his whole face had changed; it wasn't drawn and tormented anymore; there was no more pain or suffering." When there have been sudden, accidental, or violent deaths, the bereaved's fantasies of mutilation and destruction of the person are often far worse than the actual damage. The realities of the appearance of the dead person may be discussed with the bereaved beforehand, but the actual appearance may be reassuring. The recognition of the person in death provides a certain sad reality that can then be accepted. The bereaved's fantasies are often stirred by others who have suggested that he will be tormented by memories of mutilation and that he should best remember the dead person the way he was. Yet without seeing the body, the death may be very difficult to accept and resolve. Women and children are most often "protected" from the realities of the death and dead body in this way, and their fantasies afterward are often far more disturbing to them than the face of death itself would have been.

Special difficulties arise when no body is found or when the remains are no longer recognizable as a specific person or even a human, as might occur following very severe burns, major bombing, or aircraft disasters. The bereaved may still need to say good-bye and may need to talk through his or her feelings about what remains of the person and derive images of death that may be linked to these last human remnants in some other way. These issues will be discussed further in chapter 8.

Dread of the dead body, the dead person, appears in most societies and cultures. Special rituals have been evolved to deal with it and to separate it from the living. These rituals may have a medical and scientific framework as in Western society, or a magical, supernatural one, as when the dead body in some primitive cultures is still seen as having more direct power over those still living. The medicalization of death in contemporary Western society seems to have carried this ritualization to extremes. The dying are isolated behind screens, cut off from the living, who are protected from them by clinical systems. The dead are mysteriously whisked away to the mortuary, ice cold, clinical, and impersonal. Most medical institutions provide little opportunity or even a place where the bereaved can be with the dead person in privacy and closeness for last farewells.

## Funeral Rites

The rituals and ceremonies for the disposal of the dead make public the death. The affirmation of its reality, the altered state of the dead person, can no longer be denied. One level of denial is relinquished when the dead person is accepted as dead. A further engagement of reality is required to arrange the funeral and participate in it. Many bereaved people find this is a turning point where the full reality of the death hits directly home. It is a time when the numbness fades and the person seems to come out of the dream to an intensely painful real world. This is not to suggest that earlier the bereaved is out of touch with reality, but rather he is in some way dissociated, isolating the affect involved, holding at the same time a knowledge of the death yet a denial of its affects and implications.

The expected behaviors for the bereaved vary from society to society, culture to culture, yet there are many common elements in the earliest phase of bereavement and in the *rites de passage* of the funeral. The funeral serves a number of functions. Its real function is the disposal of the body. Its symbolic functions are twofold. It functions first to separate the dead person from the living and to allow the living to bid that person a farewell. This separation may be seen as complete, as in Western society, or it may be seen as the first stage of the separation of the dead person's spirit or entity from his family or tribe. It may be seen as an opportunity to experience the presence of the dead person for a further period of time before bidding him a final farewell or before sending him off on his journey to another world or state. Its second function is to provide an opportunity for reestablishment of the social group, for a reinforcement of its life and unity. The social group not only has the opportunity to pay respect to the dead person but also to express its support for the bereaved.

In contemporary Western society the funeral is usually held within a few days of the death. While in the past it was probable that the body would be held in the home for a period of time for the family and others to visit and pay their last respects to the dead, this now occurs much less frequently. The only opportunities for such direct contact may be in the hospital at the time of death, in the funeral parlor, or, if the funeral ceremonies allow, in some form of lying-in state with an open coffin.

The form of the funeral ceremony often involves a presentation about the dead person and whatever religious and cultural observances are prescribed. The behaviors expected of the principal bereaved may be laid down strictly in the prescriptions of the culture or may be quite indefinite. It is usually expected that black or a somber color will be worn. Sanctions for the expression of feeling and grief are most variable. Some cultures expect and demand a very open expression of grief at the loss and would view as shameful a funeral where tears were not shed and emotion was hidden. Many European cultures, such as those of the Greeks and Italians, have quite clear expectations of open and strong emotional release; whereas Anglo-Saxon society may view such public display of feeling as unseemly, praising the person who shows strong emotional control. Emotional expression is seen as more acceptable for women, and is indeed expected of them in most societies, where their crying and keening may carry empathic emotional release for others. Nevertheless even this release is denied to women in many societies of Anglo-Saxon origin.

The way in which the body is disposed of may have significance as well. The common practices in Western society include burial and cremation. The ritual of the lowering of the coffin in the ground and the throwing on of the earth seems to convey basic messages of the return of the body to nature and the finality of its departure. It is a concrete statement of death. The body resides in a specific place, the cemetery, the place of the dead. Cremation has a different significance. It is often perceived as "cleaner" and is increasingly popular in many Western societies. It may allow greater denial of the reality of death for some, since the body in its coffin slides away behind a curtain in an "instant" or is lowered out of sight. The ceremony is often very brief. In a moment all is over, perhaps too rapidly for the bereaved to incorporate it. Some funeral professionals prefer this because the bereaved are "less upset." The location of the deceased afterward is less certain. Has he gone up in the smoke from the funeral pyre? Are the ashes that the bereaved is given truly those of the deceased? Even when the ashes are clearly placed in an urn there may be much difficulty in reconciling them with the dead person: "He was such a *big* man, I cannot imagine him in that small box of ashes"; "When I told the children that that plaque was where their father was, I could see they could not understand and that they really found it hard to believe me." Other burial practices of other cultures may all have their own significance. They include air burials, bone burials, and mummification. In all instances these have social and psychological significance for the bereaved that may be very relevant to their adaptation to the loss (Reid 1979).

Thus the funeral brings a public and final statement of the death and separates the dead person from the living. The dead person's life may be reviewed in the ceremonies of the loss, often in an idealistic eulogy which may be difficult to reconcile with the real personality of the deceased. The bereaved may express their grief, as may others who are affected by the loss, both personally and in a societal context. And the bereaved is offered publicly the support of those who have attended, although just how much this support may be forthcoming later will depend on individual and culture.

After the funeral ceremony the bereaved returns home. In many cultures, including Western, there is a meeting together of family and friends with a wake or sharing of food and drink. This provides a further statement of support and opportunity to offer more personal condolences to the bereaved. It is also an opportunity to share thoughts, memories, and feelings about the dead person, to speak of his life and his death. The degree to which the culture or society expects and encourages such a sharing of experiences about the dead person will vary enormously. The Irish wake represents a very specific example of this however, where, with the facilitating influences of alcohol and shared emotion, much of the past experience with the deceased, both the good and the bad, may be shared by others, setting in motion early the vital aspects of the psychological mourning process. Other cultures may have extended provision for condolences to the bereaved, usually involving discussion of the deceased, as occurs with the Jewish mourning ceremony of "sitting shivah" during the first seven days following the funeral. Some cultures have special provisions for others to visit on the specific days following the ceremony. Regardless of social practice, when the deceased is buried, or his body disposed of, the bereaved must return to the empty home, the home that is now without him.

## The Absence of the Loved One: Separation Pain

Although there may be an intellectual awareness of the reality and finality of the death, the bereaved's emotional experience following the funeral ceremony is usually one of separation pain. The absence of the dead person is everywhere palpable. The home and familiar environs seem full of painful reminders. Grief breaks over the bereaved in waves of distress.

There is intense yearning, pining, and longing for the one who has died. The bereaved feels empty inside, as though torn apart or as if the dead person had been torn out of his body. With the yearning and longing there is a most intense preoccupation with the image of the deceased, as if this is held in place of him. The bereaved is alert, aroused, actively (perhaps unconsciously) scanning the environment for any clues of his presence, longing for his return. Waves of somatic distress with sighing respiration, palpitations, a deep inner pain, or often a choking feeling come over the bereaved. These are precipitated by any reminder of the deceased, any confirmation of his absence.

In all this longing there is restlessness, agitation, and a high level of psychological arousal. The environment is scanned, and the bereaved also searches, as it were, for the lost object. This may involve restless wandering to familiar places. Sleep is usually very disturbed. There is an expectant set looking for the return of the absent person. Perceptual cues may all be sorted through looking for reinforcement of the lost one's presence. Thus the bereaved may believe he hears the return at a familiar time, sees the face in a familiar place, feels the touch of a body, smells a familiar perfume, or hears a familiar sound. These perceptual misinterpretations reflect the intense longing and, like dreams, are a source of a wish fulfillment. They may be experienced as hallucinatory experiences and, as such, although comforting, may also be quite disturbing to the bereaved in their implications.

In all the bereaved's preoccupation with the absent person, there is a longing for the familiar interactions with him, the interactions that would have occurred in his presence. Each time the bereaved holds the image of the deceased and looks for the familiar interactions to turn it to reality, and this does not occur, the reality and the finality of the loss are reinforced. Thus this yearning, longing, and pining for the lost person are part of the adaptation to the loss, part of the reality testing that must slowly and painfully occur as his absence continues.

The pain and emptiness the bereaved feels is associated with anxiety and helplessness. These affects are powerful and in themselves frightening for they reawaken the earliest preverbal memories of painful separation experiences in the first year of life, the times of earliest separation anxiety. The bereaved may feel that survival is impossible without the deceased, and that the pain is too great to be tolerated. Thus there will be mitigating behaviors to shut out, at least temporarily, the acute pain of being separate from the loved one. Some mitigation may occur with repression operating to cut out the traumatically intrusive reminders of the loss, the pangs of grief (Parkes 1972b; Horowitz 1976), or there may be active endeavors on the part of the bereaved to cultivate a sense of the presence of the deceased. These behaviors are usually only temporarily successful, so that reality must be confronted once more and eventually the finality of the loss accepted. If pining and yearning are totally repressed then pathological mourning may be more likely (Bowlby 1963).

It is this separation pain for which the bereaved seeks the comfort and consolation of others. Yet they can offer no real consolation, for all that the bereaved wishes for is the return of the dead person. The only way the pain can be stilled is to have him back, something that the bereaved at one level still covertly hopes for, although at another level he fully acknowledges the futility of such a wish. When others attempt to comfort they may feel pushed away, for the bereaved wants only the dead person, and the fact that he does not come to comfort, to make things right, is a further hateful reminder that he has gone. It is, during this time, as though all of the bereaved's relating capacities are focused on the dead person, wishing as it were to draw him back, hold him, from the finality of death. All other relationships, even those that are very close and meaningful, seem to fade in comparison beside this intense focus and longing. Thus others may feel cut off by the bereaved, rejected and unwanted when the one who has gone is wanted so much.

That the bereaved is still oriented to the lost loved one and the possibility of his return is evidenced in many ways. Activities and behaviors that related to him may continue, such as the rituals of family life that were geared to his presence. He is spoken of in the present tense—"He is" not "He was"—implying his ongoing existence. His possessions may be held and treasured, awaiting his return, unless others have mistakenly taken them away to "protect" the bereaved from the pain of longing they evoke. If the bereaved can sleep, dreams may show the lost person alive, well, or returning from a holiday. The bereaved may dread awakening for the cold reality morning brings. The bereaved does indeed know intellectually, cognitively, that the lost one will not return; yet the whole assumptive world (Parkes 1972b; Woodfield and Viney 1982) is still oriented toward him and has not yet realigned to a new set of configurations and assumptions.

The affective responses of this period are intense. They comprise the intense pining and longing of grief which comes in pangs and waves; the panic, anxiety, and helplessness that are evoked when the yearning for the lost one is not requited; and the angry protests of desertion that are experienced with his absence and his failure to return and make right this loss. Bowlby (1973) sees these affects as the primary affects of separation. Anxiety and helplessness are very powerful and frightening to the bereaved. This may especially be so if traumatic or shocking circumstances of the death have already led to a helpless and overwhelmed state. These affects may be assuaged to some degree by the comforting behaviors and presence of others and also as the bereaved gradually regains control of the world and recognizes with the passage of time that, after all, he will survive.

Anger and aggression are common. The bereaved feels deserted by the deceased whose absence causes this pain. Reverberations of separation protest from infancy occur. There is anger toward the deceased, which the bereaved may or may not recognize or express. This is the essential protest at desertion. Such anger may be quite overwhelming for the bereaved who find it far more intense than everyday experience and may perceive it as irrational. It may be displaced onto those who are in some way connected with the death, who did not prevent it, or who are there in the place of the deceased. It is often displaced onto other family members, doctors, hospital staff, and God, all of whom may be seen as in some way directly or indirectly associated with what has happened. But the inner cry of the bereaved, the inner experience, is of the desertion: "Why have you left me, deserted me; how could you go when I need you so much; why won't you return?"

Anger may be heightened by circumstances of the relationship or the death. Where the bereaved was very dependent on the deceased, the sense of desertion may be great, especially if this dependence had real or symbolic aspects of infantile relationships with the mother. When there has been sudden death with little warning, anger may also be heightened by the helplessness and shock. When the deceased in some ways contributed to the desertion, for instance by ignoring health advice, the anger may be greater. With suicide, where the deceased has *chosen* to desert, anger (as well as guilt) is pronounced. Medical negligence, real or imagined, may lead to anger being focused on doctors or hospitals, and this is also likely where such personnel have related to the bereaved in an insensitive manner. Rosenblatt, Jackson, and Walsh (1972) have examined the methods of coping with anger and aggression during bereavement. They found these affects in most cultures, and found that many of these had formalized ways of recognizing and expressing such affects. They showed (Rosenblatt, Walsh, and Jackson 1976) that with women, anger was often self-directed, perhaps revealed in tearing the hair or rending their clothes, but in men it was often directed toward others. Anger may lead to action against the self or others, with further consequences for the bereaved.

With the passage of time the bereaved holds with intense longing to the image of the dead loved one who does not return. There are no interactions in reality to reinforce and continue the relationship. Each time the image is cathected yet not met by the wished for interaction, the finality of the absence and death is reinforced. These increments of reality testing accumulate as time progresses and are reinforced by the futility of interactions that were geared to the deceased. The image of the person as dead is a further reinforcement of the finality of his altered state: that he cannot and will not return. Thus recognition is initially resisted but must be confronted, unless the bereaved becomes locked into a pathological state of chronic yearning and longing. The more the bereaved fears life without the deceased, the more he may cling to the hope of return. Yet this must eventually prove futile. Where the body has not been found, or death confirmed, or even if the body was not seen, the acceptance of nonreturn may be more difficult. Where the dead person had previously been absent for significant periods, yet always returned, the bereaved may find it difficult to accept the finality of this separation until a period greater than the longest previous separation has passed. Where others collude to avoid the reality and finality of the loss, it may also be difficult for the bereaved to move to the stage of accepting that the loved one will never again return. All these and other factors make the duration of the experience of pain over the separation and absence very variable. Furthermore the bereaved may seem to accept the finality of the loss, yet later move back to a covert expectancy that the dead can return, that life can be as it was. Eventually, however, for most people there comes a time when the dead one is no longer expected back. It may come with a particular occasion or gradually, but from then on the bereaved's response will be predominantly one of acceptance and of gradually relinquishing the bonds of the relationship, finally accepting the person as lost.

## The Psychological Mourning Process

When the finality of the loss is accepted, then the work of undoing the bonds that built the relationship commences. This work, the psychological mourning process, may be seen as a reversing or undoing of the various processes that have gone into building the relationship. All the "bits" of interaction, all the many layers that were internalized into the complex multidimensional image of the loved one are now reviewed. The emotional components that made it valuable or painful are slowly sorted through. As Freud (1917) suggests, each single one of the memories that bound the bereaved to the deceased is brought up and then painfully relinquished. It is, perhaps the reverse of love (Bak 1973).

The bereaved's preoccupation with the deceased's image is no longer external, expecting and hoping for interaction with him, but internal, whereby the interactions of the past are reviewed and the emotion they carry relived. There is a very intense reexperiencing of much of the past development of the relationship, back to its earliest times. The memories may be experienced vividly, appearing, some suggest, as a moving picture before the eyes. The feelings they bring may be sadness and regret, anger and futility, guilt and relief. Pleasurable reminiscence may be followed by bitter frustration over what was lost, what was wasted, what can now never be achieved. This process of review is both private and public. The bereaved may be very driven to share memories and feelings with others, to talk of the deceased, to go over repeatedly aspects of the lost relationship, to put these memories outside, to look at them with others, to make meaning of them, to take them in again, to set them aside. In the earliest phases of his review the image and memories are often idealized, the deceased and the relationship remembered in perfection. Then, if mourning is progressing satisfactorily, more of the real memories, the positive and negative aspects representing ambivalences inevitable in human relationships are recalled. The good and the bad, the happy and the sad, of both the person and the relationship are gone through bit by bit, and these ambivalent bonds are gradually undone. If ambivalence has been pronounced and the relationship one where the bereaved nursed hating fantasies, even death wishes for the deceased, then the acceptance and working through of the more negative aspects of the relationship may be very difficult, for they may be seen, magically, as causative of the death. In such instances the bereaved may avoid the ambivalence by excessive idealization of the dead person or, alternatively, may suffer great guilt

44

which can link to the development of depression, as Freud suggests in *Mourning and Melancholia* (1917). However, with the supportive understanding of these issues by others in his family or social network, he may be able to review the positive and negative aspects, accept the ambivalence, and avoid depression (Raphael 1978*a*). For most, the loving aspects of the relationship predominate, and the review leads to sad and loving memories of the person who has gone, with only occasional negative aspects and minimal guilt.

The affects associated with the review and undoing processes will vary over time, but sadness will predominate. The bereaved is sad for what can no longer be, for the interactions of love and pleasure, anger and frustration, that can never again take place. There is sadness as the many bits of past memories are brought up, looked at, and set aside. Depressed feelings over all that has been lost are also common, over both the real and symbolic aspects of the relationship and the gratifications it provided including that of dependency. There is often a semantic confusion: many bereaved people identify their sadness as "depression," for the word "sad" seems infrequently used and little recognized in the language of much contemporary Western society. Sad or depressed feelings when labeled "depression" may lead a person to receive treatment for an illness, depression, when he may actually be experiencing only the sadness that accompanies the normal bereavement process.

Regret over what has been lost, what cannot be achieved now without the dead person, resentment for the things that were futile in the past or now seem futile in the future, are also common emotions. Anger may continue: anger at the dead person for the loneliness, the futility of the loss; anger at the self for not making the most of what one had, for not caring or loving better, or for not using the time of life that was shared to better ends. Guilt is frequent: it relates to the imperfection of human relationships. During the reviewing process of mourning, one may recall the love that was not given, the care that was not provided—the "sins" of omission. Or, one may remember the hatred he felt for the dead person, the resentment, the violence that was fantasized—the "sins" of commission. Where the relationship was basically loving, such guilt is transient; where ambivalence was high, it creates greater stress in the working through process. Relief may also be felt—relief that the illness is over, that the painful relationship is finished, that one did not die oneself—and this may be accepted or become a further cause of guilt. Despair is common, despair at what is lost and at the emptiness of the world.

Behaviorally, the bereaved is distressed, preoccupied with thinking and talking of the lost person. Crying is frequent. It seems to serve important cathartic functions and to bring a sense of relief. The person who cannot cry may feel his grief is locked inside. Sometimes the bereaved may feel that crying will never stop. Women cry more freely than men in Western society, so their distress may be overt, recognized by others, and their grief comforted. The man's loss may be borne silently by him, his sadness and tears private or contained. The bereaved usually needs to talk constantly of the lost person and the many memories of that person. He now speaks more frequently of the dead person in the past tense, although the bereaved's acceptance of this is by no means total, and he may readily slip back to the present tense again. The possessions of the dead person are gradually sorted through, like the memories. Some may be retained and treasured, others given away, as the bonds are gradually undone. Some may be held symbolically, as it were, in place of the person, or as objects linking to him (Volkan 1970). Formal duties acknowledging the death, such as letters of thanks to those who offered condolences, may now be carried out. While tears still come at the mention of the dead person, he is talked about more easily and gradually with less pain. Dreams may show the person as ill, indistinct, going away, or even dead, indicating the process of relinquishing the bond to him. Yet in a dream he may also be called back alive and joyful as he was, as though this had never happened, only to fade and become distant in later dreams.

In the earliest stage of the psychological mourning process, the bereaved's whole external world seems to be one of disorganization. It may be all that he can do to continue the basic tasks of survival. All the behaviors, the interactions that were oriented toward the deceased, are now seen as pointless, and the world that was organized around him collapses. The bereaved may rely on others to initiate actions, to help him form a coherent framework or pattern of daily activity, or the needs of others such as young children may compel him to do this himself. The bereaved's inner preoccupations also interfere with his functioning in this outer world. Gradually, however, this world becomes reintegrated. As mourning progresses, the bonds are undone, the emotions freed for reinvestment in life once more.

This psychological mourning process progresses rapidly at first, especially in the early weeks and months of the crisis period of the bereavement. After about six weeks to two months following the death, it starts to subside in many bereaved people. There is still sadness, still often an urgent need to talk of the deceased, still an ongoing review and undoing of bonds, but it is not so total. Sometimes the bereaved feels happy again, sometimes he forgets the dead person for a moment, sometimes he finds himself involved and interested in something new. The process of recovery has commenced. All through the first year following a major personal loss, mourning will continue. Each time something is done for the first time that would have been shared with the other, the bereaved mourns a little more. Birthdays, anniversaries, special holidays may painfully reawaken the full extent of the loss, bringing fresh waves of grief and mourning. The first anniversary of the death does this most powerfully, perhaps even the second. But by the end of the first year the bereaved's survival is clear. Life is going on and will continue to do so, without the loved one. There is no fixed end point of mourning during the first or even second year, but much of the work of relinquishing the bonds is accomplished in the early months and continues gradually, in steps and phases, over the first year. There are many end points, complex amalgams of feelings and memory, that now constitute the bereaved's perception and experience of the loved one as part of a life that is past. This image may still be influential in feeling and behavior, but it is not growing and active, for it is no longer nourished by the reality of human interaction.

The process of mourning may be facilitated or inhibited by factors relating to the bereaved himself, his relationship with the deceased, or his social environment. The bereaved may fear the review or be unable to tolerate its pain because of ego vulnerability or other concurrent stresses that deplete his ego resources. His ego may be vulnerable from developmental impairments or from specific earlier, infantile or child-hood, deprivations or losses. His ego may fear the affects such a review would bring and so defend against it. The relationship itself may have been so fraught with ambivalence that this cannot be faced; or the bereaved may have been so dependent that he fears if he relinquishes it with the mourning process he will not survive, so he holds onto it in blocked or distorted bereavement responses. Pedder (1982) suggests this may be linked to the ambivalence of early internalized object relations.

Perhaps, however, the most powerful influence for the majority of bereaved people will be the influence of the family and social network. If those offering support, consolation, and comfort can do so in such a way that the bereaved can accept and express, as he needs to, his affects of grief, and if they can allow and facilitate his review of the lost relationship in its positive and negative aspects, then he is likely to mourn the loss satisfactorily. He will, with such support, gradually

47

undo the bonds that bound him to the deceased and free them for investment in ongoing life and relationships. Maddison (see particularly Maddison and Walker 1967) in his valuable studies of widows shows how the widow is likely to reach a satisfactory outcome when the social network can facilitate the review, encourage the bereaved widow to talk of the good and bad aspects of the lost person and relationship, and help her express sadness, anger, and guilt. Where the social milieu interferes with the review, tries to orient the widow to the future, and denies her her affects, poor outcome is a likely consequence. Mourning in such cases may be blocked.

Thus the loss is resolved by the individual in his social context through the inner psychological processes of mourning and their facilitation through interaction with others.

Annie is twenty-nine. Her hair is disheveled. Her eyes are red from tears, endless tears. Her face is drawn in despair.

"I thought that I would never survive—that John and I could not live through it all. How could we live when they were dead? When our family was torn apart.

"At first it was some dreadful dream—a nightmare. I felt that I would wake and find it was all a mistake. The news of Pete—the hospital with Melissa—all those tubes in her tiny body and her breath so shallow and her eyes so far away. All the pain I felt for Pete I had to hang on to—I had to go, be there with her—for some faint hope that they might save her, that my love could pull her through. But I could see that wouldn't happen. I could tell from the looks in the nurses' eyes more than anything. The pity when they looked at me and then they looked away. I felt the only way I kept going was to cut off. If I let myself touch it, realize it, it would be the end. I wouldn't be able to go on.

"I wanted to die—oh how I wanted to die—but of course I couldn't: I had to keep going for John. He needed me: you could tell he was frightened; he knew in his own little way how dreadful it was—but it was so hard, so hard to tell him. He was only four: such a little boy to bear so much. So I told him, in a sort of way, and held him close and we cried—that was all we could do.

"There was the funeral—so terrible. I went through that in some sort of dream too, as though that was the only way I could survive, that if I dared, dared for a moment to let myself know, feel what had really happened, my heart would burst, my head would explode.

"It was then, after that—those days, those endless days, those empty nights—that I knew to the core of my being that they were gone. I would wander the house like a mad thing. I would go to the cupboard and pick up Pete's clothes and smell them and hold them and think to myself of his body and my heart would break and ache. I used to feel he was there around, especially at nights—that if I turned my head he'd be there, or that I heard his call, 'Hello Annie, love.' Then, then I would think Melissa, Oh Melissa, can't I grieve for you—you're gone too, my baby, my precious child, and my heart would ache for her. I kept looking for her, thinking I heard her and John chatting as they used to before they went to bed, saying as she always did, 'Mummy I must tell you.' But they weren't there, the house was empty—empty. Just John and me. Sometimes even those weeks after, I would think to myself, 'No it can't be true, God wouldn't do this to me, I haven't been bad, it's a trick, a test. I'll find they're there at home, they'll come back in the car and laugh their way through that door, just as they always did.' And for a while I'd feel better, just a little better, 'til the horror of it all came over me again.

"Oh how I hated the world. I hated that man in the truck. I hated all trucks. I hated God for making them. I hated everyone, even John sometimes because I had to stay alive for him and if he hadn't been there I could have died too: somehow I could have joined them. I longed for Pete so much. I felt so bad, and he always comforted me when things went wrong. He could put his arms about my shoulders and say 'Come on girl, have a cuddle and tell me all about it,' and everything would be right then. I willed him to come back and then I hated him too because he didn't, because he'd deserted me. It sounds crazy I know, but I felt he'd let me down. My mind kept going over the accident too—perhaps he hadn't been careful: how could he have let it happen, let them both be killed?

"Some days the panic would well up inside me. I'd be terrified. How could we exist? How could we keep going? I missed them both so much. I could think of nothing else. There was nothing, nothing left inside me, not even to comfort John anymore. I was empty, drained, and I couldn't keep going. I couldn't go another day. I was exhausted. I would try to shut them out of my mind and what had happened too—but it would come over me again in another frantic wave, and it would rise up in my throat and I'd think, 'I can't breathe—it'll choke me, and I'll die,' and I would wish it would.

"The days went on and on 'til part of me inside said: 'Look you know they're never coming back, never coming back again.' I shut that thought away at first, but I knew it was true, as I'd known all along. That they were never, never going to be with us again, that our family and our life was gone, and if there was to be anything done, John and I would have to stick together, we'd have to get through it and go on.

"All I could feel then was hopeless—and despairing, I guess. I couldn't see how we could make it. I thought so much about them. They were in my mind all the time—all the time we'd been together, all the things we did. I'd remember so much, things I hadn't thought of for years: the night Pete and I met, the fights we had; when Melissa was coming, and I thought she would be Philip; Pete and me; Pete and her; all of us together. It was too dreadful to bear, and I could do nothing but sob. I was so sad, so sad for all we had had and for them gone, gone in such a wasted way, gone forever and without us.

"I was so deep in my thoughts of them I sometimes didn't notice John at all. He'd say to me, 'Mum! Mum! Why don't Dad and Lissa come home?,' and I'd have to tell him again, and his bewildered little face would crumple up and cry. Then I'd be drawn out of my own grief, back to comfort him. Then sometimes we would hold hands and talk about them together, how when Dad did this, John did that, and how naughty Lissa was, and how much fun we had, and then we might even laugh, as though we were all doing it together again. And then we'd stop and hold one another and cry again and again.

"I am so sad. I have lost two parts of myself, of my life, of my whole being. There is a great well of sorrow inside me that will never be dry. Yet somehow, slowly, John and I are going on. We are living and we are going on."

## Anticipatory Bereavements

When there is knowledge beforehand that death is probable, or inevitable in the near future, those who are to be affected may grieve to some degree beforehand. This anticipatory grief and mourning may affect both the dying person and those close to him who will be bereaved. Research has shown that both these groups, the dying and those who will be bereaved by their deaths, may go through a number of processes with phases of denial, angry protest, and sad acceptance. Yet there is some argument as to whether these processes represent actual anticipatory bereavement or are more related to some sort of forewarning of loss, and these are considered by Fulton and Gottesman (1980). They review studies covering the responses of parents of dying children and adults losing a spouse, often widows. A most valuable contribution has also been made by Kübler-Ross's clinical study (1969) of these processes in the classic work *On Death and Dying*. There seems general agreement that the dying person and those anticipating bereavement will have a number of experiences not dissimilar to those of actual bereavement: that whatever stages there are will not be fixed or clear-cut; that the individual may fluctuate backward and forward from one stage to another; that the degree of acceptance of the inevitability of death will come at many levels and will vary greatly from time to time. Even when it is painful, life is cherished.

The first responses to news or awareness of a fatal condition are usually those of shock, numbness, disbelief, and denial. The dying person and those he loves feel stunned. There is a sense of unreality. The blow, the shock, even if suspected beforehand, must be gradually absorbed. The way in which the person is told may make a difference too. There may be a gentle, supportive, and caring communication by the physician or another person involved; or, there may be an assaultive one, leaving the individual traumatized and distressed by the experience itself as well as by information that was given. The news, however, is gradually faced. The realities of unsuccessful medical treatment, lessening body strength, pain, debility, or obvious disease contribute to the process of acknowledgment. There may be a wish to deny, to seek other diagnoses, other prognoses, which will give a different answer. And even these will contribute to the accumulating reality of the illness.

Distressed feelings can no longer be fended off. There is often then a time of fear, anxiety, even helplessness in the face of the condition and what it will mean. There is much angry protest—"Why me?" "Why my loved one?" There may be resentment toward others who are well, and toward those who have not prevented or cured this condition, and toward the self. The person is often irritable and resentful at this time; family members may be stressed and angry as well. It is a period when the support each desperately needs from the other may be alienated as each struggles to avoid facing the disease, but more particularly its fatal implications.

Denial may reappear or recur for periods. Kübler-Ross (1969) speaks of a time of bargaining where there may be fantasies that the prognosis can be magically changed by certain behaviors. Family members may all differ in their rates and degree of acceptance of the reality and nearness of death, and this can lead to difficulties of communication that further alienate support for one another at a time when it is greatly needed. There may be a "conspiracy of silence" to "protect" some family members from knowledge of the condition, or perhaps because magical thinking dictates that if the condition is not discussed it is not there or may go away.

Generally, it may be said, there is a struggle to come to terms with the condition and the prognosis. The prognosis must, because of the progress of time and the changes in body and person, be increasingly accepted. Nevertheless, hope is a very powerful element. It fuels the struggle against the knowledge of the disease, and it may also fuel a battle against the illness itself. Hope may have its origins in personal resources or may for some be linked to strong religious faith. It is the source of positive feeling for the dying person and his family that may help carry them through the painful process of facing his loss.

As the loss is acknowledged, processes of anticipatory grief and mourning may become pronounced. The dying person's grief is likely to be great (Aldrich 1963) for he grieves and mourns for the future he loses and each single one of the meaningful bonds he must relinquish. And he grieves most particularly for his primary attachment bonds. He experiences sadness and sorrow as each one of his memories is brought up and set aside, as bit by bit he undoes these bonds. There may be anger, regret, resentment, a sense of failure, a sense of being cheated of the promise of his future, especially for the younger person. There may be some feelings of relief that the battle of life will not have to continue much longer. Old guilts may be fueled, heightened, and relinquished. Depression may overwhelm with the multiplicity of losses, the ambivalences that cannot be worked through. The dying person may seem to withdraw from relationships and the world as he relinquishes them and prepares for death. His acceptance of death is very variable however. Some may reach the calm and full acceptance of the very old as did some of the patients Kübler-Ross describes. For many it may be a resignation to death. Hagglund (1981) describes the final stage of the dying process as involving a split of the mental self from the body self in the mind of the dying person. He successfully mourns and gives up his failing body and merges into a fantasy which becomes highly cathected. This fantasy world may involve an afterlife and reunion with loved ones who have died before. Or it may, as Hagglund suggests, be the fulfillment of symbiotic fantasies of closeness and care, such as have been experienced by him in the caring process of his terminal illness.

The dying person may review his life in the way the older person does in his final years (see chapter 7), but in a way that is foreshortened. Emotionally it will be a more intense and a more active mourning process. He may set his affairs in order, sort out old resentments, give and ask forgiveness, and say his good-byes (Meares 1981). His experience in all these aspects is likely, of course, to be influenced not only by his own psycholgical makeup, but also by the nature of the disease and dying process (see chapter 1) and by the quality of his attachments and relationships.

For the family members facing his death there is one major loss to be mourned—the loss of him. Many new conflicts may arise and old ones become reawakened (Maddison and Raphael 1970). At the same time the family must cathect him intensely, care for him, and maintain love and hope. The act of relinquishing the bond in mourning, while at the same time maintaining intense and often loving intimate care is extremely difficult. Sometimes a level of decathexis of the bond may be obtained with the grieving family members maintaining the caring and loving aspects of the bond in a different way (Richmond and Waisman 1955). Where withdrawal has been carried further, and anticipatory mourning been more extensive, then the bereaved may have difficulties maintaining their involvement. On the other hand there may be for some a greater intimacy, a heightened attachment in the terminal phase that allow little mourning, although the realities of the death are fully recognized. Those who grieve in this anticipatory way may have the full gambit of emotions: sadness, anger, fear, distress, guilt, sorrow, despair, depression, and relief. When the death does occur then the reality is confirmed, and further grief and mourning are set in train. The bereavement that follows may, in some cases, be little different from that following sudden losses, or, in others, it may be modified because of the opportunity to prepare beforehand, grieve a little ahead. Sometimes the bereavement is more complex, more intense, because the terminal illness and relationship cannot be easily mourned (Fulton and Gottesman 1980).

The role of faith in the bereavement response is very valuable. It may give the bereaved hope, inner resources, and a supportive social group to help him through the pain of sudden or anticipated losses; or it may drive him to guilt and despair. The bereaved may feel comforted or deserted by his god. Strong religious belief may seem the only source of survival, a cold comfort for the harsh reality of loss. In each case, the meaning and value of religious faith must be individually considered.

## Bereavement in the Family

Although bereavement has been considered thus far in terms of the dying or deceased and the bereaved, it occurs for the most part in the context of family life. The family may be considered a system and may be examined in terms of general systems theory (see, for example, Walrond-Skinner 1977). As a system, it is distinguished by its wholeness, by the relation of each subsystem to the whole system, and by its interrelationships with the broader systems of its community and society and culture. Communication is important, for this provides the mechanism whereby the components of the system interact. Communications may, through dysfunction, become blocked, distorted, or damaged. There is a tendency, however, in family theory to concentrate on the ecology of the system, on its here-and-now functioning and patterns, rather than on genesis and causality. Homeostasis concepts suggest there are also certain regularizing elements in the family system that protect its stability or facilitate its growth, but which may become dysfunctional.

The family unit may have a myth or number of myths that are powerful in dictating its functioning. These enable family members and outsiders to avoid certain themes (perhaps, in this instance, unresolved loss). The multiple interlocking role assignments in the family may be determined by such myths that involve a systematic interlocking of intrapsychic and interpersonal dynamic forces. And the psychodynamics of family members are likely to be interlocking and overdetermined in meeting needs of members to form a collusive system. This system may be primarily functional or dysfunctional.

Bereavement will affect the family system in many ways. The death of a member means the system is irrevocably changed. Interlocking roles, relationships, interactions, communications, and psychopathology and needs can no longer be fulfilled in the same way as before the death. The family unit as it was before dies, and a new family system must be constituted. The death will be a crisis for the family unit as well as for each individual member and each component subsystem. The family view of itself, the family myth, may be impossible to maintain, and all that it avoided may have to be confronted. The threat to the integrity of the family unit may come not only through the change that loss of a family member brings, but also because that member may have occupied a key role in maintaining the system, or perhaps in regulating it in a crisis. Others may be unable to take over his roles and responsibilities. While the threat to its integrity may make family boundaries close over, individual members and the system itself may, in contradiction, desperately need the support and care of other systems.

In terminal illness prior to the death there may be a focusing and reallocation of roles directed toward caring for the ill person. Systems of power and balance may change in terms of the sick role and the caring roles of different individuals. Following the death, others will be the ones in need of care. There may be a competition for the role of being the one cared for, or for being the one who is the chief bereaved. Each member may feel the need for care and the need to grieve and mourn, but the system of power balances in the family may only allow certain members such a position and outlet. Thus only the mother may be allowed to grieve the death of the child, and the father may be expected to be the strong supportive caring person. Often the children will not be seen as having a role involving grief and mourning because of their ages, or they may be "protected" from the death and grief by adults. The family myth may involve a need to believe that children cannot grieve, so as to protect one of the parents from having his own unresolved childhood separation pain and loss reawakened. There may be a myth that intense emotions such as grief will destroy the family, and so grief may be denied to family members.

The death threatens the family unit as well as each individual member. To survive as an altered but related and functional family system it would seem that several factors are important. Flexibility of role function is very significant in both the short- and long-term adjustment to the loss. Where roles relinquished by the deceased can be taken over, shared, changed as appropriate, then adjustment may be easier. Vollman and his coworkers (1971) show this in their studies of the responses of family systems to sudden unexpected deaths. Certain roles may more readily be taken over than others. For instance it may be relatively easy in some cultures for the woman to take over the instrumental role of leader and breadwinner than for the man to continue this role and also assume the emotional leadership of the family. Dysfunctional families may need to have a scapegoat, and in such instances, if the usual occupant of this role should die, the family may reallocate it to another perhaps already guilty member who accepts it because of his own interlocking pathology or need. Flexibility of roles and boundaries may also allow members of the extended family system to come in and meet needs in the time of crisis and thus maintain the family unit.

Openness of communication between members also seems to facilitate adjustment. Not only does it allow the sharing of information so essential at the time of illness and death, but it enables members to share their feelings with one another, to grieve together, and eventually to review and mourn the lost relationship. This openness is often difficult to achieve at the time of loss, for each fears setting off the other's grief. The family unit as a whole may fear the intense emotions, especially the anger and acute distress which may be perceived as disintegrative to family stability. Nevertheless, unless there is some opportunity for mutual comfort and consolation, aspects of the loss will become blocked, resolution will be incomplete, and the pathology that remains may influence family functioning adversely, even over succeeding generations (Paul and Grosser 1965).

In general terms the children are most likely to be influenced by the power systems of the surviving family members, by the role allocations and absences, and by the communication patterns and interactions that develop subsequently. They desperately need, for reassurance of survival, the stability of their ongoing life in the family. Should it become chaotic or disrupted, then their ultimate adjustment to the loss is in great jeopardy. Should they be "protected" from the grief of parents or kept from knowledge of what has happened, or should their own needs for care and mourning not be recognized because of parental bereavement and conflict, then the family system may well prove dysfunctional for them. Unresolved loss may determine patterns of relationships in the future, by dictating that some relationships (especially those with children) become replacements for those that have been lost. It may also mean that future relationships are geared to avoid or deny the possibilities of loss and death and are distorted as a consequence.

In some families difficulties arise when one member grieves in a different manner from another. For example, one may be unable to face the feelings about the death, while another may have moved on to active mourning. Much family distress may occur because of factors such as these, and lasting barriers may be created. Other families may, of course, grieve and mourn as a whole system. This functional unit will be a powerful reinforcement for individual members and may be a statement of the ongoing life of the family to the other systems with which it interlocks.

There is limited consideration of the family system response to bereavement in the psychiatric literature of loss, although some earlier sociological papers look at grief and mourning from this point of view (Eliot 1930, 1932). Lily Pincus (1974) presents a series of excellent clinical descriptions in her book *Death and the Family*, but there have been few other formal considerations of the subject since then. Most workers (for example, Parkes 1972*b*) give emphasis to the general importance of family factors in bereavement and suggest the need for support of the whole family during this time. The influence of cultural factors operating through the family and its role functioning has been highlighted by Ablon's studies (1973) of Samoan families after the deaths of family members from severe burns. She showed that the extended family's emotional support, practical assistance, and expectations helped the bereaved readjust quickly and well to the loss. Religious faith was also seen to contribute as was the ethos of commitment and hard work. The writer comments on the extraordinary emotional, social, and financial support provided to the family by its extended kinship system.

It is clear that bereavement will be a crisis for a family, and that if it can handle its loss with feeling and openness, flexibility, strength, and mutual support amongst its members, and support from others, it is likely to rebuild a powerful and unified system to face its new future.

## Longer-Term Adjustments

The longer-term adjustments to the loss involve many processes. The bereaved person may need to grieve, and mourn, and finally relinquish old roles, patterns of interaction, and sources of gratification that were once fulfilled by the person who has died. Only when these are relinquished may new and satisfying roles, interactions, and sources of gratification evolve. The social system of the bereaved may have rituals or prescriptions which facilitate such evolution, or it may be quite indefinite in its expectations and guidelines. Some cultures may have rituals and ceremonies that facilitate transition, while others, such as many Western cultures, may leave the bereaved uncertain and perhaps stressed because of this.

The bereaved person may have an altered status in society, and this may require adjustive tasks on his part. Often the status is less favorable than the one he held before the death, perhaps involving stigma or discrimination, as in the status of widow or orphan. Status may also be influenced by financial and property settlements after the death. Sometimes the change in status may be seen as favorable as when a woman gains the status of wealthy widow after she loses the status of poor wife. Many of the status transitions are negative, however.

Identity is one of the factors most powerfully affected by the death of someone close. The identity of the bereaved may have been defined by mutual roles, by the satisfaction of mutually gratifying interactions, or by the reinforcement of competence. The definition of self may rely strongly on the other, so that when he is lost, the self must find a new identity without him. This may be an immensely painful and difficult process for some, although, when it is satisfactorily worked through, the new identity may be more stable and secure and linked to the core aspects of the self.

The time taken for the longer term adaptations will vary enormously. In some instances the culture will set clear guidelines for these tasks to be finished and reintegration to occur—perhaps a year or two, or five, or ten, or never. The period of readjustment may be seen as a period of ongoing mourning. The pain and deficit of this time may be seen as a tribute paid to the dead person, a price, a sacrifice, so that in primitive terms his spirit is appeased, and the bereaved then has the right to be free of him. The period of pain and sacrifice is seen to have balanced the life that was shared. The bereaved has then suffered enough for the dead, atoned for his own survival when the other died, and thus earned his freedom from the dead person and his right to return to an enjoyment of life. The process may be clearly spelled out in some cultures by prescribed clothes and behaviors, such as the wearing of black and the avoiding of social occasions, whereas in other cultures the requirement may also be specific but covert. The process may thus influence the pattern and duration of mourning and the reintegration to new attachments and life.

It is interesting to note that there is sometimes an upsurge of distress, or even a peak of morbidity, about nine months after the death. This may, perhaps, be linked to deep inner fantasies that something left behind, some bit of the dead person, will be reborn again then. And when it is not, and his "death" continues, then fresh pain is once more experienced. Other peaks of renewed mourning, other tasks of longer term adjustment are often related to a special occasion: festivals without the deceased, where new roles must be accepted, or anniversaries of the relationship or death which reiterate that the dead person is of the past and that time must heal.

Annie is thirty. Her hair is softly curled. Her dark eyes are quiet and sad.

"Well, John and I are managing. We are just managing. I thought we never would. In those early months it was so hard for him. I was so wrapped up in my own grief, in my own feelings, that I hardly noticed him at all some days. Then one day I looked at him, and I was shocked. He was quiet and thin and withdrawn—not himself at all. That pulled me out of things, it really did. He'd needed me, and somehow I'd been away from him—elsewhere, I suppose. It was as though I was expecting him to look after himself, maybe even to look after me. I know I used to say to him, 'Hold Mummy, John, hold Mummy, that'll make you feel better,' but perhaps it was just for me.

"So I put my sorrow aside for a while. I wasn't over it by any means, and I made John my life, my whole life. I cuddled him and loved him. I spent my days with him. And he started to respond. He came back, slowly at first, but he came back to his old cheerful self. It all gave me a terrible shock, really, as though I'd let him go and I'd lose him too.

"We started to pick up the reins again then and think about what we would do with our lives. We could manage on Pete's insurance, but not with the standard of living we'd had before. I thought of going back to teaching. John could go to kindergarten; he'd like that with some friends. It would take his mind off Lissa. Then I thought, it was so long since I had taught, what if I wasn't any good any more? There would be so much to catch up to, so much to learn again—I didn't know if I could do it.

"It was like so many things in life—I'd been Pete's wife and Melissa's mother, and John's too, of course. I felt as though I'd been those things forever, and now I wasn't them anymore—so who was I? I was Annie, alright. But Annie had been different: she was the popular girl at school, the smart young schoolteacher—but not the woman. The woman had been with Pete and with Melissa. And this Annie woman without them, well, I didn't know her at all; I wasn't sure who *she* was. There were so many ways in which I felt strange, different, not myself. Being a single mother, just one child, no husband, no daughter. Filling out forms brought that home: all the spaces and headings and explanations and red tape that I'd never noticed before. My old friends, too— they changed as well. They were uncomfortable, just uncomfortable about me now—a woman without a husband. Some of them stopped asking me over, as if they were afraid of what a woman without a husband meant. Maybe they thought I'd take theirs. Some would ask me over and ask a conspicuous extra man: 'What do you do about that?' I would ask myself. Should I start to be interested again, even if I didn't feel like it. Anyway, how can you start again on all that old business of seeing if they like you, wondering if you like them, dating, whatever? That's for teenagers, not for women.

"Now the year has come and gone since his death, since Melissa died. We are finding our feet. We go out. I work. You could say I'm doing reasonably well. John and I have our own small quiet world. It's a little family. But we are a family again."

## Resolutions

### MORBID OR PATHOLOGICAL PATTERNS OF GRIEF

Numerous workers have described the disordered variants of the bereavement process. In what could be considered the first such effort, Freud (1917) describes the development of melancholia in place of mourning. Deutsch (1937) describes cases of absence of grief. Lindemann (1944) speaks of delayed reactions and distorted reactions, including among this latter group: overactivity without a sense of loss; the acquisition of symptoms of the last illness of the deceased; the development of recognized medical disease; alterations in relationships with friends and relatives; furious hostility toward specific persons such as doctors; schizophreniform behavior; lasting loss of patterns of social interaction; self-destructive behaviors; and agitated depression. Parkes (1965) describes the bereavement reaction found in psychiatric patients and classes them as stress-specific grief responses and their variants, and nonspecific responses. The stress-specific responses include typical grief, chronic grief, inhibited grief, and delayed grief. The nonspecific and mixed reactions include psychosomatic reactions, psychoneurotic reactions, and affective disorders not resembling grief. Bowlby (1980) suggests that the two main variants are prolonged absence of conscious grieving and chronic mourning, and that all other patterns described can be seen as some variant of these.

The following classification of the pathological bereavement pattern reflects these earlier formulations and the author's experience (Raphael [1975a] with many bereaved people. It does not include illnesses which are considered to represent bereavement decompensations and outcomes.

*Absence, inhibition, or delay of bereavement.* The grieving affects or mourning processes may be totally absent, partially suppressed, or inhibited. It may be that the bereaved stays in the stage of shock or denial, or that some later segment of the process is absent. The pining and yearning for the lost person may be denied, thus leading to pathological mourning, as Bowlby notes (1980). The review of the lost relationship may be avoided because of the pain entailed in relinquishing it. The bereaved may only be able to relinquish and mourn certain aspects of the lost person and not others, such as the positive but not the negative ones. Each of these inhibitions will present a different pattern of pathology and may have different sources. All basically, however, are related to the avoidance of the pain of loss.

*Distorted bereavement.* In distorted bereavement, one aspect of the loss is distorted and another often suppressed. Two common patterns are extreme anger and extreme guilt. In the case of anger, the whole bereavement response seems taken up with intense and furious rage. There is little yearning and pining and no sorrow—protest is all. This form may be most pronounced when the sense of desertion is very great, when the bereaved had intense or even infantile dependence on the deceased. In the case of extreme guilt, the whole bereavement process is obscured by the bereaved's ongoing self-blame, by his continuous and exaggerated guilty ruminations. There is little direct anger, although much hostility. There is no real mourning and sorrow, only guilt.

*Chronic grief.* With chronic grief, the bereavement picture that appeared appropriate in the early stages of loss, the intense grief, is continued unremittingly. There is continued crying, preoccupation with the lost person, angry protest, and the bereaved goes over and over the memories of the lost relationship which is often intensely idealized. Mourning does not draw to its natural conclusion, and it almost seems that the bereaved has taken on a new and special role, that of the grief-stricken one. And, it is as though the lost person lives on in the grief.

Any of these patterns may overlap, for in each there is a denial or repression of aspects of the loss and an attempt to hold onto the lost relationship.

OUTCOMES OF BEREAVEMENT

The outcomes of bereavement may be resolution of the loss, satisfactory adjustment, and a reintegration into life with new and satisfying attachments valued in their own right. Or there may be pathological patterns of resolution or the development of morbidity. Some of the general categories of pathological outcome follow:

*General symptomatology.* General ill health with increased symptomatology is widely reported both in association with bereavement and as a longer term consequence of it. This may be related to the psychophysiological stress effects especially in the earlier stages or to increased care-eliciting behavior leading to increased health care utilization. It may also be a consequence of factors such as symptomatic identification with the deceased's last illness. It may represent a general, nonspecific impairment of health through mechanisms yet to be established.

*Psychosomatic disorder.* Psychosomatic conditions may develop as a consequence of the stress or conflicts induced by the bereavement, operating through neurochemical systems. Immune-cell function change has been noted by Bartrop et al. (1977) and corticosteroid effects by Hofer et al. (1977). Other workers describe a variety of psychosomatic disorders.

*Psychiatric or other psychosocial disorder (apart from depression).* A range of psychiatric conditions including anxiety states, phobias, conversion, and dissociated reactions as well as schizophreniform conditions have been described. Mania has been reported, both acutely and as an anniversary phenomenon (Rickarby 1977). Acting-out disorders have also been described. In these, the conflict or tension generated by the bereavement is acted out in behaviors such as antisocial, delinquent, and criminal activity (for example, stealing or shoplifting); sexual behaviors including promiscuity leading sometimes to pregnancy; dependency disorders such as alcohol or drug dependence; and eating behavior disorders. Suicidal acting out is not uncommon, but it is usually associated with depression.

*Depression.* Both depressive feelings and constellations of depressive symptoms have been described in association with bereavement or subsequent to it. Vulnerability to depression may be increased, or the bereaved may develop major depression or dysthymic disorder. Suicidal thoughts and behavior are sometimes found with depression in the bereaved, as is successful suicide.

*Altered relationship patterns.* Stress or conflict generated or reawakened by the bereavement may appear in relationships following the loss. The loss may also lead to overprotectiveness in relationships, replacement relationships, relationships geared to avoiding the potential for pain of loss, compulsive care-giving relationships, or impairment of interpersonal relationships in general. It may also, of course, lead to improved interpersonal relationships through the resolution of conflict, or to a heightened investment in remaining or new relationships.

*Vulnerability to loss.* A poorly resolved bereavement, for example in childhood, may leave the individual more vulnerable to stress in the face of other future bereavements and, perhaps in some instances, make him more likely to resolve these poorly as well. In contrast, the successful resolution of an earlier bereavement may strengthen the bereaved's capacity to cope with further losses.

*Anniversary phenomena.* The anniversary of a death or other anniversaries associated with it may result in reawakened bereavement or morbidity. Correspondence phenomena (Birtchnell 1981) may also lead to distress or vulnerability when the bereaved reaches the age at which a parent died, or if his child reaches the age he was when a parent died.

*Mortality.* Although the overall outcome of bereavement may be positive, with the bereaved showing an improved ability to cope and adapt and a return to a state of physical and mental health similar to that before the death, bereavement may also be fatal. The bereaved may die as a consequence of the stress or disturbance engendered by the loss either through psychosomatic mechanisms such as death from a "broken heart" (Parkes, Benjamin, and Fitzgerald 1969), or psychogenic mechanisms, such as suicide. The levels of mortality are small but significant. Mortality following bereavement has been clearly documented (Jacobs and Ostfeld 1977), especially in certain groups, and so must be considered among the possible outcomes of loss. The bereaved's fear that he will not survive has some small basis in reality.

FACTORS AFFECTING OUTCOME

Various factors may affect the resolution of loss, increasing or decreasing the probability of pathological bereavement reactions or pathological outcome in terms of increased psychosocial morbidity. A number of different studies have shown the following factors to be important:

*The preexisting relationship between the bereaved and the deceased.* The more ambivalent and/or dependent was the relationship between the bereaved and the deceased, the more complex the mourning and the greater the probability of poor outcome.

*The type of death.* Sudden, unexpected, and untimely deaths are more likely to be associated with difficult outcomes than are anticipated deaths, although death from slow terminal illness may also in some cases lead to difficult outcomes (Fulton and Gottesman 1980). The circumstances of the death itself and comprehension of it may also be important.

*The response of the family and social network.* Where the bereaved perceives his family and social network as nonsupportive in terms of sharing in or allowing for expression of grief and the reviewing of the mourning process, poor outcome may be likely. Chaos in the family and failure of the members to support one another may also be associated with poor outcome.

*Concurrent stress or crises.* Stress or crises, especially other losses occurring during bereavement, may take up ego resources thus creating extra strain and hindering resolution.

*Previous losses.* Previous losses, especially in childhood, may increase the risk of poor resolution, especially if these losses have themselves been poorly resolved.

*Sociodemographic factors.* Age, sex, religion, culture, occupation, and economic position are other factors that may influence outcome.

The role of an individual's personality prior to bereavement as a factor in outcome remains unclear. If it is a variable, then it may operate through other factors such as the patterns of affect expression and release that defensive structure allows, the preexisting relationship with the deceased, and the quality of social support available to the bereaved. Recently Pedder (1982) has suggested that the key issue may relate to the internalization of good objects in the earliest stages of development. If the individual has such internalized objects he may cope well with mourning. The role of genetic factors is also difficult to determine; however, patients with genetic vulnerability, as, for example, manic depressive patients, may have their vulnerability triggered by a bereavement. The earliest processes of morbidity may appear in the pathological pattern of bereavement, and may themselves continue or may indeed lead to other morbid outcomes.

Despite these observations, it is clear that there are some bereaved who do not show grief and who do not progress obviously to pathological outcome, at least in the early years (Singh and Raphael 1981).

The levels of morbid outcome or pathological patterns of grief are known in only a few instances, but they may represent at least one in three bereavements. Preventive intervention may be successful in lessening the likelihood of poor outcome in highly vulnerable subjects (Raphael 1977b); and therapeutic interventions may be successful in altering pathological bereavement patterns to normal responses (Lindemann 1944; Raphael 1975a). Treatment of morbid outcomes with treatment of the bereavement is also likely to be successful in diminishing the prevalence of morbid pathology in the time following the loss. Further research is needed, however, to understand these factors and the processes through which they operate.

EXPLANATORY MODELS OF BEREAVEMENT

It is useful to look at the ways in which the processes of adaptation to loss may be understood. There are a number of conceptual frameworks that can be used to explain the observed behaviors and experiences of bereavement. Some of these models will now be outlined. It is to be noted that the model described above relies heavily on the models of Bowlby and, to a lesser degree, Freud and Melanie Klein.

*Transcultural aspects.* The phenomenon of bereavement is common across the vast majority of cultures. Rosenblatt, Walsh, and Jackson (1976) suggest that it may be basically human for emotions to be expressed by the bereaved and that the emotional responses of people in different cultures may be at least to some degree similar. In their studies of individual grief and mourning in a number of cultures, they found that almost everywhere women cry or keen following a death; that anger and aggression are common; and that fears of the dead body and spirit are present in most cultures.

Detailed descriptions of mourning in other cultures, such as Janice Reid's valuable review (1979) of practices in the Yolngu Aboriginal tribe of Australia, show how such practices may fit within the bereavement processes described in this chapter. In the Yolngu tribe, when a person is seriously ill, the close and distant relatives begin to gather at his bedside days or weeks before his death. The women care for him, and the senior men sing the sacred songs of his clan or his mother's clan to comfort him, to keep his mind alert, and to make sure that he dies in the right sacred song cycle and spirit land. Thus when he dies his spirit will be carried to its proper home and will not linger to haunt the living. Female relatives may weep or keen to match in time and tone the sacred songs of the men and the long, low notes of the didgeridoo, and lament his illness and imminent death.

With the death, there is a dramatic change. The widow and other close kin may fling themselves on the body, screaming and crying, while the others become still and quiet. The women keen and fling themselves down and may scratch themselves with weapons to bring blood to flow. The men restrain the women who then desist. The men are more likely to express the aggression of the group, seeking the sorcerer or cause of the death. The aggression may be expressed in ceremonial display, such as dances, where weapons are brandished and revenge is acted out, or in the speculations, accusations, and plans to avenge his death. The presence of the senior men directing ritual and ceremony may lessen the likelihood of overt aggression, making its expression symbolic instead. There are burial and purification rites aimed at sending away the spirit of the dead one. Several months later, further ceremonies take place to clean the house of the spirit. As Reid concludes, these ceremonies "afford the bereaved 'a time to live' and 'a time to grieve'" (p. 342).

Steele (1977) provides a similar picture for the Maya culture, and many other workers describe grief and mourning in other societies (see, for example, Bowlby 1980, chap. 8). Thus it would seem that such processes are basic to many cultures, and any explanation of them must take this into account. It is worth noting that many of the ceremonies and rituals of other cultures fit better with the emotional needs of the bereaved than do those of modern Western society. They may provide, for instance, direct and acceptable channels for the ritualized expression of anger as well as for the open expression of sadness and crying. Reid (1979) notes from the work of Rosenblatt, Walsh, and Jackson (1976) that many countries have provision for final postburial ceremonies to be held some time after the death, and these seem both to provide an adequate duration for mourning as well as a clear demarcation of its conclusion. Those societies which do have such final postburial ceremonies seldom show prolonged and chronic expressions of grief or disturbance of function, illness, and suicidal behavior following the bereavement.

While the rituals of different cultures and societies do not explain bereavement, they show its universality and also reflect the recognition of some of its basic processes. This is exemplified in the ways in which most societies provide and encourage the public expression of emotion, particularly the sadness, but also in many instances the anger. Many cultures also have a period following the death in which the spirit of the dead person is still seen as being around, and this fits well with the early experience of separation in bereavement, where the bereaved's perceptual set is to the lost person and there is still an emotional expectancy of his existence and possible return (Krupp and Klingfield 1962). Many societies then hold a final postburial ceremony which acknowledges the finality of the loss and sets the bereaved on the course of recovery and preliminary reintegration into society. It is interesting to note that in many Western communities that hold such a ceremony, it takes place about the fortieth day after the death (about six weeks), usually the time at which the bereavement crisis period is drawing to its conclusion and the bereaved shows signs of recovery and reintegration into the world. Many cultures also have a ceremony at the time of the first anniversary of the death, highlighting its significance.

*Psychodynamic aspects.* Psychodynamic explanations of mourning rather than of the whole bereavement process rely heavily on the work of Freud and his classic paper "Mourning and Melancholia" (1917). Freud draws attention to the painful psychological processes involved in relinquishing a love object. He suggests that, in this process, the loss is dealt with through *identification* with the lost object. While at first he considered such identification to occur only in pathological mourning, in later works he saw it as occurring in all object loss. Freud's description of mourning suggests that, when the loved object is lost, reality demands that the libido be withdrawn from the object. This is difficult and painful, for, as Freud notes, a love object is not readily relinquished. Initially the pain may be avoided by denying the reality of the loss, but then it is gradually accepted. The object is hypercathected, and every single one of the memories and situations of expectancy that bound the object to the ego is brought up, hypercathected, and then the tie to it dissolved. Thus the libido is withdrawn gradually, bit by bit, over time. Once the work of mourning is completed the ego becomes free and the libido may be invested in new object relationships. At first Freud distinguished between mourning and melancholia on the basis of ambivalence in the relationship to the lost object in melancholia, and suggested that here the ego identified with the lost object; but in later remarks he acknowledged the ambivalence of all human relationships and its influence on mourning, suggesting that identification is the sole condition under which the ego gives up its objects.

Other psychoanalytic theorists describe similar processes. Thus Abraham (1924) claims that the mourner introjects the lost object to preserve the relationship with it. He also acknowledges that ambivalent feelings occur in normal mourning, but in normal mourning, as opposed to melancholia, the positive feelings far outweigh the negative. Fenichel (1945) summarizes the mourning process as consisting of two acts: "The first is the establishment of an introjection; the second the loosening of the binding to the introjected object" (p. 394). Such processes of internalization have also been commented upon by Loewald (1962, 1973) who suggests that "identifications may be and often are way-stations on the road to internal psychic structure" (1973, p. 16). His view is that aspects of the relationship between the mourner and the lost object are set up within the ego and are a defense against the pain of loss. He sees this as similar to the relinquishment of oedipal objects that leads to the formation of the superego. Thus the outcome of mourning may involve something like a new intake of objects into the superego structure insofar as elements of the lost object are introjected in the form of ego ideals or more punitive aspects. Other analytic workers have also described these processes. Smith (1971) comments on the identifications of depression where the identifications are in the form of unintegrated introjects serving to deny the loss, and the identifications of grief where tentative identifications are a means of mourning. In grief the variousness of the object is experienced. Identifications with the specific aspects of the object tend to be relinquished in the process of mourning or coordinated as enduring identifications.

The different patterns of identification following loss have also been described (Krupp 1965). Thus there may be adaptive internalizations of positive aspects of the personality or interests of the lost person. These may be relatively small components. There may be transient identifications with the symptoms of the person's last illness or death. Where these become entrenched they may represent a pathological mourning process, as may strong or overwhelming identifications with punitive, negative, or powerful aspects of the dead person's character. The central place of identification in mourning has been contested by Bowlby (1980, p. 30) who sees identificatory processes as having a subordinate role, occurring sporadically, and when prominent, as indicative of pathology.

The analytic contributions to the understanding of mourning have been reviewed by Siggins (1966) and more recently Bowlby (1980, chapter 2); Kleinian theory (Klein 1948) may be seen as linking in some ways with Bowlby's in its suggestions of the importance of object loss in infancy. Klein also recognizes that the bereaved may pine for the lost object but sees the pain of mourning as being a result of guilt and paranoid fear, rather than being directly attributable to the pining. She suggests that in normal mourning early psychotic anxieties may be reactivated and that, in mourning, the subject goes through a modified, transitory manic-depressive type state. Losses that are pathogenic are seen to occur in the first year of life in association with loss of the idealized breast, rather than the mother as a whole person; and aggression in association with loss is seen as an expression of the death instinct, and anxiety a result of its projection. Bowlby (1980) is critical of these latter assumptions. However, it must be assumed that something of the Kleinian depressive position is likely to be involved in the resolution of the ambivalence experienced toward the lost object.

As Bowlby (1980) notes, much of the analytic discussion of mourning and bereavement is based on clinical studies and attempts to understand depression rather than normal processes of response to loss. Hence some of these may be difficult to generalize to normal bereavement.

*Attachment Theory.* The view of loss from the position of attachment theory was principally developed by John Bowlby (1980, chapter 3). Bowlby states that during the course of healthy development, attachment behavior leads to the development of affectional bonds or attachments, at first between child and parent and later between adult and adult. This attachment behavior is instinctive and mediated through homeostatic behavioral systems. The bond formed by attachment behavior endures of itself, and the attachment behavioral systems are activated by conditions such as strangeness, fatigue, separation from or unresponsivity of the attachment figure. When aroused, such behavioral systems may only be terminated by familiar surroundings and the availability and responsiveness of the attachment figure. When this behavior is strongly aroused, Bowlby (1977) suggests that "termination may require touching, or clinging, or actively reassuring behavior by the attachment figure" (p. 203). Bowlby goes on to state that many of the most intense emotions arise in "the formation, the maintenance, the disruption and the renewal of attachment relationships" (p. 203). He sees "falling in love" as the emotion of forming bonds, loving as the emotion of maintaining them, and grief as the emotion of losing them. Threat of loss leads to anxiety and anger, actual loss to anger and sorrow. When the attachment bond is endangered by separation, powerful attachment behaviors such as clinging, crying, and angry coercion and protest are activated, and there is acute physiological stress and emotional distress. If the protest and behavior are successful in reestablishing the bond, then they cease, and the states of stress and distress disappear. When the effort to restore the bond fails, then behaviors may fade, only to return when cues activate them, such as reminders of the lost person or unmet needs. The behavior remains, Bowlby suggests, "constantly primed" and may become reactivated. This leads to chronic stress and distress. Eventually these behaviors become extinguished, and new attachment bonds are formed, or it may be that in some instances the relationship persists in altered form in fantasy (Bowlby, p. 98), and this for some may be the preferred solution. In others it may be that the chronic stress or distress persists, leading to ill health.

*Changes in the assumptive world, personal constructs, and cognitive models.* It is suggested in Parkes's concept of psychosocial transitions (1971, 1972b) that certain events, such as bereavement, lead to major changes in the individual's life space. Parkes describes the assumptions on which an individual builds his world as his own "assumptive world." By this recognition of and response to aspects of his personal and physical environment the individual makes his life space into his own; he forms affectional bonds with the elements of this life space and labels them his own. He indicates this by his use of the words "my" and "mine." His assumptive world is made of models of these bits of his life space, past, present, and anticipated. They form his world. In grief the individual must relinquish his set of assumptions about the world that included the lost person and the self in relation to that person and then develop a new set of assumptions about this world in line with his new life circumstances. Parkes also notes how much the view of self and identity may be dependent on an assumptive world including the lost person; and he notes, too, the necessary, yet difficult, process of undoing such assumptions for a new and different view of the self.

Recently a model of bereavement involving "personal construct theory" has been suggested by Woodfield and Viney (1982). This is in some ways similar to the approach suggested by Parkes. These workers see the changes that follow bereavement as linked to the dislocation, by the death, of the bereaved's personal constructs. These personal constructs consist of the individual's system of constructed interpretations of himself and the events of his world (Kelly 1955). The psychological changes that accompany bereavement are seen by Woodfield and Viney as manifestations of changes in parts of such personal construct systems and these changes in turn as the products of "concurrent processes of personal construct dislocation and adaptation" (p. 5). Assimilation of changes may be represented by denial, hostility, and ide-alization, while accommodation to changes may be represented by change in, and elaboration of, the bereaved's personal construct system.

Linked to, and perhaps inseparable from the above two models, is the model suggested by the work of Horowitz (1976; Horowitz et al. 1980), who maintains that cognitive concepts of the world and self must be and are altered by object loss. These changes may generate intense affects. They may also activate "latent self-images" in the face of the loss as well as certain preexistent role relationship models. Horo-witz and his group consider troublesome preexistent images of the self and similar role relationship models to be common precursors of pathological grief. Many of the experiences and behaviors in bereave-ment, such as the repetitive intrusions of cognitions of images of the lost person and the intense affects generated by these, may fit with the model Horowitz provides of a stress-response syndrome (1976, p. 103).

A possible learning theory model might hypothesize that, in be-reavement, behavioral systems linked to the lost person are no longer reinforced and that behaviors geared to him are thus eventually extin-guished. This model could, of course, explain many of those outlined above (Gauthier and Marshall 1977). Phenomenological and existential approaches have not been well delineated, although Carole Smith (1976) outlines a possible model with implications for theory, as does Sunder Das (1971).

*Stress models.* Many consider bereavement to act as a stressor; and in fact the loss of the principal attachment figure is perceived as a very major stress in most cultures. Caplan (1964) describes such object loss as associated with an accidental crisis where the individual is thrown into a state of helplessness, where coping strategies are no longer successful in mastering the problem, where defenses are weakened, and the indi-vidual turns increasingly to others for help and is more susceptible to their responses. The crisis state cannot continue and is resolved over weeks, leading either to improved adaptation if the individual has strengthened his coping capacities by handling the problem satisfacto-rily, return to the previous equilibrium, or poor adaptation if coping resources have been inappropriate or have failed. Two other points of the crisis theory are important: the crisis may reawaken experiences from earlier similar crises, in this case losses, and the outcome of the crisis may be very dependent on the quality of social support available to the person during the time of the crisis. Crisis theory has proved a useful model for the study of bereavement (Maddison and Walker

1967; Raphael 1973; 1974*b*; 1977*a*; 1981), and there is much evidence to support the notion of the vital role of social supports in outcome.

The physiological stressor effects of bereavement have been indicated in a number of studies. Bartrop et al. (1977) found that the acute stress of conjugal bereavement disrupted immune response through its effects on T-cell function. Chodoff, Friedman, and Hamburg (1964) have shown the effects of anticipatory grief on corticosteroid excretion; Hofer et al. (1977) have shown the effects of bereavement on endocrine function; and Engel et al. (1971) have described the physiological responses to experimentally induced sadness.

*Illness and disease models.* In his classic description of acute grief, Lindemann (1944) describes the symptomatology and management of grief, defining this classic symptom constellation as a "syndrome." The pathognomonic factors comprising this syndrome are somatic distress, preoccupation with the image of the deceased, guilt, hostile reactions, and loss of patterns of conduct. This view of grief or bereavement is argued further by Engel (1961) in his paper "Is Grief a Disease?" He notes the correspondence between grief and other situations commonly referred to as "disease." He suggests there is a classic constellation of "symptoms" that produce suffering and impairment of capacity to function, and they have a consistent etiologic factor—loss. While many aspects of grief may be seen as normal, natural, and self-limiting, this does not necessarily exclude the consideration of grief as a disease, and many bereavement reactions cannot be classed in these categories. Engel draws attention to the usefulness of a disease concept in facilitating the scientific study of grief and perhaps the management of the grieving person.

Parkes (1972*b*) suggests that grief resembles a physical injury, a wound that gradually heals, or may heal with complications, or may fail to heal, or may reopen. He also speaks of it as the only "functional psychiatric disorder whose cause is known, whose features are distinctive, and whose course is usually predictable" (p. 6). Later workers, such as Clayton, Halikas, and Maurice (1972) also discussed the depressive-symptom complex of normal bereavement.

Pathological variants of grief may be more easily equated with an illness than may uncomplicated grief, because these processes involve greater impairment of function and are often not self-limiting. While patients are frequently diagnosed as having a pathological bereavement reaction, it is interesting to note that DSM-III, the *Diagnostic and Statistical Manual* of the *American Psychiatric Association* (1980), does not have diagnostic categories for pathological bereavement responses, but tends instead to see them classed as depression, stress disorder, or whatever may seem appropriate in terms of other diagnostic criteria. However, "Uncomplicated Bereavement" is classed as code V.62.82 under "codes for conditions that are not attributable to mental disorder, that are a focus of attention and treatment" (p. 330).

It is clear that the experience of the bereaved person is often very distressing. In response to the stress, emotional pain, or crisis, the bereaved person turns to others for care, perhaps showing evidence of heightened care-eliciting behavior, one form of attachment behavior (Henderson 1974). The medical care system is only one of many systems to which the bereaved turn (Parkes and Brown 1972), but it is indeed commonly used by many bereaved adults, as is indicated by studies showing increased health care utilization following major loss. It is interesting to note that with the provision of support for a bereaved widow during the crisis, subsequent health care utilization may be diminished (Raphael 1977b). Prescribed and nonprescribed medication is also widely used by the bereaved, but to little positive effect (Maddison and Raphael 1972; Boman, Streiner, and Perkins 1981).

Perhaps the ultimate substantiation of an illness model has been in the development of a Munchausen syndrome of bereavement. Feigned bereavement has been described by Snowdon, Solomons, and Druce (1978) who list twelve cases of patients whose supposed bereavement was thought by staff to be a major factor in their illness. These patients presented unusual pictures of grief with the supposed death having occurred in a dramatic manner. They were often referred from medical or surgical wards where staff had been sympathetic to this type of story. The present author has also seen several patients presenting a similar picture. Thus, these patients at least would accept bereavement as a medical condition of interest to doctors.

*Sociobiological model: grief in evolutionary context.* It has been suggested by Averill (1968), followed his careful review of grief and bereavement, that the stereotyped set of psychological and physiological reactions commonly called "grief" is universal among humans, and probably higher primates as well. He suggests that these grief reactions may have a biological origin and have an evolutionary function to ensure group cohesiveness in species for which the maintenance of social bonds is necessary for survival. The pain of grief makes separation from the group or individual extremely stressful and this reinforces the social group. Where loss does occur the grief has to run its "biological" course. Charles Darwin's description of the expression of emotions of grief and the responses that these evoke in others would support such a model. Darwin (1872) concludes that the facial expressions typical of adult grief are composed of tendencies to scream like an abandoned child trying to attract its mother and of an inhibition of such screaming. Thus the bereaved brings others to him. This drawing together reaffirms the social group, and the ongoing life of the species. That grief, mourning, and the bereavement reaction evolved together as a distinct biopsychosocial behavioral system to ensure the survival of the human group and the human species is an attractive concept, perhaps chiefly because it gives the pain of death and loss a purpose and an immortality.

# CHAPTER 3. The Bereaved Child

"Where is Daddy? Where is he? Why won't he come home? I want my Daddy."

*John*, age 4

"Mummy's gone, bye bye—Where's Mummy? Mummy, Oh Mummy, I want you so much."

*Joanna*, age 2½

"They are sad because their Daddy had died," said Jessica, the tears slowly running down her cheeks.

*Jessica*, age 5

This chapter attempts to tell the story of the response of younger children to the death of a significant figure. The picture that emerges comes from many sources: the author's research with bereaved children, the studies carried out by other workers, the published literature, and clinical descriptions. There are many conflicting views about children's capacity to grieve and mourn and about the possible pathogenic potential of childhood bereavement. The descriptions presented here are an attempt to present a comprehensive picture in terms of the current evidence. Throughout, the possible responses of children will be considered in terms of the nature and quality of the relationship lost; the death and its meaning for the child; the experience and behavior of the child in response to the bereavement; effects on the child through impact on the family; and longer term effects related to impact on development and possible pathogenicity. The age groups designated here are not meant to be considered in fixed chronological terms, but simply as representative of differing developmental stages relevant to these issues.

## The Young Infant

For the young infant, under six months of age, the concepts of grief and mourning are difficult to encompass. Nevertheless there are likely to be certain responses to loss, and these may represent the primordial precursors of grief and mourning.

### RELATIONSHIPS

The key relationship for the young infant is with the mother or prime attachment figure. The infant brings to this relationship certain attributes of temperament, a specific genetic constitution, and perhaps psychobiological prerequisites for attachment to the caring person so essential for his survival. The care-giver brings expectations, a representational "image," and interaction capacities. The infant brings the structural and functional patterning for these images and interactions, unless there is major impairment. With normal development, the infant-mother relationship intensifies progressively during these early months. The interactions are both rewarding, the source of good feelings, and frustrating, the source of bad. Although the infant probably has some memory span for visual information during this period, the work of Piaget (1955) and others suggests that object constancy (the ability to conceive the object as an entity with an image that is separate from the self) does not develop until during the latter part of the first year. Bowlby (1980) notes, in his careful review of the cognitive theory contributions to this field, that the development of "person permanence" may come a little earlier because of the intensity of involvement with the mother.

Mahler, Pirie, and Bergman (1975) speak of the behavioral phenomena that indicate differentiation of the infant from his mother in the first subphase of separation individuation. They note the specific smile for the mother indicating both the beginnings of this differentiation and the specificity of the bond. Thus the infant is likely, even as early as four to five months of age, to have a response to the separation or loss of this specific person. While it may be difficult for him to hold a clear representation or image of her in her absence, nevertheless her loss is likely to have impact and meaning for him in less differentiated but still important ways, perhaps even from the earliest weeks.

For the young infant, however, relationships are mostly of the interaction, the here-and-how. His relationships with people other than his principal attachment figure will be very much governed by the quality and intensity of their interactions with him.

## DEATH

It seems most unlikely that the young infant can conceptualize death. Hence, in his mother's absence, while he may be distressed in some ill-defined way, he cannot put meaning to this distress. Separation may be the same to him as death in that it equals absence, and there is no sense of time. When the death of a parent actually occurs, how it is later interpreted and presented to him may give it meaning retrospectively. For instance, at later stages, when he seeks explanation, family myths as to the cause of the death and his involvement in it may become part of his view of death and of himself. Where the death of a mother occurs suddenly and unexpectedly, there may be considerable disruption of his mothering until some new system of basic care is reestablished. Where there has been forewarning, the mother may have been able to disengage herself progressively from the infant and slowly hand over the mothering to another figure so that there will be far less abrupt withdrawal of his nurturing supplies.

## EXPERIENCE AND RESPONSE

How the infant experiences and responds to the death of a significant person is not clear. If his mother dies in the first few months of life, he may show crying and distress because of the withdrawal of vital supplies, but good mothering by a surrogate may settle this quickly. From about four or five months onward the child may show some nonspecific ongoing distress in reaction to the absence of his mother. This is probably the earliest manifestation of grief. Although he may not hold internally a true image of the mother, some part of him responds to the absence of her as a specific person. There is no evidence he can gradually undo his bonds in any sort of internal mourning process. Nor is he likely to show affects of grief, but only undifferentiated precursors of emotion such as the "primary affects of unpleasure" (Engel 1962). The effects of the death of the father or other family member are not known but are likely to have their main effects on the infant through the mother's distress and grief, which the infant may mirror.

LONGER-TERM EFFECTS

The longer-term effects of these deaths are really not known. It may be that problems arise for the child in terms of identity—not knowing who he is in terms of being part of the lost partner or not having that person as a model during development. When an infant is born during the time of a death, or a death occurs not long after his birth, the child may be consciously or unconsciously linked in identity with the dead person. The infant may be expected in some way to take the dead person's place and carry on his identity—keep him alive as it were. This may happen whether it is a parent who has died or a sibling. It seems to the bereaved family that the child's life is a replacement for the life that has been taken. There may be expectations, even molding of his identity in line with this fantasy. Sometimes the child is given the dead person's name in a way that reflects such expectations.

Although there are no systematic studies, it would seem likely that any other longer term effects or vulnerability are dependent on the quality of mothering or care that is provided should the principal care person be lost; the support for the mother's grief when another family member is lost so that she can continue to mother the infant; and the continuity and quality of the family environment available for the child subsequently. Absence of care or poor quality care over a prolonged period may lead to poor outcome, as may chaos, breakdown, discord, or disintegration of the family unit. For most young infants, it would seem that, if there is a rapid restructuring of care and its quality is reasonable, then some different but not especially pathogenic patterns of family life will ensue.

## The Older Infant

In the older infant—from six months to two years of age—the beginnings of grief and mourning are seen.

RELATIONSHIPS

Bowlby (1980, pp. 428–30) carefully delineates our current understanding of relationships in these months as they are relevant for a consideration of loss. During the latter part of the first year and the early part of the second, the infant is increasingly able to hold, in her absence, the concept of the person, his mother, as a representational image within him. He is also increasingly attached to her as a specific and separate person. He is increasingly able to search for her in her absence. Some infants will achieve these skills earlier than others, but for most they are differentiated by the second year. It seems quite clear that the infant can now yearn for this "good-enough" mother when she is away from him.

The quality of this relationship will probably depend to a great degree on the "fit" between mother and infant and the balance of rewarding "good" and frustrating "bad" affects that it has generated. The quality of the infant's relationships with others will be similar but inevitably far less intense than that with the prime attachment figure. By this stage, the infant has developed the capacity to demonstrate his anger and ambivalence with biting, hitting, and turning away; and his love, by his warm cooing and cuddling. Developmentally, the negative side of his ambivalence may be high if he has been sensitized by many frustrating separations. The relationship with the mother will be characterized by diminishing but still paramount dependence. Conflicts regarding weaning and separation, with the expression of oral aggression, are likely to emerge during this early part of this period, while struggles over control, autonomy, and anal issues become more prominent during the later part.

DEATH

While the infant cannot yet conceptualize the permanence of death, the nature of the dead state, he can certainly respond to the absence of his prime attachment figure, usually the mother. It is likely he will look for her, even search for her, in places where she might normally be seen or was last seen. Children in this age range who can verbalize may keep asking where the dead parent is. Even if they are familiar with dead objects, animals, for instance, they cannot transfer this state to the mother who is dead.

If the infant was involved in the death itself in some way, as in an accident, or was alone for some time with the dead person, the shock and the parent's nonresponsiveness may be frightening to him, but he is unlikely to make any real meaning of this altered state.

This is well exemplified in the case of David, a young man of twenty-two who saw a dead woman being taken from the site of an accident on a stretcher. Her arm was hanging over the edge and her breast partially exposed. This awakened a vivid, and previously repressed, memory of his attempts to suckle the breast of his dead mother when he was ten months old. His memory was one of the coldness, the lack of warmth and response, the fear and strangeness. The accuracy of this memory was revealed as it was carefully explored with older members of the family.

Whether the death is sudden or anticipated will have an effect on the infant in that it may influence both the transition to the next caretaker as well as the adaptation of the rest of the family.

EXPERIENCE AND BEHAVIOR

The infant experiences the death of the mother or prime attachment figure in terms of separation, absence, and the protest, despair, and detachment, so vividly described by workers such as Bowlby (1980) and the Robertsons (1952). He has an image of his mother as the source of good feelings and interactions, and he is powerfully bound to her. When she is gone he evokes this representational image and scans his world, searching for her. He is at first shocked, but he rapidly protests with loud screams and obvious anger. It is suggested that this is designed to bring her back and "punish" her, preventing future repetition of such absences. As her absence continues, and he finds his protest is to no avail, his despairing feelings supervene, as the Robertson films so vividly show. He calls up the mother's image again and again. He yearns for her, longs for her. But she does not reappear to interact with him. So there is only the image and longing and pain. His immature ego cannot tolerate this pining and longing for prolonged periods, so he may lapse into a state of withdrawal, conserving his resources and protecting himself from pain, or into distracting denying activity, sometimes aggressive or almost manic in intensity.

Eventually the infant gives up looking for the mother, expecting or hoping for her return. Despairing responses become predominant and his sadness is obvious. He becomes uninterested in toys, food, or activities. It is as though he has given up his yearning for this lost mother, as though he holds no hope in association with his image of her. This typical "separation" response persists if separation continues; and the infant becomes detached from his mother and others, unless a constant caring person takes over. Should the mother return, the infant's image and memory of her are obvious in his responses, both in his denial of her and in his eventual acceptance and reunion as he explores her face and reestablishes her presence.

When there is no return, as with death, the care offered by others in her place, or through their own love of him, as with his father or older siblings, will be the factor supporting him through this trauma, ensuring his survival. Should this care be deficient because others are too grief stricken or fail to recognize his need, perhaps because they think he is too young to be affected, then he may be left with residual vulnerabilities to separation and loss.

Affects of grief are complex, and how early they are differentiated is probably open to some question. A further issue that has been discussed by many workers is the degree to which the child's ego may be developmentally unable to tolerate these intense feelings. Most of those who hold that the infant cannot tolerate them agree that this changes with maturation. Conditions related to the bereavement may take up the ego resources of the infant or child, so that he may have few strengths left to deal with the affects of grief. When support is available to provide additional ego resources in such cases, then it seems likely the infant will be able to deal with these affects, at least to some degree, and this capacity will grow as he develops, but at all stages some support for the ego may be necessary to handle very intense affects related to loss.

The small numbers of bereaved children who have been assessed in this age group have shown a range of responses. There may be exaggerated separation responses, especially clinging, screaming, and refusing to let other attachment figures out of sight, diffuse distress, and disturbance of sleep and eating. With older infants in this age range, regression may be prominent with general return to the relative security of established earlier behaviors. Curling up in the fetal position and loss of speech may occur. It is difficult here too to tell if this is a reaction to the loss, as is most likely when the mother or principal caring person dies, or a mirroring/identification with maternal grief when a father or sibling dies. When relationships other than with the principal caring person are lost, the level of response will be very much governed by two factors: the quality and intensity of the relationship and its significance for the mother.

What bereavement responses there are in children under two years of age are likely to be overt; whereas in those over two, some control of feelings begins to be possible, and responses may become more disguised. How much the younger child can work through the loss trauma in spontaneous play is not known. Terr (1981) describes the "forbidden games" whereby children from fifteen months of age attempt, unsuccessfully, to deal with the trauma they have experienced. Playing through bereavement-relevant issues is not clear in this younger group. The degree to which high levels of ambivalence toward the person who has died will complicate mourning in this age range is really unknown. But it seems likely that the quality of parental relationships before and after the death are likely to be influential: poorer relationships correlate more with negative outcomes.

E. Furman (1974, p. 260) notes her experience with two infants who lost their mothers in the middle of their second year. She describes these children as initially showing no overt affect as they were attempting to deal with the changes brought about by the death. The children went on to sobbing episodes at night; then with comforting and talk about their hurt and the lost parent, they showed crying, sadness, and anger during the daytime. It might be that the reactions described in this age range could be seen rather as separation responses that are continued, in view of the child's inability really to conceptualize future times and his life going on without the lost parent. However, as much of the response of older children and adults is also dominated by such separation issues, this does not detract from considering the response in this group the earliest pattern of bereavement. For older children and adults, the reality testing of the finality of death comes only gradually with the repeated longing for the dead person and his failure to return, and the future without him contributes only in part to the acceptance of finality and the mourning that leads to relinquishing the relationship. Furman (p. 253) also considers the issue of whether it is possible for such infants to decathect the lost person. She believes that the cathexis for the lost person may be maintained for a number of years, and that, even as early as sixteen months of age, children may show evidence of slowly and painfully decathecting the lost person.

Jeremy was eighteen months old when his father died from acute leukemia. Mrs. K, his mother, had been aware of her husband's serious illness and probable death, and the whole family had, in some ways, prepared. Mr. and Mrs. K had decided to go on with their plans to have a child, despite his diagnosis, because they felt Mrs. K would have someone to remind her of her husband and someone to live for. When his death finally came, she was still shocked and distressed. There were times beforehand when she had found it hard to relate to Jeremy and his needs because of her preoccupation with her husband's illness, but despite this they had a warm and close bond. Jeremy had been with his father constantly as the latter had given up work as his illness progressed, so they lived an intense life in their small nuclear family group.

Following the death, Jeremy seemed to become quite distressed. He would wander around the house muttering to himself "Dad-dad, Dad-dad," seemingly searching for his absent father. After wandering a little to the rooms his father normally occupied, he would suddenly become distressed and race back to his mother, clutching her and sobbing. His sleep was disturbed at night. Mrs. K herself was very distressed, although well supported in her grief and mourning by her own family and friends. Jeremy continued to search for his father in the weeks that followed. Each morning he would come to the bedroom and trot happily to his father's side of the bed, saying "Dad-dad, Dad-dad." Disappointment would spread over his face at his father's absence and after looking about, he would crawl into the bed with his mother and hug her. He found an old shirt of his father's and carried this with him for quite a while. He would not easily let his mother out of his sight.

When he sobbed in the evening, his mother would go to him and hold him, rocking him and comforting him. "Dad-dad's gone" she would say. "He's not coming back, Dad-dad's dead," as she gently sobbed herself. Over the next few weeks, his search lessened, although he would occasionally say his father's name again, looking around expectantly. His distress gradually disappeared, except to come afresh when his mother seemed very upset. As the weeks and months continued, he seemed to have recovered.

It is with infants of this age range that the parents' and other adults' denial of childhood bereavement first commences. The empathic awakening of the parent's own separation pain and helplessness is unbearable as the parent identifies with the child. To avoid such painful memories being revived, the parent or adult may deny that the child is affected by the loss. It is at this age that the infant is first unconsolable for his "own and only mother" whom he has lost. No other person can replace her, can take away the anguish of his screams, at least initially. So that no matter how much comfort and consolation is offered, it is not what he wants. He wants simply her. In this response is the kernel of the difficulty that we face with loss. The cry of the infant's anguish awakens every fiber of our response to hold and comfort him. It reawakens the pain of our own inner experiences of separation and fear. Yet our comforting does not ease the pain, at least initially, for he wants only her. Yet it is only with our comforting that the pain will eventually ease and he will be supported to accept his loss, to relinquish the bond. This same pattern applies to bereavement throughout the life cycle, but never so poignantly as at this early stage.

## The Child from Two to Five

In Bowlby's (1980) review of loss he states that, "Between seven months and about seventeen months responses take forms that have sufficient resemblance to the responses of older children for their relation to mourning to call for careful discussion. From about seventeen months onwards responses conform even more closely to those described in older children" (p. 390). It must be recognized that none of the age spans described in this book and elsewhere is fixed and that different, earlier, later, or anomalous patterns of behavior may appear at any stage. In this sphere we lack the systematic and broad studies to make finer distinctions.

RELATIONSHIPS

The child's relationships become richer and more varied between the ages of two and five. Not only can he hold complex representational models of these relationships, especially the primary ones, but Piaget's (1955) work suggests that he is able to manipulate these images, recapitulating actions of the past and anticipating actions of the future. He recognizes different members of his family as individuals and has a different quality of relationship with each of them. He is mastering his struggles for autonomy and should by now have negotiated the phase of basic trust (E. H. Erikson, 1959). He has experienced separations and has learned to trust parents to return. He is likely to have been weaned and to have learned new patterns of gratification after relinquishing the breast. He may have experienced the birth of a sibling and may be struggling with his rivalrous hatred for this stranger who has taken away his prime love object. While dependency is still prominent he can walk away from persons he does not want, at least briefly. He can say no very forcibly, and "I love you" and "I hate you" also with great power.

By this time, he should have mastered some of his aggression in relationships, such that he may be hostile and aggressive toward those on whom he depends, yet hold at the same time intense loving bonds. Periods of struggle over issues like control may heighten the negative aspects of his relationship, as may periods of frustration and deprivation. He may also now associate his inner experiences and his behaviors with environmental and interpersonal effects—he may make causal assumptions. His view of the world is very egocentric. He may defend against his recognition of his smallness and powerlessness by omnipotent fantasies of love and destruction, and his relationships with important figures may be filled with these.

He may have experienced "good-enough" mothering (Winnicott 1949, p. 245) so that that relationship, even if fraught with a developmentally appropriate loading of ambivalence, is overall one of rewarding interactions. As these years progress, new developmental tasks may further influence levels of dependency and ambivalence in the primary relationships. For instance, nursery school entry may reawaken separation experience and anger toward the mother for what the child perceives as her desertion. He may successfully master this experience supported by her ongoing love and the rewards of other relationship experiences in the nursery. He may experience other forms of day care or baby-sitting, which now give him an extended repertoire of relationships beyond the family, lessening the vulnerability associated with a sole focus on the mother-infant dyad. On the other hand, if he has overprotective, intrusive control from his mother associated with little care, then his ambivalence may be intense within an experience that allows no separation and little recognition or expression of negative affects.

Oedipal conflicts become prominent for many children in the latter part of this phase. There may be intensification of relationships with the opposite-sex parent and a heightening of ambivalence for the same-sex parent, perhaps to the level of rivalrous hatred and death wishes. Then, ultimately, with resolution, there is enhanced identification with this same-sex parent.

Illness in child or parent may add stresses to the parent-child relationship, heightening ambivalence and/or dependence. Unresolved parental conflicts from the parent's own childhood relationships and development may also add to the complexity of the relationship. Sibling relations are frequently fraught with the ambivalence generated by envy and rivalry for those more or less powerful than the self.

The loss of a relationship, particularly a relationship with a parent, will take on the flavor of all of these pervasive developmental issues. The response will especially be modulated not only by the intensity of the relationship, but also by all these special meanings, special fantasies with the powerful threads of ambivalence and dependency running throughout.

# The Bereaved Child

Maurer (1960) discusses the maturation of the concept of death and sees its earliest precursors in the peek-a-boo games of infancy, the "all gone" phase of the first year, with the recognition increasingly in the second year that things that are "all gone" may not return. Projection of death onto others may be seen in the play of four-year-olds with games such as "Cowboys and Indians" or with the killing of insects and other creatures.

The discovery of death in childhood and the development of death concepts have also been discussed by classical workers such as Anthony (1971) and Nagy (1948). They describe stages up to the age of eight to ten years when the child is seen as developing a concept of death similar to that of adults; that death is due to natural causes and involves the cessation of life. E. Furman (1974, p. 50) notes that in her group's experience, normally developed children above the age of two are able to achieve a basic understanding of "dead" if they are assisted in doing so. Usually this first occurs with animals and birds. When parents or others are able to help the child with understanding concretely this altered and permanent state, it seems likely that the child can conceptualize the qualities of this state around the age of two to three years. Also, as Furman notes and our research appears to substantiate, it is easier for the child to comprehend death when the death is not initially associated with the loss of a loved person, and "by the same token it was easier to understand the death of a loved one when the child already had the concept of death" (p. 51). When the death of a parent or a sibling does occur, the child can be helped in his understanding if clear and realistic information is provided and if there is support to understand the facts and feelings involved. Two-year-olds may approach death not with horror but with fascination. Amongst all children in this younger age group, there may be a very matter-of-fact curiosity about death.

The younger child's understanding of death is complicated by the attempts of others, especially parents, to protect him from this knowledge, and he may struggle to reconcile his own (current) assumption and the variety of magical and evading accounts presented by others. Rochlin (1967) showed that well-developed three- to five-year-olds thought a lot about death, were well aware that it represented the end of vital functions, and were most interested in the causes of death. Nevertheless, even these accurate concepts are not necessarily fully developed, and the child's questions may reveal many conflicting views. For those children with little opportunity for accurate information, the magical thinking that can surround death at all stages of the life cycle will be most prominent.

For some of the younger children in the two-to-five age group, the permanency of death may be difficult to grasp, and the child may really expect that the dead person will return. He may believe the dead person is in another place, a place that he conceives concretely as being like another room from which he could come back. When he has been told the dead parent has gone to Heaven, he may see this as a star in the sky—again, a concrete interpretation of an adult's abstraction.

The child's view of the world continues to be very egocentric. He may equate death with killing—a consequence of his potent wish fulfillment and not unlike the destruction and havoc he wreaks with his toys. He may believe his words and thoughts: "I hate you, I wish you were dead," have succeeded. He feels powerful, yet terrified. Bowlby (1979) points out that children's fantasies about death may also be reinforced by parental comments before the death occurs. The child, when he has been behaving as parents do not wish, may be told "You'll be the death of me"—a statement that may now be seen as fulfilled.

On the whole, the child's own death anxieties do not come to the fore so much at this stage as later, when he becomes more aware of death as something that can happen to him also. Explanations given to him may bring some fears, however. When he is told death is like "going to sleep," he may become afraid of sleep, or when told that "you die as a result of sickness," he may dread becoming ill. Just how concrete some of the younger child's interpretations may be is revealed in the following vignette.

Margaret was an intelligent four-year-old whose parents had used appropriate opportunities to explain death to her. Her grandfather died, and she reacted appropriately and naturally at the funeral and burial, clarifying afterward her concerns about what would happen to his body. Among her concepts was the idea that his body would gradually rot away and go back into the earth again. She had also picked up the idea that there may be worms, bacteria, and other living creatures involved in this process. All was well until three months later when she was diagnosed as having threadworms. She became panicky and would not sleep. After careful exploration the cause of her fears—her belief that worms were part of death and dying—was revealed, and with simple explanation of the differences, the problem was resolved.

Jason, a two-and-a-half-year-old, showed an even more direct and concrete interpretation of his father's absence. He and his father used to go to a nearby airport to see planes together. When his father, to whom he had been intensely attached, died, he was told that he had "gone to Heaven to be with Jesus." In the weeks that followed he ran away on many occasions and was found, each time, in the direction of the nearby airport where he had gone to "get in a plane to go to the sky to Daddy."

What actually happens at the time of the death and what the child is told will be vitally important. Whether his comprehension is increased or, instead, he develops further elaboration of his magical conceptions will depend on this. Many young children in this age range are actively excluded from knowledge of a parent's or sibling's fatal illness, in the mistaken belief that this will protect them from the pain. The child's fantasies are likely to build on the mystery, as well as the family's fear and distress, to produce even more frightening and painful interpretations of the changes in his world. The child may even fantasize that a surviving parent (or parents) has done away with the dead person (and may also do away with him).

When word comes of the actual death, especially when it is sudden and unexpected, the child of this age range is often not told what has occurred then or, sometimes, not even later. The failure to tell the child has many origins: it may be thought he is too young to understand; or the parent may be so distraught with his or her own grief that he or she does not want to, or cannot, put into words what has happened. The parent is in a state of shock and denial, and to say the words makes real what can still be in part shut out if it is not said. Silverman and Silverman (1979) reinforce this observation from their work with widowed families where communication becomes distorted because this expectation and/or hope of return is retained and cannot be dismantled by words to the contrary.

The child's experience under such circumstances is of a shocked, distressed parent, crying and distraught; high anxiety and upheaval in the home; strangers and visitors; the absence of the dead parent or sibling; and perhaps the additional trauma of being sent away to be looked after by others. He may be told of the death by a parent or someone else in the next few days. He may be told the parent has gone away to another country, is on holiday, is sick, has gone to be in Heaven with Jesus (regardless of the family's former religious beliefs). The person who is best equipped to convey such news to him would normally be a parent, but a parent may be too shocked to put this horror into words, so it is left to others who do not know and understand him so well. There may be an additional trauma for the child when he has been involved in the circumstances of the death, for instance, the accident that caused it. His ego may be so overwhelmed by this personal trauma that it cannot take in the meaning and reality of the death.

In our prospective study of bereaved children (Raphael, 1982), 50 percent of the children aged two to eight years were told by the surviving parent or some other person that the dead parent had gone to Heaven. This proved enormously difficult for these children to comprehend, as many were not familiar with such ideas in the context of family life previously and could only interpret Heaven in concrete terms. There was also associated with this a tendency to believe the dead parent was still somewhere else in some state akin to life, yet somehow kept away from them or even deliberately staying away.

A further aspect of the child's understanding of the reality of death concerns seeing the body of the dead person, seeing him or her as a dead person, and the ritual of the funeral ceremonies. Again a great many children are actively excluded from these areas of reality testing, particularly in the younger age groups. In our study almost 60 percent of children in the two- to eight-year range were excluded from any participation in the funeral services or from seeing the parent at the time of death. Since many of these deaths were the sudden and unanticipated deaths of young parents who had often left home alive and well and had subsequently "vanished" for no reason that the child could readily understand (or was told), it was little wonder that confusion and fantasy reigned. Independent systematic assessment of these children (Raphael 1982) revealed that they had very little understanding of the nature of the parent's death, his or her whereabouts, state, or the finality of the loss. In this assessment these issues of finality of the loss were far more difficult for those in the two to five years age range. In this context it is worth noting that two children, aged three when first approached by the research team, had still not been told of the parent's death two weeks after it occurred.

Thus there is much to suggest that, when a family member dies, the young child's perception and understanding of what has happened may be very unclear, and his responses to the loss may be complicated by his struggles to comprehend the parent's or sibling's absence and his fantasies of what it means.

EXPERIENCE AND BEHAVIOR

Systematic studies of grief and mourning in early childhood are few. Van Eerdewegh et al. (1982) include children at this stage in their study of widowed parents' perceptions of children's responses to the loss, but there is no age breakdown of responses in this younger group, and the mean age of their sample was eleven years. They note the frequency of dysphoric mood in their sample one month after the death, but indicate that this diminishes by the end of the year according to parents. E. Furman (1974) in her study of children in analysis includes a number of children in this age range and seems to conclude that mourning is possible for such children following the death of a parent. Bowlby (1980, pp. 390–411) sees processes and responses in many ways similar to those of older children and states that, "provided their questions and recollections are not discouraged, the responses of children as young even as two-and-a-half differ little from those of their elders" (p. 391).

The data from the study by Raphael, Field, and Kvelde (1980) would tend to support Bowlby's view. In particular, his further comments on the need for favorable conditions to allow grief and mourning are especially applicable to this younger group. He notes that favorable conditions include what the child is told and what later opportunities are given to him to enquire about what has happened; the family relationships after the loss, especially his relationship with the surviving parent; and the patterns of relationship within the family prior to the loss (Bowlby 1980, p. 311). Favorable conditions may often fail to apply in this young age group.

In my own studies (Raphael 1982; Raphael, Field and Kvelde 1980), children in this age range are very variable in their initial response to the news of the death. According to parents' descriptions, many do not seem to understand it fully and ask some seemingly inappropriate questions immediately afterward. Commonly parents perceive the children as relatively unaffected, although there would often be comment on some change in behavior in the ensuing weeks. The younger children in this age range often show a degree of bewilderment about what has happened and some regressive clinging behavior, often with increased demandingness. The children are likely to ask again and again about the whereabouts of the dead parent: why hasn't he or she returned; what is he doing. Some children in this age group show their response to the absence of the dead parent quite directly, both in their questions and in their obvious yearning for the parent's return and their angry protest when this does not occur.

Some other common patterns emerge. Regression and clinging behaviors may persist with the child going back to wetting, soiling, wanting the bottle or even breast again, and more babyish ways of eating. Transitional objects such as soft toys and blankets are especially likely to be sought, and the child may cling to them all day, perhaps going away from family distress to a quiet corner on his or her own. Other children (in our study, more frequently boys) started to show, according to their surviving parents, much more aggressive "naughty" and "wild" behavior. It seems that the children were responding in some way to the shock of what had happened and were probably also strongly influenced by the surviving parent's distressed response.

Whether or not a child shows great distress at the parent's absence depends on the intensity and frequency of the previous interaction with that parent. Where death has been sudden, and of a mother who was previously intensely involved with the child, then there is a desperation in the child's response and in the surviving parent's attempts to fill the gap, when he himself feels so distraught.

Dave, a young father of twenty-two in our study, was shocked and grieving following his young wife's death in the intensive care unit from a fulminating infection. Danielle, three and a half, cried desperately for her mother—"I want my Mummy, where's my Mummy?" When her father attempted to hold and comfort her she pushed him away, for as with all bereaved people the only person she wanted was the one who could not comfort her, who was not there, her mother who had died. Her yearning and longing for her lost mother were intense and obvious.

In other instances where there has been some forewarning of maternal death, fathers have either increasingly taken over a mothering role or involved others such as their own mothers or sisters in the children's care. The child still yearns for the lost mother, and in our study (Raphael 1982) these younger children asked frequently for the lost parent unless actively inhibited from doing so. They were sometimes stopped by direct demands from other family members, telling them not to upset everyone by asking about the parent, or by clear messages from the father that to do so would be too distressing for him to bear. Often those involved in the child's care in the place of the mother were themselves too distressed or discomforted by their position, to tolerate the child's needy queries.

When a father dies the child's reaction will depend both on the level of his relationship with the father and on the mother's grief. The children in our study whose fathers had a special time of the day with them such as the evening when they returned home from work, were most likely to show their yearning and longing at this time as well as at times associated with special activities they had shared. At other times their distress was much more a mirror of the mother's grief.

Some were quite angry with the dead parent for what seemed to be desertion and for the chaos into which the secure world of family life had been plummeted. With others the anger was toward the surviving parent for his or her withdrawal and lack of comforting behavior. It seemed to some of these children as though they had been doubly deserted. One parent had gone away and was not coming back, while the other was removed into a world of his or her own, not appearing to perceive or respond to the child's grief. This was especially reinforced when the child was sent away from familiar surroundings or was looked after by strangers. It seemed as if the whole security of his or her world had collapsed. These traumas were so overwhelming for some children that their response was withdrawal. This may have been more maladaptive than the anger, for the quiet child was then much more likely to be seen as unaffected; as "coping," not "making a nuisance of himself," and therefore alright, so that his real pain was little comforted. Some children actively searched for the lost parent, as did Jason, the small boy described above who went toward the airport to look for his father.

Bill was a boy of three whose behavior reflected his searching. Every time a motorbike that sounded like his father's went by, he would go to the front door to see if his father were there. When out with his mother, he would search actively for a bike like his father's in the hope that he would find his father as well.

In the research interviews and assessment play sessions, these children revealed further evidence of their preoccupation with and their pining and sadness for the dead parent. Many appeared to find in these sessions the opportunity to express their fears and feelings about what had happened. A group of children who had not expressed any open pining for the dead parent according to the surviving parent, showed their responses in play. One three-and-a-half-year-old girl repeatedly played out a theme with dolls, showing a little girl crying and crying for her father who had gone away. Another girl of two and a half, whose family prohibited any discussion of the dead mother, played with the tape recorder that was still on when the interviewer was out of the room. She spoke into it saying "Mummy's gone.... Where's Mummy?... Your Mummy's not here.... Bye-bye Mummy."

Profound themes of longing for the lost parent showed in many ways; perhaps the most poignant was reflected in the large number of parent dolls that were "lost" during various play sessions—kidnapped and hidden away—not to be "found," but treasured by the children as some sort of symbolic representation of their unrequited yearnings. In this study it was quite clear that younger children in the two-to-five age range were quite able (as were those in the five-to-eight group) to express their longing and yearning for the lost person when conditions allowed. Even with unfavorable circumstances, we found this yearning and longing were quite close to the surface, and their expression could be facilitated.

Similarly, their sadness about the parent's loss was also very obvious. Many of the children were described by their parents as being "teary." They cried when discussing the absent parent and were obviously sad. This sadness tended to become more overt when the children had tested out their hopes about the dead parent's return. Often when these issues had been aired with the interviewer they seemed to be more able to accept what they had secretly dreaded and suspected, that the parent was "all gone" and would not be back.

The general anxieties many young children experience when they lose a parent are often not recognized. The family seems a secure and all-powerful world. When this basic security is totally disrupted, especially by sudden death, the child may believe his whole survival is at stake. This was reflected in our study by the children's concerns expressed in projective assessments. If the mother had died there was often great concern about who would look after them and feed them, and if the father had died, they wondered who would provide the money for food. It seemed as though these anxieties related to oral supplies representing their concerns at an even deeper level of dependency and survival.

The child's place in the family may have an influence on his experience with the death of a parent. If the child in the two-to-five age group, is the older of two siblings, the younger, an infant, may make more urgent demands, so that the older child's needs may be bypassed. Such two-child families are common in Western society. If the child is the younger of two, his older sibling may be expected to assume new responsibilities and in some instances care for and protect the younger sibling. An only child in this age range may become reabsorbed into a symbiosis with a bereaved mother, for instance, or may be rejected by a bereaved father who does not know how to relate to him. Yet most parents of young children are very concerned about their children's responses, and in our project they constantly wanted to know if their children were all right, were progressing normally, as they wished to protect them from being scarred by the loss. The parent wants to make things "right" for the child but feels the same desperation others feel when trying to help him: that of not being able to bring the dead person back.

When the death is that of a sibling, the child's reactions will again be influenced by the quality of the relationship he held with the sibling. The feelings are likely to be less intense than when a parent dies, but nevertheless powerful. No systematic studies exist, but descriptions such as those of Cain's group (Cain, Fast, and Erickson 1964) suggest these bereavements may lead to substantial and disturbed responses. Particularly mystifying to the young child is the neonatal death as well as the stillbirth. There has been preparation for the new baby, and suddenly it is not there. In the case of crib death, the sudden shock to the family, the legal ramifications, and the mystery of the cause, on top of the child's inevitable ambivalent feelings toward the baby are likely to make such deaths particularly difficult for him to understand and resolve. Such young children may even show reactions to a mother's miscarriage. The loss will have its effects, but the longer-term outcomes are not known.

With children younger than two years it is extremely difficult to assess how long the infant's response to the loss of a parent, particularly a mother, will continue. Certainly with an adequate and constant mothering surrogate or mothering care, development is likely to progress normally. Nevertheless, reports in analysis and other reports by adults who have had this experience in childhood suggest that the process of gradually giving up the bonds to the lost person may take many months and residual aspects even longer. With children in the two-to-five age group the process may continue for some time. Certainly in our study, even when the children had settled into their new life situation, and the grief of the surviving parent was less intense, there was still evidence that the children thought often of the dead parent. This was likely to go on for several months and was often quite obvious at the one-year follow-up. It was reflected in the children's preoccupations with memories of the dead parent, in their discussions of things they used to do together and of times they were together, such as holidays and Christmas. It was reflected in many of the sad statements of longing: "My mother was the most beautiful woman in the world."; "My Daddy was the biggest man in the world." Photographs of the dead person were often a trigger to these memories and an opportunity to share them. This suggests that the mourning process continued over a period of months, perhaps longer, in those circumstances when the child felt secure enough for such mourning to occur. E. Furman (1974, pp. 253–54) suggests from her experience that such decathexis during the process of mourning occurs in this young age group and may take a prolonged time, perhaps years.

In the review and remembering of the lost person, the child is even more likely than adults to idealize the lost parent. His achievement of whole object relations—whereby he may perceive good and bad in the same person—is only fragile, and splitting is a prominent defense. The child may avoid the pain of mourning, quench the fires of his longing, by a retreat into a fantasy relationship with the idealized lost parent. When this is only temporary or fluctuant, it bodes little harm. When this "safe" fantasy relationship takes over, it is at great cost to the child's other relationships as well as to his hold on reality. Further, the real remaining parent soon becomes seen as all bad and rejecting by virtue of his grief; punishing and controlling by his disciplining; and terrifying, because if one does show hostility toward him, that parent might also die and leave the child with no one. The child may fantasize this "bad" one has murdered the other, and will also do away with him.

The child's mourning processes may be reflected in active remembering and storing of his memories; by his relationship to objects representing the dead person such as clothes or photographs; by his diminishing preoccupation with him; and by his use of the past tense. His relationships with others may reflect this process too: he may start to show heightened attachment to those of the same age and sex as the dead father, such as uncles, family friends, and neighbors. As he relinquishes the lost person, these relationships, if not taken on as a replacement with avoidance of grief, become less intense, less dominated by percepts of the father, more appropriately real as partial surrogates. Surviving parents sometimes complain of the child's "embarrassing" attachments to any father figure or mother figure and may need support to recognize it as part of the child's reality testing and need. The parent's discomfort about such behavior in the child often projects fear at his or her own desperate and similar needs for attachment to caring others.

Nagera (1970) points out how it may be difficult for the younger child's ego to sustain the pain of prolonged and continuous mourning. Deutsch (1937) also stresses such a view, as does Wolfenstein (1966). This view has been used to suggest that mourning is not possible. Bowlby's work (1980), E. Furman's (1974), Kliman's (1969) and my own studies (1980, 1982) all indicate that mourning does occur. Its apparent absence may be related to unfavorable conditions such as the parent's inability to mourn or allow the child to mourn. Or it may be, as seemed to be the case for many of the children we saw, that the grief and mourning were often intermittent. The child may initially respond as if nothing of importance has happened. At another time he may show periods of intense upset and indicate that he is missing the dead parent. At other times he may carry on happily playing as if nothing has happened. At such times the child's denial is high and his ego is not preoccupied with mourning. But this does not indicate he does not or cannot mourn. His quiet periods may also be times of lingering in memory and fantasy with the dead parent, and as such constitute part of the ebb and flow of mourning. Such rests from grief, such bouts of "shutting out" what has happened also occur in adult bereavement. There is nothing to suggest they indicate a pathological response in adult or child unless they become the predominant pattern, diminishing all reality testing. This is more likely for the younger child whose fantasy life is so rich and so difficult for him, at times, to separate from reality.

Thus the risk of an inhibition of mourning growing out of this intermittent response may be greater for a child if he lacks the security of a caring environment; or if he is confused about what has happened and his part in it; or if his relationship with the dead parent was complicated by more than normal levels of ambivalence.

The child who has lost a parent or sibling at a time of heightened ambivalence may be more likely to equate death with these ambivalent fantasies. This may bring terror at his own potency, so that his bravado and behavior constantly test his environmental control and tolerance as he unconsciously seeks reassurance that he is not really so powerful. These aggressive behaviors often have strong care-eliciting overtones. Another child may show a response of regression and dependence, crying and clinging to his surviving parent. These behaviours too serve the purpose of showing his need, and hopefully eliciting the caring response of others.

Thus the child in the two-to-five-age range may experience much of the grief and mourning that adults also bear. But others may not perceive his responses as bereavement; he may lack the capacity to put into words his feelings and memories as such; and because others find his recognition of death and his painful mourning intolerable they may deny him his feelings and their expression.

Jenny and Kate were five and three when their mother died. She had been sick for a number of years with breast cancer. There had been many separations with her frequent visits to hospital. The children's father was a warm and caring man, full of concern about their needs and the effects their mother's death would have upon them. His aunt, a widow, had spent a great deal of time helping the mother during her terminal illness and had also related closely to the girls during this period. Their father was also closely involved in their day-to-day care. When Mrs. L's condition deteriorated, she was taken to hospital and died within a few days. Mr. L told both the children immediately.

Jenny was distressed and upset, crying openly. Kate seemed bewildered and quiet but after a while started crying in sympathy with her idealized big sister. In the assessment session they revealed their feelings and experience in many ways:

"Mummy was sick," said Jenny. "She had a sickness inside her. She went to the hospital and she couldn't get better so she died. Daddy told us she has gone to Heaven, and when we go to Heaven we'll see her there, but Daddy said that won't be for a long long time." In playing with the doll's house, Jenny picked up the older girl doll and said: "This is the big sister—this is me." She picked up the grandparent dolls and put them into the bed with the big-sister doll. "They're all there," she said. "This one's the Mummy now [pointing to the grandmother doll]; the Mummy's sick." She rang the doorbell of the doll's house: "Who's there?" asked the interviewer. "Why that's Mummy," said Jenny. "Hello Mummy," and all the dolls sat down to dinner.

Kate was seen by her father as being too young to really understand what had happened, although he still felt concerned that she would be alright.

Kate picked up the small boy doll. "That me," she said. Then she put it down again. "No, this baby, *that's* me," she said. She played with the dolls choosing a father and a grandmother doll as parents. The grandmother doll kept falling and was bandaged many times. "The mother is sick," said Kate. "She is going to Heaven soon." Then she put all the dolls together in bed.

Jenny drew a simple solid picture for the interviewer. It was a round face with two blue blobs and black spots. She explained: "That's Mummy. She has blue cheeks because she's sad. She doesn't want to be away from us in Heaven. She wants to come home. They're the tears. See how she's crying."

Kate looked at the test cards (the woman in a hospital bed with her family around, then the little girl on the doorstep). "They're sad," she said, "'Cos the mother's sick. She is going to die. The little girl is sad too. Her father's put her outside. He wants the mother. They are all sad."

Tony was almost four when his father died after a prolonged illness. His mother was sensitive to his needs both during that illness and following the death. She made every effort to help Tony deal with his feelings and to explain openly to him what had happened. Her in-laws did not approve of her open attitude and felt she should have protected their grandson from the pain that his father's illness and death would bring.

When Tony's father was taken to hospital for the final time, his mother told him that he would probably not come home again. His grandfather told him that if he prayed hard his Daddy would return. When the father died Mrs. J told Tony quietly that his father had died and would not be coming back. Tony's first response was to scream and kick. "My Daddy is coming home," he said. "He is coming home, I know he's coming home." In the days that followed he was alternatively sad—"My Daddy's died," he said—or angry—"My Daddy's coming home" he would say. Whenever his mother cried he tried to comfort her, saying that his father would come back. When asked by the interviewer about his father he said, "My Daddy's in Heaven. No, he's here with me; he's all around me, but he's not around Mummy." Then later he would say that his father had gone and would not be coming back. He was sensitive to separation from his mother and would follow her whenever she left the room. He had become much more regressed in his behavior following his father's death with much clinging and crying as well as returning to wetting his bed.

In his play sessions he splashed much paint around. One picture was of a lion, savage and ferocious—"a lion who killed people," he said. He drew another picture and covered it with many layers of black. The black was for the people who were "all gone, all dead." His Daddy was all dead, and he would not be coming back. In another session he played with the dolls. The mother and father doll were put into bed. Then the father doll was taken away. "The Daddy's gone," he said. "They are all sad because the Daddy's gone away."

OUTCOMES

In the crisis of bereavement following the death of a parent, the majority of young children show some "symptoms." Sleep, appetite, bowel and bladder disturbance may appear. Separation responses may be heightened. Withdrawn behavior and irritability are common. As with the grieving adult such "symptoms" appear in the "normal" response to loss and may lead to further concern about grief as an "illness" or disease. Thus the child *may* be presented with symptoms for clinical care based on what is essentially a normal response to loss.

It is suggested in Brown's work (1982) that experiencing the death of a mother before the age of five may be a vulnerability factor for severe depression. Other workers also emphasize the possible pathogenic potential of loss at this early time. No systematic prospective studies exist that clarify particular risk patterns in terms of such early bereavement. Thus possible outcomes will be considered broadly in the latter part of this chapter.

# The Child from Five to Eight

Many of the factors described for the younger child in terms of relationships and experience continue to apply for the child entering the age range of five to eight years. Some differences and developments require consideration, however, for they have relevance to the issues of death and bereavement.

RELATIONSHIPS

By this period, some of the intensity of family relationships with parents has settled, or is in the process of doing so, with gradual resolution of oedipal struggles and the broadening of the child's social field. Latency is traditionally described as beginning about this time, from about six to twelve years of age, in that it has been suggested that the child's sexual drives are lessening. The current view (see, for example, Sarnoff 1980) is that this is a time of strengthening those areas of personality that control such drives, so that the energy of the child's developmental processes is channeled into socialization and education, acculturation through the institution of the school. The child learns to know and love other adults, such as a teacher, but also learns that these adults may be frightening, powerful, and hateful. He learns to know other children apart from his siblings and playmates. Nevertheless, family relationships with parents are still his prime concern. Sarnoff suggests that the organization of ego mechanisms in the "structure of latency" acts to bind oedipal feelings into fantasies rather than actions in an attempt to master them as current stresses. Parents, in early latency, pick the myths and fantasies (for example, fairy stories or fables) that help bind these fantasies for the processes of socialization, especially in the earlier years of this period. The child learns to deal with his fantasies at this time. These fantasies are predominantly those of jealous, sexual, aggressive interrelationships with adults and siblings, especially in these early years where oedipal wishes are still being negotiated and are dealt with in defended forms for mastery.

Another important component of the child's relationships during this period is his developing capacity for feelings of guilt. The identification with parents in the oedipal resolution, as well as by a variety of other processes becomes the basis for the superego, and the child's capacity to feel guilt about what has happened or might happen. This is more specific than any earlier superego precursors from previous developmental stages.

In his relationship with others he has learned to control his feelings, be they love or hate, and has struggled with his sense of impotence in the face of others' power to make him do *their* will and not his. His personality and structural development have, however, as Sarnoff (1980) comments, produced "a state of calm, pliability and educability which can be used as the basis for the transmission of culture in a school setting" (p. 146). How close to the surface his drives and excitement really are is revealed in the wildness that can erupt in the playground at recess when he is frustrated.

DEATH

The child takes a number of cognitive and other developmental steps that will influence the meaning of death for him. His concept of causality has been developed and evolved, and this has great relevance for his understanding or interpretation of death. Field (1979) shows this in her study of the child's concept of death in relation to Piagetian theory. She found that knowledge of the causality of death was highly correlated with the child's concept of physical causality as indicated by his or her judgments about the origin of "night," although the death concept tended to lag behind the concept of physical causality. The death concept was less developed in the five-to six-year-olds but much more specifically so in the seven- to eight-year-olds and eight- to twelve-year-olds. Other workers have shown the consolidation of the child's understanding of death during these years, and most would agree that by eight years, if not before, the child's conceptualization is very much like that of the adult; that is, death is understood as a product of natural processes. It is understood that it is not reversible and that it can happen to anyone, including the child himself.

In addition to this more extensive development of causal understanding, there is the development of the child's conscience: his superego, his sense of guilt. Thus at this time even more prominently than before, the death of a parent may be linked to the child's view of his own actions or inaction as causative, but in less magical terms than his earlier associations have suggested. As his aggressive and other drives have been so recently socialized and his fantasies about parents so recently rivalrous, he may readily associate the death with his own wishes. But the child in this age range may make even more direct causal interpretations, such as feeling, for example, that his bad behavior made the parent get sick and die or that his secret transgressions against a hated younger sibling caused the injury that led to the crib death.

The child is now much more able to use words, verbal symbols, to convey and organize his memories which were previously held in "affecto-motor" dominated memory patterns. Thus, while prior to this time he may have been able to convey far more of his understanding of the death or loss in action or picture, at this stage words may become the mechanism for organizing his experience. His defense, however, may be against direct expression, and denial is prominent in his reactions, at least initially and superficially.

## EXPERIENCE AND BEHAVIOR

Children in middle childhood usually realize what has happened when told of a death and suspect its possibility when knowledge is withheld. Death has become for them more of a reality than it had been in terms of their understanding, although all its implications are not yet as clear for them as they are for older children.

Many workers (for example, Nagera 1970) note the way in which children of this age group may resort to denial as a defense in the face of the trauma of loss. They seem particularly likely to carry on as though nothing has happened, to laugh, to play and even to become almost manic in behavior. Even though this overt behavior denies the significance of the loss, the child's inner life is likely to be markedly affected. Unfortunately, because his outer response seems so at odds with the situation, he may be seen as uncaring, unaffected, and even as unloving. If this is so, he may not be comforted, and his needs to mourn may be ignored.

While the younger child, especially in the three-to-five year age group may distress others by his constant questions—"Where is Daddy?" "Why doesn't Daddy come back?"—this older child may be quiet about the topic, not wishing to ask, wishing to maintain his denial by not knowing. Nagera suggests he may strongly cathect a fantasy life that attempts to keep his relationship with the person who has died: a fantasy of the idealized lost parent with whom the real and alive parent may come to compare very poorly. Nevertheless, despite such denial and such attempts to maintain the attachment to the lost parent, the child is likely to show many reactions to the loss when these are encouraged. The child may be able to discuss directly how he feels, but because he is afraid of the helplessness this engenders, he may be unwilling to do so and may need encouragement and play to facilitate such expression.

R. A. Furman (quoted by E. Furman 1974, p. 261) notes also the way in which latency children may hide their tears, because they fear loss of control, exposure, infantile dependence, and because they have internalized parental demands for containing feelings or have identified with parents' own ways of handling their emotions. He contrasts this with the younger child for whom controls are external: with permission the younger child may keep quiet or cry; whereas the older child may only be able to express himself privately, with his own inner sanctions operating. Given the opportunity to talk about their feelings, children in the middle-childhood age range will eventually, in a trusting relationship, feel safe enough to broach their distress and sadness. However, this opportunity is often not available to them in the family because of the family's denial of their grief at this age. Within our study children in this age group showed that they yearned strongly for the dead parent but were hesitant to show this. Boys, especially in this group, had particular difficulty in expressing their sadness and longing, frequently exhibiting aggressive responses and play.

Henry, age seven, had been very distressed by his mother's prolonged illness and, finally, hospitalization and death. Although his father had explained the illness, he had not really prepared Henry for her death as he himself had been hoping it would never come. Henry was told, after his mother had been in the hospital for a week and then died, that she had gone to Heaven and would not be returning. His immediate behavior was to ignore what he had been told, running off in apparently happy and excited play. He became, however, more and more difficult to manage.

He did not cry. He had many wild and rowdy games throughout the house, crashing his toy cars into the furniture and becoming very aggressive. His father was becoming increasingly angry with him, for his own grief was great, and he was disturbed that Henry was not only distressing the family by his bad behavior, but also that he appeared to have "cared so little for his mother."

Careful exploration with Henry and an interpretation of the helplessness and need beneath his powerful and destructive games brought an open and direct discussion of how bad it felt to be a little boy without a mother. He went on to further expressions of his longing and sadness, his yearning for his mother, his confusion about her death. His behavior settled dramatically, allowing a much more natural sharing of memories and feelings amongst the family.

Another aspect of the child's response at this time may be linked to excessive guilt. The child's self-destructive behaviors, his "badness" to induce punishment, or his depressed withdrawal may all reflect his guilty assumptions that he in some way caused what happened. Again this is especially likely to be reinforced if oedipal issues were powerful for him at the time of the death, if circumstances somehow reinforced them, or if he was directly involved in the death, for instance, in the car when an accident occurred or present at the suicide. This guilt may be reinforced by accusation or innuendos from the surviving parent or family members, or if death threats and wishes were very much part of an ambivalent family scene beforehand.

The child who attends school has another stress to face. His identity in terms of being like other children is important to him. It is in these years that he may first face the trauma of being "different," singled out, because a parent has died, or because he no longer has two parents. He may even attempt to hide the fact from teachers and friends or adopt a special grandiose bravado in the vain attempt to conceal from himself and others the helplessness, stigma, and distress that he feels.

Bowlby (1980) comments on the way in which bereaved children may become compulsively care-giving and self-reliant (p. 365), perhaps because of a strong tendency to inhibit grief yet a very strong need to be cared for. In our studies, girls in this age range, especially if they had younger siblings, seemed often to show this need for care through compulsive care-giving. Their grief response was not overt, or was only transient. Yet they cared for the younger sibling in an intense, sometimes exaggerated way, with a compulsive self-reliance that was quite inappropriate to their years.

Margaret, age seven and a half, was extremely bright and almost brittle and grown-up in her behavior after her mother's death. Her father stated proudly how much of a little mother she had become. She fussed about, bathed and dressed her younger brother, even encouraging his regression to use his bottle again. In exploration it was revealed that she yearned for her mother, yet family pressures and needs were so great that she had to be the "little mother" to meet others' needs. At the same time she kept her mother alive in her identification with her, repressing her own longing for care.

Kay, a seven-year-old, had had to learn to manage at home after school during her mother's prolonged illness and had taken over some care for her younger sister at this time. Kay was able to show her grief, and when her father would return in the evening she could allow herself to be a little girl again, curling up in his arms and being babied. When her mother actually died there was a tendency to shut out her distress, but her father handled this sensitively, so that a pattern of compulsive care-giving did not appear in place of her yearning.

The nature of the mourning process over time with this age group remains to be more clearly defined. It seems from available studies and descriptions that these children will continue their grief and mourning if allowed to do so. It will be distressing for them over the weeks and months following the death unless inhibitory processes supervene. If adequate family continuity, plus surrogate or other care, is available, much of the distress will have settled by the end of the first year, although the parent will be remembered with sadness and regret. A gradual decathexis of the relationship will occur. There is still likely to be yearning for the lost parent at times, but this will be dependent on the ongoing family process. Where grief and mourning are inhibited, perhaps because the relationship with the dead parent was so ambivalent that the child cannot deal with the guilt involved, or because adequate care was not available or the child was not informed, then pathological resolutions will certainly be more likely.

It is in this age group that fear about the vulnerability of the other parent may start to appear. These children seem to realize that if one parent may be lost they are vulnerable to the loss of the other. This may induce an additional burden of anxiety that inhibits the working through of loss and also distorts the relationship with the surviving parent.

The difficulty in this age group, as with all children, of sorting out the child's reaction to the death, to the grief of the surviving parent, and to other variables, is highlighted in some of the patterns of behavior these children show.

Cathy was six when her dearly loved father died. His death was sudden, unexpected. He had gone out before dinner, and she and her mother expected him home to tuck her carefully into bed as he had always done. When the police came with the news of the fatal accident, Mrs. K could not and would not believe it. She refused to see his body, wishing to remember him as he was. Weeks later she still felt it was all "unreal," a nightmare from which she would awake. She was most distressed about Cathy's behavior, her clinging dependence and the fact that she would not let her out of her sight.

In exploring these issues with mother and child separately, it became obvious that Cathy was responding to her mother's dread of being separated from her too, and she herself was terrified of losing her mother as well as her father. Separation could only be resolved when Mrs. K came to some acceptance of the reality and finality of her husband's death, and acknowledged that she and Cathy would both survive without him.

The issue of the degree to which identification represents part of the child's normal method of resolution of loss is a complex one. Bowlby (1980) disagrees with the typical Freudian model which sees identification as a key element of mourning. He believes (p. 30) that identificatory processes occur only sporadically and that they are prominent only in pathological mourning. He suggests this is the case with children, and that much of the evidence at present explained in identification terms can be better understood as a persistent though disguised striving to recover the lost person. E. Furman (p. 257) notes that children may be "developmentally inclined to deal with loss by identification, so that this frequently presents a danger to the resolution of mourning" (1974, p. 257). She believes the proportion of decathexis and identification needs to vary according to the type of loss and the developmental stage of the bereaved, but that it is important that identification does not become the predominant means. On the other hand, where the loss is temporary or partial, the child may keep cathecting the absent person and use identification to deal with the absence. The child's identifications with loved and hated aspects of the lost person, especially a parent, are likely to be "tried out," and there may be identifications with the parent's illness. Most workers seem to see these as transient and nonpathological, unless they become prominent and entrenched. Our own experience supports these views. However, other workers disagree. For instance, Perman (1979) focuses on the importance of the child's identification with the lost love-object, linking this with narcissistic regression and autoerotic activities. He suggests this is a search for the dead parent in the self, and this view is perhaps really not so dissimilar to Bowlby's.

Johnson and Rosenblatt (1981) argue differently, suggesting that strong identifications may in some way be healthy for children, in that the child would seem to lose a much greater part of the self in giving up identifying with a parent. These workers also point out some of the possible problematic outcomes of such identifications.

Obviously the child will identify with both the dead parent and surviving parent, and there will be complex internalizations influencing his response and behavior as a consequence. The significance for the individual child can only be worked out by assessment of such factors and their operation, both before and after the death.

Tom was eight and his sister Mary was six when their father died suddenly from a heart attack. Mrs. W was overwhelmed with her grief and was intensely angry at the suddenness and desertion the death entailed for her. So preoccupied was she with her own sense of pain and hurt that she seemed little aware of her children's needs. They played quietly together much of the time, and she felt that they were little affected. However, about three weeks after the death Tom's teacher reported increasing problems with his disruptive behavior at school.

In the assessment sessions, Tom stated that he was "all right." That he was a "big boy" now and "big boys didn't cry." When the interviewer suggested that even grown-ups felt sad sometimes and cried, Tom looked at her intensely. "Dad used to cry," he said. "He was sick in his heart you know. He got so sick he died." "What happened to Daddy when he died?" the interviewer asked. "He was burned, Mummy burnt him. They had a funeral but they wouldn't let me go." He looked sad, and a tear came. He hastily brushed it away. He started to play with the paints and drew a black house. "That's where the family live," he said. "Who's in the family?" he was asked. "They have a father and a boy and a girl. Their mother died, just like our father died."

The next time he played with the dolls and doll's house. Mary came to join him. They put the dolls inside and crashed furniture down on top of them. The games became more and more violent. They then shut the doors of the doll's house and shook it furiously but, finally, after quite a while, put it down. "The children are bashing up the house," Tom said proudly. "They are bashing and smashing it. The others are all buried in the mess." When asked if the children were angry Tom said: "The mother and father go away. They don't love the children anymore. The children will find a new mother." It seemed that they were responding to their mother's angry withdrawal and their father's absence and desertion of them. But there were also elements of identifying with the anger and the desertion of the parents.

The children showed the interviewer a painting on the wall. "He's dead," said Tom pointing to a reclining figure in the picture. "See the children, they are very sad. They are crying too."

As their mother became able, with assistance, to relinquish her own angry protest and grieve and mourn her husband's death, she seemed suddenly to become aware of the children again. They talked together of the father. Tom's anger settled too, but he often seemed sad. He was able to talk about his Dad and how he missed him. Mary too was able to open up her own grief and mourning.

OUTCOMES

Although Van Eerdewegh et al. (1982) include children of this age group in their study, they draw no specific conclusions about factors of importance, or outcomes of this group. It might seem that as a group they might be especially prone to issues of guilt related to newly formed superego functions, but there is no evidence to confirm this. It might also be suggested that identifications with the parent of the same sex who has just died, so recently consolidated, may lead to some disruptions of these identificatory developments. Again no specific data exist. Thus outcomes will be considered here in general terms for the range of childhood years.

## The Child from Eight to Twelve

As with the previous age group, many issues of earlier development and patterns for younger children continue. In this latter part of latency some further issues of relevance to loss appear with the child's development.

RELATIONSHIPS

The child in this age range has left oedipal struggles well behind him and is making much more intense relationships with peers and friends. These relationships are important to him but do not supplant his family. There may be best friends with whom close intimacies, or secrets, are shared. Sarnoff (1980) notes that in these later years some children may be showing more independence from parents, rather than passivity, and may feel, especially from about nine or ten onward that they would like to be able to take over and run their own lives. Such children, as compared to those who are more passive and afraid of growing up, may object very much to parental interference. The parents may wish to keep the child obedient as he was in the earlier years of latency, and thus conflict readily arises. As Sarnoff notes "the child who is struggling for independence usually deals with a harsh, limiting and condemning parent in his fantasies, as well as the real parent" (p. 152).

There are also likely to be prepubescent developments in the later years of this age range, especially where the beginnings of physical development appear. This will mean special things to the child in terms of sexuality and sexual identity that may complicate relationships with parents, perhaps leading to a drawing apart from one parent and an intensification of identification with the other. Such factors will be relevant to the child's response should the parent die.

DEATH

The child's understanding of death is now very much equivalent to that of an adult, although abstract concepts such as Heaven may still be difficult. However, one further factor is prominent for many children from about eight years of age onward. This is the realization of the possibility of their own deaths and fearful experience as a consequence. This has been shown in a number of studies but is highlighted in the work of Turnbull (1980) and Wainwright (1980). Both of these studies confirm that not only does the child's concept of death expand to that held in adult life, but also his affective response develops, leading to fears or to defenses against them. Some children experience these fears specifically and directly, while others displace or project them; and still others use denial, reaction formation, and counterphobic defenses. Thus, when the child in this age range confronts a personal bereavement, he also faces a new and often frightening reminder of the possibility that he too could die. His concepts of death, so recently consolidated, may also be thrown into question as he struggles to accept this death—its irreversibility and its cause. As with adolescents and adults, in the stress of the crisis, the child of this age may readily revert to egocentric and magical thinking.

A further factor becomes important here. This child, more than children in the younger age groups, has a greater orientation toward and understanding of the future. Thus he will be much more likely to be aware of what the loss will mean in the future, of how it will continue, and the possibilities of years of life ahead without the lost person. This is likely to be a further stressful factor he must face in his adaptation.

EXPERIENCE AND BEHAVIOR

The child in the eight-to-twelve age range is usually shocked by news of the death if it has been sudden. He may show considerable denial or, sometimes, great anxiety and distress. Some children in this group will try to carry on as if the fact means nothing to them, insisting on going on with their play or acting in some cheerful yet obviously brittle manner. This is usually transient, and the child's tearful distress breaks through then or subsequently. The clearest aspect of the child's initial responses is that he is frightened by what has happened and does not want it to be true.

When a parent has died following a long illness the child is usually in some ways prepared and may have less need for some of the counterphobic or denying defenses that often come into play following sudden death. However, in either case, denial of some kind is likely to occur. The death of a parent is very threatening to this child. He is not so dependent on the parent as is a younger child, but the degree of independence he has achieved is still very fragile, and the parental loss reawakens his feelings of childishness and helplessness. He is likely to yearn and long for the dead parent but feel he must control such childish longings. He may feel quite unable to share these with anyone, either other family members with whom he is trying to maintain his grown-up facade or with his best friend. He does not wish to have revealed his helplessness and vulnerability. He is likely to have an independent and "coping" exterior and may seem little affected by the death. Boys are especially likely to feel that they must behave in this way, as if there is a greater social and personal expectation for them to be strong and in control. For girls, and for those who are younger children in the family this expectation is not so strong, so they may be able to share with others how desperately they miss the dead parent.

The child may find it easier to show some of his anger about the death, for this is a more powerful feeling. He is often irritable and angry, especially with the surviving parent whom he may, in some way that he doesn't fully understand, hold responsible for the loss. This anger may also come out in aggressive games or in victimizing younger siblings or friends. The general irritability may not be seen as a response to the bereavement by either the child or by those with whom he is involved, and often it is labeled instead as "difficult" behavior.

Many children in this age range are still unable to accept the finality of the loss, even though the finality and irreversibility of death in general are recognized. How could the dead parent be gone forever? It seems so incomprehensible. This, plus the fact that the yearning for him is often repressed, means that the child is at risk of failing to resolve the loss. He may hold onto the relationship with the parent in fantasy, as may the younger child, imagining in many scenes the return of the parent, his own virtue in the rescue, the love all will give him, the magic of things being right again and the way they were before the death. This fantasy relationship is often idealized, creating further problems in the child's relationship with the surviving parent or the one onto whom he may project the badness that is split off from this idealized internalization.

Where the surviving parent is sensitive to the child's grief and need to mourn, and where he has been able to retain a comfortable but nonthreatening closeness to the child during his growing independence, he may be able, gently and in private moments, to help the child share his longing. Under such circumstances the child may be able to start to mourn for the lost person, acknowledging his yearning, its hopelessness, and his sadness that he will have his relationship no more. He may also be able to share his special fears about the future, the future for his family and himself, without this person.

Many children in this age group, however, do not have their grief and mourning recognized. Several patterns of response have appeared in the children we have seen. Some children take the bereavement very quietly. They seem somewhat withdrawn. There may be little major change in their behavior, except for some withdrawal and perhaps a falling off in their schoolwork. They are not resolving their loss, but marking time, as it were, until perhaps some later favorable circumstance arises where they can acknowledge the pain of their loss and grieve and mourn for the dead parent. Sometimes this occurs when the family seems to become stable and secure again. At other times, it occurs when these children form some sort of stable relationship with a surrogate person, such as an involved teacher, uncle, or priest, who can make them feel secure enough to express their yearning and longing for the dead parent and their sadness that the parent has gone. Teachers are particularly important in this age group, because the child often has a constant class teacher with whom he forms a close relationship during the school year. Furthermore, his difficulties and stresses often appear in the class situation, because he may perceive this as a safer forum for him than the emotionality of the home. He may also be struggling with conflicts concerning his "difference" from the other children now that he is without a parent. This stigma is felt acutely by him, particularly if the children, fired by their own or their parents' anxieties, tease him or in any way make him feel anxious about his altered state.

Another pattern found in these children is that of a retreat into some symbolic or other form of behavior that is linked with the dead parent. Thus the child may become very obsessed with the dead father's special books or other cherished possessions. He may wish to carry on, to the full, activities that were shared with that parent or were specially requested of him by that parent. He may play his father's music or carry on his mother's special kitchen rituals for example. Photos and objects belonging to the dead person are particularly treasured, sometimes in secret. There may be many identifications with the dead parent's behavior or style. In all these things it is as though the child is attempting to hold onto and continue the lost relationship. This is perhaps best typified by the case of Michael, age eleven, whose father was very fond of church music. Michael, after his death, would lie in his room, his headphones on, listening for hours to a favourite hymn of his father's, which included repetitively the phrase "Oh Father, I long to be with you."

Children in this age group may also take on, as do younger adolescents, a pseudoadult type behavior. It is as though they are trying to be "grown-up" to master the pain of their loss and particularly to deny the helplessness that they equate with being a child. They may also show compulsive care-giving toward younger siblings, or attempts to do this with the mother, or a "bossiness" which is often very irritating to others and thus may alienate the support and understanding they need.

Perhaps more in this group than any other, there is a tendency toward fearfulness, phobic behaviors, and some hypochondriasis. Because these children are more acutely aware of death as a personal possibility for themselves, they may start to become fearful of sleep and darkness, equating them with times of death. Or they may search all their bodily experiences and feelings to make certain there are no symptoms of disease. Even the most minute aches and pains may become frightening, so frightening the child dares not ask about them, and his fears build inwardly He may become phobic about anything that seems in any way associated with the possibility of death. In these instances the child's grief cannot be dealt with until his death-related fears can be settled, for they are both real and a defense against the loss.

Regardless of the patterns found, the children of this age group, when seen later in life, reveal how conflicted was their inhibition of grief and mourning for the lost parent or even a lost sibling. Few seem to have the opportunity to share their longing, their feelings, and their memories with others, even those they trust. Yet when they are able to do so, there is every indication that they progress through a mourning process of decathexis very similar to that of adults.

Helen was eleven and her brother Matthew, nine, when their father died. Their mother had been extremely distressed when the father's malignant melanoma had been diagnosed eighteen months beforehand. At first she withheld the news from the children but later told them their father was very sick, although she offered little information as to the nature of the disease. In the final months of his life he was nursed at home. The whole family life became oriented toward his care. The children were distressed by this and at times resentful that their activities were curtailed, that family resources were now so scarce, and their friends no longer came to the house.

Their father seemed to be tense and irritable much of the time and often in pain. Helen was secretly shocked by his appearance, his wasting, his gray skin, and the dull, dead look in his eyes. She felt ashamed of him in some ways when her few friends did call, and did not want them to see him. This also made her feel very guilty. She knew she should love and care for him, but she found the illness and his state abhorrent. She resented him for being sick and, in a way, her mother for keeping him at home rather than sending him to a hospital. She nursed a fantasy that if he were there in the hospital they would be able to forget about him, that their lives could return to some sort of normal state. She knew that he was dying and wished he would die so that things would go back to normal. Yet she dreaded life without him. He had always been the one who seemed to understand her best in the family, and deep in her heart she felt her mother really preferred Matthew.

Matthew was very angry about his father's illness. It wasn't fair that this should happen to his Dad—it didn't happen to the other boys' fathers. He was also very frightened. How could a big strong man like his father get so sick and so thin. He kept persuading himself that his father would get better again, soon; would get big and strong again and go out to work, and the whole family would go back to being the way it used to be. He knew in his heart, of course, that this wouldn't really happen, for he could see his father getting worse and worse as the weeks went on, and he could see from his mother's worry and distress, from the quiet serious talks with the doctor, that he was not going to get better.

Two weeks before the death, their father's condition deteriorated so badly that he had to be hospitalized. He lapsed into unconsciousness during that time and then died. Their mother told them of his death with tears and some relief, for she had felt that she herself could not survive much more of his illness.

Helen was at first shocked. She became very quiet and said little. She then went away to her bedroom and locked the door and cried quietly to herself. She felt very bad about the fact that she had not visited him in those last weeks, and ashamed of her abhorrence of his physical condition. She kept feeling in her heart that if she had loved him more, if she hadn't rejected him because he was ill, that maybe, just maybe, he would have got better. Later that day, and at the funeral, she cried a little, and she and her mother comforted one another. She felt she didn't really know why she was crying, but felt that it was really for herself and perhaps in sympathy for her mother.

In the days that followed she thought about her father a lot. In her heart she didn't really believe he was gone, and for a while she nursed a fantasy that he was still there at the hospital, sick; but then she would remember the funeral. She would sometimes feel very sad, missing him in his room where he had been during his illness and almost wishing him back. She took to her room some books he had been reading before he went to hospital, some poetry books, and hid them with her other treasures.

She felt that she must not let others know how she felt, and that she could not talk about him because she had been so bad in wishing that he would go away, and even that he would die, so that it would all be over. She felt especially bad in her rejection of him. Her mother was sympathetic and talked to her about her father sometimes, but Helen kept most of her thoughts secret and to herself. They were too bad, she felt, to share, and what's more, she wanted to hold her memories of her father secretly and privately, to cherish them as she had cherished the closeness of her relationship with him before his dreadful illness.

Helen's response in the weeks and months that followed was quiet and somewhat withdrawn. She spent much of her time fantasizing about her father, his illness, and about other miraculous outcomes of his illness. Her school work suffered to a degree, but she still managed reasonably. She became a very prim "big sister" to Matthew, tucking him into bed at night against his will, looking after him in every way she could. She also felt she must take special care of her mother. Gradually family life readjusted.

Matthew, on the other hand, was much more overtly distressed by his father's death. Matthew at first protested violently. His mother must be wrong, his father was still at the hospital. His Dad wasn't going to die—no way. He kept this up for almost an hour, but then started to cry. He was obviously very frightened, for he kept asking his mother what they were going to do now they didn't have Dad anymore. He too went to the funeral but, in his mind, ignored the ceremony and spent the time imagining the great and powerful things he and his father would do together. He seemed to carry on very much as usual in the days that followed—he even seemed quite cheerful at times. Increasingly, however, his behavior became disruptive. He insisted on staying up late at night. He wanted to play wild games with his sister, but she would not cooperate, so he brought his friends home again. The aggression and violence of their play of war and battle, of shooting and destruction, created a state of uproar in the house that his mother found hard to bear.

He was frequently naughty, disobedient and aggressive toward his mother and his sister. He spoke little of his father. At school his behavior was also more difficult and rude. So the teacher arranged to meet his mother and discuss his difficulties. With this conference, both realized that his behavior might well reflect his grief and protest over his father's death. The teachers spent extra time with Matthew, and his mother sat with him in the evenings as she put him firmly to bed at an earlier hour. Matthew was then able to become the frightened little boy he felt inside. He spoke of his longing for his Dad, how much he missed him, how scared he felt, how unfair it all was. He also, in due course, voiced the worst of his fears. He knew his Dad had died from a mole. He had moles too like his Dad. He had been looking at them each day, and he was sure that they were "going bad," and deep in his heart he was very very scared that he too was going to die. His mother held and comforted him. She talked of the very special things that had made his Dad's mole "go bad," and she was able that night and later to settle his fears. They talked a lot about his father, and together they went through some of the old photos and some of his father's model kits. Matthew kept these, treasured them, and completed the ones his father had been unable to finish. It was as though both of them were helped in their grief and mourning in these processes.

This family demonstrates how the parent's sensitivity and closeness to one child may enable him or her to be aware and supportive of that child's response to the bereavement. It also shows how the child whose response is more overt and aggressive may be more successful in gaining the care he needs; and how the child who holds a loss privately and who withdraws, may readily be seen as coping and thus offered little of the special understanding that he or she needs. The child who has lost the parent he felt closest to may feel he has, in the death, suffered a total loss.

## The Child's Responses to Deaths Other than a Parent's

The responses described thus far in this chapter have principally been those following the death of a parent. The child will grieve the death of a sibling or a closely loved grandparent just as surely but by no means as intensely, unless the relationship itself was particularly close. Where a child loses a twin, or a brother or sister of near the same age, someone with whom he had shared nearly every moment of his day-to-day life, a great wound is left. This wound is always somewhat complicated by the rivalry of siblings for parent love and for power within the family and so may be the more difficult to mourn.

In an early paper exploring responses to sibling death, Cain, Fast, and Erikson (1964) describe some of the disturbed reactions they found in children presenting for psychiatric care. The children they studied showed much guilt, some of them even five years or more after the death. They kept thinking over all the nasty things they had ever thought, felt, or done to the dead sibling and felt even worse in the process. They showed as a consequence, depressive withdrawal, self-punitive and accident-prone behaviors. They tended to become especially fearful of death, because here indeed was evidence that children could die. As a consequence they often developed distorted concepts of illness and disturbed reactions to doctors and hospitals. They sometimes believed that they would die as their brothers and sisters had, and they often developed identificatory symptoms that tended to reinforce such beliefs. Some of these children also showed disturbances of cognitive functioning, almost as if by assuming ignorance they could ignore the painful realities of death and loss.

There are also effects on the child of the restructuring of the family, the mourning of the parents (Rabkin and Krell 1979), and to a lesser degree, the grief of other siblings. Parental mourning may add to the child's feelings of alienation, although it is essential for him to see parental grief; otherwise he assumes that the dead child was not cared for, and the parent would not mourn if he, himself, died. The restructuring of the family subsequent to the death of a sibling, will also have effects that will be discussed in more detail below. Common negative changes in the family structure include an overprotectiveness toward surviving children, a realignment of relationships, an attempt to relate to one of the siblings as a replacement for the dead child, and sometimes, also, unfortunately, an idealization of the dead child that leads to the living being seen as poor comparisons. Hilgard (1969) suggests some possible links between the anniversaries of the death of a sibling and psychotic and depressive states in adult life.

Because the deaths of children are so untimely and are often associated with accidents, parental guilt is high, and sometimes a surviving child may be scapegoated, as if accused of being to blame for the death to relieve guilt the parent cannot tolerate personally.

In losing a sibling the child loses a playmate, a companion, someone who is a buffer against the parents, someone who may love and comfort him, someone with whom he identifies and whom he admires. In short he loses someone dearly loved as well as perhaps envied and rivalrously hated.

A child's first experience of bereavement may be that of a grandparent. Here the response will be very dependent upon the closeness of the relationship, especially in terms of the frequency and warmth of interaction. Grief for the child is likely to be short-lived, although unresolved issues may live on in his mind, as may the impact of his parent's grief for the death of his parent.

## The Influence of the Family

The child's responses to death and loss must be viewed in the family context. Not only will the system of the family govern much of what he knows and learns about the illness and the death, but it will have laid the foundations for the patterns of relationship that existed and for the emotional response patterns that may evolve after the death. The response of the family system at the time of the death and in the early crisis period will strongly influence the response of the individual child as will the longer term adaptations the family makes to establishing a new family structure with new roles and new patterns of gratification and interaction. The family response may well govern whether or not the child achieves any successful longer term adaptation and whether or not he resolves the loss. The family system sets the tone that will determine the effects on his development of the deprivation he experiences by the death.

*The family in which death is a taboo.* Death and loss are never discussed in some families. The child knows little of them when life-threatening illness appears. The severity of the illness is denied within the family system and is certainly kept from the child. Conspiracies of silence reign. The child senses dreadful, frightening secrets, but knows that it is taboo to ask about them. His fears build, but he cannot speak out. The parents rationalize their own denial in many ways, including the beliefs that they are "protecting" their "innocent child"; and that "what he doesn't know can't hurt him"; and that he is "too young to understand" or "too young to be affected."

At the time of the death he may be told nothing. He does not see the dead body or participate in the rituals of the funeral. He experiences hushed silences and the frightening tears and hushed whispers of strangers and the extended family. If and when he is told of the death, he is told that the parent or sibling has "gone away," or "gone to Heaven." He is given the clear message that he must ask no further questions. The mystery continues. Eventually he learns that the parent or brother or sister is dead. But he has little concrete knowledge of what this means and dares not ask. This family usually has some related taboos that the strong emotions associated with loss will be damaging, and so these too are repressed. The members comfort one another with thoughts that it would be best to try to "put the past behind," "remember him as he was," and try to forget about what has happened. They believe that it would be better not to cry as it will only upset everyone more, and they try to remove all reminders of the loss. The child is bewildered, but the message of what is expected of him is quite clear. He too learns that death, bereavement, and his grief and mourning are taboo. Such a family pattern often develops from similar patterns in the parents' own families of origin, and particularly from unresolved grief at the death of the parents' own parents. It is reinforced by many views held by the broader society and the social subculture in which the family exists.

*The family in which someone must be to blame.* The whole ethos of certain families, even long before a death occurs, is one of finding fault. All behaviors in these families are viewed in cause and effect terms. "It's your fault" or "Who did this?" constitute the key themes of family interaction. Guilt is a powerful force used in socializing the children, and punishment usually takes the form of covert or overt interactions designed to increase the bad feeling. Rigidity, control, and inflexibility, as well as high or extreme expectations of behavior are common in such families. This guilty power system is usually associated with deep and unresolvable guilts in each parent, guilts that cannot be borne, accepted, or worked through because of their irrational bases; guilts that may not even be recognized as such, but must be put onto others.

When illness or death occurs, there is in these families some vague querying as to cause, but, as the family's distress increases, the search for cause and a person to blame predominates, and guilt is the main emotion that clouds the response to the death. The rigidity of the family structure makes it hard to shift roles as is necessary after the death. The more sensitive and tender feelings that the loss evokes are not natural to these family members, especially the children, so accustomed to harshness and blame. The anger that the death brings is expressed in hostility to family members. Each feels guilty and cannot tolerate it. There may be a search for a scapegoat, and a child may be called upon to fill this role. Or the family may only feel united through collective angry hostility toward and blame of some outside system. There is little room in such a response for the child's regression, his pain, and his desperate needs for care. His own bad feelings and guilt are likely to increase. If he is not the scapegoat to ease parental guilt, another family member may become it. Sometimes, in such families, when a child has died, the parents' marriage fails, because the mutual blame and projection of guilt is such that the relationship cannot continue. If it does continue, the relationship may be one of guilty hostility. The child in this family learns that death is caused by someone, that guilt and not mourning is the natural response. His future development may well be further moulded by the harshness of his experience, his need to find ways of managing his deep reservoir of bad feelings, and by the constrictions of systems of his own of power, guilt, and blame.

*The family in which relationships are avoidant.* Some families, often because the parents have themselves experienced traumatizing separations or losses, are built of "cool" relationships. The parents like and want family life, but they do not let themselves become too intimate or close. They have extensive emotional investments in other things and other people. They do not allow themselves to value their family or each other too much. The emotional tone of the family is "cool." The covert message to children, long before death occurs, is that you mustn't get to like anyone too much, because you might get hurt, you might lose the person, and the pain of such loss must be defended against at all costs.

When a death occurs in these families there is some distress and grief, but these feelings are not great, and they are rapidly covered up, for to tap them would risk opening up the parents' painful early separation experiences. This family seems little affected by the death, hurries through grief, busies itself, and gets back to work and school again. Often parents are praised for carrying on so bravely and well. The child may be bewildered by the intensity of his own feelings and by the paucity of distress in his parents. He learns to keep his own feelings low profile, because the parents cannot tolerate them. He too learns to be "cool."

*The family in which things must go on as before.*  In some families loss and change must be denied or delayed. Feelings are not faced, because the loss or absence is not really acknowledged within the family system. This system is one that has also refused to acknowledge other losses and change long before this death has occurred. There is little flexibility of roles in such families, and the roles of the system must be filled at all costs. Members are not valued or related to for their own characteristics and needs, but rather for the roles they fulfill. For instance, a mother may have a family image of her children in which one of the children is kept as her "baby" despite his growth and development. When a death occurs in the family someone else *must* take over the role of the dead person, whether it be a dead parent or dead child. Grief will be little acknowledged or expressed. The child gets the clear message that his only chance for safety and survival lies in fitting in with this picture. Another example is when a parent dies, and the other parent must have someone to care for him or her. An older child is often forced into the role of the caring one. Sometimes these families will even rapidly take in replacement or surrogate figures for the dead person. The child may resent them, but again the message is clear: there is to be no grief. At all costs the roles must be filled, even if the cost is his longing for the lost person, his own personal sorrow.

*The family for whom the loss means chaos.*  Families to which a loss brings chaos already exist in a borderline or tenuous state. They have often suffered previous parental discord, illness and loss, sometimes parental depression, and other psychiatric disorders. Their resources, both financial and personal, are few. Their networks of support share similar deprivations or are absent. They are often known to welfare and service agencies. They have, perhaps, as Vollman et al. (1971) suggest, a social network composed of professional workers, whose role it is to care for them. The child in this system is already enormously stressed by the other variables such as parental discord. The loss and consequent further disintegration of the family constitute one more tragedy. In some cases, however, where a sick parent dies, thus ending parental discord, if professional or other support is strong enough, such a family may regroup in a more stable and secure form. The child's adjustment in these instances may be facilitated, and he may feel only relief. He may not, however, have learned how to master loss and death.

In other families where adjustment in general has been marginal but adequate, the loss may be the final straw. Chaos reigns in the family from then on with high levels of discord, or the family unit may disintegrate. This is sometimes an outcome for families with few financial resources where, when the mother dies, the father can no longer work and maintain the home. Children are farmed out to different relatives or institutions. They lose not only their family life, stressful and familiar, but also any ongoing family relationships and also their home. Fortunately such outcomes are less common where there are adequate welfare and support systems, as there are in many Western societies, or extended family systems of care as in less developed countries.

*The family that must do the right thing.* Some families seem unable to handle family relationships or crises with ease. However, the parents are aware enough of their own difficulties in such areas to try to learn what is the right thing to do. And their skills do indeed increase, so that they handle many problems reasonably well. There is sometimes a certain intellectualization about this in the beginning, but often, where the parents start to feel comfortable about it, some more natural emotional responses emerge. Such families have often learned the right things about child development and improved their systems of communicating and sharing feelings. Where there is serious illness, possibly fatal, they try to take the right steps to deal with it and handle communicating in a fairly natural way. They usually tell the children what has happened, perhaps providing them with books or other concrete guidance. They have often found out how to handle death and loss from workshops on such topics or their own reading. They may take the children along to the funeral and will do their best to explain what has happened to them. Sometimes they find this is very difficult, because despite all their knowledge of the right thing to do, their own impulses or fear and deprivation break through, and despite their rational approach, the more primitive feelings drive their responses. After the death the same tone continues. For the most part, such families do handle the loss reasonably well, for they are consciously geared to the child's needs and search for his responses. However, there is sometimes the difficulty that the things they defend so strongly against, dominate and alter their behaviors. The child in this family learns a pattern of response to loss that is fairly adaptive, although he often picks up and responds to the other, more covert message, that this is a fearful and terrible thing that is neither understandable nor controllable. Nevertheless, the genuine concern of the parents makes it most likely that such a child will have opportunities to grieve and mourn this loss.

*The family that functions with openness and sharing of real feelings.* In the family that has developed its relationships with openness and shared feelings, the relationships are those of worth, where, for the most part, positive and negative affects can be tolerated. Members of this family can tell one another how they feel. The pains of separation and loss in earlier stages of development have been borne. The child has already learned that he may yearn and be angry and be sad, and that his affects will be tolerated and he will be comforted. The crisis of loss is very painful in this family, for there is much intimacy. Yet the resources and patterns are there so that family members will be able to express their various affects: their yearning for the loss, their grief, their anger, their guilt, and their sadness. The relationship with the lost person can gradually be mourned, and a new family system, with patterns of warmth and closeness, will grow from this. Sometimes there will be barriers and periods of difficulty, but overall there will be a gradual progress toward a new adaptation. If family members grieve at different rates, with one still denying the loss, another experiencing separation pain, and another gradually recovering, then frictions may arise. If there were particular conflicts at the time of the death that heightened splits or ambivalences that would otherwise have been resolved in the passage of time, then resolution may be difficult. But on the whole the basic patterns and strengths of the family facilitate resolution of such issues over time. The child will suffer pain with the loss. His development may be different because of the deprivation. But he learns that loss can be mastered and that the care and consolation offered by others in times of pain are very healing. He is hurt by the loss, but not scarred, and he does not fear life because of it.

## Special Bereavements

*Suicide.* The child who survives the suicide of a parent may have special difficulties. There is the shame and stigma of the death and the mystery that often surrounds it. The nature of such deaths is even less likely to be explained to the child. He senses mystery and guilt, yet does not know the reason. These deaths frequently come on the background of parental ambivalence and much family discord. Nevertheless, they are often sudden and unexpected, and even when they are not, they seem the fulfillment of threats that had been going on for a long time and seemed to have lost their meaning. Some children are involved in the deaths, in that the suicide, such as a shooting, takes place in the child's presence. A careful study of responses in children was carried out by Shepherd and Barraclough (1976). They found that 50 percent of parents in their study failed to tell the children anything about the suicide and the remainder gave varying amounts of information, despite their good intentions. The mean age of children told of the suicide was ten, of those told something about the death was eight, and of those told nothing was four. None of the children orphaned by shooting or drowning was told of the specific circumstances. Not surprisingly, as a consequence of the suicide there were changes in family living circumstances and some reallocation of roles. These did not seem to have a major disruptive effect, perhaps because many of the families had been so discordant beforehand. Some of the children showed guilty responses after the suicide, and most showed anger, sorrow, and some distress, except where there had been some prolonged separation from the parent beforehand. Some of the children showed longer term responses of anxiety, but other major psychological consequences were not apparent, either early on or at the time of study five to seven years after the deaths. However, as the authors note, these conclusions were drawn from parents' reports and not from contact with the children themselves, and they may have reflected parents' failure to recognize their children's grief and other disturbances.

Other workers (for example, Cain and Fast 1966; E. Furman 1974) would seem to suggest that such bereavements are in fact more difficult to resolve. Our own studies substantiate this. For children of suicides there is not only the uncertainty of what has happened, but the long-standing pain that was often linked to the relationship that is difficult to resolve. The shame and guilt in the surviving parent, and the fact that the surviving parent's mourning is often disturbed, will also have reverberations for the child. He is particularly likely to carry a burden of nameless guilt, some feeling that his inner badness must have caused the parent to desert and reject him in this way. He may have fantasies of reunion and may actively fantasize or contemplate suicide himself. In the child there may still be a concept that death is akin to a reversible state, like sleep. Orbach and Glaubman (1979) show how the child's cognitive concept may lead him to believe he can undergo lifelike experiences after death. The child may have two conceptions of death: impersonal death, referring to other people; and personal death, referring to himself. This latter form may be seen as reversible. He may long to go to be with the dead and often idealized parent. Depression is common. His identification with the dead parent may also lead to other self-destructive behaviors, or it may form the foundation for suicidal thoughts in adult life. Bowlby (1980, chapter 22) reviews studies of children's responses to parental suicide. He quotes Cain and Fast's work (1972) showing two main types of reaction in the children: one is that of sad guilt-laden withdrawal and inhibition; the other is of angry, hostile, defiant, and ill-organized behavior. The role of parental threats before the death is emphasized as a source of guilt, particularly where the child has been told he is upsetting a parent or "driving him crazy." The child may also feel that all that went wrong between his parents and seemed to lead to the suicide is his fault. There are, of course, special problems when in the height of repeated threats and arguments, the parent has told his spouse to "go ahead and get it over with" or suggested, as did one of our subjects, "Why don't you shoot yourself?"

Hamish was six when his father died. His father had been depressed for about six months, but the family had struggled to cope with this, and his mother had colluded with his father to avoid psychiatric care. Mr. P's depressive episode was his first major attack, but there was a strong family history of depressive illness, and an uncle had suicided.

Mr. P's depression had been so bad that he had ceased work a few weeks before and had spent the days lying around the house, worrying about the family's debts and the black state of the world. He had normally had a fairly good relationship with his only son, although tending to be rather strict and full of very high expectations for him. Hamish, his mother, and two sisters had gone out to a school fête. When they returned, as Mrs. P entered the house she found her husband's body lying where he had fallen, a gun beside him and a wound in his head. In great distress she hurried the children into the back room and called for help. Neighbors, the ambulance, and police arrived. Mrs. P was distraught, already blaming herself for leaving her husband and for what had happened.

She explained to the children that their father was sick and had been hurt and that the ambulance would take him away. She could not bring herself to respond to Hamish's frightened queries as to what had happened or why the police were there, but brushed him aside. Neighbors then took the children to their own homes, and Mrs. P went to her sister's place.

In the days that followed Hamish became very afraid. He was separated from his mother most of the time, and when he saw her she was very distraught. Finally she told him his father had died and that he had been buried. She explained nothing more.

The family returned home and resumed life, but without Mr. P. Hamish returned to school. It was there that he heard from his friends that his father had "committed suicide." He did not fully understand what it meant but knew that it was very bad. As the days went on he felt the other children were avoiding him, and he felt different and frightened. His teachers were kind but seemed to treat him in some special way. He tried to ask his mother to tell him more about his father's death, but she seemed unable to help him and only became more distressed when he brought the topic up with her. He then heard two boys saying that his father had "shot himself" and he "must have been some kind of nut." Hamish was deeply shocked, remembering suddenly and now understanding the blood and the gun he had glimpsed as they entered the house that day.

He could not sleep that night and lay in bed very frightened and sobbing to himself quietly. His father must not have loved them. His father must not have cared. He himself must have been very bad for his father to do this. Perhaps it was to punish him. His sadness overwhelmed him.

He thought more and more of his father in the days and weeks that followed. He dreamed of him somewhere else, and of the happy times they had shared. He paid less and less attention to school and to the world of his family. His mother seemed so preoccupied with her own grief and the distress of his younger sisters that she did not seem to notice him.

It was only after several weeks that his depression and despair became obvious to her and to his teacher. He was referred for assessment. It took several weeks to draw him into a relationship with a child psychotherapist, and then, through a number of sessions, the depth of his hurt, anger, and despair was revealed. He felt his father had deserted him, that he was bad and unlovable, and that his mother could not love him either. He was extremely angry over his father's action, and as he was able to play through some of his affect his mood started to improve. In the weeks that followed he gradually started to become involved in his school and family again and moved toward mourning and relinquishing his relationship with his father. He still had periods of sadness and anger when he thought of the circumstances of his father's death, but his guilt had lessened and his capacity to love had returned.

*Divorce.* Children who experience a parental divorce have many losses to work through. There is the loss of idealization of parent figures and the loss of idealization of the mother-father relationship. They can no longer feel they are loved and cherished above all else, because parental needs and feelings have obviously been given priority. They lose as well the whole family they knew, becoming part of a different family unit. They find a closeness and intimacy with one parent, the one who has custodial care, and a different and perhaps not quite satisfying relationship with the other. They do, as Wallerstein and Kelly suggest (1980), go through processes of grief and mourning which are in many ways similar to those of bereaved children. Capacities of the child to recognize the finality of the loss and to express affects vary with age ranges as in bereavement. These children, like bereaved children, often nurture a fantasy relationship with the idealized absent parent. They also long for a magical reunion of the parents and return of the family to its earlier state of wholeness. They frequently blame themselves for the loss and the parent's unhappiness. They often adopt defenses of denial, reaction formation, and pseudo-adult behavior in their attempts to cope with their hurt, pain, and helplessness. They are also very angry, for they feel that the parent has chosen to desert and reject them. In cases of divorce, resolution of the loss is often complicated, because it comes on the background of such high levels of parental ambivalence and discord. As with children who have been bereaved by the death of a parent, these children take some time to settle into the new and different life circumstance. While much of their overt distress may be settled after the end of the first year, nevertheless, much of the loss may not be resolved, but may instead be secretly locked away, influencing their emotional life and relationships.

It might be said that, like bereaved children, these children go through denial, through grief, and mourning. They have fears of abandonment and are often harrowed by issues of guilt and blame. They may respond to the divorce with regression and immaturity; or they may respond with a hyperactivity that is not always adaptive. Anger is prominent and may lead to neurotic reactions in projection and phobias, compulsive behavior and depression; it may also be acted out, either in identification with parents or through superego lacunae and with parental sanctions. It may also be used to compensate for feelings of powerlessness and to test out relationships. Gardner (1976) outlines many of these problems in his useful book on the psychotherapy of children of divorce, suggesting techniques for dealing with the affects and conflicts that arise. He also highlights the importance of the child's ongoing fantasies of parental reconciliation and the implications of the loss of a parent by divorce for the child's self-esteem and role identifications, taking into account the impact on resolution of oedipal conflicts. As with bereavement, the child's depression, and altered behaviors, or other symptoms may be strongly linked to identification with the response of the remaining parent, or with the absent one when he attempts to hold on in this way.

Many of the issues highlighted by these workers in relation to divorce are similar to those of bereavement by death. Yet the divorced parent remains, in fantasy or reality, a living force in the child's life in a way that is quite different from the situation after a death. The child here has to resolve the complex issues of this different relationship and the role it may play in the ongoing life of his family.

## Family Life after Loss

As highlighted by workers in the field of childhood bereavement as well as divorce, the nature and quality of family life after the crisis will be very important to the child. The loss of a particular parent may have consequences in a number of ways. Effects on identification by the lack of role models are possible. These may be linked to issues of oedipal conflict resolution. For instance, Arthur and Kemme (1964) found guilt reactions in the majority of children who suffered the death of a same-sex parent. Fast and Cain (1964) observed that sons who lost their fathers tried to avoid positive feelings to their mothers and showed very strong loyalty to the dead father. Girls in Arthur and Kemme's study tended to idealize their dead fathers. Birtchnell (1969) suggests also that oedipal resolution may be impaired by subsequent relationships that develop between the child and the remaining parent. He sees some homosexual conflicts arising in such situations as well as heterosexual ones. Similarly, Gardner (1976) highlights such factors for children of divorce. In both instances the occurrence of the loss during the oedipal phase may seem a consequence of oedipal wishes. Furthermore, care-seeking or seductive behavior on the part of the parent may reinforce difficulties. The special problem for the child of divorce may be the way in which one parent vilifies the other, perhaps leading to difficulties for the child in maintaining identification with an absent and apparently evil father, for instance.

The particular effects for the child of either sex of the death of one or the other parent have yet to be fully delineated and must take into account individual dynamic factors. However, Newman and Denman

(1971) suggest the death of a father may have some associations with later felony type behavior, and Lifshitz (1976) found that fatherless subjects, especially those orphaned before the age of seven, tended to show significant constriction in awareness and differentiation in their broader social milieu, as well as a narrowing of a number of psychological indices. The National Family Study (Douglas 1970) suggests too that the childhood death of a father may be associated with later antisocial behavior, and that of a mother with adolescent pregnancy in girls.

The stability of family life after the loss is another important factor both in responses to bereavement (Birtchnell 1969; Bowlby 1980) and to divorce (Gardner 1976; Wallerstein and Kelly 1980). A one-parent family is likely to be particularly vulnerable, as is a new family with a new parent figure if there is remarriage. Wallerstein and Kelly point out the conflicts for the child after divorce, especially with issues of maintaining attachments to the absent parent. Despite this, many remarriages for divorced parents prove rewarding, and a good family life may result for the children. These issues are not so well understood following bereavement. The child often longs for the regularity and security of a full family life again, yet may enjoy special privileges when he has only one parent and does not have to share him or her with another adult. He feels vulnerable in the single-parent household, because he knows that he might also lose this parent, and because he now has no balancing effect from the other. Yet once he is used to this situation he may strongly resist his parent's attempts to establish new relationships. Where these are reestablished successfully, there is much to suggest that the child finds them valuable and rewarding in many instances. There may be an initial rejection of the new parent and a renewal of loyalty and grief for the one who has been lost. If these further levels of grief can be supported sympathetically then there is much to suggest that he may establish new and rewarding bonds.

## Pathological Patterns of Bereavement in Childhood

There is no clear definition, as yet, of what may be normal or pathological in terms of patterns of childhood response to loss. It may be suggested that, just as with an adult, there may be an absence or inhibition of bereavement. This seems common in children who have no opportunity to grieve or have their response to the loss recognized. The yearning may be repressed and unconscious as Bowlby (1963) notes, or it may be that the child's ego cannot tolerate the pain of relinquishing the lost object or the intensity of the affects involved. In fact, in his early works Bowlby tends to equate pathological mourning with childhood mourning. It seems also likely that distorted patterns may appear, although exaggerated protest is more likely than pronounced guilt. It is only in the later years of childhood that this type of distortion may occur. Chronic grief is not common. Bowlby (1980) divides disordered variants of children's responses to loss into those with persisting anxieties, which may include fears of further loss or a fear that the child himself will die; those with hopes of reunion and a desire to die; and those with persisting blame and guilt. He also notes patterns of overactivity with aggressive and destructive outbursts, and as well those patterns which he calls compulsive care-giving and self-reliance. Euphoria with depersonalization and identificatory symptoms, and accident proneness, are also included in his list. Whether the response of a child is considered disordered or not can only be understood by a full evaluation of the loss he has experienced, the way it occurred, and the nature of his family life. All these factors will strongly influence responses in childhood and the adaptations and outcomes that are achieved.

## Possible Outcomes of Bereavement in Childhood

Many possible consequences have been hypothesized for major bereavements affecting young children. Immediate traumatic effects are suggested. The possibility of impaired development has been inferred. The creation of a vulnerability state leaving the child at risk for disorders such as alcoholism, depression, or suicide in adult life have all been suggested. A higher rate of childhood bereavement found in a group considered to show creative genius could lead to assumptions of positive developmental effects. Specific influences depending on the sex of the parent who died, or of the sibling who died, have been inferred. Yet despite all these possibilities, no clear-cut findings have really emerged, for the vast majority of studies have been retrospective, and the variables are many and complex.

# The Bereaved Child

*General symptomatology.* In childhood, the general symptoms of bereavement manifest themselves especially in the sphere of sleep, appetite, and habit disturbance. Van Eerdewegh et al. (1982) found that parents (surviving the death of the other parent) reported that their children (ranging from two to seventeen years of age) showed a significant increase in symptoms one month after the death when compared to a control group of children who were not bereaved. While all symptoms they assessed but three were more frequent in bereaved children than in controls, increases were significant only for dysphoric mood, sadness, crying, irritability, sleep difficulties, decreased appetite, withdrawn behaviors, tempers, and bedwetting. At thirteen months follow-up (to avoid the twelve-month anniversary effect) the authors noted a significant decrease in dysphoric mood, but a significant increase in abdominal pain and fights with siblings, with lack of interest in school but increased interest in general nonacademic activities.

Our own prospective oriented study of bereaved children looked at both parental reports and child assessment (Raphael, Field, and Kvelde 1980; Raphael 1982). We noted a very high level of behavioral symptoms in the early weeks and months following the parent's death, as compared to symptomatology reported for these children prior to the death. In this nonselected sample, up to 20 percent of children may have shown two or more symptoms from the checklist prior to the death, but 86 percent were noted as having two or more symptoms after the death. These symptoms included withdrawal, aggression, clinging, and severe separation responses as well as sleep, appetite, and habit disturbances.

Arthur and Kemme (1964) describe high levels of symptomatology in their uncontrolled study of eighty-four bereaved children attending a child-guidance clinic. They reported feelings of hopelessness (29 percent), impaired appetite (19 percent), phobic separation responses (45 percent), and nightmares and night terrors (23 percent). Increased crying (13 percent) and noticeable sadness (35 percent) were also reported. The children were often fearful about illness and sleep as well as separation. Some tended toward inhibited and withdrawing behaviors, others to impulsive and aggressive responses.

There are no specific reports of health care utilization patterns by the children after the death, as compared to adult's responses where increased health care utilization has been reported by a number of workers (Parkes 1964b; Maddison and Viola 1968; Raphael 1977b). It is of interest that in Van Eerdewegh's study there were in fact fewer physician visits in the bereaved group than in the control group. This may fit with the parent's being too preoccupied with his or her own grief to seek care for the child's symptoms or the parent's failure to perceive the child's symptoms or recognize their significance. For instance, fathers have been shown to be relatively unaware of many of their children's difficulties following the mother's death (Bedell 1973). Certainly in our study many parents seemed only to become aware of changes in the child when directly queried about them. They often could not relate them to the bereavement or see them as evidence of the child's needs. This was particularly likely to be the situation when the parent's own grief was inhibited or when he had other pathological bereavement responses.

A further complicating factor in terms of the child's behavioral responses may be the parent's perception of these in terms of his or her own bereavement responses. Thus, in a number of our studies the mother was likely to present the child for care with complaints or concerns about the child's aggressive feelings and behaviors, the child's dependent needs, the child's sleep disturbance, and the child's sexuality. On closer assessment it would become obvious that the mother was in fact presenting the child vicariously as representing some problem area or unmet need of her own. The child's needs *might* coincide, but his response was more often in a different sphere.

The child cannot take himself to systems of health care for the comfort and support he may need to deal with the loss, unless he is an independent adolescent, and even then it is unlikely he will do so. Thus an additional support system used frequently by adults to deal with the pain of loss in a socially acceptable way is not so readily available to him. If his parent's grief is such that the parent is unable to provide the support he requires, and there is not anyone else easily available, it is obvious that his risk of malresolution of the loss may be heightened.

*Psychosomatic effects.* Childhood parent loss has been suggested as a factor in the etiology of a number of conditions. Studies have shown a higher incidence of parent loss in children who develop juvenile diabetes, although the losses reported were more frequently those of divorce rather than death. The earlier the loss, the greater the stress, these workers suggest, perhaps because of its effects on the surviving parent (Leaverton et al. 1980). Stein and Charles (1978) make similar observations. A possible role of loss in the precipitation of thyrotoxicosis is suggested by Morillo and Gardener (1980). Parental loss has also been described as a factor prior to the onset of juvenile rheumatoid arthritis (Herioch, Batson, and Baum 1978). In these disorders the loss is suggested as being one factor in a multifactorial etiology, and further loss factors are also described in association with the course of the disorders.

*Adjustment disorders, neuroses, and conduct disorders.* Felner et al. (1981) show that children dealing with crises of death and separation or divorce showed greater overall school maladaptation than children without such histories. The children who had experienced parental death had more socialization problems than did controls, while those who had experienced separation and divorce had socialization and acting-out problems. Van Eerdewegh et al. (1982) show an increased disinterest in school at thirteen months follow-up for a significant group of bereaved children compared with controls. School refusal was noted as a common presenting problem in school-aged bereaved children in Black's study (1974) of child guidance clinic children.

Rutter (1966) notes the role of parental death in the presentation of some children to child psychiatric clinics and comments on the vulnerability of children in the three- to four-year-old age group.

Cain, Fast, and Erickson (1964) describe a variety of disturbed reactions in children to the death of a sibling. Binger (1973) notes that in a sample of children who had lost a sibling from acute leukemia, more than a half showed altered behavior patterns that indicated considerable difficulty in coping. Some reactions appeared during the terminal illness, but the more severe followed the death and persisted. These included enuresis, headaches, poor school performance, school refusal, depression, severe anxieties, and persistent abdominal pain.

Bedell (1973) notes that children surviving the mother's death may have a cluster of difficulties; for instance, a child may have nail-biting, bed-wetting, and poor school performance. About 20 percent of the children in this study were perceived by their fathers as having difficulties, but Bedell recognized that a variety of factors, including the surviving father's level of involvement with the child before the death, could influence the accuracy of this estimate.

The range of adjustment disorders varies. There may be conduct disorders, described in some groups, while neurotic symptomatology patterns seem predominant in others. As noted by Arthur and Kemme (1964), regressive behaviors, disorganization of play, excessive eating, soiling, and masturbation appeared early, and later major adjustment disorders, such as defiant manipulation, self-punitive problems, and inhibited withdrawal reactions, were more prominent.

Recently Elizure and Kaffman (1982) have found emotional disturbance in 40 percent of the normal kibbutz children (N = 25) they studied during the four years following their fathers' deaths. The two common types of behavior disturbance were over-anxious dependence and antisocial aggressiveness leading to high levels of pathology.

*Depression.* Depression as a possible outcome of childhood deprivation caused by the loss of a parent was suggested by Spitz's model of anaclitic depression in severely deprived infants in institutional settings. Similar depressions have been described since in human infants separated from their mothers as well as in experimental monkeys (Harlow 1962). It is obvious however that many children do not suffer more than temporary depression responses to the loss of a parent, so a number of influencing factors are likely to operate.

Rutter (1981) points out that misery and unhappiness occur in childhood, as does depression, but unhappiness as a symptom and depressive illness as a syndrome are certainly not synonymous. Caplan and Douglas (1969) studied children presenting to a psychiatric out-patient clinic. They compared those with a primary diagnosis of depression with a control "mixed neurotic group." Ages were from five to sixteen years. They found that the depressed group had experienced a much higher level of separation and/or losses including bereavement than the control group, and that there were often multiple losses for the bereaved children. Van Eerdewegh's group (1982) found depressive symptoms to be highly significant for bereaved children, especially sadness, crying, withdrawal. These were characteristic of the bereaved group, but the dysphoric symptoms tended to decrease significantly over time. The mild form of depression was present in nine of the fifteen depressed children in the study, but in none of the control children. These workers suggest that this could be typical of the bereavement process whereas the more severe depression, of similar incidence in the control group, represented another clinical entity in which the bereavement had perhaps acted as a precipitant. This severely depressed group was similar to that described by Rutter (1966) in that they both comprised mostly adolescent boys who had lost their fathers. Also, all but one of the mothers of the severely depressed group had at one time had a diagnosis of primary or secondary depression.

In our own preliminary studies (Raphael, Singh, and Adler 1980), 25 percent of the children assessed (N = 20) prospectively had a clinical picture that could be classed as childhood depression in terms of the criteria of Schulterbrandt and Raskin (1977) when assessed by a skilled clinical psychologist. Independent assessment of parents revealed that all the parents of these children were suffering from obvious and severe depression at the time of assessment during the first few months following the other parent's death. In some instances this depression was long standing; in others it had apparently been precipitated by the bereavement.

EFFECTS OF CHILDHOOD BEREAVEMENT DURING LATER LIFE

Childhood bereavement has been suggested to be a vulnerability factor for a variety of disorders in adult life. For the most part the studies are retrospective, and many methodological problems exist so conclusions are nondefinitive. The effects described are, for the most part, nonspecific, although several groups of disorders have been suggested as relevant.

*General symptomatology and ill health.* A number of studies suggest those who have experienced parental loss in childhood are more likely to present with general symptomatology, increased health care utilization, and vague or specific complaints of ill health in adult life. These studies also suggest that such a group may experience greater general psychological distress or ill health, such as "demoralization." Seligman et al. (1974) suggest that loss of a parent in childhood may play some role in presentation of adolescents to general medical services. The Midtown Manhattan Survey in New York (Langer and Michael 1963) showed an increased risk of psychiatric disorder in those who had lost a mother before the age of sixteen, but this held only for "lower class" women. These studies are certainly not conclusive and may reflect social variables more than loss.

*Psychosomatic effects.* Workers such as Schmale and Iker (1971) suggest that those who as adults develop cancer may be more likely to have had childhood experiences of deprivation and loss. It is inferred by most of these workers that the childhood experiences are likely to leave some vulnerability which may then be triggered by subsequent losses which act as precipitants creating an environment favorable for the development of disease through immune and endocrine systems.

*Psychiatric disorder (excluding depression).* The loss of a parent in childhood has been suggested as an etiological factor in alcoholism and other addictions. Sholnick (1979) presents a model of the "craving" for the substance as representing a craving or longing for the lost object, and the addictive substance is taken to deal with this craving and/or pain.

Watt and Nicholi (1979) suggest from three separate studies comparing adult schizophrenic patients with other psychiatric patients, that the premature death of a parent may be a contributing factor in the etiology of schizophrenia. The high frequency of parental death among schizophrenics was not attributable to a genetically linked tendency to suicide. The deaths tended to be earlier than average in the lives of schizophrenics and more common in those with paranoid symptoms. Some workers in the past, such as Dennehy (1966) and Hilgard (1969) also support such findings, while others, such as Granville-Grossman (1966) disagree.

Markusen and Fulton (1971) in an anterospective examination of a population suggest a relationship between childhood bereavement and offenses against the law, but they recognize the methodological shortcomings of their study. A further study (Bendiksen and Fulton 1975) fails to show a connection between childhood bereavement and disorders such as divorce or arrest in adult life.

*Depression.* There has probably been most interest and controversy about the possible relationship between bereavement in childhood and adult depression. It is impossible to review all the conflicting findings here, but some of the most significant studies will be presented.

Brown (1982) reviews his group's work on the relationships between early loss and depression in adult life. His Camberwell study showed loss by death of the mother before the age of eleven was significantly greater for depressed women in the community than for a matched nondepressed control-group of women. Brown was able to show the vulnerability-factor nature of the association by demonstrating that there was increased risk of disorder (in the year of the study) for the bereaved woman, *only* when a provoking factor operated in the year before. There was no raised risk for the early bereaved women when there was no provoking agent. Other vulnerability factors could increase the risk of depression. These included having three or more children under fourteen living at home and low intimacy with a husband. Brown then goes on to discuss the association found by himself and other workers between early loss of a parent and severity of depression. In his subsequent Walthamton study (Brown 1982) these same factors appeared. Of women who had lost a mother by death before seventeen years of age, 24 percent had experienced affective disorder in the twelve months prior to the interview, and in those experiencing such maternal bereavement before the age of eleven the rate was almost double that of those experiencing it after eleven. A further interesting intervening variable appears in this study: namely, that those women with early loss of a mother are more prone to premarital pregnancy, and those with premarital pregnancy are particularly predisposed to later depression, a further variable independent of lack of intimacy with their husbands.

Birtchnell (1972) in an early study shows similar findings of the possible pathogenic potential of the loss of a mother before ten years of age, but in more recent work based on community samples (Birtchnell 1980) he fails to show such associations. He notes in the later work that those bereaved women who had bad relationships with their replacement mothers had certain clinical characteristics: they were more likely to break down at an early age with neurotic rather than endogenous type depression, and they were more prone to severe and chronic anxiety type symptoms, often being diagnosed as hysterical or inadequate. He suggests that such effects of inadequate replacement mothering could often be mitigated by a satisfactory marriage and family. His subsequent work with these subjects (Birtchnell and Kennard 1982) suggests that, while these early bereaved women had marriages that were no different from those of controls, they had more difficulty with child rearing especially when their children reached adolescence. They tended to be more possessive and overprotective. There was also some tendency for them to marry younger men, perhaps carrying on the maternal role they may have had to adopt in their own families following the mother's death. An interesting related finding was that men who had lost their mothers early tended to marry older women, perhaps as mother substitutes.

Other workers negate potential roles for early parent loss in creating a vulnerability to depression in adult life. For instance, Tennant, Bebbington, and Hurry (1980) reviewed studies that attempted to link parental death in childhood to adult depressive disorders. They comment on the inconsistency of findings which they link to the methodological limitations. They conclude from the studies they reviewed that, with rigorous matching of experimental and control samples, no association could be found between childhood parental bereavement and depression in adult life.

Suicidal ideation and behavior have also been linked to childhood bereavement in the work of Adam et al. (1982). Adam compared subjects with a history of parental loss before the age of sixteen with a matched control group from intact homes. Early parent loss subjects demonstrated significantly more suicidal ideation and attempts, and this relationship was even more marked when the loss had resulted in chaos and disruption of family life: findings which were significant for loss by death and separation or divorce. However, Adam's findings were not directly linked to diagnosis of depression.

*Relationship patterns.* As noted previously there are some studies suggesting an influence of early parent loss on the relationship styles of the bereaved in adult life. Birtchnell and Kennard (1982) note the influence on marital patterns. Earlier workers such as Jacobsen and Ryder (1969) also note an inability to sustain intimacy in the early years of marriage, although the marriages were sometimes rated as closer.

*Sensitivity to loss.* Bowlby's work (1980) would suggest that unresolved bereavement in childhood might make the adult more likely to handle bereavement poorly in adult life. The Caplan model (Caplan 1964) of crisis would reinforce such a view. Brown's data (1982) lend some support to this. Our own studies of bereaved adults also suggest that this may be a mechanism, but statistical evidence is lacking because of the small numbers of subjects in most studies.

*"Anniversary" or "age-correspondence" phenomena.* It has been suggested that anniversaries of a death may be times of increased vulnerability to disorder or decompensation, perhaps acting as precipitating factors. Bornstein and Clayton (1972) describe intensification of symptoms in widows and widowers one year after their partner's death. Pollock (1970; 1971*a*; 1971*b*) also describes a range of similar anniversary vulnerabilities and notes that they may recur each year. Pollock believes that such reactions result from incomplete or pathological mourning. Depression is not an uncommon presentation (Hilgard 1969) in such cases, and even manic symptoms have been described (Rickarby 1977). However, the relevance of such phenomena in children is unclear.

Birtchnell (1981) explores the other type of anniversary phenomenon which he labels a "correspondence" phenomenon, in which a breakdown occurs when the patient's child reaches the same age he was when his parent died. Similarly, it may also be that the breakdown occurs when the patient reaches the age the parent was when he or she died, and these two correspondences may concur. Hilgard and Newman (1959) had described these phenomena earlier, finding them to be frequent in the clinical sample they examined. In Birtchnell's group of patients, the phenomenon occurred but had no specific clinical features. The observed number of cases was small, no greater than would have been expected by chance. He did feel, however, that the correspondence could have accounted in some measure for the time of onset of the symptom and the clinical characteristics, which might reflect symptoms like those associated with the death.

FACTORS INFLUENCING THE OUTCOME OF CHILDHOOD BEREAVEMENT

Bowlby (1980) outlines the factors he believes to be associated with the more favorable outcome of childhood bereavement. He lists the influencing variables as follows:

1. The causes and circumstances of the death, including what the child is told and what opportunities are given to him subsequently to enquire about what has happened
2.. The family relationships after the loss, especially whether or not the child remains with the surviving parent and the quality of those relationships and family life following the loss
3. The patterns of relationship within the family prior to the loss, particularly the relationships between the parents and between each of them and the bereaved child (p. 311)

In Bowlby's work and the work of others, these variables are elaborated, as is the evidence in support of them. It is of particular relevance to this volume how closely these factors reflect the key variables influencing the outcome of bereavement generally (as outlined in chapter 2) and the bereavement of adults (as outlined in chapters 5 and 6). It is apparent from a variety of sources, outlined below, that the general framework of factors can be delineated for childhood bereavement outcome along similar lines for both children and adults.

*The preexisting relationship between the bereaved and the dead person.* Where high levels of ambivalence or dependence exist the mourning process and reaction to the loss are likely to be more complex and more difficult to resolve. As noted by Bowlby (1980), these preexisting levels of ambivalence make it difficult for the child to deal with the loss. In childhood such difficulties may add a further load to the attempts to resolve the bereavement, in that the child may already be suffering impairment in his ego functioning and development, even to the level of symptomatology prior to the death. This fits with the finding of the effects of disturbed relationships with parents on child development and, as well, the effects of parental discord on child psychiatric symptomatology (Rutter 1981).

The child's particular dependence on the parent for survival is a key issue that may interfere with the process of mourning. It is only when either the surviving parent or surrogate figure takes over tasks that ensure the child's survival that he eventually feels secure enough to grieve and mourn. R. A. Furman (1973) notes that "a child has physical and emotional needs that must be met for his survival, and if his loss is that of a parent, he must be certain, before he loosens his attachment to this internal representative of the lost one, that these needs will be met" (p. 228).

E. Furman (1974) also reviews the essential nature of certain narcissistic supplies for ensuring the child's survival, and the upset of the bereavement to the narcissistic equilibrium (p. 248). She also notes the role of ambivalence (p. 248). Thus she also supports the importance of the child's dependent needs and his ambivalence to the parent lost, in the difficulties that may arise in the mourning process.

*The death: circumstances and understanding of it.*    Bowlby, Nagera, R. A. Furman, and a great many other workers cited above all comment on the importance of the child's understanding of what has happened—in terms both of his capacity to conceptualize the nature of death generally, and this death in particular, as well as what he is told at the time. E. Furman (1974, pp. 235–39, 246–48) reinforces the importance of these issues, as do our own studies (Raphael 1982; Raphael, Field, and Kvelde (1980). The child's involvement in the death may also be important, as may the degree to which he is excluded from further reality testing about it, because he is unable to see the body, is "protected" from the funeral, and is denied the opportunity for questioning.

A further point of importance is that for the young child the death of a parent, or even a sibling, is always premature and untimely, be it from illness or accident. Bowlby (1979, 1980) also points out the higher percentage of suicidal deaths in the parents of young children. Deaths of parents of young children are not only untimely, but often sudden and unexpected. Thus the potential for trauma in the death itself is greatly increased. It is even more likely that these deaths will be poorly explained to the child, thus enhancing his fantasies and diminishing his capacity to understand them.

*The availability of supportive care after the death.*    When supportive care is available, the child, like the adult, may be comforted and consoled so that his grief may be expressed and his mourning progress satisfactorily. The supportiveness of the surviving parent may provide such a background as noted in a number of Bowlby's cases. Adam's work (1982) pointing out the importance of family stability after the death and Brown's recent work (1982) showing similar trends support this. Birtchnell (1971) shows the protective effect of an older sibling on a

younger sibling in terms of pathological outcomes of childhood bereavement. The detrimental effects of lack of supportive care for the
bereavement are also suggested by Silverman and Silverman's study
(1959) and by Rutter's findings (1966) that discord and multiple shifts
of home are more likely to be the factors influencing outcome than
simply the bereavement itself. Lifshitz et al. (1977) found that, following the father's death, the mother's approach and the social system
were important variables in short-range outcome. Kibbutz children
were less affected. The more concretely affectionate the mother's approach, the more adjusted the child appeared to be.

Our own studies also suggest this view. Thus when the child lacks
support for expression of grief and for his mourning his outcome is
further at risk. The difficulty for the child may relate to the fact that
there may be no one with whom he can share his feelings (E. Furman
1974, p. 261; Kliman et al. 1969) and who can comfort him. The inability of the surviving parent to perceive and respond to the child's grief
because of his or her own need or pathology is highlighted in Silverman and Silverman's work and detailed in our own studies (Raphael
1982; Raphael, Field, and Kvelde 1980). Similarly social support has
been found to be a factor in the adjustment of poor children (Sandler,
1980).

*Additional stresses.* There may be additional stresses that operate to
make the burden for the child's ego too great. For example, when the
family disintegrates or the child suffers the many additional losses that
the bereavement may bring, this may constitute too great a strain for
the child's ego. Similarly if his ego resources are taken up with issues
of survival, it may only be when this is assured that he is free to grieve
and mourn. These issues too are relevant at all ages, for as E. Furman
(1974) notes "at all ages, specific conditions related to a bereavement
may weaken the mourner's ego or absorb energies in such a way as to
impair his tolerance for affects" (p. 259).


## Conclusions


There are, thus, many stresses to be faced by the child who loses someone with whom he has strong bonds of attachment. The death itself is
often bewildering and frightening for him. The threat to family life

brings further insecurity. Yet with the sensitive support of his parent or parents he will master this trauma. His life and development within the family will go on.

Jessica was five. She showed her mother the picture she had painted. There were black clouds, dark trees, and large red splashes.

"My," said her mother. "Tell me all about this, Jess." Jessica pointed to the red splashes. "That's blood," she said. "And these are clouds." "Oh," said her mother. "See," said Jessica, "the trees are very sad. The clouds are black. They are sad too." "Why are they sad?" asked her mother. "They are sad because their Daddy has died," said Jessica, the tears slowly running down her cheeks. "Sad like us since Daddy died," said her mother and held her closely, and they wept.

# CHAPTER 4.
# The Adolescent's
# Grief and Mourning

"A policeman at your house at night has to be bad news. . . . This icy feeling came over me . . . and my heart started thumping and I thought, 'something dreadful's happened—it must be Dad.'"

*Ron*, age 15

"I felt so alone, as though I had no one, no one of my own."

*Nancy*, age 15

"My whole world was empty and blank without her. I wanted her back, but they all kept saying how grateful we must be that she was with Our Lord and not suffering anymore. I felt so selfish that I wanted her so much. I knew that I shouldn't—that that was bad."

*Mary*, age 14

"Jenny was my girl. She was special and private, and she was mine. When she died, they wouldn't even let me go to the funeral. I loved her and she loved me . . . and *them* . . . *they* knew nothing, nothing, about what it was like for us. *They* were too old to know. They treated me as though she was theirs and as though I didn't care."

*Steve*, age 16

For the adolescent, death is an anathema. Everything emphasizes life, change, growth. His body's development, the excitement of his developing thought processes, the enticing world of adulthood and power that is now so near: all these things make death seem impossible. The adolescent faces bereavement unwillingly, as though he has been assaulted by a confrontation with reality that has no place in his world.

There are a great many developmental changes in adolescence which may bring their own levels of psychic upheaval. The stress of bereavement is superimposed upon these. Thus, to understand its impact, some review of this developmental period is essential, for it will be the background that influences grief and mourning. Conceptually, from a variety of theoretical frameworks, there are several strands of biopsychosocial functioning to be considered:

*139*

1.  Bodily changes such as growth in height, weight, and the development of secondary sexual characteristics require changes in body image and lead to a high level of concern with the self as these changes are accommodated gradually into the new self: "man" or "woman" rather than "boy" or "girl."

2.  Linked to body changes are major endocrine changes. These lead to powerful sexual feelings and drives which must become accommodated into the emotional world and the affective sense of self. Often associated with this is a general impact on mood produced by hormonal changes, leading to the "moodiness" that is common among adolescents. Most girls achieve biological maturity by fifteen years of age and boys by their sixteenth birthday. Most adult levels of hormones are reached by the age of sixteen.

3.  These changes lead to a revival of oedipal conflicts from childhood development. Such conflicts may or may not have been satisfactorily dealt with previously. Now they come up with fresh intensity and added libidinal threat, in that the adolescent has a potentially sexually active body.

4.  Cognitive developmental changes as outlined in Piaget's theories (Inhelder and Piaget, 1958) suggest that adolescent thought processes now reach the phase of formal operations allowing for abstraction, reasoning about reasoning, and the separation of form from content. This cognitive step makes possible the development of the reflective self which can consider the self as it is, be critical of it, and preoccupied with it. These processes may also be involved in the adolescent's tendency to self-centeredness with the belief in the self as unique (and perhaps also as special so that the self will not grow old or die). Critical attitudes toward others, such as parents, with the construction in fantasy of idealized others are another characteristic feature of adolescence. Recent studies reviewed by Offer (1980) suggest that many adolescents do not reach this stage of cognitive development at least until the end of high school. He suggests that only 35 percent may in fact do so by then. The implications of this for the understanding of adolescent development are not clear.

5.  Social development occurs requiring the adolescent to accomplish certain social or psychosocial tasks as demanded by his culture and society. These commonly include the development of relationships outside the family, usually with peers, ultimately culminating in the development of or capacity for establishing adult dyadic and family relationships of his own; the growth of

independence from the family of origin; the development of work/occupation/career training and skills so that he is able to be or become self-supporting. These are relevant to the self as a social person.

These major changes that the adolescent must accommodate are changes he must also have a part in accomplishing. There will be some psychic upheaval associated with them, but whether or not this reaches the level of a developmental crisis for all adolescents is not clear. E. H. Erikson (1959) suggests that the period of adolescence is a developmental crisis of "identity" versus "identity diffusion." More recent work on the ongoing development that takes place throughout adulthood would seem to suggest that some aspects of identity development continue well beyond adolescence into much later life-cycle stages. Anna Freud (1958) suggests that some upheaval may be an essential part of normal adolescence, although workers such as Masterson (1967) have shown that much adolescent turmoil does not have a benign resolution.

It has been suggested by Sugar (1968) that adolescents may go through a period of what he calls "normal adolescent mourning." He believes that this involves the adolescent recognizing the imperfections of his parents, the loss of his idealizations of them, and his view of their omnipotence; the loss of childhood; the loss of the dependent intimacies of family life; and the loss of an ideal world. This awareness may lead to much grief with associated affects of anxiety, helplessness, anger, and yearning for what has been lost. Sadness may reflect the mourning for the lost ideals of parents and childhood. These affects may interweave with the other emotionality of adolescence. It may be that such emotions also motivate the adolescent search for ideals.

In terms of a more systematic study of this phase there are Offer and Offer's (1975) studies of normal adolescent boys. These workers suggest that there may be three types of growth: continuous with well-adjusted development; surgent with periodic spurts and regressions; and "tumultuous-chaotic" and disturbed. Rutter (1979) has reviewed the scientific underpinning of our understanding of adolescence drawing on his own work and a wide range of other research. He concludes that adolescence may be a time of disturbance and upheaval for some, but it is certainly not necessarily so, and that the concept of developmental crisis of identity cannot be substantiated from data presently available. Rutter suggests that a percentage of adolescents may be disturbed (maybe 10 to 15 percent), perhaps a level of disturbance comparable to the tumultuous growth group of Offer and Offer (1975). He also notes that depression, misery, and unhappiness are common in adolescents and are often not recognized by parents or teachers. Similarly loneliness is a frequent complaint (Ostrov and Offer 1978). The recognition of these real and painful levels of distress amongst the adolescent population is important, for it is upon such baselines that the distress of bereavement may be superimposed, making the adolescent indeed vulnerable.

A further variable that must be taken into account when considering the impact of loss in adolescence is the role that the adolescent has in terms of the dynamics of his family system. He may be a delegate (Stierlin 1973) or a scapegoat, for example, or he may fill any one of many roles of significance to the stability and functioning of an adaptive or maladaptive family group. Indeed there is much to suggest that the family itself reverberates with adolescent development (Sharp 1980). It is as though adolescence reawakens identifications and issues from each parent's own adolescence as well as these aspects of the family system. Temporary family regression and instability are likely. To quote Sharp, "In normal families this regression provides the empathic interpersonal framework within which family members can recognize, share and facilitate adolescent development" (p. 199).

Adolescence is also a phase that evokes strong response in many societies and cultures. Certainly in Western society many of the community's conflicts are projected onto adolescents who are stereotyped in many negative ways as being violent, aggressive, sexual, and threatening. The adolescent's responses and actions, or people's perception of them, may be determined by such attitudes.

The adolescent's response to major bereavement will then be influenced by such variables as well as by the nature of the relationship lost and aspects of his response to death.

## Relationships in Adolescence

The key relationships for adolescents are those with the family of origin, with particular friends, and with peer-group members. There are thus a variety of relationship patterns that may potentially be lost.

Relationships with parents pass through many phases. Thus in Offer and Offer's studies (1975) of adolescent boys the continuous-growth group showed affection and respect, yet separateness from parents. Crises were handled with flexibility on both sides, good sense, and a "free flow of emotional expression" (Sharp, 1980, p. 177). In his surgent-growth group the young men had conflicting, often poor, self-images. Relationships with parents were more likely to be conflictual, especially over independence. These boys were aware of many feelings but controlled their expression carefully, although at times they showed ongoing disappointment and repudiation of their parents. Offer and Offer (1975) suggest that this group, when confronted with a crisis such as the death of a close relative, would "repress their feelings and rigidly control their conduct." Their backgrounds often already had a high level of severe illness, death, separation, physical limitation, and financial hardship. It would seem likely that the negative self-images these young men had might be easily reawakened and come to the fore with bereavement. The tumultuous-growth group's high levels of distress and chaos came on the background of marked disadvantage, major parental conflict, mental illness in a parent, and vague and contradictory parent values. The young men in this group had great difficulty separating from their parents, doing so only with painful conflict, otherwise staying bound and immature. They often lacked trust for potentially supportive relationships. They were sensitive and vulnerable about their feelings.

Unfortunately there are to date no similar systematic studies of adolescent girls, although there are some in progress (for example, Raphael and Cubis 1982). Some factors researchers perceive to be relevant to adjustment in adolescent girls include the influence or relationships with parents, sexual development, bodily change, the capacity to bear children (Deutsch 1967), and the adjustment to one's "identity as woman" with all of its implications (Raphael 1978b). As yet, however, there is no description of the patterns that such female adolescent development may take, nor their outcomes in terms of coping and adjustment.

These considerations are important, for they link to some of Rutter's findings (1979) with the adolescents he studied. Almost half the disturbed adolescents in his group had pictures of parental discord linking with problems that had their origins in childhood. Although some rebellion against parental values was common in the general group of adolescents, this usually related to fairly superficial issues such as clothing and hair styles. Basically most of these adolescents, though they at times had difficulties with their parents, perhaps going through periods of rebellion and repudiation of parental values, nevertheless made the transition to adulthood with reasonably positive relationships and identifications with these parents.

Important in the context of the possible loss of such key relationships is the way in which adolescents may go through crests and troughs in their ambivalence to their parents. They may switch backward and forward between hatred and love, dependence and independence, powerful feelings and calm. As Sharp (1980) notes, the adolescent's ego may go back to earlier modes of gratification, focusing and gathering strength for the next thrust toward adulthood.

Development will bring up many psychodynamic issues of importance in relation to parents. Not only may earlier themes of orality, anality, and genitality be revised, but so also may the related themes of trust, autonomy, and initiative. The oedipal conflict takes on a new meaning with the instinctual drives of sexual maturation. For the adolescent boy this will mean longing and conflict in his relationships with his mother, conflict and resentment in his relationships with his father, yet a further reinforcement of identification with him. For the girl, longing and conflict will occur in relation to the father; conflict, resentment, and identification with the mother. The incest taboo operates in most cultures to block expression of these oedipal drives, so that they may instead appear in fantasy or be disguised in relations with parent figures, leading to the acting out of the incestuously derived longings with others outside the family. Many of the battles between the adolescent and his parents may have their origins in such longings for affection and intimacy, which are defended against by setting up a situation of conflict that seems to make love, childhood gratifications, and incest impossible. These revived conflicts of this oedipal stage will be influenced by the mourning process should death of a parent occur, because guilt is likely to be high. Also, the loss may be great because of the intensity with which the relationship may be cathected, especially when the reworking of the conflicts is at its height in the early or middle part of adolescence.

Aggression is another theme of importance in adolescent relationships, especially with parents. Not only are there many frustrations that can lead to anger, but the body is bigger, more powerful, and thus has the capacity to act violently toward those who produce such feelings. Adolescent boys particularly experience upsurges of aggressive drives and may long to test them, yet dread the consequences. There may be a redirection of these urges to fantasy, or they may be acted out within the family, or displaced onto others outside it. Such feelings may also constitute powerful components of the ambivalence the adolescent feels in relationships, especially with parents. Feelings that are turned against the self may contribute to some of the depression and misery common at this time. Should the death of a parent, or of another toward whom such aggression has been felt, occur, then the death may be seen as a consequence of the aggression. Fear of one's power, as well as guilt at its effects, are likely to complicate such bereavements.

Dependency themes are also common in the adolescent's relationships. Early in adolescence there may be a longing for the symbiotic closeness and protection of childhood, yet externally the adolescent may try to repudiate this, vehemently insisting on his independence. Later there may be a genuine relinquishing of childlike dependent ties for an easier mutual dependence that is realistically based in mutual need and friendship. For some, this type of independence may never be achieved, leading to outcomes of either anxious attachment or compulsive self-reliance (Bowlby 1978). In the former outcome, there is a clinging dependence that resists separation, which the adolescent finds difficult to handle, while in the latter, the attachment needs are inhibited and disclaimed or projected onto others who are cared for compulsively. Death, separation, and mourning are difficult for young people in both these groups. Thus the death of a parent may occur at a time when the adolescent is attempting to deal with such complex themes as sexuality, ambivalence, and dependence, perhaps on the background of a level of despair that may be associated with long-standing parental discord.

The death of a parent is likely to be the greatest loss for the adolescent, especially in the earlier years when he has not completed his separation. However, at this time he is more likely to experience other deaths. The death of a grandparent, for instance, is often the adolescent's first encounter with a significant death. In their study of fifteen hundred Melbourne high school students Tobin and Treloar (1979) found that 38 percent reported their first encounter with death as having been that of a grandparent. This produced significant distress and grief for a great many of those who experienced it, whether it occurred in childhood or during adolescence itself. The relationships an adolescent has with the grandparent may be distant. Then the loss may take on more symbolic meaning, such as the theme that the line from which he descends, his parents and thus ultimately himself, are all vulnerable. In other instances, however, the grandparents may be the source of vital, highly cathected relationships. They may be figures with whom he has related in a safer way than with parents, or they may have been his source of security in an otherwise turbulent world of family discord. When family breakup has occurred the adolescent may have lived with the grandparent as a true parent figure. Thus, the loss may be very painful though little recognized as such by others. The impact of the grandparent's death on the parent may also be substantial (see chapter 7), and this may in turn have secondary effects on the adolescent.

Relationships with siblings may take on many different styles and have many complex components. Ambivalent feelings are frequent. There may be considerable dependence, especially with older siblings, who may also be a source of pride and envy. With younger siblings, rivalry and competition are likely, especially, if they are now enjoying the recently yet ambivalently relinquished dependent intimacies with parents. Where the adolescent loses an older sibling, this may be seen as the loss of someone who represented a source of secure identifications as a pathway to adult life. The loss may lead to great insecurity in this sphere. On the other hand, a much younger sibling may be a fantasy baby to the adolescent, and may be grieved as such.

Many adolescents will have intense relationships with peers, such as best friends, boyfriends, and girlfriends. These young people may die in motor vehicle accidents, by suicide, or less frequently from other causes. The adolescents who loved and valued those who died are likely to be deeply affected yet are not readily recognized as the bereaved, since the bereavement of the families takes precedence. Conflicts or acting out which have been transferred to such relationships from the family of origin will make the grief and mourning the adolescent experiences most complex.

There are other less obvious losses that are important to adolescents. The adolescent girl may lose her first pregnancy in termination, miscarriage, or through adoption. The first pregnancy, as Deutsch (1945) suggests, has enormous psychological significance for the girl. Even though the girl may choose to relinquish the pregnancy or the baby, she is still likely to mourn and grieve for it (see chapter 6). However, because others expect her to feel pleased that she has dealt with her "problem," she may receive little emotional support to work through the loss. Boys who father a child in adolescence may suffer a similar grief and mourning which is even less likely to be recognized and supported.

The death of a pet is often highly significant to the adolescent. If his pet has been a valued source of attachment, as well as serving symbolic needs, he is likely to grieve and mourn for him. Similarly, the deaths of idealized public figures will bring great grief and mourning for the adolescent, as exemplified by President Kennedy's assassination and the death of John Lennon.

## Death and Adolescence

In adolescence, the understanding of death becomes much more like that of adulthood. Those adolescents who attain formal operational thought may become able to grapple with the abstractions of death as well as build on their understanding of its reality and finality gained in the earlier years. However, the magical thinking of childhood is easily reawakened for the adolescent as it is for adults facing a bereavement. The adolescent wants to deny death, shut it out, for he does not wish to know that he too can die.

There are not many studies of adolescents' understanding of death per se and the meaning they make of it. Alexander and Alderstein (1958) show the ubiquity of distressed and fearful responses. In their studies of adolescent boys they found that thirteen- to eighteen-year-olds showed strong affective responses to death words (as measured by the Galvanic Skin Response [GSR] and response times). The authors link this to an ego instability associated with development at this time. Maurer (1964) studied late high school girls and found that maturity and high achievement were associated with a greater sophistication and acknowledgement of the inevitability of death as well as with enjoyment of life and altruistic concerns. The immature and poor achievers tended to show greater fear, which was often pervasive and communicated indirectly. Separation anxiety, belief in spirits, violent concepts of causality, and concepts of the dead as "feeling" and "asleep" all pointed to responses similar to those of earlier developmental levels. Fear and death were linked concepts appearing frequently in the productions of these younger girls. Sarwer-Foner (1972) comments on his observations of adolescents, particularly in the terminal phase of adolescence, suggesting that their behavior often demonstrates "a yearning for and an insistence on immortality and indestructibility—a need for being able to guarantee forever their current state of physical alertness and well-being" (p. 52). Turnbull (1980) carried out a more systematic exploration in structured clinical interviews of the levels of attainment of both the cognitive and affective concepts of death in latency and adolescent children. She concludes that until adolescence few children have adequate concepts of death. The latency aged children in her study accepted the finality and irreversibility of death but tended to attribute death to some purpose or motivation. The adolescent showed the capacity to introspect regarding feelings as well as regarding thoughts about death. The adolescent's concepts were still often concrete but were based less on ubiquitous causality and more on the uniformity of nature. In adolescents, but not in the younger age group, there was accommodation to the inevitability of the natural process. The adolescents' emotional responses also indicated such accommodation. Those adolescents who had at some time experienced a bereavement showed a greater attainment of the concept of death, as did those of higher socioeconomic status. Children from working-class families seemed to be less able or less sophisticated in acknowledging the inevitability of death. Turnbull suggests that the experience of bereavement aids the adolescent's eventual acceptance of personal death.

Responses to death experiences as described by adolescents surveyed in a death education program in Melbourne, Australia, (Tobin and Treloar 1979) bring further insights. The following list shows the responses of these adolescents (N = 1421) when queried about their own deaths and gives sample comments.

1. The aspects of their own deaths that were most distasteful to them were: that death might be painful (about 43 percent); that it would cause grief to friends and relatives (41 percent); that they were uncertain about what might happen to them after death (29 percent); and that they would feel cheated out of experiences of life not yet enjoyed (26 percent).

   "It scares me not to have everything and everyone you know not there—to just have it happen at any time."
   "I am lonely about my life, so if I did die I avoid the pressure and problems of my life, and I can see God. Sometimes I want to die. I think it will be peaceful when I die."
   "I wouldn't be able to have any more sex or enjoy my money."
   "I hate the thought of being closed up in a coffin."
   "For a while I have been thinking late at nights what happens after death, and it has confused and frightened me."
   "I haven't yet developed into the person I want to be, so I'm not prepared for my death but I'm afraid of it."
   "I know how upset my Mum would be, and I hate to see her cry."

2. Death meant to them: the beginning of a new life after death (35 percent); a kind of endless sleep or peace (37 percent); the end, the final experience (22 percent); and don't know (23 percent).

"Death is nothing in my life."
"Although I'm an atheist, I still believe when someone dies a part of them still lives."
"I am scared of the uncertainty involved with death."
" ... the time when you are useless and the time to go."
"God has promised me eternal life, and I'm confident in His promise."
"I have avoided the thought of death."
"I'm too scared to experience it."
"Death is the end."
"Hopefully it is not the end."
"I think there might be another asteroid, somewhere you could go."

3.  The kind of death they would prefer was: a quiet dignified death (39 percent); sudden and not violent (33 percent); death after a great achievement (18 percent); and there is no appropriate death (15 percent).

    "I would get up and fight to survive like people who have been told they are going to die and go on great events like extremely long walks and survive (It has happened.)."
    "I would like to die in my sleep with no pain."
    "I don't care if I went quickly or was machine gunned. I would still die anyway."
    "Surfing and my surfboard knocks me out—my amps blew up and electrocuted me."
    "I would like to die peacefully in my sleep or in my armchair watching TV. I would like to die in old age."
    "There is no proper way to die."

4.  They would prefer to die in the age range of: seventy to eighty (31 percent); eighty to ninety (29 percent); ninety to one hundred (23 percent).

    "I don't want to die."
    "Eighty to ninety—I wouldn't like to die very old because I have seen old people suffer."
    "Zero to twenty-five—I have no wish to grow old."

The comments of these adolescents reflect some of their many spontaneous views on death. They show the wide spectrum of fear, denial, curiosity, rejection, and even acceptance. The aspects of death that may be frightening to adolescents are the lack of control they have over it, the fact that it may cheat one of life, and that it is uncertain, unknown. The adolescent is especially threatened in that goals of adulthood are now so close, and he is likely to feel he cannot bear being frustrated in reaching them. He may do much to deny the reality of death; he may attempt to denigrate its power by pretending to himself and others that he is not afraid of it, sometimes taking wild risks in desperate counterphobic endeavours to play games with death and win.

For some young people, there may even be a romanticization of death, as, for instance, when a breakdown of the idealized view of the parents and the world is an aspect of splitting of good and bad—the world is all bad, and death is all good. Suicide is one potential outcome of this, particularly when the romanticization is linked with depression or despair and with magical fantasies of return from the dead. The fragility with which concepts of the finality and irreversibility of death are held, even in adulthood, means that the adolescent often inwardly believes that reunion with the dead person may in fact be possible, just as he fantasizes a return from his own death.

Sudden violent deaths are readily associated with the adolescent's own violent aggression or destructive fantasies. In combination with a powerful and idealistic superego he is likely to suffer much guilt. Anger over the world for its badness (and his own badness, split off and reprojected) is likely to be prominent. Prolonged illness and suffering may seem especially poignant to him in his identification of his own adolescent suffering with that of the terminally ill person. He may ruminate on the unfairness of the world and God in allowing such pain. This may be one reason why an adolescent rejects religious beliefs. Other adolescents will try to deal with their fears and the reality of death and loss by intense religious involvement, which may or may not help them with their struggle to come to terms with their own mortality.

Inevitably, the death of someone close to the adolescent is a hated reminder of his own mortality. "I don't want to know about death," he says. "I don't want to think about it." Yet the occurrence of the death forces him to do so. As Rutter points out (1979, p. 35) anxieties about the future seem greater in adolescence: death, separation, and loss confirm the worst fears.

## Adolescent Bereavement: Grief and Mourning

There are few systematic studies of adolescent responses to bereavement and only a few case descriptions or peripheral references to them in general works. Bowlby's work on loss (1980) tends to consider responses for children, especially older children, and adolescents together. A small study of adolescents by Gapes (1982) reflects patterns not dissimilar to those described below. A study of parental loss in college students by Werner and Jones (1979) also reports on this field.

The description that follows comes chiefly from the author's observations of normal adolescents seen during the assessment of bereaved families in outreach programs; from the reports of school children and teachers about adolescents' reactions to bereavement; from observations of adolescents referred as disturbed following bereavement; and from the findings of bereavement problems among adolescents assessed for other purposes in research or clinical studies.

The most intense response (at least in early adolescence) seems to be associated with the death of a parent and this usually leads to major changes in family life. The patterns of adolescent response to other bereavements are, on the whole, likely to be similar. As with other age groups, the initial response is of shock, numbness, and disbelief. Death was thought to be something that happened to other families. The adolescent may feel helpless and frightened and wish to carry on as though nothing had happened. When a parent dies he may long to be a child again, to be protected from the death and all it may mean. His inner response is to wish to deny it in every way. The adolescent, however, so sensitive to social cues and expectations, finds himself "expected" to behave in certain ways. He may be expected to be "grown up" and to comfort other family members, especially the surviving parent and his younger siblings. This may be gratifying in that it offers a sense of usefulness and a positive role in the face of helplessness. But he may have great doubts about his ability to fulfill such needs when he feels so childlike and frightened himself. At other times he may be expected to be like a child and be treated as one; he may be excluded from what is happening; he may be told little about the terminal illness or death; and he may be kept from seeing the body or going to the funeral. He may bitterly resent this attitude, even though he secretly longs for the protection and security of childhood. Through all these expectations and his own fearful helplessness, his overwhelming experience is of bewilderment.

The experience of the absence of the dead person brings yearning and longing for that person. The level of yearning may be determined by the intensity of interaction that existed beforehand and, for older adolescents, by the degree to which some separation from parent figures had occurred. In younger adolescents the yearning for a return to closeness with parents is quite intense, so that with the death of a parent there is preoccupation with the parent's image, a pining and longing for him or her. Where the relationship is less physically close, there is still a sense of emptiness and a wish for the return of the dead person. The typical waves of distress (Lindemann 1944) may also appear. The adolescent finds it very difficult to accept the intensity of his longing for a lost parent. So often his recent rebellion and steps toward independence had led him to believe that he no longer needed his parents in any close way. In pining for them, he may feel he is being sucked back into childhood again, to its symbiosis and powerlessness, and so he may very actively resist the yearning he feels, denying it or repressing it. It may be easier for girls to acknowledge their longing, and acceptable that they should do so in many cultures. For boys and young men, this is much more difficult, for they may see the longing for a father or mother as childish or unmasculine. Thus the yearning is often repressed, producing a vulnerability to pathological mourning.

Angry protest is usually much more easily expressed. There is anger at the world, in many instances long before the death occurs, and this anger is now given an extra fire and meaning. "They" should not have let this happen. The death proves the adolescent's righteousness in his idealism and his criticism of life. The anger serves the purpose also of giving the adolescent some sense of power when he feels helpless. It may be turned inward when fueled by guilt or in those circumstances when no expression is possible and may lead thus to a despairing black view of the world. Sometimes there is angry acting out, partly to elicit care from those who do not otherwise seem to recognize the adolescent's distress and partly to punish the self and others for what has happened. There is a great sense of desertion too when a parent dies. The parent who should have been there to comfort and protect has gone. The "growing up" should have been protected for a little longer. The parent should have stayed around. The adolescent's orientation toward the future, compared with that of younger children, is such that he has some awareness of the deprivation that will be involved in the times to come. He is frightened of this and resents it. His world will change, not as he wants it but in ways that are outside his control. Repeatedly he will say how "unfair" it all is—that death should come—that his parent should die.

When the adolescent has been able to recognize and express some of these affects he starts to progress toward a greater acceptance of the finality of the absence of the lost person. He has known this intellectually before, but it is only with realities such as the funeral or the fact that the person does not return, that interactions that would normally have been carried on with them have no meaning, that life has obviously altered, that he starts to mourn and relinquish the person he has lost.

Tobin and Treloar's studies (1979*a*) vividly document some adolescent experiences.

"When my father died I was very depressed. I felt lonely and empty inside. I didn't want to believe Dad was gone. I felt saddest at night, because that's the time I would be with Dad. I hated the doctors and nurses because they wouldn't let me see Dad before he died. I often felt like screaming and I liked to lock myself away from people."

"My mother died of leukemia. I felt sad, very unhappy, and alone. I still can't believe that she is dead."

"When my father died I was unsure how to act, whether to cry or what."

The patterns with other deaths may be similar.

"When my uncle died I didn't want to accept it. Everybody else cried except me, and I thought there was something wrong with me. I really thought it was all a nightmare. It seemed like Uncle Bill was just on holidays and we wouldn't be able to visit. After about two weeks the truth finally got me and I cried and cried. Then I could finally accept the fact that I would never see him again."

"I just kept saying it wasn't true, that Nana couldn't just go like that without saying anything. When the second phone call came through to say she'd died, I sat on the stairs but I couldn't cry; I just sat, as though she was close to me. My sisters hated me because I hadn't cried, so I felt angry and confused and still in disbelief."

"My brother died in an accident. I felt it was all my fault because of all the things I called him. And that if we didn't go there in the first place it wouldn't of happened. We should have stayed home."

"A car had run over my cat plus another one. I felt angry, and I wanted to have the two drivers smash their faces into my fist and ram them into the wall."

"I refused to believe my boyfriend had been killed. After a while I became confused and was in a deep depression for about three months. I stayed at home at night and couldn't concentrate on my homework, which made me even more depressed, but after a while I began to accept his death, and I now enjoy myself, but I still get depressed occasionally."

The uncertainty outlined in these responses, the gradual acceptance, the nonacceptance are common patterns in adolescence. The adolescent's overt grief may be less intense or it may be suppressed, because he is uncertain of how his responses will be perceived by others. His fears of loss of emotional control may be a further inhibiting factor, for he may be already struggling with the increased emotionality of his adolescent years. The threat to his own mortality may make him even less ready to acknowledge the death. Some adolescents will also be struggling with major developmental conflicts as well, often on the background of stresses and perhaps chaotic family relationships, so it may be no surprise that they have few ego resources available to deal with major bereavement.

In a small but detailed study of adolescents' responses to bereavement, Gapes (1982) defines the typical adolescent response as one of "escape," compared to that of their mothers which was defined as "preoccupied." Gapes found that while there were some responses—guilt, anger, depression, disorientation, and insecurity—the adolescents frequently suppressed or repressed their emotional responses. They often felt that their emotions were unacceptable to their social environment, especially their peers. Their peers, they felt, were evasive, unable to discuss with them their loss, and these adolescents fully empathized with this response as they themselves avoided the topic of death. They often had little knowledge of what was normal in a grief reaction and so were most hesitant to show their natural responses for fear they might be noticed, considered different or abnormal, which would be abhorrent to them in their adolescent sensitivity to the views of others. In the stresses of expression of emotion, in coming to terms with the meaning of death, and in reviewing the past for the mourning process, they felt themselves to be deficient, uncertain, and unsupported by others.

In a study of college students (La Grand 1981) an older group of adolescents shows many similar patterns to those of Gapes's study. These students described their responses to the loss of a loved one. Depression was their most common response occurring in 75.3 percent of respondents with feelings of emptiness also being frequent (58.1 percent of subjects). Crying, headaches, insomnia, digestive upsets, and exhaustion were also prevalent, reflecting patterns similar to those described by adults. In coping with the loss, they felt that the availability of a friend, family member, or significant other was of vital importance to help them talk about what had happened and express feelings. Women were more willing to talk about their losses in this way than men. Students wanted unbiased friends with whom they could discuss their loss and feelings, without the friends becoming too upset or making comparisons with his own losses. They felt that they were very vulnerable immediately after a major loss, that they needed significant others to whom to voice their fears, angers, woes, and guilts. They acknowledged that they needed solitude at times as well. There was also a need for family support in working through the loss. It was often helpful to talk to others who had been through similar experiences. Openness and honesty were valued above all in these communications. Where there was an opportunity to prepare beforehand for the loss, this was helpful; and they also found it helpful to have their parents or others as good models for how to handle loss. Knowledge of loss as a condition of human existence, and the various patterns of response to it, was also helpful to many students who felt reassured about their own experience and behavior.

Thus there is much to suggest that grief and mourning may constitute a number of difficulties for adolescents, and that the outcome may often be complex. The painful work of mourning can occur, but the adolescent's ego may defend against it in a number of ways.

MOURNING: CONTINUOUS AND INTERMITTENT

The adolescent who is reasonably secure, who can be comforted by a surviving parent or older sibling, who has avenues for expression of his grief will start to review the lost relationship, to remember its many aspects, to talk these through or quietly reminisce upon them; in short he will start to mourn the person he has lost. In this reviewing process, his memories are often intensely idealized, the ideals of adolescence reinforcing this process. It may be difficult for this idealism to be relinquished, because the ambivalence so commonly experienced in this developmental phase may link the negative aspects to the death, producing much guilt and self-blame. He may vociferously criticize himself for not loving the person enough, for not appreciating his worth while he was alive. He may feel that his lack of consideration or rebellious behavior have in some way caused the death, especially if he has little real acceptance that death is a result of natural processes but sees it instead as at an earlier developmental level, in concrete causal terms. The higher the developmental levels of ambivalence in the preexisting relationship, the more complex the tasks of mourning, especially the working through of guilt. Occasionally the lost person is vilified initially for the pain he is causing the adolescent and his family, especially the mother. This usually gives way to sadness and longing for the dead person and a gradual mourning for him.

The ongoing tasks of adolescence, the pressures of school, the sanctions against emotional expression, and the difficulties others have in perceiving his needs and supporting them, may all mean that the process of mourning is a rather private one for many adolescents; or that it occurs in bursts, intermittently, when circumstances are favorable and the ego allows this regression. The mourning is thus likely to extend over a considerable period as the loss is slowly resolved. Where normal adolescent mourning has been in progress, the forced special mourning of bereavement may be resisted, for the adolescent had much more control over his relinquishment of parents before and many more rationalizations to support him. These are taken away by parent death, making it difficult for him to progress with this task.

Sometimes mourning may be delayed until secure relationships facilitate it—for instance, the surviving parent is able to respond to the adolescent's needs, or a sensitive and involved teacher provides the opportunity for the adolescent to share his memories and his feelings.

Ron, fifteen, described his father's death, his own reaction to it, and how he began to recover.

"When Dad died it was a terrible blow to us all. We knew he'd had a bit of blood pressure trouble, but it wasn't anything really serious. The night he died he was out at a Rotary meeting. He had a heart attack in the car while he was coming home. The policemen came to the door to tell Mum about midnight. It was terrible. There was the policeman, and Mum was crying and sobbing, and he was looking helpless and funny and didn't seem to know what to do. A policeman at your house at night has to be bad news. At first when I saw him I thought, Gee, what had I done; then I saw Mum and knew it was something terrible. This icy feeling came over me and my heart started thumping and I thought, 'something dreadful's happened—it must be Dad.'

"The policeman looked up and saw me. 'Come on,' he said, 'you've got to help your mother. You look after her. Get your uncle to come; I've got to go now.' I felt as though my whole world was crumbling. There was Mum in tears, I was scared shitless, and they were expecting me to do something. Well, somehow I managed. I got her a cup of tea—I put my arm around her. I even made her feel better for a moment, and that made me feel better too. I was in charge, and even though I was scared, I was coping.

"Then my uncle came, and Mum turned to him. I was relieved in a way and angry too—they started treating me like a kid then. My uncle took over all the arrangements, the cremation and everything. I hated that, burning him instead of burying him. They had to go to identify his body, and my uncle did that—said Mum and I couldn't see him. We'd be too upset. We'd better remember him the way he was. I wanted to see him for myself. He was my dad, and even though we'd had a few rows, I still loved him a lot. They even wanted to keep us kids away from the funeral. The younger ones—I could understand that—but not me, I was near enough to grown-up. Anyway, as Mum had said, I'd have to be the 'man in the house now Dad was gone.'

"Our whole family was in a mess for weeks. It was as though we all still really thought Dad would come back. There were always visitors and we'd have to be polite to them, and sometimes they'd talk about Dad and sometimes they'd avoid the subject. We were all uncomfortable. It was worst at nighttime.

That's when he should have come home—we always expected him to come in the door, and of course he never did. We were afraid to talk about him together for quite a while, as though we'd upset one another and that would make everything even worse.

"For a while I'd pretend to myself that everything would be all right, that we didn't really see that much of Dad when he was alive—he was always so busy with work, so we really wouldn't miss him that much. I used to pretend to myself that he was away on business. I kept myself going with that one for quite a while. Then I'd get scared stiff, because, of course, I really knew he was gone, that he wouldn't be coming back, that our lives were different now.

"I was scared with all the responsibility that seemed to be on my shoulders now. I didn't know how we'd be financially—if I'd be able to finish school, or I'd have to go out and get a job—but that turned out to be alright as he'd had a good insurance policy and we could manage. I was afraid of being different in any way—I'd always been a bit that way. I could remember the times I had a go at other kids—like Peter when his dad and mum split up, and I didn't want them to be having a go at me. Being without Dad, fatherless, like an orphan or something seemed really bad.

"When I realized that that was all right, and maybe our lives would still go on in some sort of way as a family, I started to let myself think about him. I used to miss him a lot at nights—that was the time we spent together. I used to long for him to come back, make things alright again, just as they were before. But as time went on, of course I was getting used to the way things were and accepting he was gone.

"I used to be in bed at night thinking about him, about fathers, about what he'd meant to me. I remembered the times we used to spend together, the great times we had. He was a pretty good father, I thought. A lot of things went through my mind about the past as well as a lot of thoughts about the future. I could talk to Mum about some of them, but not many, really, because she seemed to need to lean on me. That was what the family expected. They kept saying it was good I was the man now, how lucky I'd grown up enough to be able to help her.

"Sometimes it all seemed stuck inside. I felt really bad about the arguments I'd had with him, especially the bad blowup the week before he died. I used to wonder if that sort of strain had made his blood pressure worse or affected his heart. I tried asking my biology teacher about it. He was a great guy, and he seemed to sense there was something more in what I was asking, and he asked me about my dad. Well I really felt a fool at first—there I was crying and telling him all. But he didn't seem to think there was anything wrong with that. He made me feel good about it. In fact, I felt a lot better, like a burden had been lifted. I talked to him on and off after that, and it was a great help. He made me feel that what I felt and thought about Dad was normal, and after a while I started to feel a lot better. I still felt sad about Dad, and we talked about him quite a lot at home. It was good to have a man like my teacher to lean on sometimes, but on the whole I felt I was getting over it all right and that there weren't too many problems. Life was going on."

Some adolescents appear to express yearning and protest, yet when the time comes to mourn for and relinquish the dead person, or a parent, the young person is unable to do so. He becomes "bossy," adult in behavior, presenting himself as in control and powerful. Some of this behavior may be understood as a reaction formation against the helplessness and fear. It may also be a partial identification with the dead person to keep alive the "adult" as it were in the child. The pseudoadult behavior is often in bizarre caricature and may be very difficult for the family to manage, even if it covertly seems to meet some of their needs.

Damien was fourteen when his father, who had been something of an invalid, died suddenly. His parents' marriage had been filled with violence and discord. His father he saw as an aggressive, powerful, and frightening man. In the early weeks after the death he felt frightened and upset and longed to have his dad back, even his violence. His mother's weeping and disintegration frightened him. His little sister seemed to be the only one who was looked after. Damien started to become very aggressive, ordering his mother and sister around, and became a little Hitler in his demands on both of them. He insisted he was not missing his father anymore and that the family would now be alright because he was in charge. He suggested his name be changed to that of one of his television heroes—an aggressive and violent model for his action—a man who solved everything by power and fighting and who never showed feelings.

His mother's chronic grief and inability to mourn her husband reinforced his behavior even further. It reached a crescendo when, with various rationalizations, she took him to her bed , to hold and cuddle, just to comfort her. The family dysfunction then became so marked that they were referred for therapy. It was only when his mother's mourning progressed more adaptively and he himself had his helpless longing, fears, sadness, and guilts recognized that he started to relinquish this role. His younger sister was also then able to give up being the "baby" and express some of her own anger at her father and mother.

IDENTIFICATION WITH THE DEAD PERSON

The adolescent clings to mannerisms, ideals, and behavior of the dead person. This may be obvious, pronounced, and deliberate after the death of a pop hero. More frequently, it is subtle and unconscious. When transient it may reflect part of the mourning for the deceased, but when prolonged and exaggerated it usually represents a block to mourning, as though the dead person and the relationship with him is being kept alive inside the self. Thus the adolescent is temporarily at least protected from the painful affects of grief and mourning. Such identifications are usually gradually given up in the face of reality, particularly if greater feelings of security occur and relationships stabilize.

This pattern of response to bereavement may be reinforced by adolescent identity issues. If there is great uncertainty within the self about who and what one is or will become, there may be strong ego pressures to consolidate *some* identity choice. The threat to the ego that major object loss brings in bereavement heightens the uncertainty about who one is now that one is "fatherless" or "motherless" or who one is without the one who has died. The adolescent may seek an identity, any identity to resolve this anxiety. It is also likely that strong pressures may operate within the dynamics of the family system to push the young person further to take over the role of "father" or "mother" to help the family system avoid the pain of mourning and the stresses of the deprivation of this role. An extreme example of this is seen in the case of James, age eighteen.

James was eighteen and in his last year of high school when his father died from a myocardial infarction. James was shocked and overcome by his powerful mother's distress and regression. He had many guilty feelings about his father whom he had hated. On the day following his father's death, his mother laid out for him his father's clothes and informed him that he should leave school now—he was the man in the house, and he must take over his father's business. James followed his mother's directions. Each day he found himself behaving and talking more and more like the man he had hated. Yet he could not stop. "It's as though I've got him inside me," he said. "He's there and I can't be rid of him. I suppose you could say I'm afraid to let him go. I feel that there would be nothing there if he went—I'm nothing and nobody. I don't know who I am. So I may as well be him."

## WITHDRAWAL AND DEPRESSION

Some adolescents show marked withdrawal from relationships when they have lost someone close to them. They may fear closeness and avoid it, for they fear their sensitivity and being hurt again. They may feel different and wish to avoid others who remind them of this difference. They may be preoccupied with fantasies of the relationship they have lost, ruminating over it, longing to have it back so they can make it different, or relishing its fantasy gratifications to the denial of reality. There may be great suffering with this if the relationship or the death has been a source of guilt. The adolescent may "delight" in torturing himself with remorse as his asceticism feeds his suffering.

"There were lots of times I felt bad," said Mary, age fourteen, "long before

Mum got sick. Growing up really frightened me. The girls at school used to snigger and laugh about sex. They used to talk about the things boys do to you. I hated it. I hated them. I just didn't want to know about it. My grandmother told me it was all bad, that you had to watch out for boys, that you would get into terrible trouble if you didn't. I knew my Mum had been in some sort of trouble when she was having me. The family wouldn't talk about it. It was some kind of secret. I think though that Grandma made her and Dad get married. Whatever it was, it was bad because you could tell how upset they were if anyone talked about things like that and the look they'd give one another.

"When my breasts started to grow and I started to get hair on my body, I felt really bad. It was as though something could happen to me now like had happened to Mum. They talked to me about growing up and periods and boys, and that made me even worse. You could tell they thought that I'd do something bad, too, like Mum had, and that they'd have to watch me.

"Mum started to change; she was in pain a lot, and I could see something was wrong with her. We were very close, and she used to cry sometimes and tell me she was very sick. Then one day she told me she had cancer inside her, in her woman's parts, and she didn't think she was going to get better. I was scared—scared like I'd never been before. How could she have something like that inside her, something you couldn't see. How did she get it—what would we do without her—what would I do?

"We seemed to get even closer after that. She seemed to turn to me. I used to sit beside her bed in the afternoons after school and we would talk and talk. She would talk to me about being a woman, and she'd seem terribly sad. She'd keep telling me to be good, be her 'good girl,' and I'd be all right—I wouldn't have to suffer like she did. The cancer got worse and worse. They couldn't do anything to stop it. It was in her ovaries, I think. Then she used to get this bad discharge—it would smell terrible and she'd hardly let Dad into the room at all—she got me to do everything for her. I kept thinking why couldn't the doctors make her better, but they'd just come and give her needles and go again and nothing would change. When the pain got bad I would really worry that I wasn't helping her more, but she kept saying she was all right and that all she wanted was me with her.

"Then one day she seemed to fade. I could tell she was going to die, and I felt desperate. I was so close to her now—I couldn't bear to lose her. The doctors came, and they said she would have to go to hospital, and an ambulance came and took her away. They wouldn't let me go—they said it was no time for children. Dad went with her. He didn't come back that night, and we all stayed up and worried and worried. He came the next morning—he looked dreadful. He said, 'Children, your mother's at peace now. She has died and gone to be with God. We must all be grateful.'

"I was sick and frightened. There was a funeral and we went to that, but I felt as though I wasn't there. I went home and I went into Mum's room and it was just as it was when she'd left. I sat beside the bed and I thought I would will her back, she must be back, she can't be gone—look how I cared for her and loved her—how could God do this—she's my Mum and I need her.

"Then it was like some sort of nightmare. I wanted her back so much. My whole world was empty and black without her. I wanted her back, but they all kept saying how grateful we must be now she was with Our Lord and not suffering anymore. I felt so selfish because I wanted her so much and I knew I shouldn't—that that was bad and selfish.

"I would lie awake for hours at night thinking about her—why she had to die. They wouldn't really tell me much about her illness, but I read in a magazine that you got those diseases when you were 'promiscuous', so I knew it had to do with sex. It was some sort of punishment for her, but she wasn't bad—not to me anyway. Then I started to think of badness and sin: I knew if anyone should have been punished, it should have been me. That feeling got stronger and stronger: somehow I was something to do with her trouble—she'd been in trouble having me, I knew, and the thoughts I used to have at night, I knew they were bad too, the thoughts about the things the girls said about boys and what they do to you and all the things I used to imagine.

"I knew how bad I had been; I felt as though I had made her die—it was to punish me that God had taken her. I almost felt better when I accepted that; it made sense, because she wasn't bad—*she* couldn't be—and I knew *I* was. The more I thought about it the more I felt bad too; and I knew it was my punishment as well, that I had to suffer as she did. I thought about her and me all the time. It was as though she was still there with me—thinking about her seemed to take up my whole life. I used to wish I would die too, to join her, but I knew God wouldn't let me, that would be too easy. I had to suffer; I had to make up for it, so I had to go on living."

Mary became progressively more withdrawn and depressed. She was obsessed with her "dirty mind" and her "punishment." Her withdrawal increased until her schoolwork became impaired and her problems were obvious in the home and school environment. It was only with prolonged and intensive therapy that Mary became able to mourn her mother and come to some better adjustment in her psychological world.

Many adolescents who are bereaved experience depressed feelings. These add to the general levels of misery and unhappiness that are common in their age period (Rutter 1979) and may reach the severity of depressive illness. Even if this does not occur, the world may seem a black, depressing place, and the future may seem to have little hope. Van Eerdewegh et al. (1982) suggest from their prospectively oriented study of bereaved children's symptoms as reported by parents, that depression following bereavement was most frequent in adolescent boys who had lost a father. This fits with Rutter's (1966) earlier findings that depression in adolescence may often follow a loss and may be more common for adolescent boys who have lost a father, perhaps precipitating psychiatric presentation. The more recent study (Van Eerdewegh et al. 1982) suggests that severe depressions are more likely in those who had mothers suffering from a primary or secondary depression that began prior to the death. Thus it may be that a vulnerability exists, that the loss acts as a precipitant, and identification with a depressed grieving parent may further shape the response of the adolescent into a depressive picture.

### CARE-ELICITING BEHAVIORS

Henderson's (1974) concept of "care eliciting" in man has much relevance to bereavement. Adolescents, rather than expressing their loss-induced distress directly in grief and mourning, may express it in behaviors that may be seen as having care-eliciting goals. The nature of such behaviors may be overdetermined, involving not only motivations for care, but also tension release, hostile and self-punitive functions, and, in some instances, may represent an attempt to replace the lost object.

The care-eliciting pattern may be different for boys and girls. In general terms, it is difficult for either to seek care directly from others at this time, because to do so suggests weaknesses that the adolescent wishes to deny as well as a need for others, which is an anathema to him. While care-eliciting behaviors may be a source of increased turning to care services and increased medical care utilization, such sources of care are rarely acceptable to the adolescent. This was a significant finding in Gapes's study (1982) of bereaved adolescents, namely, that there was no evidence of symptoms of health deterioration and no evidence of heightened health care use. The adolescent often does not wish to draw attention to himself or his body in this way, nor does he trust such systems of care, as he often sees them as representing adult value systems that he rejects. His needs for care to facilitate his grief and mourning are often not met by his peers, for they too avoid such subjects and feelings with him because of their own fears and uncertainties. Some adolescents may have a heightened fear of death that may lead them to anxiety about any body experience or symptoms. For a few there may be some hypochondriacal preoccupation or some generally phobic avoidance of any situation that might possibly be connected with ill health or death.

A much commoner picture is of acting out of the bereavement-generated distress and conflict. For the girl, the distress of the loss may generate a longing for comforting and reassurance, a diffuse need to be held, to be consoled. This need may be acted out with those outside her family in sexualized relationships which give her a transitory reassurance of body comforting as well as a sense of wholeness, of ego fusion with another. These relationships do not solve the loss, although they may temporarily assuage the pain. Sometimes she may become promiscuous as she searches for the lost part of herself that is gone. She may become pregnant, unconsciously desiring someone of her own to love, someone who will not die and desert her and who will in some way replace the lost person. This acting out may be a temporary phase. One of her relationships may provide the opportunity for grief and mourning that may help her resolve the loss. Or, her family may stabilize sufficiently to perceive and respond to her need, so that acting out becomes unnecessary. The acting out may add to the girl's bad feelings, serving the purpose of punishing her for the guilt she feels about the death, yet enabling her to deny this as she consciously links it to her sexual behavior. Or it may be a phase that she passes through without negative sequelae.

The boy who acts out bereavement-generated stresses to seek care and relieve tension often does so in a much more aggressive manner. The comforting through body contact he may long for in his emotional pain is, in many cultures, even less ego-syntonic. His anger and action-oriented behaviors are nearer the models of masculinity. Thus delinquent acts, activities such as risk-taking in fights, driving, or drug-taking, and testing out authority systems, are more common. These too serve the ends of punishment, release of tension, and eliciting the involvement of others. Unless he is in some way "held" from further acting out by a system of control or by involvement in a secure, caring relationship, this pattern may have many negative outcomes for him. When he is so held, then he may be able to face and deal with the pain of this grief as he mourns the loss.

Other acting-out patterns may occur in relation to systems in which the adolescent is involved. For example, examination failure, dropping out from school, or school refusal may appear. These responses seem linked to the anger of the loss, the need for care. They may also be related to the dread of competing, because competing is equated with aggression which is equated with "killing" the opposition, and this is equated with death. Stealing may also appear at this time, perhaps as shoplifting for girls and petty theft or car stealing for boys. It serves the same aims as other forms of acting out but may also symbolically in some way represent an attempt to steal back the person who has gone.

Nancy's Dad died just before her fifteenth birthday. He had been ill for three months and had died from rapidly progressive liver disease. Nancy and her mother had been going through a very ambivalent phase in their relationship for the past year in that Nancy felt her mother controlled her too much and would not allow her the freedom a girl of her age should have. She and her father had been close. She always felt that she was "his girl." She had helped her mother a lot during her father's terminal illness but felt that she had been excluded at the end and resented her mother even more because of this. She was the youngest of three girls and felt her mother had favored her two older twin sisters while she had been her father's "pet."

"After he died I felt I just couldn't believe it. I was terrible. I felt so alone, as though I had no one, no one of my own. Everyone came to visit, and they all spent a lot of time with Mum and my older sisters too. It seemed as though all the grown-ups cared for each other, but they didn't notice me. Mum was really 'queening it up' too—getting all the sympathy, crying, and saying how much she loved Dad. That was what really upset me, when you thought about how she used to nag him and carry on all the time.

"The thing that hurt me most, though, was when I heard someone ask her how I was taking it. She laughed and said that I'd be all right—I was young, that I was a cold little thing that never showed much affection, so it wasn't likely I'd be affected at all.

"I cried that night as though my heart would break. I felt that none of them cared, and I was right, they didn't. I thought I'd really show them—if that's how they thought I was, that's how I'd be, even if my heart was breaking inside. So the next day I was all bright and gay, and said I'd be home late that night, I had a date. They all looked at me as though that was what they expected and just let me go.

"The boys really thought I was great—I really turned it on for them—everything I had. I'd be all excited, and they thought I was pretty sexy. I'd feel good at first, especially when they would hold me afterward, but then it would wear off and I'd feel bad and dirty. They used to tell me they loved me. I knew they didn't mean it, but it made me feel good, because at least for a while I'd feel someone did—someone cared, now I didn't have Dad."

Obviously Nancy's family was nonsupportive, and there were long-term problems. The bereavement acted as a precipitant for behaviors that may have reflected her underlying vulnerability. There were few supports available to her to support her ego with the stress of a major loss or its resolution.

SEXUALITY AND BEREAVEMENT

The sexual development of the adolescent is a very important part of his life. It marks his change into an adult person, into a biologically different individual who can never again be as he was as a child. Loss may have significance to him in this sphere. He may link themes from his sexual fantasy and experience to the loss, or the loss may have effects on his developing sexual life. Also, because adolescent sexual relationships are very prevalent in many societies, often involving at least 50 percent of adolescents, the adolescent may also be vulnerable to the loss of someone who is sexually important to him, and the society may provide little overt recognition or acceptance of this.

*Loss and oedipal conflicts.* With the revival of oedipal issues that occurs in adolescence, there may be heightened libidinal investment in the opposite-sex parent and antagonism toward the same-sex parent. These longings are strongly defended against in terms of powerful incest taboos, which take on an added power with the maturing of the sexual body. The death of the same-sex parent may seem a fulfillment of oedipal wishes, both frightening and exciting. Death of the opposite-sex parent may be seen as linked to the desire the adolescent harbored for him or her and thus a punishment and a consequence. Guilt is likely in either case. The wish to avoid such guilt and superego recrimination may prove a block to relinquishing the lost relationship. Thus mourning may be inhibited. This is particularly likely in that the adolescent may feel totally unable to share the feelings and fantasies he has had with others, for he frequently perceives them as either bad or abnormal.

Transient experiences of this kind may occur in many adolescent bereavements and are usually worked through with little long-term effect. Where there have been major oedipal difficulties going back to earlier oedipal development, then the adolescent may be more vulnerable. Thus the bereaved girl who has lost an oedipally loved father may seek only such "oedipal" relationships in the future. There develops a repetition compulsion when she seeks to replace the loved father and work through the oedipal conflict, usually unsuccessfully, in further relationships with older father figures.

In families where there have previously been problems of psychosexual development, where there is family disorder with exaggerated and sexualized cross-generational relationships, the outlook may be even more difficult. The adolescent may have problems resolving the conflict, the loss, and the pressures of the surviving family unit to continue his sexualized role. All this may be heightened by the not uncommon tendency of a surviving parent to turn to an older, adolescent son or daughter both for comfort and for fulfilling certain roles such as that of "the man of the house," or "the woman of the house." Thus, the boy may be taken to his mother's bed because she longs for the warmth of a human body beside her, to be held affectionately as a barrier against her grief. The parent may see little or no sexuality in the relationship, but a much more primitive and basic body need. Nevertheless, for the adolescent, acutely aware of every tiny sexual change in his body, the sexual overtones may at once be prominent, exciting, and threatening. The adolescent may flee from such stimulation with rejection of the parent's needs and his own. He may act out his arousal in other spheres, he may develop sexual inhibitions. He might also, as a consequence, develop an incestuous relationship with that parent.

*Loss of a source of sexual identification.* The death of the same-sex parent may deprive the adolescent of a source of sexual identification that may be important to him. He or she may have been consolidating adult sexual identity and still have certain important steps to take in the adoption of his or her identity of "man" or "woman." Some steps of this may be blocked by the deprivation from this object loss. Alternatively there may be an identification with the lost person which produces inflexible sexual roles rather than the range that might have otherwise been available. Another issue that arises is when the adolescent equates maleness or femaleness with vulnerability, possibly death. For example, a boy may fear manhood, believing that men are vulnerable and die, as did his father. Or, a girl may fear womanhood, for to become a woman is to be destroyed by disease, as perhaps her mother was. The illness or disease of the parent may be perceived as having a sexual etiology, as with the example of genital cancer noted above, and this may have further implications for future sexuality.

An interesting corollary to this is the finding of a high level of parental loss in those with gender-identity disturbance. Thus Bernstein et al. (1981) found a high level of parental loss in children between the ages of ten and nineteen in a group of patients with gender-identity disturbance. The authors noted a dramatic increase in cross-gender orientation following the loss, even to the degree of seeking sex reassignment within one or two years. The loss of a father was particularly significant in these cases. The authors do not suggest that the loss caused the gender-identity disturbance, but simply that it acted as a precipitant to further difficulties in this area.

*Loss of a sexual relationship.* The adolescent may lose someone who is sexually important to him, with whom he is having his first intimate relationship. It may be someone with whom his sexual relating is exciting and rewarding, conflictual, guilt provoking, or meeting other needs. It is rarely a sexual relationship that is acknowledged in formal social terms by his family or community, and thus his loss, and what it means to him, will not have recognition. The loss of such a relationship may well indeed evoke many negative attitudes and responses in others, and perhaps in himself. Thus he may not be able to share what he has lost with others, neither the intensity of his physical longing for the lost person nor the various conflicts and ambivalences the relationship might have generated. Although it might be a strong pair bond, both he and his partner might be seen by society as still having their primary bonds with their families of origin. This problem is greatest in earlier adolescence when such relationships are even less sanctioned.

In the older years, the sexuality of boyfriend-girlfriend relationships may be accepted to a greater degree, with some opportunity openly provided for mourning. Where adolescents live together in monogamous relationships, there may be intense attachment as well as sexuality, even though this may not ultimately become a permanent relationship for the couple. Its loss at such a time of intensity is likely to produce great grief. Added to this is the fact that many deaths of young people occur suddenly and even violently in accidents or suicide, for example. The lack of a social framework for many, the inability of others to provide support because of their own vulnerability and fear of loss, all make it likely that such bereavements may be poorly resolved.

Steve, sixteen, was proud of his growth and development, and of his prowess at sport. He had fallen passionately in love with Jenny, one year his junior, at a school dance. They had been dating constantly for three months and had found every opportunity they could to be alone together. Both sets of parents thought the relationship was a "little too intense" but shut their eyes to its possible sexuality. Steve's parents were very busily involved in their own social life which centered on his father's upwardly mobile executive career. They were disappointed that Steve did not show more academic ability, but otherwise left him to his own devices. His younger siblings admired him, but he considered them "juveniles" and a bit of a nuisance.

His relationship with Jenny had rapidly developed into a sexual one. His sexual needs were very intense and many days he could think of little else but when he might see her next and how he would make love to her. She had been hesitant at first and was worried they were "doing the wrong thing." She would constantly ask him what would happen if her Mum found out, or his parents, but Steve always managed to persuade her it would be all right. Her affection for him was great and made him feel all the warmth he perceived as lacking in his own family life.

Jenny was killed one afternoon as she was riding home from the park where they often met. Steve heard nothing of her death until the next day at school when one of his friends said to him, "Hey man, wasn't it tough about Jen?" Steve felt as though he had been hit and angrily demanded to know what the guy meant. "Didn't you know," he said. "She was killed yesterday—knocked off that bike of hers down near the park."

Steve felt numb, disbelieving. It couldn't possibly be true. He would have had to hear about it. Why hadn't someone told him? Why had they left him vulnerable—to hear like this? His parents—they should have known, should have told him. They were too busy with their own damn affairs—what did they care?—they knew nothing about him and what mattered to him anyway. He felt angry, like smashing someone. What could he do—how could he get out of school? He couldn't stay there. He had to find out what had happened. He had to see her. They'd have to let him see her—she was his, not theirs. They couldn't stop him. He felt like crying, but he couldn't. He thought this was just as well; what would the guys think if they saw him in tears? He was some kind of hero to them now, and they'd soon lose their respect if they thought he was a "sis." He stayed the morning at school and left in the lunch hour. He went to Jenny's mother's place, hoping he could see Jenny perhaps—hoping he could find out what had happened. A stranger opened the door to him asking him what he wanted. He managed to get out that he had been a friend of Jenny's and had come to see about it. The stranger looked at him coldly saying couldn't he see this was a bad time to come—this was the family's time. He'd tell them that Steve had called and repeated it was a private time. As the door was shutting Steve managed to ask about the funeral. The man said clearly it was to be a private ceremony, just for the family, that was all Jenny's mother could take.

Steve wandered the streets in misery that afternoon. He went back to the park where they had last met, and in a private corner broke into tears. His longing for Jenny was intense. He felt as though it couldn't be true—perhaps it was even some fantastic story they were putting around to keep them apart. He kept expecting she would ride up a little later, as she often had, full of excitement and modesty. His anger broke through again and again. He hit out at the trees, the bench, 'til he hurt his hands.

That night his parents casually remarked they were sorry to hear of Jenny's death—she'd been a "nice little thing." His father said he was sorry, he supposed Steve must be a bit upset, but at least now his mind might be off girls for a bit, and his work at school might improve. Steve's anger and hurt was enormous and he stormed out of the house.

Steve was unable to attend Jenny's funeral. Nobody realized the extent of his grief, or the depth of their relationship. He was unable to share his feelings with friends. He could tell no one of his longing for Jenny's affectionate warmth and how empty and futile his life seemed without it. He felt angry and guilty most of the time. His alienation from his parents increased. As the months went on he thought less of Jenny and no longer cried himself to sleep at night. But his relationships with others took on an angry and tough defensiveness in which he demanded control and avoided closeness. In his heart he felt he would "show them"—that he would never allow himself to be made vulnerable to this sort of pain again.

*Sexual acting out.* Sexual acting out may occur as a consequence of bereavement. As noted previously this may occur as an attempt for body comfort and care, as a discharge of tension, as the acting out of particular conflicts, or as an escape from incestuous pressures in the home. It may also represent an attempt to achieve adulthood by unconsciously equating sexual behavior with adult behavior. This may be in response to underlying identity conflicts in the adolescent that are intensified by the identity uncertainty of the bereavement. It can represent a form of identity foreclosure. Studies such as those of Greenberg, Loesch, and Lakin (1959) and Coddington (1979) highlight the frequency of loss in the background of instances of adolescent pregnancy which may be one consequence (overdetermined), of such actions. Impulsive, sometimes perverse, sexual acting out may also occur.

## Bereavement from Childhood Appearing in Adolescent Loss Responses

Sometimes earlier losses, for instance the death of a parent in childhood, may reappear with grief and mourning or some other form of distress in adolescence. It may be that a relatively minor loss in adolescence triggers an unexpected level of grief, because the childhood loss is reawakened by it. This may occur with the adolescent leaving home, for instance to go to college or university. It may be that the developments of adolescence open up earlier memories, because there are lowered ego defenses with the developmental crisis. Blos (1962) has seen adolescence as a time of "second chance," perhaps for reworking of earlier conflicts more successfully. There may be restorative and healing processes with the maturation of adolescence. The growth of concepts of death, the greater security in family life that may have evolved by this time, and the evolution of surrogate relationships may all contribute to a readiness to face again the childhood loss and master it. The adolescent has more resources to grieve and mourn than he had in childhood. Indeed some workers such as Wolfenstein (1966) have suggested that it is only with adolescence that mourning is possible. Although recent work would not seem to support this contention, it is certainly true that some children may not have the opportunity, ego resources, or support to grieve and mourn for losses they experienced during childhood, and this may only come with adolescence or, for some, with adulthood. Thus the appearance of grief and mourning in adolescence may provide an opportunity for reworking of these losses.

It has also been noted (Seligman et al. 1974) that there may be a high level of parental loss in childhood or adolescents presenting for psychiatric care. The earlier loss may produce a vulnerability in the adolescent as well.

## Longer-Term Adaptation to Bereavement

Little is known about the longer-term patterns of adjustment of bereaved adolescents. With the death of a parent there will be a number of adjustive tasks. The adolescent will have new roles in his family, as the roles and tasks filled by the dead parent are shared and reallocated. There may be, as was noted above, strong pressures for him to fulfill the role of the absent parent to maintain family stability, especially if he is the oldest child. If he should totally take over such a role, it is likely to have many negative implications for his subsequent development, forcing him to premature identity foreclosure. However, in most families there is likely to be some increased responsibility for adolescent children after the death of a parent. The adolescent may resent this, or he may successfully grieve for his loss of childhood privileges and find greater strength and maturity through successfully coping with the changes. On the other hand, when given a disciplinary role over children, the adolescent may vent old hostility, lack judgment and be merciless, giving rise to depression in the younger children.

Where he was closely involved in interaction with the person who has died there will be a need to establish new patterns of interaction that gratify the same needs. The adolescent may find these through a remaining parent, a friend, or often a supportive parent surrogate such as an uncle, priest, or teacher. These surrogate relationships are a useful transition until he matures beyond the need for them. They may be problematic if they are taken on as replacements for the lost person, for the loss is then not adequately mourned and the new relationship is likely to be conflictual in the many areas in which it differs from the one that was lost. The loss of specific gratifications that the relationship with the person who died provided may also need to be worked through so that new sources of similar rewarding gratification may be developed. These may be dependent, affectional, narcissistic, or sexual. Finding new sources of gratification may take quite a time, for the adolescent may be hesitant to trust again for fear of fresh loss or hurt.

One other area of longer-term adaptation relates to altered status. The adolescent may now be different because he is fatherless or motherless. He is in an age group in which he is particularly sensitive to the norms of his peers. He may bitterly resent any perceived stigma associated with his altered status, particularly any pity or shame. As well, he grieves the loss of his intact whole family and may see his family as different and incomplete, and so may have to adjust to a new image of himself as part of this. The effects of the deprivation the loss brings will only become obvious after some time has elapsed.

There is one further area in which he may be sensitive, and that is to any altered financial status of the family. He is now, as he was not earlier in childhood, realistically aware of financial needs. His own may be quite substantial as he tries to keep up with a peer group culture. Thus he may perceive a change in his financial status as a very significant additional loss, one that he resents yet must adapt to.

Should his parent remarry, he may have many strong feelings about a new parent figure, seeing such marriage as disloyalty to the dead father or mother, yet at the same time longing for the return to the normalcy of an intact family. These are progressive adaptations that he may be called upon to make in the years that follow a death.


## Pathological Patterns of Bereavement


The adolescent's grief and mourning may readily take on a pathological course. The developmental stresses already existing at the time of the loss may create a level of ego vulnerability. The levels of ambivalence in relationships with parents may be developmentally heightened. There is often envy, rivalry, and ambivalence in relationships with siblings. Intrapsychic factors such as fears of regression or loss of emotional control may inhibit the capacities to be comforted by others and to grieve for the loss. Interpersonal networks may be fragmented, with conflicting expectations for behavior and communication: some, for instance, may expect adult behavior from the adolescent, while others may expect child behavior; but most will expect the avoidance of grief. There is, as well, the special vulnerability experience of the threat of death now so personally close. Playing out or acting out solutions to inner stress are often the chosen ones in adolescence, so that grief affects may go unrecognized and undischarged. The acting out may lead to consequences, for instance pregnancy or trouble with the law, that in themselves become further blocks to grief and mourning. Furthermore the adolescent fulfills many functions for his family: he may speak for their grief or be their scapegoat; he may be their "delegate"; or he may be required to replace the person who is lost and is often the family choice to do so. He would be free of his family, yet the bereavement brings back his needs for them at a time when he feels most fragile about such needs.

Some of the pathological patterns of bereavement that may appear are not dissimilar to those of adulthood. Their frequency in adolescence is simply not known.

*Suppressed or inhibited bereavement response.* The apparent absence of grief is frequent. The adolescent may be grieving privately, or he may simply be unable to cry or mourn for the person who has gone: the loss is too overwhelming, his own emotions too frightening.

*Distorted grief and mourning.* Extreme guilty ruminations are not uncommon, especially when there were high preexisting levels of ambivalence and many hostile fantasies about the deceased. Extreme anger may also appear as a distortion of grief. This is most likely when the adolescent's sense of desertion and helplessness are very great as may also be his fears of personal mortality. He rages at the world in angry protest to demonstrate his power, to protect against further loss, and perhaps even covertly to call back the dead. Whatever his reason, he does not mourn, and his anger continues.

*Chronic Grief.* It is uncommon for adolescents to experience chronic grief. They have difficulty expressing grief and are extremely unlikely to take on the role of the chronic grief-stricken one. Their unresolved losses will appear in other ways such as in acting out or in some other of the patterns described above.

## Outcomes of Adolescent Bereavement

There are to date, to the author's knowledge, no systematic studies of the morbidity levels, or the nature of the morbidity, that may follow adolescent bereavements. The following comments are derived from the limited information available.

1. General health impairment does not seem to occur in the same way as it does in adults.
2. Psychosomatic disorder has not been clearly associated with adolescent bereavement.
3. Psychiatric disorder other than depression has sometimes been suggested by clinical reports. Delinquency is one pattern that has been described. Some workers believe there may be increased drug and alcohol intake and that the adolescent may be precipitated into problem behav-

ior in these spheres by the death. Phobias appear occasionally, and there have been some cases of obsessional neurosis that appear to have been precipitated by major loss.

4. Depressive complaints are common in adolescents and common following bereavement. Rutter (1979) believes that depressive illness may be precipitated by parental bereavement, especially in adolescent boys. The study by Van Eerdewegh et al. (1982) supports this but notes also the role of major depressive illness in the other parent as a contributing factor. Stone (1981) suggests that psychological precipitants of an overwhelming nature, such as death of a parent or loss of a love relationship, may precipitate certain adolescents who are at risk for manic-depressive psychosis (depressive type) toward both borderline-level integration and depressive disorder. He further suggests that adolescents not so at risk may similarly succumb to such precipitants, developing a psychological picture with overt signs of depression. Clinical experience suggests that fairly severe depression may be quite common after many types of bereavement in these years, and that suicidal ideation or behavior may also be an outcome. Systematic studies are necessary to clarify this further.

5. Acting our disorders may not be transient, but consolidate into major ongoing neurotic or character problems. This is more likely to occur on the basis of other unfavorable factors including parental difficulties. Shoor and Speed (1976) describe patterns of delinquency in fourteen adolescents. They link these to bereavements over the deaths of close family members and hypothesize that these adolescents were unable to face the loss and death and so their grief "exploded in antisocial ways." Psychiatric intervention was useful in resolving some of the grief and led to improvement in several cases.

6. Relationship patterns may be influenced by a death. The adolescent may become afraid of closeness or may attempt to build relationships in which he is protected from loss in the future. He may attempt to replace the lost person in his new relationship patterns. He may also be forced into a replacement relationship to meet the needs of other family members. The grief of some disturbed adolescents following their psychiatrist's suicide is described by Graves (1978). He vividly describes some of the relationship difficulties involved in his therapy with them, and their painful attempts to rework earlier deprivation with this further relationship failure.

7. Loss in adolescence may contribute to adult vulnerability: perhaps to depression, suicide, or alcohol problems. Information regarding this is presently inadequate.

"My big brother, John, was a hero," recalled thirteen-year-old Ken. "Everyone in the whole family thought he was the greatest. My mum and dad thought the sun and stars shone out of him. I guess I just trailed around like his little shadow. I wanted to be like him, to do everything just like he did. He was good at sport; the guys at school liked him; he was school captain the year he was to leave. He was popular with everyone. He was good looking; he was 'with it.' I used to copy everything he did—the clothes, the music—I wanted to be the way it was for him.

"We never knew why he killed himself or if it was an accident. He was a great sport, and he knew all about guns. Maybe he meant to do it; maybe it was an accident. The coroner said we'd never really know.

"When he died, it changed our whole life. My mum and dad never got over it. They wouldn't talk about it: 'It was such a disgrace,' they said. They'd 'always been such respectable people—there had never been anything like this in the family before.' They kept saying, 'We must remember him the way he was'; 'We must not talk about it'—that we should just pretend to ourselves and it would be alright.

"I was so confused. The kids at school avoided me for a while. I didn't know what to say, and they didn't either. The teachers would always be comparing me to him though, and they'd say 'You're getting on well—like your brother.' But I got the message I wasn't really as good as him.

"After a while Mum and Dad seemed to take notice of me again; it was as though they only had one son now and they'd better make the most of him. They started to treat me like they used to treat John. They'd boast about the things I did. Sometimes they even slipped and called me John. That felt strange but I really didn't mind. It was good to have them care about me. We all seemed to carry on as though nothing had happened after that. I felt a bit strange at first, but I soon got used to it. I had been John's shadow before, so there wasn't much difference now. I felt as though I had taken over and was being him and that was better for everybody.

"It would have been all right I expect, except sometimes I felt miserable for no special reason. I should have been happy because I had everything, but I wasn't. When I looked back I used to think the real me had died when John died—that I'd taken over John's personality. I felt sad for *that* me, the real me. Then I thought 'What did it matter anyway; I was only a shadow of John.' I was sad, really sad, because no one missed me—all they wanted was John. I was gone—the real me, that is—and no one seemed to care."

Despite the possible pathologies outlined above, it is quite clear that many adolescents resolve their loss quite adequately, usually over a period of time. Pathology is by no means inevitable, and in assessing the bereaved adolescent every attempt must be made to look for strengths which may be activated to facilitate grief and mourning as well as the longer term adaptational tasks.

FACTORS AFFECTING OUTCOMES

The same basic factors will influence the outcome of adolescent bereavement as they will the outcome at other life stages. These include

1.  The quality of the relationship that was lost. The intensity of the attachment, the ambivalence and dependence, and the libidinal investment in it will influence the severity of the loss and the mourning processes.

Heightened ambivalence and dependence, either through development or current circumstances, will be more difficult to resolve, giving a loading for more pathological outcomes.

2. The kind of deaths. These deaths are often sudden and unexpected. Death itself is only beginning to be understood by the adolescent and is a threat in personal terms.

3. The nature and quality of family and social support. Adequate support is often lacking, because the adolescent may not be perceived in need, or those who would offer support are themselves too grief stricken, or his peers are themselves too avoidant and fearful.

4. Concurrent crises. Adolescent development itself may, for some young people, be a crisis to be resolved, taking up ego resources, which are not thus available for the bereavement.

5. Attitudes of the community and culture. The cultural stereotype of the adolescent may result in his being denied his rightful rituals of grief and mourning.

The La Grand (1981) study of older adolescents cited above also supports the importance of these factors. It is also worthy of note that a knowledge of normal bereavement patterns is helpful for the adolescent; the adolescent who is so afraid that his intense and strange feelings may be abnormal is very reassured by such information. This would support the value of high school educational programs in this sphere.

LOSSES OTHER THAN DEATHS

A much more frequent loss than parent or sibling death is that of parental divorce. The adolescent here forcibly loses his idealization of parents and often perceives himself as traumatized by the circumstances of their divorce. Wallerstein and Kelly (1974) describe this adolescent experience. Like younger children, the adolescent longs for his parents not to have separated; yearns for the status quo, the intact family; pines for the absent parent; and is often angry and guilty. While some adolescents mature and gain strength through this experience, many do not. They often become depressed and perhaps fearful of new relationships. It is quite clear that they experience the divorce as a major loss but one that is not easily resolved, even over time.

Many other losses may cause grief and mourning in adolescence: parental rejection may occur and the young person may be turned out of the home, or a parent may simple leave. Abortions and miscarriages are also important sources of grief. The death of a pet may be the first loss and may be most painfully felt as will any first encounter with death and bereavement.

"In the morning I left for school, and I didn't know but I'd seen my cat for the last time. When I arrived home I didn't realize he was gone. Later on Mum told me he had died. I knew he was old, but I couldn't take that he was dead. He had already been buried so I couldn't see him. I felt very sad, but I didn't want to cry in front of Mum. Mum told me not to tell my brothers and sisters. That night, when I went to bed, I just burst out crying, and I felt like going and unburying him. I was so mad that he was buried because I wanted to see him. I felt very sad for days after that" (from Tobin and Treloar 1979).

CONCLUSIONS

Loss is painful for adolescents—and death frightening. Life is changed when a family member dies, especially if it is a parent. The adolescent is aware of this. He receives little comfort for the grief he feels and may have few opportunities to share his memories and mourning for the lost person with significant others. He may act out his distress. He may become depressed. He may struggle on to maturity, consolidating his identity, perhaps foreclosing it prematurely. The crisis may strengthen his coping or leave him vulnerable to the crises and developments of adult life.

"When my mother died I thought my heart would break," recalled Geoffrey, age fourteen. "Yet I couldn't cry. It was locked inside. It was private and tender and sensitive like the way I loved her. They said to me, 'You're cool man, real cool, the way you've taken it,' but I wasn't cool at all. I was hot—hot and raging. All my anger, all my sadness was building up inside me. But I just didn't know any way to let it out."

# CHAPTER 5. Loss in Adult Life: The Death of a Spouse

"I was stunned, numb with shock. It couldn't be true. It must be a dream."

*Jennifer, age 35*

"My whole being ached for her—I wanted her back—I could think of nothing else. Every minute I thought she'd come through the door again—that lilt in her walk. Again and again I'd hear her voice, see her in the crowd. Each time I thought of her it was like a knife in my heart."

*Peter, age 30*

"I was so angry I wanted to hit out at God and the world. I wanted to hurt everyone just like I'd been hurt. I wanted to destroy. He'd left me and I hated him for it."

*Alice, age 45*

"Our lives together flowed past me like a river of time. I'd stop some places and remember how it was—all we shared, the good and the bad—and my heart seemed as if it would break I missed her so much. And I thought the tears would never stop."

*Jake, age 50*

Although there are many losses the adult may experience, two stand out as the most disruptive and potentially stressful: the death of a spouse and the death of a child. These losses have such great impact because of the intensity with which the relationships are held and the core themes they represent in the person's existence. The death of a spouse, or a partner of an adult pair-bond relationship, leads to a painful bereavement response. The marital pair have, in most instances, such closely interwoven lives that the loss of one partner may cut across the very meaning of the other's existence.

## The Relationship

The relationship between the married couple takes many complex forms. It is built upon many levels, It is, as well, a special subsystem of the family group, and it is influenced by and reflective of the broader social system. Yet, it represents the interaction of individual dynamic forces in each partner.

The way in which such relationships are built was outlined in chapter 1. However, it is useful to recapitulate briefly here. Each partner brings to the relationship an internalized pattern of earlier relationships and fantasies. This pattern, or image, will be composed of perceptions, based upon parental relationships, of each parent as the ideal or nonideal partner; experiences of each parent as a loving or hating person; internalization of the parents' relationship as a whole; internalizations of other partnership relationships, and of societal and subcultural models of "ideal partner" and "ideal relationship." Some of these perceptions will be conscious, but some will be built in terms of unconscious dynamic forces within the individual. This condensation also contains projections of the good and bad parts of the self.

The image that has been brought to the adult-to-adult pair bond will be molded by the realities of the partners as well as by their interactions as the relationship between the two adults progresses. Although initially there is much idealization, eventually the partner is related to in his good and bad aspects as a real person. The internal image of the relationship changes as a consequence. At any point the relationship will be composed of this internalized image that represents both the current feeling state and the symbolic meaning of the relationship, as well as similar factors internalized from the past and the interactions which contribute to its reality on a day-to-day basis. To understand the quality and nature of a marital relationship at a particular time, it is necessary to consider various aspects in the development of such a relationship.

Early in the development of the adult pair-bond the relationship may be one of ideal selves. But, as time progresses, with increasing knowledge of each other and self-disclosure, the relationship becomes more one of real selves, each partner being accepted and related to increasingly in terms of his real qualities. The internalized image held of the relationship represents both the early phases of perfectionism and the progressive changes to accommodate reality. A key aspect of this development is the degree to which the good and bad parts of the self and others are integrated and the inevitable ambivalence dealt with. Some theoretical models suggest a number of developmental stages for the relationship and have equated them with E. H. Erikson's life-cycle stages (1959), such as "trust versus mistrust"; "autonomy versus shame and doubt"; and "initiative versus guilt." This may prove useful in understanding the love and conflicts of a particular dyad at a particular time but has not really been validated in any other way.

Some distortions may appear in the dyad that influence its quality and style. For instance the partners may not readily accept the nonideal parts of the other. These may be rejected and attempts made to retain the relationship of ideals, each partner trying to change the other to "fit" his needs. This may lead to the breakdown of the relationship or a mating of idealized but "false" selves. Another common distortion (as noted by Dicks 1967) is that of mutual projection, where the partners project onto each other the unwanted and denied parts of the self and attach to these. This type of relationship is usually one with a conscious image of the partner as "bad," together with hostile interactions. The whole quality of the relationship may be influenced by this, or it may only occur periodically, for instance, in crisis.

The partners as individuals grow, develop, and change in the progress of this relationship. Some conflicts may be worked through. Greater personality maturity is likely, both because of adult development and the psychological makeup of the relationship. The nature and quality of the relationship will be governed by, and will govern, the intensity and intimacy it involves.

There are many different patterns of closeness in such dyads, which will lead to very different responses if lost. In some marriages each partner has a distinct and relatively separate life-style. The couple may share family life but not a great deal of closeness. The wife may have her own circle of friends, and her matriarchal kinship network from which she derives her gratifications, and the husband, his working place, his friends from work, drinking, and sport. The couple's interaction, although familiar and valued by each, is minimal: the meal, the bed, and perhaps little of the latter as the years progress. When a partner dies in this dyad the loss is great, but it affects far fewer areas of the bereaved's existence than it might in another dyad. In other relationships, the dyad may take precedence. The social life of the couple is shared. All experience is brought back to and takes reference from the dyad. Values, interests, feelings are very closely shared, and sexuality is intense. Interactions are frequent and prolonged and bring increasing self-disclosure and closeness. The loss of a partner in this type of relationship will bring much greater distress because so many of the interactions and meanings to life centered on that person. These are two extremes of dyadic patterns; most dyads fall along the spectrum between them.

Sexuality brings a special intimacy to dyadic bonds. The closeness and knowledge of the other's body, the gratifications, the pain, the shared ego and fusion of intimate sexuality all mean that there will be an intense physical parameter of loss should a partner die.

The relationship may be a source not only of reliable attachment, but also of identity and self-worth. The more the identity of each partner relies on that bond, the roles it involves, and the sense of identity provided by the interactions with the other, the greater the loss of identity and threat to identity should a partner die.

There are a number of patterns, or styles, of dyadic relationships which may become factors in the nature of the bereavement response should a partner die and which may also influence the longer term outcome. Symbiotic dependence between the partners may be extreme and may represent more aspects of the mother-infant relationship than adult to adult relating. Also, the ways of handling ambivalence will create certain patterns: a relationship may depend on denial of anger and aggression, or there may be intense bonds that are chiefly maintained by the aggressive charge that fuels interactions. It may also be that sadistic and masochistic drives are fully indulged in bitter physical and/or verbal interchange. The marriage style may be governed by certain interlocking dynamics in each partner: the hystero-obsessional marriage and the melancholy marriage (Hooper et al. 1977) are examples.

The social frameworks and set of the relationship will also be significant. The relationship may represent symbolic social functions and needs. The husband may represent to the wife security, power, status; the wife may represent a beautiful possession or a safe haven from the world of work. The social framework may see such dyads as very important or may place little importance on them.

The role of the dyadic partner as parent will contribute to the nature and quality of the relationship. There may be positive aspects such as when each partner values the other for the parenting role with children; or negative ones, as when one partner envies the closeness between the other and a child. The dyad may take precedence in the family, or crossgenerational dyads may seem to have more potency, leading to schism and other family dysfunction.

The dyad changes gradually over time in its longitudinal development, but also undergoes intense ebb and flow in the flux of everyday life. Thus its various qualities such as ambivalence and dependence may be heightened at one stage, only to fade within a few hours or days when another parameter will take on greater importance. This flux forms the relationship and is absorbed into its overall flavor, unless, of course, a loss cuts across a particular phase and highlights it—leaving it in frozen frames.

Marriage is many things to many people: excitement and love; stability and change; pain and hatred; intimacy and distance. When the partner is lost, all the meanings of the marriage, all its memories, will be thrown into relief.

## Death and Deaths

While it may be assumed that the adult has gained full conceptual understanding of death as a final and irreversible process, it is important to realize that this is sometimes a thin veneer, barely covering the concrete or fantasy conceptualizations that evolved through his childhood. Even for adults, the crisis of death may reawaken these earlier and more primitive processes, and they may strongly influence his thinking and response at this time. There may be magical thinking: fantasies of killing and blame; magical rituals of what might have been "if only"; dread of the words of death as well as contamination by death. Deaths that are of killing and violence, such as accident, suicide, or murder, may make such fantasies all the more pronounced. The way in which a death occurred at a special time—for example, during sexual intercourse, following a dream, or after having been discussed—may reinforce the magical fantasies of personal destructiveness that the bereaved harbors. Death of the marital partner, or the dyadic partner of an intimate bond, brings death very close and, inevitably, touches the bereaved personally, reminding him that he too may die.

Deaths during young adult life when these pair bonds are intense are often sudden and unexpected, and not infrequently violent, with all the consequences of traumatic stress and guilt that these may bring. For instance, it is reported that violent deaths such as suicide, homicide, and accident are the leading cause of death for people aged one to thirty-nine, and a third leading cause of death for people of all ages (Holinger 1980). Major cardiovascular diseases and neoplasms are the principal causes in the older group. Bowlby (1980), among others, draws attention to the frequency of violent deaths, especially suicide, in younger adults with such bonds. Such deaths are associated with greater shock effects and often many other difficulties that hamper their resolution.

Mrs. Bernice C was forty, and her husband, forty-five. He started to collapse at the steering wheel of their car, but managed to pull to the side of the freeway, then became unconscious, gasping for breath. Mrs. C could not drive and tried desperately over the next half-hour to stop cars on the freeway while she was attempting to resuscitate him. He was dead when assistance finally came. Her mind was filled with her panic-stricken memories of the scene, and she could think of nothing else. Her dreams repeated the events. The intruding images of the death brought panic and helplessness and she could not grieve.

The many ways in which sudden deaths are difficult include the extra effects of shock, anger, the difficulties with mutilating-destructive fantasies, the helplessness, and the legal and other processes with which the bereaved must become involved.

Slow, lingering deaths also have their stresses. The burden of the illness, the pain and distress of the dying person, the heightened intimacy of the relationship if the bereaved is constantly with the sick person and caring for his body functions, the ambivalence that debilitating illness and personality change may bring can all create difficulties for the bereaved spouse. The partner may feel guilty both because (though he has done all he could) his partner still suffered and died, and because he is finally released and free and glad he did not die himself. Malignant disease may cause many distressing deaths of this kind.

Clive S nursed his wife Lois, age thirty-eight, through her terminal illness from cancer of the breast. He felt committed to care for her until the end but was appalled and repulsed by the changes in her body and terrified of her neediness and suffering. He bathed her daily and thought with distress of the times when her body had been so stimulating and exciting to him. He dreaded that she would sense his revulsion and so tried desperately to provide her with everything she wished for. Her irritability at his intrusive care and the pain she experienced constantly made her a difficult patient. She knew this but found she could not contain her feelings. He longed for her death but dreaded it, as he could not imagine life without her. Yet he identified and empathized with her suffering, but quietly rejoiced at his own health and survival.

The complexities of illness and death will also have meaning in terms of each partner's past experience and present fantasies. Thus the death has many meanings and many feelings attached to it.

# Loss in Adult Life: The Death of a Spouse

## The Experience of Conjugal Bereavement

The processes and experience of bereavement are common to widow and widower, but the expression may be very different, dependent on culturally sanctioned behaviors for each sex. The discussion that follows will describe conjugal bereavement in terms of the woman's response, commenting where appropriate, on the differences for a man. The response resembles the typical pattern described in chapter 2.

The initial reaction is of shock, numbness, and disbelief. How can the partner who filled so much of life, so much of the bereaved's reason for existence, be dead? The death is a blow. The anguish may break through. The whole aura of this grief-stricken person is such as to evoke the intense, empathic response of others.

The bereaved may be with the partner during the death, feeling helpless as he seems to fade away despite all efforts to hold him, keep him alive. She may sit holding the body, rocking back and forth with it, willing it to life. If she was not with her partner when he died, there is likely to be a strong need to touch or hold the body when she sees it, perhaps to affirm the death, finally hold and comfort him and herself, and say her good-byes. Where there has been prolonged illness, the end point of death may seen indistinct, for the wasting and withdrawal of life from the body in the dying process has given many cues to the nature of death itself and the ultimate loss.

Following the news of the death, those most intimately involved, the nuclear family, make efforts to comfort and support the bereaved spouse. Family members, neighbors, and friends all come to offer their condolences and practical assistance. Two key issues must be dealt with: the necessity for carrying out those tasks essential for survival, the meals and other mundane needs of family life; and the arrangements for the disposal of the body. There are often culturally prescribed behaviors or rituals to deal with both these essentials. It often happens that the widow, seen as the "prime bereaved," may be treated, because of her shock, as though she cannot participate in either of these tasks, especially the funeral arrangements. Others, perhaps male relatives, may take over. The widow may wish a part in such planning but may be too distressed to insist on her wishes.

In contemporary Western society the funeral usually takes place within a few days of the death. The family gathers. A service, secular or religious, is planned. Burial or cremation occurs. The shock, numbness, and denial may continue throughout this period, but, for most, the funeral is a further specific confrontation with the reality of the death; weeping is likely, and the waves of anguish and despair that the bereaved has been fighting off are likely to break through. The extent to which this open expression of grief is possible is dependent on circumstance, social situation, and personal variables. The bereaved may feel the need to "keep up a good front," a facade of control, because the deceased or society would have expected this. Or her own internalized expectations may demand constraint of feeling. Others may feel it shameful not to cry. The widower in many Anglo-Saxon cultures would feel womanly or weak if he displayed such feelings. Yet his European counterpart from Italy or Greece would consider that he and the deceased were demeaned if there was not the proper show of grief.

Some funeral services—for instance, cremation in some societies—may be so deritualized and brief that there is little time for realization. It is all over before the impact is felt and the grief released. Other practices fully reinforce the reality and solemnity of death and the passage of the deceased to another state. His departure is quite clear. The return home from the services may be a family gathering or formal wake. But after the guests depart the confrontation with the dead person's absence is inevitably stated: the empty place at the table, the empty half of the bed.

SEPARATION PAIN

As the numbness starts to fade, the first intense experiences of grief center on the absence of the loved partner—the experience of living apart and being separated from him. All the woman wants is to have her man back. All the man wishes and longs for is his dead wife, her presence near him, with him. This physical experience of the absence of the dead partner, this "separation pain," is extremely intense for the conjugally bereaved. The partner was so much a basic, accepted part of everyday existence in terms of interactions, feeling, and behaviors, and in terms of the bodily need for closeness, let alone sexuality, that it may not be until his absence, his death, that the partner realizes how completely life was integrated with him.

There is intense longing for the lost person. The bereaved yearns for the sound of his voice, the sight of his face, the smell of his body. Every fiber of her being calls out for him. All emotion is focused on his image, as if to draw him back. Reminders of him are sought eagerly: he is looked for in all familiar places—desperately. Yet reminders of him precipitate fresh pangs of longing. Each time he is sought and not found it is as though the bereaved were pierced by a knife, for the pain of his absence is so great. Arousal is high. The lost person is expected at familiar times, looked for, listened for. Yet he does not return. His image is held intensely for comparison with all cues that might indicate his presence. At one level, it is clearly recognized that he is dead and gone, but at another there is the belief in the possibility of his return.

There are waves, or pangs, of grief as the partner's absence continues. The longing (and covert belief in the possibility of return) may be reflected in many behaviors still organized around familiar things, and suggesting the possibility of life continuing as it was. The bereaved may be unable to resist the urge to prepare and set out her husband's clothes or to set his accustomed place at the table. The yearning leads to a perceptual set for the absent person. His image is held intensely. There is the longing for the reality of interaction to disprove the loss. The bereaved may see or hear the lost person or feel his touch. Dreams may also reflect such longing. Primitive and preverbal reverberations of earlier separation experiences are reawakened, leading to waves of panic when the lost person fails to reappear.

Regression is a common and natural response in the face of the shock of loss, the pain of separation. The bereaved may curl up in the fetal position. He or she may long to be held, comforted, looked after. This is difficult for many adults, especially men who fear such regression is evidence of weakness and femininity and who therefore cannot allow it. Many of those men and women who are overindependent as a reaction against more childlike dependent needs are especially threatened and may attempt to repress regression urges along with their sorrow and tears.

The other powerful emotion associated with being separated from a loved one is anger. There is a sense of being deserted by the dead person. The bereaved feels "Why did this have to happen to him—to me? Why not someone else? Why didn't someone stop it, prevent it?" and, "Why did he leave me? Why isn't he here when I need him most?" The anger may appear as irritability with all those who offer help, all those who seem to be there instead of the dead person, and with those associated with the death. There may be rage, more intense than the bereaved has felt before, seemingly irrational. This anger is often displaced. This may be reinforced by the behavior of others at the time of the death. For instance, when a person dies in a hospital emergency room the family may be told the news abruptly, brusquely. It is quite likely that their natural anger at the loss, the "desertion," will be heightened and displaced onto the hospital or the doctor who did not save the dead husband.

Anger toward the dead is difficult to acknowledge, for it seems "crazy": the bereaved recognizes that he, the deceased, did not mean to leave, could not help it. It is unconsciously linked to fantasies of destructiveness and killing, stirring up feelings of guilt. Its basic purpose is to call back the deceased, to punish him, to prevent him from deserting again. This too seems madness, for the bereaved knows full well he is dead. In private, or in her fantasies, she may call out to him, "Why did you desert me?" But there is no answer.

The intensity and irrationality of the anger, the helplessness of the separation anxiety, and the perceptual experiences may all lead the bereaved to feel she is indeed becoming insane. The present is terrifying, the future filled with dread.

## Finality and Mourning

"Secretly I was really expecting he would come back—I knew it couldn't really be true. I would turn to the door each evening, thinking I heard his key. Each time he didn't come in my heart sank—it was eating away at my hope, my belief. Yet I couldn't let go—to accept he was gone for good was somehow disloyal. Occasionally the despair would break over me: for a moment I'd know it was real, he wasn't coming back, he was there in the ground. But most of the time it wasn't like that. In my heart I felt longing for him, and he was so alive there. He just had to come back; he was always such a vital person; he just couldn't be dead. The weeks went on like that. They all came to offer sympathy, but it was as though I was in another world. He'd been away for weeks before, anyway, and he'd always come back. Then one day I knew it was real, that he wasn't coming back again, and that this was all there was. It wasn't what I wanted, but that's what it was."

Each time the bereaved wife longs for her dead husband, each time the image is not met with the reality of interaction, the finality and permanence of the absence is reinforced. When there are also images of the person as dead, and of the ceremonies of death, there is further affirmation. With increasing realization of the finality of the loss the bereaved starts to give up any expectation of return of the dead person. She becomes preoccupied internally with the "image" of the person and memories of the relationship. It is as though this is held in place of the person until the bonds to him are gradually undone. Many powerful feelings well up as memories of the relationship are sifted through: regret that more was not valued when the partner was alive; resentment over those things that were not made right or over being cheated by death of what was hoped for the future; ineffable sadness over what was and can no longer be; sorrow for the lost past and the younger years that are gone with it; anger at life, the dead person, the self for what one did not have and now may never have—perhaps children, perhaps love; guilt for the love that was not perfect, for the hate that was nurtured, the care that failed; release from the suffering of illness, from the suffering of relationship; triumph that one did not die oneself, guilt that such a feeling could appear; depression at the emptiness of self and world; and envy of those who have not lost, who live unscathed by death.

The psychological mourning process involves the review of these and many other aspects of the lost relationship in order that the bonds binding the bereaved to the dead partner may gradually be relinquished, freeing the emotional investment for ongoing life and further relationships. Thus the bereaved reviews, piece by piece, memories, thoughts, and feelings associated with the image of the dead partner. Sadness and other feelings relevant to each of those memories are experienced intensely as each is faced, treasured, and reluctantly put aside. The process is inevitably painful, yet must progress. S. Freud (1917) describes this clearly in dynamic terms.

Initially as the relationship is reviewed the lost partner may be idealized. The bereaved paints a picture of a perfect man, a perfect woman, a perfect love, a perfect relationship. As the review extends and if circumstances are favorable, more real memories surface. The dead person's more negative qualities are remembered, perhaps a little ruefully, perhaps with some anger, but at least with some acceptance that that was how he was. When levels of ambivalence were high, rather than accepting the negative aspects, there may be much bitterness and regret, especially if the bereaved sees no chance to do things differently in the future. Thus the woman whose husband dies leaving her childless and menopausal may have lost not only him, but also any hope of things being different. A young widower whose wife dies after a bitter marital relationship may feel there is hope for a better relationship in the future; bitterness and regret are not so great except for the loss of what may be seen as "wasted" years. Critical to the issue of resolving the loss is the way in which the average of the good and bad of human relationships is accepted and balanced.

When the bereaved remembers the dead person as the "real" person he was to her, then mourning is progressing successfully. Marked distortion, either by idealization or vilification of the memory indicates that mourning may be skewed and resolution difficult. Perhaps guilt as the intrapsychic force is the variable that interferes: the bereaved may be too guilty because of her ambivalence, even her death wishes for that partner to remember the real and negative aspects that seem so clearly linked to the fulfillment of such wishes. And social forces eulogizing the dead person, advising her not to remember the bad, only the good, may make these negative aspects even more difficult to face. As all human relationships have some ambivalence, and marital dyads are very complex human relationships, it is inevitable there will be some guilt. Where the relationship is basically loving these transient feelings will pass rapidly in the mourning process. When favorable support is available, allowing the bereaved to express those ambivalent feelings, these too will be resolved (Raphael 1978a). But intense ambivalence and the absence of appropriate support may make this aspect of mourning very difficult so that the bereaved clings to the relationship, will not relinquish it, or will only mourn and hold to an intensely idealized and distorted view of the lost person.

The process of review and all the many feelings associated with it are most intense in the early weeks and months following the partner's death. The bereaved seems obsessed, totally preoccupied in her focus on the dead person. Life seems disorganized and all else meaningless beside the death. Behavior is purposeless, despair overwhelming. The future seems black and empty; the years ahead without the dead partner, endless and unwanted. The bereaved may wish to die, resenting life and those things that reinforce existence. In the complex web of the marital dyad, it is only when one half is torn away that the other realizes how constantly, intensely, and unconsciously the most minute interactions and thoughts seemed to have purpose in terms of the deceased and are now purposeless. The bereaved may say how little she feels; she may be unable to initiate activity and may need others to do this for her; or she may carry on automatically feeding the children, going to bed, carrying on only because she feels she must do these tasks. But her whole interest and involvement are elsewhere—with her dead husband. Her children, others in the family, may all feel excluded by this preoccupation, yet it is essential for her mourning process.

As the lost relationship is remembered, reviewed, there is often an intense need to talk through, to share the memories with others. Just as the person in love talks obsessively of the loved one, so does the bereaved wish to discuss, look at, relive, make meaning of each one of these memories. It may also be part of the reality testing of the relationship and its loss: talking about it, testing it out with another, putting it outside the self. The bereaved weeps and cries as she does so, for it is very sad. She will share different memories and their affects with different friends and family members. She will wish, too, to sort through the partner's clothes and possessions in the same sad and gradual way, sharing some, treasuring some, keeping the most intimate privately to herself. Those with whom she is involved may be able to accept, facilitate, and share this bonding review; or, because of their own anxieties or society's rules, they may be unable to do so. For the most part the support of others to encourage and facilitate these processes is very critical to her resolution of mourning (Maddison and Walker 1967).

The progress of the mourning process is revealed in many ways: in the ease, yet sadness, with which the bereaved can talk of the dead person; in her capacity to complete the associated social tasks, such as making a decision about the headstone and participating in legal arrangements; in her use of the past tense over present and future tenses when speaking about the dead person; in her remembering of the deceased as a separate relinquished part of her life; when her dreams represent the partner as ill or distant; when she starts to smile and again feel the warmth of human interest in the outside world and her future in it; and when she realizes with surprise, perhaps a little guilt, that she has not thought of the dead person for a while, that her grief has been momentarily forgotten. This is the beginning of reintegration into life. The emotional cathexis that had been turned into the task of mourning now begins to become available for reinvestment in the external world. Although the bereaved still does not really wish to go on in time without the dead partner there is now a certain acceptance that she will, and that she will even again find some pleasurable experiences in life.

The time taken to reach this stage varies enormously. The first six weeks following the death are usually the most intense and painful. Some lessening of grief and mourning seem to occur after that period. This turning point seems recognized in many societies where there is some sort of memorial service held about the fortieth day after the death. Yet for most of the first three to four months the bereaved may still be very distressed. And there may be times, as with acute reminders of the person, that all the grief seems to come back again with its original intensity, and a fresh wave of mourning over newly reawakened losses takes place.

One widow said, "I have my good days when I really feel I am coping; then I have my bad days—everything feels just as terrible as ever, and it's as though I've made no progress at all. Then things improve again: I realize I can and will go on. Even though I know life will never be the same again, there will be good things, and there is a future."

Anniversaries may bring fresh bursts of grief and mourning. Sometimes the bereaved will find that the day of the week or month that was the day of the death will be especially distressing. Anniversaries of the wedding, special occasions, birthdays, and holidays such as Easter or Christmas are likely to bring painful exacerbations (Pollock 1971a). The first anniversary of the death is particularly hard for most bereaved, with all the memories of the death and the loss vividly relived. Yet at the end of this first year the bereaved feels she has survived; she can and will exist without the lost partner; she had achieved some goal that seemed impossible in the early months—survival. Life is going on.

Patterns of "normal" bereavement for widows and widowers are essentially the same. The external manifestations, however, may differ because of sex role differences in behavior. The widow may more readily express her feelings openly and elicit care—her tears and sorrow are easily accepted as womanly. The widower may be expected to control his distress—tears and need are seen as unmanly in many Western societies. His grief may be more hidden, and constrained; hers more open. The degree to which life has been organized around the lost person may make a difference also. The man may have been the central core of the woman's existence; his loss deprives her life of all meaning. The woman may have been the comforting haven of love, but secondary to the excitement and challenge of the man's life or work. The intensity of grief may be different, for more sources of loss may exist in the woman's bereavement than in the man's. But these differences may be very superficial, bringing misleading assumptions about the needs of the widower and of the widow.

Peter was thirty when his wife Ellen, twenty-eight, died from a subarachnoid hemorrhage. They had two children, a girl, six, and a boy, four. Ellen had collapsed suddenly with a severe headache. She was rushed to hospital but died despite resuscitative attempts. Peter was shocked and numb for the first few days. She had always seemed so well and full of happiness, so he found her death unbelievable. His family and Ellen's were both very distressed, but rallied immediately. Peter's widowed mother moved into the house to take care of the children to whom she had always been close. Peter felt he arranged the funeral "as in a dream." He had seen Ellen's body after the death and was stunned by its peacefulness—she had always been so actively, noisily alive. He explained carefully to the children what had happened, but they, too, seemed stunned and unable to comprehend. They kept asking him questions about why she had died that he felt were unanswerable. Over the two weeks following the funeral he felt as though he were in a state of "suspended animation." He took this time off from work but found he could do little with it. He wandered around the house restlessly, startling at the slightest noise or reminder of Ellen.

"It was as though I was waiting for someone—her—I was waiting for her to come back. I kept thinking I saw her out of the corner of my eye, and I'd turn my head quickly to catch her, but of course she was gone—she wasn't there. Then I'd catch a whiff of her perfume when I opened the wardrobe door to get out my clothes, and I felt I would die. It was like a knife going through me— the pain was so great I thought my heart would burst. Then I'd get angry, so angry. It was crazy, I know, but I thought 'Why did she go?' She had no right to go and leave me like that—we needed her; the children were too little to lose a mother. They needed her, and I needed her too. Why did she have to die? Why didn't we know there was something like this wrong with her? Why didn't we get her checked up? How could she look so healthy when she had something like this lurking in her head? Why didn't the doctors know? Why didn't they fix her? And at night then, it was terrible: the bed was so empty and white. She used to curl up beside me and her skin would thrill me again each time it touched mine. I don't want to sleep, yet I do—then I wake with a start. I'm sure she's there. I *feel* her beside me as real and warm as ever, and I lean over to touch, to make love—my body's longing for her—and it's like a slap across the face. She's not there—there's nothing, nothing. All I want is her—no one, nothing else.

"I yearned and yearned for her to come back. It was as though I expected her to materialize, to come floating down the stairs in that old dressing gown, as she does each morning and say 'Hi,' just as she always has. Then one morning I looked up the stairs waiting as usual, then I turned away. 'No,' I said to myself, 'No she's really gone; she's never coming back.' I felt like my heart was sinking, that I had black lead in me. I knew then, I *really* knew that it was for good. And I sat at the table and sobbed and sobbed, and the kids said 'What is it Daddy?' and I said 'It's Mummy, I want her so much and she's never coming back.' So we sat and held one another and they cried too, though I don't know if it was for them or me.

"I thought about her all the time in those weeks: all the things we used to do together; the day we met; the fun we had; the fights; how we nearly broke up; the trouble I gave her in the beginning; how stubborn she was; when the kids were born; that cute look on her face—all the little things and the big ones too. It was as though they were my treasures. Some of them I wanted to keep to myself, they were so private, but some I had to talk about and talk about. I talked to Mum and to my brother and to Ellen's sister and to some good mates. Sometimes I cried and they'd put an arm around me and say 'OK, get it out' and that helped a lot. Sometimes I was angry, angry that life had cheated us of all those years we'd planned together, angry that she hadn't looked after herself better—but that passed. I was a bit guilty too, sorry I hadn't helped her more with the kids, hadn't told her more often how much I loved her—God knows I did, but really she knew that too—she used to tease me about it sometimes. It seemed as though my life was filled with her in those first months, no one else. I'd lost her, but I was hanging on to what was left, my memories. Then it seemed to come to a time when I realized I couldn't hang on to her like that, that I had to get on with life. I still thought about her most of the time, but it didn't hurt so much; it was easier to talk about, and the tears didn't come so often. Somehow or other I started to feel interested in life again. I felt guilty about that at first—disloyal—as though I was letting her go. Then one day I found myself smiling and laughing. That stopped me. 'There,' I thought, 'That's what she would have wanted. She was like that herself.' So life went on.

"All that first year was difficult. Never a week went by without something we would have done together, some secret thing we would have laughed at or shared. At first I thought I'd never make it, and in the beginning I felt like dying myself, but I couldn't. I loved life too, and there were the kids; they were part of both of us, and they needed me so much. When her birthday came, and our wedding anniversary, and the kid's birthdays, it was terrible: they'd been such special times for us; it seemed obscene she wasn't there, and it would all come over me again. It was the same on the anniversary of her death. That was a turning point, though, because we had made it; we all had, and we would keep on going. It was a different life without her, but it was life."

## THE INFLUENCE OF FAMILY AND SOCIAL GROUP

The death occurs not only for the bereaved partner, but also for the family group, nuclear and extended. The family members are usually mobilized during the terminal illness and immediately following the death. They come together to offer mutual emotional support, solidarity, and practical assistance, as well as for a reaffirmation of the family. Roles are defined for the different family members during the illness and immediately following the death, depending on the power distribution in the family system and the perceived needs of individuals. The widow or widower is usually considered the principal bereaved person, with an acceptance that she or he will grieve. The family unit may give clear messages as to how and when that grief should appear, but at least it is usually positively sanctioned for this person. It may be very distressing to the bereaved spouse when this does not occur. For instance, when the man dies, his mother may see herself as the central person, having the greatest grief, because she has lost her son. The wife may feel she should rightly hold the central grieving role for she has lost her husband. Such "competition" for grief may be intensely distressing to both parties and may interfere with their capacity to grieve as they wish.

When a man loses his wife there may be expectations from his family group that he will be the "strong one" who supports the rest of the family through their loss of mother, daughter, or sister, for example, so that his own needs to be comforted and consoled may not be met. This is often the dilemma within family units: each member is bereaved, yet each needs also to fulfill the role of comforter to others. Such dual roles are very difficult to meet.

Another issue for the bereaved adult in the family with dependent children may be the need to ensure the family's survival. The widower or widow may feel that he or she has to contain his or her feelings and set aside needs to look after children, provide food and shelter, and secure a source of income. This is particularly likely if the family is under threat of losing its home or may not in fact survive because its material resources are so poor. Once survival is ensured the surviving parent should be able to let her feelings go if other circumstances, internal and social, are favorable, so that grief is only delayed. More frequently the needs of the children may be used as a rationalization for avoiding the pain of grief. In such circumstances the widow, for instance, may stop herself from crying for fear that it will "only upset the children more." She mistakenly attempts to protect them in this way, not recognizing that her lack of grief may be much more threatening for them, particularly in the long term.

Within the family there may be different patterns and levels of grief. The bereavement may progress at different rates. Thus when the husband or wife is in the acute crisis, the children may be showing little response, perhaps because they have not fully taken in what has happened. Later when parental grief is lessening the child's disturbed behavior may indicate that his grief and mourning are *now*, instead of earlier, reaching their peak. These differing patterns and rates often lead to misunderstanding and resentment, because the other does not seem to appreciate either the bereaved's grief or how bad the situation seems. There may be a fear of sharing feelings and memories lest they bring distress to others, particularly as one family member's view of a happy intimacy shared with the dead person may be another's view of remembrance of envy, exclusion, and resentment. Easier to share are the memories of joint family occasions, times of shared pleasures, but these may have been few and far apart in a dysfunctional family.

Family patterns of supporting and comforting one another in the family before the loss may set the scene for what is expected. It may be that one person is the one who is always cared for, and that others cannot grieve, because they must continue caring for that person despite their own intense needs. Power patterns within the family will be quite important in defining who takes charge, who is allowed to grieve, and perhaps even who is scapegoated and blamed for the death. The functional family with flexible roles and the capacity to express and share feelings is likely to weather the crisis of death better (Vollman et al. 1971) than the family with rigidity and poor methods of handling feelings. Gross family pathology is usually linked to gross pathology between the marital partners, and so the resolution of such bereavements is likely to be very problematic.

A further complicating issue for the family, especially the older family, may be the division of property after the death. The widow or widower may find that the spouse died intestate, or left the property entailed, or did not bequeath all as had been anticipated. Bitter resentments over such perceived inequities may alienate those from whom support is needed, as well as interfere with the bereavement by the intensity of emotion that becomes invested in the sense of injustice. Even the informal distribution of treasured possessions amongst family members may be seen as having hurtful consequences. The bereaved spouse is likely to feel, because of the intimate bond shared, that all such treasures are rightfully his. Bearing in mind that such objects may in ways symbolically represent the dead person, may be linking objects (Volkan 1970) to him, the reasons they are so emotionally important to the bereaved becomes obvious. The sharing of personal effects, all that is left of the dead person, often takes place in the early weeks after the death. The old rivalries and frictions that may be highlighted in this process may well interfere with the crisis resolution.

The bereaved widow is very dependent on the support of other adults at the time of the crisis. In terms of Caplan's crisis theory (1964), not only does she turn to others for support, but she is also much more influenced by the responses of others to her than she would be at a noncrisis time. The recently bereaved widow and widower often sense others' reluctance for involvement and fear of the bereaved's need and dependence. They often feel that they must follow the overt or covert expectations for behavior given by those on whom they are so dependent at this crisis time for fear that if they do not, they will lose their vitally needed support. Thus they may feel impelled to behave in certain ways in terms of expression of grief, review of the lost relationship, and discussion of the deceased that may be contrary to their real feelings. This is often pronounced in their relationships with adult children, who may be afraid of the parent's potential dependence upon them now that the partner has died, and who thus may wish the bereaved to deny, lessen, shut out the grief, to continue coping as though nothing had happened. Such adult children may have specific views of the longer-term adaptation of the parent, perhaps encouraging a new partnership for the bereaved or actively negating one.

In-laws are another group with whom similar patterns of difficulty arise. Many widows claim that their husband's families lose all interest in them after the death, fearing dependent demands they might make, yet later are antagonistic toward any ideas the widow might have about forming a new relationship. Such failures of support are often a grave disappointment to the bereaved.

The general properties of social and kinship networks as they influence bereavement have been described by Walker, McBride, and Vachon (1977). These workers suggest that the dense social networks may offer best support for the crisis time in their opportunities for emotional and practical assistance, while the less dense networks may be more facilitative of longer-term adjustments through the bridges they offer to new role and relationship development.

However, the most careful and detailed study of the specific interaction of the widow with her social network and its influence on the bereavement process comes from Maddison's work (Maddison and Walker 1967; Maddison, Viola, and Walker 1969). He was able to show how the widow's perception of specific aspects of her social-network interaction in terms of her expression of grief, her review of the lost relationship in the mourning process, and other general crisis issues, was one of the critical factors in outcome. He explored widows' perceptions of their social-network interactions in quite specific terms of actual interactions (for example, what others said or did), their perceived helpfulness or unhelpfulness, and needed interactions that did not occur. He also investigated the particular relationships involved.

The findings were as follows: widows who went on to poor outcome (in terms of their health in the postbereavement year) perceived themselves as having many more unsatisfied needs in interpersonal exchanges during the bereavement crisis than did those with good outcome. The widows felt that they needed more encouragement and support in expressing their affects, such as grief and anger. They needed more opportunity to talk actively, particularly about the husband and their life together (reviewing the lost relationship in the mourning process). These widows often needed specific support to talk of the negative as well as positive aspects of the lost relationship, and they needed nonjudgmental acceptance of the expression of their feelings of guilt, especially when the relationship had been a particularly ambivalent one. They also felt they needed more practical help and general support.

Poor outcome was also associated with interactions perceived as unhelpful in that they blocked the widow's expression of affects: others may have been shocked by her feelings; told her to control herself and pull herself together; suggested that she minimize her grief by thinking of the suffering of others; advised her not to be angry or guilty; or told her not to cry because she would upset others. Other unhelpful interactions were those that were perceived as blocking her mourning process by advising her not to think of the past but to focus on the future, to take up new friendships or activities, or suggesting that she should think, even at this crisis time, of remarriage.

Maddison (Maddison, and Walker 1967) concludes that these perceptions of unhelpful interactions were often accurate. Others were frequently well-meaning in their attempts to support the widow, but their efforts produced only "clichés of comfort" and were often defensive or even overtly or covertly hostile. The social network, including family and friends, was often perceived as inadequate in the face of the crisis adversity, and when this was the case the outcome for the widow was often poor. More recently Vachon et al. (1982) have also found that deficits of social support correlate with enduring high distress in bereaved widows. These findings are supported by Henderson, Byrne, and Duncan-Jones's findings (1981) in epidemiological surveys where perceived inadequacy of attachment at the time of an adversity such as loss may correlate with subsequent morbidity. Furthermore, my own studies (Raphael 1977b; Raphael 1978a) show that where social support is perceived as inadequate, therapeutic intervention in the form of supportive interactions, aimed at modifying the perceived areas of deficiency, is likely substantially to improve outcome, suggesting some etiological association. In these studies it was found that women who had perceived their social networks as failing to encourage or support their talk of the dead husband were helped by interventions that facilitated this. Where the widow had previously had an ambivalent relationship, her social network may have failed her by denying that she should express her guilt or review the positive and negative memories she had of their relationship. Specific facilitation of these areas lessened the likelihood that her mourning would develop into melancholia.

Jane S, age thirty-two, showed many of the ways in which such family and social-network variables may operate. Three weeks after her husband's death she felt that the fact he had really "gone" hit her fully. That day she received a small check from his place of work, his final pay. Her husband Bill, a "truckie," had been killed in an accident. It appeared that he went to sleep at the wheel, but no one was sure. The police came with the news and asked whether she or anyone could identify the body. Immediately, her mother who had been called in, took over. Although Jane wanted desperately to see if it was Bill and was filled with dreadful fantasies as to what might have happened to him, her mother insisted her father go instead to the identification. She emphasized that Jane should not see the body; it would only upset her if she did and thus make it more difficult for her family to help her, and, "after all, they were all she had now." When Jane persisted in with her wish, Mrs. K (her mother) made it quite clear that she found this unbearable—that Jane must "remember him as he was."

In the days that followed, Jane's sisters and friends called to see her. They all seemed very upset and obviously wished to be helpful. They advised her "not to think about the past, only to think about the future." Whenever Jane brought up her concerns about how Bill had died she was told not to think about it, because "he couldn't have suffered anything." She wanted desperately to talk about how guilty she felt, as they had had an argument the night before and she had refused to have intercourse with him. She felt that he may still have been upset when he left early the next morning and that this may have interfered with his concentration while driving, leading to the accident. No one would let her express her guilty feelings; each time she tried to do so she was told that she had been a "good wife," "the best," and she had nothing to feel bad about.

She felt angry with Bill, deserted by him, especially as he had left that morning without saying good-bye. Yet the moment she started to show any anger, her family and friends became very uncomfortable, changed the subject, and told her not to upset herself. Her mother told her she'd never cope if she let herself feel things like that. When she wanted to cry, as she often did, especially in the evenings when she missed him so much, she was told she should remember how lucky she was—she had had a good husband and had lovely children, and she shouldn't break down or she'd hurt them. Each time she started to talk of her memories of Bill—of the things they had shared—her family and friends said she must put the past behind her, she should just think of the good things about him and plan for the future: she was young and attractive—she'd soon be remarried. It is hardly surprising that this well-meant advice was perceived by her as blocking her expression of grief and stopping her mourning for her husband.

## LONGER-TERM PATTERNS OF ADAPTATION TO THE LOSS

After the initial crisis of the early weeks and months, the intensity of grief and preoccupation with the mourning process lessen. The dead partner is still thought of constantly, but the bereaved is reoriented again to life. The memories of the dead partner are loving, sad, regretful, angry, perhaps even relieved. What he would have liked, how he would have thought about a particular problem is often taken into account, but the bereaved has basically come to some acceptance of her life going on independently without the partner. Many times in that first year she will have to make a decision, carry out a task, follow a course that would normally have been shared with him, but she now carries the responsibilities and their consequences without him. Her life has inevitably taken a different course. Each time she must confront an issue of this kind, she again may feel grief, perhaps anger, sadness, or helplessness, and she may mourn a little more as she remembers times when these things were shared, when she was comforted and supported. Her memories of him are a complex amalgam of the past of the relationship and the distillation of this in the current stage of the mourning process.

Sometimes the lost relationship may continue to exert a major influence. The widow or widower may have "conversations" with the spouse, perhaps when sorting out problems, or just for the comfort of some sense of the other's ongoing presence. But reality testing is maintained, and these episodes represent only a small element of the bereaved's overall functioning. Cultural and social factors may reinforce the continuing reliance on the partner. Yamamoto et al. (1969) describe how the tie between the Japanese widow and her husband is maintained through the cultural "cultivation of the idea of the presence of the deceased" (p. 1665). The husband's photograph is kept at the family altar in the home, and his presence is felt and used as a support. This does not represent a break with reality testing, for the widow can "look at the picture and feel he is alive and look at the urn and ashes and realize he is dead" (p. 1665). In fact the evidence suggests that this helps her bereavement. Moss and Moss (1979) describe the role of the continued presence of the image of the dead spouse in the elderly widowed.

Regardless, however, of the support that may be derived from such thoughts, the bereaved widow or widower has a number of tasks for longer-term adaptation that must be negotiated. There is a necessity to find new sources of adult to adult interaction that will meet needs now unfulfilled with the loss of the spouse. The needs within relationships are defined by Weiss (1974a) and have been discussed here. They include: attachment, social integration, nurturance, alliance, guidance, and reassurance of worth. Although the marital relationship may not satisfy all of these needs, it does seem different from other relationships in that it does not simply specialize in one or two of these areas, but is based on the assumption that any or all of the partners' needs will be met within the relationship. As a minimum, the marital relationship makes a number of provisions, including a sense of reliable attachment. Thus the spouse may need to grieve and mourn for what is lost in terms of the fulfillment of these needs. And, when he or she has relinquished the former source of gratification—the dead partner as a source of fulfillment—then steps must be taken to find other ways by which the needs may be met.

Most painful for the bereaved person is the loneliness he or she feels after the death of the partner. Weiss (1974a) sees the complaint of "loneliness" as the emotional response to the loss of the adult attachment bond. It is not lessened by other companionship, except temporarily, and it is, he believes, quite specific for the adult pair bond. It only settles when a new adult attachment is made. While many would not use the term quite so specifically, it is certainly true that loneliness, unrequited loneliness, is one of the prime themes for the widow or widower in the months, perhaps years, following the death. Parkes and Brown (1972) found such loneliness frequently in their younger widows and widowers. Maddison and Walker (1967) noted it frequently in their subjects, and our own studies document it as a frequent and distressing complaint. Clayton (1975) found that living alone did not influence the occurrence of depressive symptoms in widows and widowers at one month, but, at both one month and one year after death, those living alone were significantly more likely to be using medication. Weiss (1974a) views the loneliness as a reaction to the absence of the loved one rather than to the bereavement itself. Thus the loneliness is likely to continue over a period until the deficit state is resolved. Bahr and Harvey (1979) studied widows following a mining disaster and found that they manifested very high levels of personal loneliness but not of perceived community underinvolvement. Glick, Weiss, and Parkes (1974, pp. 212, 242–43) in a series of interviews during the year following bereavement found that loneliness did not fade unless the widow had "reaffiliated." Sixty percent were still lonely at the end of twelve months. Two to four years later those who remarried or were engaged were no more lonely than the average woman, but those who had not moved to form such relationships tended to still be very lonely. Lopata's study (1979) of Chicago widows shows that even though many had been bereaved for an average of eleven years, half said loneliness was their most serious problem, and a third said it was their second most serious problem.

This loneliness can be the source of great emotional distress and despair for the widow. Children, even though they may need her, may stay constantly with her, and are a source of attachment and love, do not usually help diminish the widow's sense of loneliness. Nor do her friends. It may be very difficult for this need for adult attachment to be met. Early in widowhood, both her own distress and social expectations make it difficult for the bereaved to seek a new partner. Indeed it has been shown that premature suggestions about remarriage are perceived as unhelpful and may interfere with the resolution of her bereavement (Maddison and Walker 1967). Yet, even later, there may be few avenues open to her to meet potential mates or even partners for shorter term relationships. Her loneliness may drive her to unsatisfactory liaisons, further lowering her self-esteem and diminishing her view of herself as a potential partner. The situation for widowers is less clear. Many may be lonely and, indeed, report it as a great problem. Social sanctions may make it easier for the man to seek a partner, even remarry, and there are likely to be more women available than men to provide such opportunities because of the earlier deaths of men in most societies.

Younger widows and widowers may have intense needs for a partner yet dread the adjustments this may require for the children and feel they must protect them from any further trauma. Children may be quite ambivalent about the parent finding a new mate: on the one hand they may desperately want a new father or mother; yet, on the other, they may resent this stranger taking over the parent's emotional life. They may actively intrude to break up potential relationships or frighten off potential partners by their neediness. There have been few investigations of the levels of remarriage in the widowed and the degree to which such relationships are satisfactory. Schlesinger's findings (1971) suggest that for the most part they are satisfactory. Widowers with young children are particularly likely to move into some form of pairbond relationships because of their need for assistance with the rearing of the children while they maintain incomes through work.

Cultural and subcultural variables are likely to play a major part in the opportunities the widow or widower may have to find a new mate and hence ease loneliness. Many societies, for example, sections of Indian and Greek society, have strict prohibitions about any future remarriage for widows. Rules tend to be less stringent for widowers, although there may be clear guidelines as to possible partners. As a rule, male partners have wider opportunities and women fewer, both because there is a greater availability of possible women partners and there are more sanctions against women remarrying.

Sexuality and sexual needs are a very important consideration for the married person who has lost a partner, especially the younger and sexually active person. In the bereavement crisis there is an intense longing for the lost partner. For some bereaved people this may manifest itself as an intense sexual longing as well. Yet for others, all thought of drive or need related to sexuality may be totally inhibited: the "last thing" that is thought of. All desire may be absent and may take a long time to return. For those women whose longing for their husbands is experienced sexually as well as emotionally, the situation may be quite distressing.

Elizabeth, a quiet and demure thirty-year-old widow, was staggered at the intensity of her sexual need. It was far greater than she had felt for her husband during his life, and this made her embarrassed and regretful. It was, as she said, that she longed for him to be back, making love to her, as though she hoped to call him back by her very bodily need and her frustration.

Kay was thirty-five, distressed and guilty in her bereavement following her ambivalently loved husband's sudden death. She was, she said, "on fire, red hot. Now I know what they mean about widows—if you put a man near me I'd set him alight." Her need was less specific but represented her longing for her man with whom she had had an intense and highly satisfying sexual relationship.

Little is really known about the "normal" sexual response pattern of widows or widowers following their partner's deaths. Experience in our own studies suggests these patterns are varied and individual. Much is projected onto the bereaved in this situation: the legends about widows and their sexuality are ample evidence of this. They are, in most community myths, seen as highly sexual, especially in secret, yet expected to be bland asexual women in their day-to-day life. The widower is seen as a man inevitably in search of a new partner. Such stereotypes make it even more difficult for each to express his or her real sexual feelings at the time of bereavement and often for a long time afterward. Loyalty to the dead partner, and the acceptability of their sexuality within their social group, may also interfere with the reestablishment of such relationships, as Glick, Weiss, and Parkes note in their study (1974).

Confusing the picture further is the need of the widowed person for nurturance, body comforting, and contact. It may seem that this is only available through sexual liaison, so that when relationships occur they may be more dominated by this need than by sexuality. Many women feel the longing to be held in someone's arms and believe they can only find it sexually. Men too may see this as the only acceptable framework in which their longings for closeness can be met. Sometimes impulsive sexual acting out, or promiscuity (Segal 1963), may be the way in which such needs appear.

The need for nurturance, someone to care for one, and for one to care for, is very important to both widows and widowers. The loss of the partner for whom they cared may make them feel quite worthless without such a role, especially if there are no children. Sometimes an outlet is found in the woman's caring for others, as described by Bowlby (1980). Here the widow, particularly, is likely to become obsessed with caring for others, such as her children, who are helpless, grief stricken, or dependent. She cares for them as she would be cared for herself, gaining some vicarious but limited satisfaction in the process. This is particularly likely with the woman who has been involved for a long time in caring for her dependent and/or ill husband, and perhaps others as well. She may very rapidly take on further "lame dogs" in a series, if this is the critical need the relationship served for her. Some take on nursing roles to fulfill similar bereavement needs. Or such secondary nurturance may be the prime motivating force for some in self-help movements.

The opportunities for social integration available to the bereaved person may be different from those open to him or her before the death. While many bereaved are distressed by premature attempts to involve them socially during the earliest crisis phase of the bereavement, as the weeks and months progress the reintegration into the social field becomes increasingly important. The first time out in a social situation as a single person is an anxiety-provoking and significant experience, seen as a vital step in the process of recovery. Lopata (1971) points out how much society is oriented to couples. The widow, used to couple-relationship socializing, may find herself the "odd one out" at dinner parties with former friends of herself and her husband. She may find herself traumatized by her solo status and may suspect that others do not feel comfortable with her although they previously shared familiar patterns of social interaction. She may have to establish new patterns, perhaps with other women in a similar situation. This may occur through informal groupings of other friendly widows, or formally through widows' organizations, or through single-parent and singles' groups. Cultural and subcultural variables within the society may determine the possible channels of social integration open to her. The avenues open to the widower tend to be wider, in that he may be seen as an "eligible" partner in a group, rather than a threat. On the other hand there are fewer informal systems open to him to meet those in similar situations. If his wife has been the principal socializing force for the dyad he may become very isolated following her death. The nature of this process in the dyad prior to the loss of the partner is an important variable. If most socialization involved friends known through the husband's business, the widow may find few of these relevant for her after the death. Similarly, if the couple's social activities centered on the wife's girlhood friends, then the husband may lose this network with his wife's death.

Roles and identity are further very important aspects of longer term adjustment. Early in the bereavement many of the roles carried out by the dead partner will have to be reallocated so that basic family functions can continue. The flexibility of role assumption in the family unit is adaptive in terms of carrying on functions necessary for its survival. Vollman et al. (1971) describe families with rigid role structure who had difficulty in adapting following sudden and unexpected deaths. Ablon (1973) describes flexibility of roles in Samoan families following loss and how this enabled a smooth transition in bereavement. Where there is prolonged illness with warning of the death, there may be more opportunities to make gradual role change, the partner perhaps gradually taking over roles the ill person fulfilled, or others, such as children or extended family, coming in to share such roles. There may be an active resistance to reallocation of roles in the beginning, while some faint hope is still entertained of the possibility of return. There may be a fear at slipping into the other's shoes, even a feeling of disloyalty. But many functions must be continued: the breadwinner must be replaced by some source of income; and the family, if it is to survive as a group, must have some emotional focus. And such roles as cook, must all be at least partially filled. These "new" roles for the bereaved widow or widower may be difficult to accommodate alongside old roles. Conflict may occur, but eventually some new equilibrium will be established, unless actual breakdown of the family system occurs.

The identity of a partner in a marital dyad may be critically bound to traditional roles of wife and mother. In much of Western society a woman who marries takes on her husband's name, and is frequently introduced only as his wife, for example, as Bill Roe's wife. Similarly the man may be introduced as Jane Roe's husband. More frequently the emphasis is on the side of "This is Bill Roe's wife." The widow may see her identity entirely in terms of her role as wife, or roles as wife and mother. She may define herself by these roles. They may be the sources of her sense of worth, her self-esteem. Similarly a man's principal source of self-esteem may be his work. The loss of such a role through retirement or unemployment may bring consequences similar to those of the widow who loses her role of wife. When the role is lost she may become quite uncertain of her identity and have few sources of gratification that reassure her of her worth and that provide self-esteem. Also, the role of "widow" may be stigmatized within her society.

Women may have many roles which are linked to their concept of identity: roles within work situations, within community groups, within friendship networks. Thus for some, although the role of wife may be primary, other roles may contribute very significantly to satisfaction and view of the self. Recent work suggests that the presence of other role investments that are sources of self-esteem and satisfaction may facilitate adjustment after the bereavement. The widow with only one role, the one she has lost, which is her sole source of her sense of identity, may have a more complicated or delayed adjustment.

The old roles and identity must be grieved for and relinquished before the new can be established. The bereaved may be reluctant to do this, resentful of the loss and the society that imposes it. Many widows comment bitterly on the first letters they receive indicating their widowed state. There is often resentment at being called a widow: the word is avoided. The woman may try to escape the label and its implications.

Joan S, age forty-five, was bitterly resentful over her husband's prolonged death from cardiac disease. Months after he died she stated firmly to the therapist providing bereavement counseling, "You will *not* make me into John's widow. I was his wife, and I'll stay his wife. Widow is a black word—a nothing—that's not me."

The eventual identity of the woman following the death of her husband may only evolve over the many months and years that follow. This is especially obvious with women who have married young; whose very marriage, often in adolescence, was an attempt to escape the identity crisis of adolescence by a pseudoresolution equating role, that of a "married person," with adult identity. Some women repeatedly comment, "I don't know who I am; I've got to find myself, to find out who I am." It seems that on top of the bereavement crisis, a delayed developmental crisis is often superimposed. This may be quite satisfactorily worked through the later stages of bereavement: the woman may take on a rich and personally satisfying identity through her growth in competence (handling the crisis and managing by herself); through her career development (commencing or completing training or work in a career she values); and through her capacity to make new and rewarding social and personal relationships by using her own interpersonal abilities. Some widows do not have such satisfactory resolutions, becoming instead anxiously dependent, taking on such a role or identity as "the grief-stricken one" who lives her chronic grief. Others may rapidly find a replacement for the dead partner so that they do not relinquish the only role and identity they know. While there are likely to be complications to this in dyadic terms, for a few it is surprisingly successful, suggesting that perhaps the original relationship was one of complementary roles rather than an intense bond between individuals.

The bereaved's sense of worth may be intimately bound to the roles and identity that the relationship entailed. The loss of the partner, even if he or she were ambivalently valued, is thus a blow to the self and to the esteem of the self. It may take the bereaved widow or widower some time to rebuild this after the death.

PATHOLOGICAL PATTERNS OF BEREAVEMENT

While there are no statistical guidelines as to exactly what is normal bereavement, the above descriptions fit most commonly accepted assumptions of what is normal for conjugal bereavement. A variety of pathological patterns have been described for bereavement in general and may be applied to this loss.

*Absent grief.* Deutsch (1937) uses the term "absent grief" to describe grief that does not appear at all. It may be difficult to distinguish from delayed grief in the early months following the loss. The bereaved seems to show no response to the death of the partner and often carries on "as though nothing had happened." Such a pattern has been seen as evidence of strength and coping by many, rather than pathology, but recent understanding suggests that it is probably related clearly to morbidity, except in a few instances. The grief may be absent for many reasons: the loss cannot be acknowledged, or feelings cannot be expressed because these are somehow fantasized to have disastrous consequences for the bereaved. Like the other pathological patterns and outcomes that will be described here, this may be clearly linked to some of the vulnerability factors for poor bereavement resolution. Some cases of absent grief are not clearly related to pathology, however, at least in the short term (Singh and Raphael 1981). Perhaps a rapid replacement is found, perhaps some of the preexisting relationships were purely narcissistic with little recognition of the real person who was lost. In such cases there is little need for grief, so long as the narcissistic needs are met from other sources. The bereaved may have little capacity for the expression of feelings, so that whatever internal adaptive processes of grief and mourning are, there are no external manifestations. Or there may be other unknown variables.

A typical pattern of absent grief was that of Mrs. J, whose husband died at fifty-eight from cardiac disease. Mrs. J was praised by her children for her bravery, for she did not shed a tear at the funeral and returned to her secretarial job the next day. Her friends marveled at her composure. It was "wonderful how she coped." No one wanted to mention her husband's name for fear of upsetting this ideal picture. At night, in the years that followed, she set his place at the table, discussed her problems at work with him, and put on the light over his chair. She cultivated a belief in his presence to keep her from breaking down. At the fifth anniversary of his death she became severely, and to outsiders, "inexplicably" depressed. Careful evaluation revealed her unresolved grief which was explored therapeutically, leading to a delayed but ultimately satisfactory resolution of the loss.

*Delayed grief.* The bereavement process may easily be delayed. This is particularly likely if there have been survival issues at the time of the loss crisis. For instance when the bereaved has been seriously injured in an accident in which the partner died, and her own life is at stake, all her emotional energy may be taken up with the battle to live. It is only later, when the danger is past, that the grief can appear. If she is pregnant and near term, this too may delay the grief, for her emotional cathexis is geared to the child and the birth. If the grief and mourning progress normally after relatively short delays, then the outcome is unlikely to be pathological. Where delay is related to avoidance of the pain of the loss, or a setting aside of grief because of fears related to loss of emotional control or fear of guilt and anger, then more pathological outcomes are likely. Also the bereavement response may be delayed when the death is not really accepted, because the body was not found or seen. The risk factors for poor bereavement resolution may be the etiological factors in such delayed grief.

*Inhibited grief and mourning.* In some cases, the expressions of grief are in some way or another toned down or shut off. This may represent an overall inhibition of response or a partial inhibition. For instance the whole response may seem very slight and short-lived compared to the intensity of the relationship. Part of the bereavement response may be inhibited, such as the angry protest. Or the yearning may be unconsciously repressed in the manner Bowlby (1980) so clearly links to pathological outcomes. The review of the lost relationship may not occur, for the bereaved stays locked in the stage of grieving separation, always yearning and angry, but with a covert belief that the dead spouse can and will return some day. There is thus an unwillingness and inability to relinquish the relationship in the mourning process.

Elaine P was forty-five when her husband Ken died from advanced malignant disease. The latter years of their marriage had been very intimate as she nursed him devotedly through his terminal illness. Her whole life came to revolve round his care. She resented his death bitterly, although she said "he had to be free—he could not have gone on suffering like that." But she felt her own life had no meaning now without him, that she had no other role or use in life. They had no children because of his sterility. She never worked. She had done little anticipatory grieving, for in her heart she nursed the belief that if she cared for him enough she would somehow keep him alive. She was shocked and disbelieving when he finally "passed away" beside her in the hospital.

She went home and carried on with her usual tasks. At the funeral she felt like an onlooker, not really part of what was going on. As the weeks went on she thought of "nothing but Ken." At first she persuaded herself that she should believe he was still at the hospital and would eventually come home, but this did not help for long. She longed for him "every minute of day." She felt his presence and thought she saw him, heard his voice. She was chronically angry with God. "Why did he take my Ken: I look at those others, they didn't love one another—they didn't care like I did. Why won't God give him back." It might be said that part of her bereavement became intensified in the separation phase, that she became blocked, locked into that response, and it became chronic to the point of inhibition and exclusion of mourning.

Inhibition of some aspect of mourning is a very common pathology of bereavement. Intense idealization of the dead partner with little review, acceptance, or relinquishing of the more negative aspects of the relationship is one such pattern. It commonly relates to a difficulty in facing the ambivalence toward and perhaps dependence on the dead person, as though to acknowledge the negative would bring forth anger and guilt too painful to bear.

Jack, forty-nine, spoke of Mabel in this way: "She was the greatest little woman ever. She was the best cook, the best wife in the world. She did everything for me." He could say nothing negative of her and insisted their life together had been perfect in every way. The intensity of his insistence on this was harsh and aggressive, as though he dared anyone to prove otherwise. It was only after careful exploration that he revealed his resentment toward her for her coddling and intrusive control of his life, and how much he had longed for his freedom. He then became able to talk in a more realistic way, cheerfully, yet sadly, talking of the good and the bad, and taking a positive orientation toward his new found freedom instead of an obsessive preoccupation with all he had lost.

*Distorted bereavement.* Distorted bereavement reactions have also been described (Raphael 1975*b*). These are usually linked to some inhibitions of other areas of grief and mourning. Common patterns include intense pervasive anger in the absence of sadness and mourning, and overwhelming guilt. Other distorted patterns may lead to manic response (Rickarby 1977) and symptom development which will be discussed in more detail below.

Extreme anger in the bereavement response to the exclusion of all else is often associated with pathological dependence on the dead partner. The relationship was often more like that of mother and child than of two adults—one of powerful symbiotic themes. The sense of desertion is great, and the bereaved feels her very survival threatened by what has happened. She wants to punish those who leave her so deprived: the deserting husband who died and left her as well as those who will not fill his place and meet her immense dependent needs. These often link to earlier losses, such as the death or departure of a parent in childhood. Sudden death that has "cheated" her of her security is especially likely to lead to such anger. If it is caused by manmade disaster or accident this is even more pronounced. Someone is to blame, must be punished, and perhaps the law has failed to do so.

Margaret, age thirty, had married Robert when she was in her teens to escape the poverty of her home life. Her mother had died when she was ten but had had little time for her with her frequent childbearing. Her father was alcoholic and expected incestuous intimacies of her as she grew to adolescence. She had had to care for her six younger siblings up to the time she left, when pregnant, to marry Robert, ten years her senior and a "gentle, really caring man." "He idolized me," she said. "I was everything to him, and he did everything for me; I never had to lift a finger. He was the father I'd never had. And a mother too in a way," she added as an afterthought. Her response to his death following the collapse of the building on which he was working was one of bitter rage.
"He was the only one who ever cared for me. They took him away from me. They killed him. They may as well have knocked the building down on him, it's just the same. I'll never get over it. I hate the whole world. What do they know about what it's like. What do you know. Nobody cares about me. I hate everyone—the people in the street—all those silly women who've still got *their* men. I hate the lot."

Such feelings may appear transiently in the early phases of any bereavement, but they are associated with other responses, such as yearning, and they eventually pass. In these distorted grief situations, however, they do not pass. The anger goes on and on, eventually disrupting the bereaved's whole life, destroying systems of support and most other relationships.

Extreme guilt is often linked to intense ambivalence in the lost relationship, often to the level where death fantasies were actively nurtured toward the dead person. Even though the bonds were strong and the couple could not separate, the hate was the motivating force, perhaps in a sadomasochistic way, that fired the relationship. The death seems a fulfillment, and the bereaved must punish herself eternally. This is often associated with severe depression evolving out of the loss.

Beryl P, age thirty-eight, tormented herself constantly with thoughts of what she might have done to save her husband John's life. He had had diabetes, but he suddenly died of a myocardial infarction despite his long illness. She had bitterly resented his illness and his alcoholism. Yet she had had a certain satisfaction in provoking him to the physical violence that so frequently characterized their relationship. She had told him frequently he'd be better off dead, that his violence would be the death of him. She constantly thought about the ways he might die and what she would do with her life when she was free of him. She had never been able to leave him despite the bad relationship, for he said it would kill him if she ever did. Her ambivalence appeared in her inability to provide a diabetic diet for him, as she always made some special sweet, "because he couldn't be expected to eat that other awful stuff all the time," and "what harm would such a little bit do anyway?" She was also hesitant to call help on the day of his death, delaying ringing the doctor for some hours after his chest pain commenced.

After the death she thought of nothing but his blue face as he "gasped for his last breath," and the "helpless bewildered look in his eyes." Her dreams and waking hours were filled with her guilty ruminations. There was no anger, no sadness, no mourning, just guilt.

*Chronic grief.* Perhaps the most difficult pattern to understand and manage is the picture of prolonged, intense, chronic grief. This may appear either as the full range of the bereavement response or as a chronic picture of one of the disturbed patterns discussed above. Months or years later the bereaved still appears actively grief stricken, is still preoccupied with the lost person, visits the grave again and again daily or weekly; talks, thinks, feels nothing that doesn't relate to the death and the dead; cries at the slightest reminder; and is chronically angry, perhaps guilty. The widower or widow seems to keep the dead spouse alive by chronic grief, and soon seems to alienate all other relationships. Often life is maintained as if he or she will return: The room is kept as a memorial, the clothes untouched. The role of the chronically grief stricken seems to be all the bereaved knows.

Alan K was fifty-five when his wife Mary died from carcinoma of the breast. She had been ill for some months. Even though her condition was serious, he really believed she would recover. Up until a few days before her final hospitalization she struggled to look after him as she always had. When she went to the hospital he called to see her daily but did not really think she would die. The word of her death left him stunned. He did not see her body after death, and went through the funeral in a "state of shock." When he went home to the empty house he felt he had lost his "whole life." He cried for her repeatedly. He reminisced constantly over their marriage, idealizing what had been a reasonable but average relationship.

Three years later the picture was unchanged. He was angry with the world that such a good woman should die. He seemed unable to look after himself properly and resented the fact that he was no longer cared for. He could not orient himself toward anything but his wife. His married children offered every support, but it seemed to have no effect. He visited her grave regularly twice a week taking flowers each time. His life was one of chronic grief and he did not seem able or willing to change this.

*Anniversary reactions.* A variant of pathological bereavement may appear in anniversary reactions. Some anniversary response is normal, but in other cases it may take on the form of symptoms or behaviors that recur regularly and represent unresolved aspects of the original bereavement.

## THE SYMPTOMATOLOGY OF BEREAVEMENT

A number of workers have now studied the patterns of symptoms that appear following the death of a spouse with fairly consistent findings. There are many "symptoms" that appear in the early crisis months, representing perhaps simply the autonomic and psychological distress of the bereavement crisis. Others are longer lasting and obviously represent a spectrum of morbidity.

*General symptomatology.* Complaints about sleep, appetite and weight disturbance are common after bereavement, both in the early months and during the following year. Maddison and Viola (1968) found that 40 percent of the widows they studied, aged sixty and under, had major difficulties with symptoms such as insomnia and nervousness in the thirteen months following the death. Headaches, indigestion, chest pains, palpitations, and dysphoria were also common as were appetite and weight loss. General aching and fatigue and reduced capacity to work were also noted. In their subsample of Sydney, Australia, widows, more than 32 percent reported major deterioration in health in the year following bereavement, as did more than 21 percent of Boston, Massachusetts, widows. Both these levels were very significantly higher than the relative control population. These workers note however that 36 percent of widows they studied experienced virtually no symptoms at all, and a further 36 percent had few persisting complaints after the crisis period had passed. Calvert, Northeast, and Cunningham-Dax (1977) in another Australian study found increased general health impairment in bereaved people aged fifty and older, as measured in terms of doctor visits, but only about 26 percent of the subjects were widows or widowers. These findings are in general agreement with those of other workers such as Parkes (1966*b*) who report that widows under age sixty-five consulted their general practitioners more frequently for psychiatric and other symptoms in the six months following bereavement than in the control period before.

Whether these "symptoms" represent actual ill health or a greater dependence on doctors has been questioned. Maddison and Viola (1968) note that workers were unable to differentiate the relative contributions of painful affects; demonstrable somatic change; and a motivated assumption of the sick role. Certainly most workers agree that the "symptoms" at this time are predominantly psychological or psychosomatic in nature. Clayton, Halikas, and Maurice (1971) have carefully viewed symptomatology during the first month in bereaved widows and widowers (mean age sixty-one). These workers conclude that crying (94 percent), depressed mood (84 percent), and sleep disturbance (80 percent) were the cardinal symptoms of bereavement. Anorexia, weight loss, tiredness, difficulty concentrating, poor memory, and loss of interest in television and friends were frequent. Guilt ideas occurred but were not common. Only 15 percent saw or called a physician for these symptoms. Parkes (1972*b*) also describes weight loss and insomnia as frequent in his London widows during the first month and Marris (1958) found it in 79 percent of his widows. Clayton's group notes that these symptoms were more frequent in widows than in widowers.

Thus it would seem that many distressing experiences occur during the "crisis" time of bereavement, especially the early months: these include bodily experiences as well as psychological. They are often experienced as symptoms and may lead bereaved widows and widowers to seek medical care. For the most part such symptoms lessen during the remainder of the year following the loss, but for some subjects they persist, causing the bereaved to experience significant health impairment during that time.

*Psychosomatic reactions.* Many of the physical symptoms described above could be classed as psychosomatic reactions to the bereavement. Maddison and Viola (1968), however, found no specific increase in major psychosomatic disorders following the loss. A direct stress and psychosomatic effect might be reflected in physiological changes. Bartrop et al. (1977) showed a "measurable abnormality in immune function" in bereaved spouses compared to control subjects. They demonstrated that T-cell function was significantly depressed after bereavement but found no change in hormone concentrations, and so concluded that the immune-function change was not mediated hormonally. Such changes would provide evidence of a mechanism for the increased numbers of infections reported after bereavement by workers such as Maddison and Viola (1968).

Parkes, Benjamin, and Fitzgerald (1969) describe an increased mortality from cardiovascular disease in widowers aged fifty-five and older during the first six months following the death of the spouse, and conclude this is a psychosomatic consequence of the bereavement, that these men died from a "broken heart." Greenblatt (1978) also comments on higher mortality in widows resulting from heart disease and arteriosclerosis but does not comment on the time relationship to the bereavement. Yamamoto et al. (1969) comment on the frequency of object loss prior to medical admission in Japan. Schmale (1958) also comments on such losses, as does Engel (1961) in his description of the giving-up/given-up state prior to disease onset. Jacobs and Ostfeld (1977) review epidemiological literature to comment on the excess mortality in the newly widowed. Although, as they note, there are methodological problems in many studies, these findings are consistent and replicated. Younger persons and men are more at risk. They conclude such mortality may be mediated by psychosomatic mechanisms, such as physiological changes associated with the loss response and behavioral changes that compromise health maintenance or chronic disease management. They conclude that the duration of elevated risk varies by sex and is no more than two years for men and women: the peak for men is the first six months, and the elevated risk greatest in the young. Heart disease and neoplasm are common causes of death in which psychosomatic mechanisms may play a part. Cottington et al. (1980) recently studied sudden cardiac death in women aged twenty-five to sixty-four. They found that these women were six times as likely as the control population to have experienced the death of a significant other within the preceding six months.

Specific psychosomatic disorders have been linked to bereavement in some clinical case descriptions, but the validity of these findings in epidemiological terms is uncertain. Bereavement has been suggested as a precipitant for ulcerative colitis (Lindemann 1944); neoplastic disease, such as carcinoma of the breast, carcinoma of the cervix, and leukemia (Klerman and Izen, 1977); thyrotoxicosis (Lidz 1949); and asthma (McDermott and Cobb 1939). Breslin (1977) comments on the role of unresolved grief in psychosomatic disorders in general terms.

Thus it may be concluded that there is much to suggest an impairment of physical health in the bereaved, even to the degree of an increased mortality risk in close relationship to the bereavement. In psychosomatic terms, however, the evidence as to potential mechanisms by which this may occur is very limited, apart from Bartrop's study suggesting acute stress effects on the immune-system response.

*Psychological symptoms and disorder (excluding depression).* Psychological symptoms, which are prominent among the general symptomatology present following conjugal bereavement, represent the main thrust of complaints. Parkes and Brown (1972) note that sleep, appetite, and weight disturbances were common psychological symptoms in bereaved widows and widowers under forty-five years of age, but other psychological symptoms apart from depression were not more common among this group than among others. Psychological symptoms predominated in Maddison and Viola's study (1968) and were frequent among the widows of my own study (Raphael 1977b). Clayton's reports (Clayton, Halikas, and Maurice 1972) also reflected very high levels, although she sees many of the symptoms as related to the "reactive depression" of widowhood. Crisp and Priest (1972) found some psychological patterns higher among the bereaved, but they do not comment on the specific patterns for widowhood. Bereavement has been significantly associated with first entry into psychiatric care (Stein and Susser 1969), or psychiatric admission (Parkes 1965). While specific disorders described are most frequently depression, neurotic disorders such as phobias, obsessions, hypochondriasis, and conversions have been described as well.

Psychological symptomatology is not only reflected in the search for health care but in the use of psychotropic drugs. Tranquilizer use increased significantly in Parkes and Brown's bereaved widows and widowers (1972), Maddison and Viola's widows (1967), and antidepressant use in 52 percent of Clayton's study (Clayton, Halikas, and Maurice 1972). Many of these widows and widowers commenced such drug use for the first time following the bereavement, and for many it was maintained for a long period afterward, becoming part of a pattern of chronic drug use that appeared to do little for the bereaved's condition and adjustment. Many bereaved widows have commented on the way they had been sedated immediately after their husbands' deaths. This is particularly likely to occur if the woman demonstrates any behavior that is seen as "hysterical." She may be given injections of sedatives or tran-quilizers in the first few hours, especially when family members call the doctor to give her something to "settle her down." Most women resent this enormously, seeing it as dampening their natural outpour-ing of grief. Often this initial sedation is followed up by prescription of other sedative or tranquilizing medication with the message that it should be taken to ease or block out all emotional pain. Many of these women describe themselves as having "a straight jacket" around their emotions as a consequence of these drugs and as unable to grieve as they would wish because of them. Although it is difficult to sort out cause and effect relationships, studies suggest that such drugs do little to improve outcome in such bereavements (Maddison and Raphael 1972; Boman, Streimer, and Perkins 1981), and may even become a further factor hampering resolution. Even when such drugs are not prescribed, a surprising number of bereaved people self-medicate ei-ther with the pills of other people or substances available without pre-scription. Self-medication may also be one of the reasons for the in-creased use of alcohol described by Maddison and Viola (1968), and Clayton's group (Clayton, Halikas, and Maurice 1971). Alcohol may be taken to induce sleep and block out pain and loneliness, or, may be a form of acting out in a self-destructive manner in response to guilt and conflicts aroused by the loss.

Other acting out behaviors have been described in response to loss. Impulsive sexual behavior may appear (Segal 1963). This sexual impul-sivity may be difficult to separate from depression, but it usually repre-sents a desperate measure to reestablish the symbiotic relationship on which the ego integrity depends. There is a need for comfort, bodily contact, and reassurance against the pain of the loss, the rejection, and the fear of being alone. Pregnancy may be another outcome in adults as in adolescents. Accidents have been described as being precipitated by bereavement, but no systematic studies of this outcome exist. Shoplift-ing has also been noted in clinical reports.

It is interesting to look at the patterns found by Parkes (1965) in his study of bereaved psychiatric patients. These patients were those likely to be diagnosed as having affective disorder, but they showed other manifestations at various times, including anxiety, phobia, and hypo-chondriacal symptoms. Grief in these cases tended to be atypical with abnormal prolongation, undue intensity of the bereavement process, and hypochondriacal symptoms resembling those suffered by the de-ceased during the last illness, as well as panic attacks. Difficulty in accepting the fact of the loss and ideas of self-blame were significantly more frequent in this psychiatric group as compared to controls. This work lead Parkes to conclude that bereavement reactions could be classified into two groups: grief and its variants; and nonspecific and mixed reactions which included the symptomatic states described here. Such a picture of the association of psychiatric disorder with poorly resolved bereavements involving extreme preoccupation with the lost object and ideas of self-blame is also noted in Wretmark's study (1959). The bereavement response itself has been classified as "neurotic" by some workers (for example, Wahl 1976) when it is excessive, protracted, associated with irrational despair and hopelessness, and preoccupied with the fear of personal death, and when there is prolonged irritability, aimless hyperactivity, or apathy.

It is in the area of conversion reactions, hypochondriasis, and illness behavior that there seems ample clinical evidence of some of the symptomatic patterns associated with bereavement, although there are no systematic studies of this area. Many bereaved widows and widowers experience transiently body symptoms reflecting the dead partner's terminal illness. Chest pain is a frequent complaint after the death of a partner from heart attack; also headache, when the death has involved a cerebral condition or episode. For the most part such symptoms are fairly transient, but still distressing. They may be linked to identification with the lost person, unconsciously representing an attempt to hold part of the person within, perhaps even to punish the self for surviving the loss, by suffering his pain. There may also be fantasies of reunion with the dead person. Where such symptoms become prolonged they may be linked to a need for punishment of the self, related to guilt and ambivalence about the dead person (Krupp 1965). There may be real difficulties in diagnosis, for, of course, the bereaved is more vulnerable psychosomatically: the chest pain may be identificatory *or* may represent cardiac disease. The picture is further confused by the fact that it may be easier to experience the physical than the emotional pain and to ask for help for it rather than for the distress.

No distinct pattern of conversion disorder has been described, but conditions such as spasmodic torticollis, paralysis, and chronic pain are manifestations found frequently in the clinical situation. General hypochondriacal complaints may reflect the bereaved's preoccupation with his suffering or his fear of death. Each body perception may become focused upon, in case it represents some dread disease, such as that which has "carried off" the dead partner. Such complaints are more frequent where there has been prolonged nursing of the terminally ill person, perhaps through very distressing final stages of malignancy. So much has the bereaved absorbed the cancer and its manifestations that it is almost as though she feels she has taken it within her, and that she too will be contaminated by it. Dependence on the lost person and heightened but denied ambivalence about caring for him, tend to reinforce this further. Secondary gain from the role of "the sick one" may lead to a continuation of such complaints, particularly when the time is well past for care to be gained for the bereaved role.

*Depressed mood.*    One of the common experiences after bereavement is depressed mood. This may appear transiently or be more profound and continuous. There is often a semantic confusion: the bereaved widow states her feeling as depression when she really means sadness, for the word sadness has become little used, particularly when speaking of personal feelings which are more frequently labeled depression.

Mrs. K described the difference between sadness and depression. "Sometimes I feel very sad—there's an empty feeling inside me and tears come to my eyes and I miss him terribly, especially when I remember all the things we did together—even the fights we had. Then there are other times when I feel black and depressed—worthless somehow, as if it's all for nothing and there's no future worthwhile; I'm empty then, but I'm empty of all my feelings except this blackness and I don't know if I can go on living."

Most widows and widowers are likely to experience some sadness and some depressed feelings. Parkes and Brown (1972) found depression scores significantly higher in bereaved widows and widowers under age forty-five (average age thirty-six) than in matched control subjects. Clayton, Halikas, and Maurice (1972) assessed older widows and widowers (average age sixty-one). They found that 35 percent of those studied had a collection of depressive symptoms similar to those found in psychiatric patients. However, thirteen months later only 17 percent were depressed in this way (Bornstein et al. 1973). Crisp and Priest (1972) failed to find much difference in psychoneurotic status, including depression, in the year following bereavement in a mixed bereaved group. Maddison and Viola (1968) found, in their studies of Boston and Sydney widows (under sixty years of age) carried out during the thirteen months after the death, that one in eight subjects had consulted a physician to seek treatment for depression, and as many as two in five had problems with insomnia and nervousness.

Unfortunately, because many bereaved people, especially women, complain of their depressed, possibly sad, feelings, they are often given antidepressants without there being evidence of the type of depressive syndrome for which these are likely to be an appropriate therapy.

In such instances inappropriate antidepressant medication is often perceived by such patients as blocking their grief and doing nothing to assist with their resolution of the loss (Maddison and Raphael 1972).

Depressed mood may lead to depressive illness of the more severe kind requiring psychiatric assessment and intervention. This may immediately follow or complicate the bereavement crisis. Differentiation of the depressed feelings of bereavement [termed by Clayton, Halikas, and Maurice (1972) the "reactive depression" of bereavement] from the depressive syndrome at the time of bereavement is difficult. Typical symptoms such as anorexia, weight loss, and sleep disturbance are common to both. Clayton et al. (1974) comment on the difficulty of differentiating the symptoms of a bereaved population from those of a matched, hospitalized group suffering from diagnosed depressive illness. They did find that the hospitalized depressed subjects had more symptoms (an average of fifteen compared to an average of seven) from a list of depressive symptoms. Despite these conclusions the data they present show a number of significant differences. Freud in his original distinction between mourning and melancholia described the lowering of self-esteem he felt to be typical of depression rather than mourning. The depressed patients in Clayton's study, as compared to the bereaved, believed they were a burden on others and had marked feelings of worthlessness and hopelessness. Suicidal thoughts and the wish to be dead were much more frequent among the depressed patients, fitting with Freud's concept of the anger toward the ambivalently loved object being turned against the self in melancholia, with the wish to murder the introject. Guilt was also more frequent in the depressed. The symptoms of the depressive syndrome, such as terminal insomnia, anorexia, weight loss, fatigue, psychomotor retardation, and poor concentration were significantly more frequent in the depressed group, although they did appear amongst the bereaved. Of particular interest in this discussion was the finding that the bereaved were very significantly more likely to cry easily than the depressed.

Clinically the differentiation may be difficult in the individual case. However, a picture of a recently bereaved person showing severe and persistent depressed feelings; marked hopelessness, worthlessness, and possibly self-blame; persisting anorexia, weight loss, and early morning awakening; fantasies of death, suicide, or reunion with the dead person, should call for thorough assessment, as depressive illness is likely. Psychomotor retardation with a picture of frozen emotions, perhaps an inability to cry, may predominate; but some bereaved adults have the restless, despairing, agitated depression which may be even more like the picture of intense normal grief. Should depressive illness be diagnosed, management may need to be instituted rapidly, while maintaining efforts to facilitate the expression of grief and promote the mourning process, especially taking into account the ambivalence to the lost person that may need to be resolved. Most workers suggest that it is possible to treat the severe depressions pharmacologically or physically (Lynn and Racy 1969), while continuing grief work with the patient, and that it is in fact essential to do so.

Should the lost relationship have been one of ambivalence, there is a greater risk of depression. This is heightened much further if the social network is unable to facilitate the bereaved's review of both the positive and negative aspects of the lost relationship or the expression of affects of anger, sadness, and guilt; or reinforce his self-esteem (Raphael 1977b). Where the risk of such depression can be detected beforehand, preventive intervention geared at resolving the ambivalence and promoting self-esteem may lessen the risk of subsequent severe depression (Raphael 1978a).

Suicide is, of course, a possibility for those who are so severely depressed, and its incidence is high for the widowed (McMahon and Pugh 1964), especially in the first year and following any further major loss. Preoccupation with possibilities of reunion with the dead person, severity of depression, as well as the usual indicators of risk for suicide such as planning, previous attempts, and isolation among others all need to be assessed in this context.

The relationship between the development of depressive illness following bereavement and preexisting genetic vulnerability to this is not known. It may be that this outcome is more common for those with a personal or family history of affective disorder, but evidence to support or refute this is lacking. Paradoxical response to the death of the spouse has been reported for some patients with depression. For example, Friedman and Zaris (1964) report three patients already in treatment who had a flight into health when their spouses died. In these cases, they attributed the response to the freeing of the patient from dependent and ambivalent issues in the marriage. Why such factors should lead to "cure" in some cases and illness in others is not clear.

Rickarby (1977) describes four cases of mania associated with bereavement. One of these occurred in a widow eight days after the death of her husband, while the others were much longer term complications of other losses. The widow's relationship with her spouse had been a very ambivalent one, and she had a prior history of affective disorder with a depressive illness three years earlier. Her switch to mania seemed to occur as part of her reaction against her overwhelming rage and guilt; it was postulated that it was precipitated by her response to the persistent stress she was undergoing during her attempts to avoid the affects and realities of the loss.

EFFECTS OF BEREAVEMENT ON RELATIONSHIP PATTERNS

Following the bereavement, patterns in other relationships are likely to be changed in some ways. The family, for instance, will be restructured with new balances of interaction, power, and emotional investment within that system. The family unit and the bereaved will have new relationships with others outside the family system, and there will be some restructuring in waves throughout the social group. Some totally new relationships may also be formed, as when the widow or widower commences reintegration into social functioning. Many of the new relationship patterns may be positive and adaptive. Others may be on a spectrum that extends into gross abnormality. Some patterns and styles in the pathological continuum follow.

*Fantasy relationship with the lost idealized partner.* The bereaved may continue a relationship with the dead spouse in fantasy. In this relationship, the partner is ever-loving, perfect, unable to desert or die. The bereaved cannot be rejected, and the partner is always with her, manifestable at will. Splitting occurs: all the good is with the imagined person, and all the bad is with real persons. The bereaved starts to find fault with all other relationships, projecting onto them the negative and denied parts of the self and the other. There is an increasing withdrawal from reality, although psychosis is unlikely. Other relationships progressively fail because they cannot tolerate the negativity and hostility.

*Replacement relationships.* The bereaved may become attached to someone who is seen symbolically, unconsciously, or actively as a replacement for the lost person. In the most gross examples, the widow or widower rapidly, perhaps within a few months of the death, becomes closely involved with another partner who is chosen because he or she is exactly like the lost spouse in age, job, appearance, manner, or some other quality. Such relationships are usually doomed. The partner is valued only in terms of his similarity to the dead spouse. As soon as his real and different attributes start to appear they are either rejected or attempts are made to force him into the familiar mold. Eventually many such relationships break down. If not, they continue with painful distortion.

Another form of replacement relationship may develop within the family system where the widow or widower chooses one of the children as a replacement for the lost spouse. There are strong pressures on the child to fill this role which may well fit with his or her own poorly resolved oedipal wishes. Often social pressures reinforce this type of solution, praising the boy or girl in younger families, or reinforcing the "duty" that must be fulfilled by an older child in taking over the care of the widowed parent. These children may present for child psychiatry much later when a potential stepparent appears on the scene and their new role is required to change once again. Sometimes an adult single child, who sacrifices opportunities for a family life of his or her own to form a close tie with a widowed mother or father, may then go on to develop a pathological intimacy and dependency filled with ambivalence in this new partnership.

Replacement relationships may also develop with those involved in the care of the bereaved person, for instance, a clergyman, counselor, social worker, neighbor, or friend. This is not common, but it does sometimes occur if the person keeps "filling the gaps" left by the dead person without encouraging the bereaved's grief and mourning as well as the assumption of new roles.

*Self-destructive relationships.* When the bereaved is guilty about the previous partner and the death, this guilt may operate unconsciously to ensure that no satisfying relationships develop. Instead, these relationships bring pain, punishment, proof of worthlessness, and unlovableness. They seem to take the bereaved on a downhill course, further damaging self-esteem and fulfilling the unconscious desire for destruction as punishment for the ambivalence felt toward the dead person.

*Avoidant relationships.* Sometimes the bereaved is only able to form relationships that avoid intimacy. The theme of these relationships is that the bereaved will never again take the risk of getting close to someone for fear of suffering again the pain of loss. Relationships are deliberately made brief, transient, and persons are chosen who will not be able to give intimacy themselves. The bereaved feels protected from possible future pain, but this choice is usually basically unsatisfying.

*Compulsive care-giving relationships.* As with children, bereaved adults may become compulsive care givers, devoting themselves only to relationships with the very dependent, ill, or helpless, caring for them as they would be cared for themselves. These relationships have the additional advantage that the helpless person may need the bereaved so much that desertion is impossible except by death. When death does occur a new person is found for the bereaved's compulsive caring.

*Power and aggression relationships.* The bereaved's sense of helplessness in the face of death and loss may be so great that behavior is dominated by the need for power and control in the future. The bereaved may become aggressive and power-seeking in family and other relationships as a defense against the terrifying experiences of dependence and helplessness. This issue may arise decades later during family therapy.

*Relationships where old repetition-compulsions continue.* Old remote relating styles that were manifest prior to the death, such as sadomasochism or hyperdependency may continue unabated or exaggerated following the loss.

All of these patterns represent some areas in which the bereavement has been poorly resolved, in particular ways in which the deceased was not mourned, and these now influence present relating styles.


## Factors Affecting the Outcome of Conjugal Bereavement


There is now considerable concurrence in studies from different sources about the factors that are relevant to the outcome of conjugal bereavement. The classic early paper was that of Maddison and Walker (1967) followed by replicating studies (Maddison, Viola, and Walker 1969) looking at the influence of social-network variables.

Parkes (1975b) defines social and illness variables, and my own work (Raphael 1977b) independently refines similar factors. Volkan (1970) notes many similar variables in his review of typical findings in pathological grief. The principal variables include the preexisting relationship, the circumstances of the death, concurrent crises, social network support, socio-demographic variables, and personality.

### THE NATURE AND QUALITY OF THE LOST RELATIONSHIP

High levels of ambivalence and dependence in the preexisting relationship with the partner create greater problems in the mourning process. The bereaved at risk of bad outcome has greater guilt, greater anger at the desertion. These feelings may be more difficult to express. Our own studies have highlighted the role of ambivalence and dependence as themes of the preexisting marriage (Raphael 1977b; 1978a). These may lead to greater risk of inhibited or distorted grief, chronic grief, and depression, as well as other possible negative outcomes. In our own studies these are highlighted by descriptions of the past relationship. The ambivalence is reflected in intense negative aspects of the relationship, such as violence and anger, that are usually denied or minimized by the bereaved. Sometimes the denial is very great, and intense exaggerated idealization presents. Careful exploration of the day-to-day nature of the relationship reveals its true ambivalence. Dependence in such relationships is usually of the symbiotic kind, reflected in comments such as: "He was like a father to me"; or "He did everything for me." Such relationships usually exclude others by the very intensity of the closeness and mutual dependence. Where the ambivalence can be worked through with social-network support to face the guilt, anger, and negative aspects, and with reassurance of the bereaved's own self-worth, negative outcomes such as depression may be avoided (Raphael 1978a). Parkes (1975b) has picked up similar variables. He describes the "clinging" relationships which lead to severe, extreme pathological yearning in the bereavement itself and perhaps aimless depression, idealization of the dead, and chronic grief subsequently. His highly "ambivalent" group was also at risk, being more likely to be anxious, depressed, withdrawn, and self-reproachful. Reflecting this ambivalence, self-reproach and anger were likely to be great early in the bereavement and to correlate strongly with pathology in the form of guilt and anger and anxiety and/or depression subsequently. Such findings are in line with many of Freud's (1917) earlier psychodynamic concepts about the role of ambivalence in mourning and melancholia. More recently, Horowitz et al. (1980) suggest processes whereby pathological grief may evolve with the activation of latent negative self-images. Often these are seen as coming from pre-existing relationship models which include dependence with paranoid-schizoid splitting, frequently with primitive ambivalence.

THE NATURE AND CIRCUMSTANCES OF THE DEATH

Studies evaluating bereavement both retrospectively and prospectively (Raphael and Maddison 1976) delineate the importance of the nature of the death in defining the outcome of conjugal bereavement. Sudden, unexpected, and unanticipated deaths, especially deaths of the young, that are perceived as untimely are more likely to be associated with pathological outcome. Such deaths are more likely to produce traumatic effects of the traumatic stress-syndrome type, so that the bereaved's ego is taken up with the shock effects of the death, the news of the death, and its circumstances. It then becomes difficult for the bereaved to deal with the grief and mourning. Deaths of this kind find the bereaved unprepared. They are more likely to involve violence, accidents, mutilation, destruction, killing, stirring the worst of such fantasies in the bereaved. They are associated with a greater sense of helplessness and the omnipotence of death, so that the bereaved feels personally threatened and vulnerable. Often much psychic energy goes into trying to make meaning of the death, finding out why it happened, who is to blame, perhaps because the bereaved hopes to prevent such shock in the future, or undo what had happened. This may be further complicated by a failure to see the body of the dead partner, adding to the problem faced by this group in general of accepting the finality of the loss (Singh and Raphael 1981). Others (Lehrman 1956; Levinson 1972; Volkan 1970) all reinforce the possible pathological potential of sudden deaths. Bedell (1973) notes a similar effect in the adjustment of widowers, reinforcing Parkes's data (1975b) for this group also. Such deaths may also be associated with increased mortality in the bereaved because they are more likely to occur in hospitals, by the roadside, and other places than at home (Rees and Lutkin 1967). When the death occurs immediately, shock effects are likely to be great, but even a few days warning may leave the bereaved ill prepared. These deaths may also cut across periods of heightened ambivalence in everyday life thus leaving a greater burden of mixed feelings to be resolved in the mourning process.

Anticipation of the death, as with terminal illness, seems to give a greater chance for preparation. There may be anticipatory grief and mourning. However, Clayton et al. (1973) found no difference in outcome at one year between widows and widowers who had experienced anticipatory grieving and those who had not. Fulton and Gottesman (1980) also support this view. Clayton's sample was an older one, where death may well have been anticipated because of age, so that even when sudden it was not totally unexpected. Certainly Parkes's studies (1975b), as well as our own, suggest that pathological outcome is less likely with this group, but that the issue is complicated. The prolonged suffering of the terminal illness and the nursing care required may emotionally drain the bereaved and heighten ambivalence and dependence in the relationship. Where there has been an inability to discuss the terminal nature of the condition, a conspiracy of silence, or the bereaved has not really accepted the terminality, poor outcome is more likely.

CONCURRENT CRISES

The presence of concurrent life crises, at or around the time of the death, adds to the stress experienced by the bereaved and heightens the risk of morbidity. Parkes (1965) and our own studies (for example, Raphael and Maddison 1976) support this finding. Some such crises may be coincident upon the loss—for instance, moving or a daughter getting pregnant. Others may be involved with the loss, such as being involved in the accident in which the bereaved was killed. Or still others may simply occur at the same time, such as losing a job, serious illness, or death of another family member. Sometimes it is often difficult to tell whether or not these other crises occurred as a consequence of the death, but the stress effect is still significant either way. Particularly difficult are multiple concurrent bereavements, as with a woman in our study who lost her husband and two daughters in one motor vehicle accident. Her whole nuclear family was wiped out in one blow. Other crises may cluster in the weeks around the death. Such situations are particularly difficult to resolve, being so overwhelming that they lead to inhibition of grief or chronicity, or clear psychiatric decompensation.

SOCIAL-NETWORK SUPPORT

As outlined earlier in this chapter, the variable of social-network support may be critical to outcome. Those who, during the crisis, perceive their social network as nonsupportive are likely to do badly. This lack of support may be in terms of specific needs for encouragement of grief, facilitation of mourning, or special aspects of mourning, such as dealing with ambivalence. Unhelpful social-network interactions may block grief. The bereaved is often disappointed by the lack of practical assistance and reassurance of worth (Maddison and Walker 1967; Maddison, Viola, and Walker 1969). This variable may interact with the variable of the preexisting relationship with the deceased, especially ambivalence. Vachon et al. (1982) in their recent study also indicate that deficient social support correlates with poor outcome for bereaved widows. Parkes (1975b) has not specifically explored this variable but notes that similar types of feelings, such as "nobody understands or cares," were expressed at the first interview by those who did badly subsequently. As mentioned earlier in this chapter, Henderson, Byrne, and Duncan-Jones's recent findings (1981) strongly indicate that "perceived social support" in the face of adversity is a mitigating factor against morbidity.

## Loss in Adult Life: The Death of a Spouse

Societal expectations may also be important in providing support of certain kinds. The culture may allow support for the expression of grief for some but not for others. Thus a recent study of the Huli people of New Guinea suggests that in this culture wives are encouraged to grieve, but husbands, who have a passive role, may not mourn their wives' deaths. These widowers tend to show a higher mortality (Frankel and Smith 1982).

### SOCIODEMOGRAPHIC VARIABLES

Parkes's studies (1972*b*, 1975*b*) suggest that the lower socioeconomic groups were likely to do badly compared to other socioeconomic groups, but it was not clear how much this may have related to a higher prevalence of disorder in this group anyway, or perhaps a higher general loading of life stress. Socioeconomic factors may lead to greater "survival" problems for the widow or widower and her or his family. Certainly high social status groups are also vulnerable. Harrari (1981) shows how doctors' wives may be at risk of pathological outcome for many reasons that include ambivalence in their relationships with their husbands, overinvolvement in the care of their husbands during the terminal illness, and lack of appropriate support.

### PERSONALITY VARIABLES IN THE BEREAVED

Although no specific risk factors have been demonstrated, it may be suggested that people with personal characteristics that lead them to form dependent, clinging, ambivalent relationships with their spouses are at greater risk of having a poor outcome. Those who, perhaps because of their own personality styles, make relationships with others who are unable to accept the expression of feeling and review of the lost relationship may be at greater risk, as perhaps may be those with a "plaintive set" that leads them to perceive their social group as inadequate and nonsupportive. It may also be that those who have difficulty with the acceptance of the expression of negative affects or of powerful feelings generally may be more likely to inhibit their grief and mourning. To date, the evidence relating personality characteristics to outcome remains inconclusive.

Earlier personal experience of bereavement, especially childhood parent loss may contribute to vulnerability, either through its influence on personality development or by leaving a pathogenic focus. The degree of this contribution to morbidity is uncertain, though it has been suggested by Brown (1982), for example, that further loss such as that of a spouse, *may* be more likely to lead to depressive outcome.

They *key* variables influencing outcome are thus the preexisting relationship, the death, other crises, and perceived social-network support. A knowledge of these factors can be used to provide preventive counseling for those conjugally bereaved, thus lessening the risk of pathological outcome (Raphael 1977; Singh and Raphael 1981).

Karen L was twenty-five when her husband Luke was killed. He had been heavily involved in bike racing and was a local champion. Karen both resented his riding yet was excited by it. She was torn between watching at the speedway to see the "spills," yet dreading Luke would one day be the one to "go." Luke made his living through bike repairs. He led a fairly "wild" life between races and was closely involved with the local bike group "The Golden Glories." The group had started with this name, but was locally referred to as "The Gories" because of their preoccupation with blood and violence. Karen's relationship was characterized by violence, both physical and verbal. She nevertheless felt she loved Luke deeply. They had been living together since her pregnancy at the age of sixteen, when both had been glad to escape their alcoholic families of origin. Karen's relationship with Luke gave her status amongst her friends, and her family had been closer now that she had proven herself some sort of adult or equal. She was expecting their third child when Luke died.

The night before Luke's death, Karen had a dream, one she had had previously, that he was violently injured and died calling for her. In the dream she was covered in blood, yet could not reach him. She begged him not to race the following day, but he laughed and told her that she was nagging, no good, just like her mother. Luke's accident occurred the next day on the track, and he died following severe injuries.

Karen went to the hospital but was not allowed to see him during his last hours as the surgeons struggled to save him. She was not allowed to see his body, being told it was "too smashed." She was tortured by thoughts of his death, by guilt that she did not stop him from riding that day, by memories of the savage fantasies she'd entertained during his episodes of violence.

Her family told her she was "better off without him," that he was "no good," and now she should come back to be with them because no one else would want her anyway. Her friends avoided all discussion of bikes or his death, telling her she should remember his as "The Champ," that she was young, attractive, and she'd soon find someone else. The youger children seemed endless in their demands. The pregnancy drained her physically and emotionally. Financially she had few resources to manage their rented home. On every parameter she seemed likely to be at risk in terms of this bereavement.

She commenced bereavement counseling with a community nurse, but her mother competed with this relationship, putting heavy pressure on her, both in her grief and her management of the children. She dropped out of counseling, and when the nurse tried to follow her up, she found that Karen had gone off with one of her late husband's friends leaving the children with her mother, who had called in the department of welfare to take the children. The nurse was persistent and eventually found her. Karen reacted guiltily and said her boyfriend wouldn't allow visits from people like the nurse and that she was "all right" and would manage.

## Other Partnerships in Adult Life

There may be other dyadic partnership relations in adult life that may show patterns similar to the conjugal ones, among them, the young couple intensely, even secretly, in love; the de facto relationship; the extramarital relationship; and the homosexual couple. For all these people, bereavement may bring the same painful sorrow, the same needs for support. Perhaps they run a greater risk in that the relationship and the loss may not be so readily recognized, ambivalence may complicate it, and support may be less available.

Less intimate partnerships of close friends, working mates, and business associates, may have similar patterns of grief and mourning, but they are likely to be attenuated.

Special sibling relationships may produce intense bereavement, such as that described by George Engel (1975) following the death of his identical twin—the other half of self. Twin death has been described as producing great grief and sometimes highly pathological outcomes (Holland, Harris, and Holmes 1971), although this was not the case of Engel.

"Pathological" adult partnerships, such as the intense symbiotic closeness that develops between some adult children and a parent, are likely to lead to a major and often pathological pattern of grief and mourning. The maiden daughter who has dutifully devoted her life to the care of her aging, controlling mother is typical. Depressive illness is common following such bereavements, indicating a need to consider this group at high risk.

## Loss by Divorce

Many marriages are broken by divorce rather than death. The spouse's grief may be intense here too, but it is inevitably more complicated because of the preexisting ambivalence and the perceived desertion. Guilt levels are high in such bereavements. Often the partner vilifies rather than idealizes the other. These people may become blocked in the bereavement, angry and protesting, longing as their children do for a return of the lost person and secretly nurturing a fantasy that all can be as it was. Wallerstein and Kelly (1980) suggest that this may take at least a year to resolve, and may go on much longer in some cases. The special difficulty in divorce is that the "bereaved" must mourn someone who has not died and may have to mourn one type of relationship with the partner to reestablish a different one. This is difficult to do at the best of times and the more so when guilt and anger are pronounced. Nevertheless, this loss too is resolved, although as recent findings suggest, perhaps with more long-term role difficulties for the divorced than the widowed (Kitson et al. 1980).

## Conclusions

The loss of the intimate partner, always imperfectly loved, will inevitably be painful. Not only is there the crisis of loss, but also the difficult longer term social adjustments to new roles, identity, and interaction. The support of significant others will be vital to most of those who are so bereaved, particularly when the loss is sudden and untimely. Where supportive relationships exist with family and friends the bereaved widow or widower can grieve and mourn, and, for the most part, resolve such losses adequately.

# CHAPTER 6. Loss in Adult Life: The Death of a Child

"They said it was nothing ... just a miscarriage. I was only a few weeks overdue. I had seen those pictures and I knew it was only tiny, but it was *my* baby, and it counted for a real baby."

*Sandra, age 24*

"Then I said, 'I want to see my baby, doctor.' He said, 'No you can't Mrs. King—it's no good, the baby's dead—it will only give you bad memories to take away. It would be better if you put it out of your mind.' Then he hurried away as though he were ashamed, or something—maybe so he wouldn't see me cry."

*Lena, age 30*

"I was so sad, so empty, I thought I'd never feel whole again. I used to think about the funeral, and think about him. It was such a tiny casket. He was such a little person to die."

*Margaret, age 22*

"We knew something dreadful was wrong. I felt as though I'd been hit—I was going to be sick. I knew it was no good."

*Nathan, age 40*

"I still hate the world. They took everything away from me—all that counted. I'll never get over it, never, never, I know."

*Ruth, age 32*

A child is many things: a part of the self, and of the loved partner; a representation of the generations past; the genes of the forebears; the hope of the future; a source of love, pleasure, even narcissistic delight; a tie or a burden; and sometimes a symbol of the worst parts of the self and others.

The loss of a child will always be painful, for it is in some way a loss of part of the self. The death is likely to be complex: the death of babies and children are not expected in Western society, are even denied. In any society, the death of a young child seems to represent some failure of family or society and some loss of hope.

In this chapter, the death of the child and its impact for parents and family will be considered from the point of view of the different developmental stages at which the loss may occur; the attachments of each stage; the types of loss; as well as the patterns of grief and mourning that may follow. Where specific patterns of morbidity are known to follow particular losses, they will be dealt with; otherwise morbidity will be considered in general terms as will the factors influencing outcome.

## Attachments

As noted in chapter 1, the relationship of the parent with the child begins long before birth. For each parent, there is the fantasy child he or she will have. There are, in fact, often many fantasy children, perhaps representing parts of the family of origin or the hoped-for parts of the self. Any particular child may have meaning to the parents in that he or she may specially represent the self, perhaps by occupying the same place in the sibship, or perhaps because of the attributes or the circumstances of his or her conception or life which make him or her a special focus for identification.

From the time of conception, the child becomes a source of fantasy, a fantasy that builds on the pre-conception images of what a baby, this baby, will be. The relationship with the developing unborn child commences from the time of the conception or when the pregnancy is first acknowledged. It builds upon the image or anlage of the potential child that each parent brings to its making. Women usually, and men often, relate to this developing but as yet unborn child as their growing baby. In this presentation the fetus will be discussed as the baby, because this is how the relationship is usually perceived by the parents.

Many pregnancies are, of course, unplanned and initially, or even throughout, unwanted. In such instances, the ambivalence of the attachment is obvious. It is likely that many pregnancies will evoke ambivalence, for, while there are positive, loving, and hopeful aspects of the fantasies about the developing child, there are also fantasies about the negative, intruding, or dependent aspects as well.

In the earliest months of the pregnancy the mother's attachment to the developing baby is usually intense, for the baby is harbored and nurtured by her body. The father's attachment is less intense, for the unborn baby is less real to him, and he knows it only through fantasy and identification with the mother. In the early months, it may not seem a human life to him, whereas to the woman it is likely to seem so from the moment of conception. Nevertheless, as he lies beside his wife the warmth of the baby within draws his attachment closer to this fantasy child.

As the unborn baby's presence becomes more distinct through the changes in the mother's body, the lack of menstruation, the changing breasts, the physiological and psychological responses it provokes, the woman's fantasy grows richly. That fantasy is a fabric of many threads, representing the balance of positive, loving, fearful, and destructive feelings, the pattern of which will vary over the course of the pregnancy. When the balance is essentially positive, the baby wanted, the woman's own interpersonal environment loving and supportive of her, then these affects predominate. Where the baby is unwanted, the woman's own resources so inadequate or her needs so poorly met that she has little to give to the baby, then the negative, destructive fantasies may be prominent. These usually become repressed, leaving only guilty residues.

The baby may be conceived, perhaps "accidentally" for unconscious needs, in an attempt to solve interpersonal stress or actual intrapsychic conflicts (Raphael 1972a). There may be conscious or unconscious fantasies that the unborn baby will replace someone who has been lost; provide someone who will need and love her; be someone with whom she can make up for her own deprived childhood; be a way of showing others she is grown-up, mature, sexually attractive, a woman; or be a source of power, control, or punishment in her relationship with her family or the father. Where such issues cloud the conception of the child, such themes are likely to come into the fantasy relationship with the developing baby, influencing the outcome of the pregnancy itself and the future bond between the mother and that child.

When the baby's quickening and later first movements are clearly felt, the fantasy relationship with this fantasy child intensifies. The naming of the baby, the rehearsal for parenting, the fantasies shared with the father, the reality of the child, come to the fore. The baby seems now a living entity, a third person in what was before a twosome, a constant real presence. The baby is more real to the father from this time on, not only because of its presence in the mother's womb, but also because it moves, can be felt, can even be heard clearly and distinctly by him. The bonding of the parents to the unborn baby grows daily. Still, ambivalent feelings may appear: fears of damage to the baby or self in the birth process; concerns about the possibility of abnormality; and regret about the things that will have to be sacrificed for it. Negative feelings may be seen as murderous and rapidly repressed, particularly if the parents have reached the level of wishing the baby were not really going to come.

With the birth, the real baby appears. For attachment to him, the fantasies must be relinquished and mourned so that the emotional investment is free to know and love him as he really is. The mother is sad briefly, for he is not exactly as she had hoped or expected him to be, but her grief is momentary unless the discrepancy is very great. Where the baby is the "wrong" sex, premature, imperfect, the grief may be more prolonged or inhibited, thus interfering with the bonding to the baby.

The parents' involvement together, listening to the baby, knowing of it beforehand, and sharing the birth experience are all likely to enhance the bonding that does occur, especially for the father. The rewarding interactions he has with the baby, the time spent, involvement with its care, will all define his emotional attachment to it. These factors will influence the intensity of the relationship each parent has with the baby, and hence the impact for them at various stages should they experience its loss.

The attachment to the baby in early infancy to six months grows with his care. The mother and father look for signs of his individuality, his response, his particular behaviors. His temperament, interaction, capacities, and responsiveness will all feed the attachment. Increasingly he will be related to as the real personality he is seen as being. The baby's helplessness and need are evocative to the parents, and will involve them inevitably, but the relationship will also be built on feelings toward him for his real or fantasized attributes. If the birth has been a painful or negative experience, the experience may become associated with the baby who may be seen as causing it. If disappointment is great with this real baby, the baby may be seen as the disappointing one. If the "fit" between mother and baby is poor, the mother may see herself as a bad mother and unconsciously blame the baby for her bad feelings. If the mother's own mothering has been deficient, she may find herself unable to respond to the baby's demandingness, hating him as a cause of her failure to prove that she could love him as she herself was never loved. If she herself cannot tolerate the good and bad in others or herself, and has not resolved such issues of ambivalence, she may cut the badness off, projecting it onto the child.

The threads of ambivalence will vary as the relationship develops in the early months of infancy. This is a time of intense relating between mother and infant, but often less intense between father and infant. With the first baby, the parents must adjust to parenthood, to the dyad becoming a three-person relationship that may leave each parent feeling his or her needs are not being met. This may present a further and common source of ambivalence toward the young baby. For most, however, the basically loving aspects far outweigh the negative, the baby is cherished, and less loving feelings are repressed.

In the latter part of infancy (from six months to two years), the baby is increasingly able to respond as an individual to specific persons. He can register distress at their departure and punish them with his anger on their return. They, too, may feel separation pain when they are apart from him. Now he can bite, spit out, turn away, and, later in this period, say no or walk away when he wishes to deny the parent control. These developments, even when viewed with pride, may heighten parental ambivalence.

One of the key problems for the parents is that societal attitudes strongly suggest that all parents must be perfectly loving, and all babies are perfectly lovable. Thus, even the most natural and transient anger with the child—rejecting him, hating him, wishing he were not there—or moments of failure to care are sources of guilt. The negative feelings cannot easily be shared with others, are enhanced by the guilt, and thus may increase, forming a stronger part of the relationship with the child. Nevertheless, they may have relatively little overall significance unless the child is lost. With the death of the child these feelings are thrown painfully, tormentingly, to the fore.

During the childhood years, after the age of two, the child is related to more and more as a real and separate person. The fabric of ambivalence may have an increased number of negative threads, perhaps because parts of this individual are neither liked nor accepted by the parents, are even hated or rejected, or perhaps because developmental issues of autonomy, independence, and oedipal relationships may lead to temporarily high levels of ambivalence. The image each parent holds of the child will be constantly modified and molded by the real interactions with him. It will be a complex amalgam of the thoughts, feelings, and memories that encompass the relationship's past as well as the projections for the future. It will include both positive and negative aspects and will encompass mutually dependent needs of parents and child.

With adolescence, the relationship becomes even more complex.

Here the reworking of the parent's own adolescent issues strongly colors the relationship, bringing transferred aspects, projections, and fears. While at earlier stages a similar reworking may occur, adding an extra parameter, especially during the oedipal period, for example, this is most pronounced in adolescence. At the same time, the adolescent is growing physically and mentally, separating from the parents, threatening them with developing sexuality, at a time when parental sexuality may be on the wane. Not only does the adolescent carry the parental projections, but also those of society. He is seen as uncontrollable, aggressive, sexual, even violent, and many will act out in such ways. Ambivalence is very high in these intense, yet separating, years. Loss at this time is especially difficult to resolve, even though some loss of the child from the intimacy of childhood bonds has inevitably commenced and would inevitably have progressed.

In adult life, the relationship of parents to child is likely to be less intense but still strong. The child still represents all he meant during the childhood years, all he carries of the hoped-for future. He is a representative of the parent beyond the parent's death, symbolic of the parent's immortality—the only way the parent can go on into the future as he ages. So to lose this adult child would be to lose the continuity of the line, the denial of death that he meant for that parent.

The loss of the child affects both parents and is likely to throw open the whole dyadic relationship or the relationships of the family unit. Where the child holds a crucial role in the balance of such dynamics—is perhaps an emotional focus, a *raison d'être*, a healing of family and/or dyad difficulties—then his loss may represent the loss of the marriage and the family as well.

## Deaths

The death of the child is always untimely. In most developed societies, he is expected to reach adult life. So, inevitably, the parent will feel cheated of the child's life, the child's future. Often the death is sudden and unexpected, from accident, injury, or medical emergency. Much less frequently, it is caused by progressive, debilitating, or malignant conditions with opportunities for preparative, anticipatory grief. Many of the slowly progressive conditions have congenital factors in their etiology so that the death may be complicated by the extra burden of shame and guilt such illnesses bring. Malignant disease in childhood brings images of horror: the fantasies of small and helpless bodies being taken over by cancer. All the deaths of childhood are abhorrent and so especially stressful. Futhermore, there is societal expectation that children should not die. Parents are likely to feel they somehow failed, that society will condemn them when death does occur. When the death is a consequence of accident, say drowning, burns, or poisoning, or there has already been a background of ambivalent neglect, then the condemnation may be profound. The parent's condemnation of the self or partner is likely to be even more judgmental, so guilt is prominent.

Although the death may be understood intellectually, it is nevertheless difficult to accept, because it "should not have happened" in the parents' minds. There may be much preoccupation with possible causes, both to settle issues of fault and blame and to attempt to gain control in the future to prevent such a thing happening again. Magical thinking is often prominent in the interpretation of possible causes or in the development of protective ritual with other children subsequently.

The death of a child is evocative for the whole social group. The tragedy of lost life and future, the fears for other children and the self, make these deaths particularly significant.

## Bereavement at Different Stages of Development

### MISCARRIAGE

The woman who spontaneously miscarries may experience significant grief, may mourn the lost, hoped-for child. This loss is poorly recognized by others, especially if the pregnancy is lost in early weeks or months before the fetus is considered viable. The special meaning of the pregnancy to her, whether it is wanted or not, will influence her level of grief. A later pregnancy, when the baby's movements have been felt, is more likely to be seen as the loss of a person, a baby, even if it has not reached the legal limit of twenty weeks for being considered so. If the pregnancy is accompanied by a desperate hope for childbirth, then its loss with be most painfully felt and perhaps be considered as a personal failure. Fearfulness is common after miscarriage, even where there is a sense of relief that the baby will not come after all. The grief may appear immediately or may be delayed until the time the baby's movements would have been felt, or some other trigger reminds the mother of the loss, such as the date the baby would have been born. Sadness is the predominant affect, although there may be anger if the mother feels it should not have happened, either because she wanted the baby so much, or because she perceived medical or personal care as failing. There may be guilt if her wish not to have the baby had been significant at some point, especially if it had reached the level of thinking or planning for an abortion. The woman may have little support for her feelings in such instances, since she is expected to be relieved. Where the pregnancy had been gained after a long period of infertility, it may seem that all hopes are dashed. Despair is substantial. Long after the event, the woman may dwell on the details, allocating blame to herself or others for what went wrong. Her failure to rest, undue activity, sexual intercourse, or medical mismanagement may all be seen as at fault. The whole episode may become a focus of unresolved grief.

In her mourning for the lost pregnancy, the woman may have many fantasies about the state of development, the sex, any abnormality, damage to, or disposal of the fetus. An opportunity to share these thoughts and feelings is often of great value to her in assisting her to relinquish the dead baby and her hopes for it. She may seek rationalizations about the loss, such as "it would have been abnormal anyway," which are only partly reassuring, for they carry the covert message that her body produces bad and damaged things. Nevertheless, with support, such issues are usually worked through.

The loss is significant to the woman and will be stated as such by her. For her it is not "nothing," "just a scrape," or "not a life." It is the beginning of a baby. Years later, she may recall it not just as a miscarriage but also as a baby that was lost.

Sandra, age twenty-four, spoke of her grief after miscarrying.

"They said it was nothing . . . just a miscarriage. I was only a few weeks overdue. I had seen those pictures, and I know it was only tiny, but it was *my baby*, and it counted as a real baby.

"I wanted to see it, but really all there was was blood. They said I couldn't see anything in that. When I got home I cried and cried and they couldn't understand. Jim tried to comfort me. He kept on saying it would be alright because we could have another baby right away. But that was another baby—it wasn't the same at all. It was *this* baby I was crying for, and there'd never be another one just the same as it. Jim said we hadn't really been ready for it anyway, that it was just as well. That only made me feel worse, as though we'd got rid of it. Then I wanted it all the more, just to show it that we loved it and cared for it. Some days I would think of how it would have been—a little boy or a little girl.

"Anyway, my tears went. I was a bit sad again now and then. Each month I used to think, *now* the baby would have been this big; *now* I would have been feeling the movements; *now* it would have been due. I felt a failure until I became pregnant again and then it faded. Really, I got over it alright when you look back. But it wasn't 'nothing.' For me I really did lose a baby—not just a miscarriage."

The father may also feel some sadness, but it is likely to be less intense than the mother's, unless he had particular hopes and fantasies invested in the pregnancy. First pregnancies have a unique significance (Deutsch 1945) for both the uniqueness of the fantasized baby and the changes it induces for the first time in the woman's body. Pregnancies lost to the couple whose fertility is unproven are also a more painful loss. The grief from previous miscarriages may also be reawakened with new losses. In each instance, the grief and mourning need recognition, perhaps support, to facilitate resolution.

A case of pathological grief following spontaneous abortion is described by Corney and Horton (1974). Their patient presented with irritability, explosive behavior, and episodes of crying. She complained of "empty feelings, like there had been a death in the family." During history taking, it became obvious that the death was a spontaneous miscarriage at four-and-a-half months, that had occurred four months previously. The loss was sudden and unexpected, the pregnancy had been viewed ambivalently, support was not available at the time, and the patient's response then had been suppressed. These typical features of pathological bereavement seemed to indicate the factors that had led to pathological response in this situation. This woman was able to work through these feelings in her therapy. The authors also note that Freundt's study of Danish women (1964) found that 15 percent of women showed some kind of "nervous symptoms" following abortion. They also quote Simon et al. (1969) who found that two-thirds of women they studied suffered transient (lasting a few days to a week) feelings of depression and/or disappointment following spontaneous abortion. Obviously morbidity is not necessarily high or severe but can have pathological consequences for some.

TERMINATION BY INDUCED ABORTION

The reaction to induced abortion highlights the dilemma of loss of a pregnancy. Here is a pregnancy, at least to some degree "unwanted."

237

The decision to terminate is often conflictual, forced on the girl or woman by social circumstances, her needs of the moment, or the wishes of others. The pregnancy that ends in termination may, in the first place, have been more likely to be a consequence of unresolved conflicts, such as those discussed previously. The girl's personality may be vulnerable because of earlier deprivations, and, in some instances, she may have characteristics that are self-destructive or accident prone. The pregnancy itself, and the choice of termination as a solution, may indicate the girl lacks necessary support from her family and social group (Raphael 1972a). It is only in relatively recent years that termination has become socially acceptable as a solution to unwanted pregnancy in some societies. However, stigma, shame, and secrecy may still remain. Religious background may make the choice even more conflictual if the girl has had a strong Catholic upbringing. Family moral values may reinforce the "wrong" of such a solution to her pregnancy.

For many, the abortion may consciously or unconsciously be equated with murder. Even women with attested liberal views and strong beliefs in the freedom of a woman to do what she will with her own body, are likely to nurse deep inside them something they deny—a feeling that they have somehow "killed" the baby. The termination may be the obvious, the only, solution seen as appropriate for the pregnancy. And the procedure may be simple, painless, and conducted under the best medical conditions. Yet for many women there will be grief to follow and often an undue burden of guilt as well. It is particularly difficult for the woman that she seeks on one hand to be rid of the pregnancy, yet at the same time mourns its loss. Often she is expected to feel grateful that she had been able to obtain the termination, as well she may. Those to whom she might turn for support give her a covert message that her affects should be of pleasure and relief rather than sadness, failing to recognize that the two may coexist. The woman may have required a high level of defensive denial of her tender feelings for the baby to allow her to make the decision for termination. This denial often carries her through the procedure and the hours immediately afterward, so that she seems cheerful, accepting, but unwilling to talk at that time when supportive counseling may be offered by the clinic. She is notorious in avoiding follow-up because she wishes no painful reminders of her loss, such as the place or people with whom it occurred.

In the decision-making process before termination, many clinics offer the opportunity for counseling for the decision. Most young women are afraid to face their ambivalence about the decision at this stage for fear the abortion will be denied them, or because they fear they will not have the strength to carry it through if they do. Often they are far along the pathway of decision making because of the pressures others place on them, especially their mothers, families, and boyfriends. When the decision is strongly influenced in this way, making the girl's ambivalence even higher, she is more likely to do badly afterward in psychological terms.

Thus, there may be a picture of a highly ambivalent attachment to the baby, beginning, but denied; strong pressures to deny the attachment and the ambivalent feelings; an environment that expects a positive rather than negative feeling after the termination, and gratitude rather than sorrow; and a conflicted person with a pregnancy that was unconsciously designed to solve a conflict, but will now, it seems, only add to it. Furthermore, society informs the girl that it is really "a minor thing" that is happening to her, "just like having a tooth pulled," so that she may feel her reaction and distress are signs of her own abnormality, something she might already suspect. Her self-esteem is often low, the abortion itself and the guilt she feels in her decision to have it further reinforcing such negative views of herself.

Not every woman who presents for termination may have done so as a result of conflict about pregnancy. Contraceptive practice may have failed, or termination may be the method of that society for fertility control. Ambivalence toward the pregnancy may not be great, and the choice to terminate it may be clear and simple for the woman. In these circumstances, grief may be minimal, simply resolved, unlikely to lead to pathological outcomes. Just what proportion of women presenting for termination resolve the issue easily is not really known. Most studies are simple short-term follow-ups with little recognition of some of the complexities that may be involved in outcome. There is often little recognition of grief and mourning in the surveys, which ask if the woman is pleased with her decision, which in most cases she is. Most studies suggest that the younger age group (especially first pregnancies), those persuaded to termination by others, those lacking social support, those having it under socially negative or illegal circumstances, are most likely to be at risk. To this list would be added those for whom the pregnancy represents an attempted, yet failed, solution to conflict.

The pattern of grief and mourning is not dissimilar to that for spontaneous abortion, except that suppression and inhibition of grief and mourning are much more likely. The first appearance of sadness is often noted six weeks or so after the termination, when defenses are

down or the loss of the baby is obvious because of the failure of anticipated body changes. Anger is more likely to be directed toward the self
or toward those who are seen as pressing the girl to have the termination. Guilt is not shown. There are many anxious, querying rationalizations that it was "the only thing to do, so why should I feel like this?"
Thoughts about what the baby might have been like and fears about
possible negative effects on future pregnancies may appear. Many
women are curious about what has happened to the fetus, but this does
not necessarily block mourning. Some grief and mourning may appear
when the baby would have been born. The woman may find herself
depressed and tearful some months later "for no good reason," she
says—then she remembers that this is when the aborted baby would
have been born.

The girl or woman who has support to accept and work through
these negative feelings may set them aside. How the whole issue is
handled by the father of the baby may be important in this regard also.
He may be involved in a joint decision which feels right for both of
them, in which case there are likely to be few untoward consequences.
The younger girl, especially if she does not have a steady, long-standing monogamous relationship with the boy may find herself unable to
tell him about it, but rejecting of him because he has in some way
failed her. Such relationships may break down at that time. The older,
married woman, who has had other pregnancies or terminations and
who has children, is less likely to be so personally disturbed, and consequently there may be few negative effects on her relationship. Some
fathers will feel angry and cheated by the woman's decision to terminate their child, whether or not they would be prepared to care for it as
a father. Many men involved in the termination of a pregnancy they
have fathered will experience grief too and may need recognition of
their mourning for the lost child. When the pregnancy has reached an
advanced stage before termination decisions are made, it is likely that
underlying feelings will be even more ambivalent. This and the advanced development of the baby make this loss more difficult to
resolve.

The failure to resolve the loss of the baby in termination may appear
in a number of ways. There may be repeated "unwanted" pregnancies
going on to termination in a "repetition compulsion" which attempts
to undo the "trauma," to rework the experience satisfactorily. Repeat
terminations and unplanned pregnancies are of high incidence, especially in the young unmarried group. Clinical evidence suggests that
these girls are embarrassed and distressed on each occasion, and are not

really consciously choosing this form of birth control. The woman who finds difficulty in becoming pregnant at later stages, who does not conceive, or who repeatedly loses wanted pregnancies may become obsessed with guilt over an earlier abortion, seeing her current problems as "God's punishment" for the "wrong" she did then. In depressions later in life, the theme of guilt over an abortion is common, but it is impossible to draw a cause and effect relationship in such instances. Some young women seem to follow self-destructive, nonfulfilling lifestyles after a termination as though determined to punish themselves.

When Julie, age sixteen, found out she was pregnant, she didn't know what to do.

"I knew Mum and Dad would take it badly. They didn't like Ken, and Mum had told me not to 'get into trouble.' Dad thought kids like us had no moral values anyway. I kept it to myself for a while—I think I really felt that if I didn't talk about it, it might go away. Then I started to get frightened. I was putting on weight, and Mum kept asking me questions. In the end I told her. She cried and screamed and said she should never have trusted me, that Ken was no good either. That really hurt because I loved him, and I knew if I told him about it, he'd be great. She said I wasn't to tell anyone. We'd get it 'fixed up.' She wasn't going to be made a disgrace of in front of her friends. I was to keep quiet, tell no one.

"So she took me to the clinic. They were very nice there, kind and understanding. They asked me what I wanted, but how could I tell them? I thought about the baby. I knew I couldn't manage it. I couldn't put Mum through anything more. I had to go through with it. So I said it was OK, it was fine with me. It was over quickly. Mum seemed so relieved, so pleased. She got busy right away, got me back to school again.

"I couldn't look at Ken—I couldn't tell him what had happened. It was his baby too. I felt black and dirty inside, so I made some excuse and we just broke up. I went on at school and I guess you could say everything was alright—in a way."

Julie presented for another two terminations before having her first baby as a single mother at nineteen. She had a series of unsatisfactory relationships with boys, was chronically depressed, and tended to drink too much on occasions. She had broken with the baby's father but was determined to keep the child. "This one's mine," she said. "No one's going to take him away from me."

During her supportive session with the social worker assisting her with the arrangements for the pregnancy, Julie was able to work through much of her grief and mourning for the loss both of her first baby and of Ken. The role of family dynamics in the pregnancy, her attempts to escape from her mother's intrusive control, and her acting out of her mother's sexual difficulties became clear. The way in which the second pregnancy had "accidentally" occurred as Julie attempted to do things properly that time, was dealt with. The role of Julie's motivation in this pregnancy, her determination to deal with it successfully, and its role in restitution of the earlier loss, were all discussed in her therapy. Her self-destructive behavior and its guilty origins were worked through to some degree. She went on to manage the baby reasonably well and to lead a more rewarding life-style. It was interesting to note that the baby's birthday was the third anniversary of the day that the first baby would have been born.

Psychopathological sequelae of induced abortion are not inevitable, but they occur for many women, especially in the younger group. The grief and mourning may well be resolved with support that recognizes the importance of the loss for the girl.

STILLBIRTH

When there is a stillbirth, the loss is not a chosen one. It seems to come tragically when the fulfillment of pregnancy seems at hand. It may be quite unexpected, often sudden. Hopes built during the months of pregnancy are dashed. The psychology of stillbirth has been recently reviewed by Kirkley-Best and Kellner (1982).

The relationship of the mother to the baby that is stillborn may fall anywhere on the spectrum. Some of these pregnancies will have been unwanted, the attachments highly ambivalent, and abortion contemplated. Some will have experienced transient ambivalence, the baby wanted sometimes and not others. Some babies will have been longed for, ardently desired. The father's developing attachment to the baby is likely to be similar to the mother's. He may be present at the baby's birth.

The baby's death may occur with some forewarning. Either through congenital abnormality or intrauterine event, it may become obvious that the baby will not be viable, or that it has already died. This is immensely painful for the parents, particularly if they must wait for the natural onset of labor to produce the dead baby. Some anticipatory grieving may commence when the death is discovered or when diagnosis is made of a nonviable deformity such as anencephaly. The knowledge of the baby's death may come to the parents in such a way. However, on many occasions, the mother senses something wrong— cessation of movements, unexpected sensations, something not quite right—that leads her to have the matter investigated. She may have kept this concern to herself or shared it with her husband. This may be the beginning of her working through her loss.

In some instances, it may be that "a dull, sad quietness pervades the labor ward as the baby emerges, and its floppy body is hurriedly wrapped in a sheet and whisked away" (*British Medical Journal*, January

1977, p. 126). In others, when the stillbirth is unexpected, there may be "frantic efforts at resuscitation as the silence becomes increasingly oppressive, raising everyone's anxiety, especially the mother's" (p.126). The cause of the death may be difficult to ascertain and even more difficult to explain to the distressed mother. The borderline between natural causes and some sort of medical mismanagement may be a narrow one in some instances. The doctor's sense of guilt and failure may add to the mother's belief that the baby should not have died. It may be easier for her to believe that someone is to blame than to face some of her own feelings of guilt and failure. In her fantasy, the death is likely to be seen as a punishment for the ambivalence in her relationship with the baby, for the times she did not fully want or love it, for past misdeeds, such as abortions. And congenital abnormalities, birth trauma, intrauterine defects might all be interpreted by her as evidence of her damaging and destructive body and womb.

The mother's comprehension of the death, and her mourning for the baby she has lost, are often further complicated by the fact that she has been prevented from seeing and touching the baby. Medical assistants and hospital systems are frequently extremely reluctant to let her have any sight or contact at all, in the mistaken belief that this policy will aid in her recovery. But the majority of mothers are more anxious to see their babies, to touch, hold, name them, and take part in the arrangements for the burial. They may find photos of the baby helpful, especially as evidence that the whole pregnancy produced something: a baby that was real and can be remembered.

A most valuable description of the experiences of some of these mothers is provided in Rosemary Montgomery's unpublished study (1978) of forty mothers in an Australian hospital. She notes how frequently mothers were shocked to find that the baby they had been delivered of was whisked away, taken from them, with no explanation; how distressed they were when they were refused the opportunity to see their baby; how important the naming and burial were for them, as they often feared the baby would be disposed of in the garbage or the hospital incinerator; and how difficult it was when husbands were told to take over all these responsibilities and protect the wife from them. These women found it almost impossible to see their babies if the doctor did not agree, and even if they wished for it they were often too distressed to insist. Staff fantasies about the state of the stillborn babies appeared in descriptions such as: "he had no skin"; "he was grossly deformed"; "he had no head" (anencephaly). To the parents who saw these babies this was far from the reality. Montgomery notes: "The observed pattern was for parents to examine their baby closely and in detail, often noting familial resemblances: the process of identification in fact observed to follow live births. It seemed that seeing the baby often enabled the parents to enact two processes necessary for grief: to incorporate the baby as a tangible love object, part of themselves, and as well, to separate from it" (p. 8). She notes the case of Mrs. J, who, rather than seeing the anencephaly as monstrous, as she had been told, was "struck by how normal the body and face were and felt love and pity for her own baby, instead of fear" (p. 9).

The fathers' needs in these circumstances are so often ignored. As Peppers and Knapp (1980) point out in their excellent book *Motherhood and Mourning*, the husband is often rapidly pushed into the role of protector and decision maker and must suppress his own grief. These authors point out that this process may well interfere with the wife seeing the baby. They emphasize the critical importance of sharing the experience of seeing the baby together for the stability of the couple subsequently, for doing so gives them a chance to grieve together. It allows for the husband's expression of his loss too, and its recognition by the wife.

Many women are heavily sedated through the stillbirth experience and afterward. This may not only interfere with opportunities for seeing the baby but may also suppress their grieving response. Further suppression may result from the fact that the women and their whole milieu have been geared to the joyous welcoming of a live baby. Anger and disappointment, impotence and failure, may be the responses of staff. The woman's grief, her longing for the baby, her crying for it, and her wish to see and hold it, may be seen as evidence of disturbance rather than a natural response. No one seems to know what to do to help and support her, for all she wants is her baby and her baby is dead. Nobody knows which ward to place her in after the birth. In the ward with other mothers and babies, her distress is intense—she has no baby of her own, envies the others, and longs to take one of their babies, anything to have a baby to take home. In Montgomery's study the women were often placed in the ward with hysterectomy and cancer patients. They saw themselves as destroyed women, too, because of their failure in the task of womanhood.

The grief following stillbirth is likely to show in intense yearning and longing for the lost baby, in the need to see, touch, and bury it before the finality of its loss can be accepted. The mourning process with all its sadness, anger, memories, and despair takes place over the many weeks that follow. The mourning is especially difficult because there are so few concrete reminders of the baby. The review, as with all losses of children, goes back over the relationship, back to the beginning of pregnancy, the special times that are remembered, such as the baby's first movements, the names that were chosen, the hopes that were nurtured, the boy it might have been, the girl it was. The positive and negative aspects may all be recalled: the negative, with guilt, since those aspects now appear to have been dread forebodings. Montgomery notes how many women saw such foreboding of the death in retrospect. The hoped-for futures also have to be reviewed and relinquished, maybe set aside for another baby, another time.

When the time comes for the woman to go home empty-handed, her sense of failure and despair may peak. There is "nothing to show for all those months," "nothing to show for the labor and the pain." She may dread the explanations to well-wishers, to family, and particularly to children. She may dread the empty cot, the prepared nursery. The inability of others to comprehend her loss makes it a lot more difficult. People may be well-meaning, but when they make comments such as "You shouldn't be upset; you were lucky, you never knew the baby anyway, so there was nothing to lose," she knows they have little understanding of her feelings. Many avoid her because they don't know what to say, what to do with the presents they had for the baby, or whether to send flowers or not. The lack of support from hospital and social network often complicates the woman's recovery. The breakdown of communication and misunderstandings with husband and family may create further problems. She runs a substantial risk of failing to resolve this bereavement satisfactorily. Her mourning and grief are likely to continue for a considerable time, so support may be lacking at later stages because everyone expects her to be "over it by now."

Lena, age thirty, told of her experience: "I wanted this baby so desperately. We'd tried so hard to get pregnant again. I'd had two miscarriages, so we were specially careful. I hardly dared hope. But when I got to sixteen weeks, twenty weeks, I started to believe that it might be all right. I started to think about the baby. Joe was so thrilled. We didn't mind if it was a boy or a girl—as long as it was all right. I was scared to get clothes or even to get the room ready—I had been so disappointed before. I didn't want to tempt fate. When it started to move we'd lie in bed at night feeling it. Joe was so proud. I was scared. I didn't know how I'd be as a mother. I was so worried something might go wrong. I kept hearing stories of women who had deformed babies and hadn't realized anything was wrong. I worried so much about that that the doctor got a scan—just to be sure. I could see the baby and there wasn't anything wrong. It was a wonderful feeling. I took the 'pictures' home to Joe and said, 'That's our baby's first photo—we'll put it in the book.'

"When I got to thirty-six weeks, I started to feel strange, worried—I was sure something was wrong. They kept telling me the baby had to be alright—nothing could happen now. Then my water broke. Everything started to happen at once. Joe came home and took me to the hospital. They listened to the baby and they all seemed worried, but they kept telling me it would be fine. I *knew* things were terribly wrong. Then everything happened so quickly. The baby came. I was in a daze—full of drugs they gave me. I kept calling out 'Where's my baby, I want my baby—my baby's dead isn't it?' They all said 'Sh', 'sh,' and gave me another injection. But I saw them taking her away—all wrapped up in a blanket.

"The next few days were like a nightmare. There were drips in my arms. I kept asking about the baby, but no one told me anything. I was so drugged. I slept most of the time. Sometimes when I woke Joe was there beside me. He looked terrible. I'd say to him, 'Our baby's dead isn't she?' and all he'd say was 'Shush, shush,' just like the rest of them, and keep telling me I was very sick and had to rest.

"Then I seemed to come out of it. The doctor came and told me: 'Your baby was born dead Mrs. King. We don't know why, but it was probably for the best—it might not have lived long anyway. You'll be well enough to go home soon.' Then I said, 'I want to see my baby, Doctor.' He said, 'No you can't Mrs. King—it's no good, the baby's dead. It will only give you bad memories to take away. It would be better if you put it out of your mind.' Then he hurried away as though he was ashamed or something—maybe so he wouldn't see me cry. They kept telling me not to cry or they'd have to give me something to settle me down. I was upsetting the other women. The nurses couldn't bear me crying. They didn't seem to know how I felt. When Joe came in at visiting hours, I told him I had to see the baby. He said, 'It's no good, Love, I've had to bury her. We couldn't put you through that.' I felt as though I could die—she was gone—as though there had never been anything there—like a puff of smoke—phantom pregnancy. It was nothing. All I had was nothing. That's all there was. All those months of longing and fear, all those years of wanting my baby—all gone for nothing.

"I hated Joe for a while. It was as though he'd been part of it all. At first he wouldn't tell me where she was buried or what name he'd given her. They thought it would only make me morbid. After a while he took me there—that made all the difference in the world. Somehow it said she had been real, that the milk in my breasts, the swelling in my stomach had all been real, not just a dream. Then I realized Joe felt so bad too. He'd been trying to be strong for me all the time and he was really hurting as well. I'd felt such a failure until then—not a proper woman at all. But I could see Joe needed me, too, and I loved him. Somehow when I could comfort him, and we could both talk about it together things seemed to come right. I was sad for a long time after, especially the first anniversary of her death. Sometimes I'd get out that little picture from the scan and say, 'Well, Mary Jane, we didn't really know you for long but we loved you.' "

Joe, thirty-two, told the story from his perspective: "It hit me in the guts when they told me our baby was born dead: how can a baby be born dead when it was alive and well before? Then they told me Lena was to know nothing about it. I was to arrange the funeral and all that. I was nearly sick inside. Somehow I managed to do it, but it was like a nightmare. Then Lena looked at me and I could feel all the blame in her eyes. It was as though we were miles apart and we'd never be together again. My heart was breaking for her, for the baby, for me. But I had to keep it to myself—they'd told me she had to be protected and it was up to me. If we hadn't gone to the grave together, I think it would have been the end of our relationship. It seemed to lift a black load off my shoulders. She seemed to see me again as a person too. She seemed to love me like she used to. It was all that saved us both. We can go on now with a bit of hope for the future."

Various consequences may follow stillbirth. Wolff, Nielson, and Schiller (1970) carried out a three-year follow-up of fifty bereaved mothers. They found that half had resolved their grief with another pregnancy, but that the other half was adamantly opposed to having another child, and half of this group had chosen to become permanently sterilized. Lewis and Page (1978) describe a profound disturbance of mothering with a subsequent live baby. The "replacement child syndrome" may develop as a continuation of this lost pregnancy, especially when it is considered as a nonevent. Abnormalities of bonding to subsequent pregnancies and children are common. Overprotection of the remaining child or children may occur and may be a feature of bonding to subsequent children (Rickarby, Single, and Raphael 1982). A particular problem occurs for the mother who has one stillborn twin. Her grief may be inhibited by the attachment to the live baby, or conversely, her attachment to the live baby may be inhibited by her grief for the twin who has died.

Marital and sexual difficulties are common after stillbirth. These are frequently linked to the differing patterns and levels of grief in each parent and the consequent incongruity of parental grief. Somatic symptoms are also frequent. The distortion or loss of "body part," in this case, the baby, may be experienced as phantom sensations of the baby kicking, as though the mother were still pregnant. There may be a sense of deformity or defectiveness that she could have produced such a "bad" thing as the dead baby, perhaps associated with the activation of earlier negative self-images, such as those described by Horowitz et al. (1980). Anniversary reactions may appear each year at the time of the baby's death, often in the form of depression. There may be extreme fear during future pregnancies, but the incidence of pathological outcome is not known.

The risk of poor outcome may be increased if the mother is heavily sedated; if she is prevented from seeing the baby; if the parents are unable to communicate and share grief or recognize its different patterns for each other; if the mother's previous self-image was poor; and if support is lacking. This latter variable is unfortunately often present in that medical systems find stillbirth extremely difficult to handle (and may even deny the extent of its effects), and family and friendship networks are unsure how to respond to what seems to them a "nonevent." Women repeatedly note that they often only feel supported by others who have been through the same or a similar experience.

NEONATAL DEATH

Many of the characteristics of the bereavement following neonatal death are similar to those following stillbirth, except in neonatal death the parents have some opportunity, even if limited, to know and attach to the real child. The two conditions have been studied together by many workers, under the heading "perinatal death" (see, for example, Peppers and Knapp 1980). Although the bonding to the sick neonate may be inhibited by the threat to the child's life, its prematurity or illness, in most instances, with modern obstetric practices, the attachment to the real baby has time to consolidate.

When the parents realize their newborn child has some life-threatening condition they experience the typical responses to loss. Initially there may be shock, numbness, and disbelief, particularly if there has been nothing to foreshadow the threat. Then there follows an acute longing for the baby, more pronounced in mothers. Where there is a period of illness the baby is usually cared for in a neonatal intensive care unit where the parents are actively involved in its care. The mother's bonding will be enhanced by the tactile contact and seeing her child, but she may have already commenced anticipatory grieving for it. The extent of her anticipatory grief may be determined by the degree of forewarning of the baby's death or serious condition, with the more sudden and unexpected deaths of otherwise healthy neonates being associated with the greatest shock effects for both parents. Whatever his condition, there is an intense longing to hold and cuddle the baby, which is likely to be quite impossible because of his physical condition. As anticipatory grief and mourning progress, the parents may find themselves withdrawing from the child. The dilemma and distress of the parents in such instances is most sensitively described in Wendy Bowie's story of the life and death of her firstborn (Bowie 1977).

When the death has occurred the mother may have intense yearning and longing to "hold, cuddle and rock" her baby (Helmrath and Steinitz 1978). There may be feelings of being cheated or frustrated by not having a baby to care for and a resentment and envy of those who have. This is followed by sadness, prolonged crying, and feelings of emptiness as the finality of the loss is accepted. There appears to be little anger or hostility toward the infant, but there may be some toward the hospital, those who did not prevent the death, as well as toward the self. Guilt is common as the parents seek some explanation or understanding. There is often an intense need to talk of the baby, its physical appearance, all that happened with it, and of the lost hopes for the future. This mourning process may involve the parents going over and over, again and again, details of the pregnancy, birth, and subsequent events. This is part of the catharsis of their helplessness over what has happened, a working through of guilt, and a review and relinquishment of the lost baby.

The asynchronous pattern and intensity of grief for each parent is described by all those who have studied this group. Some (Helmrath and Steinitz 1978; Clyman et al. 1980) note how the fathers recover earlier, and often cannot comprehend or support the wife's prolonged mourning or depression. Kennell, Slyter, and Klaus (1970) and Peppers and Knapp (1980) note that, while this is true in some instances, in others the fathers may be more affected because they had been more actively involved in relating to the baby in the intensive care unit while the mother was confined to her hospital bed. This does not appear common in clinical situations at present, although the father's grief is often not recognized, because, as with stillbirth, he is expected to be the strong protective one.

The cause of the death is very important to these parents. Clyman's group found in their study (1980) that, even though 74 percent of the thirty-five families interviewed understood the causes of the deaths and the risk of their recurring in subsequent children, they still wanted to ask questions about this information and discuss the autopsy reports. Families often use the autopsy reports as reassurance about the healthy aspects of the baby as well as to confirm the cause of death. It is important to parents to be told about the death immediately after it occurs and to be allowed to hold the baby, as this helps bring reality to the loss. Clinical experience suggests that parents do not regret having seen the baby but greatly value the experience and memories. Although this may be upsetting for them, such upset is a natural response to the loss. The parents should *not* be sedated to stop this. The importance for the whole family of seeing the baby is suggested by many researchers in the field. Western practice may negate the baby as a person who has died, but other cultures such as Hispanic Latin Americans place great emphasis on the family seeing the baby and on proper mourning and funeral practices.

Guilt is another force that motivates the parents' queries about the baby. There may be bizarre fantasies as to their own actions that might have caused the death, and the parents are only reassured when these can be voiced. The levels of ambivalence toward the pregnancy, and again toward the baby during its illness, may be further sources of guilt that the parents need to work through.

According to Helmrath and Steinitz (1978), the acute grief may last six months to a year, but paternal grief is likely to have a much more rapid resolution. This may cause difficulties, but on the other hand, the relationship between the couple may be deepened or improved. Patients describe many problems in their family and social field following the death (Clyman et al. 1980). The parents may be preoccupied with their own distress. There may be difficulties in explaining to the children what has happened, in understanding their different grief and mourning, and in responding to their questions and needs. There is the problem of what to do with the things they got for the baby. This may only be resolved as they gradually mourn the loss and feel able to relinquish them. Parents often feel very unsupported by family and friends. Few can let them talk of the baby and their fears and sadness as they need to, to mourn their loss. Parents often feel they require ongoing assistance, but this may not be readily available to them. In Clyman's subjects 80 percent felt they needed continuing follow-up because of "inability to resume previous responsibilities." Yet for many, such support is not available.

Kennell, Slyter, and Klaus (1970) found all of the mothers in their study reported definite sadness and preoccupation with the baby, insomnia, general disturbance of sleep, and increased irritability. Those whose mourning was particularly intense were more likely to have suffered the previous loss of a baby, to have had positive feelings about the pregnancy, and to have touched the baby before his death. Only one of the mothers had pathological grief, however, and she had suffered a previous postpartum depressive psychosis. These findings suggest that grief and mourning may be intense for mothers following neonatal death, but such intensity relates to the loss, and the attachment to the baby. It is by no means indicative of pathology. Pathological outcome, it would seem, is much more likely to arise from a highly ambivalent attachment, a failure to come to terms with the realities of the death (perhaps by not seeing the body), suppression of grief and mourning (perhaps by sedation), and failure of social support. Support may fail in that it blocks or fails to facilitate the natural but intense experiences of grief and mourning at this time. Taylor and Gideon (1980) and Gilson (1976) emphasize the valuable role of the physician and other hospital staff in providing support to facilitate resolution. Such support may be best provided alongside the routine procedures and care of the parents at this time.

Unresolved grief may be more common with this type of bereavement. It often occurs when the loss of the child reawakens a parent's unresolved feelings of helplessness, inadequacy, as well as irrational guilt. The mother may resort to maladaptive behavior of the dependent, learned-helplessness type. This may be difficult for others to handle. Other forms of pathological outcome have not been systematically studied but appear to be very similar to those following stillbirth (Peppers and Knapp 1980).

Margaret was twenty-two when she lost her baby.

"Our baby was so small. He was premature, six weeks premature and just so tiny. At first I thought he wouldn't live at all when I came into labor so early. But the doctors told me that they had saved babies smaller than this, so that there was every hope that he would be all right. The intensive care nursery was a strange place—like somewhere from outer space. There were all those tiny little things looking more like mice or tiny monkeys than real babies. And there was our Justin, he was one of them.

"Bill and I would go there all the time. They'd let us touch him through that little plastic cabinet, but he looked so fragile—all those tubes and his skinny little arms. We loved him very much, although when we first knew we were having him, we hadn't really wanted him at all. Then we got used to the idea and it was terrible to think of anything happening to him. When he was born too soon, I was really frightened. I felt God was punishing me for not wanting him in the first place. . . . When he was so sick, all I wanted to do was hold him close, breathe my warmth and life into him. But I couldn't do that. I would touch him, and look into his little face and hope that all my love would somehow make him better.

"He wasn't growing, so even though they kept telling me he was all right, I didn't really believe them in my heart.

"The day he died seemed like any other day, warm and sunny. It just didn't seem possible that a little baby like that should die. He hadn't had any life yet—how could God let it happen? I couldn't cry at first—I felt dry, drained, as though there wasn't a tear left in me. For a long time I tried to believe he was still there at the hospital.

"Then there was the empty room at home, and it all came over me like a great tidal wave of grief. I was so sad, so empty, I thought I'd never feel whole again. I used to think about the funeral, and think about him. It was such a tiny casket. He was such a little person to die."

OTHER LOSSES OF THE NEWBORN BABY

There are two other major kinds of losses of a newborn child that may occur. They are not deaths, yet the mother and possibly the father, where he is involved, may mourn extensively. The grief is intense yet it may not readily be recognized and supported by others.

*Adoption: relinquishment.* It has long been recognized that the mother who relinquishes a child for adoption may be distressed. Yet until recent years it was felt that she should be discouraged from all thought or review of her loss and that her feelings should be suppressed. The powerful longings of mothers for their relinquished children have always been present, but it is only now with increased public understanding of their loss that they are able to express these.

Typically, when the mother intends to relinquish the baby, she may try to inhibit her attachment to it during its intrauterine development. This may be successful to a degree, but, with the birth, the biological and psychological processes inevitably lead her to the beginnings of attachment and an interest and involvement in it. Furthermore, because of the processes outlined in the beginning of this chapter, she is likely already to have considerable psychological bonding to the image of this, her fantasy baby.

With the birth she faces the reality of a loss that she had previously only imagined. For most women there is a period of sadness and often great doubt and ambivalence. Modern adoption counseling allows some opportunity for the working through of these issues. Some grief counseling is also frequently provided. Nevertheless the woman often represses or suppresses much of her longing for her baby so as to have the strength to go on with her plans to relinquish it. Social pressures may reinforce this further. For these reasons, and because the baby is indeed not dead but separated from her and alive elsewhere, the grief is usually very poorly resolved. The image of the baby is kept alive and active in the woman's mind. It is very often part of her fantasy in which it has a life and development of its own. Thus, even with an understanding of her needs and her bereavement for this loss of her child, it is often difficult to facilitate a resolution.

The mother's grief and distress were, of course, prominent features of adoptions that took place before the current, more enlightened approaches. The stigma of pregnancy for the unmarried, the unavailability of abortion, the pressures on the woman to relinquish the child rather than raise it as a sole parent, and the systems of care that denied her her feelings of grief, all led to a very traumatic experience for most young women. Additionally, the loss would be poorly resolved. In a study of twenty psychiatric patients suffering from depression or anxiety who had a history of relinquishing a child during their adolescence, approximately fifteen to nineteen years prior to the study, Rynearson (1982) describes the painful experiences of these women, experiences that were probably representative of those of a much larger group. The trauma of the circumstances of delivery, the signing of papers and relinquishment of the child was remembered by the woman as a time of loneliness and panic. In the following years the women showed much evidence of their repressed maternity, in recurring dreams concerning the loss of the baby with contrasting themes of traumatic separation and joyful reunion; preoccupation with babies and their possible resemblance to the lost child; obsessive fears about infertility; the urge to become pregnant; "an overdetermined need to undo the act of relinquishment" (p. 340); anger and disillusionment toward men; and some sexual dysfunction. Longer-term adjustments involved a particularly anxious and protective attachment to subsequent children and a concern for these, especially girls as they reached maturity, that they not suffer as the mother had. Mourning continued a long time, lessening gradually, but always intense at anniversaries of the loss.

Helen, twenty-two, described her feelings before and after giving up her baby for adoption.

"I could feel the baby growing in me all the time. I kept thinking—how will I ever give it up. I tried to stop myself from getting attached to it. I called it 'it' and tried not to think whether it was a boy or a girl. I tried to be firm with myself. There was no way I could keep it. I couldn't manage. A baby needs a family, and some family wanted my baby. They'd give it all the love and affection and proper family life. All the things I'd wanted. I used to think a lot about the family—what they might be like. I wondered what the baby would think when he found out his real mother had given him up. So I prayed that he'd know it was really because I loved him and I wanted him to have all the good things I couldn't give him. The closer it got to the time the harder it was. I was frightened about the birth, worried if he'd be all right. I knew it would be hard to adopt him out if he wasn't perfect.

"The labor was all right. The hospital was really good, and they were very nice to me. When I looked at him I knew he was mine. I loved him right away. I had to be very strong; I wanted so much to hold him and keep him. I had to keep telling myself all the time that I was doing the right thing, that it would be best for him in the long run and best for me too—I wasn't ready to be tied down yet. There were too many things I had to do. I was very strong the day I signed the papers. They told me he was going to a very good home: a couple who could give him everything, who couldn't have one of their own, who had waited years for him. So that made me pleased. But when I was by myself it was as though they'd taken away part of me. I couldn't cry; I thought if I did I'd never stop. I had to keep it to myself, because no one understood. They all thought it was the only thing to do.

"That's five years ago now. I think about him such a lot: I see a child in the street, and I think that must be about Peter's age. I wonder if it's him, and I look at the parents and search all their faces, but of course I don't know. It's really just a dream. Each year I celebrate his birthday. I make a little cake and put the candles on and blow them out one, two, three, four, five. Sometimes I imagine what he might be doing, what he's like now—if he knows about me, what he thinks about me. Then I think how it will be when he gets bigger. I wonder if he'll try to find me. Sometimes I think I'll find out where he is. I know you can't, but somehow I would and I'd go and watch and make sure he's all right. I gave him up, but he's still part of me away there somewhere—he's my child."

*The birth of a defective or handicapped child.* When the baby is born, or shortly after, it may be recognized that the real baby is indeed very different from the fantasy baby. The differences may be immediately apparent, as with Down's syndrome, or obvious a little later. Even the very premature baby, so different from the image of an ideal baby, may in some ways be seen as being "defective." The very obviously handicapped child is, of course, different from what the parents desired, different from the baby to which they were attaching before its birth. The grief for the relinquishment of this fantasy baby, the perfect baby they had hoped for, may be very great and difficult to resolve.

There may be an initial wave of grief followed by some denial of the disability. Then with the growing awareness that developmental milestones are not reached and that the infant does not respond, fresh waves of grief and mourning occur. The grief in such circumstances is likely to occur at progressive stages of development as the new losses of potential are faced in each phase. The grief for this lost child is complicated further by ambivalence, guilt, and sometimes lack of support. It is difficult for the parents to relinquish the fantasy and attach to a baby so far from their ideal. And both the grief and the attachment are likely to be inhibited and complicated as a consequence (Solnit and Stark 1961; Emde and Brown 1978).

# Loss in Adult Life: The Death of a Child

The sudden infant death syndrome (SIDS) is one of the commonest causes of death in the early months and first year of life. Bluglass (1981) notes that it may account for up to two thousand deaths per annum in England and Wales; and May and Breme (1982-83) note eight to ten thousand deaths annually in the United States. It occurs in two to three thousand live births. Other causes of death in early infancy are much less frequent and are more likely to be associated with gross conditions such as severe congenital abnormality or overwhelming disease. The cause of SIDS is unknown, although recent studies suggest it is a syndrome of multifactorial etiology, with prolonged apnea (often associated with sleep apnea), as part of the final common pathway leading to the sudden death.

Epidemiological and case studies now make it quite clear that this condition leads to a major crisis for the bereaved family. Distress is extreme and outcome often problematic, although systematic data on levels of morbidity following SIDS are not yet available from current work (see, for example, Bluglass 1981).

*The attachments.* There is no information available as to the nature of the attachments between the mother or other family members and baby before the death. Some sociodemographic factors may suggest there could be problems in a few of the relationships. The SIDS baby is often born to much younger parents, and incidence increases with lower socioeconomic class (Bluglass 1981). SIDS can occur in any level of the population and in all cultural and social groups. Loving, involved, sensitive parents have been just as shocked by this tragedy as have those whose ambivalence toward the baby is obvious.

An important difference between deaths at this stage and the other losses discussed above in this chapter, is the degree to which parents have a chance to attach to and know the baby as a real person. If the father was present at the birth and actively involved with it, his "engrossment" with the baby will be considerable. The mother is usually very intensely involved with "primary maternal preoccupation," so that most of her behavior and responses are likely to be oriented toward the baby in these early months when these deaths are most common. These factors make the loss more intensely experienced, and the absence of the baby and the futility of the parenting roles make the loss so overwhelming.

*The deaths.* The nature of SIDS is still so shrouded in mystery, so shocking and unanticipated, that these circumstances in themselves

255

make it much harder for bereaved families to cope. Typically the baby had been well, perhaps even checked by the doctor that day in a routine way, or occasionally for minimal symptoms. He is put to bed in the normal manner and found dead in his crib either during the night or the following morning. These infants may die in other circumstances, for example, in the room with other children or parents. The death is usually silent, with no agonal crying or evidence of undue movement or distress. The parents have no warning, although sometimes, in retrospect, perhaps with their attempts to master the experience, they seem to feel that they had some sense of foreboding that they felt should have alerted them. For many of the parents the syndrome is unknown, until it happens to them. The circumstances of sudden, quiet death in a healthy baby seem inexplicable. The legal requirements in many societies are a further terrifying factor, for some kind of investigation is usually required, and the parents are carefully questioned as to possible causes by the police. Both this procedure and the parents' own inability to comprehend the death make it seem as though some cause must be found. Parents may feel that others believe they were responsible through injury or neglect, and they themselves often feel that this must be so. This is particularly likely when the deaths occur in societies where infant death rates are low and where all children are expected to live.

The suddenness, the mystery of the cause, make the death difficult to explain to others. Associations with guilt multiply. Children in the family find it most difficult to understand, sometimes blaming the parents for getting rid of the baby, or feeling that, in some way, they themselves must have been responsible. The specter of the death seems to haunt the family for a long time. Parents try to find all the information they can about the syndrome. The autopsy report is part of this information process, although its contents may be ill understood by the parents. When it *is* understood, the death may seem even more frightening. Parents realize that doctors cannot specify or control it. Thus it comes to symbolize the omnipotence of death, making them feel vulnerable in themselves and their relationships. Finding a cause is seen as a way of protecting against such trauma in the future, gaining some control to negate the powerlessness that is otherwise felt. So sudden, so unexpected, so untimely is the death of such a young infant that it constitutes a trauma that may intensify and complicate resolution of the loss.

*Experience and behavior.* The response of the parents to the death tends to follow a typical pattern, confirmed by a number of researchers in this field (Cornwell, Nurcomb, and Stevens 1977; Lowman 1979; S. Lewis 1981; Mandell, McAulty, and Reece 1980; Watson 1981; K. Bluglass 1980, 1981; May and Breme 1982-83). When the mother finds her baby dead in the crib she screams. This scream may be a primitive response to bring the assistance of others as well as the first manifestation of her grief. The father, a neighbor, or a sibling of the dead baby may come to her aid. There may be attempts to resusciatate the infant, but these are of no avail. Medical assistance is called but can do nothing. As Cornwell notes, in the first hours after the death the parents simultaneously know and deny that their baby has died.

Feelings toward the dead baby are intense. The mother, and often the father, wish to hold the baby's body. The mother may hold it to herself, rock with it, walk with it, perhaps at the same time calling out with her sorrow and despair, begging God for it not to be true. When the body is taken away, perhaps for legal reasons, the parents may feel intensely resentful and even resist this.

The mother's anguish at separation from her infant is most powerful. That, as in other bereavements, is the first part of her process of adaptation to the death. Because she has been so intensely interacting with her infant it seems to her as though the whole purpose for her existence, her *raison d'être*, has been taken away. She longs for the baby with every fiber of her body. She looks, searches for him in his room, in all the familiar places, at all the familiar times. She feels empty inside, as though he has been torn out of her. Her arms feel empty, and she yearns for a baby, her own baby, to hold. The feeling of losing part of herself is intense. This may be particularly so with such young infants, for as E. Furman (1980) suggests, and Cornwell's observations bear out, the mother may still psychologically feel the baby to be part of her, within her. He may indeed have been inside her in his development longer than he had been without.

The image of the baby is before her as she yearns and longs for him. Reminders of him send painful surges, pangs of grief throughout her body. She is so preoccupied with cues, so alert to all possible stimuli that may indicate the baby, that she hears his cry, sees his face. Her preoccupation seems to cut out all other stimuli from the environment. This may be part of the numbness many parents describe, which may last beyond the early weeks to the first two to three months. It may be so great as to interfere with her "survival" tasks for the family.

The search for the baby, the preoccupation with the image of him, may lead to restless, distressed, motor behavior. Dreams may be filled with the search for the baby or concern about him. The parent may secretly or overtly nurse fantasies of his return, relinquishing these only when reality forces through. Parenting tasks may be continued as if anticipating his return, the mother preparing bottles, the baby's bed, and clothes. The baby's possessions may be cherished as reminders, handled, and put away. The powerful nature of the fantasy of getting her baby back is clear in Ellen K's story.

She came to see me for "bereavement counseling," two weeks after her infant son's death. She had been told that this would "fix her up." Her first session was one of history taking, during which she was distant and withdrawn throughout, constantly looking around the room. She left prematurely, agreeing to a second appointment reluctantly. Twenty-four hours later I was called to the local hospital where she had been admitted following a massive overdose. As she gained consciousness she stated angrily in response to queries about what had happened,

"When I went to see you I expected that you would give me back my baby. You were the expert. That's what you were supposed to do. There was nothing else I wanted from you. There was no other reason to go. When you didn't bring him back it was as though the whole horrible reality of it hit me—he was dead—he was gone forever. I hated you. I hated God, I hated the world—so this was all I could do."

Anger is common in sudden unanticipated deaths, especially the deaths of such young children. There is anger at God, doctors, the marital partner, other children, family, friends, the social network, and the lost baby. Frustration and irritability are common and often projected onto others, perhaps with scapegoating. The distress is extreme in the early weeks: highest for the mother, but also intense for the father, especially if he has been intimately involved with the baby. The parents may be incoherent, little able to give an account of what has happened or their feelings, and unable to believe they can survive. The grief may be cut out temporarily by exhaustion or by deliberately avoiding reminders and thoughts of the baby. Agonizing sadness breaks through, sometimes early, sometimes after a period of time, as the reality and finality of the baby's loss is acknowledged. The longing for the baby is unrequited. The realities of the inquest, the funeral, the baby's absence, the futility of the caring role, all go to reinforce the finality of the loss, setting the grounds for the parents' acceptance and mourning.

There is an increasing preoccupation with memories of the baby and pregnancy and a sad relinquishment of parental roles. But the mourning is inevitably complicated in this type of death by the issue of guilt. All workers in this field describe the overwhelming nature of parental guilt and blame. The parents search desperately for a cause. While the findings of the autopsy and careful explanation by others are indeed helpful and reassuring, nevertheless the unknown etiology powers the guilty search for causes. The mother goes over and over everything she did in the child's care, searching for some cue, some slight difference in ritual. The father too may search her behavior or his own. Sometimes he may give covert or overt messages that she must have done something different, and hence, by inference, something wrong. He may state emphatically, repeatedly, persuading neither her nor himself, that he does not blame her. Both are angry and guilty, and it is easy to project this onto each other. Communication may also be blocked, each fearing to set off the other's grief if the loss is discussed. It is hardly surprising that problems in the marital relationship are found frequently in both the short and the long term. This angry, guilty response may be projected onto others: doctors who feel a sense of failure; friends who do not help. It is most difficult when it is projected onto a child. The child may have been present when the baby was found, or even minding him. His own guilty frightened response, linked to his rivalrous thoughts about this new arrival in the family, may make him respond as though he were to blame. He may accept the scapegoating because he is powerless, or because somehow his so doing seems to assuage parental distress. Either way this will not help resolve family grief and mourning and is usually very destructive for ultimate family functioning.

The feelings of the parents are most intense in the earliest weeks. Watson (1981) found that 70 percent of 308 families studied in Great Britain showed acute distress with anger, bewilderment, self-blame, and anxiety when seen in the first few days. A second interview three weeks later showed this distress has lessened to some degree for over 50 percent of families, although it was still very apparent. It seems that by two to three weeks families are still in a state of crisis but, at this stage, more able to verbalize their feelings and concerns. Lowman (1979) found that while a bereavement-index score was high for the parents of his study in the first two months, it had settled to much lower levels by the follow-up visit at four to five months. Cornwell, Nurcombe, and Stevens (1977) noted this acute peak of distress, lessening over the weeks and months that followed but still very intense during the first year, especially at times such as the days around the baby's birthday. They observed that many parents still seemed primed to their baby's image, even twelve months after the death. The parents were alert for signs of babies, constantly thinking of them, and cued to possible similarities to their own.

It is quite clear that the response of father and mother differ for many couples. The mother tends to be more depressed, withdrawn. Her grief seems more intense, prolonged. She weeps. Her life seems more disrupted by her loss. The father's response style tends to be more like that described for perinatal deaths. He takes over protective, management functions, suppresses his feelings, deals with his distress by keeping himself busy and active. He seems to get over his grief more quickly and cannot understand his wife's continuing preoccupation with it. Cornwell, Nurcombe, and Stevens (1977) found the average time of return to normal function was 10.3 months for the mother, 3.6 months for the father. These observations from Cornwell's study and clinical experience are reinforced by the findings of Mandell, McAulty, and Reece (1980). They studied paternal response in twenty-eight fathers and found that they had: a necessity to "keep busy" with increased work; feelings of diminishing self-worth; self-blame because of lack of care and involvement; and a limited ability to ask for help. It seemed that in well over half the cases they were attempting to deny the reality of their child's death and avoid the pain of mourning. Denial was also evidenced by their wish to have other children as soon as possible and by their avoidance of professional help that would involve acceptance of the loss. On the whole the fathers tended to be more angry and aggressive than the mothers. Clinical experience suggests that rather than rapidly working through the loss as the father suggests, he instead puts it "under the carpet." It is a painful focus that is often discussed only hesitantly, or avoided. Sometimes a realization that other men have had intense feelings about such as loss (as in self-help group discussions) may make it possible for the father to face for the first time the extent of his own grief.

The family unit itself is disrupted. Many of these children are first-borns according to Lowman (1979). Their deaths in the first few months of life (two to four months of age is a peak period) mean that the transformation of dyad to family unit is interrupted at a stage when it was only just consolidating. The loss of the baby seems to cut at the heart of the family life. The mother's intense grief may interfere with her capacity to sense or respond to the grief of her husband and children. The children are bewildered by such a death. Family communication is disrupted. Nobody can explain the inexplicable. Nobody dares talk of the dead baby for the distress it brings. Unless the family system is flexible in its capacity to express feelings of sadness, loss, anger, guilt, it may have great difficulty adapting to such a traumatic and sudden death. If blame and guilt are difficult to handle and must be put onto someone else, then scapegoating of some member is a likely consequence. Family difficulties may well extend into the other generation, to the grandparents. They may have a personal emotional investment in the grandchild who has died and may see one of the parents (especially the son or daughter-in-law) as somehow responsible for this blow to the ongoing family of posterity. Their grief is often not recognized, and their critical role in the adjustment of young parents who often turn to them for support may be ignored.

The broader social network may be affected by the loss and be unable to support the family as required. The members are often perceived as nonsupportive in their critical attitudes toward parents, their wish to avoid any discussion of the dead baby, their attempts to suppress parental grief, and their general discomfort and ignorance about such deaths. Doctors and other helpers are unfortunately often included in this category, although parents feel that they are the people from whom help is very important. Where the doctor arrives quickly, explains to the parents, follows them up, and offers emotional support, this role is greatly valued.

*Outcomes.* There are a number of areas of personal and family function in which difficulties have been reported.

1. General symptomatology and distress are said to be high, with mothers reporting many somatic complaints. Insomnia, nervousness, tension, and lack of appetite are common (Defrain and Ernst 1978). Cornwell, Nurcombe, and Stevens (1977) describe a general deterioration of health.

2. Psychosomatic reactions have not been clearly documented, but there are findings that fertility is diminished after the SIDS, perhaps through psychosomatic mechanisms. Thus, Mandell and Wolfe (1975) noted a higher rate of spontaneous miscarriage and lowered fertility following SIDS.

3. Some individual cases of depression and psychiatric admission have been described, but there are no studies of specific symptoms, disorders, or their levels. K. Bluglass (1980) describes some patients in his broader group under study who presented with psychiatric illness and pathological grief. He also quotes Cornwell as finding three cases who sought psychiatric help for delusional hypochondriasis, depression, and severe anxiety. Clinical experience suggests that depression is common for many of the women and also anxiety, particularly in relation to future children. It has also been noticed that increased smoking and drinking behaviors may be found. Psychiatric morbidity has also been described in other children in the crib-death family, as have fears,

sleeping difficulties including nightmares, and angry aggressive behaviors. Some of this response may be transient. Some may be specifically related to parental withdrawal resulting in deprivation for the child.

4. Interpersonal relationships may suffer not only at the time of the crisis but also subsequent to it. Strain on marital relationships (30 percent of the subjects in the Cornwell group's study) may extend to frank marital breakdown. Many workers suggest that these problems are most likely in relationships that have already shown difficulties prior to the loss (Lowman 1979). Marital and sexual problems are described frequently in the clinical literature. Indeed some marriages seem strengthened by the crisis shared and worked through together, the couples' compassionate intimacy bringing them much closer than before.

Relationships with surviving children may be strained to the level of pathology. Halpern (1972) reports three cases where the mother's panicked accusations against a child at the time of the infant sibling's death led to the mother and that child being locked into a pathological relationship marked by fearful doubt, guilt, and hostile dependency. Outright rejection of other children may sometimes occur. A surviving child may also be forced into a replacement-child role with all its possible pathological implications.

Special problems arise for the mother and to a lesser degree the father with future pregnancies. There is intense anxiety which is heightened into a phobic overprotectiveness. The baby must be watched over "morning, noon, and night" for fear it will suffer a similar fate. This anxiety climaxes when the baby reaches the age at which the SIDS infant died and tends to subside subsequently. It may recur with other births, though it is likely to diminish once the mother has succeeded in rearing a live child after the death. This phobic overprotectiveness may also appear with older siblings.

The whole issue of future children, or the next baby, is one of importance. Some parents may feel an intense desire for another baby, even in the height of the bereavement crisis. Often this is a wish to avoid the pain of grief. There may be great fear of future pregnancies because the bereaved believe they could not bear again the possibility of such anguish. It is sometimes the fathers who press most for another baby, perhaps in some cases to deal with their grief and in some to assure themselves of their virility despite this blow to their image of themselves. There is a sense of making good, a reassurance of worth in being able to produce a good, whole, live baby again. The risk of replacement-child pathology (Cain and Cain 1964; Poznanski 1972) exists with subsequent children but seems unlikely if parents have grieved and mourned the lost child and relinquished it. This is best achieved if pregnancy does not occur too soon after, if the parents are encouraged to recognize the importance of this issue, and if they mourn the lost child. Parents are now well aware of this problem and often comment how "when I held him in may arms I thought of the baby I lost, and I thought for a moment it was him, but then I knew it was a *new baby*—and a *different* one."

*Factors affecting outcome.* As with other bereavements, key factors may be associated with the outcome of the SIDS bereavement crisis. May and Breme's study (1982/83) provides a useful review which fits with this model. The following factors are those most frequently observed:

1. The role of the preexisting relationship with the baby is considerable. The relationship is usually intensely idealized by the parents irrespective of its previous affect. Where the background for ambivalence exists, most workers suggest there are more problems to resolution. Thus, in the very young parents, where the baby was born out of wedlock or to a single parent, or where abortion was contemplated, the guilt aspect will be more pronounced making poor outcome more likely. May and Breme also note that some infants may be central to the bereaved in every way. The parent may attempt to hold onto the relationship through some form of chronic grief, perhaps acting as though the infant were still alive. In other cases the infant may have a functional role in the family. Such relationships and roles with the infant are likely to create extra problems for resolution in the bereavement.

2. The sudden, traumatic, and inexplicable nature of the death is itself an extra risk factor for outcome. Legal requirements complicate this further. May and Breme suggest that views about the preventability of death will also contribute. There may be greater guilt if the death is perceived as preventable and the parent assumes responsibility. Misinformation or misunderstanding may contribute to this. The parents' knowledge and understanding of SIDS is rated as an important variable (May and Breme 1982–83).

3. The kind of support parents receive is another variable. Social and professional networks are frequently perceived as nonsupportive at this time. Most of the workers who have been cited here (for example, Watson; Bluglass; Cornwell; Mandell, McAulty and Reece; and Lowman) all comment on the frequency with which crib-death families find others unable to respond to them with either information or emotional support for grief and mourning. Cornwell reported that more

than 50 percent of doctors felt themselves unable to handle parents with this syndrome. Reports from other workers are similar. Lowman's study (1979) shows how professional support persons (specially trained community nurses) can facilitate better support for the bereaved. Self-help organizations are also of immense value in this regard (Bluglass 1981). May and Breme also consider this issue important. Family and friends often mean well, but seem unable to support the bereaved as they would wish.

4. Other stresses may hamper resolution. Moving to a new home, the stresses of a coroner's inquiry, and financial difficulties may all create further strain on ego resources. Evidences of blocked or inhibited grief may appear, but they seem far less frequent than the extreme prolonged form of grief, except for men who may suppress their responses. Disruption of function may also be indicative of pathological outcome.

May and Breme (1982/83) in their valuable presentation delineate factors to be assessed as significant variables in the SIDS Family Adjustment Scale. (These items are scored by interviewers on a 1–5 scale, with 1 indicating the most negative and 5 the most positive association.) They are as follows:

- Communication of feelings
- Life-style resumption
- Use and perception of family support
- SIDS information
- Perception of preventability of death
- Careful decision-making about future children
- Religion (strong religious orientation)
- Family morbidity
- Infant centrality
- Family emotional health
- Functional role of the infant in the family
- Family solidarity

These workers are using this scale to predict those families most at risk and provide appropriate specific intervention programs. Limerick (1976) and K. Bluglass (1979) describe some such counseling techniques, while Lowman's (1979) study provides a very valuable community intervention model. These and other workers (for example, Watson 1981) note the therapeutic value for many families of even a single research interview, which, though painful, is usually perceived as positive. It seems that these programs may facilitate the first expressions and sharing of grief that will allow the gradual mourning and resolution of this immensely painful loss.

"She was our first baby," said Alice, twenty-three. "She was so beautiful and so healthy. Richard and I simply doted on her. She was all we had ever dreamed about.

"I'll never forget that night. We went to bed normally, I tucked her up on her little sheepskin rug. They were the thing to have for your baby. I've often wondered since if maybe it had something to do with her death. My sleep was very disturbed, as though I sensed something was going to happen. I woke at 2:00 A.M. and went in to check that she was all right, to pull the covers up. As soon as I got to the door I seemed to realize something was wrong. I screamed and screamed. She was cold and dead, and I knew right away it was too late. Richard rushed in and we tried to save her. We called the ambulance. All the neighbors came. But nothing did any good.

"I'd never heard about such things before. I always thought the parents must have neglected the child. The police came. They were nice, but they told me there would have to be a coroner's inquest. I know now they were only doing their duty, but at the time it seemed as though they were accusing us of doing something to her. It was like a terrible nightmare. I wanted to hold onto her, not to let her go, but they took her away. For days I couldn't understand it. I thought I'd never survive.

"Everyone was very kind, but you could see they thought it was strange. They kept asking me what I'd done—going through everything, as though I must have done something that caused it. Even Richard and my family kept asking me what I'd done with her that day. . . . I felt so guilty myself. I was inclined to agree that I must have done something wrong. I'd go over things again. But there were no answers. It was only when I met another parent who had been through the same thing, who'd survived it all, that I knew I wasn't going mad, that maybe I would get through it some day. God knows when."


"That night will be sketched on my mind forever. I will never forget it," Alice's husband Richard recalled.

"Even now when I go into the baby's room, it all comes back to me— every single detail—in slow motion. I thought help would never come. When it did, it was useless. It just confirmed what we really knew—that she was dead. After that everything was chaos. Alice was in a dreadful state. She would hold the baby's things to her and rock and moan 'I want my baby, I want my baby'; I wanted her too, although somehow I couldn't say it, couldn't let anyone know. It was frozen inside me.

"Anyway I had to take charge, keep busy, make all the arrangements. I did it somehow or other. I couldn't understand how it could have happened. I kept wondering what we did differently, or if Alice had done something. She seemed to sense this—as though I blamed her. I didn't really, I simply couldn't understand it. That was all. She seemed so deeply grief-stricken for so long. As though nothing would console her ever again. I felt it badly too—she was my baby as well. I couldn't show my feelings like Alice. In my family the men had to be strong, in control—no tears. I think she thought I didn't care. I did. It hurt me deep inside, but I had to keep going, and I had my work. I had to get on with life. Alice's whole life was centered about the baby. That made it so much harder for her. She spent all day every day doing things for her, with her, and now she was gone there seemed to be no point in anything.

"I tried to comfort her—the one way I knew how—in bed. She couldn't see that I was being loving. She just turned away from me and sobbed. That hurt me too. It seemed that I meant nothing to her and the baby meant all. She couldn't see I needed to be comforted too. She said I didn't care—how could I think of sex at a time like this—that I must be callous and cold.

"It went on for months like that. I tried to help her. I thought if we had another baby we might feel better. She couldn't bear the thought of that—though she wanted one desperately, I know: she used to look at other people's babies so longingly, as if she would like to take them for her own. She was afraid if she had another baby she could lose it too. She was afraid of something else happening, she said, so she simply couldn't take it. I wanted to hold her, to comfort her so much, but somehow it didn't work. She couldn't comfort me either. Then I took to staying out late—there seemed no point in coming home. Really that's how our marriage ended—it faded out. You would have said it was quite a good marriage—before this happened."

*Other Deaths in Infancy.* Other deaths in infancy may show a similar pattern if they are sudden and unexpected. Accidental deaths (for example, drowning and car accidents) frequently have similar sequelae, with maybe more parental projection, blame, and guilt. This is likely to be related to the higher background levels of ambivalence that exist in some cases, perhaps contributing in some way to the neglect of care which led to the death. This is not the situation for many families, whose grief will still be intense. Nonaccidental injuries, such as battering and abuse, may lead to death. Parental grief and mourning are often ignored alongside society's enormous anger toward parents who cause the deaths of their children. These parents are usually deprived, inadequate people whose relationship with the dead infant had been full of projections from their own unhappy childhoods. They are likely to need extensive support. It is worth noting that when a parent insists during bereavement counseling sessions that she is a "murderess" it may be that indeed she is, even if this was not obvious in the death. Such patients are in need of expert psychiatric care.

Deaths in infancy from malignant or other disease are likely to be associated with anticipatory grieving as in the older group of children with malignant disease. Parental grief is still great, but adjustment is more gradual with the warning they receive.

All these deaths of the very young are difficult to resolve. Pepper and Knapp (1980) suggest that for many mothers something remains; portions of the grief are tucked away, appearing from time to time when least expected. They call this "shadow grief"—a burden that mothers may bear for the rest of their lives. It may intrude on special occasions with a painful memory of the loss, a dull aching reminder that shuts out joy for a moment. It is a transient reminder of the loss that comes like a shadow across life.

DEATH IN THE CHILDHOOD YEARS

Death in the childhood years takes on a new significance. The child in these years is known and related to as a real person. The family unit it established in its own particular system. There will be many shared pasts to be lost when the child dies, as well as hoped-for futures.

*Attachments.* The parents will have progressively developed the relationship with the child through the various and/or conflictual phases that have arisen up until the time of the terminal illness or death. Although the child's physical dependence on the parents lessens with age there may still be intense emotional dependence of one upon the other. The child may, in some families, become central to parents' emotional life, either in a role of maintaining the marital dyad or as one parent's chief attachment figure. In such families the children are often allocated to a parent—one child may "belong," as it were, to one particular parent. This may be the case from the beginning, or it may develop as the marital relationship lessens or life fails to provide the hoped-for rewards, and the parents' dreams of satisfaction and achievement become heavily invested in a particular child and his future. The loss of a child may also take on extra significance if there are multiple overdetermined levels of identification with him: he occupied the same place in the sibship the parent did; he was the same sex as the parent; he carried similarities and roles that the parent had as a child; and he fit in with the parent's needs for neurotic conflict resolution through some identificatory pathway.

Naturally many families will not have such a pathological pattern of parent-child relationships, especially where the relationship between the parents themselves is strong. Nevertheless, many of these elements may operate in some lesser way in the quality of the parent-child bond, thus creating difficulties in the mourning process. The "image" that is the condensed representation of such a bond at any particular time will include the past and present gratifications and frustrations, the ambivalence and dependence that have been woven into it during the processes of development, as well as the effects of the particular personalities and needs of the parents and child. The quality of the bond will be further influenced by the place of the child among other siblings who may be favored above him, or above whom he seems more important.

*The deaths.*   Deaths are not common in this age group. The two main causative elements are accidental deaths (by far the commonest) and malignant disease. A third smaller group includes the congenitally fatal conditions such as cystic fibrosis or fulminating infection or disease.

Accidental deaths in this age range are complex and traumatic. Motor vehicle accidents are likely to involve other family members in many instances, unless the child is hit as a pedestrian. The shocking unexpected nature of these deaths, their "killing" aspects all lead to great problems of adjustment which will be heightened if the parent was in any way involved. If the mother or father was driving the car in which the child was killed or, as sometimes happens, backed the car out of the garage over the young child and fatally injured him, guilt and recrimination are overwhelming. Blame from the other parent and family members is also very great. Other very traumatic accident situations occur, such as drowning and burns. While many of these deaths are truly accidental, in others there seems some elements of unconscious or even perhaps conscious parental rejection.

Studies of drowning and near drowning covering 111 Brisbane, Australia, children (Pearn and Nixon 1977*a*, 1977*b*) show that these commonly occurred in the backyard swimming pools of the upper class or the bathtubs of lower-class families. These pools were often inadequately fenced and supervised. Pearn and Nixon indicate that a small group of bath drownings or near drownings could have been deliberate immersions, representing an unsuspected form of child abuse. Deaths were more frequent in large families, perhaps because it was thought older sibs were supervising the child, or because the child was not easily missed in the larger group. They were also more frequent among older parents. Common parent-related factors associated with vulnerability to such deaths included: lack of supervision; a parental "vulnerable period" where the parent switches off, perhaps because of marital disharmony, tiredness, or involvement in other activities; child neglect or nonaccidental injury; and unrealistic disciplinary expectations, for instance, allowing a child under five to supervise and/or discipline a younger sibling.

Burns are another common group of accidental deaths that are traumatic in every sense of the word. Martin, Lawries, and Wilkinson's report (1968) describes some of the types of burns as well as the impact on the family. In many of their cases parental neglect seems obvious, as with young children found alone in a burning house and children with exploding petrol tanks. Clinical experience reinforces the view that a proportion of deaths from childhood burns occurs in chaotic families with parental alcoholism and neglect as common features. Nevertheless, many others do not. Parents often risk or give their own lives in attempts to save children from burning homes or cars or other sorts of fires, and there has been no background of ambivalence or failure of care. Often burn deaths are complicated in several ways. Not only are they shocking, but they seem to touch off some of the worst fantasies of pain and destruction. This is in marked contradistinction to drowning, often rationalized as a peaceful, painless way to die. The child may die at the time of the burns. In such cases the body may be very charred and difficult to recognize. Perhaps the child may live for a period, suspended between life and death. The burns, charring, infection, and resuscitative equipment may make him seem unrecognizable to parents, so that they are often repulsed and terrified, wishing to comfort him yet unable to do so. Parents seen clinically in such situations discuss hesitantly with great shame their horror and repugnance about the child's appearance. Modern resuscitation may mean the child, near death, holds onto life of a kind much longer. The parents are torn between the longing for recovery and the wish for him to die, something they sense as inevitable. The techniques of modern burn care may mean that they, the parents, have little they can do for him and so they feel especially inadequate. The child may seem as though he is no longer theirs but, rather, is claimed and owned by the nursing staff who care for him.

Staff are themselves very distressed by the management of severe burns, so may have little chance of emotionally supporting the parents. Sometimes they mistakenly try to protect them from the sight of the child or involvement with him, or from seeing his body. Wherever possible parents should be allowed and supported to do so. However, in some burn cases, where death is immediate, the body may be burned beyond all recognition. In such instances parental wishes must be respected, but careful discussion may help resolve the issue, allowing the parents to accept the death and the unidentifiable remains as those of their child.

Deaths from malignant disease in childhood involve a different type of stress. There is likely to be a process of gradual adaptation to the reality of the child's illness and fatal prognosis. Although childhood malignancy, especially leukemia, is viewed with abhorrence, nevertheless it is seen as a disease state, not the outcome of personal action. Some parents actively seek to blame some factor in themselves or others, but this usually occurs when there are other sources of guilt, perhaps in ambivalence to the child or over past perceived sins for which the child's illness is seen as a punishment. Malignant disease is seen as untimely in this age group. The child and parent are cheated of life by something that they feel should not have happened. This theme is common to bereavements within the childhood age range, for it is assumed in present-day society that children should not die. Deaths from leukemia create special problems, for this condition, which was previously seen as inevitably fatal may now achieve prolonged remission (perhaps cure?). Parents and children may feel they dare not hope for the child's survival, yet the evidence is clear that he is not dying. Such diseases may lead to an orientation of "living each day as it comes," not investing in the unpredictable future.

Where death occurs from some inherited disorder there may be an extra element to it. There is likely to be a sense of shame—inadequacy at having produced the damaged child—for the "bad," destructive genetic inheritance. Guilty feelings about such disorders in the family are also likely to complicate the anticipatory grief and mourning as well as the subsequent bereavements.

*Experience and Behavior.*    Where the death is sudden, a typical pattern of adult grief and mourning may follow. There will be a large element of shock, however, in accidental deaths, and all these deaths will be perceived as untimely, making them especially difficult for the bereaved to accept. Where the parents do not see the body the death may be even more unreal. Extreme anger about the accident—a hatred of the driver of the car, for example, a desire to hit out and get revenge—may dominate the parents' response. This may be directed toward other agencies or toward the husband or wife. A traumatic neurosis effect is common if the parent was present at the death or in any way involved.

Mr. and Mrs. L were at home when they heard a loud crash. Mrs. L suddenly realized Melissa, her four-year-old, was not playing in the house where she had been a moment earlier. She ran, but said she felt almost paralyzed because she "knew it was her; she was hit." Vividly etched in her memory, replayed in slow motion are the details of the scene as she passed through her front door and out onto the street—the gathering crowd, the blood, the small still body.

This replayed constantly, in repetitive cognitions, with periods of repression over the two years following the death. There was all the helplessness, dread, and panic she felt at that moment—powerless rage at God and the driver. Her life had become disorganized and purposeless. She had not mourned but had become fixed in that time and place, neither having her child nor relinquishing her.

The parents' thoughts are filled with "if only." All the events leading up to the death are gone over, revised. What could have been done differently, actions that might have contributed, omissions, are all sought in these attempts at mastery, and perhaps also allocation of blame. The bereaved parent may become locked into the angry "if only" stage of separation from the dead child. There is yearning for the child, restless searching, helplessness, but no real acceptance. There may be little overt grief, just restless agitated distress. In other instances, some level of acceptance is achieved but only with guilty recriminations, sometimes bordering on the delusional. It is as though such parents recognize a connection between their ambivalence to the child and the death, and seek atonement in their *mea culpa*. For many of these parents the grief becomes pathological and chronic, continuing many years after the death with little abatement. They may be preoccupied with the image and the presence of the lost child, keeping his room untouched, visiting the grave daily, and talking to him.

Mrs. S told of how the only place she "felt all right, whole" after her son of three was run over, was by the grave. She would visit daily, or on alternate days, and leave flowers. She could feel him there with her, and she no longer felt distressed. She would tend the grave, feeling reassured that she was mothering, protecting him. She would tell him she loved him. Her interest in her other children became vague and secondary. Her husband's support enabled her to keep up this ritual, which she said was "all that kept me from going mad."

Where there is the diagnosis of terminal disease, a process of anticipatory grief and mourning follows. Typically the initial reaction is of numbness and unreality. Bozeman, Orbach, and Sutherland (1955) vividly describe the mothers in their study and their reaction to the diagnosis of their child's leukemia. These women found it was impossible to believe that one day their child could be well and the next day, through the diagnosis, dying. All the mothers in the series attempted to deny the implications of the prognosis in this initial period.

When the initial denial is relinquished the parents of children with a fatal disease seem to pass to a new phase. All energy is devoted to attempts to make sure of the diagnosis, to understand the condition, to push for the "best" available treatment. The disease is accepted, as is to some degree its threat, but its prognosis is not yet assimilated emotionally. There is still hope of cure, reversal, miracle. Emotionally the parents still hold to the child, the bonding is intensified, and most of the emotional cathexis is focused on the child as if to hold him back from death. If the child is hospitalized and the parents separated, separation pain may be quite intense, especially so because of this focusing. The parents' thoughts are with the child the whole time. The child's image is strongly held. Powerful healing fantasies develop. There may be magical thinking, prayers, bargaining with God—"Let him live"; "Give him back"—with promises to do this, sacrifice that, or be good in return.

Angry protest may well up in the parents: Why *their* child, why *this* loved child when so many other children are unloved? This may lead to anger with staff, rejection of diagnosis, or sometimes displacement of anger onto the husband or wife, or onto doctors who cannot cure. The doctor's manner in providing the diagnosis and discussion about it contribute to this if he seems unsympathetic to parent needs.

Changes in family dynamics are likely to follow the diagnosis. The family integrity is under threat. The other children may or may not be told. Parents often withhold or modify information they give young children in the early stages, because they do not themselves accept it sufficiently to put it into words. The children sense the threat and consequent distress and build their own fantasies of it. As the child's illness becomes obvious and debilitating, the other children know even if not told of the threat to his life. The sick child and his care become the center of family life. The mother's mothering intensifies toward him, often to the exclusion of the father and others. This may distort family adaptation. Siblings and father may resent their exclusion and may guiltily envy the sick child his abundance of care. Deprivation of love as well as of resources, which have been taken up by the disease, lead to further friction. These issues are best resolved when open communication of feelings is possible in the family, and caring roles can be shared.

As the condition progresses the changes in the child are an inevitable confrontation with the reality of the fatal prognosis. These changes are twofold: the child weakens physically, and the disease marks him. And, psychologically, the child shows an awareness of his failing, sometimes a withdrawal, a recognition that he is dying. As this becomes more obvious, it is threatening to the family. The mother may start a fresh battle to retain hope, to deny. She may demand new treatments, different doctors. She may, in an almost manic way, talk of what he and any other child will do in the future, insisting that all will be well. The parent who has tried to "protect" the sick child by not discussing the seriousness of his illness with him may be forced into further elaborations to explain these negative changes, to deny their meaning. This is painful for the child who may sense that his mother cannot deal with his dying. He may then have to share his loneliness and needs with hospital professionals rather than his family.

Gradually the reality becomes more acknowledged. Treatments are only palliative. Comfort and care are the essentials. The parents' anticipatory mourning for the child may have commenced some time before this, but now it accelerates. There are memories of his earlier childhood—bittersweet; memories of the pregnancy and the birth; cherished fragments of the happy shared times; and regretted fragments of unhappiness and ambivalence. There are times of great sadness over what has been lost, a longing that it should not be so, yet a recognition that it is. The lost futures are also mourned—all the hopes that were held for the child, including the fruition of parental desires. Sadness is the predominant affect: parents weep often and long. There may be guilt too, as they search for some meaning in why *their* child should die. The inevitable ambivalences of parent-child relationship will heighten this. The special ambivalences of the particular relationships at this stage will color feelings, again reinforcing guilt. Not only is the child mourned as a person, but his role and meaning for each family member are mourned too. Within the family unit it may be that only some will be allowed their grief, some will carry the guilt, some will be the "strong" who protect. Communication will have to involve sharing of memories and sadness, the relinquishment of blame, and guilt, a giving up of scapegoat and "strong" roles, to avoid difficulties that would interfere with the ultimate adjustment of the family unit.

Whether the child dies at home, as may be preferable, or in the hospital, it is a time when each of the family will need to have individual opportunities to say good-bye. There will be personal feelings to sort out, special private memories to cherish, love to pass on, and forgiveness to seek. The child usually dies with peace. Then there is peace, even relief for the family in the early moments of acceptance.

The duration of the illness may influence the progress of the anticipatory bereavement. Sometimes parents will mourn the child, relinquishing the most intimate bonds so that they become able to care for the child but are less painfully involved (Chodoff, Friedman, and Hamburg 1964). This gradual detachment over a three to four month period may be their way of coping. For others the grief and mourning will only be intermittent, reflecting the course of exacerbations and remissions in the illness. When the death actually occurs there is still some brief numbness now that it is real. In the days that follow a great emptiness is experienced, for the sick child had been the emotional focus for family functioning. The pain of separation is likely to be very great as interactions with the child had filled so much of the bereaved's life. There seems so little purpose in everyday tasks. For a while the bereaved still thinks of the child as being in the sickroom or the hospital, hears his call, sees his face. There is also a sense of being emotionally drained now that the long process of dying is finished. Often the bereaved feels that she just managed to keep going to meet the child's needs and now has nothing left. For many this is a quiet sad time with further levels of grief and mourning. Anger may appear that this young life was lost in such a futile way, but in many cases it has been worked through before and is less intense. Where bitterness appears early it may indicate the pathological nature of the bereavement. The bereaved must punish the world and herself for all that she has lost in this child. The symbolic losses are very significant in such cases, including narcissistic gratifications and future achievements, for example. There is often an irrational sense of failure as a parent, which brings further feelings of misery with the child's death.

One common theme pervades the mourning for children. The child who has died is usually intensely idealized. The parental memories of him or her are of a perfect, beautiful, brilliant individual against whom all others pale in comparison. The child's real nature is lost. This is a way in which the parent tries to hold onto the child despite his death. Where this splitting leads to comparison, it leads to many problems for the surviving children who seem so imperfect. Because the mourning is thus incomplete it may mean that the bereaved parents, or particularly the mother who is most likely to follow this course, do not free their emotions for ongoing life. Thus hostility and deprivation become common in the family milieu. The system may adjust to a new homeostasis that centers on the idealized memories with overt or covert chronic grief, or, the system may break down.

Through the crisis of prolonged illness and death, or sudden death, the family is likely to need not only one another's support, but also that of the extended family and social network. Friends are needed for tangible practical assistance as well as emotional support (Bozeman, Orbach, and Sutherland 1959). Mothers may be disappointed in their own mothers for their failure to understand and offer emotional assistance. Grief of the grandparents, especially anger and disappointment over the child's illness and death, may contribute to this (Gyulay 1975). The support offered by others may be impaired by their own identification with mother or father. Professional support may be reasonable, although there is much to suggest that professionals find this area a painful one also. The greatest support often comes from sharing with other parents experiencing the same crisis. Such experiences have been found to be very helpful to mothers with leukemic children, children with cancer, and through bereaved parent groups such as "Compassionate Friends," a self-help group for bereaved parents. The fathers' responses are similar to the mothers', but usually less prolonged and intense.

Ruth was thirty-two and her husband Nathan, forty, when Rachel, eight, their only daughter, was drowned in a boating accident. They were holidaying with friends at a lakeside resort. Rachel had joined the friends' children in a junior sailing regatta. Ruth and Nathan were on the hotel terrace for afternoon drinks watching the children's races when a speedboat cut through the small sailing dinghies. Several capsized, including the one manned by Rachel and her friend. Although both girls were good swimmers and had on life jackets, Rachel sank.

Help came rapidly as Ruth and Nathan watched, paralyzed, from the shore. Rachel could not be found. That evening her body was washed ashore. Her life jacket was not on and she had a slight head wound that had possibly knocked her unconscious at the time of the accident. It seemed, as events were reconstructed, that she had not bothered to tie on her life jacket, boasting to her friend that she did not need it, as she was such a good swimmer anyway.

"Ruth was like a mad thing," Nathan said. "She could not contain herself. She screamed. She raged. It seemed as though she blamed the whole world—me too. We could never get that scene from our minds; it played over and over like a cracked record. It all happened so quickly, and yet so slowly. It was all happiness—then this fast boat cut through those kids, cut them up. It was all upheaval—water, sails, kids everywhere. We could see a boat was over: it couldn't be Rachel's. Even if it was it had to be alright; she'd been in spills before. She was a good swimmer and a good little sailor. Everyone, all the other boats, came to help. Then it all seemed to get frantic. We knew something dreadful was wrong. I felt as though I'd been hit; I was going to be sick. There was a great pain in my guts. What could we do. I raced down to get a boat, but I knew it was no good, I could feel it was no good."

Ruth described their relationship with Rachel. "Rachel was everything for me. She was all I'd never been. My own family was not much; I was one of five, and my mother never seemed to have time for me. When she did, all she could do was criticize. I was too fat; my skin was no good; I wasn't bright enough. Nothing about me was ever good enough for her.

"Nat and I had awful trouble having Rachel—we tried so hard. Then when I was pregnant I kept having these bleeds. I spent three months of that pregnancy in bed. The birth was difficult too, and the doctor told me I was very lucky to get her, that I'd be most unlikely to be able to have any more. . . . Well, from the moment we got her home we just doted on her. She was so pretty and so sweet and so good. Everyone loved her. She was so bright at school too—she could have been anything she wanted. I loved her so much. It was as though I poured over her all the love I'd wanted myself and never been able to get. We just gave her everything; we couldn't deny her anything. She was the most precious thing we had.

"I think the thing about her death was that it was so pointless. I am so filled with hate about it. At first I hated Nat, too. We'd had this argument beforehand about letting her go. I hadn't wanted to; he laughed. He said I was overprotective, that she'd never live if she was tied to me like a baby and that I had to let her go sometimes. He said it was safe. Of course it wasn't safe. I blamed him for weeks; maybe I still do in a way. Then I could see that it wasn't just that. I hated the man in the boat. They never punished him as they should have. I still hate the world. They took everything away from me—all that counted. I'll never get over it. Never! Never! I know!"

Grief and mourning are enormously difficult in such cases, for the bereaved does not wish to relinquish the lost relationship when there seems so little hope of replacing it. Therapy with Ruth and Nathan improved matters to some degree, as their anger and longing lessened and they were able to commence their gradual undoing of the bonds. After reaching a plateau they became heavily involved in a service organization fostering children. At a later stage further therapeutic working through was accomplished, although Ruth always retained some core of bitterness about her life.

*Outcomes.* Systematic studies of outcomes for bereavements at this stage are few. Nixon and Pearn (1977) found that families after the drowning or near drowning of a child showed sleep disorders, nightmares, anxiety states, and increased drinking, all sometimes extending over many years. Nineteen percent of these parents received specialist psychiatric treatment following the drowning, whereas none had done so before. Overprotection of remaining children was common, and the siblings of one-third of the fatal cases were significantly affected with sleep disorders and feelings of guilt. Many clinicians have described similar patterns in families following other accidents, and in burn families (Martin, Lawries, and Wilkinson 1968; Martin 1970).

Specific psychiatric disorders have not been defined, although seeking psychiatric care is common. Clinical experience suggests that depression is a frequent symptom, often complicating a severe chronic grief reaction. In their study of families who had lost a child with cystic fibrosis, Kerner, Harvey, and Lewiston (1979) found that almost half of the families showed depression. It is a frequent presentation after motor vehicle accidents, burns, and other accidental deaths, as well as after some deaths from fatal illness. While it might be expected that psychosomatic reactions could appear there is no clear-cut evidence linking such illness to these bereavements.

Relationships are often affected. The family members may become alienated from one another or from a social group. Marital breakdown is frequent; Nixon and Pearn (1977) found it to occur in 24 percent of the families they studied following fatal drowning, and it also occurs among some burn families. This is most likely when marital difficulties existed before the death, and these may in themselves have contributed to it. Sometimes the parents are drawn closer together and their relationship improves with greater intimacy consequent upon the stress faced together. In other instances, the couple is held together by mutual blame. They cannot separate as each cannot bear to carry the guilt of the death but must have another on whom to project it.

Deaths during this childhood period were those most likely to lead to the replacement-child syndrome of Cain and Cain (1964). In their description, the parents grieved but could not relinquish the need for the child. The dead child was enshrined, his image maintained, and then (contrary to their previous plans) they had a new baby on whom they imposed the identity of the dead child. They attempted to shape the child into a very idealized and often unrealistic image of the child who had died. Continual unfavorable comparisons were made between the substitute child and the dead child. The children described in this study were overprotected, yet given clear messages that they would die too. Much hostility was displaced onto these replacement children, almost as though they were responsible for the death. It is not surprising that the children described in this series suffered gross psychopathology. While the replacement-child syndrome described in this clinic study may well occur, it is by no means inevitable. Furthermore, it may not involve a new child, but one of the surviving children may be taken on in the dead child's place.

Other substitute themes that may appear in family dynamics include the "haunted," "bound," or "resurrected" child selected from the survivors. The child may be scapegoated (Tooley 1975). A family that has had some relative homeostasis with a child for each parent (as discussed on p. 267) may go into a stage of disequilibrium when one parent loses his or her child (Rickarby 1976). Anger and envy may eat into family relationships so that they become untenable. Envy of other parents with children may disrupt friendship networks as well.

*Reparative outcomes.* Apart from strengthened family bonds as a consequence of successful crisis resolution, another positive outcome may arise. The pain of the experience, the desire to understand and control it, the wish to make something worthwhile that will continue on after the death may be among the motivating factors that lead to the formation of not only successful selfhelp organizations, such as Compassionate Friends, but also to research foundations such as those to investigate leukemia and childhood cancer, and to political action programs such as those that promote legislation for greater safety measures to protect children from accidents. It is recognized that many overdetermined factors may contribute to the powerful motivation that mobilizes such outcomes. While some may represent vicarious grieving or other processes, they may still have significant healing effects for those involved as well as benefits to the society.

## DEATH OF THE ADOLESCENT

Deaths in younger adolescents are likely to have very similar outcomes to those of the childhood years. Resolution may be complicated, however, because of the heightened ambivalence and struggles for independence that occur at this time. The deaths are often accidental and may be the consequence of premature attempts to be involved with adult pursuits, such as car driving, bike riding, and drinking. There has often been a family conflict in the background. Deaths from illness during adolescence have many of the patterns described for children. All of these deaths seem particularly bitter, since the young person was just stepping onto the threshold of life.

Deaths of older adolescents perhaps reflect most clearly some of the issues for the family. Typically the death occurs in a motor vehicle accident of some kind. It is sudden and unexpected. It frequently occurs on a background of substantial family conflict. Alcohol is often involved. The child is an emotional focus for parental conflict where ambivalence is high; or perhaps is a greatly loved child still living at home, with a role of fulfilling parental hopes. He or she may be out with other young people in a car, or alone on a motorbike, when fatally injured. (Some injuries are not fatal, of course, but may for many reasons become a source of grief, as when there is severe disability.) There has often been an argument beforehand about whether or not the adolescent should go. The whole outing may have been intended as an act of defiance of parental wishes, or simply for the thrill of risk taking. Police officers bring the message of the death. The shocked mother and father may have to identify the body. Sometimes the mother is prevented from seeing it, so that she has an additional problem in accepting the reality and finality of her loss. Grief appears for the mother, but the father is frequently "strong and silent," suppressing his feelings. Maternal grief continues unabated, often for many years. There is great anger: anger at the son for deserting her in this way, though it is usually denied; anger at those involved with the accident; anger at the husband because of the arguments and noninvolvement in the circumstances that lead up to the death. The bereaved feels cheated and rages at the world because all her hopes are lost. She cannot replace this child. She feels she has nothing. Her background may be one of deprivation, so that all her earlier losses are reawakened. She resents her husband because he is there and not the son, and he does not seem to grieve. She is often bitter toward her surviving children, in the early days at least, because they are there and "the most loved one" is not. She may alienate their support. She may take over one of them as an emotional replacement. But nothing assuages the pain. She grieves. She visits the grave. She enshrines his room, his possessions. She hates others who have not lost their children. She turns away his friends because she cannot bear to see them in his place. She hangs onto his memory, idealizing him, bitter toward the world. She will not give up her grief, for she feels she has nothing else. She may continue thus for years, her grief unabated, or eventually and very slowly time may heal to some degree.

This sad picture is not inevitable. Some parents do painfully, yet slowly, resolve such losses. They are more likely to do so if there are other children and the investment in the dead child was not too neurotically overdetermined. The extent of chronic grief as opposed to resolution is unknown, for no systematic studies have been undertaken. However, the follow-up of bereaved parents whose late adolescent children were killed in a major rail disaster confirmed that this group was very severely affected, particularly the mothers (Singh and Raphael 1981).

Alan was seventeen and had been working a year when he finally bought his motorbike. His mother, Mary, was apprehensive about its dangers. She had always been anxious and overprotective toward him. Her relationship with his father was fraught with provocations, alcohol, and verbal and physical violence. She had asked Alan not to go out that night, but his father had abused her and Alan had laughingly said he'd be all right. The night went on and he failed to return. She worried and would not sleep, but kept reasoning to herself that he would be with his mates.

At 3:00 A.M., the police arrived to inform her that "there had been an accident," and they "thought it was her son involved. Did she have a picture of him." Her husband, Wal, finally woke. Identification proved that it was indeed Alan. He had run his bike into a car on the opposite side of the road. Blood alcohol levels were high. Mary wept profusely in the hours and days that followed, bemoaning her fate and the death of her son. Her doctor gave her heavy sedation, but to little avail. Wal took to drinking more, as he felt useless at home and heartbroken in his own way about Alan's death. He was deeply hurt and felt his wife gave him no support but was instead "wallowing in self-pity."

Mary's grief continued unabated until she was referred for psychiatric assessment two years later following an overdose of barbiturates which she had been using excessively over that time. Some specific work promoting mourning by going with her to the grave, going over photos and memories, helped lessen some of the intensity of her grief. She progressed slowly to a baseline of some periods of depression and many sad memories. She did not return to her premorbid level of functioning.

Deaths during adolescence are common. They are often traumatic and on the background of ambivalence. It is likely the bereaved parents are a high-risk group requiring further research assessment and preventive management.

Suicide is an increasingly common cause of death in this age range. It too occurs on a family background high in ambivalence, with open hostility and unresolved dependence. The death itself brings shame, stigma, and guilt. Complicated, maybe pathological, bereavements seem a likely outcome for the survivors. This painful legacy has been described in the case of a younger child (Whitis 1968), and findings are similar in this age group.

DEATH OF THE ADULT CHILD

The older parent who experiences the death of an adult child is likely to be deeply disturbed by it. Such a person is likely to feel that his or her own death would have been far preferable to that of the son or daughter. The parent adjusts, for there has usually been a degree of separation from the adult child already. Nevertheless, grief is intense. The parent may also be expected to take on parenting roles for the child's children at a time when emotional resources seem drained. Despite their own grief many parents do this successfully. There is little known of the patterns of grief and mourning in this group. They seem from clinical experience to follow the usual pattern of shock, separation pain, and mourning. The deaths are difficult to adjust to because they are untimely. Like other deaths they may be harder to resolve if ambivalence and dependence levels were unduly high. One study of parents who had lost sons in the 1969–70 war of attrition in Israel, found that most resolved this loss reasonably well, and that good family relationships and education beforehand facilitated this (Purisman and Maoz 1977).

Sometimes parents in this older age group will be resentful of the child's family who have "taken" him from them. There may be competition for the role of the most bereaved between, for example, the mother of a son and his younger widow, each claiming her loss is the greater. Resentment may arise at the needs of the surviving in-laws, fear of their dependency and that of the grandchildren. Survivor guilt may be another problem faced by these bereaved parents. They feel they should not have survived, fantasize dying instead, yet are glad to be alive and guilty at that feeling.

Helen and Ross, both age fifty, were grief stricken when their daughter Jenny, age twenty-five, died from malignant melanoma. The condition had been rapidly fatal over the six-month period following diagnosis. At that time they moved closer to where Jenny lived with her husband Stan and two young children, girls of five and three. Helen helped care for the children as Jenny's illness progressed, but, as she confessed to Ross, it was all she could do to attend to the children's needs, so great was her distress at her daughter's condition. She constantly thought of Helen and prayed for her cure, although as the weeks progressed she could see this was impossible.

Following Helen's death she and Ross moved in with Stan. There was often friction between them, yet they felt bound to "do the best they could" for the children. Helen loved them but at another level resented the sacrifice she and Ross were now forced to make for them, and, as she kept telling herself, "for Jenny." She was recurrently depressed over the next two years until they moved back to their own home when Stan remarried. Helen felt that it was only then that she and Ross could really "let go" their grief for their daughter. They had "done their duty," but now faced the terrible loss it meant for them.

## Conclusions

Whatever the age, the death of the child is seen as untimely by his parents. They often feel that their care has somehow failed, no matter how loving and adequate it was. In mourning the child the parent will go back to the child's earliest beginnings, his conception. Yet it will be difficult to give the child up. Patterns of chronic grief are common and irrational guilt may prevail. In losing the child the parent loses not only the relationship but a part of the self and a hope for the future. Even when mourned, the child is not forgotten. He is always counted as one of the children. And such a loss may alter, forever, the course of the parents' life and even of the parents' relationship to one another.

As Sanders (1979/80) points out, for adults, the death of a child when compared to the death of a spouse or parent, evokes the highest intensities of bereavement and the widest range of reactions. Sanders's study showed death anxiety to be higher for this group, with despair prominent. Somatic symptoms were multiple. Their lives seemed not to make sense. Sanders suggests that most of the parents "gave the appearance of individuals who have suffered a physical blow [which] left them with no strength or will to fight, hence *totally vulnerable*" (p. 317).

# CHAPTER 7. The Griefs of Growing Old

---

"After all, what can a man expect, when he's getting on in years, when he's not quite up to it anymore?"

*Malcolm, age 64*

"When I did look it was dreadful, red, angry, ugly, destroyed." And later, "Each scar was fading. It was still horrible, but I was getting used to it."

*Brenda, age 48*

"I longed for the days when I was young and fit—when I didn't need to carry anything around with me—just myself. Sometimes I would wonder if it was all worth it. I was just a walking pill factory, that was all."

*Mary, age 65*

"My retirement, well, you know . . . there is a certain sorrow in it."

*Ernie, age 60*

"It's been a good life—not always easy—but I'm satisfied with it."

*Gordon, age 79*

The griefs of growing old begin with the first realization that one cannot do, with ease, something that one had previously been able to accomplish without thought; that one will not, now, achieve the fullness of one's hopes and dreams; that one's life is not limitless, but finite, and the time remaining is not great. Eliot Jacques (1965) describes the mid-life crisis as a time when, about halfway through our lives as we anticipate them, perhaps around our mid-thirties, when we are half our three-score years and ten, we face the inevitability of our own deaths. This, he postulates, leads to an ill-defined crisis state. But the individual may make major changes in his life which are likely to reflect this turning point. He may try to deny the inevitability of his own death by a return to youthful behavior and dress. He may take up a life-style that reflects more his true needs, recognizing his limited time to fulfill these. Creativity changes, Jacques believes, so that it is more the molded, measured production than previously. Before the mid-life crisis, what was created was considered whole and good; it had been created and could not be changed.

The key element of this mid-life crisis, regardless of outcome, is the recognition, emotionally, that one day one will die. It may be that the presence of an older generation, or the longevity of eighty- or ninety-year-old parents, still protects one from that to a degree. It may be that one has faced death closely through serious life-threatening illness or threat of war or disaster. The idea of one's own death is difficult to encompass, perhaps unacceptable to the unconscious, yet some level of recognition that one will die, that one will relinquish one's life, is confronted.

At the time of the mid-life crisis there may be some grief and mourning for growing old. There are sad, perhaps angry, feelings at the realization that one has not fulfilled one's ambitions in relationships or work and now may not be able to do so. There are many thoughts of what has gone before. Changes to new relationships through divorce and remarriage may represent an attempt to accomplish these interpersonal life tasks satisfactorily in the time left. Change to new work may reflect the wish for satisfying achievement in this sphere in the time that remains. Guilts and regrets at "wasted" years may be powerful factors in motivating these new life directions. Sexual activity may also increase or change its form and direction. There may be affairs, experimentation with what was previously considered perverse, promiscuity, or new and passionate loves. Then, gradually the man or woman settles into a pattern for the years that follow: this pattern may be rich and rewarding with fulfillments of his or her real abilities; but sometimes it is a pathological continuation of the denial of death, unrealistic for the body, the age, and the capabilities.

Grief and mourning for the loss of unfulfilled hopes and wishes, with the acceptance of what can realistically be fulfilled, have been described elsewhere (Grayson 1970). The expression of sadness, anger, and guilt, and the gradual going over and giving up of such hopes and wishes will be critical to resolution. If this does not occur, futility and frustration will follow, energies will be directed toward impossible infantile wishes and dreams of youth which lead to the dissatisfaction of an ineffective life-style. This is rather like the woman who dreams of the perfect lover and rejects all real men and real relationships for what is nonattainable. Fantasy is essential and can be rich and stimulating, but if it denies real action and gratification it ultimately leaves the individual's life empty.

The kinds of losses that will be discussed in this chapter may be faced at many different stages of life: during childhood, adolescence, or young adulthood through illness or dying. Sometimes the elderly who are healthy may not meet them with advanced old age. The same processes of bereavement, with grief and mourning, are likely to follow such psychosocial transitions (Parkes 1971) regardless of the age at which they occur. But when they come to the young, there is likely to be more shock and trauma, more intense grief, greater mourning. In the older years they are often anticipated, their inevitability recognized and so prepared for. They bring grief and mourning of a gentler kind.

## Impairment of Function

It may be that from perhaps the late thirties or early forties, the man or woman starts to become aware of lessening efficiency of some normal body functions. The early signs may be subtle, easily attributed to tiredness, but they come progressively as gentle reminders that our bodies someday will die. Physical fitness and health may enable the individual to deny such recognition longer, but there comes a time when it is inevitable. The first gray hairs, the need for reading glasses, a little shortness of breath, a slowness of erection are some of the subtle changes of aging that will mark the beginning of a cumulative series of minor impairments of function. It is worth looking at some of these in detail.

### LOSS OF VISION

Visual loss may be gradual or sudden. There is usually a progressive impairment of visual capacity from the age of forty onward which first manifests itself in the need for glasses for reading or fine work. The individual whose vision has previously been good may be little affected, but as the years progress he may find he cannot do without spectacles for certain essential tasks. He is a little sad, but accepting of this gentle reminder that he will not see forever. Visual impairment in the older years may simply be this, the need for glasses. Severe disorders with much greater visual impairment such as glaucoma and cataracts are likely to produce a greater distress. Although, with the "blindness" that may come with cataracts, the older person has considerable warning, it is still a frightening transition to make. There is anger, sadness for the loss of the easy visual ability, regret, and remembering of things that were seen so clearly and beautifully, accomplished so easily. Medical technology is of great assistance in minimizing many of these visual losses but reinforces the person's dependence on good doctors or good aids. Retinal detachment may threaten sudden blindness, and, as with other losses, the adjustment is more difficult because of the added shock element; the inability to prepare oneself gradually for the altered world. Where the loss is not resolved, it may result in chronic anger, depression, or denial of impairment with failure to readjust to an altered life-style and the need for aids or care. Some people will, for fear of dependence, or because of the narcissistic blow involved, deny to themselves or others the extent of their disability, trying to build life-styles that avoid the use of the lost function.

LOSS OF HEARING

While hearing loss may occur in the younger years as a consequence of disease or occasionally injury, it is of course much more frequent in the elderly. Its onset is gradual and little recognized by the affected person. Denial may reinforce the delay of recognition. Finally, others, especially adult children, may have to confront the person with the severity of this loss of function. Many elderly people resent this bitterly and deny that it has occurred. Even when diagnosis is confirmed and aids provided they may fail to use them, for they have not grieved and mourned the loss. Anger is a common response, as is clinging to the belief that hearing is as adequate as in the past. Anger is projected onto others who provide the aids which "don't work" or who don't "talk up" so that they can be heard. As the hearing impairment worsens there is increased difficulty of communication, with increasing isolation from others leading sometimes to a paranoid misinterpretation of their interactions. Where the loss is mourned, the feelings worked through, the deaf person is able to readjust to his new and different interpersonal world.

LOSS OF SEXUAL FUNCTION

Sexual function is variable in the older years. It may be lost earlier as a consequence of physical or psychological disorder, and grief may be intense as a consequence. Sexuality is so closely bound with the sense of self, the body, and intimacy that it may bring losses in all these areas as well. Regardless of this possibility of loss earlier in life, the older person shows progressive dimunition in sexual function at a rate that will vary with sex, relationship, physiology, health, and social factors. Although reports vary, some common patterns apply (George and Weiler 1981; Sadock, Kaplan, and Freedman 1976). Both men and women show some gradual dimunition of sexual interest, arousal, and activity from their forties or fifties onward. While many of the elderly may maintain satisfactory and stable sexual activity even into their eighties the general trend is one of cessation or decline. Sadock, Kaplan, and Freedman (1976) suggest that aging affects a man's capability more than a woman's. From his thirties on, the man may sense a reduction of sexual interest and urgency. By his late thirties, although his erection is still attained quickly, his refractory period is lengthened. The two physical indices that are most sensitive to aging in men are the frequency of orgasm and the length of the refractory period. Nevertheless, as George and Weiler (1981) point out in their study of aging married couples in the community, 58.2 percent reported a stable pattern of sexual activity, and of these more than half engaged in sexual activity once or twice a week. Once over sixty-five, the level of stable activity was less, with significant numbers going from some activity to no activity. As with earlier studies, both men and women attributed this cessation of sexual activity to the physical condition or attitudes of the male partner. Sadock, Kaplan, and Freedman describe a similar picture, emphasizing that the woman's orgasmic response may continue well beyond her partner's, given favorable circumstances, but for many women, inclination and circumstances may limit the likelihood of such intensity of activity. Studies of the biology of aging show the physical background for such changes in men: falling levels of testosterone, reduction in spermatogenic function, and rising levels of gonadotrophins (Hudson and Baker 1980). In women, menopausal changes lead to a gradual change of ovarian function, from predominantly estrogen to predominantly androgen function, and are associated with alteration in the sensitivity of target organs to sex steroids (Quinn 1980).

The level of female responsiveness may be decreased by vaginal mucosal atrophy with decreased lubrication and less response from vaginal contractile musculature. Obviously partner availability, quality of relationship with partner, opportunity, health and social attitudes, will all be influential. Loss of sexual function may commonly be precipitat-

287

ed by ill health, or surgical trauma, or by a psychological cycle of anxiety built around fear of failure, perhaps following an episode of failure induced by alcohol or tiredness.

The loss, the realization that sexuality does not now and will not again have the joyful thrust and urgency of youthful desire, brings sadness. It is a very clear indication of change, of what must be given up. This sadness, perhaps depression, may further interfere with function that is not irrevocably gone. If the loss of the sexuality of youth can be accepted and mourned many older couples settle into a pattern of altered but satisfying sexual intimacy. The total loss of sexual function is by no means inevitable: some people maintain a stable and fairly active pattern into their eighties and nineties, but these are a minority. Furthermore, for many women the loss occurs with the death of the husband, and there may be few psychologically and socially acceptable avenues open for sexual satisfaction after that time. In many instances the loss of sexual function is complicated by psychological conflicts, so that these factors may interfere with the grief and mourning that occur at relinquishing it. Some may experience bitter regrets that they did not ever enjoy sex to the full, that relationships were limited or futile, that they missed opportunities and did not have the freedom of today's youth. This bitter resolution may manifest itself in a type of chronic grief over sexual experience that is destructive to marital and other relationships.

The loss of sexual ability may be most externally obvious to the couple in the man's erectile failure, leaving him with a greater sense of grief, and perhaps his wife with resentment as well as sadness, for this gratification that will no longer be a source of shared pleasure. The woman's loss may be more experienced by her in the body changes that define her as"old," even "middle aged" and therefore not seen by society as sexually desirable. In early response to these losses either partner may try to increase activity or try to find outside sources of reassurance in other partners or behaviors. This may transiently delay or deny the loss, leaving greater ambivalence to work through when it is eventually faced.

Malcolm and Joan were in their early sixties. Their marriage had been a comfortable one with no major stresses. The children had grown up, left home, and were married. There were young grandchildren. Joan presented to her general practitioner, seeking his advice about her health. She had been "tired, fatigued, feeling her age, getting old," she said. Perhaps she needed a tonic. The doctor carefully explored her history and physical status. After some discussion Joan revealed that she was constantly "irritable" with Malcolm and often "depressed." She could not understand why.

The doctor arranged a joint consultation to clarify marital dynamics. Malcolm said he was fine but concerned about Joan: maybe drinking a bit much, but nothing else. "After all," he said, "what could a man expect?" He was "getting on in years now," even though he didn't really "feel old." The doctor asked the couple what they meant by 'old'. They responded in general terms: "not able to do all the things you used to"; "not quite up to it anymore." The doctor picked up these words and asked about their sexual activity recently. Both were hesitant, slightly embarrassed. Malcom said, "You really don't expect 'oldies' like us to be up to that stuff, do you doctor?" When the doctor noted that many older people were still sexually active and often did have sexual difficulties, the atmosphere between the couple changed. A story of some loss of interest and arousal over two years was given. This had led to Malcolm feeling that his masculinity was failing and to Joan's angry resentment that this part of her life might now be finished forever.

Careful counseling from the doctor allowed them to ventilate their sadness about the loss of their previous "lusty" sexuality, and he provided information about the different physiological responses in the latter years Joan's words were: "I was so sad, I cried a little, and often. It had been such a good part of our lives. It brought us close when we'd had a row. It healed things. It comforted me. At first I was so angry. I thought he was rejecting me—I even thought he had another woman. Then, when he stayed out late drinking I thought he didn't care, didn't want me anymore. I didn't realize it was his loss too and that it could be close and all right in other ways. . . . "But life is different now. We are no longer young. I think we've both come to accept it at last and can make the most of the good things we've still got going for us."

LOSS OF FERTILITY

Linked to the loss of sexual interest, arousal, and activity, but not solely dependent on it, is the loss of fertility. When the capacity to conceive ever again or bear children is lost, a major segment of a person's life is set in the past. This loss is most pronounced for the woman for whom childbearing is the most central function and for whom the loss is distinctively marked by the cessation of menstruation with the menopause. Menopause may involve many perceived losses for her: youth; attractiveness; the regular reminder of her womanhood in menstruation, which may be seen as having revitalizing functions; and loss of childbearing capacity (Raphael 1975b). Or she may have experienced these losses earlier through hysterectomy [(Raphael 1972b)], or medical disorder, or the loss of childbearing through sterilization. Regardless of the cause, this is a significant loss. Even women who seek sterilization to limit their families, who may feel they have more children than they wish, experience some sadness with the acceptance that they can never again bear children. This sense of loss is greater after hysterectomy for there can be no fantasy of reversibility such as that used by the woman who has been sterilized (Barglow et al. 1965). Similarly, menopause brings this same painful regret. Deutsch (1945) highlights the importance of childbearing in the woman's view of herself as woman and suggests that its loss may be felt as the death of part of the self. Grief may be intense where the woman is childless or has not been able to have the family of her dreams (perhaps she wanted one with more children, or a child of a particular sex, or a family constellation reflecting her own family of origin and could not achieve it, or she wanted to make up for a lost pregnancy or child). Anger, sadness, regret, and guilt are felt; depressed feelings or depressive illness may appear. The woman thinks back over her past, especially her pregnancies and her children, and dwells on the dreams that she has lost. She may blame herself or others for what has been lost, or be angry at the world. Those who offer her well-meaning advice telling her she will be free, that she must not think of the past, only the future, may be perceived as nonsupportive, for they interfere with her grief and mourning.

Clinical experience suggests that with good marital relationships, a sense of her own self-worth, and other sources of self-esteem she will resolve this developmental loss satisfactorily. The woman who lacks a satisfactory marriage, whose only source of power and self-worth has come from her children may not do so. The loss of fertility is a marked crisis for the woman; it may not be to the same degree for the man, unless he has been unable to father children and strongly desired to do so. His capacity to fertilize may continue into his aging years, even into his eighties should sexual functioning continue. Where he is in a stable marital relationship he will suffer the loss of the dyad's childbearing years along with his wife, thus sharing her grief and mourning. One of the adjustments that may secondarily fill such needs will come through the adoption of grandparent roles (Gorlitz and Gutmann 1981).

LOSS OF LIMB, BODY PART, OR BODY FUNCTION

The reaction to loss of a limb following amputation has been described by Parkes (1972a; 1975a) who makes a clear comparison between the grief experience of amputees and that of widowhood and the grief following loss of a home. The mean age of his amputee subjects was fifty-four. The amputees showed a bereavement response, with a typical period of numbness followed by restless pining and preoccupation with thoughts of the loss, as well as clear visual image of the lost limb and a sense of its presence. He noted defensive procedures such as a difficulty believing in the loss and the avoidance of reminders. When he compared amputees with widows he found that the grief of the widows was more intense initially but diminished subsequently, while similar features in the amputees persisted unchanged over the next year.

Amputees show the same separation pain as widows in their yearning and longing, and the same anger and urge to search. They may often wish to know the fate of the amputated part, and some may even wish ceremonially to bury it. They hope at least it goes to "science" rather than their fantasies of the hospital rubbish bin or incinerator. The phantom limb may in part represent this powerfully cathected image. In their anger, there may be anger toward the self, or others may be seen to be to blame or otherwise connected with the loss. Gradually, as the part no longer fulfills its real function, the finality of the loss is accepted. The amputee mourns what is lost, remembering its function, its pleasures, and its pains. His emotional energy then becomes free for reinvestment in his new body, his new way of functioning, including his prosthesis. Thus, the loss of body part will lead to grief and mourning for that part, its function, and the whole body image. The loss may be poorly resolved in those with rigid and/or compulsively self-reliant personalities; or where there is prolonged illness leading up to the amputation and severe or life-threatening illness following it; or when others are dependent on the amputee; or where there are other associated losses such as unemployment, retirement, or medical complications with the stump (Parkes 1972a).

The grief for the loss of a body part may be complicated by anger over the need for the surgery and guilt over the role one's own behavior may have had in the condition (for example, smoking, neglect of diet, delay in presentation and hence diagnosis). Anxiety may be high in association with the surgical procedure, the threat to life, the envisaged helplessness, pain, and dependence. Thus this grief is often difficult to resolve. Psychiatric sequelae have been described for many amputees, as in the study by Shukla et al. (1982) who found that depression, crying spells, insomnia, loss of appetite, and suicidal ideas were common.

While Parkes's work (1972a) concentrates on loss of a limb, other forms of "amputations" may lead to the loss of a highly significant body part. Thus the loss of the uterus in hysterectomy may be followed by a period of grief (Raphael 1972*b*). The loss of the breast in mastectomy is a loss to the woman's body image, her views of herself as a woman, and her perception of her attractiveness to others, as well as a threat to her life itself in the malignant diagnosis associated with it. Carcinoma of the breast is a common disease for women, and mastectomy is its usual treatment. There is shock and numbness which is disturbing initially. Yearning and longing for the lost breast and a preoccupation with it and one's body is common. At first the woman dares not look, for she wishes no reminder of the loss. But as time progresses she is inevitably forced to confront this reality. The first time she looks is highly significant for her: the beginning of her acceptance of the finality of the loss and her altered state. She looks hesitantly, looks again, and covers the area. Gradually she comes to accept this as her different body. At first it may be perceived as mutilated, but gradually this perception lessens to allow its incorporation into her sense of self. At first there are feelings of despair and fear that she will be unacceptable to others. She may hide her mutilation from her husband. Her own acceptance will be greatly facilitated by his acceptance of her body, especially by his capacity to see her as a sexually attractive woman again. Prosthesis and mammoplasty may also assist. She may remember in her mourning the uncertainties of the early growth of her breast in adolescence, the pleasures it brought her in sexual arousal, the delight of feeding her babies, the fear and pain with the discovery of a lump. It is part of her self and is mourned as such (Schoenberg and Carr 1970; Maguire 1976; Jamison, Wallace, and Pasnau 1978*a*, 1978*b*).

Brenda was forty-eight when she first noticed the small lump in her breast. She left it for a few days, hoping it would go away, not discussing it with her husband in the hope that she was "imagining" it. After three days her anxiety rose; she told him, saw her doctor, and was referred immediately to the surgeon. His response was serious and urgent. She was hospitalized the next day, and a mastectomy was performed the following day.

"At first I was in a state of shock—it all happened so quickly. I just couldn't really believe it was happening to me, but I went along with it anyway. I was rushed to the hospital. That in itself was terrifying because it made me realize that they really thought it was very serious and I knew my life was in danger. After the operation I was still in a state of shock. That lasted for days. I didn't want to know about my breast at all; I didn't even want to touch it. When the nurse came in to look at the dressing I would turn away. I kept thinking about it all the time. I felt as though it was still there anyway, and I used to think to myself, "Perhaps they didn't really take it away." I wouldn't ask the doctor about it because I didn't want to know—not then anyway. All the time I would think about it—wanting to turn the clock back, longing for it still to be there. I was angry too. Why did it have to happen to me—what did I do to deserve it?

"Then the day came when I had to see it. As each day went past, I really knew it wasn't there and I had to look. I knew it would shock me and I dreaded it, but I had to see the reality for myself. When I did look, it was dreadful, red and angry, ugly, destroyed. I turned away quickly—all I wanted was to forget what I had seen.

"Each day I looked a little bit more. The scar was fading. It was still horrible, but I was getting used to it. At first I was full of despair; I thought I'd never survive. I thought Don would leave me, that he wouldn't be able to stand it. I'd be all alone. Nobody would ever want me again with something like this. I didn't even want the girls to see it. I felt I wasn't a proper woman anymore, that they'd be shocked and would want to back away. It seemed as though I could think of nothing else but that breast. I wondered what they had done with it—whether it had been burnt in the hospital incinerator, or what they did with such things. I thought about how I used to look. I was always so proud of my breasts. Don was proud of me too. He always said I had such a good figure. He used to laugh and say he was a 'breast man'—some of the fellows liked legs and some liked 'bums,' but he liked a 'good pair of tits,' and that was what he had got, with me.

"I remembered the babies too—feeding them, them sucking away. Of course that was all behind me a long time ago, but it was something I thought about then. My feelings were so mixed up—I was ashamed even though I knew it wasn't my fault. I was frightened too. In a way I was glad to be rid of it because it had that cancer in it and maybe I'd have a chance with it gone. I was guilty. I kept wondering if something I had done had caused it. Maybe it was a bump. I wondered if the abortion I'd had had something to do with it. Or if I was too 'sexy' and what Don had done with my breasts had made it happen. Most of all though I was afraid—afraid that I might die, but more afraid that *he* wouldn't want me anymore after I came home from the hospital. I kept it away from him. Then one day he came in on me in the shower. I could see he was shocked—he almost stepped back. But he was very nice to me too. He was all tender and loving. I was glad of that. But more than anything I wanted him to want me as a woman, and that seemed to be the last thing in his mind.

"When I met Anne from the Mastectomy Association I thought her visit would be a waste of time—that the last thing I would want was to get involved with other women who had something like this. She was really helpful. She started to talk about some of the difficulties that women in their group had brought up. I found I couldn't keep quiet. I had to talk. It all poured out—all I felt. She really understood, not like the others who were sympathetic and kind but just couldn't know. She knew. She'd been through it too. Her husband had found it difficult and she had too, but they'd got together again. She really looked good too; and she told me about her other operation and the clothes she wore. I felt as though some great burden had been lifted. I told Don all about her that night, and it seemed to break down the barriers between us too. That was the beginning of the time I started to believe I might have some sort of life again after all."

The outcome of the bereavement for the loss of a body part may be satisfactory, or, like other losses, it may be associated with chronic grief or health impairment. The failures of rehabilitation and chronic pain after limb amputation are examples. Maguire (1976) reports that, for mastectomy patients, depression, anxiety, difficulties with sex and work that were high during the early months, were lower but still significant one year later. After that time, 20 percent of the women were still depressed and 28 percent still had sexual difficulties. Nevertheless 75 percent reached satisfactory levels of psychological adjustment. Jamison, Wallace, and Pashau (1978a, 1978b) found 10 percent of women and their husbands had poor adjustment to mastectomy one year later.

In losses such as those of amputation or mastectomy, there is usually a threat to life through the seriousness of the condition as well as the stress of the surgical procedure. These are additional stresses to deal with which may hamper working through the loss. Social support will also be a key factor as will the acceptability of the altered self to others, especially the partner. These variables will be important in defining outcome.

Amputations of other sexual organs, such as the penis or testes, are likely to be associated with similar complicated processes of grief and mourning in that not only is a body part lost, but also a highly valued part of the self and a highly cathected function is lost as well.

Hysterectomy is a further crisis of loss experienced by many women (Raphael 1972b, 1974a, 1976a). In the early weeks there may be a longing for the situation as it was before. Sadness is common, found in 60 percent of cases in my studies, reflecting perhaps the grief for loss of body part, loss of childbearing capacity, perceived loss of attractiveness, and perceived loss of some core aspect of the feminine self. A significant percentage of women fail to resolve this adequately and go on to experience depression (30 percent), general health impairment (24.7 percent), or deterioration of sexual function (16.5 percent) (Raphael 1976a). Others will resolve the crisis very satisfactorily. Factors affecting outcome include preexisting psychiatric problems such as Briquet's syndrome or depression; the threat to life involved; other stresses present at the time of surgery; and the perception of the social network as supportive; and particularly the acceptability of the altered self to the prime attachment figure, the husband.

Colostomy and ileostomy are procedures where there is loss of an internal body part and altered function to follow. The effects on body image are more through the altered site of bowel action and the appliances than through the internal changes. These procedures too are often associated with life-threatening illness and the stress of the surgical procedure. Acceptability of the altered self to others will be a critical part of the longer term adjustment. Here too the individual needs to grieve for the functions lost, mourn for what must be relinquished before he or she can make the adaptation to the new state. If grief is not expressed and mourning does not occur, readjustment will be delayed.

In all these instances the loss is clear-cut and associated with the additional stresses of threat to life and surgical procedures. Grief is likely. Those affected need support to express this grief—the sadness, anger, guilt, and, particularly, anxieties about the altered self and its acceptability to others. Anxiety about the procedures involved as well as the threat to life may be prominent. With acceptance the individual mourns what he has lost, goes over his feelings and memories about the body part, its functions, its symbolic meaning, its part in his wholeness as a person. He remembers the good pleasurable aspects of the impaired part; the wish to be rid of the badness from the self, the fear of loss of whole body integrity. His mourning includes the search for understanding of the cause of the condition and a knowledge of the changes treatment will bring. There is likely to be guilt over behavior that is imagined to have contributed to the disease, or, in fact, did; regret over what cannot be changed; fear of the changes to come; and dread as to the dependency that may be involved. The support of his prime attachment figures and others to help him with his feelings and his acceptance of his new state will be paramount. Others who have experienced similar losses may offer a special support, a message of survival and coping, that is invaluable.

OTHER LOSSES OF BODY FUNCTION

Some losses of body function are not necessarily associated with loss of body part or replacement procedures. Loss of respiratory function in chronic obstructive-airways disease, loss of mobility in arthritis, loss of cardiovascular function in cardiac disease, loss of movement and sensation in cerebrovascular disease, loss of gastrointestinal function in diseases of the gastrointestinal tract and bowel are all examples. These losses tend to be gradual, and the grief over them not intense, perhaps not even recognized. Irritability, sadness, a difficulty in accepting that one can no longer do many of the things that were previously easy and pleasurable may reflect the reaction to the loss. The patient who seems preoccupied with his body functions, what he can and cannot do, may in some ways be showing his chronic grief and mourning for what he cannot accept. Respiratory, cardiac, and locomotor system impairments are extremely common in elderly populations, as are indigestion and constipation. The losses may be so subtle as to be accepted as an inevitable part of the aging process. When mobility and independence are severely hampered by such conditions then they may produce a greater sense of loss with more intense grief and mourning, as is often seen in stroke patients, leading to difficulties in rehabilitation. If such issues are poorly resolved, the chronically angry, resentful, older person, demandingly dependent, may alienate the support of those whose care he so desperately needs. The functional impairment may be related to factors such as alcohol abuse, and in these cases the patient's guilt and also the resentment of those involved in his care may create further problems in his management.

Loss of function of bowel and bladder deserve special mention as they are frequent concomitants of old age. Prostatic hypertrophy and genitourinary disease may make the man feel he is failing in a basic function. Loss of the capacity to urinate or loss of control over it and over bowel action, is a source of embarrassment and distress as well as grief.

LOSS OF HEALTH AND WELL-BEING

With aging there is often a general impairment of health and well-being. The loss of health makes the individual dependent on systems of medical care, in need of medication, or impaired in one or more areas of his function. It may threaten his independence as well as his financial security. It is not surprising therefore that he may suffer some grief on this account. Nevertheless many older people, especially those who are physically well and have a confidant, have a high level of psychological well-being (Larson 1978). It is very easy to stereotype these losses as inevitably followed by psychological impairment. Although they may bring grief and mourning, many are resolved satisfactorily so that most of the elderly people in the community accept their impairment, its management, and the changes it brings, living with a sense of well-being and satisfaction.

Mary K was sixty-five. She had had, she felt, a "pretty good life." However, these days things were difficult for her.

"It's as though every little bit of me is folding up, giving in. First it was my eyes—needing glasses all the time. Then it was my hearing. I kept missing out on important things in the conversation—I started to feel isolated, as though things weren't getting through to me. In the mornings my joints would ache. I just didn't seem to have the strength I had before, so there were quite a lot of things I couldn't manage. When I came up the stairs I was always just a bit short of breath, and going out to get the shopping would make me very tired. Meals didn't interest me anymore; they seemed to have lost their taste. The doctor said there really wasn't a great deal wrong. I had a little heart trouble, and he gave me pills for that. I had a little arthritis and he gave me pills for that. I was constipated too, and I wasn't sleeping much: he gave me pills for those things as well. Sometimes I felt a bit depressed so he felt I should take some nerve tablets. By the end of it all I thought I would rattle. I had twenty-four tablets I had to take every day. It was not as though I was very sick: I wasn't. I could still do most of the things I wanted to. But just the thought of all those tablets made me feel sick. I longed for the days when I was young and fit—when I didn't need to carry anything around with me—just myself. Sometimes I would wonder if it was all worth it. I was just a walking pill factory, that was all. I suppose the tablets were necessary, maybe they kept me going. All I wanted though was to be without them, for things to be the way they were. I was irritable all the time too—trying to remember if I had taken my tablets or not, having to have them with me wherever I went. Maybe it's just as the doctor says: old age is catching up with me after all. I've got to accept it even if I don't like it. That's the way it is."

## LOSS OF BRAIN FUNCTION

One of the great sadnesses for many people as they age is the loss of cerebral function. This may be quite subtle and first noticed in a little difficulty of memory, a hesitancy and loss of quickness in certain mental functions. It may be quite gross, following cerebral damage with a cerebrovascular accident, or with intracerebral lesion such as tumor. There may be the subtle minimal losses normal with aging, or the progressive destruction of higher cerebral functions with dementia. When damage is such that sufficient cerebral function remains for awareness there is often a great deal of grief. Angry, irritable feelings are common, followed by sadness and depression as the reality and finality of the loss are recognized. The person may go to great lengths in attempting to hide his impairment from himself and others, because of his shame and fear. There are associated anxieties about loss of control, particularly when there is emotional lability and, as well, fear of dependence on others and of their acceptance of his altered self. This loss may be most difficult for those who have highly valued their mental functions and seen these as a key element of the self.

## Loss of Work

In a recent valuable review, Singh (1982) examines the psychological place of work in man's life. Most people consider work in terms of its functional value in providing financial supplies that can be used for other needs or that can be primary sources of satisfaction in themselves. But work has psychological significance as well, serving as a possible source of self-esteem and achievement or as an outlet for creativity. It may be a key element of identity in that the self may be narrowly defined by functions such as the work role. A man (or woman) may identify himself by his trade or profession—he is a plumber, a doctor, a foreman. Women who have not "worked" outside the home often feel a lack of identity when they cannot state themselves in terms of a work role apart from mothering and domestic tasks.

Work may provide a structural system within which the individual can identify himself by a place in a hierarchy or an organization. It may be perceived as a guarantee of an entire system of interpersonal relationships, which may be rewarding or a source of conflict. Work may be a source of activity, an escape from thoughts or circumstances; a source of pleasure and pride; or it may be perceived as a burdensome drudgery that is bitterly resented.

The psychodynamic significance to the individual of work and choice of work has not been systematically studied, which is, as Singh (1982) notes, surprising in that it plays such a central role in human life. The choice of work may well be determined by powerful unconscious forces so that work fills certain inner needs or reflects certain intrapsychic conflicts. An example of this may be seen in the way in which some of those who have experienced deprivation and loss in childhood may be strongly driven to work in caring professions where, by vicarious identification with those for whom they care, they may gain secondhand some of the care of which they feel so deprived. Financial insecurity in the early years may drive some to work situations which ensure a high level of monetary gain, as if to protect against this feared deprivation. Identifications with powerful childhood figures, including aggressors, may be another determining factor.

The hours and style of work rather than the choice may reflect certain personality features. The well-known Type A personality may be driven to overcommitment, long hours, and deadlines. The obsessional may relish careful, detailed application to highly specific tasks. Those with strong narcissistic or histrionic traits may only flourish in work situations that provide drama and narcissistic supplies. Work may be the only place where the individual feels valued and gratified; or it may be the place where he feels inadequate and frustrated. People may long to work, or they may dream only of the freedom from it. It is viewed most ambivalently.

We frequently know the name of a person's occupation but very little about what that kind of work may entail. Yet most people spend an average of eight hours per day, five days per week, forty-eight weeks per year working, perhaps for fifty years of their lives. We consider people have the "right to work," yet we are only just beginning to consider what they may experience if they lose the opportunity or ability to do so.

One recent review (Warr 1982) looks at the psychological meanings of paid employment as well as the psychological impact of unemployment. This author suggests that work itself may be associated with considerable stress so that at any one time 5 percent of employees may suffer from work-related strain severe enough to warrant health care. He then goes on to document the "suffering" of unemployment, noting the psychiatric morbidity found in many groups. The variables he believes may be important in determining outcome include: length of employment; level of work involvement; perception of the self as being on the labor market; occupational status; financial position; family employment; social support network; local levels of unemployment; and hobbies and personal interests. He emphasizes the need for a great deal of further research to clarify many of the psychological aspects of work and lack of work.

As with other losses, the loss of work may be sudden, as when a worker is unexpectedly fired or laid off. Or it may be gradual with careful planned cessation at the expected age. With technological and economic changes some people may have difficulty in ever gaining work in the form of rewarding employment, or they may have difficulty gaining the sort of work they would ideally wish for, or the type of work that would meet intrapsychic needs. These latter are special types of losses and bring a special type of grief—the grief for what one has never had—for unfulfilled wishes.

SUDDEN OR UNANTICIPATED LOSS OF WORK

The sudden, unexpected loss of work through forced unemployment brings a crisis for many individuals. When a person is "sacked" or laid off, his initial response, as in any bereavement, may be one of shock, numbness, and disbelief. If it is known that other similar work is easily available, these feelings may be transient and soon replaced by rationalizations that it was "all for the best anyway" and blame directed toward the employer. Even so there is likely to be some sense of loss: workmates, security, self-esteem. Where the job was valued and cannot be easily replaced, the bereavement response is likely to be much more intense.

The shock period may last several days, perhaps longer, the stunned apathy sometimes merging into depressed, hopeless withdrawal. Feelings of helplessness, shame, and inadequacy are common. Panic-like attacks of anxiety may appear. There is often a sense of unreality, a strong wish for things as they were, a yearning to have the familiar situation back again. All the negative aspects of the work may be temporarily forgotten. It now seems only desirable and is desperately wanted. Action in terms of job seeking may be temporarily paralyzed. The more unexpected the job loss the greater the shock effect and the greater the difficulties of accepting it.

Feelings of helplessness, inadequacy, anxiety, and angry protest may appear. Anger may be directed toward the organization, the employers, the specific person who did the firing, those who should have prevented it, the bosses, God, and the government. Anger may be displaced onto others connected with the loss, onto the family whose needs are reminders of one's inability to provide, or onto the self, held responsible for actual or fantasized failures. With sudden unanticipated deaths the bereaved desperately goes over events that led up to and surrounded the loss. Similarly with this sudden loss, the affected person goes over and talks through what has happened, attempting to make meaning of it and gain mastery and control over the situation, with the ultimate aim of undoing the helplessness and preventing recurrence in the future.

The loss of a job may result in many other losses including financial security; the job's contribution to personal identity; the symbolic meanings of that job for that person; the friendship network of the working place; the sense of achievement and self-esteem that the work provided; and the inner psychological needs met by the nature and style of the work itself. The degree to which each of these factors contributed to the meaning of work for that individual will determine the level of grief experienced at their loss. The degree to which such needs may be satisfactorily met from other available sources or may be readily replaced will also be a factor in the severity of the bereavement response.

The older man or woman who loses a job suddenly or unexpectedly is less likely to be able to find another or to have the motivation or abilities to retrain for a different occupation. The blow of job loss followed by the message from potential employers that they are looking for "someone younger" may make the person feel he is only "fit for the scrap heap." The loss of self-esteem with the firing or layoff may be added to by the humiliation of failures in further job-seeking, so that the individual's view of himself sinks lower and lower.

Bearing in mind the ambivalent relationship many people have with their work, it is likely that anger and guilt will also be prominent: anger at the deprivation and at the self; guilt over anything real or imagined that one did to contribute to the loss; or about the fantasies one had about "doing away with" one's work. With the loss of work, interactions and behaviors that were geared to that end become meaningless. There is no motivation to initiate activities, and behavior may take on the same purposelessness and disorganization found in other bereaved people whose actions have no significance now that their object in gone.

Hope may be difficult to maintain and indeed may be unrealistic in terms of future equivalent employment. For a proportion of people this crisis may resolve itself positively with new satisfying employment opportunities or the successful initiation in business. For many it does not. Chronic despair follows the repeated failures. The longing for the lost work and opportunities may be great yet not mourned and resolved. Often the person is "stuck" with wanting work as he knew it, being unable to relinquish the positive and negative aspects of what it meant to him. Frequently he is blocked in a phase of angry resentment and blame. So often the outcome is one of chronic despair, unresolved loss, and failing self-esteem. The anger he feels toward employers must be held in if he is to seek further work, yet doing this increases his depression.

Chronic grief for the lost work, of a bitter and angry kind, is a possible outcome. Another is depression. Many men affected in this way, especially those without deep and gratifying relationships with their family, pass into a bitter apathetic and chronic depression that is difficult to shift. They "give up." The giving up may also be such as to lead either to disease onset in psychosomatic terms or to alcohol and drug dependence. Clinical experiences suggest this is frequent following unexpected and unwanted loss of job in the older group, but systematic studies are lacking. The increased health care utilization may sometimes result from a worsening of general health, but on other occasions it may represent a motivated assumption of the sick role. Recompensable injury may occur at times when the person suspects he will be laid off so that financial and dependency needs may be met through care for this condition (Hamilton 1977). Relatively minor conditions may lead to great invalidity, again through the unconscious or conscious desire to be cared for by others. Work in the compensation field suggests this is particularly likely for those who started work when young, worked hard and long for others, and who now feel it is "their turn" to be looked after.

Alec S was forty-five. He had been working at the big steel company for thirty years, from the time he left school. In the industrial city in which he lived the steelworks were the chief employers. The city's prosperity was dependent on the company. Working there was part of Alec's identity. His father had worked there before him and had got him his first and only job there when he left school at fifteen. The men at Steel Co. prided themselves on their company and were strongly identified with its prestige and power. Conditions there were tough, but the men prided themselves that only the tough *real* men got and held jobs with such a company. Alec worked in heavy laboring work, as he had no trade but felt that his strength and reliability made him one of the firm's best workers.

His friendship network was composed entirely of his mates from work. They drank together at the end of shifts and went to the races together. His was a world of men. He was fond of his wife May in a general sort of way, but their relationship lacked warmth and intimacy. He had prided himself on the fact that she had never worked, but kept the house—that was "a woman's place." She was a background factor in a life in which the working place and the friendships of it were central. There were two children, a daughter who had married and left home and a son of eighteen who had had trouble getting a job, being unwilling to take on a laboring role like that of his father's at Steel Co.

Alec resented his son's refusal to take up the job he had got for him with the company two years before and the fact that he had worked little since, living on the "dole" (unemployment benefits) and on his parents' goodwill. Alec accused him bitterly of being a "no-good bludger" (Australian phrase of a derogatory nature for a loafer: someone who wants to take it easy and live off others). Alec knew things were bad in business generally but thought that this would have no significance for him. Steel Co. was too big for that: "Why if it went down, the whole country would be on its knees." He was therefore totally unprepared when one month after his forty-fifth birthday, he opened his pay packet to pull out with his money a form from the management stating that they regretted to inform him that he was being given a month's notice and a termination bonus.

His first response was of disbelief—they must have made a mistake. They must have meant this for some other "bloke"—not for him—not with his thirty years of loyalty to the company. He went back to the paymaster: "There must be some mistake," he started to say. The paymaster looked down at his work, shook his head, and called for the next man. Alec still could not believe it. A couple of good friends nearby had also received notices, but several others had not. Their discomfort was obvious. Alec felt they wanted nothing to do with those who had lost their jobs, and that they were turning away from them. They were good "mates" and he felt that already something terrible had come between them all, that there was some great barrier between him and his friends who still had their jobs. He felt hurt and rejected by their change, even at this early time, yet he was still in a state of shock. Somehow their attitude hit home to him that this had really happened—that he had really lost his job.

That day he did not go with his friends to their regular drinking place. Instead he headed for home. May was dismayed by his early arrival and shocked by the way he looked. She asked him what had happened—was he sick? He could hardly answer her at first, but got himself a beer out of the refrigerator and started to spill out the story. Anger welled up in him at the unfairness of it all. He raged at the bosses; at the union for letting the men down; at the government; at the men who had their jobs and had turned away from him. He was near to tears and ashamed of this for he perceived it as a weakness for a man to cry. When May tried to comfort him he pushed her away: "What do you think I am, an old woman or something? I'll show them who's the tough one; I'll have them crawling to me." He feared his need to be cared for, for it reinforced his sense of helplessness and inadequacy in the face of what had happened.

In the weeks that followed after he stopped work his life took on a regular pattern. He would get up late in the morning, "hung over" from heavy drinking the night before. He would dwell constantly on thoughts of work—what he would normally be doing, what his mates would be up to, how they'd go together to the pub when they finished a shift. The tough times he had had at work were forgotten; he lovingly idealized every memory of it from the first days to the recent past. He looked back on his complaints and thought that he had been stupid. He would give anything, anything, to have it back now. He roamed the house restlessly, looked halfheartedly at the job ads; and for the most part ignored May. He threatened his son with violence if he said one word about work or the company. So, the atmosphere was one of anger and tension.

About the tenth day he pulled himself together enough to start seeking a new job. He wasn't used to presenting himself as a supplicant and resented every moment of it. All the jobs had many applicants. Always the response was the same. Yes, he was obviously a good worker, *but* they were looking for someone a "little younger," "trained," "with more experience," and so forth. Each day of failure made him angrier, more humiliated. He would go home to a night's solid drinking. May suggested that she could get a cleaning job at the local hospital "to help out 'til things got better." He abused her violently, saying no woman of his was going to make a fool of him, he'd show her, she wasn't going to shame him by doing something like that.

His chronic anger continued. He had occasional short-lived laboring jobs. His drinking increased. Six months after his job loss, he was hospitalized for medical disorders related to his heavy alcohol intake.

Alec lost not only his job, his source of income, but his identity, his friendship network, his sense of power, and perhaps even his sense of masculinity. He could not grieve these sudden losses; he lost or lacked the social network that might have supported him to do so. Morbidity of this kind is not an inevitable consequence, but it is certainly a possibility for many of those affected. Systematic studies of this are yet to be provided.

ANTICIPATED LOSS OF WORK

*Retirement.*   There is much more research about and understanding of the process of retirement than about sudden job loss. While some individuals who retire do suffer a crisis experience which they may or may not resolve satisfactorily, many make this transition in a careful, measured way without undue psychological upheaval. Modern preretirement planning programs give opportunities for anticipatory guidance to deal with the various adjustment tasks involved. The preretirement worker is assisted into new patterns of interaction: methods of attaining financial security, retirement incomes, or pensions; socialization opportunities and how to use them; and how to develop activities that may prove rewarding in place of work skills. The person who retires in such circumstances may look forward to his freedom from work, filled with hope and enthusiasm for his excitingly planned future. For the more affluent retired group, many commercial resources are available with a whole leisure industry seeking to facilitate the dispersement of retirement capital.

Even in the most positive of situations, however, some loss is involved. For those who cannot look forward to living comfortably in financial security but who are reliant on a small pension the situation is far from glowing. For those whose lives seem without meaning when work was all that gave meaning, the future does not seem positive. For those without family or social network the picture may seem grim.

Losses accompanying retirement may include those of finances, personal identity, meaning to life, and sources of gratification, among others. Even though it is seen as inevitable by most people, retirement may feel very unacceptable at a particular stage in life when, for instance, a person sees himself as "too young" to stop work. While it may in some situations be within the person's control to decide the time of his retirement, in others it is totally decided by administrative systems which cannot accommodate individual needs. More than this, however, is the loss of an everyday, regular, ritualized pattern of behavior from one's life. The retiring person may not realize this until close to the time of retirement or afterward. The comfortable familiarity of the place of work, the people at work, the times of day spent there, the tasks—all contribute to the fabric of the individual's existence. When these are gone there will be, for quite a while, a feeling of great emptiness. The work and all it meant will be gradually mourned. Other things will assume its place in the fabric of life.

Ernie, a coal miner, reflected, "It only hit me last week. I've been looking forward to finishing: no more shifts and that long drive. But I'm going to miss going down that hole. There's something special about it down there. I'll miss my mates too. . . . You know . . . there is a certain sorrow in it."

While shock and disbelief about retirement are infrequent, there are some people who have used exclusive denial, and for whom realization of what retirement means comes only on the first days home from work. The full meaning of the change in their lives "hits" them only then. For most, the early weeks are full, the freedom celebrated, and only as the months progress does the emptiness seem boring, frustrating. The man may find himself thinking constantly of his work, feeling "useless," because he cannot fulfill those tasks he did before. There is often an angry irritable response to the world. It may be difficult to admit the discontent, for others expect the retired person to be enjoying his freedom, especially those who find their current work burdensome and envy him his presumed life of ease.

A difficulty many couples face in retirement is the adjustment to increased time spent together. Often the wife has organized her life around friends and the husband's absences. She may be forced into including him in these activities or in relinquishing them to spend time with him. This adjustment together may take many months. It may not be well resolved by couples whose marriages have had previous strain and for whom such intimacies are untenable.

Many retired people compound the crisis of retirement by a move to a retirement settlement or to some new home or El Dorado. A very great sense of loss is likely to follow such a move. As Fried (1962) points out in his early paper "Grieving for a Lost Home," not only is there the loss of the familiar surroundings to which each person is attached, but also the loss of friendship and neighborhood networks that are likely to be important in crisis resolution. People who make this double step are likely to take some years to align themselves with new friendship groups and to bond to a new dwelling and life-style.

The early stages of retirement for the "young old" who have no major financial or health problems may be quite satisfactory once the loss of work is grieved. A recent paper (Portnoi 1981) suggests that the current literature does not indicate a major negative effect on health, although obviously there may be such an effect in some instances. In a valuable review of the psychiatric aspects of retirement, Wasylenki and McBride (1981) note that retirement is scored in many life-event schedules because of the number of changes it involves. In the Holmes and Rahe scale it is rated ninth in significance, only two points below "being fired at work," whereas Paykel places it many points below being fired, inferring that it is far less distressing. The review suggests that researchers view a range of processes as influencing adjustment to such loss. Activity theory concentrates on the activity side of work and suggests that adjustment will be facilitated by the individual substituting other activities that will give him satisfaction. Disengagement may also be seen as a way the individual adjusts to loss of work in that he may wish to withdraw from high-energy, full-time work to redistribute his declining energies. Accommodation to work loss may be influenced by factors including socialization, psychological resources, social support, income, health, meaning of work, and preparation for retirement.

As far as outcome of retirement in health terms there are many negative stereotypes but little scientific support for most of them (Wasylenki and McBride 1981). Thus there is a common stereotype that retirement has negative effects on physical health, even leading to increased mortality. Studies making such inferences may not have taken into account preretirement health. Poor health may lead to early retirement and higher morbidity and/or mortality. Aging and socioeconomic factors may also not have been accounted for. When these variables are controlled in methodologically careful studies (Tyhurst, Salk, and Kennedy 1957; Ryser and Sheldon 1969; Thompson and Strieb 1958), findings support an *improvement* in health after retirement. There are even fewer studies of the effects of retirement on mental health. Those that exist do not seem to support the assumption that retirement precipitates mental illness in the elderly. Some of these studies citing high rates of psychiatric impairment in the retired associate the impairment with deprivation factors such as lower socioeconomic status and poor physical health, rather than retirement itself. General life satisfaction and well-being have also been investigated postretirement. While most people do not seem to show impairment, some are severely affected by retirement, and their health or health-preserving behavior may be severely affected. There is a need for more systematic studies which control for relevant variables and which commence before retirement occurs. Outcome may be affected by previous health status, income level, preretirement attitudes, socioeconomic status, cultural and national differences, sex, individual personality structures, and life histories. The factors that will define the individual at risk of postretirement morbidity have yet to be systematized. At present, however, the available evidence suggests that most people resolve this type of loss of work satisfactorily.

## Loss of Relationships

*Disengagement.* There is hardly a psychosocial writing on the older years that does not speak of the concept of disengagement. Cumming and Henry (1961) describe disengagement as a process in which many of the relationships between an older person and members of his social group are relinquished and others attenuated so that there is a mutual withdrawal. Consequently there is decreased interaction between the older person and his social group. Brody (1974), reviewing other workers, suggests that psychological disengagement may precede social disengagement; and that disengagement may proceed at different rates and in different patterns for different people, and may have a variety of outcomes. Engagement with the family however is likely to remain substantial into the very late years.

Most workers seem to agree that there may be some process of disengagement for many elderly people. Some also suggest that it may not always be desirable. Whether disengagement is an active process of withdrawal or occurs as a passive consequence of lessened mobility, smaller financial resources for social interactions, ill health and debility interfering with the desire for social interaction, or societal expectations of diminished interaction in the older years, is not known. Regardless of the cause, the older person is often very sad about the lessened social contacts. Loneliness and isolation are frequent complaints. Often there is sorrow over old friends who no longer call, irritable complaints about the young who are "so taken up with their own interests" that they seem to have no time. The eagerness with which company is sought by many who are aging; the enjoyment that the companionship of social groups brings; the reluctance of letting someone leave: all seem to indicate that relationships are needed and wanted. The older person yearns and longs for others. He may be irritable or cross with them, protesting that his needs for relationships are great and that they are not adequately met. There is much time spent in mourning for those that are lost: the aging man or woman goes over and over old relationships that were important and are now gone. Sometimes they are idealized, other times vilified, and yet other times remembered realistically. There is sorrow that they are no more.

*Special losses.* Quite apart from such general losses, there are special losses of importance. The person who reaches sixty-five, seventy, or eighty has survived many others of his own peer group and even a significant number who are younger. He has suffered grief for the deaths of his own parents in most instances, or will soon do so. Friends, perhaps siblings, have died. He has lived through the loss of many intimate relationships by this time, even if those most important to him such as spouse and children are still intact. Each death may remind him of his vulnerability, yet make him glad he has survived. He will have handled these losses in various ways, resolving many satisfactorily, perhaps others less so.

With aging, the world of the the elderly becomes increasingly a world of women. Wasylenki and McBride (1981) suggest that in North America two-thirds of people over seventy-five are women. The average life expectancy of men and women is increasing gradually, but the increase is greatest for women, so that losses leave the older population progressively more female than male. This in itself brings a sadness of deprivation of relationships with the opposite sex.

*The "empty nest" syndrome.* Before even reaching the older years a couple may face the first loss of a child leaving home. The postparental transition to the "empty nest" when children leave is now a most frequent family development among those in the middle-age range. There is a loss of a clearly defined role when the children leave which may have marked repercussions for the mother, and perhaps to a lesser degree for the father (Roberts and Lewis 1981). The degree to which the loss is expected or unexpected, timely or untimely, and the ambivalence and/or dependence of the relationships with the child or children will be factors influencing outcome. Roberts and Lewis (1981) quote numerous studies documenting the sense of loss that many women experience, particularly when their identity has centered on mothering (Spence and Lonner 1971). Similarly fathers may experience a loss when they perceive their roles in nurturing their children and wives as no longer necessary (Lewis, Freeman, and Roberts 1979; Lewis and Roberts 1979). Roberts and Lewis (1981) suggest that the loss may be poorly resolved for some individuals or couples, leading to psychosocial morbidity. Increased divorce rates may reflect a failure to resolve such a crisis. Alcoholism in women has been described in clinical studies (Curlee 1969). Depression is said to be common, but since most studies are on clinical populations they are difficult to generalize from (Powell 1977; Oliver 1977). Other studies can find no clear correlation between the empty nest and the onset of psychiatric disorder. Nevertheless, there will be a period of grief for many mothers and fathers when the children leave home. Those parents with role transition difficulties, lack of other roles, and ambivalent conflicts with the children, or those for whom the loss is considered untimely or associated with other crises, or for whom support is lacking (for example, through divorce or widowhood) are the ones least likely to resolve the bereavement satisfactorily and therefore are more at risk of subsequent morbidity.

*Death of the parent.* In adult life the death of a parent has previously been viewed as something that should be accepted, a source of grief but not of difficulty. The valuable work of Horowitz et al. (1981) shows how stressful the bereavements following such deaths may be for many adults. They found that the death of a parent was "a serious life event leading to measurable symptomatic distress" in many persons, including those who did not seek therapy. Those who sought treatment in their study tended to experience many more intense symptoms and adjustment difficulties than those who did not. While both the bereaved who sought treatment and those who did not felt sad, symptoms were more prevalent in the patient group. The patient group tended to cite more negative life events both before and after the death, such as the failures of relationships with friends and lovers, car accidents, and work difficulties. While both groups were actively mourning the lost relationship, this seemed much more complex for the patient subjects who seemed to experience many more negative self-images as a consequence. When the patients had turned to others, particularly primary attachment figures, for support with their distress and working through the loss, the intensity of their need often proved too much for their social network, with the consequence that primary and other relationships were disrupted, producing further stress and difficulty in working through the loss. On the other hand those who were coping better, the control group, were able to use their social supports more positively. Whether the death was anticipated or not did not prove a significant factor in this study. Horowitz and his group (1981) concluded that, in terms of global adjustment and depression, the patient group suffered significantly more illness than the control group, often with a stress-response syndrome, and required care. Within these groups, younger female subjects and the unmarried were more at risk, perhaps suggesting that they may still have been in some intense "partnership" relationship with the dead parent, as suggested in chapter 5.

Other workers have also suggested the possibility of pathology after the death of a parent in adult life. Suicidal ideation and attempts, depressive morbidity (Birtchnell 1975), stress-response syndrome, and identifications related to positive and negative aspects of the lost parent (Malinak, Hoyt, and Patterson 1979) have been described.

GRIEF FOR THE YOUNG-OLD

The "young-old" in the age range of about sixty to seventy-five may have a fuller world of relationships than the old-old (over age seventy-five). They may still have parents and may be actively involved in "parenting" them. This may bring conflicts with siblings or with a spouse which can complicate these relationships as well as those with the elderly parent. The relationship with the elderly parent may often be fraught with resentment over dependency and other ambivalence. The loss of the parent may therefore bring relief but may be complex to resolve, often leaving residual guilts. Deaths of siblings may revive old rivalries. The untimely deaths of adult children lead to a painful bereavement. The adjustment to such losses is likely to be influenced by the same core variables as other bereavements: to what degree is the loss sudden or unexpected; how ambivalent is the relationship; what is the quality of support available to facilitate grief and mourning; and what other stresses or crises may interfere with adaptation? The elderly person in current Western society will have grown up in a society which frowned on the expression of emotion during grief and which also encouraged denial. This person may be afraid of grieving openly and hence may be blocked from channels of resolution. The disengagement from the social network may mean there are few opportunities for support. The loss of those with whom memories of the dead can be meaningfully shared may inhibit the mourning review of the relationship. Illness and/or economic difficulty may produce further stresses. And there may be many losses occurring over a relatively short time span. Thus, because of such variables, many of these losses may be inadequately resolved.

BEREAVEMENT IN THE ELDERLY

A systematic study of bereavement in the elderly has been carried out by Weiner et al. (1975) looking at responses to the death of a close family member and the effectiveness of psychotherapeutic type treatments for those bereaved. They showed increased health care utilization by the bereaved, especially by the fifth and eighth months after the bereavement. There was a worsening of health for those whose health had previously been bad, and an increased use of tranquilizers and antidepressants. They did not find an increase in major hospitalization, psychiatric decompensation, or deaths in the fifteen months following the loss. Services to help with their grief seemed very acceptable to this group. The patterns of bereavement—namely, feelings of emptiness, sad and happy memories of the deceased, crying spells, fears, anger, loneliness, discomfort—were very similar to those described by other workers in the bereavement field.

Another pattern of loss that sometimes occurs in the older age group is a severe bereavement following the death of a pet. This is most likely to happen when the pet somehow symbolizes (or is) a primary attachment figure. Sometimes a person who has failed to resolve a previous loss may transfer attachment needs to a pet, which becomes a replacement, or link, to the dead person. Or for the very isolated and lonely elderly person, the pet may be the chief source and receptacle of nondemanding affection. Whatever the cause, the death of the pet may lead to grief and mourning requiring just as much support and understanding as other more obvious losses.

Katherine White was sixty-two when she presented with severe and chronic complaints of depression. She and her husband had recently moved into a retirement village. Neither could understand why she felt so bad when they now had "everything they had ever planned for and wanted."

Careful history taking revealed the following series of losses. Two years earlier Mrs. White had left the retail store in which she had worked for twenty years, a job she had taken to help her cope with her depression at the time the children left home. She missed the friendly atmosphere and the customers "dreadfully," yet would not tell her husband about this because she felt he would be disappointed in her since he had been so excited about their planned time together in retirement.

Eighteen months prior to presentation her best friend had died from cancer. This had been a "dreadful shock" to her because the illness had been a short one, and she, this friend, and the friend's husband, had intended to spend much time together after retirement.

Twelve months prior to presentation her younger sister died from a heart attack. The two had "never been close," because Mrs. White had felt that her sister had been spoiled by her parents. Nevertheless the death was a "great shock." She felt guilty and depressed for a while, but "pulled herself together" as she had to take over the care of her aging mother who had taken her sister's death very badly. She resented this burden, feeling it was all her sister's fault and that it was most unfair she should have to care for her mother when the latter had so obviously favored her sister. Her mother died nine months prior to presentation. Mrs. White was relieved, but guilty that she should feel that way. She showed no grief at that time.

Six months prior to presentation, she and her husband had moved to the new retirement unit that had just been completed. She felt very sad at leaving her own old home which she had treasured and cared for since early in their marriage. The new unit was "very beautiful" and she felt she could not complain. She missed her old home and thought of it constantly. She missed the chats with neighbors and the friendly people in the corner store. The new neighborhood seemed full of strangers, raw and brash. She found she was having increasing difficulty sleeping and that her days were filled with depression and despair. Her depression had no "biological" features.

It is easy to see all the hallmarks of unresolved loss in this history—a history that is not atypical in the older years. Psychotherapy geared to gradual working through of some of these losses and promoting social support helped lessen the depression over the next three months, and by two years Mrs. White was reasonably happy in her new environment, although still subject to some bouts of "misery."

## Death of a Spouse

While the general pattern of bereavement following the death of a spouse, as described in chapter 5, may be the same as for a younger person, there are specific considerations that complicate grief and mourning for the elderly.

The older person has usually spent a long, long time with the marital partner. There is a comfortable relationship in which the day-to-day ritual is regular and secure. Each knows the other very well; knows "all his little ways." Outside worlds are less cathected. Work has been relinquished. Socialization is diminished. There is a focusing on family life and the things of importance to the couple, on children and grandchildren. Where there is ill health, there may be much mutual dependence: the partner may be needed for the care he or she can give as well as for the personal communication. The partner may be the only really close relationship that is left, the only remaining source of physical affection, and the only one who sees value and worth in the individual. The need for the partner may be very great even when there has been long-term ambivalence. The likelihood of replacing him should he be lost is very small. (Cleveland and Giantureo [1976] suggest that, of widows aged over sixty-five, fewer than 1 percent will remarry.)

The death of a spouse at this time is usually much more anticipated than in younger conjugal relationships. Death may be rehearsed as the couple talks about what each would do if the other "goes first." Quite frequently there is a progressive failure of health or obvious serious illness. Women in the older years anticipate widowhood and may carry out some of the psychological working through the bereavement beforehand. Nevertheless, when the death does occur, there is still a sense of shock and disbelief. The bereaved feels very alone. Anger and irritability are prominent. Helplessness may be very great, especially if the bereaved spouse feels that he or she will not survive without the one who died. The threat to physical survival seems much greater for some of the very old in such circumstances, as though indeed they will not survive. Women often see themselves as surviving better than men, for they believe they will somehow be able to carry on the basic survival tasks of eating and keeping the house in ways that men may not.

The grief may seem diffuse, with little focus. The widow seems to show weeping, agitation and care-eliciting behavior. The widower may show angry withdrawal. Initially, both are more likely to exclaim, "What will I do without him (or her)?" than to express yearning for the spouse's return. Underneath this helpless distress is an intense longing for things to be as they were and a great fear of the future. If there was prolonged illness and suffering, these emotions may be tinged with relief. Hallucinatory experiences are frequent, so great is the wish for the dead person to return. The elderly bereaved cling to this image and may derive great comfort from it.

As the reality of loss is gradually accepted, some mourning for the lost relationship may commence. But it is in this area more than any other that there can be a marked difference from the younger conjugally bereaved. The younger person has a whole future of reality ahead to force him or her toward a surrender of the relationship with the dead person who will not share that future. The older the person is when the spouse dies, the less the future he or she perceives. There are fewer years left, and thus so much less motivation to suffer the pain of the mourning process and relinquish the spouse. There is a tendency, secretly or publicly, to continue the relationship, to hold to it in fantasy or in behavior, because the pain cannot be borne and the bereaved sees no future anyway without the dead partner.

Thus the older widow or widower will continue a style of life that may be strongly governed by what the spouse would have done or wished. There may be private conversations with him; he may be asked for guidance. Moss and Moss (1979) have sensitively outlined the vital role this "image" of the dead spouse plays in the life of elderly widows and widowers, including the effects it may have on remarriage. They note too how this tie to the image may be reinforced by personal and social expectations, by loyalty, and/or by the expectations of children. The widow(er) holds on for the few years left, living on together with the lost person, maybe cherishing this image while awaiting reunion in some form of afterlife. There may be some expression of grief, some pain at separation, irritability, anxiety, and helplessness. There may be some sadness as parts of the relationship are reviewed. In the young-old the relationship may be in part given up, but in the very old it is likely to be cherished and retained, and in so doing, grief and mourning are partly denied.

The helplessness of the older bereaved person may be frightening to others who fear they will have to meet long-term dependency needs for this person now the spouse has gone. In addition to these needs the bereaved often may express marked hostility toward those who offer help, especially when they are of the same sex as the deceased. These factors may continue to alienate the very support the older bereaved person needs at such a time.

Many of the older bereaved may not show their grief directly, but rather through an impairment in their physical health. The general or specific health impairment may follow stress effects of the bereavement or represent increased care-seeking behavior. Social functioning may deteriorate too as the person seems less able to manage alone, and poverty is common (Pihlblad, Adams, and Rosencranz 1972). The increased mortality rates for older widowers in the first six months after the death of the spouse have been documented by Parkes, Benjamin, and Fitzgerald (1969). Clinical observations suggest that some of the bereaved elderly just give up and die. Depression has been said to be common. The studies from Clayton's group (Clayton, Halikas, and Maurice 1972) describe a "depressive symptom complex" rather than a significant morbidity in terms of other depressive illness. Shulman (1978) notes the higher risks of suicide and parasuicide in old age, highlighting the role of a recent bereavement in increasing the risk.

One of the few studies of conjugal bereavement among the elderly (those over sixty-five) has been carried out by New Zealand researchers Richards and McCallum (1979). They interviewed one hundred bereaved spouses in their own homes six months after the deaths. These showed many symptoms, and almost 30 percent were depressed by generally agreed criteria. Depression did not increase with age and tended to be less in those who had had warning of the death and who had had an opportunity to discuss it with the spouse beforehand. Thirty-two percent felt their health was poor, and, when depression was included, the authors found that the incidence of illness in this age group in the six months after bereavement was closer to 40 percent. Unfortunately the authors had no matched control group for comparison and were not really able to state the degree to which their sample was representative of the general group of aged bereaved. However, one of their interesting findings in terms of factors correlating with depression was that when the bereaved individual perceived himself as having regular reliable family support he was significantly less likely to become depressed. This, they felt, could be used to define people at risk and provide necessary services for them, perhaps through the general practitioner whom the bereaved often perceived as helpful at this stage. On the whole this study supports the observation of many that bereavement has an impact on physical health in this age group.

Few of the elderly bereaved remarry (25 percent of widowers and only 1 percent of widows in a study by Moss and Moss 1979), despite the findings that "remarriage seems to have positive effects on support systems and life evaluation of former widows" (Lopata 1979, p. 170). Social sanctions and the strength of the bond to the dead spouse seem to influence that pattern.

Following a period of bereavement, the elderly widow or widower may move, perhaps to be nearer to children from whom she or he seeks support, or into some society of the widowed, perhaps a retirement complex. The reintegration into a social group may be easy or difficult. One powerful determinant will be cultural and social attitudes toward the role of and importance of the older person: whether he is seen as the repository of tribal wisdom and culture, as with the Pintjantjatjana Australian aborigines (Hope 1981), or as a burden to be tolerated as in many Western societies. The elderly may lack status and resources, or they may be supported and valued by others. Ultimately such factors may be critical to the longer term adjustments to a greater degree than the bereavement itself.

Mick and Joan had been married fifty years. Their large family had gathered from around the country to celebrate the occasion and had departed to their widely scattered homes. Mick was seventy-five and Joan sixty-nine. The relationship had been a fiery one in the early days, with Mick drinking a bit too much and "playing up" with the girls. Joan had nearly left him once. Then in their middle years the relationship seemed to settle into a reasonably happy and comfortable one for both. After Mick had retired, they had settled down to interests in their home, interspersed with frequent holidays with the children and grandchildren. As the years went on they talked a little about dying: what each would do if the other "went first." There was a covert understanding between them, never really verbalized, that Mick, being the older and a man, would probably "go" first, and that this would be just as well as he had never done much to look after himself, had never even "got himself a meal." Joan had always met his every need. Both had a degree of cardiac failure, but it was well controlled with medication. Their days were spent together in quiet reverie or in the simple and basic day-to-day tasks of family life.

They were sitting together on the veranda one day when Joan suddenly collapsed. Mick tried to resuscitate her and called the neighbors to help. She died from myocardial infarction on the way to the hospital.

At first Mick was totally stunned. This was not what they had expected, what he had anticipated. Sure, he realized, they were both "not chickens" any longer, but he was older than she was. He kept thinking it couldn't be true. The days that followed were like a nightmare. The children came and were busy. They organized everything, even the funeral. He sat around in a state of shock, the tears pouring down his face from time to time. He kept feeling that she must come back. The house was full with *their* children, *their* friends, visitors—all full of advice and goodwill but far away from him and his feelings.

After the funeral the children stayed for a week. They organized friends to come in and visit him and then flew back to their respective homes. They seemed angry with him, he thought, as though they thought he should have died, not their mother. They made it quite clear what they expected him to do, and that was to cope. They told him to ring them if he needed anything but gave quite clear messages that they thought he should not.

When they left, the house was empty, "like a tomb," he said. He wandered from room to room thinking of Joan, longing for her presence, the comfort of her teasing and bustling. His bed was empty at night. Her comfortable bulk and warmth were gone. Nothing consoled him as he wandered the house. Sometimes he would think he heard her calling his name. Sometimes he would smell her smell. He cried to himself a lot but covered this up when anyone came. The neighbors brought him a meal each night, and after a while friends came to jostle him, jovially telling him it was time he got out. He resisted this for a while, but eventually complied "just to get a bit of peace." He enjoyed nothing, but he kept on going. All his thoughts were of Joan.

He found that it helped him to pretend to himself she was still there—busy in the kitchen, pottering in that bit of garden of hers, coming in the gate from her shopping. He would "talk" to her in the evenings just as he used to. This comforted him even more. He felt in his mind that this was strange, so he kept it as his secret. It kept him going for all the things others expected from him, so he could not give it up. He would say to himself, and to her, as he went to bed in the evening, "Not long now girl—I'll be joining you soon—just hang on there—childhood sweethearts like us—soon we'll be together." He died quietly in his sleep nine months after Joan's death.

## Death of the Self

As life draws to its end, the aging person faces another death. He experiences even more clearly the knowledge of his own death—the death of the "self." There may be many partial deaths along the way. The loss of sexuality may seem the death of a vital part of the self. The failing of the brain with its dementing processes is another partial death of self that may have to be endured. Just as there was some confrontation with the finitude of life in the mid-life period, there is now an ever-increasing reinforcement of this with the many partial losses, with the deaths of others, and with the passage of years.

This sense of personal finitude leads the older person to an increasing preoccupation with death. Death starts to be thought of personally: how it will come? when will it come? Sometimes there are fears, a wish to turn away from it, and a shutting out and denial of reminders. At other times there is a desperate wish to talk about it, to share the fears, to find out more about the unknown. There is a growing perception of the aloneness of death. There is a wish for it to come quietly, silently, without pain, a wish to meet it with courage. Sometimes it is looked for as a friend: "I am ready for death," says the old man. The processes leading up to this preparedness for death in old age are really those of anticipatory grief. The premonitory mourning processes that those with terminal illness work through have been most sensitively described by Elisabeth Kübler-Ross (1969) and Knight Aldrich (1963).

Those in the older years who are not so clearly suffering from terminal disease but who are rather approaching death through age tend to show a gentler extended grief and mourning. Subtly, the awareness that one's life is not infinite is personally confronted. In an interesting study and review of this concept, Marshall (1975) suggests that many individuals perform a "crude form of calculus" in estimating their own life expectancy. This involves evaluating such variables as the age to which one's family members, especially parents (but also siblings), lived; one's own age; one's health; and one's social environment. Marshall's study found that the older the individual is, the less time he believes he has left. If he is younger than the age at which both of his parents died he may perceive he has more time left than he would believe if he had exceeded their ages. If he has outlived all or most of his own siblings, he becomes more aware that his own life is nearing its end. If his health is bad he may feel he has not long to live, unless he has already lived a long time with bad health and feels he can survive it. If many of his friends have died, or he is in a retirement center where deaths are frequent, he may feel his own death cannot be far away. If he has recently lost someone close to him, such as his spouse, he may become acutely aware of his own finitude.

The influence of this concept on the older person's feelings and behaviors may take many forms. It may, for instance, as Marshall believes, have an influence leading the individual to focus more on the self. Also reminiscing is a frequent finding, especially in the very old. It may represent a going over, review, making meaning of, and sorting through the experiences of the past in all their good and bad aspects. In truth it has much in common with the mourning process and, as such, represents at least in part a mourning for the life, the self, that will be relinquished with the death. As in other mourning processes, memories of old losses may appear. Often the past is idealized, then made ego-syntonic, and this too is like many bereavement processes. Marshall's work suggests that these past memories that are reviewed may be more important for those who have five to ten years left to live than for those with fewer than five years. It may be that the more extensive life review enables the giving up of the past so that the self moves to some stage of acceptance and preparedness for personal death. This varies enormously from person to person, however. For life is very sweet and not easily relinquished, even for those to whom it has brought much pain.

The concept of the life review in old age is an important one, suggested initially by Butler (1963). It may be equated with a process of anticipatory mourning for the elderly. It may involve a review of many of their memories and all the powerful feelings attached to them. This is the time, as Marshall notes, where the individual is actively involved in bringing past conflicts to consciousness, in reviewing them, and coming to terms with his past life. This personalized reminiscence is most likely in the phase of "middle awareness" of finitude. At this time a person is most likely to be able to express his dissatisfactions with his life. It may be that by sharing his reminiscence with others, he comes to view his past as appropriate and acceptable.

Thus it may be that through this mourning for the lost selves of the past, in the reminiscence of the life review, the individual resolves this final crisis of his development; that he comes to what E. H. Erikson (1959) calls the sense of "ego integrity," rather than the pain of personal despair. As Brody (1974) suggests, "It involves in part 'acceptance of one's one and only life cycle,' and comes only to him 'who in some way has taken care of things and people.' One who successfully masters this stage has a 'new, a different love of their parents.'" In Erickson's words (1959), "The lack or loss of this accrued ego integration is signified by fear of death. . . . Despair indicates a sense that the time is now too short for an attempt to start life anew and try out alternate roads to integrity." One could "paraphrase the relation to adult integrity and infantile trust by saying that healthy children will not fear life if their elders have integrity enough not to fear death" (pp. 28–29). Thus the older person accepts this final loss: the loss of the self in his own death.

Gordon R was seventy-nine. His health had been progressively failing over a number of years. There was a cardiac condition, kidney disease, and some arthritis. He had had a number of hospitalizations and was getting progressively weaker. He sat quietly on the veranda three weeks before his death talking to his son-in-law with whom he had a warm and mutually respectful relationship.

"You know, when I look back over my life and think of how it's gone, I feel pleased with it. Sure, there were things I would have liked to do differently, better. I always wished I had a chance to be a pilot—to fly—but that wasn't to be. I often used to think I should have taken the opportunity to be in my own business, but it didn't work out that way. The things that really count in my life—well I have what I wanted and I made the right choices.

"I've loved her always. She was my girl from the beginning, and I love her now. She's been the best wife a man could have. We went through some really bad times, when the children were sick, especially all that illness with Jim, but she came out on top. The doctor said she was a wonderful woman the way she handled it and he was right.

"And the things I haven't been able to do myself, well, that doesn't matter. When I look at my kids I feel really proud. They've done so well—even Jim who was so sick for so long. They're part of me and I'm proud of them. They're going on. It's been a good life—not always easy—but I'm satisfied with it."

# CHAPTER 8. Death and Disaster

"We lost so many things that were part of us. My wedding dress, Alan's trophies, Martha's old teddy bear. I used to cry for those little things night after night, them and all we had lost."

*Susan J*

"She was such a beautiful city. She had looked her best that Christmas eve. It was almost as though she'd been raped."

*Jack L*

"There lay all those bodies, crushed and neat—like sardines in a can—or prawns in a pizza. I'll remember all those dead as long as I live."

*Onlooker at the disaster site, Granville, 1977*

"Then in all this death was a voice, a girl's voice. She said, 'I'm alive! I'm alive, here!' and I could see her face and she smiled."

*Rescue worker at Granville*

Death may come peacefully, at the end of a good life. It may also come awesomely, perhaps violently, in the course of natural or man-made disaster. Disaster may be personal, striking only a small number of people, even just one family. Or it may be widespread involving the community or the nation. Disasters may come suddenly, with little warning, through the turbulent forces of nature or the failing of man-made devices. Or they may come gradually, growing to massive proportions and destructiveness, almost before the community is aware and can recognize their disastrous nature. Famine is a natural disaster of this type and pollution perhaps a man-made one. The greatest of disasters may, of course, be the disaster of war, for it is both acute and violent, chronic and debilitating. It is a disaster of human aggression on a massive scale. Other smaller scale disasters of this kind, such as civilian violence, riots, and terrorism may also have their toll, but they cannot match the destructiveness and inhumanity of war.

Disaster symbolizes many things to people (Raphael 1975c, 1979/80; Kinston and Rosser 1974). The powerful forces involved, the massive nature of many disasters, and the physical realities of life-threatening circumstances, may bring individuals into direct personal encounter with death. Disaster also symbolizes death. It may evoke death fantasies in those who view it or who read of it. It may provoke death related anxieties and defenses against them. The powerful nature of this interest in death, and wish to explore and master it, is attested to by the enormous popularity of disaster literature, films, and other media productions.

Disaster also threatens and frequently brings massive destruction of man-made edifices and even of natural formations. The destruction may occur violently. It fulfills the most primitive of destructive fantasies and reawakens the most primitive fears. Those affected by the disaster may be called upon to master such stresses. Many others less directly affected may unconsciously indulge their destructive fantasies before reconstituting their defenses of denial and repression.

Disaster may bring many deaths and many losses. The numbers of the bereaved are then very great. Their grief and mourning may be intense. There may be many other losses for them as well, such as loss of home and treasured possessions, loss of community, and loss of security in the world as it was known. All these losses must be grieved and mourned. Not only may there be the acute stresses of such losses, but also deprivations may continue for a long time afterward, acting as a chronic stressor.

Survival themes are common in association with disasters. Those who did not die are elated that they have met with death and defeated it. Yet they may also feel guilt, equating their safety to another's demise. The theme of survival may alter the survivors' subsequent lifestyles in positive or negative ways.

Disasters are not forgotten. They stay in the minds of those involved and may do so for a long, long time. They become a significant reference point around which other experiences are organized.

It is worthwhile to consider several different types of disaster; the death, destruction, and loss they involve; and how those affected come to cope with the trauma, grieve, and mourn.

## Natural Disasters

Common causes of natural disaster include hurricanes, tornados, and cyclones; earthquakes; erupting volcanoes; floods and tidal surges; and bush and forest fires. These represent all the violence of powerful natural forces, unleashed and uncontrollable. They reinforce man's frailty and impotence, his insignificance in the face of nature. Also, they throw in question the whole framework of his physical environment, which he may have been accustomed to view as secure and stable. While man-made disasters are seen as a consequence of man's negligence or failure, these disasters are seen as beyond the control of man and are very often interpreted as acts of God. Thus the causes have been seen, from the earliest times, as representing the gods deciding man's fate, punishing man, reminding him of his proper humility in the face of their power. Although these myths are not widely acknowledged in "civilized" and scientific communities, they constitute a deep and primitive theme that recurs as those affected by a disaster try to make meaning of it and gain mastery over it.

The phases of response to natural disaster have been described as follows:

1. There is the phase of warning. There may be some knowledge or awareness that a disaster is likely, perhaps probable. Community or personal warnings may be issued. Often they are ignored or denied, because the sense of personal invulnerability remains. Each person cannot really believe he will be affected.

2. There is the phase of threat that occurs when disaster is close and will obviously strike. Most people relinquish denial in the face of the obvious threat. They may then take appropriate actions to deal with the disaster, such as physical protection and ensuring the presence of loved ones.

3. Finally, there is the impact of the disaster when it strikes. There is often a great sense of shock. The individual and the group feel frightened, helpless, and overwhelmed. Intense fear, anxiety, and helplessness may be the main experiences. If the individual is unable to act during this phase he may feel even more paralyzed and powerless. His needs to mobilize all ego resources to personal survival may make him feel he is the only one affected. The stunned affect may lead to the beginning of what is called the "disaster syndrome," where the individual sits shocked or wanders in a daze, not taking in what has happened and not apparently responding. This numbing may be a protec-

tive mechanism whereby the ego shuts out the trauma that threatens to overwhelm it. It is usually transient.

4. Following the impact is the phase of inventory or assessment. At this stage, the victims start to make an assessment of what has happened. The impact has lessened. They are not so stunned. There is a growing awareness that others have also been affected, perhaps the whole community. They begin to recognize their losses. There is a high level of anxiety about the whereabouts or fate of those who are most important to them, their primary attachment figures. There may be an intense preoccupation with images of these figures and a powerful drive to search for them, even though this is personally dangerous or inappropriate. This separation anxiety may rise even further if search is impossible because of injury or situation. Another strong affective experience may be the elation of personal survival: the feeling that death came close, but one did not die—even if many others did. This may generate a temporary "high," often seen by others as disturbed and inappropriate, but driving the person to action. It may become a source of guilt at some later time. Angry protest about the disaster and the losses may start to appear: "Why did this have to happen"; "Why to me, to my family?"

5. The rescue phase merges with the assessment phase. Those affected may start to rescue others or commence the task of their own rescue and removal from the disaster site. Many other systems of assistance may start to converge, offering help to all those affected. In affluent societies, those converging may, temporarily, overwhelm the victims, forcing them back into roles of helplessness and passivity, but this is unlikely in societies where the level of disaster exceeds community resources. In this phase the losses of the disaster are realized more fully. The multiple losses involved may induce a fresh sense of shock and numbness as the individual attempts to deal with them. Separation anxiety may continue if the safety of family members is still uncertain, reaching a crescendo during this time when they are not found or the likelihood of their deaths starts to be realized. The arousal generated by the need to search or by the excitement of survival may lead those involved to great heights of physical and emotional achievement, to levels or tasks that would be beyond their capacity at another time. This "high" may push people for several days, even to seemingly superhuman goals. Later it may be followed by exhaustion, but the winding-down processes may take a considerable time. Natural leaders may arise in the community at such a time facilitating the tasks of rescue, aiding in the formation of groups to deal with the issues in-

volved. Much natural grouping also occurs, both for practical need and because of the emotional need to share the experience, to gain information and understanding, and to assist in working through the psychological trauma.

6. The recovery phase is a prolonged one where the affected individuals and community regroup, attempt to reconstitute the physical environment, at least in habitable form, and gradually reestablish the social processes that existed before the disaster. The degree to which this is possible may depend on the extent of the disaster, the degree to which losses can be replaced, and the resources available. This is the period where grief and mourning for what has been lost are greatest. It is the time when the effects of the deprivations induced by the disaster begin to be felt. And it is the period when the chronic stresses of ongoing difficulties may constitute the greatest problem of adaptation. The absence of basic services, the breakdown of community networks, the problems of evacuation may all complicate this phase, as may the conflict as to the pattern of renewal.

A TROPICAL CYCLONE: TRACY IN DARWIN, CHRISTMAS 1974

Darwin is a city on the northern fringes of the Australian continent. It was, in 1974, something of a frontier city, isolated from the southern capitals and from any of the densely populated parts of the country. A city of about 45,000 people, the character of Darwin was typified at that time by a tropical life-style, a tough frontier personality, an avoidance of people's past histories (for many had gone there to escape them), a friendly warmth, and an abounding capacity for drinking Australian beer. The city had a basically Anglo-Saxon Australian background, but also strong Asian and Greek communities. There was also an Australian aboriginal population which was formed by and interchanged with the aboriginal groups of the Northern Territory. This multiracial mix and isolation led to a casual life-style. Darwin's isolation is typified by the fact that other major cities and the national capital are 4,000 kilometers away and the nearest town (a population less than 3,000) is almost 400 kilometers away.

There were warnings of tropical cyclone Tracy for some days before. At 9:00 A.M. on Christmas eve a prerecorded cyclone warning alarm was issued over local radio stations. There was little evidence that any of those in authority, or the local population, heeded this warning. It was repeated later during that day with increasing frequency until radio stations went off the air with the full impact of the cyclone in the early hours of Christmas morning.

This cyclone struck in full fury with winds that probably exceeded 250 kilometers per hour. Nearly 200 millimeters of rain fell in a nine-hour period. Families who were quietly in their homes awaiting Christmas, those who were partying, members of the community in all their different activities were all affected by its violence. Most houses were torn apart. Sheets of iron from their roofs were hurled through the air. Cars were overturned. Solid objects were carried distances through the air. Homes disintegrated, leaving families huddled together in cupboards, toilets, bathrooms, or any solid place that seemed to give them a chance of survival. The rain pelted down in the pitch black and shrieking gale. Children were pulled from the arms of their parents by its force. People huddled in the rubble of their homes and prayed, sometimes with others dead and injured around them. Some died, crushed in their homes; some suffocated as rubble collapsed around them; some were killed by flying debris; some were killed in their cars as they tried to escape.

In Alan Stretton's book about the disaster (1976, pp. 19–20), some of those who survived described their experience:

"We could hear roofs being ripped around us as though they were made of paper. It was like bombs going off. In minutes our home was blown apart. . . . God knows how we survived."

"Everything is gone—the whole house collapsed. All that remain are the floor boards."

"We ran from room to room as the house folded up around us. The walls were just ripped open."

"The edge of the cyclone came back with an unbelievable roar. When our place started to disintegrate it was even worse. There was nothing we could do."

"It looks as though an Atom Bomb has hit."

From my own contact with those affected come many stories such as the following:

Alan and Susan J were at home together on Christmas eve preparing the Christmas dinner and preparing for the celebrations on that day. Their two children Martha, five, and Bill, three, were put to bed early in anticipation of Christmas morning. The winds increased dramatically, tearing at the light tropical house with savage violence, ripping off shutters. Alan and Susan woke the children, bundled them into warm clothes and blankets, and took shelter with them in the bathroom, as the cyclone warning had advised. They spent the most terrifying night of their lives as their house disintegrated around them. The parents sheltered their children by lying with their own bodies across them. Yet every minute they were terrified for their own lives. The eye of the cyclone came with a period of quiet, but they dared not go outside for the warning had specified that there would be strong winds again as the other side of the cyclone went through. As it did, the small bathroom shook, but somehow, in what Alan felt was a miracle, it remained. Eventually the winds settled. Slowly, hesitantly, after waiting a little, they found their way out. Alan's experience during the cyclone was one of terror. It brought back to him with frightening reality his fears during his time in Vietnam. Susan, too, felt terror, but also an overwhelming and desperate wish to save and protect the children. She wondered vaguely if many others had been affected, and thought regretfully that they should have bought a solid house, not this open and tropical one they had both loved.

As they found their way through the rubble of the house, they emerged into the light and saw before them a sight that stunned them to silence. For the city around them, the houses, the buildings, and the trees, were devastated. All was flat, empty, terribly quiet. It was many minutes before either of them could talk, and as they tried to do so they both started to cry. The children clung to them in bewilderment. They felt as though they were all in a state of shock— that this could not have really happened; that it was a dream from which they would all awake.

Then they started to notice some movement and saw their neighbor next door making his way through the ruins. A great sense of relief and joy flooded over them. They rushed to one another, confirming both families had survived. Then started the process of taking stock, seeing where others were, wondering where to go to find out, and looking for the remnants of their world of personal possessions. The Christmas tree stood pathetically in the ruins of their living room—stripped and shattered. The toys were spread across the yard. There was no feeling of Christmas. Their experience was a typical one and that of most of the families.

In the weeks and months that followed they grieved for many losses. Susan and the children were evacuated to a southern city where they stayed with her parents. Alan stayed on as an essential worker in the city to repair and rebuild. This separation stressed their marriage greatly. Their home, for which they had struggled, was gone. Their neighborhood was lost, for most of their friends left Darwin never to return. Their dog was nowhere to be found. Susan said, "There were so many losses, yet I felt I shouldn't grieve, we were so lucky to be alive. There were so many worse off than we were. The children hadn't been hurt. I knew I should just feel grateful. Every time I went to talk about it, people would say how fortunate we were and that was that. I couldn't really tell them how I felt. Sometimes it seemed they were such little things I cared about, such silly things to feel a loss for. I wept and wept over our photograph albums. They were all ruined. They were our past—there in pictures, our wedding, the children as babies, our first house—and they were gone. It was as though our past was gone too. There were all our treasures—the china vase my grandmother gave me, my wedding dress, the books I won at school, Alan's trophies, Martha's old teddy bear. We had lost so many things that were part of us. I used to cry for those little things night after night: them and all we had lost."

In the days that followed the disaster, most of the population left Darwin. Over 25,000 people were evacuated in a massive airlift to southern cities. Many others set off on the long journey south by road, carrying with them what they could of family goods and possessions. The decision to evacuate was made by the commander of the National Disaster Organization because of the total devastation of the city and its services. Many of the people of Darwin were desperate to leave. Yet others resented being torn away from what was left of their possessions and their homes. This massive airlift in itself was extremely stressful: the relocation to other, often strange, cities made the people feel as though they were refugees. Even with the great human kindness extended by the shocked Australian population, this could not help being a traumatic experience for those who were separated from family and home. In one instance, several members of one family were evacuated to different cities, each hundreds of miles apart. The mother was injured and cared for in one hospital, the children and husband in another. Often there was great uncertainty about the whereabouts of relatives and friends.

Jack, a sixty-year-old man, evacuated to a southern city, explained what the loss of his community meant to him:

"I felt as though I was deserting her. She was my city, and I didn't want to go. I wanted to stay there and be with her and help fix her up. They told me I wasn't young and fit enough, that my bad heart had to be looked after, and there would be no medical attention to spare. They made me go, so I had to. Well, Mum and I came here, and they put us in one of those migrant hostels. It was comfortable enough, and people were very kind. All I could think about was Darwin. I'd lived there all my life. I knew those streets inside out. I'd seen her grow from a sprawling country town to the place she was today, a fine city.

"When the cyclone hit, we all knew things would be pretty bad. There hadn't been a bluster like that in years. At first I thought it was just like the bombing again [Darwin had been bombed in the Second World War in February 1942, killing 243 people and devastating the town.]. In fact my mate said he thought that that was what was happening at first. Anyway, when I saw what had happened that morning my heart felt as though it would break. She was such a beautiful city. She'd looked her best that Christmas eve. It was almost as though she'd been raped.

"Right away I started to help with things—trying to help the others, getting together with some of my mates to see what we could do. We went down to the school and found a lot of the folks had gathered there. It was something of a first aid station. There were people lying around everywhere so we got stuck into making cups of tea, hot water, and cleaning the place up a bit. I felt I was doing a job and helping. That made me feel better I guess.

"Well, when they said I had to go, I felt old and useless. A lot of my friends stayed behind to do their bit, and I wanted to be with them. When we got down south I kept thinking of all the things I could have done, and what my friends would be doing, and I wanted to be with them there. It was really hard too, because we didn't get much news out at first. We knew things were very bad and the damage was dreadful. There was even some talk that they'd abandon the whole place and rebuild somewhere else. That really threw me. The few of us that were here would get together over a beer and talk about it all. We felt so useless being so far away. Then they started to get more information back. The rebuilding was starting soon. A lot of people weren't going back though. I felt I'd lost her—my old girl Darwin that I knew so well.

"Sure they'd promised us a new and gleaming city—that was fine. But she wasn't going to be the same, and a lot of the people I cared about weren't going to be there either. I was going back, but things would be different. I suppose, you could say they wouldn't be bad, but the Darwin that I loved had gone."

A total of forty-nine people died and sixteen others were missing presumed dead. It was probably fortunate that the death toll wasn't higher. There were many who were bereaved by those deaths, but who the bereaved were and where they were was difficult to know. No services were aware of them specifically in Darwin, and following evacuation, they proved almost impossible to locate. There were many myths about them. How true and representative these myths are of their experiences is difficult to state.

It was said that a man's body was found high in the telegraph wires on Christmas day. Little is known, however, of the family who mourned his loss. One young woman who had been injured and knocked unconscious as their home was torn apart, was said to be mourning her husband who was dragged away from her in the winds exceeding 200 kilometers per hour in the height of the cyclone. Later his body was found nearby by neighbors. She never saw his body, and that cyclone night holds her last memories of him. Another story is of a couple who sat stunned in a corner of the hostel to which they were evacuated. It was said that both their children had been killed in the disaster. Who was to know? There were bodies found in the rubble of the city. Some were husbands, some fathers, some wives and mothers. What happened to their families is simply not known.

Stretton (1976, p. 46) describes some of this experience of death during his first few days in the city: "We passed a large room that had been pressed into service as a mortuary, and we were all shocked and saddened to see the broken and mutilated bodies of men, women and children laid out in neat rows on the wet floor." He noted how the wet floor was becoming covered in an ever-widening, pinkish stain of blood, as the "blood mixed with water from rain dripping from the ceiling." In this room and in the tropical city, with its heat and humidity there was the "sickening, pervading odor of decomposition and death."

This theme of death and decomposition filled the memories of those who experienced the cyclone or who came to the city in that period immediately afterward. The newspaper reports were filled with words of death and decay. Myths and stories of death spread rapidly. The human deaths were there—not a great number in a city of 45,000, but deaths still. This theme of death was pervasive in so many other ways. Dead animals, the deaths and decay of their bodies, the death of plant matter, and the heat promoting decomposition, all fed the aura of a city, as one of the newspapers said, "filled with the stench of decay and death."

As with any other event, with little warning the cyclone cut across many stresses and crises of everyday life. Thus, some people suffered a double trauma. There were a number of women in the maternity ward of the hospital that Christmas eve and night. Some had their babies in the period of the cyclone. Some struggled to protect them, care for them, and feed them under appalling circumstances as the hurricane raged. Power, water, and other essential services were lost. One woman went out of labor after having started, was evacuated to a southern city, and did not come into labor again until she returned to Darwin two weeks later. As the women recovered from childbirth they were evacuated with their new babies, in the days that followed, to strange southern cities. Their husbands often stayed behind to help in the cleaning up and rebuilding of the city.

Disasters such as this cyclone produce many stressful memories. Many people suffered a "traumatic stress syndrome." They were haunted by traumatic and intrusive memories of the disaster and nightmares in the weeks and months that followed.

Pat and her children were evacuated south. Her husband Rob stayed behind, for he was a builder and much in demand. Pat stayed with her parents with whom she had always had a difficult relationship. The friction between them rose as the months progressed. She wanted desperately to go back to Rob, but the authorities said they could not, as there would be nowhere for them to live. Stories filtered back of the wild lives the men of Darwin were leading in the absence of their wives and of the young women who'd somehow managed to get to Darwin and help them. Pat was angry and distressed, missing her husband, having difficulties with the children. She said: "They were so edgy all the time that it made me even worse. The moment a wind would come up, even a little bit of a storm, they'd both be terrified. I felt bad myself too; I was afraid I would panic. All the feeling of that terrible night came back again and again. I couldn't sleep. It was as though we were all still awaiting, expecting the damn cyclone to return. I knew it wasn't all due to the cyclone, but that was the part that stayed with me. Even when I wasn't expecting it, memories would come back. It seemed to be etched in my mind forever. The screaming winds, the pouring rain, and then in the morning when it was all quiet and the sun was even out—everything empty and still and broken. I don't think any of us will every get over it fully. It's something that will haunt us until we die."

Darwin has been rebuilt in the eight years since the cyclone. Modern, cyclone-proof buildings have replaced many of the old establishments. She is a charming and attractive modern city. But like the bereaved she is a different city. She has a new identity, and that identity includes a reference point to the cyclone of Christmas 1974.

The themes of death, destruction, and loss following this cyclone are very similar to those described in other studies of natural disaster. The experience of death was massive, even for those not directly involved. There was an aura of death about the disaster even though the numbers who died were not great. The massive destruction created further losses of place, neighborhood, and city. It stirred the destructive fantasies of those who would save it. Newspapers spoke of the "undeniable fascination" with the totality of the disaster. The networks of support that would normally have facilitated resolution were broken by the disaster and the evacuation. The psychic trauma of the event itself had effects which lived on in memory, and which altered the identity of the city. Themes of survival generated the energies for recovery but sometimes made it hard to grieve.

While there is little information about those who were bereaved in this disaster, there has been considerable follow-up of some of the community and those evacuated. The findings substantiate Stretton's comment that *"the damage to the minds of the survivors can never be fully calculated"* (Stretton, 1976, p. 21). Thus Milne (1977a, 1977b) reports on emotional disturbances in children and adults following the disaster and notes that these appeared worse in those who were evacuated. Parker (1977), in an interesting study of those who were evacuated showed that there was a high level of psychological dysfunction (58 percent) initially, which fell to 41 percent at ten weeks, and to a basic population level of about 22 percent fourteen months later. He hypothesized that initial morbidity was associated with the experience of thinking one might die, whereas morbidity at ten weeks was more closely associated with relocation stresses. Western and Doube's study

(1979) refines some of these issues further. These workers found that the most important contribution to later stress experienced by those exposed to the cyclone was disruption of the familiar and valued social environment and separation from the immediate family and friends. Such losses seemed to exaggerate the multiple other losses experienced and at the same time remove a factor that was important in their resolution. There is an extensive literature looking at psychological and social outcomes of disasters (Kinston and Rosser 1974) which generally substantiates such findings.

OTHER NATURAL DISASTERS

Earthquake disaster has been poignantly described in all its devastation by a number of workers. Rennie (1970) describes his experience assisting after the 1970 earthquake in Peru. He speaks of how "peculiar" was the devastation of the earthquake; of the dead far outnumbering the wounded; and of the lingering shock, the vast, hopeless disruption of communication. A report from a psychiatric team following an earthquake in Macedonia in 1963 spoke of similar massive destruction. They described patterns of psychological response that have been delineated elsewhere, including initially a mild stupor in more than half the population, and depressive reactions on the second and third days after. There was some childish behavior noted but little panic (Popovic and Petrovic 1964). The traumatic experiences of children following a Los Angeles earthquake are discussed by Epps (1972) who notes how traumatized some of them had been by the frightening experience. In major earthquakes death and destruction are both very great.

Descriptions of reactions to flood disasters show the same patterns: initial denial, the shock and helplessness of the impact, the painful adjustments to loss subsequently. General health impairment is one of the morbid health outcomes described by Bennet (1970) and Abrahams et al. (1976).

Bushfire disasters have been a terrifying part of Australian heritage. The same patterns of responses have been described for these as for those above: shock, helplessness, fear of personal death, and later overwhelming grief for the losses involved. Reports of fires in Hobart, the Blue Mountains, and other areas of Australia all speak of the great fear generated by the uncontrollable fires, the fire storms when there are high winds, and of the painful grief that has followed personal bereavements in such circumstances. One bushfire in Victoria trapped and burned motorists in their cars on a wide highway; another wiped out suburbs; another trapped and burned a group of volunteer rescue workers. Each of these, and others like them, brought intense disaster experience and painful bereavement to the communities and families involved. As I complete this book a series of disastrous bushfires have exploded across the drought-stricken southern states of Australia, claiming sixty-seven deaths in a matter of hours.

## Man-Made Disasters

Man-made disasters are those that may occur as a consequence of the failure of some man-made structure or as a consequence of human failure in the performance of a function that involves many lives. They may also involve an interaction of powerful natural forces with human-related inadequacies. The bursting of a dam is typically the type of disaster that is seen as a consequence of some structure failing, as would be the collapse of a building or bridge. Human failure may make its effects known through pilot error, for example, in the crash of an aircraft, or through the failure of the machine.

While natural disasters generate anger—anger at God, at the world, at nature—a much greater anger appears in response to disasters that are seen as somehow the consequence of human frailty or error. These disasters seem to awaken all the primitive causal logic that someone must be to blame for death and destruction. Here blame is allocated either by formal inquiry into the disaster or in the minds of the bereaved and others affected.

In some instances there may be warnings of a man-made disaster, just as with a natural one. The same patterns of response are likely to apply. Sometimes there may be ample warning of the collapse of a dam, or of a fire, or a wartime disaster, for example. In other cases however warning is minimal so that often the disaster is only experienced from the phase of impact. The suddenness of such disasters often means that there is little opportunity for escape. Should circumstances combine this with a density of population at the place of disaster, then the death toll is likely to be high. Factors in the physical environment also affect the toll, as when the disaster occurs in a hostile or extreme environment. In such cases, destruction of person and property may be great, and rescue and recovery very difficult.

Survival has a special meaning too and is often associated in people's

minds with chance and luck. There may be survivor guilt or a reaffirmation of the values of life.

Some of the different types of man-made disasters that have been
studied from the point of view of the deaths, losses, and destruction
involved, will now be considered.

## A DAM BURSTS

The Buffalo Creek Disaster occurred in 1972 when a slag-pile dam,
swollen by heavy rains, burst and poured down the narrow Buffalo
Creek valley in Man, West Virginia, where a mining community lived.
One hundred and eighteen people were killed, and four thousand ren-
dered homeless. Psychiatric assessment of survivors showed that they
continued to suffer from symptoms of anxiety, depression, hostility,
somatic symptoms, and social isolation two years after the disaster.
Their symptoms were comparable in severity to those of a psychiatric
out-patient population (Gleser, Green, and Winget 1978). Those who
survived described their horror at seeing their families and friends
swept away in the "black tide" of water; their shock and helplessness;
the overwhelming nature of the destructive force of the water, from
which they struggled for their very lives to escape; the loss of their
homes, their communities, and their life-styles (K. Erikson 1976); their
relief at their survival, yet guilt that they had survived where others
had not and that they had been unable to save them; the way in which
their memories and experience of the disaster intruded and stayed with
them, and how, when they attempted to repress them, they often could
not; the anger and search for retribution and compensation; and how
they felt the impact of the disaster was with them forever, and their
lives would never be the same because of it (Church 1974; Tichener
and Kapp 1976).

## AN AVALANCHE

The deaths of children in a disaster seem especially poignant and
painful. In 1966 the mining village of Aberfan, Wales, was devastated
by an avalanche of coal, mud, and rocks that engulfed 116 young children as they sat in their classrooms. The descriptions of this disaster are
enormously painful: the shock of the community; the desperate, hopeless attempts to rescue the children and others from the black slime of
the slag heap; the laying out of the bodies; the grief of the whole
township for the loss of its children; the grief of whole families for the

loss of all their young ones; how the village closed over to deal with its own pain; the anger and guilt over the heap that everyone had known would some day cause trouble; the ongoing pain and the never ending grief that seemed so great it could not be resolved; the anger and demands for retribution; and the regrowth and rebirth of the community (Williams and Parkes 1975), with a new identity but one always associated with the disaster.

A NIGHTCLUB FIRE

Nightclub or hotel fires have been among the serious fire disasters that have occurred in recent times. Lindemann's classic account (1944) of his work with survivors of the Cocoanut Grove nightclub fire that occurred in Boston, Massachusetts, in 1942, provided the basis for his description of the syndrome of acute grief. With Cobb (Cobb and Lindemann 1944) he studied those who were injured, and found that as well as bereavement problems there were levels of severe emotional distress. More recently however Tichener and Lindy (1978) have produced a valuable account of this same experience from their perspective as psychiatrists involved in immediate work with the aftermath of the disaster. This nightclub, with 2,500 guests inside caught fire at 9:00 P.M., and within an hour the club was gone, and 168 people were dead. Tichener and Lindy describe the experience of those who survived: their anguish and terror as parts of the building exploded; their guilt for those they could not help escape; the panic as opportunities for escape lessened and the fighting when available exits became jammed; and the resignation and hopelessness of some who believed they would surely die and yet miraculously escaped. The experiences following the disaster reflect the massive death and destruction involved. Tichener and Lindy tell of the old gymnasium converted to a morgue, describing first the "one hundred and twenty-five bodies in rows on stretchers covered with white cloths and uniformly gray faces"; then, the "less recognizable corpses"; and, on the third and fourth days, "those remains which came in plastic bags, the only chance of identification being dental charts and the possibility of finding a finger from which to take a print" (pp. 6–7). They describe the families walking slowly up and down the rows of bodies, "looking to find and identify a wife, a son, husband, daughter, friend or relative," and afterward, as these families remained, trying to absorb the shock and decide what to do. There was "fear in the presence of so much death—made grotesque by the gray faces in neat rows—and the immense grief impressed upon us" (pp. 8–9). The authors' responses to this massive death included denial and disbelief; psychic numbing; protest and rage; fatigue and traumatic overload; helplessness; and the experience of the grotesqueness of death.

The frightening experiences of maritime disasters have been described (Leopold and Dillon 1963; Carlton 1980) and popularized in real and fictional accounts such as those concerning the sinking of the Titanic. Leopold and Dillon describe a very high level of posttraumatic neurosis among survivors of such disasters, even after four years, and note that this increases in association with compensation claims. Carlton notes the anger, grief, and survivor guilt. The most detailed account in recent literature is that of Henderson and Bostock (1975) on the survivors of the *Belle Star* sinking near Tasmania. These workers describe the survival mechanisms of the men who drifted on a raft for many days. They found that intense attachment ideation and a drive to survive kept these men going despite the deaths of their comrades and the appalling conditions. It was the intense preoccupation with the images of those they loved that seemed to give them the power to do this when exhaustion, and possibly death, threatened.

AN AIRLINE DISASTER

Airline disasters usually occur without warning and in the most tragic circumstances. There are often large numbers of people involved and very few survivors. It is only in recent years that any systematic attempt has been made to assess the psychological effects of such disasters and provide support for the survivors. Major air disasters highlight certain other aspects of disaster.

There is an element of "chance" in who is involved in these disasters. When those affected come from many different walks of life and many geographically separated areas, it is hard to follow-up and provide support for the survivors subsequently, and it in some ways diffuses the aftereffects of the disaster. When those involved come from a particular group, or the same community, perhaps on some organized tour of mutual interest, the impact of the deaths is added to by the destruction of a segment of the community. It may be easier to organize support in a local area or with a specific group, but the need may be so great that it is difficult to fill, especially as the social resources that would have buffered the bereavement are likely to be so depleted. There is the element of chance, too, in why an individual may have chosen to take one particular flight over another, or in his luck in having perhaps missed the ill-fated flight on this occasion. The hand of fate or God is often seen as playing some part in this.

The place of death may be very strange, hostile in the extreme, and a long way from the homes of the injured, the dead, and the bereaved families. The crash of an airliner in Washington, D.C., into the icy Potomac River, and the disastrous crash of the Air New Zealand DC-10 in the desolate wastes of Antarctica highlight the hostility of environment and distance. These factors add to the trauma of death for the bereaved and the stresses experienced by the rescuers.

The bodies of air disaster victims may be mutilated and destroyed such that they lack any human or identifiable appearance. The bereaved may find their mourning complicated by this, and it poses the most painful stresses for rescue teams (Taylor and Frazer 1980; Davidson 1979; O'Brien 1979). The bereaved are further distressed by the suffering they imagine occurred for those who died with such a total annihilation of their physical structure.

The destruction is massive and sudden, and it is vividly portrayed in the media. It cannot be denied, because it is so publicly stated. Thus it is very difficult for those involved and the bereaved to shut out, even temporarily, the trauma and its implications.

Because these deaths receive a great deal of publicity, there is public sympathy and support, but there is also public curiosity and perhaps a vicarious fascination with these public deaths. Then the disaster passes from the front pages rapidly, as the community's interest wanes and a new disaster takes its place. Those affected may feel there is little support in the later weeks and months following the deaths, at the time when it may be most needed. In the acute phase of the crisis there is often also much promise from governments and community of money, services, compensation, and assistance for those affected. There is often great disillusionment as these "promises" seem to fade or the bureaucratic systems block their provision. Thus the public nature of these deaths, while offering public affirmation of the loss and grief of those affected, may also create extra sources of stress.

These deaths may involve many other people who are not directly related to the deceased and who would not normally be classed among the victims or survivors. For example, many identify with those who have been killed and their families through the public presentations of the death and the fantasies involved. But even more than this, those who are involved formally or informally in the operations of rescue and recovery are affected by the massive confrontation with injury, death, and destruction in such disasters. This may be little recognized since the rescuers, especially the professionals, are often seen as being accustomed to handling injury, blood, and death: the degree to which they are distressed, grieving, and affected may not be recognized. Often they are sensitive and caring people who become intensely involved with the victims and survivors. Where there are injured, there may be an intense and personal attachment between the rescuer and the person he works with and keeps alive. There maybe an intense emotional and physical investment in heroic deeds of rescue. There may be a great and painful distress at the destruction of human bodies and the waste of precious lives. There may be a fellow feeling and empathy for the grief-stricken families. The trauma of the disaster, of the destruction, or the death and the dead bodies, may stay with these involved others for a long time (Raphael, Singh, and Bradbury 1980; Taylor and Frazer 1980; Raphael 1981).

Just what a disaster may involve in these terms is highlighted by the descriptions and media presentations of the Mt. Erebus air disaster and particularly by Taylor and Frazer's valuable and careful studies. The following description owes much to their work.

In November 1979 an Air New Zealand DC-10 aircraft taking sightseers to the Antarctic to view, from the plane, the icy continent, crashed without warning into Mt. Erebus. It appeared that all aboard were killed instantly. The passengers included a Japanese tourist contingent as well as local New Zealanders. The bodies were scattered widely by the impact, and many disintegrated. Rescue teams and disaster victim identification workers had to be flown in from New Zealand. The physical conditions under which they worked were extreme and in themselves very stressful. The state of the bodies made it necessary for workers to build defenses to enable them to handle the many dismembered remains. A number were physically sick and had to force themselves to continue. The bodies had to be collected together as well as possible, "completed," and attempts made to find personal possessions which might assist identification. The bodies had to be transported, through the very difficult physical conditions, back to the base and eventually back to New Zealand. In the course of a week, these workers recovered 204 complete bodies and 139 incomplete bodies. The experience was stressful for them: they reported psychological and physical tension, irritability, fatigue, anxiety, despair, and a heightened sensitivity to and a preoccupation with death. Taylor and Frazer note that these symptoms settled to some degree with the opportunity to talk the experience through with others, and as time passed. Psychological debriefing was also of assistance, but even so, stressful memories of the gruesome sights intruded for a considerable time. Much of the experience was such that it could not readily be talked about with family members, and thus there was a special need to share it either with those who had also been through the experience or those who were more professionally equipped to deal with what they heard. The mortuary assistants who attended to the remains back in New Zealand were also very stressed as they attempted to maintain defenses so that they could deal with the bodies. They found that traumatic perceptions intruded in their thoughts and in their sleep. They had little opportunity to talk through their stress and so were often unable to come to terms with their feelings. To do their jobs, disaster workers may have to shut off some of their feelings, yet even so they are often left with imprinted and traumatic memories of their experience. They are likely to be a further group of "victims" of the disaster.

A RAIL DISASTER

Train crashes are another form of disaster which may involve a disparate group of people, together at a particular time, in major destruction and death. The destruction is often not as great as in air disasters, but other circumstances may add to the horror.

In January 1977, in Granville, New South Wales, an early morning commuter train from the outer Blue Mountain region outside Sydney became derailed and crashed into the stanchions of an overhead cement bridge. This brought down the giant cement slab of the bridge, crushing some of the carriages and their occupants underneath. Emergency and rescue workers were rapidly on the scene, assisting the injured from the other carriages. They were confronted with the problem of trying to rescue those who were still alive and trapped beneath the slab as well as remove the bodies of those who had died. The slab threatened to collapse further during the rescue operations. The carriages were crushed to almost forty-five centimeters at some points. The train contained gas cylinders so that welding and cutting instruments could not be used. Over that day and night and the following day, police, volunteer rescue workers, ambulance and medical teams, and other groups, worked intensely to free those still alive, to lift the slab, and to remove the dead bodies. I was personally involved in the provision of support services at the city morgue for families identifying the bodies of the eighty-three who died; in education about stress and bereavement for those who would be working with the injured and bereaved subsequently (Raphael 1977*a*, 1979/80); in provision of support for the bereaved and injured in the weeks following the disaster; in psychological debriefing of some of the rescue groups; and in conducting a survey of the effects on rescuers of the disaster (Singh, Raphael, and Bradbury 1980; Raphael 1981); and with a colleague in follow-up investigation of the longer-term effects on health and the effectiveness of preventive intervention for those who had been bereaved (Singh and Raphael 1981). Some of our observations of the disaster experience follow.

A total of eighty-three people died in this disaster. This confrontation with death was reflected in newspaper and media reports at the time of the disaster; in the experiences of those who dreaded that a member of the family might be involved; in the feelings of those who knew a loved one to be on the train and in the crushed carriages; in the frustration of the rescue workers as they struggled to free the injured and dying; in the fears of those who felt the slab sinking further down upon them as they crawled along the narrow space trying to find those still alive; and in the many many bodies that were recovered and lay in neat rows at the city morgue.

"I rushed to the place where the wreck had occurred. I knew my daughter always caught that train, and I knew she always rode in the same carriage. I prayed with all my heart that she would be all right. I couldn't get near the place. No one seemed to know what was going on. I was desperate. There were so many victims. They said we would have to phone to find out—to go to the morgue. I kept praying that it wouldn't be her, that it wouldn't be true, that she would be all right."

"We crawled along on our stomachs—it was dreadful in there. There were arms hanging out—some people you could see were dead, others it was hard to tell. They were crushed down so badly. There was this smell of blood and their bodies—their bowels had let go.

"Then in all this death there was a voice, a girl's voice. She said, 'I'm alive! I'm alive here,' and I could see her face and she smiled."

"I wondered so much, so much, how they died—did they suffer? Surely they must have suffered. Someone said that my husband must have died instantly, from asphyxiation, but how could that have happened? They were all crushed. You could see the dreadful slab and they were all crushed under it. They *must* have suffered."

"I was scared stiff in there, but I had to go—there was no way I couldn't. It was my job and I wanted to. But it was really bad—all those dead. And then the slab started sinking. I thought I'd had it—that this was it. That this was the end.

*339*

Then it settled again and I got out. ı had to go back under there again and again. And I did. And every time I thought it might be my last."

"I had never seen a dead person before. It was a sort of a shock. They are so cold. There they were in the morgue—not just one of them, but row and row."

"It still looked like him, but it was hard to tell—it was swollen and different. But they were his clothes. I think it was him, and it must have been him. But so many dead—how could you ever know?"

"Well, I thought I was hardened to it all. I thought I could take anything. It was part of my work to see dead bodies, and some of them badly knocked about too. But this really hit me. Some of them were so young. It seemed so pointless and futile. There were so many. They stayed etched in my mind, all those faces, all those bodies, for a long long time."

"When they lifted that slab, that was the worst time of it all. Up it came, and there they lay—all those bodies crushed and neat, like sardines in a can or prawns on a pizza. I'll remember all those dead as long as I live."

The personal confrontation with death was stressful to all those involved: the injured and the bereaved; those who would normally have been on the train and in the crushed carriages but who were not on that day; the rescue workers; and the community. Exploration of the experience of the rescue and disaster workers later revealed that those who had felt that their own lives had been in danger were often particularly stressed. But for some there were also positive effects. They felt that they realized the value and importance of life and relationships and saw things differently from that time on, ordering their priorities in human terms. Those who had been stressed by the experience found the opportunity to talk through the stress to be very helpful in their subsequent adjustment. Some took advantage of the informal debriefing sessions held at the local pub after the disaster, but for others, it was worked through formally in psychological debriefing sessions arranged by the support team. As is frequently the case, workers found a special benefit in sharing their emotions and experience with others who had been through the same experience. While, for the most part, this helped them, the process also on occasion produced family stress when the family members felt excluded. Nevertheless, this did not usually lead to longterm difficulties, since some sharing with families eventually took place.

And for all the stress and distress that this massive and personal confrontation with death meant, the response of most people was one of great human courage.

The awesome nature of the concrete slab, the smashed and crushed train carriages, produced an aura of destruction that was for many of the onlookers both frightening and fascinating. However, while some of the bodies were crushed, for the most part, those who died were clearly recognizable. In reality, the destruction was not the principal theme of this disaster, although it was so in many people's fantasies.

The bereavements of the family members who lost relatives in this disaster were intense. In the first day they went through a period of great distress waiting for news of their loved ones. They rang the places of work of those who might have been on the train and the police information coordination center. They went to the disaster site. They came to the city morgue and waited in quiet, sad crowds for the bodies to be brought in. Some waited there for two days for the last bodies to be removed from the wreckage. They waited, filled with dread. Then there was the process of identification. The city morgue had little provision for a personal atmosphere, although all those involved were considerate and caring. In many instances women were actively advised against seeing and identifying the bodies of their menfolk, with the message it would be too distressing to do so. Yet subsequently these women were even more distressed by their fantasies of the possible mutilation their husbands or others had suffered. The bodies were released for burial within a few days.

The mountain community and outer western suburbs from which the dead had come were still in a state of shock in the early days. On some streets many women had lost their husbands. On others a number of different family members had been affected. The funerals took place over the next few days. The newspapers were full of the disaster, and many people offered help to the bereaved. Government response was dramatic, with offers for compensation and financial support, the promise of a full inquiry, and the mobilization of support services. Much was done for those affected in the early weeks. Then response waned and, as many of the bereaved were facing the full impact of their loss, it seemed that others expected them to be recovered. Compensation apparently offered so freely in the beginning would now have to be contested in court. Support services were withdrawn to their everyday tasks. In the months following the disaster, the pain of personal bereavement was felt by many families.

"My daughter was so young and full of life. She was going in to work as usual that morning, and I'd taken her to the train as I always did. She used to sit in the first carriage and when I heard about the crash, I thanked God because I thought she'd be alright. Then I rang her work just to check and they said she wasn't in yet. I felt my heart start to thump and a feeling of panic was rising inside me. I left my work and went to the bridge; but you couldn't get near the place, so I went to the police but they couldn't help. That day seemed never ending. I kept ringing, and then they said to go the morgue, so I did.

"It was her all right—I knew from her dress, although it was all torn and bloodstained, and part of her face was crushed, and she was sort of swollen all over. I just broke down. I felt my heart was breaking. There she was dead. It was such a waste. She was so young and full of life. She'd had everything ahead of her, all her life going for her, and this had to happen.

"I hated the world and the railways, and everyone. We had the funeral, but it didn't seem real. We kept thinking she would come back to the house as she always had. It seemed so dead and empty without her. Our lives seemed to have no point anymore—there was nothing to go on for. All the weeks that followed, all the months, I could think of nothing else but her. I gave up all interest in life and still feel that way now."

"When I heard the news of the crash, I nearly went mad. My son never caught that train as a rule; he always caught an earlier one. But that morning we had an argument, and he asked me to drive him to the train, and I wouldn't. I said, 'You can walk. You can find out how tough life's meant to be.' So he did, and he missed his train and caught that one instead. I've killed him just as surely as if I'd put the gun to his head and fired the bullet."

"My husband was a good man. We had a pretty good marriage. He always caught that train to work and that morning was just like any other; that is, until I heard the news—they announced it in a news flash. It hit me like some terrible blow. At first I couldn't believe it. I rang my sister and she came to be with me and we rang up to find out what we could. But most of the time there was little information. The day went on. We watched the television. They had it all on that. It was something like a nightmare. It didn't feel real. I couldn't convince myself he was there. I kept thinking he must be at work, although I really knew he wasn't. Then, the next time I rang, they said a male relative should come into the morgue, there was a possible identification. I wanted to go myself, but everyone said I shouldn't. I was frightened, so I didn't go. Afterwards I regretted that. I kept thinking to myself, perhaps it really wasn't him, perhaps they made a mistake. I was just trying to hope really, because I knew inside me that it was."

"For the first few weeks I just seemed to be in a daze. The boys would ask about their father. I explained it all to them, but I really didn't believe it myself. The days were empty, and the nights worse. There was no one I could turn to. Other women in our street had lost their husbands and they were just as desperate as I was. There were lots of people to help and lots of forms to fill. Everyone was very kind. I know they meant well. But all I could think of was that it was such a terrible way to die.

"One of the worst things that happened was when I saw this man outside, sitting in a parked car, watching the house. I was frightened. I looked out again and he had gone. He was there again several times in the evening, so I finally called the police, and he went away. Then when I was talking to my friend who'd lost her husband too, I found out he'd been at her place as well. Then we talked to some of the other women, and it turned out he was an investigator. He was to see if we had other men living with us so they wouldn't have to pay us the compensation for our husbands' deaths. That was terrible. Well they stopped it, but it was something I'll never forget. How could any of us have been interested in other men when our husbands had only just died. It made us feel so cynical about all they'd promised in the beginning, all the help they were going to provide. It simply made things worse.

"After that we used to get together, a group of us who all lost our husbands in the disaster. We used to talk about it together. That helped a lot. We knew how one another felt, and that made the world of difference."

"I was so angry about my son's death. It should never have happened. The railways had been in a shocking state for years—everyone knew that. Then they said it was no one's fault. It had to be. He should never have died. I felt like smashing them all, punishing them. I would sue them for everything I could. There was no other way to get back at them for what they had done."

"I've been visiting the grave each day for months now. I feel all right while I'm there—as though I'm with her. But the rest of the time, my life is empty. I can't believe she'll never come back."

"I thought that I could manage things—just manage them—until the children started playing trains. They had this big train. They used to play with their father before he was killed. But now they played a game they called the bridge smash. They'd smash the train into everything. They'd knock everything over. It was quite violent really. I couldn't bear it. It was like my nightmares, and it brought them all back—that day, the television playing it all, the waiting, the bridge, the train. That picture will never go from my mind. It torments me always."

The bereaved were offered support and counseling through local services in the health and welfare area. In some instances there were specialist counselors; in others, bereavement counseling was provided by local clergy, community nurses, and other personnel. An independent follow-up study of the effects of the disaster and the counseling provided was carried out fifteen to eighteen months later (Singh and Raphael 1981). Many of those who were bereaved were still suffering greatly at this time. Mothers who had lost children (usually young adult children) tended to do the worst. They had not had much counseling, and they presented pictures of chronic grief with desolation. They would frequently comment that their lives were devastated. Widows did badly as well, but not so badly as the mothers and fathers. Widowers, although often still distressed, seemed to have made the best adjustments. Outcome was better in those who had seen the body and in those who had supportive networks that helped them with their grief. It may be, of course, that those who choose not to see the body have ego vulnerabilities that make their personalities such that they are more likely to be prone to bad outcome anyway. Those who had received bereavement counseling did better than those who had not, particularly if this had been provided by skilled workers and if they had perceived it as helpful.

It was quite clear from this project that many people developed a substantial morbidity as a consequence of their disaster loss. Their grief and mourning were complicated by the shock and trauma of the disaster, by failing to see the body and say their farewells, and by the ambivalence and inadequacy of the support provided for them afterward. For some, the loss was irreplaceable and their own personal destruction by the death irrevocable.

Survivor feelings had various effects. A number of people who would usually have been in the carriages that were crushed were elated, yet felt guilty as though they had condemned the occupants of the seats to death. It is probable that these survivor feelings motivated many of the people who came to view the disaster and who seemed vicariously elated by their encounter with death. A great many of those who escaped from the front carriages felt guilty that they had not been able to save others. The workers at a nearby health center shared such feelings. It may be that survivor feelings powered some of the early community response.

Those directly involved—both the victims and the helpers—still have extensive memories of the disaster and see it as a turning point in their lives. Each year, on the anniversary, a man lays a wreath of roses at the place where the train left the rails. Granville was a relatively unknown suburb, until it made its name with the disaster.

DISASTERS OF PEACE

Civilian violence and terrorism have sometimes reached disaster proportions in recent years, both for entire communities and for those experiencing them personally. Violence, terror, and death are the hallmarks of such situations. There is a developing psychiatric literature, highlighting some of the responses that are associated with them.

The ongoing conflicts and riots in Belfast have been shown to be associated with temporary "normal fear and anxiety responses" (Lyons 1971, p. 272). Lyons (1971, 1972) found no increase in psychotic illness. In the areas of greatest aggression there was a decrease in depression, which could be linked to the externalization of aggressive behavior. These general findings, however, speak little to the issue of individual

344

terror and confrontation with death in this city, or for that matter, in others similarly affected, such as Beirut. Morris Fraser's sensitive book *Children in Conflict* (1974) paints a bitter picture of the children of Belfast, their fears, the disruption of their lives and experience, by the violence of the street. He quotes an eight-year-old boy who says how the guns keep him awake all night, how sometimes he can't stop crying because his house will be burned or his father shot. This author concludes these children are very dependent on the supporting responses of significant adults, who may protect them to some degree on some occasions, but who often cannot. These children are thrust into worlds and lives of violence that are damaging and difficult to tolerate.

Massacres are another form of civilian violence that may have disastrous repercussions. The 1978 mass suicide in Jonestown, Guyana, will come into this category, but little is known at present of the effect of such disasters on the bereaved and other survivors.

Lenore Terr (1981) examined twenty-three children involved in a school-bus kidnapping. She found that all these children suffered from post-traumatic emotional sequelae. The children experienced a sense of there having been omens of the disaster, in that they looked back both during and after the kidnapping to specific events they saw as connected with it. The children were fearful of further trauma during the disaster, and experienced disturbances of cognition such as misperceptions, hallucinations, or time-sense disturbances. Repetitive phenomena occurred as with adult traumatic-stress syndromes, but in the children's cases, they involved traumatic dreams, posttraumatic play of the kidnapping experienced (which was not realized as this consciously), and reenactment of the disaster. There were few repetitive intrusions of the scenes or flashbacks, such as in adults' experience. The children suffered from many fears afterward, even in the most ordinary circumstances. In particular, they believed they could be kidnapped again and were tense and anxious as a consequence. It appeared that this disaster had traumatized them so that they could no longer trust the world.

A recognition of the traumatic effects of such disasters is now well established, and hostages rescued from similar circumstances do, for the most part, receive supportive psychological intervention afterward, aimed at helping them resolve the experience.

DISASTERS OF WAR

Disasters of civilian life pale in comparison to the disasters of war. The massive numbers involved, the threat to person and country, the violence of modern weapons, all lead to massive threat of death and destruction for large numbers of the population.

Combat disorders have been well documented as a response to involvement in battle, where death and violence threaten personally and intensely. In a recent and valuable review, Boman (1982) describes some of the sequelae for the victims of the Vietnam conflict. He highlights the primacy of battle stress in causing later psychiatric disorders and the lesser importance of premorbid personality. He points out how these men faced the threat of mutilation and death in so many ways: each Vietnamese man, woman, or child was seen as a potential harbinger of death or mutilation; booby traps and mines were everywhere and produced hideous injuries and deaths; their world was full of the violence that they must do to others or others would do to them. Many lost their comrades but had little opportunity to mourn them. While psychic numbing and other repressive defenses were used to deal with the feelings aroused by the environment of death and violence, these were often only temporarily successful. Overall the long-term effects involved three main areas. There were significant post-traumatic stress disorders and personality changes, often with continued psychic numbing, emotional constriction, and alienation from feelings and people. Depression was common, as was substance abuse. While many of the stresses could be supported and worked through in the strong social group of the unit, some soldiers were either moved from their group or lacked such resources. Boman concludes that the Vietnam veteran often continued in a state of psychic numbing, relying heavily on denial and repression to master painful affects, memories, and impulses; yet the sequelae were like "buried dragon's teeth" now "bringing forth their baneful crop of depression, anger, guilt, resentment and psychopathology" (p. 124). These findings reflect, in condensed form, the inevitable sequelae, even for the soldier, of the disastrous violence and death of war.

*Extreme stressors.* Concentration camps and atomic warfare are examples of extreme environmental stressors. Hocking (1965, 1970) describes some of the longer-term effects of extreme environmental situations such as wartime concentration camp experience, demonstrating their effects in impairment of health. There is also an extensive literature of the Holocaust, indicating the lasting impairment experienced by many of the survivors and the effects on their children. The level of death, destruction, threat, and loss in such circumstances is so overwhelming as to call forth the most powerful responses, and it can be of little surprise that there are many psychiatric sequelae. Lifton's sensitive account (1967) of the experiences of survivors of the atomic blast at Hiroshima can leave no one who reads it untouched.

## Surviving Disaster: The Survivor Syndrome

In his study of the survivors of Hiroshima, Lifton (1967) suggests that those who survive such disasters experience much "end-of-the-world" imagery which seems a reactivation of their sense of psychic death. These people experience primarily what Lifton calls the "imprint of death." This imprint occurs whatever one's previous psychological traits and relates the extremes of confrontation with death experienced in circumstances such as those of the bombing of Hiroshima and the Nazi concentration camps. For the bomb survivors, its effects were most strongly felt in death imagery in preoccupation with the event in a "spellbound fascination." These people also lived a life of grief, not only mourning those they had lost, but also all the losses of the catastrophe and the loss of their innocence about death.

"Death guilt" is also described by Lifton as part of the survivor syndrome. In this, the survivor feels that in some way he was given a priority to survive that was purchased at the cost of another's life. Lifton found this guilt to be especially intense, when for instance, parents survived their children. This type of guilt is also reinforced when there is competition for survival, as in the Nazi concentration camps, where survivors may have felt they contributed actively to the deaths of others. Nevertheless, even without any apparently "rational" cause, such guilts over survival were intense in the survivors of both the Hiroshima bomb and the concentration camp disasters and were felt by survivors to have created a "living Hell." These same guilts may appear in other disasters, but they are most pronounced in disasters of this type. They also seem reinforced by ongoing thoughts of the dead and links with them. The survivors' suffering, rather than expiating deeper guilts, seemed to reinforce them.

The survivors' major defense against death anxiety and death guilt becomes the cessation of feelings. Such "psychic numbing" is an extension of the sort of shutting-out process that occurs in the disaster syndrome, where the victim appears stunned and dazed. This process may serve an adaptive function at the time of encountering death, for the denial may protect the person from the terrible reality of the death threat for him, or his identification with the death of others. This numbing also suppresses rage and resistance. It may give way, allowing the person to open up his feelings again, or it may continue making the person into some sort of "living dead." The numbing may appear in more adaptive forms, allowing the person to continue necessary tasks in the face of death-related stresses, somewhat in the way described for parents of children with malignant disease in Chodoff, Friedman, and Hamburg's work (1964) or for disaster workers (Tichener and Lindy 1978). Lifton also notes that this phenomenon of psychic numbing may have operated in some degree in allowing the world to contemplate and live with the horrors of disaster that the Holocaust and Hiroshima produced.

Survivors Lifton studied experienced "nurturance conflicts." They were likely to be very suspicious of the "false" nurturance of others. They were "touchy" and sensitive to the responses of others and developed a form of severe victim-consciousness which sometimes reached the level of paranoia. Lifton also found that the survivor tends to make a "formulation" of his death-immersion experience in his attempts to explain and gain mastery over it. It is part of his rebuilding of the world he has lost and his comprehension and control of it and is in some ways similar to the mourning process.

The importance of the survivor concept and the survivor response spreads far beyond those affected directly by the Holocaust and the atomic bomb. It extends to the experiences of those who have survived many other disasters. The extent of feeling may vary, and the qualities of the survivor syndrome may fluctuate. In some instances psychic numbing may predominate, in others the death imprint, in others death guilt. The pattern will depend on the individual and the disaster experience. Psychic numbing may be a process that enables those working in a disaster situation to handle their feelings. Survivor guilts and death imprints may also affect these people because of their massive immersion in death, their encounters with the "endless rows of gray bodies." Tichener and Lindy (1978) describe the core of this experience in their work with victims following the Kentucky nightclub fire, and a similar experience was found with those working at the disaster site and morgue in the Granville rail disaster and with the Mt. Erebus team. These experiences are small by comparison with the massive numbers of deaths of the Holocaust, but the same themes of dealing with death appear. Similarly, those working with the daily disasters of motor vehicle accidents may find that the same processes apply:

psychic numbing to handle the death, with death imprint and guilt perhaps to follow. For the most part, the numbing is transient and relinquished after the period where it has served an adaptive function. Sometimes it may continue, leading to ongoing impairment in personality and functioning, as suggested by the difficulties of some Vietnam veterans.

The role of survivor behavior in other areas of life has been addressed by Ironside (1980). He describes the survivor behavior that develops in certain chronic medical conditions, such as end-stage renal failure, and how this may lead to a pattern of conservation-withdrawal behavior. He notes the same responses in patients in long-term psychoanalytic psychotherapy when they are facing an overwhelming stress, and he sees it as a mechanism of survival.

The theme of the survivor, whatever the context, is twofold. He is special because he has survived the massive death or trauma. He has used certain mechanisms which have aided his survival, such as denial or psychic numbing. He wants to survive yet he feels his survival has been bought at the price of the lives of the others who died. So he feels guilt. This guilt may be hard to expiate, and the role of survivor, or some of the behaviors it involves, may continue long beyond the acute threat-survival period.

## Personal Disaster

The individual may experience disaster in the most personal terms, either through his own passage through a community disaster such as those outlined above, or because of disastrous, calamitous events in his own life (Raphael 1981). Catastrophic events of this kind may include personal involvement in major disaster, the death of a child or spouse, the death of a very close family member or friend, and serious life-threatening illness. These events are the more disastrous as they all undeniably bring losses and high distress, or they bring great change, or they are unable to be prevented or controlled, or they are sudden and unanticipated.

A young man of twenty-eight died suddenly in coronary care from a myocardial infarction. His wife was pregnant with twins. Her father was dying from malignant disease.

A young woman was killed in a car accident. Her husband was severely injured in the same accident and one of their two young children severely brain damaged.

A young woman's husband and two children were burnt to death in an amusement park fire while she watched, helplessly.

The concept of personal disaster is useful in considering individual response for it provides a framework for looking at the issues of special relevance. In personal disasters the individual experiences a close encounter with the death either through the threat of injury or death to himself or through the death of others close to him. If he himself has encountered life-threatening danger, he may experience high death anxiety, with arousal and even excitement generated by this. At such a time there is often a panoramic memory with vivid recall of significant past experiences often spanning a lifetime. These memories are relived very briefly and intensely with the emotion attached to them, as if they represent a condensed and brief life review (Noyes and Kletti 1977). Helplessness and shock are also part of such an encounter with death. The death threat may leave its imprint in the memories of the scene, which may lead to a traumatic neurosis, or in the memories of the death of the other. The sense of personal invulnerability has been breached and the person's defenses have responded. His life may be different thereafter, because he can no longer be innocent of death. He must acknowledge its power and to some degree the inevitability of the loss of his own life and the lives of those he loves. His longer term adjustments to this personal death encounter may be maladaptive, with closing off and denial, a continuation of psychic numbing; or they may be adaptive, leading him to reevaluate his life and live it in ways he believes to be ultimately more worthwhile.

The personal disaster experience may also bring some encounter with destruction, perhaps also with violence and destructiveness. The forces of accident or illness destroy or threaten to destroy the human body; either a person's own or that of one he loves. The individual's own fantasies and explanations of destructiveness and his own guilt about destruction must inevitably be stirred. This confrontation with the destructiveness of man and nature may be defended against with defenses that are adaptive, so that it may be encompassed as only one facet of human behavior, but one that must be accepted as part of the self. There may be grief here too for the loss of innocence that makes one no longer able to deny this component of man and self. Or, the defenses that are adopted may lead to denial; splitting projection; seeing destructiveness only as part of others; or to internalization with depression, self-destructive life-style, or even suicide; or to acting out of rage, violence, and destruction because impulses can no longer be controlled. These patterns have all been described for the war veteran, but they are also found in those whose encounter with personal disaster is the battle field of accident, injury, illness, assault, or bereavement.

Personal disasters involve the personal experience of loss. They follow events such as the loss of the primary attachment figure in calamitous and unexpected circumstances, at a time when death should not have come. They involve a loss of belief in the security of the personal and sometimes physical world, and in one's own immortality. These losses must be grieved in the adaptation to personal disaster, and the very traumatic nature of the experience, with the threat to the individual's own survival, may make this exceptionally difficult. Grief and mourning are often delayed, blocked, and when they occur exceptionally painful.

Survival is an issue. The fact that the individual survived when another did not, that he nearly died and did not, may lead to a sense of elation and excitement. Yet this cannot be considered alongside the deaths of others, and so guilt rapidly appears. If the survival seems unfair, if the individual survived when it seems that another should have been saved or if he was unable to rescue or save that person, then this guilt is reinforced. The numbing that allows him to face death and survive, the imprint of death memories, the guilt of death itself may all be strong themes for personal disasters as they are for more massive ones.

Personal disaster is not forgotten but stays with the individual as a reference point in his existence. He may change his life following it, he may attempt to repress it, but in anniversary phenomena, in his memory and attempts to interpret it, the disaster remains an ongoing part of his experience. When confronted by a community disaster, a group or society may be imprinted by it; deny, incorporate, or even relish its destructiveness; mourn the losses it brings; survive it with guilt; and memorialize it. So also may the individual in the personal disasters of his own life.

# CHAPTER 9. Caring for the Bereaved

---

"I'm sorry Mrs. Jones, but I'm afraid I bring you some sad news," Constable Pearce said gently.

"It's terrible for you, I know," Donna said. "You must both miss her dreadfully." David looked shocked as the tears started to roll down his face. Sally cried softly, "Oh, we do, we do," she said.

"I'm sure you must be very busy doctor; there must be a lot of sick people who need you more than I do."

"You certainly had some happy times together," said Dr. K, "but I suppose, like us all, you two had your ups and downs as well. Jack was a very real person, so I guess you must have had a pretty real relationship."

He put his arm around her and patted her gently. And she cried.

The pain and suffering of grief has been known to human society for a long, long time. Just as it has been suggested that this distress may have evolutionary significance for the human group, it might also be hypothesized that the comfort and consolation human beings offer to each other at such times are powerful reinforcers of the bonds so essential for family and community life. Much of the healing of bereavement takes place in the warmth of family life and friendship. Yet the bereaved also, in their distress, turn to or contact many other people. This chapter attempts to provide a framework from which care may be offered to the bereaved by those who have contact with them in the processes of terminal illness before the death; during the bereavement crisis; or subsequently in the months and years that follow, where bereavement seems still to be the most relevant issue.

## Comfort

The most basic of human responses to those who are grief-stricken and distressed involve the offering of comfort and consolation. The appearance and behavior of the bereaved person is usually such as to evoke caring responses from others. The head lowered, the shoulders hunched, the weeping, the agony in all the body language—all this says "Hold me, help my pain, I have been hurt—comfort me." The natural response is to hold, touch, and murmur sympathy to this person. When holding him, the comforter may rock gently backward and forward. Frequently he will pat the person gently and regularly with one hand while holding him. Darwin (1872) notes how the facial expressions of grief are like those of the distressed infant abandoned by his mother. It may be that such comforting responses are automatic and, in some senses, representative of the comforting of mother for child. The comforter may murmur gentle, nonspecific sounds or words of reassurance. "There, there," he may say. Such comforting may be offered automatically in empathic response to the distress. Those caring for the bereaved may in other instances feel hesitant, not able to touch, because they fear it would break some personal barrier, suggest some intimacy, or even assault. In these cases the caring person may best offer comfort with his quiet and continuing presence, indicating he is prepared to stay with the bereaved until the shock has been absorbed and the bereaved can in some way reintegrate his defenses to cope with the life tasks required at that moment. Often the bereaved may then be supported by family members or relevant others.

This comforting is usually most necessary at the acute times of loss, when the bereaved receives the news of the terminal illness or of the death, or when the reality of the death and loss finally breaks through the initial shocked denial. Those who have been professionally trained to other models may find it difficult to offer comfort because it represents the human side of their response, something they may have learned to detach or dissociate in some therapeutic frameworks. For the bereaved, even the simplest touch may convey much more than formal words: the very humanity and empathy of the caring person's involvement with his pain, something that is vitally important to the bereaved at such a time.

In the phase of acute acknowledgment of the loss or threatened loss, the bereaved's obvious anguish may be very great. It calls out to the kin to offer comfort. In most societies they will come together with the bereaved for this purpose. The concept of care-eliciting behavior as a form of attachment behavior has been elaborated by Henderson (1974). Much of the bereaved's natural response in this time is such as to elicit the care of others. His needs for care may or may not be adequately met by his interpersonal systems. If he is with a professional system (at a hospital or clinic) as he well may be when he receives the news of the terminal illness or of the death of a loved one, then his responses will elicit care from these individuals as well. It is at this time that attempts are often made to deal with his natural distress by the techniques familiar to that professional system, which are perhaps the very techniques inappropriate to the natural pain. This is best exemplified by inappropriate attempts to have the distressed or bereaved person heavily sedated.

Maria L was in the emergency room when the doctor came out to tell her that her husband Joseph had died despite all the attempts to resuscitate him and save his life. She collapsed into the seat, weeping loudly and calling out in great cries of anguish, "Oh my Joe! Oh my Joe! He's dead! He's dead!" All the other people in the outer room shifted uncomfortably and looked very disturbed. They did not want to know about Joe and Maria at all. It was all too upsetting. A nursing sister hurried along the corridor to the young medical intern who had broken the news to Maria and who was standing around helplessly, not quite knowing what to do and wishing he were somewhere else. Why did they always give him these rotten jobs to do, telling people bad news like this. He couldn't do anything for them.

The nurse, an older woman, was firm. "You must do something for her, doctor," she said. "You must do something right away. I've rung the relatives and they'll be here as quickly as they can. You can't let her keep up that noise. It's disturbing all the other patients too much. You must give her something to settle her down—you can't let her go on suffering like that. If you don't stop her she'll get really hysterical soon, and then what will we do? You know I'm short-staffed here, and we haven't got anyone who can stay with her; they're all too busy. You've got to do something for her doctor, and quickly. Can't you see she's getting worse? You've got no right to leave the poor woman in a state like that."

It can hardly be surprising that Dr. X responded by the immediate administration of intravenous sedation for the distressed and bewildered woman, and a hastily written prescription to follow on. She little understood the reason for the injection, but in her shocked state felt that the doctor must be doing what was best. In the terms of her own humanity and her own culture, her response had been natural. During the days and weeks that followed she felt dazed, not only by what had happened, but by the "heaviness" of her emotions. She felt drowsy and in a different world. Her grief would well up inside her and she longed for the catharsis of its outpouring. This did not seem to come. "They have made me sleep," she said. "It is very bad. I should not sleep. Now is the time to grieve for my Joe."

The natural comforting responses may come more easily between women. They are part of the repertoire of behaviors for the comforting of hurt children and for the day-to-day crises of their lives. Men may be hesitant, because the tenderness of the comforting response is frightening to some, perhaps because it is equated with weakness or, if offered to a woman, suggestive in some way of sexuality.

Wal was a policeman, a big man, renowned for his toughness in the force. Over the years he had often had the job of going to give families bad news, and it was something he never liked to do, but something he saw as his duty. The other men would sometimes talk of the difficulties involved in this task and how they hated it; how they got it over as quickly as possible; what a tough part it was of the policeman's life. Wal kept silent on such occasions, because he knew he was different and not sure whether to be ashamed. If the men knew what an old "softie" he was, he would never live it down.

He went on one of these calls later that week. "Mrs. Jones?" he said. And when she answered "Yes," and he had further checked her identity, he asked gently: "Could I come in? I'm afraid I bring you some sad news." He suggested that she sit down and then he said: "I am sorry, but your son, Jim, has been badly hurt in an accident, and I have to tell you that they've not been able to save his life. He has died." Mrs. Jones sat still and shocked for fully five minutes. Wal sat quietly beside her, his big hand gently on her arm. Then she started crying, "Oh what will I do, what *will* I do?" she sobbed bitterly and with great anguish. He patted her shoulder with his big hand. "There, there, my dear," he said. "There, there." He stayed with her, sitting quietly beside her as she wept a little longer. After a while he said, "Now, my dear, can I get you someone who can be here with you when I have to leave?" He carefully arranged for others to come. When they did, he explained quickly to them and her the legal processes that would be required. He patted her on the arm, said he would call the next day to see that all was well, and quietly left.

Dr. P had known the Long family for several years. He had brought their two small children into the world and had looked after their everyday illnesses. When Mrs. Long presented to him for a routine checkup because she was tired, he thought little of it. With the return of the blood test results, however, he was shocked to learn that she had every evidence of acute leukemia. The appointment at which he had to tell her of this was distressing to them both. He liked this young woman and her husband very much. He felt personally involved with them. He did not want them to have to face this dreadful thing, and yet face it they must.

She sat down and said brightly, "Well, what is it, Doctor, some iron tablets again for my anemia?" Dr. P hesitated a moment then went on, putting his hand across the desk to touch her as he spoke: "I'm sorry, Jane," he said, "but I'm afraid the tests were not too good." He paused while she absorbed this. "What's wrong?" she asked with a frightened look on her face. "Well," said Dr. P slowly, "it seems that the blood cell balance is not as it should be. The pathologist thinks that there are a very large number of abnormal white cells, and he believes you may have leukemia." Jane Long sat shocked and silent for several minutes. The doctor gently patted her hand. She then started to cry. She asked angrily, "Are you sure, how could you be sure of something like that, from a little blood test?" He went on over the next half hour to explain the test, its meaning, the further investigations they must do immediately, and some of the implications. He touched very briefly on the treatments that would be necessary. He spoke of the importance of seeing her and her husband together that evening and of the explanations the children would need.

He paused and sat quietly with her as she cried at times throughout the interview. He explained simply and patiently, the most important facts. From time to time he touched her gently or held her hand as he explained things earnestly to her. She gradually settled her initial distress and left his office with some sort of containment of what she had heard. He felt distressed for her—seeing ahead much more clearly than she could the many problems that would have to be faced in the months to follow. He felt angry and helpless that he and medicine had so little to offer in terms of cure. He felt somewhat drained by his own involvement in the interview, but grateful and relieved that he had been able to comfort her.

Practical support is also sometimes a critical issue in the earliest stages of contact with those who are bereaved. Of special importance is the need of the bereaved person to see the body of the deceased. Thus those who are helping at this time may need to help the bereaved see the body, as is his right. This may involve going with him to see the body. Or it may mean helping family members understand and share this final farewell; or it may be that the person's fears about the state of death and the body need to be dealt with so that he can be supported to take this step. Afterward he may need to share his feelings and experience as he comes to terms with it.

While obviously no one should be forced to take this step, it is clear that most bereaved people, including children, are greatly helped by doing so. Death itself is not so bad as their fears and is more readily integrated when it has been seen and known and the farewells made.

## Consolation

Several problems emerge in trying to help and console the bereaved.

*Helping the bereaved bear separation pain.* In the days and weeks that follow, the bereaved longs for the dead person. How can others help him at this time? Whereas initially the distress of the bereaved is nonspecific, that of someone wounded, now the anguish is quite specific:

focusing on and yearning for the absent person. Those offering care may find the picture confusing. There is hurt and distress, yet the bereaved hardly seems to notice or respond to the person offering care. He wants only the dead person. Others are only really valued if they seem to provide a link with that person, or if in fantasy they offer some hope for his return. The role of the caring person now is to be with the bereaved as needed, to accept the focus on the lost person, and to facilitate the bereaved's expression of the yearning and protest he feels because of the person's absence. The caring person may need to help the bereaved recognize the cause of his distress: the absence of the person. He may need to help the bereaved test out again and again the reality of this absence, the death and its circumstances, the finality of the loss. He may need to help prevent the bereaved from using nonadaptive means to deal with his loss. And, he may also have a role in facilitating the understanding and response of others involved in the bereavement.

Donna M was a community nurse, in the local health center. She was calling to see a young couple, Sally and David W, five days after the crib death of their four-month-old baby. It was her role to acquaint them with the findings from the postmortem and to tell them of the local self-help group, as well as to offer them support during the crisis period. She called in the evening so she would find them both at home together. Sally sat on the lounge, sobbing unconsolably. David looked young and frightened, with his arm around his wife, trying to appear strong and in control. His questions came first: Why did it have to happen, why their baby? Had they done something wrong? Why hadn't the doctor known there was something when they'd taken her for a checkup? Why had the police come? Why was *she* here now? Couldn't everyone leave them alone? Couldn't they see that they'd been through enough?

Donna sat quietly accepting his outburst without comment, except an occasional encouraging nod. There was quietness for a moment. Then she replied: Yes it was terrible. She knew that they must both feel dreadful. Yes, it was such a sudden death and very hard for them to bear. Something like this was so difficult to understand, she knew, especially when doctors could not say what had caused it. She paused a while again. Both were listening intensely, Sally with occasional sobs.

Sally's questions came next. How did people ever get over this? She never would—she knew she never would. All she could think about was Lisa, her baby. Why did she have to die? She kept going over and over in her mind, wondering if she had missed something. She thought she was going mad. She kept thinking she heard her cry. She kept going to the room just as though she were still there. Sally broke into sobs again. David looked more angry and helpless than ever. Donna leaned forward and touched Sally's hand. "It's terrible for you, I know," Donna said. "You must both miss her so dreadfully." David looked shocked as the tears started to roll down his face. Sally cried softly. "Oh we do, we do," she said. "I can't believe she has gone. She was so little and perfect. She filled every minute of my day; I don't know what to do. I want her back, that's all. I want . . . I just want her back so much."

Donna said softly, "Yes, I know." She said little else for a while as Sally sobbed quietly but with lessening intensity. She then went on to explain in a little more detail the nature of the death. She responded to their questions for clarification. They talked some more of the baby and how much both parents missed her. It seemed then, too, as if Sally suddenly realized that David was as disturbed as she was, and she turned to comfort him a little as well. Donna suggested that she would call again to see how things were going, because she knew there would be lots of painful times to come. She then explained about the self-help group before she left. She sat in her car a few minutes to regather her own defenses. They had been so angry. She wondered if she'd done the right thing. These deaths were so terrible and so unfair. When you thought of all the families she saw where they didn't want the children, even abused them, and then for this poor young couple to lose theirs. She would see them again in a few days. They were still in some state of shock. They'd perhaps need a bit more help when it really hit them again.

In this description, the caring person has fulfilled the chief goals of care necessary at this stage: to facilitate the emotional release; to assist the bereaved in recognizing and expressing their yearning for the lost person; to facilitate reality testing by a review of the death and its meaning; to promote other social support; and to initiate the basis for an ongoing caring relationship should this be needed. It is important that the carer doesn't collude with distorting defenses. There is often, for instance, anger toward those who were associated with the death. There may often be a need to help the bereaved recognize the sense of anger toward the deceased associated with feelings of being deserted by him. There may also be a need for ventilation of anger at those who have been perceived as failing the bereaved person at this time.

It is important to realize that support offered at this time does not and cannot really stop the bereaved's feelings of loss. Rather, it can help him know, and name, and express the pain that the dead person's absence causes. The bereavement resolution will be hampered if those offering support try to block this, for instance, by trying to prevent the bereaved from dealing with the reality, by pretending the death has not happened, or by avoiding talking about it. The same will be true if they try to keep the bereaved from acknowledging the absence of the dead person by taking him away from reminders of it, by blocking talk of it, by false reassurance that it can be fixed, or by trying to block it out with some other means such as drugs or alcohol. The difficulties for the person offering support at this time lie in the intense angry protest, which the carer may often feel is directed toward him; in the painful empathy that the separation pain evokes; and in the bereaved's clear message that all he wants is the dead person back, and, if the carer cannot provide that, he is not wanted.

*Helping the bereaved accept the finality of the loss and relinquish the lost relationship.* As there is a growing acceptance of the finality of the loss, there is an increasing preoccupation with memories and a review of the lost relationship. At this stage, the support person's role is to facilitate the acceptance of finality, the review of both negative and positive aspects of the lost relationship, and the expression of affects that this evokes. The caring worker may be called upon to encourage these processes himself, or he may be able to help the bereaved's social group to do so.

Dr. K had been the family's general practitioner for a long time. He looked after Mr. Q in his final fatal heart attack, and had been kindly and supportive to Mrs. Q in the two weeks following the death. He recognized that now that her family had returned to their homes, she would be feeling the loss most greatly. From his past experience with other widows he knew, too, that this was the time that they most seemed to need to start talking out their relationship with their husbands. He called around to the house, recognizing that this was the place where the loss was most real to Mrs. Q, and this, although painful for her, might help her talk through her feelings better than if she came to his office. So, two-and-a-half weeks after the death he called to see her. "How are you today?" he asked. "I thought I would just drop in and see how you were doing. She looked at him hesitantly. "I'm fine," she protested rather too quickly. "I'm sure you must be very busy, doctor; there must be a lot of sick people who need you more than I do."

Many bereaved people are hesitant to let others know they need help and often rationalize it by suggesting that others are more needy than they. This suggestion may also be a mechanism to see if the person offering care really understands and to see if he can bear to share their distress. They're giving him an easy way out at this stage. Then, too, it may reflect their fear of the pain that will be involved in talking about their bereavement and is thus an avoidant pathway. Maddison and Walker's work (1967) shows clearly how bereaved widows often need gentle but active encouragement to help them review the lost relationship and express their feelings about their marriage.

Dr. K hesitates, but only for a moment. After all, he thinks to himself, it would be so much easier to leave things be. He's got a busy day, and he knows from past experience that once Elsie "lets go" she may need to talk for an hour or more. Part of him doesn't want to talk about it either. He misses her husband, Jack, too. He was a good friend as well as a patient, and they often enjoyed a game of golf together. It will be painful for him as well. But then, of course, he knows at another level how much more difficult it will be if he misses this opportunity, leaves it until later. He knows Mrs. Q was very dependent on her husband and also that things were not easy between them. Her social network, he knows, although well meaning, would probably not be able to encourage her grief. They were all the sort of women who believed it was better not to talk of these things. "You mustn't speak ill of the dead." "It's God's will." That was the sort of thing they would say to her, and she'd be left with it.

So he said, "Well, Elsie, I thought you might be feeling a little low now that everyone's gone, and it just might be the time you needed a friend to talk to, a shoulder to cry on maybe. Anyway, if it's alright I'd like to come in and have a chat with you about Jack, and how you're coping." Mrs. Q welcomed him with tears and they sat down on the lounge to reminisce together.

"I miss him so much you know," she said. She poured forth her story of the shock his death had been, despite knowing how sick he was; how she kept thinking he'd walk in the door and how it hit her just a few days ago, with terrible reality, that he would never be back. She talked about how sick and upset she felt; how she couldn't sleep; how she didn't know how she'd manage without him.

"He was such a good man," she said, "the very best. He was so good to me. He did everything for me. He never let me lift a hand if he was there." Her idealization continued for some minutes, until Dr. K said gently, something of a twinkle in his eye, "Come on now, you're making him sound like a Saint or something." "Well," she said, "he was." "You certainly had some happy times together," said Dr. K, "but I suppose, like us all, you two had your ups and downs as well. Jack was a very real person, so I guess you must have had a pretty real relationship."

She looked shocked. "We were very happy," she insisted. "Oh yes, I know," he said. "But I suppose you had your difficult times as well." She smiled shakily, and went on to talk of some of the difficulties over these years.

"Sometimes I feel very guilty," she said later. "I keep thinking I should have made him go to see you earlier." They talked that through. She went on to talk about the time she had nearly left him and the arguments they'd had recently over their children. She wondered if the tension might have made his health worse, and she talked as well about all the things he used to do for her. Dr. K let her talk through these guilts, neither agreeing nor disagreeing with what she said. At the end he said it seemed that she and Jack had had the sort of problems in their marriage that most people had. He knew people often felt guilty about these things afterward, but it seemed to him that they really didn't need to; that these things were just part of life. After all, he said, he imagined it wasn't always easy for her now. She must sometimes feel pretty angry with Jack—it was almost as though he'd left her, just when she needed him most, just when they'd got things they wanted in life.

"Yes," she said, "funny you should say that. I've felt so angry with him. It is as though he'd walked out on me. He should have been here to look after me just as he always had. I was ashamed of feeling that. None of my other friends have ever said anything bad about their husbands. I felt it was so irrational, so crazy—after all, he couldn't help dying. But I have felt that way so much of the time."

They talked a little longer about Jack. She cried on and off, remembering some of the things they'd done together; a little rueful about some of the bad times; very sad that she hadn't really told him how she loved him; guilty that she'd never enjoyed the sexual side of their marriage; pleased about the good time they'd had on their last holiday. She finished her talk by the comment, "Yes, it was as you said. He was a great man, Jack was, but he could be difficult sometimes. He was a real man, you know."

Dr. K left quietly, promising to call again in a week or so's time and suggesting she call him if anything worried her. He felt relieved that she'd been able to talk so freely and also that she'd been able to remember Jack a bit more the way he was. There was still a way to go, however, and he'd have to go back again. She was a very dependent lady, and he'd have to be careful she didn't start relying too heavily on him. In this crisis time he could offer her support, but he'd have to make sure she worked toward some links with her friends and perhaps some of the community groups. It had been a bit difficult, hearing all those things about the other side of Jack. Still, that was life.

In the case of Dr. K and Mrs. Q the goals of support were fulfilled. The bereaved's grief and mourning were encouraged. Possible blocks to these, such as intense idealization, were lessened. The review of the real person and the real relationship was set in motion. This process may be accomplished in one contact or several. In line with crisis theory, such support is best offered and most effective in the earliest weeks to the two to three months following the death.

## Facilitating Recovery

The longer term adjustment of the bereaved may best be supported by facilitating reintegration into the social group. Here the caring person may have to help the bereaved grieve and mourn the old roles that have been lost, the previous status and identity that must be relinquished, the lost forms of gratification. It is probably in this area particularly that the bereaved is helped by the role models offered by others who have passed through these processes, such as members of self-help groups; and by those who can assist with tasks linked to the social structure of reintegration, for instance, training for new roles or work; and by those who offer realistic opportunities for socialization. The building of self-esteem is important. So also is the assistance of social agencies in providing practical resources for those who must take over the role and functions left by the deceased's death. Thus, those in contact with the bereaved individual, either personally or professionally, may be able to offer support, comfort, and consolation to the bereaved in a number of ways.

### THERAPEUTIC ASSESSMENT OF THE BEREAVED

In the process of contact with a bereaved person it may be important to determine whether or not the bereavement process is progressing; whether or not there are risk factors for poor resolution; and whether or not there is already some sign of pathological bereavement processes or other morbid outcomes. I have developed a broad format for assessing these factors that explores certain aspects of the bereavement. This format is so designed that, in itself, it has goals of facilitating the expression of grieving affects and promoting the mourning processes; in other words, it is a therapeutic assessment.

Discussion of bereavement throughout this book has shown that several factors are associated with a greater risk of morbid grief processes, failure of mourning, and pathological outcomes. These include the particular circumstances of the death; the patterns in the preexisting relationship with the deceased; the capacity of family and other social network members to support and encourage grief and mourning; the occurrence of multiple crises or stressors at the time of the bereavement crisis; and, in some instances, earlier unresolved vulnerabilities such as previous loss or childhood bereavement.

The therapeutic assessment is designed to explore a number of areas of grief. These are framed below as specific questions, but they might be framed in many other forms. Furthermore, the information they seek may be produced spontaneously by the bereaved. These areas of query and their rationale are set out as follows:

1. *Can you tell me a little about the death? What happened? What happened that day?*

The caring person gives the bereaved a clear indication that he is willing to talk about the death, is indeed interested in doing so, and sees it as of great importance to the bereaved. The very use of the word death, or the direct opening up of this area, is often most reassuring to the bereaved. He may have had a great urge to talk about it but found that most others avoid the topic or rely on evasions and euphemisms. The exploration of this area serves further purposes, apart from indicating to the bereaved that it is a natural and appropriate area for discussion.

362

It provides information about the nature and circumstances of the death and the bereaved's involvement in it: how he heard of the death; whether it was expected or unexpected, timely or untimely; whether there were particular and shocking circumstances; how it may have produced a further traumatic-stress syndrome for the bereaved; how his presence or absence at the time of the death may have been a source of guilt; whether it occurred at a time that cut across and highlighted special conflicts or stresses in the relationship with the deceased that may complicate resolution of the loss.

The bereaved's capacity to talk of the death and his pattern of emotional responsiveness about it, indicating his anger, his helplessness, any personal fears of vulnerability through his association with it, may start to become obvious. Defenses of denial and avoidance may also be evident.

Whether or not the bereaved was able to see the body of the person as a dead person and say his own private good-byes will also become clear or may be explored. Also, the bereaved's acceptance of, involvement in, and feelings about the funeral may become apparent. Whether this is something that will be helpful in facilitating resolution or will in fact be a block to mourning may be assessed. Thus there is information about the circumstances of the death that may indicate greater risk and also indicate some areas of the bereaved's emotional response to the death and their implications, such as indicators of denial or blocking, on the one hand, or the presence of grief, on the other.

Aaron was nineteen. His response to this first area of query about his sister's death provided a great deal of information. "She died in a car accident," he said. "It was very sudden and a terrible shock to the whole family." He then hastily went on to insist how well they were coping now and what a wonderful girl his sister had been. He was asked if he could tell the interviewer a little bit more about her death. "Well," he said, "she was just smashed up; that was all"—again without much display of emotion. He then changed the topic. The interviewer went on to discuss the funeral with him. He had attended and "coped very well." He was then gently asked about the day of the death—what had they been doing, how had his sister been in the car, where had she been going? He angrily burst out: "What do you want to know all that stuff for; haven't I told you enough?"

Then he started crying: "I suppose I may as well tell you all about it—it would be a great relief, really, to talk about it to someone. We'd had this terrible fight that morning. We were often fighting, but that day was really bad. I told her to 'go and get stuffed,' that I was fed up with her, that all she was was a burden to the family—that was that. I didn't really mean it; she was a great kid most of the time. Well she dashed out and got in the car, my old bomb, and off she went. I thought she shouldn't be driving it—I knew the brakes were only so-so, but I thought to myself, 'What do I care? Serves her right if she does have a prang.' I never thought she'd have a smash really, and I never thought she'd die. I'll never forget the sound when she hit that truck right outside. I dashed to the door, and there it was like some nightmare. I tried to get her out, but she was dying then, I'm sure. I felt as though I was paralyzed. I couldn't get her out. I couldn't stop her dying. And it was all my fault."

The shocking circumstances of the death and the guilt and the ambivalence that were heightened at the time of the death were all revealed as risk factors for problems with resolution. The apparent lack of affect in the early discussions suggests some block to grief, and the query served some therapeutic purpose in allowing discussion of the death and some catharsis.

2. *Can you tell me about him, about your relationship from the beginning?*

This second area of query opens up the whole *history* of the lost relationship as it is intended to do. The caring person queries the history of the relationship back to its earliest beginnings: the expectations, hopes, and disillusionments that went into making it and the images and interactions it involved. This area of query conveys to the bereaved the fact that the interviewer sees this too as an important and vital area to the bereaved, and that he is prepared to talk of it and share the bereaved's emotions about it. This may be in marked contradistinction to those who shied away from this topic, afraid of what to say or afraid of the bereaved's yearning and anger. Also, this query serves to elicit information from the bereaved.

It may reveal the quality of the preexisting relationship with the dead person and the level of ambivalence and dependence it involved. This will indicate the degree to which the bereaved may be at risk of problems of resolution because of the relationship, perhaps running the risk of distorted or chronic grief reactions or subsequent depression.

The degree to which the bereaved is denying the loss, still perhaps experiencing it emotionally in terms of the absence of the lost person, or is in the process of relinquishing it may become apparent. Thus the bereaved's yearning for the lost person may be obvious in his preoccupation with hopes of return, in his responses, his behavior, or even in his use of the present tense. The degree to which he avoids mention of the dead person and the emotion the use of his name entails may all provide cues as to the stage of resolution that has been reached, and whether or not it seems appropriate for this bereaved person in these life circumstances, at this time.

Information on the progress of mourning and relinquishing of the lost relationship, as a whole, real relationship rather than an idealized one, may be gleaned. The degree to which the bereaved can talk of the person in real terms, recall negative as well as positive memories and recall the unhappy as well as happy aspects of the lost relationship will be important. This would not, of course, be expected in most bereavements in the early weeks, but would be after that time, as the mourning process sets in course. Where the bereaved presents only positive aspects, the negative are also carefully explored, perhaps through further query such as: "You've told me a lot about the happy times you shared. Can you tell me a little about the times that were not so good?" The bereaved's response to this may indicate blocks, or in fact the question may serve the therapeutic purpose of opening up this area.

The grief affects associated with mourning may also be assessed. The levels of sadness, anger, particular guilts or abnormal levels of guilt may be noted for the possibility that they may create difficulties with resolution.

Thus this exploration may provide evidence of risk factors from the relationship as well as indications of the progress and quality of mourning, as appropriate for this stage after the loss. At the same time the exploration provides the review of the relationship from its beginnings, in both its positive and negative aspects, and thus acts therapeutically to facilitate the mourning process.

When queried about her son Steven, who had died five weeks ago at the age of nine from a cerebral tumor, Cynthia R insisted he was the most perfect child, perfect in every way. He was bright and happy and never let his illness get him down. He had been cheerful to the end, and she had cared for him and loved him every minute of the day. She didn't know what she would do without him now that he had gone, and she still found it hard to believe. The more she was asked to talk of Steven the more intense became her idealization, and the reaction formation it involved became increasingly obvious.

The interviewer then inquired back to the time of her pregnancy with Steven and his early years, encouraging her to discuss the day-to-day details of their lives. It became increasingly obvious that Steven had been conceived at a time of great marital conflict. Mrs. R had contemplated having an abortion during her pregnancy and had had great difficulty bonding to Steven in the early months. His temperament and hers had not fitted well together, and she often saw him as being like his father, for whom she sometimes felt intense hatred. With the onset of his illness she had become extremely guilty and had overcompensated with an intense, overprotective, and somewhat artificial involvement in her child's care.

This assessment achieved the goals of understanding her underlying ambivalence in the relationship and of promoting a more realistic mourning process for the real rather than the idealized relationship.

*3. What has been happening since the death? How have things been with you and your family and friends?*

This area of query explores the pattern of response since the time of the death and the quality of family and social-network support perceived to be available. At the same time, it provides a clear indication to the bereaved of the importance of his feelings and relationships in the time since the death.

It may yield information about the experience of the bereaved, including his levels of emotion about, and resolution of, the absence of the lost person and the finality of the death, as well as reveal any problems of social living. Particular aspects may be explored to assess the degree to which the bereaved perceives his social network as facilitating his review of the lost relationship and his expression of grief, as well as providing support for his coping and other needs. Specific aspects may be explored as relevant: for instance, the ways in which the family or friends may allow, encourage, or block the review of negative aspects of the relationship as well as anger and guilt, especially when the relationship was a particularly ambivalent one.

This area of query may yield evidence of risk factors, such as perceived inadequacy of social support or other crises or stresses that may have occurred. It may also indicate blocks to resolution or a delayed, inhibited, or distorted pattern of bereavement.

Mrs. Joyce B was twenty-nine when her husband Evan died. He had had severe renal disease for many years, but Mrs. B had nursed him devotedly. His death was unexpected at the time he died, despite his chronic and debilitating illness. Exploration of this area with Mrs. B revealed that she felt she was coping reasonably—indeed, her friends said so. But she had been unable to cry and had found herself thinking that her husband would soon come home from the hospital again. Her friends, she said, had been very kind, and also her brother and sister. She knew they meant well. However, they kept telling her she should feel pleased, that she was now relieved of the burden of her husband's illness. She was told she should forget about the past and think only of the future; that she was young and she would soon remarry; that she should accept her husband's death as God's will. She found these comments very distressing, for she thought constantly of her dead husband and missed him very much. They had been particularly close because he was home so much with his illness. Her friends also told her she should only remember the good things about her husband, and that she should think of his good points and the good times in the relationship. She remembered some of the unhappiness with his irritability and demandingness and felt herself to be bad and guilty as a consequence. She knew her family and friends to be helpful; but, in fact, on careful assessment, she perceived their interactions as nonsupportive and interfering with her grief.

This assessment achieved the goals of understanding the possible risk factors for nonresolution and perception of nonsupportiveness; it showed some blocking of her grief and some failure of her family and friends to facilitate the mourning process. The interview itself provided some opportunity for working through.

4. *Have you been through any other bad times like this recently or when you were young?*

This area of query seeks more specifically signs of any other concurrent crises or stressors and their effects as possible risk factors for bereavement malresolution. It also enables the evaluation of earlier losses, especially childhood bereavement, and their possible pathogenic potential. These are not necessarily frequently occurring variables, but they are important when they are present.

Mr. C, for example, had lost his job five weeks before his wife's death. He had also had a drunk-driving charge about which he felt very humiliated. His childhood had been one of frequent separations, and his mother had died tragically when he was five. He was immensely vulnerable to loss and had tried to avoid closeness as a consequence, although he finally succumbed to his wife's warmth and love. This loss, her death, brought back all the unresolved anguish of his mother's suicide. He was at risk of problems with this current bereavement, and the assessment enabled those working with him to provide sensitive, specific, and skilled assistance.

The kind of therapeutic assessment described here may be used for several purposes:

1. To facilitate and consolidate a satisfactorily resolving bereavement
2. To provide a framework for specific preventive intervention with bereaved who are at high risk of malresolution
3. To provide a framework for specific intervention with pathological bereavements so that these may possibly be diverted to a more adaptive course

The second and third of these will now be dealt with in more detail.

PREVENTIVE INTERVENTION WITH THE BEREAVED AT RISK OF MALRESOLUTION

From the framework provided by the therapeutic assessment, a "risk profile" may be drawn up for each bereaved person, delineating the specific areas in which he may have difficulty. Specific-crisis or short-term bereavement counseling may then be provided for him. In the model of Caplan (1964) this is most appropriately dealt with in the crisis period of the first weeks and months following the loss. Experience suggests that, during the first two weeks, many bereaved people are still so taken up with the necessary practical tasks and family matters that they are not so ready to talk and work through the various aspects as they are from about the third week onward. After about six to eight weeks some of the urgency of the crisis settles and old defenses come into play, so that the optimal time for such preventive intervention is probably between the first two to eight weeks or slightly later, perhaps even up to three months after the death.

The format (which I describe elsewhere; for example, Raphael 1976b, 1977b, 1978a, 1980a; Raphael and Maddison 1976) is that of short-term focal psychotherapy, with the focus in this instance on the recent loss crisis and the particular parameters of risk. It is carried out over one to six or even eight sessions, usually in the bereaved's own home. Sessions are often one and a half to two hours in duration, since this time seems to fit with the bereaved's needs in the crisis period. Longer-term issues of entrenched psychopathology are avoided except insofar as they appear specifically relevant for the bereavement and its resolution.

*Goals.* The goals of the intervention are generally to encourage the expression of grieving affects and promote the mourning process. Particular goals are defined for each individual as well and reflect his risk profile. Thus they may include the working through of traumatic-stress-syndrome effects related to the circumstances of the death. Here the bereaved would be helped to face the affects of helplessness and anxiety generated at that time and to gain a new mastery so that the preoccupation with memories of the death scene or situation can be relinquished, and the bereaved can carry on the work of mourning. Sometimes there may be a need to deal with guilt linked to ambivalence in the lost relationship. Or, it may be that the angry sense of desertion with the death of a partner in a very dependent relationship may have to be dealt with. The perceived inadequacy of the family and social-network support may also be a risk factor requiring work with the bereaved and probably his family to facilitate greater mutual support.

*Techniques.* The techniques used depend on the establishment of rapport and the use of the interpersonal relationship with the bereaved person to move toward the goals outlined. There is a focus on the bereavement and the emotions it has generated. The bereaved is encouraged to express the yearning for the lost person and the angry protest at the desertion his death seems to represent. Where anger is displaced onto others, every attempt is made to help the bereaved face its origins in his anger at the deceased, although ventilation at other realistic causes of anger is also accepted. The review of the lost relationship is encouraged with an opening up of negative factors if these are denied. The various affects such as sadness, relief, regret, or anger are dealt with as appropriate.

The counseling relationship usually develops quickly as there is increased attachment behavior at this time, and the bereaved is highly motivated to seek help for his distress. The lowered defensiveness of the crisis period allows for a free flow of material and expression of affects. Psychodynamic connections are readily understood and often produced spontaneously with some insight by the bereaved. Earlier unresolved losses that were not obvious at the time of assessment often come to the surface and may become available for working through. The termination of this short focal therapeutic encounter is particularly important, as many of the intense and true affects of separation and loss appear at this time in the transference, and may assume greater meaning with respect to the bereaved's real life experience of loss. It is often only then that the intense yearning and intense protest can really be expressed and internally accepted.

The interpretation of transference aspects is also very important, for these may reflect very significant parameters of the bereavement process. The bereaved's anger at unmet dependent needs, that the caring person cannot or will not take away the pain of the loss, may be usefully dealt with. The persecuting, hostile parts of the dead person may be projected onto the carer and may make the relationship uncomfortable. Nevertheless, it is critically important that such negative projections are dealt with and recognized in the transference.

Resistances to the painful work involved in relinquishing the lost relationship may appear in a number of ways. The bereaved may suggest he is coping well and does not need help: others are sicker and need the counselor's valuable time. He may infer that the counselor cannot really understand because he has not been through such a loss himself. There is often a resentment and envy of those who have not lost a spouse or child as has the bereaved, with a message to the therapist that the bereaved's envy may destroy him if he persists with his counseling. There may be more direct attempts at avoidance by changing the subject, denying a problem, or bringing in reinforcements by asking others to be present at the time of the counseling sessions. There may be a preoccupation with the needs of others, as a defense against recognizing the needs of the self. The person may attempt to find a replacement relationship or someone he can care for and grieve through vicariously. He may try to seduce the counselor into becoming a replacement for the lost person so that they do not have to do the painful work of mourning together. He may produce the most fascinating (but entrenched and probably unchangeable) psychopathology to mislead the counselor and avoid the loss issues. All these resistances may be dealt with by interpreting for the bereaved his wish to avoid facing the pain and loss, yet stressing for him the importance of doing so.

When there are difficulties with the expression of affects, they are frequently associated with fears of disintegration, loss of control, and breakdown. This may have to be interpreted for him, as may the fears that the bereaved has about survival and identity, when he starts to give up the lost relationship.

With the counselor's communication of his recognition of the pain involved, with some opportunities provided to express the affects involved and the beginnings of review of the real good-bad relationship, the important first steps have been taken toward an adaptive as opposed to maladaptive resolution. Much of the further work of relinquishing the relationship will continue beyond the early crisis months, yet its adaptive course can be set at this early time and a high-risk maladaptive course averted.

*Outcome.* Such specific crisis intervention is assessed by the degree to which the bereaved moves on to more normal grief and mourning processes and, in particular, the degree to which the risk factors have been dealt with or reduced.

Elizabeth S was thirty-eight when her husband Jason, forty-nine, died. He had been an invalid for some years and on a pension but had been able to play a quiet game of bowls and manage his garden. They were close as a couple, because he had spent much time at home with his wife. There was a relationship of mutual but pleasant dependency, for he had fulfilled her needs for care that she felt had been lacking in her own, unhappy childhood. She had compulsively worried about his health and insisted on looking after him carefully, in line with her training as a nurse. She always gave him his tablets, and made sure he had the right diet. She had recently been concerned that he was not so well and insisted he see the local doctor who prescribed some new medication. Jason took this somewhat irritably and collapsed not long afterward. She tried desperately to resuscitate him as she waited for the doctor to come, but her efforts were in vain. Her mind was filled with memories of his blue, cold face as she tried to give him mouth-to-mouth resuscitation.

In the weeks that followed the death she and their two daughters were intensely distressed. She was filled with guilt over his death, both because she could not save him when she thought she should have been able to, and because, at her urging, he had taken the new medication to which, it now seemed, he had been fatally sensitive. Her mother could offer little support. She kept telling her daughter that she was lucky to have had such a good marriage, and that she hadn't deserved such a good man—she couldn't even look after him properly. She advised Elizabeth to think of the future and to get a new job and all would be well; she'd soon get over it. Mrs. S perceived her mother's comments as very distressing and unhelpful and as blocking her capacity to cry or to talk about her guilt. She showed no evidence of psychiatric illness and no past history of such. She was seen by the counselor in her own home for four sessions in the third, fourth, fifth, and sixth weeks after the death.

The first session dealt with the death, the circumstances of the day, and the many complex feelings Mrs. S had as a consequence. Her fears of loss, the ways they had reinforced her compulsive concern for her husband's health, and their origins in her frequent separations from her mother were explored. She worked through much sadness over these early deprivations and losses. She relived some of her experience of the day of the death and the helplessness and panic she had felt. She came to an acknowledgement that she had done her best to save him, and her preoccupation with memories of the death started to lessen. Her anger at the doctor for the tablets he prescribed and at the futility of attempts to save her husband's life was ventilated. This was then opened up to deal with her feelings of desertion. Her intense rage that her husband should somehow "desert," "reject," her when she had cared for him so well, and when she secretly believed he could never leave her, was expressed. She spent a considerable part of that two-hour session in angry tears and resentment that somehow, despite all her care and plans, she should once again face the pain of being separated from someone she needed so desperately.

The second session was spent exploring further her longing and yearning for her husband and the quality of their relationship. Her dreams about him were discussed, as were her horror and panic when she would awake to find he was not there beside her. The yearning to have someone who loved her and who would not, or could not, leave her led to further sad and painful memories of her mother's harshness and rejection. She then went on to talk more of the realities of what she had lost, and her mother as the real person she was, and the finality of her husband's death.

In the third session she talked more of their relationship. She remembered and reviewed the special closeness it had involved and their warmth and affection for each other. Yet she also recalled the disappointment and frustration she felt at the inadequacies of their sexual life. She was angry at the lost opportunities her husband's illness had meant. She resented his jovial good humor with others and his irritability with her. She recalled the earliest days of their relationship, the good times of their marriage, the disappointments, and the adjustments they had made. She talked somewhat resentfully of "people you start to trust, who let you down, go off and leave you." The counselor interpreted these feelings in terms of her sense of loss at her husband's desertion and the fact that he too would be going after their final session the following week. Mrs. S expressed further her sadness and frustration.

In the fourth session she spoke of her concerns for her family. These were explored. There was anger and resentment toward her mother, whose assistance she now needed to help with the girls while she went out to work and whose support in the crisis had been so inappropriate. She was concerned for her daughters having to grow up without a "father to care for them." This reflected much of her own anger toward her own father for leaving her care so totally to her mother and also her anger toward her husband, for the fathering he failed to give now that he had died, for she had in many ways seen him as both the father and the mother she had longed for in childhood. Like them, he too was now proved imperfect. At the end of the interview she spoke of him in real terms and of some hopes for the future. She said to the counselor, "It's been helpful to talk about these things, and I don't feel so guilty now. I know I've still got a long way to go. I'll always find it hard that life dealt me this blow. I needed him so much." Then she smiled: "Well," she said, "I needed you so much in the beginning too, but I've got to do without you as well. You men are all the same—always off to something else or someone else. I'd like to say I couldn't manage, but really, I expect I will, without either of you." And with a slightly hostile but aware smile she said good-bye.

This patient had achieved some goals. Her risk factors were lessened and her bereavement process set on a more normal course. At follow-up a year later, she was coping reasonably well.

### EFFECTIVENESS OF SPECIFIC PREVENTIVE-INTERVENTION PROGRAMS FOR THE BEREAVED AT RISK

In a controlled trial I was able to demonstrate the effectiveness of a program of crisis intervention using the model described above (Raphael 1977b; Raphael and Maddison 1976). Nonselected widows in a large city (Sydney) were contacted in the early weeks following their husband's deaths. All who were willing (the vast majority) were interviewed and assessed in a semistructured nondirective interview to define the nature of the bereavement response and the level of risk in terms of the quality of their preexisting relationships with their husbands, the circumstances of the death, the presence of concurrent crises, and their perception of social support. Those who were, on the predetermined criteria of high levels of perceived nonsupportiveness (or lower levels, plus other criteria), at risk of poor resolution were then randomly allocated to preventive intervention with a separate intervention worker and to nonintervention control groups. Those receiving intervention were contacted and provided with specific counseling, usually in their own homes. Sessions averaged two hours' duration, and the average number of sessions was four, though they ranged from one to eight. The intervention was toward general goals of encouraging grief and promoting mourning, but also, specific areas of risk for the individual widow were dealt with. The interventions were recorded and rated by an independent rater for the degree of achievement of these goals. Subjects were then followed up thirteen months after the death (to avoid the twelve-month anniversary phenomenon) and their outcome independently evaluated in general health and adjustment terms. At follow-up, those high-risk subjects who had received preventive intervention (N=27) were significantly more likely to have a better outcome, and those high-risk subjects who had not received it (N=29) were more likely to show substantial health impairment. Their health was in fact much worse than that of a non-high-risk control group from whom they differed very significantly. The health of the intervention group was equivalent to that of the non-high-risk subjects. The degree to which the intervention had been rated as facilitating grief and mourning also correlated with the likelihood of good outcome. Subjects rated as nearing these intermediate goals were likely to go on to better health and adjustment than those who dropped out or whose intervention did not seem to achieve these ends. Within the subgroup of risk factors those who were considered at risk because they perceived their social networks as nonsupportive of their grief and mourning were especially likely to benefit from this type of intervention (p <0.001). Thus it would seem that a specific intervention of this type can be effective in lessening post bereavement morbidity through its role in facilitating the normal bereavement process.

Similarly, in a subgroup and study of further subjects (Raphael 1978a) the author was able to demonstrate the effectiveness of supportive intervention for those at risk of malresolution through difficulties resulting from an ambivalent and/or dependent relationship with the deceased. Here, where the social network was unable to provide support for dealing with the ambivalent aspects, the bereaved was significantly more likely to suffer depression, as Freud (1917) had originally hypothesized. Preventive intervention aimed at working this through lessened the risk of depressive outcomes.

The same sort of methodology and techniques, although not applied in a random control trial manner, when provided for those bereaved in a major disaster was also shown to be effective in lessening the risk of malresolution and poor outcome, at least for those who perceived them as helpful and felt able to use them (Singh and Raphael 1981).

Williams and Polak (1979) provided nonspecific programs of intervention to bereaved families. These were not selected for their risk category, except that the deaths were all sudden and there was a high refusal rate. These authors concluded that their intervention had little or no effect and may have been detrimental. This fits perhaps with the findings from a review of the literature in primary prevention, where it has been shown that nonspecific programs with broad populations are unlikely to show demonstrable effectiveness, whereas specific programs on high risk populations are more likely to be able to demonstrate an effect if one exists (Raphael 1980*b*).

Another study of such bereavement counseling is that of Gerber's group (1975). They found that those offered such support received significantly fewer prescriptions of drugs, reported fewer consultations with physicians, and less of a general feeling of ill health. Vachon et al. (1980) have also shown the effectiveness of self-help intervention with bereaved widows in lessening the degree of morbid outcome.

Parkes's group (1979) carried out a study of the effectiveness of services for relatives of patients dying at St. Christopher's Hospice, London. This study also focused on those defined as at high risk, and the risk variables were defined by a questionnaire evolved by Parkes previously, but including variables such as the preexisting relationship with the deceased (especially clinging relationships), anger and self-reproach, and the perception of inadequate social support. This group also included low socioeconomic status and young age as further risk variables. When the counselors became more skilled, but not in the first year of the service, there were significant differences in outcome favoring the group that received the specific support. As with my own study, people in the high-risk group were helped with intervention to achieve a reduced level of risk equivalent to that of the low-risk group, while the high-risk nonintervention subjects showed very significant morbidity.

In a valuable review, Parkes (1980) concludes that professional and professionally supported services and self-help services are capable of reducing the risk of postbereavement morbidity. He suggests it may take a counselor one year to become proficient in providing this. The goals for most of these effective programs are as outlined above: the encouragement of grief and the promotion of mourning. Not only may the bereaved person be comforted and consoled, but he may, sensitively and appropriately, be assisted in the resolution of his loss.

## Bereavement Counseling: The Management
## of Pathological Grief

The therapeutic assessment of the bereaved individual may indicate that bereavement is already taking a pathological course or indeed has done so for some time. The care of those showing evidence of such a morbid grief reaction will then devolve from the type of deviant reaction and the etiological processes (perhaps risk variables) that have contributed to the development of this "abnormal" pattern.

The following models will be examined here:

1.  The psychotherapeutic and bereavement counseling model to deal with this type of response during the crisis and subsequent to it (Lindemann, 1944; Raphael 1975*a*, 1975*d*, 1975*e*)
2.  "Re-grief therapy" used in psychotherapy to resolve such pathological bereavements subsequent to the crisis (Volkan and Showalter 1968; Volkan 1971)
3.  Behavioral treatments for the bereaved, both in the early times following the loss when pathology appears (see, for example, Ramsay and Happei 1977, 1979; Gauthier and Marshall 1977; Gauthier and Pye 1979), and subsequently with procedures such as "guided mourning" used for morbid grief (Mawson et al. 1981)
4.  Other therapies for resolution of pathological bereavement that may include aspects of the above approaches (for example, Hodgkinson 1982; Melges and DeMaso 1980) and may also include an existential approach or Gestalt therapy.

### FOCAL PSYCHOTHERAPY

The model of focal psychotherapy involves an assessment of the particular form of pathological bereavement response and management specific to it as well as to the etiological processes involved. The goals are the conversion of the response to a more normal pattern in which the patient is able to grieve and mourn. This therapy may be carried out either in the crisis or subsequently.

*Inhibited, suppressed, or absent grief.*  Where grief is inhibited, suppressed, or absent, the reasons why the bereaved cannot accept the death or the loss are explored indirectly. The dependence on the deceased, the guilt about the death, and the fear of bereavement affects are among the possibilities. The counselor's principal task will be to go over repeatedly the bereaved's relationship with the deceased, for in so doing, the bereaved's defenses to the loss will be revealed and some aspects of the mourning will be facilitated. Where affect does not appear, and would seem appropriate as these issues are discussed, the counselor may interpret this as the bereaved's fear of affect release. At another stage, he might observe the beginnings of emotional release which are quickly covered up and interpret this behavior as the bereaved's fear of loss of control. The fear of the disintegrative effects of affect is a frequent dynamic in such patients. When it seems that guilt over the lost relationship interferes with the acceptance of the death, the counselor may interpret this as the bereaved's concern that the "killing" fantasies now seem so fulfilled.

The elements that are intrinsic to this work involve the following: a general recognition of the bereaved's inner pain which is obviously difficult for him to bear and express; a general recognition that this and his other fears are common amongst bereaved people and thus understood by the counselor; a recognition that his defenses serve some psychological purpose and therefore will not be torn down harshly or without due consideration of their function; a recognition that he is reluctant, probably for a variety of reasons, to relinquish the person who has died, and that, *together*, the bereaved and the counselor may be able to explore and understand the reasons and feelings involved in this; and a recognition that he, like many other bereaved people, dreads and wishes to avoid the pain of loss and other intense emotions that occur naturally at this time, especially anger, sadness, and guilt. Such understandings may be made explicit in interpretation, or they may be more gradually worked toward with the bereaved. The counselor may return again and again to this lost relationship and its history; the death and its circumstances; the social field, especially the family, and its response. Direct confrontation with the denial of absent or inhibited grief is rarely successful and instead often leads to a stalemate or battle between the bereaved and the counselor: the counselor believing he must get the bereaved to grieve and the bereaved, tenaciously holding on to his denial and suppression, because for reasons neither has discovered, he cannot tolerate the loss or affective release. It is in the exploration of the death and the relationship that these reasons will be discovered and the denial thus able to be relinquished.

Sarah B was thirty-five when her husband Brian, thirty-eight, died. He had been the center of her life in every way, from the time of their marriage when she was seventeen and pregnant with their first and only child, Kim. Kim had left home a year previously after a bitter struggle for independence from the parents. Mrs. B did not know where she had gone and was still deeply grieving her daughter's angry departure. She felt she had failed because she had tried so hard to give Kim the love and affection her own childhood had lacked. Brian had also had a deprived childhood. He and Sarah had been, as she said, "everything to one another." "We never thought of anyone else; we were complete the way we were. We never needed anyone else. When Kim left he made me feel all right about it. At first I blamed myself, but he kept reassuring me. He told me it wasn't my fault and he made me believe in myself again."

"I felt as though I was just getting over it, this last month. We were doing so many things together again, and in a way I was almost pleased she'd gone. She sometimes used to come between us, and now we had no one to please but ourselves. Neither of us had any family, and we wouldn't have wanted them if we had. They'd never been any help to us. We just had each other, and that was all we needed."

Brian died from a myocardial infarction. He suffered one severe attack and was admitted to coronary care. He seemed to be recovering, and Sarah spent each day with him. They felt hopeful and planned the holiday they would take together. She spent her evenings imagining how she would look after and protect him because he was "all she had," and they "only had one another now." Ten days after the first attack Brian suffered a second major episode and died before she could reach the hospital to see him. She would not see his body, although supported by the hospital staff to do so, because she wished to "remember him the way he was."

She seemed in a daze from that time on. She made all the practical arrangements about the funeral. She tried to find Kim and eventually contacted her. Kim came home to the funeral but left immediately afterward. In the days and weeks that followed she carried on with little emotional display or change in her pattern of life. She went to work in the business she and Brian had shared and seemed to their few friends there to be "bearing up and managing well." She did not cry. She did not talk of Brian and avoided all mention and reminders of him. At home she shut up his study and put away his things and continued her life in a wooden and frozen manner.

She was contacted in a survey from the hospital eight weeks after the death. The assessment of her adjustment at this time was as follows: "Mrs. B is in a state of frozen or absent grief. She avoids all discussion of her dead husband or his death. She shows little overt emotional response. Her social network is sparse. She has a pathological bereavement response and requires counseling."

She was contacted in an outreach program offering support for bereaved families by a local clergyman. She was at first very unwilling to be involved, stating she was coping well, and they "couldn't bring him back, so what was the point." The contact counselor sensitively suggested that this was surely the most painful thing of all, and that they couldn't bring him back. Mrs. B looked startled at this comment and thought quietly for a moment. Then she said that she had felt it was strange—that she just "couldn't cry for Brian, and yet it didn't seem right," because she "loved him so much." She agreed to a further session before she would commit herself to counseling.

In the next session in her own home one evening a few days later, she seemed to regret having agreed to see the worker. "I don't know why you've come," she said irritably. "There's nothing you can do. It's up to me—that's all." The counselor agreed that it was hard to see what might come of their discussions, but that many bereaved people did find it helpful to talk to some-one outside the family. Mrs. B accepted this to some degree. The counselor then went on to an exploration of the relationship in general terms, and in the recent months leading up to Mr. B's illness and death. Mrs. B's first show of emotion came as she described their problems with Kim and how hurt she had been by her daughter's departure and by her coldness at the time of her fa-ther's death. The counselor recognized that Mrs. B might also be hurt by her own "coldness" of response since her husband's death, so rather than joining in the condemnation of Kim, he used it as an opportunity to suggest that perhaps like lots of people, and probably Mrs. B too, Kim might have found it hard to bear the feelings she had inside; perhaps they were so painful she felt she had to hang on to them. Mrs. B struggled to contain her own tears for the first time, but swallowed, regained control, and said, "Yes," she could see what the counselor meant. She then hastily changed the subject and asked quite direct questions about the counselor's own family, becoming cheerful and in control of herself again.

The counselor saw that Mrs. B's defenses were a little less fixed than before, but that she was indeed very afraid of her affect about her loss. He recognized from past experiences that this might be connected with deprivations and sepa-rations in childhood. He then encouraged Mrs. B to talk of her own experi-ences in her early years, and the picture of loss and rejection unfolded. The counselor commented after a while that having gone through so much as a little girl must have made it especially difficult for her now; that it must have seemed specially unfair to lose someone when you'd already suffered such a lot of losses—that of her parents, and then Kim, and now Brian, her husband. "Yes," it was so unfair; she couldn't let him go, she needed him so much—he was all she had. She'd never find anyone else, never. She still couldn't believe he was gone. She kept thinking he would come back. She would never survive if she accepted his death. She'd have to give up and die herself—that was all she wanted to do anyway.

Over the weeks that followed the counselor saw her for ten sessions, on an average of two sessions per week. Mrs. B's intense anger at the desertion she felt, her hopelessness about life without her husband and about herself, her anger with her daughter, her guilt that she may have in some way contributed to her daughter's difficulties and may have pushed her husband too far, thus contributing to his death, were all discussed. The bereavement response was converted from a pathological, absent pattern of grief to a normal one, and she was assisted with the inevitably painful resolution of this.

*Distorted grief.* With distorted grief, some levels of inhibition or suppression of grief may operate alongside powerful distortions. Com-mon patterns are extreme anger and extreme guilt. Angry distortion is often found following the loss of a dependent relationship or when there are sudden or unexpected deaths for which someone is blamed. It is the sort of pattern that appears when medical care systems have failed or been negligent, or when the deceased died violently perhaps through murder, accident, or disaster. The counselor's aims and techniques will be similar to those described for inhibited, suppressed, or absent grief, but there will be particular emphasis on assisting with the working through of the displacement aspects of the anger and the problems created by the loss of a very dependent relationship, or one that symbolized something special and irreplaceable for the bereaved.

Harry K was forty-nine when his son died. They had had a close relationship generally, but with his son's recent independence with a new car and job, he felt he "couldn't understand the younger generation anymore." His son died after a car accident. He was taken to a small country hospital and then transferred to the city where he died after seven days. Mr. K believed that the doctor in the local hospital had been incompetent, and subsequent findings suggested this was so. It seemed to him that his son "need not have died." He was intensely angry and obsessed with plans to sue the country doctor and hospital. There was no evidence of grief or mourning, just intense anger. It seemed that he almost believed that if he could punish those involved he would bring his son back again. He did not talk of him, but simply of what "they" had done to him. He did not see his son's body after the death. His wife kept telling him it was God's will, and they must accept it and remember Ray as he was. Harry was little consoled by this. His local doctor saw him ten weeks after the death, when he presented, asking for something to help him sleep. The doctor recognized the pathology of his angry response and referred him for psychiatric assessment and management.

The counselor, a psychiatrist in this case, followed the general principles of finding out about the death and exploring the lost relationship. He could see that a direct interpretation or attempt to diffuse the anger at this stage might well be intolerable for Mr. K who desperately needed this defense. Harry K had, in fact, invested all his hopes for the future in his son. All that he had not achieved in his own life was invested in what he believed Ray would accomplish for him. In the months before the death he had sensed that these hopes could be disappointed, but he continued to believe he could win his son over and had bought him the car with this in mind.

His anger at those who were associated with the death had some basis in reality, and he was allowed ventilation of this. After he had spoken angrily and at length about his rage, the psychiatrist commented that this must make it difficult for him to relate to him, too, and to doctors generally, and that this was especially hard when he was feeling so bad about his son's death and needed to share those feelings with someone. Mr. K said that it was so, and he hadn't wanted to come, but he knew he had to; he felt he was going crazy, and he couldn't talk to anyone about it: his wife had gone "all religious" and couldn't understand how he felt. The psychiatrist then explored further about the death and found out that Ray had been drinking heavily according to the police report, and that this probably caused the accident.

In the sessions that followed, he was able to help Mr. K express his anger at his son for "letting him down" in so many ways, both by his behavior and by the dashed hopes for the future. As this anger was faced, Mr. K became able to grieve for his son and acknowledge how desperately he missed him. At later stages he was encouraged with further review of the relationship which initial-ly he idealized, but later remembered in real terms. After five sessions he had made considerable progress in his mourning and came for only another two sessions: one, three months later and the other, at the anniversary of the death. This man's loss was not only that of his son, but also of his hopes for his own future relived in his son. His loss was irreplaceable, but he was able to come to some terms with it.

In the distorted pattern of extreme guilt, there is also usually partial suppression and inhibition of other aspects of grief. Extreme guilt is most likely to occur when the relationship between the bereaved and the deceased had been one of marked ambivalence, perhaps even filled with overt or covert wishes for the other's departure or death. As well as hostile fantasies, there may have been overt or covert destructive-ness toward the dead person before the death. This is the type of re-sponse that may be seen with the death of a child where there had been abuse before the death, even if the abuse was not directly caus-ative. The circumstances of the death may reinforce such guilt further, as for instance when the bereaved was driving the car at the time the other was killed. In some instances the guilt cannot be borne personal-ly and is denied and projected onto others who are blamed, especially other family members. This sort of distortion may then resemble the angry distortion described above, but will have more of its dynamics in denied ambivalence and guilt.

The counselor's goals here too, will be the encouragement of grief and promotion of mourning. He will follow the same general guide-lines described for unexpressed grief and angry distortion, exploring the circumstances of the death, the lost relationship, and the support available to help with the resolution of ambivalence. There is a special need here to explore the origins of the ambivalence in the relationship, its links to earlier repetition compulsions, and the bereaved's parent-child relationships. The "death wish" toward the dead person may be found, and when this can be voiced by the bereaved and faced with the counselor, a major step is taken toward resolution. This group of be-reaved may relish the painful nature of the guilt, hanging on to it in attempts to propitiate the dead. If it becomes unmanageable, they will be at risk of sinking into a more clear-cut depression, and if they also fantasize reunion with the dead person, then suicidal preoccupations will have to be carefully dealt with in therapy. A difficulty for the therapist is to abstain from too early a reassurance that the bereaved "did his best" or "did all he could" for the dead person. The bereaved knows full well, consciously or unconsciously, the extent of his murderous fantasy and is only really reassured when this is brought out in the open and faced with the counselor or significant other who can help him come to some terms with it in a nonjudgmental way. When the guilt is linked to real behaviors and does not have its origins purely in fantasy, then the counselor's role may be to help the bereaved accept and live with it as a reality in terms of the part he had in the deceased's death. However, for the most part, such guilts have their origin in fantasy, and this is the arena of much of the psychotherapeutic working through.

Lorraine F was forty-two. Her upbringing had been been harsh, with strict parents and an intense religious orientation. Her husband Colin had been an aggressive man and intensely sexually demanding. She was very dependent on him, however, and the marriage was one of strong bonds. He had had numerous affairs with other women, which she bitterly resented. He often tormented her about her frigidity and told her vivid stories of his other women's sexual responsiveness to him. They had five children ranging from eighteen to nine years of age. Many times, when he was away with one of the other women, Lorraine had lain in bed, lonely and angry, fantasizing the things she would like to see happen to him. She imagined him injured, violently beaten up, in great pain, and always crawling back to her for care and support. On some occasions she imagined him dying as a result of the violence which others, with whom she identified, would inflict on him.

Colin became ill eighteen months prior to his death with a carcinoma of the bowel. Mrs. F nursed him through his terminal illness with rapidly advancing metastases and a poorly functioning colostomy. He was angry and resentful about the disease and about his dependence on her, yet desperately needing her care. She looked after him meticulously, nursing him at home until the day of his death. Following this she developed an intense guilty preoccupation with his illness and her care of him, seeing many doctors, to make sure she had done the right things with his colostomy and that she had not contributed to his death in any way. Despite this repeated reassurance that she had done "more than any man could wish for," she relentlessly tortured herself with thoughts that she had failed him. There was no grief or mourning, only guilty rumination. One doctor, recognizing the pathological nature of her response when he saw her six weeks after the death, referred her to the local bereavement counselor.

Mrs. F was angry at the referral but felt that the counselor, a community social worker, might be able to help her by telling her what she should have done in the care of her husband, and that she would surely agree that she had not cared for him properly. The counselor listened to her bitter self-recrimination and then suggested it would help her understand the situation better if Mrs. F could tell her a bit about her husband. She herself had not known him at all, and she might get a clearer picture if Mrs. F could go back over the relationship, how they met, the years they had known one another, and so forth.

In this carefully explored review Mrs. F at first intensely idealized her dead husband, repeating what a wonderful man he had been, "the best of husbands." The counselor waited patiently until this was all said and then queried back to the earlier days of the relationship. She would occasionally throw in a comment that some particular episode or behavior "must have been hard to take at times." At first Mrs. F ignored these comments, but after a while started to say, yes, there were times when it was difficult for her. Then she would quickly move away from them. With persistence, however, the counselor was able to get her to face more and more of these until Mrs. F's angry tears broke through and she started to cry and speak of the terrible times she had had with his affairs.

Over the five sessions that followed, Mrs. F's feelings were explored in greater detail. Her own guilty contribution to their sexual difficulties, its relationship to earlier inhibitions in her family life, and her father's incestuous overtures were worked through. The bitterness of her feelings toward her husband and her dependence on him came up as themes again and again. The counselor said quietly that, when people felt hurt in relationships, as she obviously had, they often felt that they wanted to hit out and hurt back. She imagined Mrs. F must have felt that way often, as most people would have, and she wondered if she could tell her more about just the sorts of things she had thought. Mrs. F denied at first, but then went on gradually to pour out her many hostile fantasies.

The turning point of the therapy came in the third session when in the midst of one burst of emotion about this she said: "I could have killed him." There was a stunned silence for a moment, and then she hastily added, "I didn't really mean that, I just meant I was very angry with him." The counselor nodded. She thought Mrs. F must have been very angry with him indeed. People sometimes did feel so angry, as she had, that they really did feel like killing the other person, and that made it especially hard when that person died—it made them feel as though they'd caused it, or somehow had something to do with it. Mrs. F nodded and cried quietly through all this. "Yes," she said, she did feel terribly bad, terribly bad. She'd wanted revenge so much, for all the hurt that she suffered, but she loved him too, and he had had such a terrible illness and died in such a terrible way. The counselor encouraged her to talk through some of the aspects of his final illness and what it had meant for her and more guilty fantasies were dealt with. She had, at times during that illness, thought that he was being punished, but her guilt was immediate and great, and she compensated by caring for his every wish.

In the remaining sessions she worked through further levels of her ambivalence in the relationship and her needs to have someone on whom she could depend. She made several appeals to the counselor to keep seeing her, but when given reassurance that the counselor would be available when and if needed, she went on to work through further aspects of the loss. Her anger that needs could not be met, and that she would have to manage alone, were dealt with, but she seemed to have mastered an extreme guilt. She said at the end, "I don't feel so bad now. It was a good marriage in some ways, but a hard one in others. I suppose I managed the best way I could, all things considered. Perhaps I'll be able to make a new life now and a better one. Things will be easier for me in some ways and for the children too. I suppose I'll be lonely, because I miss him, but a lot of the pain has gone,"

In these instances of pathological grief a psychotherapeutic model has proved useful for achieving more adaptive resolutions. The lowered defensiveness of the crisis seems to facilitate such working through. Often the bereaved person is reassured by the model of short-term therapy, with the clear message inherent in it that the counselor or other supporting person believes in his or her ultimate ability to cope with the loss and to manage without ongoing therapeutic support. Also helpful, perhaps, is the communication that there is an appropriate end point to grief, as is suggested by the rituals and ceremonies that spell out an end point in some cultures. The same models and techniques can be used at a later time if such pathological patterns become set and continue after the crisis. However, defenses are more rigid then, and working through is more difficult, and some other techniques of the re-grief methods may be necessary to facilitate this delayed resolution, unless some other crisis of loss or concurrent crisis opens up the defensive structure and motivates change. The shorter term models are also helpful in preventing the counselor from becoming a replacement for the lost person, although this issue may also need to be actively dealt with, for it is no ultimate solution for the bereaved.

Chronic grief presents quite a different picture, however—inevitably a more difficult one. It may indeed arise because no proper end to grief and mourning in the bereavement response has occurred. It is not, by its very nature, diagnosed or even suspected until a considerable time after the loss. The pathological defensive pattern and the entrenched role, with all their secondary gains, are by then very well established and difficult to shift. Often the bereaved is not motivated to relinquish either the chronic grief or the ongoing relationship with the dead person that it symbolizes.

In these cases there is an ongoing picture that is similar to acute grief, but that extends well beyond the normal time. It is severe and extreme. It links to an inability to relinquish the dead person who is, as it were, kept alive in the grief. It comes often in dependent and irreplaceable relationships, and where deaths are unexpected, and following the deaths of children. It usually indicates that the bereaved had an extraordinary and possibly pathological emotional investment in the dead person.

The aims of counseling here, too, focus on the quality of the lost relationship, the nature of the death, and the perception of social support. The particular work of counseling in these cases is to explore why the relationship has such special meaning to the bereaved and why it cannot be relinquished. It is also important to explore what roles and identity the bereaved had in terms of the deceased, because it may only be with new roles and identity that the dead person can be given up. Sometimes the chronic grief develops a secondary gain of controlling and punishing others as well as eliciting their care. Very often, however, it ultimately alienates all sources of care, including professional systems.

It is often helpful to set a series of concrete tasks, akin to the behavior therapy model procedures. These may involve, for example, sorting through the dead person's possessions or making fewer visits to the grave. With clear tasks, the bereaved may make some gains. If other sources of gratification can be developed and an alternate role to that of the "chronic griever," then eventually a more positive outcome may be achieved. This group of patients are, however, notoriously difficult to treat and frequently retain unremittingly their morbid picture.

*Bereavement counseling concurrent with the management of other pathological syndromes.* Bereavement may have many pathological outcomes and these may also require management. Counseling may continue in any of the above frameworks simultaneous with the management of psychiatric disorders and psychosomatic complaints and still have the same goals. The counseling may be a critical part of therapy where the bereavement has been a precipitating or perpetuating factor in psychiatric morbidity. Thus bereavement therapy has been used to resolve such issues in neurotic conditions such as agoraphobia, conversion and dissociative conditions, panic and anxiety states, and hypochondriases (Jennings and France 1979). It is also important to deal with any such unresolved issues in the acting-out disorders or dependency conditions such as increased alcohol or drug taking. The importance of bereavement counseling in psychosomatic disorders where the bereavement plays a stressor role has been described for asthma (see, for example, Stamm and Drapkin 1966), and ulcerative colitis. In line with the work of Bartrop et al. (1977), its management should also be considered important from the point of view of prevention of stress-induced immune disorders.

The role of bereavement counseling in depression requires special mention. While antidepressants are unsuitable as therapy for normal grief (Maddison and Raphael 1972; Boman, Streimer, and Perkins

1981), they should be used as appropriate for depressive syndromes found in association with bereavement. In such instances, bereavement counseling should be continued to facilitate resolution of the loss, taking special care with the aspects of ambivalence and the risk of suicide. Where depression is very severe and nonresponsive to such therapy, then electroconvulsive therapy may be used (Lynn and Racy 1969; Davis and Franklin 1970), but the resolution of bereavement must still be dealt with, and counseling, such as that described in this chapter, seems the most appropriate model for doing so.

RE-GRIEF THERAPIES

The theme of reworking a poorly resolved bereavement at a later time had been touched upon by a number of psychoanalytic writers (Fleming and Altschul 1963; Wetmore 1963), but it was Volkan's concept of "re-grief" therapy that defined this mode of therapy specifically (Volkan and Showalter 1968; Volkan 1971). According to Volkan, the goal of therapy is limited to two specific outcomes. The patient is helped to understand why he has not in the past been able to to complete his mourning. He is then assisted to complete it in the present and to experience and express his grieving emotion. The initial stage of treatment is the phase of "demarcation." Through detailed history taking about the lost person and the lost relationship, the patient is helped to make boundaries demarcating him from the dead individual. The patient may be asked to bring in a photo of the dead person to facilitate this focused consideration and differentiation. The circumstances of the death are carefully examined. The patient is helped to externalize the lost person by drawing "affective" boundaries between them, and by abreaction. He is helped to recognize that his experience with the lost person has ceased.

The patient is seen perhaps three to four times a week over about three months in Volkan's model. There is some interpretation of the transference, but the therapy does not rely on the development of a full transference neurosis. After the initial phase of therapy, the therapist focuses on the linking objects that the patient uses as his symbols of, and contact with, the lost person (Volkan 1972). This tends to open up the patient's emotional response to the loss, and he becomes able to experience the grief that has been postponed from the time of the death. Knowledge of what is condensed and symbolized in the "linking object" helps the therapist make interpretations to loosen the patient's contact with the lost person. In this way frozen emotions are stimulated and reawakened. The therapist may ask the patient to bring his linking object to sessions with him, and the handling of this object may further free blocked emotions. With his knowledge of the particular dynamics associated with the failure to resolve this loss previously, the therapist is able to make further interpretations which facilitate resolution. Dreams may also be interpreted. Volkan provides case examples of his technique.

This technique is obviously somewhat similar to the focal psychotherapy described previously. Both these methods involve intensive review of the relationship and the death, with the aims of promoting grief and mourning. The techniques of using photographs and dreams as well as linking objects may prove useful stimuli to therapy. In the absence of other crises or distress motivating the bereaved, these procedures make the process of working through much easier.

The therapy for pathological grief is always more difficult at this later stage when defensive processes are consolidated in a pathological way, and motivation for change may not be great. Barry (1981) suggests this may be because many of the chronic and entrenched bereavement problems tend to occur in those with underlying personality disorders which have interfered with their grief work. Treatment of such underlying disorders is then required as well.

BEHAVIORAL THERAPY

Some of the behavioral approaches to prolonged and morbid grief reactions were first suggested by Ramsey and Happee (1977, 1979). They see the unresolved grief reaction as something like a phobic reaction. The technique they suggest for approaching it is one of forced confrontation with the facts of the loss and all that it entails. The aims are to break down denial and to evoke depression, guilt, anger, and anxiety until these affects of grief are extinguished, and there are no further reactions to the loss.

This is usually done in lengthy sessions (two hours) from which the patient cannot escape. The therapist presents items he expects to evoke a reaction in imagination until one "hits home." When the patient reacts, with perhaps a crying or aggressive outburst, the therapist allows the emotional release to take its course and then subside. He then keeps on presenting that item again and again until finally no further emotional release occurs. Then he tries other items and continues the process. Ramsay and Happee say that both the therapist and bereaved must be prepared for extremely painful emotional outbursts. The distress may be so great that the therapist may have to alternate between being a hard taskmaster and a gentle supportive caring person. Ramsay sees the therapist-client relationship as of vital importance. He also notes that tranquilizers and antidepressants may obstruct the process. Gauthier and Marshall (1977) and Gauthier and Pye (1979) also describe behavioral approaches.

Although this therapy may be seen to have much in common with other models, Ramsay and Happee deny that it is a "forced Freudian approach." They see it as being most applicable for those bereaved who are unable to work through their loss verbally with family or friends or in other verbal therapies.

The most recent and detailed trial of the behavioral method is that of Mawson et al. (1981) in their controlled study of "guided mourning" for morbid grief. Psychiatrists or nurse therapists were used to provide sessions in which the patients were exposed to avoided or painful memories, ideas, or situations, both in imagination and reality. The morbid grief reaction was equated to a phobic avoidance response. Where the loss was the main factor, the patient was encouraged to say good-bye to the person in sessions, in writing, and by visiting the cemetery. There was also an emphasis on facing factors related to the death if these had been phobically avoided. Whatever the distressing situations were, the patient was encouraged to describe them repeatedly or confront them repeatedly until his distress was diminished. There was an intense reliving of painful memories and feelings associated with the bereavement. Patients were also given written instructions to force themselves to face the loss, for instance, by looking at the photo of the dead person each day. The control group was encouraged to *avoid* thinking about the death or dead person or any reminders. In this small pilot study a significant difference was found in the direction of improvement, on all indices, for those patients who received guided mourning. This improvement was maintained at ten and twenty-eight weeks. The authors conclude that this approach is most likely to be effective for the sort of morbid grief that involves some form of phobic avoidance.

Thus these behavioral therapies appear to have some success for those patients suffering from chronic pathological bereavements with strong phobic avoidance aspects. They represent a useful modality for some of these difficult problems.

OTHER APPROACHES

Most other approaches to pathological bereavement seem to rely on some elements of the models described above. Hodgkinson (1982) describes a therapy of abnormal grief in which there was emphasis on the bereaved telling the story of the loved one's death. The therapist facilitated the emotional release in association with this, and the writer saw the initial emotional outburst as very important. He suggests there may also be some elements of "response prevention" in encouraging the patient to lessen responses that were geared to the dead person. When the emotional blocks are released, conflicts related to "unfinished business" with guilt and anger are worked through. He suggests that the use of Gestalt techniques, such as talking to the "third chair," could be helpful in this regard. In the cases he describes, the bereaved seemed to go through a change toward the end of the therapy. They actively relinquished the dead person and recovered from then on.

Melges and DeMaso (1980) suggest that there are three interrelated phases of grief resolution therapy: cognitive structuring for the decisions to regrieve and for clarification of the procedures; guided imagery for reliving, revising, and revisiting scenes of the loss; and future oriented identity reconstruction. These authors concentrate on the guided imagery with the objectives of helping the bereaved to relive, in imagination, sequences of the loss; to revise these scenes to remove barriers to grieving; and to revisit the scene, again in the imagination, as if it were really taking place in the here and now. They consider that changing the patient's construction of reality is central to the therapy.

A slightly different approach is that of Alexy (in press) who describes a technique using what he calls the "principal theme postulate." This involves the counselor and bereaved working out the principal theme that is relevant in the bereavement as well as secondary themes. When they are agreed upon, they work together exclusively on the principal theme. This is in contrast to other models, which tend to explore broadly the various themes of the loss. Alexy believes that the concentration on a single, principal theme is likely to be most effective. This same worker has also investigated which counseling dimensions bereaved parents prefer in support offered to them following their children's deaths. He found that different techniques were preferred in different phases, with cognition dimensions being more important initially and insight orientation later (Alexy 1982). Such findings may prove useful in integrating different counseling systems and styles.

A range of other counseling models is also described in Schoenberg's

(1980) book of bereavement counseling. They differ little, however, from those outlined here.

## Management of Bereaved Families

Although the models described here have all dealt with the bereaved person as an individual, it is obviously critical that the family aspects of bereavement be considered and managed, both preventively and therapeutically. Not only do the bereaved family members depend on one another for practical and emotional support, but family systems may be such as to actively interfere with grief. The differential rates of grieving of the various members may also lead to friction, further pain, and misunderstanding. And finally, the family as a whole system is hurt and wounded, and perhaps even broken, by the loss.

Work with the family at the time of the bereavement crisis needs to meet several goals. It should facilitate a simple, open, and honest communication about the facts of the death and loss. It should emphasize the importance for family members of sharing their feelings and the pain this may involve as well as the different experiences each may have in the weeks and months that follow the death. Facilitating of the review of the lost relationship, in its positive and negative aspects, may also be part of the work a counselor carries out with the family system. Some communication to the family as a system that its pain and loss are recognized and empathized with is also likely to be helpful.

Family members may find it very difficult at first to show their feelings and concerns to one another following the death, and they sometimes require the supportive presence of some other person to help them do this. Each fears his grief will upset the others; and there is often, too, a fantasy of the whole system disintegrating in tears and distress. This is particularly frightening when each member already feels bereft and insecure.

Most attempts to work with bereaved families have come from efforts to assist bereaved children, and thus their approach is from a child psychiatry model. Although the value of such therapy seems obvious, its difficulties should not be underestimated. Each person at the time of the crisis feels his loss to be greatest, his pain the worst, and his need for support and comfort from family members or therapist to be the greatest. Nevertheless, such a family approach with the bereaved

(Nunn, personal communication) has proved most helpful in families at the time of a death and subsequently to it.

Dora Black (1982) has made a most valuable contribution to understanding in this field. She has developed a project to work with bereaved children and their families following the death of a parent. Her study aims at testing the efficacy of brief family therapy intervention in promoting the processes of mourning in children and the surviving parents, and in helping the family make a healthy adaptation to the loss. In a controlled study, experimental group families were offered counseling by a family therapist for six sessions about one to three months after the bereavement. One and two years after the bereavement both the experimental group and control group, who had not received intervention, were followed up independently and assessed for family functioning and child adjustment. The results of this project are currently being evaluated and will be of immense interest to those in the fields of bereavement and family therapy.

An earlier presentation of the value of family therapy in bereavement is that of Paul and Grosser (1965) who discussed "operational mourning" and its role in conjoint family therapy. However, their model refers more specifically to belated mourning for earlier unresolved loss. It involves repeated review of recollected details surrounding the loss, with the therapist's encouragement to express feeling. These workers believed that during such mourning the other family members could be helped to acquire greater empathy for the feelings of the others, and that this would help with the resolution of the loss as well as with the family's subsequent adjustment and functioning. Paul (1967), in a later paper, reinforces the significance of this empathic approach in the family therapy of grief, showing how family members could gain empathy with the others' grief as it was being expressed. Such empathic sharing, either at the time of bereavement, or subsequently, is of great importance to family members and the system as a whole.

In a discussion of death and living, Slivkin (1977) takes a family therapy approach. He notes the value of family work when a member suffers from terminal illness and in the crisis following the death. Schneiderman (1971) talks of intervention therapy for families following unexpected death. Williams and Polak's (1979) preventive intervention is also directed toward families. These workers (for example, Polak et al. 1975) note that, when the dead person had been a scapegoat for the family, then painful and extensive role reallocation was needed after the death, and if this did not succeed the family system tended to collapse. The healthier the roles of family members prior to the death, the more likely they were to have support systems to help them. Where the dead person had generated conflict prior to the death, the family tone could become better afterward. These findings all have implications for possible family therapy interactions following bereavement. Caroff and Dobrof (1975) also reinforce the significance of working with the whole family as a unit of service both during terminal illness and after the death.

The emphasis on family work and the various approaches to it grew out of a recognition of the specific needs of some families stressed by terminal illness or acute deaths. All of these approaches emphasize shared communication and feelings plus a discussion of the death and the relationship that has been lost. All recognize the differential rates of grief and the various readjustments of the family system that may follow the death, both adaptive and nonadaptive, with suggestions for reinforcing the more adaptive outcomes.

## The Care of Bereaved Children

Although the needs of bereaved children seem at one level very obvious, they have only in recent times been considered as possible indications for providing care. Much of the work done with children has been carried out in the course of psychoanalysis, where children were helped to rework earlier losses or deal with those that arose in the course of therapy (E. Furman 1974). Perhaps little was provided for bereaved children in other formats, because it was felt that they were unaffected by loss, or that if they did need help, the adults of their families would automatically provide it. Recently, in systematic studies such as our own (Raphael, Field, and Kvelde 1980; Raphael 1982) some of the grief and mourning of younger children has been recognized.

Children show needs for care in terms of the bereavement crisis in a number of ways. They may require recognition of their pain and fear in an insecure world. They may require opportunities to grieve and mourn. They may be at risk for problems of resolution, because they are told little of the death. They may be given little chance to express their feelings about the death or about the person they have lost. They may be distressed because their family world threatens to collapse into chaos. The following are key elements in the care of bereaved children.

1. There should be support for the surviving parent or parents to facilitate their own grief and mourning, so that they may have ego resources available to perceive and respond to their children's needs. Sometimes support is provided by the parent's extended family and social group. Other times it is not available, and professional assistance may be required. Our studies showed clearly that when parents were themselves very grief stricken, or suffering a pathological bereavement response, even though they were concerned for their children, they often seemed unable to perceive their distress and grief and respond to their needs to mourn. Care for parents should follow the models outlined above in this chapter.

2. There should be an opportunity for family members to share feelings and memories about the death and the dead person. This frees feeling in the family system, so that there are opportunities for mutual and empathic comforting and consolation. This shows that the strong affects of grief will not destroy the family system. It conveys to the child the naturalness of feelings at this time and offers a model of their expression.

3. The child himself may need specific and individual support for the particular issues the bereavement brings for him. With older children and adolescents this may be provided in a nondirective interview and counseling framework. With younger children, play and projective techniques are of value. Our experience suggests the value of a doll house, with family from which the child can choose; some of the other usual paraphernalia of more aggressive play, such as cars and guns; and painting and drawing equipment. With a number of sessions in the period of the crisis, perhaps four to eight, the child develops enough trust to express much of his longing for the lost parent or sibling, talk or play through some of his anger at the loss, and express some of his guilt when this is a factor. Uncertainties about the death and what has happened to the dead person are common in younger children, with guilt and personal fears appearing in those who are older. As well there may be conflicts or stresses dependent on the child's development level and relationship with the lost person that can further complicate the bereavement.

Anna H was twenty-nine when her husband Fred's cancer, a seminoma of the testis, was diagnosed. Their children were James, eight, and Penny, five. Anna felt she could not really tell the children about Fred's condition, because at one level she herself could not believe it was so serious, and, at another, she thought that it might upset them or disturb their sexual development if they knew that it affected that part of their father's body. She told them he was sick, but little else. The children were both somewhat mystified by their mother's obvious distress. Their father seemed to change also and became thin and moody. He always seemed cross with them and was often away at the hospital. It was during one of these visits to the hospital that their father died.

Anna, their mother, was shocked. She had not really accepted that this illness was likely to kill her husband. She felt frightened and helpless, not knowing what to do or whom to turn to for help. Her own parents lived far away, and Fred's family was all dead. Her neighbors were good friends but not especially close, as was usual in city life. After going to the hospital and seeing the doctor she returned home the the children. She knew she must tell them but recognized that she simply didn't know what to say. She said that their father had "gone away" and then broke into tears. It was not until the next day she could bring herself to say he had died and would not be coming back. In the weeks that followed she seemed still in a daze. Sometimes she would be filled with panic, wondering how she would ever manage, either financially or emotionally, "alone" as she now saw herself. She would come out of her dreamlike state to get the children's meals and put them to bed, but at other times, she seemed almost unaware of them. Penny was showing increased clinging and demandingness which her mother found difficult to tolerate. James was being aggressive and destructive and occasionally wetting his bed again at nights.

Anna was provided with support from a skilled bereavement counselor, a clinical psychologist, who saw her the first four weeks after the death. He worked with her to help her deal with her anger about her husband's illness, the fears she had of his cancer, and her lack of any support system. He also discussed with her the children's needs and arranged for another worker to see them. The sessions he had with her over the next few weeks covered her relationship with her husband; some of the difficulties in their marriage; her isolation so far from her own family; her fears of having to grow up suddenly, because she had been a girl when she met Fred and had known no one else, and he had always looked after her. A session with the family all together enabled Anna to tell the children a little about their father's illness and death. They were also able to share some of their feelings.

A skilled child-care worker saw James and Penny together and then individually for a total of six sessions each in their own home. James was very untrusting of the counselor at first and wanted to know why she had come. They were all right, he said. "I am big now. I will look after Mummy and Penny, now that Daddy's gone away." The counsellor asked if he knew where his father was. James looked very confused. "Yes, Daddy has gone to Heaven," he said proudly. "He is up there watching us. He won't be coming back. Mummy said he would like to come back but he can't." The counselor asked how James felt about this. "When I grow up I will be a big man like Daddy. I will drive trucks all around Australia. I will have hundreds of trucks." James became more and more excited and started to pick up the play things throwing them grandly down onto the floor. "The trucks will have many smashes," he said, "and I will get new ones, bigger trucks. I will have the biggest trucks. I will have more than anyone else." The counselor suggested that James was growing into a big boy now and one day he would be a big man. But she also wondered if, perhaps, he felt a bit scared sometimes too, now that Daddy wasn't there anymore. James started to talk more about his father following this. He missed him very much, he said. He wished so much he would come back. The counselor helped him to talk through this longing for his father on a number of different occasions in the sessions.

In the fourth session James drew some families. One of the figures had a big penis. The counselor asked James who this was. He said it was his father. His father had a big "dick" he said, "because he was sick." The counselor asked him if he knew about his father's sickness. His fears about this tumbled out. His daddy had got sick because he played with it too much. He knew. He was very afraid when he grew up his might get big too, and he might die like his father. The counselor was able to explain something of the father's illness and reassure him that he would grow up safely to be a big man.

In the sixth session James drew black pictures of his mother. She was going to die too he said. All grown-ups died. The counselor asked him if he was afraid she, the counselor, would die too, because she was going away now, as this was the last time they were going to work together to talk of his feelings. James cried sadly. He would miss her too. But he had his own mummy, she was better now, and she loved him again. He knew the counselor had to look after lots of other children.

Penny was shy at first and did not want to leave her mother to spend her time playing with the counselor. With gentle persuasion, she eventually did so. She chose a family of dolls with a father and played happily with these, going through the family routines. This continued for two sessions, with no clear communication from her. The therapist talked gently, asking her each time what each doll was doing. Penny started beating the little girl doll, the one she identified with herself. When the counselor asked about this, she insisted the little girl was "very bad, very bad." She would have to be put to bed with no supper. The counselor asked about the other dolls, what did the mother and father think about this? "They know she is bad," said Penny emphatically. "See the father is going away. He's *never* going to come back." The counselor asked if Penny thought her Daddy had gone away like that. "Yes," said Penny, "Penny was very bad." With further exploration, Penny's communication that her father had left because of her naughtiness was reiterated. The counselor explained something of his death and said that it was often hard for children to understand when someone died, because they didn't know where he was. Perhaps it would help, she suggested, if they talked to Mummy about this and found out where Daddy was. They talked about the funeral and that he was dead and had been buried, just like Penny's cat when he had died last year. Penny seemed very reassured by this, and her mother agreed to take her to see the grave.

In the sessions that followed she played many games with the father and little girl doll together. She told the counselor how much she missed her father and how she was afraid her mother would go away too. Sometimes she would take the little girl doll and put her to bed. "She's very sad," she would say. "Her Daddy's gone away." Another day she threw the dolls around wildly. The father doll was bashed against the other dolls. "He's bad," she said angrily. "He hurt the Mummy; he didn't love her anymore." This led to a discussion of her fantasies that perhaps her father had left them and had not died. She became even angrier with him. "He's a bad Daddy," she said. "They will send him away." She seemed to gain increasing acceptance of his death following this and was less fearful of separation from her mother. Both her anger toward her father and her sadness appeared at times.

In the final session she played through a party with the doll family. "It's a good-bye party," she said. "It's a good-bye for Daddy." "And perhaps for me too?" asked the counselor. "Yes," said Penny joyfully, "Good-bye for you too."

These issues were not fully resolved for either the children or their mother; however all three were helped considerably with their grief and mourning.

Several workers have described their work facilitating mourning in childhood. Kliman's group (1969) has had extensive experience with double orphans. Black and Urbanowitz (1982) have used a family therapy model. The effectiveness of such counseling in preventing subsequent morbidity remains to be established, but it seems successful for assisting with the child's bereavement process. Work with adolescents will involve models much more like those of adult counseling but will also emphasize family factors.

## Management of Anticipatory Bereavement Reactions

When there is knowledge beforehand of the terminal nature of illness and the impending death, psychotherapy, counseling, and anticipatory guidance can help the family's adjustment, both during the illness and subsequent to it. The counselor's role here is similar to that with bereavement. He will try to help the dying person express his grief and mourn his many losses, and he will provide the same sort of care for family members. The critical nature of family interactions at this time means that some orientation to family sessions will be helpful, although both the dying person and his family members may wish for support for themselves as individuals. Cramond (1970), Kübler-Ross (1969) and many other workers have outlined the relevant issues in considerable detail. The following points should be noted:

1. The patient and his family need support to deal with the diagnosis itself. Most patients and their families need to know the nature of the condition and its prognosis, but they will vary in the degree to which they take this in initially and will need to ask questions on many occasions.

2. Each may need help with the various feelings the terminal illness evokes. Anger, sadness, regret, resentment, or guilt may be prominent.
3. Hope is usually maintained for a good part of the illness, and neither the patient or his family will be preoccupied with the possible death all the time. There may be many other realistic concerns that need to be dealt with.
4. Children are usually able to comprehend and come to terms with death and dying and should be given an opportunity to know of the illness and its prognosis in simple terms.
5. Fears of the pain and the "aloneness" of death are often the most distressing aspects, and the patient may need support in dealing with these.

With these general considerations in mind, the dying person and his family may be supported and cared for during the terminal illness and the bereavement that follows it.

## Self-Help in Bereavement

Some of the earliest attempts to deal with the distress of bereaved people and provide better support for them arose in a number of self-help organizations for the bereaved. These organizations were often developed by people who had experienced a particular loss and saw the deficiencies of care within health care systems, and who then became instrumental in group formation. Some of these groups are run purely by, and for, those who have experienced a particular bereavement crisis; others are linked to professionals or other associations.

Widow-to-widow programs evolved in clubs such as the Cruse Club in England and a variety of similar organizations in other countries. The importance of such groups in providing support for members was recognized by P. R. Silverman (1969), who has promoted, in the United States, a number of widow-to-widow support programs for the bereaved. These have proved to be extremely valuable in the provision of counseling and practical support. The bereaved widow who has recovered at least to some degree from her loss is perceived as being particularly empathic and understanding by other widows. These women speak of the great relief that came from sharing their distress and problems with "someone else who had been through the same thing." Not only does there seem to be this special understanding, but also there is often a message of successful coping and survival—something the woman now starts to identify with and see as possible for herself. The organization can also offer practical assistance, opportunities for friendship and socialization, and in some instances it can act as a lobbying force to push for legal or political changes that are of benefit to the bereaved.

P. R. Silverman reports on the functioning and perceived benefits of widow-to-widow programs (Silverman 1967, 1969, 1971, 1972). She suggests they offer a valuable form of preventive intervention. However, the only systematic comparative study is that by Vachon et al. (1980). In a study of 162 Toronto, Canada, widows under seventy years of age, 68 randomly selected widows were offered one-to-one and later group support from other widows. These helping widows had resolved their own bereavements and were trained by Vachon's team to "reach out with an offer of help." The widows who received help and a control group were followed up six, twelve, and twenty-four months after the death. While there were no significant differences in general health measures between the groups, there were three measures of psychological change that favored the group that had received support. Those widows who had high scores on the general health questionnaire (GHQ) at one month, before the offer of help was made, and who were assumed to be a high-risk group, seemed to be particularly likely to be helped by the program in that they were much better at follow-up than high-risk subjects who had received no support. Although there were some methodological difficulties in this study, its findings do seem to indicate the value of such programs.

Other reports of self-help groups in this field include those of Barrett (1978) and McCourt et al. (1976). These lack systematic external evaluation, but suggest that, at least to participants, these programs seemed helpful. As Parkes (1980) points out, these programs are backed by professionals with considerable experience with the bereaved, and most helpers undergo some training before they carry out their support roles. Under such circumstances their work is usually of considerable assistance to bereaved widows and widowers.

A number of different organizations have developed for bereaved parents. Compassionate Friends is a general outreach group for bereaved parents and usually functions with a backup of professional support and may be very successful (Videka-Sherman 1982). Sudden infant death groups are also well developed and offer very valuable mutual support for parents experiencing this crisis. A variety of other groups, such as those offering support for parents of children with cancer and burns, have also been described, but they are far less extensive and well developed than the bereaved parent and sudden infant death groups. Stillbirth, miscarriage, and neonatal death support groups have also been of great assistance to many affected by these losses.

Support groups and organizations for terminally ill patients and their families, such as Make Today Count, have also proved of value.

These various groups seem to serve many different functions. They may, for instance, simply act as a forum for sharing practical difficulties and resources. They may provide general support and friendship. Most are valued because of the special empathy members feel toward each other, with the common distress that all share. Those organizations that offer counseling and emotional support, over and above their friendship and sharing of feelings, make a very significant contribution to the care of the bereaved. They are best able to fulfill this function when the helping members are well trained and backed by ongoing professional support from those skilled in the area of bereavement.

## Bereavement and Prevention of Morbidity

While it is clear that bereavement may act as a precipitant or vulnerability factor in the development of morbidity, it is also clear that many bereaved people do not suffer pathological outcome after their loss, even though their distress and deprivation may be very great. Nevertheless the field of bereavement has provided a fertile ground on which to suggest, develop, implement, and sometimes test preventive programs aimed at lessening the risk of postbereavement morbidity.

Some of these programs have been general in approach, directed toward educating the community on the more adaptive methods of dealing with death and loss. These adaptive methods include the open expression of grief and the mourning for and discussion of the dead person in all his good and bad aspects. They emphasize the value of support from others at the time of the crisis; the special needs and vulnerabilities of bereaved children; the importance of honest and open attitudes; and the other losses, such as disability and aging, which may also involve grief and mourning.

The educational methods have sometimes been broad based, aimed at heightening community awareness. Dr. Elisabeth Kübler-Ross's extensive lecture tours addressed to the needs of the dying, constitute an example. Other times they have been more specific, directed, for example, toward those groups that have contact with the dying and bereaved, such as doctors, nurses, health care professionals, and funeral professionals. There have also been educational programs for schools, which have had the aim of teaching children and adolescents more about the natural aspects of death and dying and the processes of adapting to loss.

There has been a general increase in public awareness of the importance of these issues as a consequence of many such programs, and as a consequence of the increasing interest the media have shown in the areas of death and loss. While this heightened awareness is obviously of significance, whether or not it has fulfilled a role in preventing morbidity or pathological bereavement patterns is unclear. It seems likely that it has made the general public more attuned to the support that others need at such times and thus is likely to have been beneficial. As is so often the case (Raphael 1980) it is difficult to evaluate the effectiveness of these broad-based programs.

There have also been specific programs directed toward particular groups of bereaved people which have been aimed at lessening the risk status of these people. The programs may be directed toward, for instance, widows and widowers (P. R. Silverman 1972; Raphael 1977*b*; Vachon et al. 1980); the parents of stillborn children or of children who have died; or toward children who are bereaved (Gilson 1976; Lowman 1979; Black and Urbanowitz 1982; Black 1976). The programs may themselves be general, even though directed toward a particular group, or they may be specific for that group. A further specificity may be the provision of preventive intervention which is directed toward those at high risk and specifically tailored for the particular risk factors (Raphael 1977*b*; Parkes 1980). These more specific programs have been shown to have demonstrable effectiveness in lessening postbereavement morbidity and thus represent one of the few positive outcomes in preventive psychiatry. Much further work is necessary, however, replicating such studies and devising and implementing more specific preventive services for other bereaved who are at risk.

The stress of the bereavement crisis, the clear-cut nature of the stressor, and the effectiveness of a goal oriented approach, mean that bereavement offers a very useful point of entry for preventive services. Some bereaved, however, will not wish to utilize support at such times and some will not need it. Preventive programs that are developed will have to be sensitive to such issues.

## The Ending of Grief

Sometimes in work with the bereaved it is necessary to recognize that the time has come for an ending of grief, at least in its most acute and disturbing forms. Because Western society is often deritualized, the bereaved and those who support him may be uncertain as to the ending of grief. While it may be distressing and inhibitory of grief for the bereaved person to have his period of bereavement cut off in the early weeks, it is also difficult when its end is uncertain. Reid (1979, chap. 2) notes how there is a time to grieve and a time to live. The bereaved person may need support from those caring for him to give up his acute grief after the early months or, at least, not to feel guilty as his grief lessens and he starts to reinvolve himself in life again. The counselor working with him may need to provide some interpretation or permission for this, while recognizing at the same time that some grief and mourning will continue to reappear over the months and years to follow.

Because each bereaved person takes his own time to grieve, this is a delicate area, but, as the bereaved person and those helping him recognize the reawakening of life and libido, it is important to nurture their development gently.

## Counselors for Bereavement

Many people will have contact with the bereaved and in the process may comfort them and console them. These people may also be called upon to provide counseling alongside whatever other roles they may fulfill.

As Parkes has noted from his studies (Parkes 1980), it takes some time, perhaps a year, for the nonprofessional or volunteer person to develop adequate skills to work with the bereaved. He believes that the "value of services that lack the support of trained and experienced members of the care-giving professionals, remains to be established" (p. 6). It is also quite clear from our own experience that a bereavement may open up many sensitive issues, the handling of which may require considerable psychotherapeutic skills. Thus, knowledge of bereavement patterns and associated dynamics is critical, as is training in the skills required to deal with them. Case supervision to help with further development of competence in this field is also important. Such supervision helps the counselor deal with the stresses of work and avoid problems induced by the counselor's own unconscious dynamic vulnerabilities in this area.

Those offered help may find it most acceptable when it is offered concurrent with other services such as medical and nursing care or welfare (Singh and Raphael 1981). Here it is possible to use some of the processes outlined in this chapter to comfort or console the bereaved, or to assess therapeutically and provide more specific support for them. Those bereaved at high risk, or those already showing signs of pathological bereavement or poor outcome, are likely, however, to require the intervention of a skilled and well-trained counselor. This role may be filled by a nurse, social worker, clergyman, psychologist, doctor, psychiatrist, or other professional, who has the appropriate abilities. The core attribute, however, of anyone offering support for the bereaved, is the capacity for empathy. This brings special difficulties for the counselor, since empathy with the bereaved in their encounters with loss and death touches off in each one of us the most personal of terrors. We all have to learn to live with loss, but the person who works in this sphere must confront it every day.

# CHAPTER 10. Living with Loss: Passion, Compassion, and Defense

"I care for you," she said, "but what if we lose one another?"

"Well," he said, "that is the price we must pay."

Each person must make his way through life encompassing two important facts. If he loves, there will be the great rewards of human intimacy, in its broadest sense; and yet when he does so, he becomes vulnerable to the exquisite agony of loss. And one day—he knows not when or how—he will die.

This knowledge of the possibility of loss may strongly influence the patterning of human relationships. Some dare not involve themselves intimately with others, because they cannot bear the thought of the pain of separating from them or of eventually losing them. They may be especially vulnerable, perhaps, because they suffered and did not resolve such pain in early childhood. Or, the fear may be deep within them, implanted there by fearful parents, themselves scarred by childhood pain. Others will build relationships in which they hope to prevent loss. They may do this by taking on those whom they sense are likely to be too dependent to leave them. Or it may be that they themselves reject others so that they seem to themselves to gain mastery of the pain by being the aggressors, the more powerful, the deserters and not the deserted.

The infant's earliest experience of separation pain and grief may come with his first separation from his mother. When he is comforted after this, when his mother consoles him on her return, he learns, for the first time, of both pain and survival: that the pain can be borne and life will go on. When he is comforted and consoled, this experience will be incorporated in his overall development. When he is not comforted or consoled, this may lead to a painful vulnerability that becomes locked within him. If it represents increasing deprivation, for which he receives little care, then the vulnerability to separation and loss may become a powerful focus. It may influence his pattern of relationships, leading him to avoid those who may reawaken the feelings of vulnerability, or, aggressively reject those who could evoke them. It may also influence his expression of emotion, for he may have learned that others will not accept his anxiety and anger or his sadness and despair. Thus he may build for himself a way of living that denies these affects or prohibits their release.

These early experiences and the ways in which they were dealt with are readily awakened in the process of facing loss or separation in adult life. They are also triggered as the individual empathizes with another's loss. If his own experiences have been traumatically painful, then repression defenses may come into play, blocking the resolution of personal loss or the capacity to empathize with others. Even in ordinary circumstances this reawakened early pain may be distressing, because, for the infant, it seemed to threaten survival. It may be felt as the primitive and preverbal distress that was the infant's first experience of separation pain, so that those in contact with personal loss or the losses of others may wish at any price to escape reexperiencing that early pain.

It is useful to consider this early, internalized, primitive, and usually repressed focus of separation and loss as the "inner bereaved child" inside each one of us. This inner bereaved child is reawakened when we lose someone we love or when we share someone else's loss and attempt to comfort and console him. It is intensely relived when we identify with the child's experience of bereavement. It is part of our empathy, yet it is difficult to bear.

When this separation or loss pain is touched upon in the losses that are encountered in everyday life, then the individual may respond in a number of ways. He may flee from the pain, either by leaving the person who triggers it or by trying to escape the situation by other means. He may stay, but defend strongly against his affects. These defenses may be those of denial and repression leading to some psychic numbing. The numbing may be minor or transient, allowing him to continue without major distortions of his personal experience and response. This behavior may even serve an adaptive function in that it may allow him to bear what would otherwise be overwhelming and give him time to master it gradually. The numbing and denial may be massive, to the point of excluding all real experience of the situation and thus distorting it. This distortion may remain rather than occur transiently, so as to become a permanent maladaptive part of the individual's behavior. Or, the individual may allow himself to experience the pain, this loss of others. In so doing, he identifies with the affected person and his feeling state, yet is not totally overwhelmed by the affects of the other, nor his own reawakened earlier experience. In this latter response he has developed the capacity for compassion: "suffering together with another."

This compassion allows us to empathize with the distress of others and to offer them comfort and consolation. Yet it may also bring distress for us, proportionate to the severity of their loss, the closeness of our identification with their situation, and the degree to which our own earlier pain has been revived. For this distress we also may need the support and care of others, our families, those with whom we work, and others who share this experience.

For some people, in the course of life, there may not be a great many losses to be faced in this way. Their compassion may only need to be felt for the distanced distress of others, the accident victims, the dead of war and violence in another country. Some may in fact try to order their lives so that little demand is placed upon them to share or experience the feelings of others. Other individuals seem to have lives filled with loss and death. They may struggle from one personal crisis to the next. They may retain their capacity to respond, their compassion for others, or they may seem to become numbed or defended, because it is, for them, the only way to survive. The majority of people encounter a number of personal losses in their lives and bear the grief these bring. They also share the losses of many others, of family friends, and the human race. They feel compassion.

The person who works in the field of bereavement will be called upon to experience, in close and empathic encounter, a great many of the losses of others. The person who undertakes such work may well have had sustained early loss himself; indeed, a number of studies suggest that those in the caring professions, for instance, doctors and nurses, may have higher than average levels of perceived deprivation in their childhoods. There are also the heightened attachment and closeness that crises of loss and disaster involve. There are also, in some instances, very strong identifications with those for whom the caring person cares. To retain his compassion, the caring person in this field may need considerable support from others, both his family and his colleagues. He needs, for instance, to share the burden of cases in supervisory sessions. He needs backup and relief for the cases he finds hard to bear. He needs to take clear breaks from such work, which are officially sanctioned, and indeed required, by his system of work. He needs, in short, care and consolation from others to bear the enormity of much of the pain and loss and death he helps others encompass. If this is not available for him, he may develop defensive pathology in the form of dehumanization, distancing of interpersonal relationships, or isolation of affect, so that cold mechanical relating and care is all that he can give (Raphael 1981). Denial may, of course, be used temporarily or partially by the worker, allowing a rest from the stress of his empathy and permitting the integration of what would otherwise be intolerable. It is only when it becomes extensive and continuing that defensive pathology may result. Without adequate support and care for himself, the worker may also run the risk of "burnout," where psychosomatic symptoms, exhaustion, and disturbed involvement appear. Or, as those who work in such situations recognize, he may try to console himself and to mitigate the stress, perhaps by acting out in his interpersonal relationships or by self-consoling behaviors, such as eating or drinking. Most empathic involvement can be stressful, but this stress can usually be managed with the support of others and with systems of work that make provision for it.

Thus, it would seem that a key issue for the individual, and indeed his society, is to learn to bear the pain of loss that must inevitably be faced; to keep his passionate involvement in humanity and human relationships; to learn to comfort and console others with compassion; and to seek and accept for himself the compassionate concern of other members of his human society.

# REFERENCES

Ablon, J. 1973. Reactions of Samoan burns patients and families to severe burns. *Social Science and Medicine* 7:167–78.

Abraham, K. 1924. A short study of the development of the libido; viewed in the light of mental disorders. In *Selected papers on psychoanalysis.* London: Hogarth Press.

Abrahams, M. J.; Price, J.; Whitlock, F. A.; and Williams, G. 1976. The Brisbane Floods, January 1974: Their impact on health. *Medical Journal of Australia* 2:936–40.

Adam, K. S. 1982. Loss, suicide, and attachment. In *The Place of Attachment In Human Behavior,* ed. C. M. Parkes and Joan Stevenson-Hinde. New York: Basic Books.

Adam, K. S.; Lohrenz, J. G.; Harper, D.; and Streiner, D. 1982. Early parental loss and suicidal ideation in university students. *Canadian Journal of Psychiatry* 27:275–81.

Aldrich, E. Knight. 1963. The dying patient's grief. *Journal of the American Medical Association* 184(5):329–31.

Alexander, I. E., and Adlerstein, A. M. 1958. Affective responses to the concept of death in a population of children and early adolescents. *Journal of Genetic Psychology* 93:167–77.

Alexy, W. D. 1980. Coping with loss: The principal theme postulate. *Rehabilitation Literature* 41 (3–4):66–71.

Alexy, W. D. In press. Dimensions of psychological counseling that facilitate the growing process of bereaved parents. *Journal of Counseling Psychology.*

American Psychiatric Association. *Diagnostic and Statistical Manual of Mental Disorders,* 3rd ed. 1980. Washington, D.C.: American Psychiatric Association.

Anthony, S. 1981. *The discovery of death in childhood and after.* Sydney, Australia: Penguin.

Aries, P. 1974. *Western Attitudes Toward Death: From the Middle Ages to the Present.* Baltimore: John Hopkins University Press.

Arthur, B., and Kemme, M. 1964. Bereavement in childhood. *Journal of Child Psychology and Psychiatry* 5:37–49.

Averill, J. 1968. Grief: Its nature and significance. *Psychological Bulletin* 70:721–48.

Bahr, H. M., and Harvey, C. D. 1979. Correlates of loneliness among widows bereaved in a mining disaster. *Psychological Reports* 44:367–85.

Bak, R. C. 1973. Being in love and object loss. *International Journal of Psychoanalysis* 54: 1–8.

Barglow, P.; Gunther, M.S.; Johnson, A.; and Meltzer, H. J. 1965. Hysterectomy and tubal ligation: A psychiatric comparison. *Obstetrics and Gynecology,* 25:520–25.

Barrett, C. J. 1978. The effectiveness of widows' groups in facilitating change. *Journal of Consulting and Clinical Psychology* 46(1):20–31.

Barry, M. J. 1981. Therapeutic experience with patients referred for "prolonged grief reaction": Some second thoughts. *Proceedings of the Mayo Clinic* 56(12):744–48.

Bart, P. B. 1971. Depression in middle-aged women in *Women In Sexist Society,* ed. V. Gormick and B. R. Moran. New York: Basic Books.

Bartrop, R. W.; Lazarus, L.; Luckhurst, E.; Kiloh, L. G.; and Penny, R. 1977. Depressed lymphocyte function after bereavement. *Lancet* (16 April): 834–36.

Bedell, J. 1973. The maternal orphan: Paternal perception of mother loss. Paper presented at the Annual Meeting of the Foundation of Thanatology, November 1973: New York.

Bendiksen, R., and Fulton, R. 1975. Death and the child: An anterospective test of the childhood bereavement and later behaviour disorder hypothesis. *Omega* 6(1):45–59.

Bennet, G. 1970. Bristol Floods 1968: Controlled survey of effects of health on local community disaster. *British Medical Journal* 3:454–58.

Bernstein, S. M.; Steiner, B. W.; Glaister, J. T. D.; and Muir, C. F. 1981. Changes in patients with gender-identity problems after parental death. *American Journal of Psychiatry* 138(1):41–45.

Binger, C. M. 1973. Childhood leukemia: Emotional impact on siblings. p. 195–209 In *The Child in His Family: The Impact of Disease and Death*, ed. E. J. Anthony and C. Koupernik. vol. 2. New York: John Wiley.

Birtchnell, J. 1969. Parent death in relation to age and parental age at birth in psychiatric patients and general population controls. *British Journal of Preventive and Social Medicine* 23:244–50.

———. 1971. Early parent death, in relation to size and constitution of sibship, in psychiatric patients and general population controls. *Acta Psychiatrica Scandinavica* 47:250–70.

———. 1972. Early parent death and psychiatric diagnosis. *Social Psychiatry* 7:202–10.

———. 1975. Psychiatric breakdown following recent parent death. *British Journal of Medical Psychology* 48:379–90.

———. 1980. Women whose mothers died in childhood: An outcome study. *Psychological Medicine* 10:699–713.

———. 1981. In search of correspondences between age at psychiatric breakdown and age at death: Anniversary reactions. *British Journal of Medical Psychology* 54(2):111–21.

Birtchnell, J., and Kennard, J. 1982. Some marital and child-rearing characteristics of early mother-bereaved women. *British Journal of Medical Psychology* 55(2):177–86.

Black, D. 1974. What happens to bereaved children? *Proceedings of Royal Society of Medicine* 69:38–40.

Black, D., and Urbanowitz, M. 1982. Intervention in bereaved families. Abstract, Tenth International Congress of the International Association for Child and Adolescent Psychiatry and Allied Professions, Dublin, Ireland, July 1982.

Blos, P. 1962. *On Adolescence: A Psychoanalytic Interpretation.* New York: Free Press of Glencoe.

Bluglass, K. 1979. Counseling families after a baby dies. *Modern Medicine* 24:6–12.

———. 1980. Psychiatric morbidity after cot death. *Practitioner* 224:533–39.

———. 1981. Annotation: Psychosocial aspects of the Sudden Infant Death Syndrome. *Journal of Child Psychology and Psychiatry* 22:411–21.

Boman, B. 1982. The Vietnam veteran ten years on. *Australian & New Zealand Journal of Psychiatry* 16:107–27.

Boman, B.; Streimer, J.; and Perkins, M. 1981. Crisis intervention and pharmacotherapy. *Crisis,* 2:41–49.

Bornstein, P. E., and Clayton, P. J. 1972. The anniversary reaction. *Diseases of the Nervous System* 33:447–472.

Bornstein, P.; Clayton, P. J.; Halikas, N. L.; and Robins, E. 1973. The depression of widowhood after thirteen months. *British Journal of Psychiatry* 122:561–66.

Bowie, W. K. 1977. Story of a first-born. *Omega* 8(1):1–17.

Bowlby, J. 1963. Pathological mourning and childhood mourning. *Journal of the American Psychoanalytic Association* 11:500-541.

———. 1969. *Attachment.* Vol. 1 in *Attachment and Loss,* ed. M. Masud R. Khan. London: The Hogarth Press.

———. 1973. *Attachment and Loss.* Vol. 2 in *Separation: Anxiety and Anger* London: Hogarth Press.

———. 1977. The making and breaking of affectional bonds: I: Aetiology and psychopathology in the light of attachment theory (the fiftieth Maudsley Lecture). *The British Journal of Psychiatry* 130:201–10.

———. 1978. Attachment theory and its therapeutic implications. pp. 5–33. Vol. 6 of *Adolescent Psychiatry: Developmental and Clinical Studies,* ed. S. C. Feinstein and P. L. Giovacchini. Chicago: University of Chicago Press.

# References

————. 1979. Personal Communication.

————. 1980. *Loss: Sadness and Depression.* Vol. 3 in *Attachment and Loss.* London: Hogarth Press.

Bozeman, M.; Orbach, C. E.; Sutherland, A. M. 1955. Psychological impact of cancer and its treatment: The adaptation of mothers to threatened loss of their children through leukemia I. *Cancer* 8:1–19.

Breslin, M. 1977. Unresolved grief in psychosomatic disorders. Mimeographed. North Carolina: Duke University Medical Center.

*British Medical Journal* 1(January):126. *1977.* Annotation: Grief and stillbirth.

Brody, E. M. 1974. Ageing and family personality: A developmental view. *Family Process* 13(1):23–37.

Brown, G. 1982. Early loss and depression. In *The Place of Attachment in Human Behavior,* ed. C. M. Parkes and Joan Stevenson-Hinde. New York: Basic Books.

Butler, R. 1963. The life review: An interpretation of reminiscence in the aged. *Psychiatry* 26:65–76.

Cain, A. C. 1966. The legacy of suicide: Observations on the pathogenic impact of suicide upon marital partners. *Psychiatry* 29:873–80.

Cain, A. C., and Cain, B. S. 1964. On replacing a child. *Journal of the American Academy of Child Psychiatry* 3:433–56.

Cain, A. C., and Fast, I. 1966. Children's disturbed reactions to parent suicide. *American Journal of Orthopsychiatry* 5:873–80.

Cain, A. C., and Fast, I. 1972. Children's disturbed reactions to parent suicide. In *Survivors of Suicide,* ed. A. C. Cain. Springfield, Ill.: Charles C Thomas.

Cain, A. C.; Fast, I.; and Erickson, M. E. 1964. Children's disturbed reactions to the death of a sibling. *American Journal of Orthopsychiatry* 34:741–52.

Calvert, P.; Northeast, J.; and Dax, E. Cunningham, 1977. Death in a country area and its effects on the health of relatives. *Medical Journal of Australia* 2:635–36.

Caplan, G. 1964. *Principles of Preventive Psychiatry.* New York: Basic Books.

Caplan, M. G., and Douglas, V. I. 1969. *Journal of Child Psychology and Psychiatry* 10:225–236.

Carlton, I. G. 1980. Early psychiatric intervention following a maritime disaster. *Military Medicine* 145(2):114–16.

Caroff, P., and Dobrof, R. 1973. The helping process with bereaved families. Paper presented at the Annual Meeting of the Foundation of Thanatology, November 1973, New York.

Chodoff, P.; Friedman, S. B.; Hamburg, D. 1964. Stress, defenses and coping behavior: Observations in parents of children with malignant disease. *American Journal of Psychiatry* 120(8):743–49.

Church, J. S. 1974. The Buffalo Creek disaster: Extent and range of emotional problems and/or behavioural problems. *Omega* 5(11):61–63.

Clayton, P. J. 1975. The effects of living alone on bereavement symptoms. *American Journal of Psychiatry* 132:133–37.

Clayton, P. J.; Halikas, J. A.; and Maurice, W. L. 1971. The bereavement of the widowed. *Diseases of the Nervous System* 32(9):592–604.

————. 1972. The depression of widowhood. *British Journal of Psychiatry* 121:71–78.

Clayton, P. J.; Halikas, J. A.; Maurice, W. L.; and Robins, E. 1973. Anticipatory grief and widowhood. *British Journal of Psychiatry* 122:47–51.

Clayton, P. J.; Herjanic, M.; Murphy, G.; and Woodruff, R. 1974. Mourning and depression: Their similarities and differences. *Canadian Psychiatric Association Journal* 19:309–12.

Cleveland. W. P., and Giantureo, D. T. 1976. Remarriage probability after widowhood: A retrospective method. *Journal of Gerontology* 31:99–103.

Clyman, R.; Green, C.; Rowe, J.; Mikkelsen, C.; and Ataide, L. 1980. Issues concerning parents after the death of their newborn. *Critical Care Medicine* 8(4):215–18.

Cobb, S., and Lindemann, E. 1944. Neuropsychiatric observations during the Cocoanut Grove Fire. *Annals of Surgery* 117:814–18.

Coddington, R. D. 1979. Life events associated with adolescent pregnancies. *Journal of Clinical Psychiatry* 40:180–85.

Corney, R. J., and Horton, F. T. 1974. Pathological grief following spontaneous abortion. *American Journal of Psychiatry* 131:825–27.

Cornwell, J.; Nurcombe, B.; and Stevens, L. 1977. Family response to loss of a child by sudden infant death syndrome. *Medical Journal of Australia,* [30 April] pp. 656-58.

Cottington, E. M.; Mathew, K. A.; Talbott, E.; and Kuller, L. H. 1980. Environmental events preceding sudden death in women. *Psychosomatic Medicine* 42(6):567-74.

Crisp, A. H., and Priest, R. G. 1972. Psychoneurotic status during the year following bereavement. *Journal of Psychosomatic Research* 16:351-55.

Cumming, E., and Henry, W. E. 1961. *Growing Old: The Process of Disengagement.* New York: Basic Books.

Curlee, J. 1969. Alcoholism and the "empty-nest." *Bulletin of the Menninger Clinic* 33:165-71.

Darwin, Charles 1872. *The Expression of Emotion in Men and Animals.* London: Murray.

Davidson, A. D. 1979. Disaster: coping with stress. A program that worked. *Police Stress* 1:20-22.

Davis, H. K., and Franklin, R. W. 1970. "Continuing grief" as a method of psychotherapy following E.S.T. *Diseases of the Nervous System* 31:626-30.

Defrain, J. D., and Ernst, L. 1978. The psychological effects of sudden infant death syndrome on surviving family members. *Journal of Family Practice* 6:985-89.

Dennehy, C. 1966. Childhood bereavement and psychiatric illness. *British Journal of Psychiatry* 112:1049-69.

Deutsch, H. 1937. The absence of grief. *Psychoanalytic Quarterly* 6:12-22.

——. 1945. *The Psychology of Women.* New York: Grune & Stratton.

——. 1967. *Selected problems of adolescence.* New York: International Universities Press.

Dicks, H. V. 1967. *Marital Tensions.* London: Routledge & Kegan Paul.

Douglas, J. W. B. 1970. Broken families and child behavior. *Journal Royal College of Physicians of London* 8:203-10.

Eliot, T. D. 1930. The adjustive behavior of bereaved families: A new field for research. *Social Forces* 8:543-49.

——. 1932. The bereaved family. *Annals of the American Academy of Political and Social Sciences* 160:184-90.

Elizure, E., and Kattman, M. 1982. Children's bereavement reactions following the death of the father: II. *Journal of the American Academy of Child Psychiatry* 21(5):414-80.

Emde, R. N., and Brown, C. 1978. Adaptation to the birth of a Down's syndrome infant. *Journal of the American Academy of Child Psychiatry* 17(2):299-323.

Engel, G. L. 1961. Is grief a disease? *Psychosomatic Medicine* 23:18-22.

——. 1962. Anxiety and depression-withdrawal: The primary affects of unpleasure. *International Journal of Psychoanalysis* 43:89-97.

——. 1975. The death of a twin: Mourning and anniversary reactions—Fragments of ten years of self-analysis. *International Journal of Psychoanalysis* 56:23-40.

Engel, G. L.; Frader, M.; Barry, C. J.; and Schalch, D. S. 1971. Changes during experimentally induced sadness. *Psychosomatic Medicine* 33:471.

Epps, L. S. 1972. Application of behavior therapy techniques in treating children severely traumatized by earthquake. Proceedings of the Eightieth Annual Convention, American Psychological Association pp. 347-48.

Erikson, E. H. 1959. Identity and the life cycle. In *Psychological Issues,* vol. 1 New York: International University Press.

Erikson, K. 1976. Loss of communality at Buffalo Creek. *American Journal of Psychiatry* 133:302-5.

Fast, I. and Cain, A. 1964. Fears of death in bereaved children and adults. *American Journal of Orthopsychiatry* 34:278-79

Felner, R. D.; Genter, M. A.; Bocke, M. F; and Cowen, E. L. 1981. Parental death or divorce and the school adjustment of young children. *American Journal of Community Psychology* 9(2):181-91.

Fenichel, O. 1945. *The Psychoanalytic Theory of Neurosis* New York: Norton.

Field, J. 1979. The Development of the Concept of Death in Children. M.A. Thesis, University of New South Wales.

Fisher, S.; Andrews, G. R.; Harris, S; and Martin, S. 1976. *Cancer patients and their families.* Sydney: Health Commission of New South Wales.

# References

Fleming, J., and Altschul, S. 1963. Activation of mourning and growth by psychoanalysis. *International Journal of Psychoanalysis* 44:419–31.

Franke, S., and Smith, D. 1982. Conjugal bereavement among the Huli people of Papua, New Guinea. *British Journal of Psychiatry* 141:302–305.

Fraser, M. 1974. *Children in Conflict.* Sydney, Australia: Pelican.

Freud, A. 1958. Adolescence. *Psychoanalytic study of the child* 13:255–68.

Freud, S. 1915. Thoughts for the times on war and death. In *The Complete Psychological Works: Standard Edition*, vol. 14. London: Hogarth Press.

Freud, S. 1917. Mourning and melancholia. In *Sigmund Freud: Collected Papers*, vol. 4. New York: Basic Books.

Freundt, L. 1964. Surveys in induced and spontaneous abortions in the Copenhagen area. *Acta Psychiatrica Scandinavica*, 180 (supplement):235–37.

Fried, M. 1962. Grieving for a lost home. In *The Environment of the Metropolis*, ed. L. J. Dahl. New York: Basic Books.

Friedman, J. H., and Zaris, D. 1964. Paradoxical response to death of a spouse. *Diseases of the Nervous System* 25:480–83.

Fulton, R., and Gottesman, D. J. 1980. Anticipatory grief: A psychosocial concept reconsidered. *British Journal of Psychiatry* 137:45–54.

Furman, E. 1974. *A Child's Parent Dies.* New Haven: Yale University Press.

———. 1980. The death of a newborn: assistance to parents. In *The child and his family: preventive psychiatry in the age of transition*, ed. E. J. Anthony and C. Chiland. New York: Wiley.

Furman, R. A. 1973. A child's capacity for mourning. In *The child in his family: The impact of disease and death*, ed. E. J. Anthony and C. Koupernik. New York: Wiley.

Gapes, C. 1982. A study of bereaved adolescents and their church group. Unpublished manuscript.

Gardner, R. A. 1976. *Psychotherapy with children of divorce.* New York: Jason Aronson.

Gauthier, Y., and Marshall, W. L. 1977. Grief: A cognitive-behavioral analysis. *Cognitive Therapy and Research* 1:39–44.

Gauthier, Y., and Pye, C. 1979. Graduated self-exposure in the management of grief. *Behaviour Analysis and Modification* 3:202–8.

George, L. K., and Weiler, S. J. 1981. Sexuality in middle and later life. *Archives of General Psychiatry* 38:919–23.

Gerber, I.; Rusalem, R.; Hannon, N.; 1975. Anticipatory grief and aged widows and widowers. *Journal of Gerontology* 30:225–29.

Gilson, G. 1976. Care of the family who has lost a newborn. *Postgraduate Medicine* 60(6):67–70.

Gleser, G. C.; Green, B. L.; and Winget, C. N. 1978. Quantifying interview data on psychic impairment of disaster survivors. *Journal of Nervous and Mental Disease* 166:209–16.

Glick, I. O.; Weiss, R. S.; and Parkes, C. M. 1974. *The first year of bereavement.* New York: Wiley Interscience.

Gorer, G. 1959. The pornography of death. In *Modern Writing*, ed. W. Phillips and P. Rahv. New York: McGraw-Hill.

Gorlitz, P., and Gutmann, D. 1981. The psychological transition into grandparenting. In *Modern perspectives in the psychiatry of middle age*, ed. John G. Howells. New York: Brunner/Mazel.

Granville-Grossman, K. L. 1966. Early bereavement and schizophrenia. *British Journal of Psychiatry* 112:1027–34.

Graves, J. S. 1978. Adolescents and their psychiatrist's suicide: A study of shared grief and mourning. *Journal of the American Academy of Child Psychiatry* 17:521–32.

Grayson, J. 1970. Grief reactions to the relinquishing of unfulfilled wishes. *American Journal of Psychotherapy* 24(2):287–95.

Greenberg, N.H.; Loesch, J. C.; and Lakin, M. 1959. Life situation associated with the onset of pregnancy. *Psychosomatic Medicine* 21:296–300.

Greenblatt, M. 1978. The grieving spouse. *American Journal of Psychiatry* 135:43–46.

Gyulay, J. 1975. The forgotten grievers. *American Journal of Nursing* 75(9):1476–79.

Hafner, J. 1982. Personal communication.

Hagglund, J. B. 1981. The final stage of the dying process. *International Journal of Psychoanalytics* 62:45–49.

Halpern, W. 1972. Some psychiatric sequence to crib death. *American Journal of Psychiatry* 129(4):398–402.

Hamilton, J. W. 1977. The significance of object loss in individual response to accidental trauma. *Comprehensive Psychiatry* 18(2):189–99.

Harlow, H. F. 1962. The heterosexual affectional system in monkeys. *American Psychologist* 17:1–9.

Harrari, E. 1981. Pathological grief in doctors' wives. *British Medical Journal* 282:33–34.

Helmrath, T. A., and Steinitz, E. M. 1978. Parental grieving and the failure of social support. *Journal of Family Practice* 6:785–90.

Henderson, A. S. 1974. Care-eliciting behaviour in man. *Journal of Nervous and Mental Disease* 159:172–81.

Henderson, S., and Bostock, F. T. 1975. Coping behaviour: Correlates of survival on a raft. *Australian & New Zealand Journal of Psychiatry* 9(4):221–24.

Henderson, S.; Byrne, D. G.; and Duncan-Jones, P. 1981. *Neurosis and the social environment.* Sydney: Academic Press.

Hendrick, C., and Brown, S. 1971. Introversion, extraversion and interpersonal attraction. *Journal Personal Social Psychology* 20:31–36.

Herioch, M. J.; Batson, J. W.; and Baum, J. 1978. Psychosocial factors in juvenile rheumatoid arthritis. *Arthritis and Rheumatism* 21:229–33.

Hilgard, J. R. 1969. Depressive and psychotic states as anniversaries of sibling death in childhood. *International Psychiatry Clinics* 6:197–211.

Hilgard, J. R., and Newman, M. F. 1959. Anniversaries and mental illness. *Psychiatry* 22:113–21.

Hinde, R. A. 1979. *Towards Understanding Relationships.* London: Academic Press.

Hocking, F. 1965. Human reactions to extreme environmental stress. *Medical Journal of Australia* 2:477–83.

———. 1970. Extreme environmental stress and its significance for psychopathology. *American Journal of Psychotherapy* 24:4–26.

Hodgkinson, P. E. 1982. Abnormal grief: the problem of therapy. *British Journal of Medical Psychology* 55(1)29–34.

Hofer, M.; Wolff, C.; Friedman, S.; and Mason, J. W. 1977. A psychoendocrine study of bereavement. *Psychosomatic Medicine* 39:481–504.

Holinger, D. C. 1980. Violent deaths as a leading cause of mortality. *American Journal of Psychiatry* 137:472–476.

Holland, J.; Harris, S.; and Holmes, J. 1971. Psychological response to the death of a twin by the surviving twin with the same disease. *Omega* 2:160–67.

Hooper, D.; Roberts, F.; Hinchcliffe, M.; and Vaughan, P. W. 1977. The melancholy marriage: An inquiry into the interaction of depression. I: Introduction. *British Journal of Medical Psychology* 50:113–24.

Hope, D. 1981. Pintjantjatjana and the aged. In *The Crisis of the Ageing Mind.* Proceedings of the South Australian Post Graduate Medical Education Association, 8-10, April 1981, Adelaide, S. A.

Horowitz, M. J. 1976. *Stress response syndromes.* New York: Jason Aronson.

Horowitz, M. J.; Wilner, N.; Kaltreider, N. 1980. Signs and symptoms of post-traumatic stress disorder. *Archives of General Psychiatry* 37:85–92.

Horowitz, M. J.; Wilner, N.; Marmar, C.; and Krupnick, J. 1980. Pathological grief and the activation of latent self images. *American Journal of Psychiatry* 137(10):1157–62.

Horowitz, M. J.; Krupnick, J.; Kaltreider, N.; Wilner, N.; Leong, A.; and Marmar, C. 1981. Initial psychological response to parental death. *Archives of General Psychiatry* 38:316–23.

Hudson, B., and Baker, H. W. G. 1980. Endocrinology of ageing: Men in their twilight years. In *The Biology of Ageing in Man*, pp. 115–30. Report of a Workshop on Biomedical Research into Ageing. National Research Council, Australia.

Inhelder, B., and Piaget, J. 1958. *The Growth of Logical Thinking from Childhood to Adolescence.* New York: Basic Books.

Ironside, W. 1980. Conservation withdrawal and action engagement in a theory of survivor behavior. *Psychosomatic Medicine* 42:1–14.

# References

Jacobs, S., and Ostfeld, A. 1977. An epidemiological review of the mortality of bereavement. *Psychosomatic Medicine* 39:344–57.

Jacobsen, G., and Ryder, R. 1969. Parental loss and some characteristics of the early marriage relationship. *American Journal of Orthopsychiatry* 39:779–87.

Jacques, E. 1965. Death and the mid-life crisis. *International Journal of Psychoanalysis* 46:502–14.

Jamison, K. R.; Wallace, D. K.; and Pasnau, R. O. 1978a. Psychosocial aspects of mastectomy: The woman's perspective. *American Journal of Psychiatry* 135:432–36.

———. 1978b. Psychosocial aspects of mastectomy: The man's perspective. *American Journal of Psychiatry* 135:543–46.

Jennings, L. E., and France, R. D. 1979. Management of grief in the hypochondriac. *Journal of Family Practice* 8:957–60.

Johnson, P., and Rosenblatt, P. C. 1981. Grief following childhood loss of a parent. *American Journal of Psychotherapy* 35(3):419–25.

Jung, C. G. 1934. The structure and dynamics of the Psyche. In Vol. 8 of *The Collected Works of C. G. Jung*. London: Routledge & Kegan Paul.

Kastenbaum, R. 1965. Time and death in adolescence. In *The meaning of death*, ed. H. Feitel. New York: McGraw-Hill.

Kellehear, A. 1983. Research into near-death experiences. *New Doctor* (in press).

Kelly, G. A. 1955. *The psychology of personal constructs.* New York: Norton.

Kennell, J. H.; Slyter, H.; and Klaus, M. K. 1970. The mourning response of parents to the death of a newborn infant. *New England Journal of Medicine* 283:344–49.

Kerner, J.; Harvey, B.; and Lewiston, N. 1979. The impact of grief: A retrospective study of family function following loss of a child with cystic fibrosis. *Journal of Chronic Disease* 32:221–25.

Kinston, W., and Rosser, R. 1974. Disaster: Effects on mental and physical state. *Journal of Psychosomatic Research* 18:437–56.

Kirkley-Best, E., and Kellner, K. R. 1982. The forgotten grief: A review of the psychology of stillbirth. *American Journal of Orthopsychiatry* 52:420–29.

Kitson, G.; Lopata, H. Z.; Holmes, W.; and Meyering, S. 1980. Divorcees and widows: similarities and differences. *American Journal of Orthopsychiatry.* 50:291–301.

Klein, M. 1948. Mourning and its relation to manic depressive states. In *Contributions to Psychoanalysis*. London: Hogarth Press.

Klerman, G. L., and Izen, J. E. 1977. The effects of bereavement and grief on physical health and general well being. *Advances in Psychosomatic Medicine* 9:63–68.

Kliman, G.; Feinberg, D.; Buchsbaum, B.; Kliman, A.; Lubin, H.; Ronald, D.; and Stein, M. 1969. Facilitation of mourning during childhood. *American Journal of Orthopsychiatry* 39:247–48.

Kreitman, N.; Collins, J.; Nelson, B.; and Troop, J. 1970. Neurosis and marital interaction. I: Personality and symptoms. *British Journal of Psychiatry* 117:33–46.

Krell, R., and Rabkin, L. 1979. The effects of sibling death on the surviving child: a family perspective. *Family Process* 18:471–77.

Krupp, G. R. 1965. Identification as a defense against anxiety in coping with loss. *International Journal of Psychoanalysis* 46:303–14.

Krupp, G. R., and Klingfield, B. 1962. The bereavement reaction: A cross-cultural evaluation. *Journal of Religion and Health* 1:222–46.

Kübler-Ross, E. 1969. *On Death and Dying*. London: Tavistock.

La Grand, L. E. 1981. Loss reactions of college students: A descriptive analysis. *Death Education* 5:235–48.

Langer, T. S., and Michael, S. E. 1963. *Life stress and mental health*. New York: Free Press.

Larson, R. 1978. Thirty years of research on the subjective well being of older Americans. *Journal of Gerontology* 33:109–25.

Leaverton, D. R.; White, C. A.; McCormick; C. R.; Smith, P.; and Sheikholislam, B. 1980. Parental loss antecedent to childhood diabetes mellitus. *Journal of the American Academy of Child Psychiatry* 19(4):678–89.

Lehrman, R. 1956. Reactions to untimely death. *Psychiatric Quarterly* 30:567–69.

Leopold, R. L., and Dillon, H. 1963. Psychoanatomy of a disaster: A long-term study of post-traumatic neurosis in survivors of a marine explosion. *American Journal of Psychiatry* 19:913–21.

Levinson, P. 1972. On sudden death. *Psychiatry* 35:160-73.

Lewis, C. S. 1961. *A Grief Observed.* London: Faber.

Lewis, E., and Page, A. 1978. Failure to mourn a stillbirth: An overlooked catastrophe. *British Journal of Medical Psychology* 51:237-41.

Lewis, R. A.; Freeman, P. J.; and Roberts, C. L. 1979. Fathers and the post-parental transition. *Family Co-ordinator* 28:514-20.

Lewis, R. A., and Roberts, C. L. 1979. Post-parental fathers in distress. *Psychiatric Opinion* [November/December], pp. 27-30.

Lewis, S. 1981. Some psychological consequences of bereavement by sudden infant death syndrome. *Health Visitor* 54:322-25.

Lidz, R. 1949. Emotional factors in hyperthyroidism. *Psychosomatic Medicine* 11:2-9.

Lifshitz, M. 1976. Long range effects of father's loss: The cognitive complexity of bereaved children and their school adjustment. *British Journal of Medical Psychology* 49:189-97.

Lifshitz, M.; Berman, D.; Galili, A.; and Gilad, D. 1977. Bereaved children: The effect of mother's perceptions and social system organization on their short-range adjustment. *Journal of the American Academy of Child Psychiatry* 16(2):272-84.

Lifton, R. J. 1967. *Death in life: Survivors of Hiroshima.* New York: Simon & Schuster.

———. 1975. On death and the continuity of life: A psychohistorical perspective. *Omega* 6:143-59.

Lifton, R. J., and Olson, E. 1976. The human meaning of total disaster: The Buffalo Creek experience. *Psychiatry* 39:1-18.

Limerick, L. 1976. Support and counselling needs of families following a cot death bereavement. *Proceedings of the Royal Society of Medicine* 69:839-41.

Lindemann, E. 1944. Symptomatology and management of acute grief. *American Journal of Psychiatry* 101:141-48.

Lipson, C. T. 1963. Denial and mourning. *International Journal of Psychoanalysis* 44:104-7.

Loewald, H. W. 1962. Internalization, separation, mourning and the superego. *Psychoanalytic Quarterly* 31:483-504.

———. (1973). On internalization. *International Journal of Psychoanalysis* 54:9-17.

Lopata, H. Z. 1971. Widows as a minority group. *Gerontologist* (supplement)11:67-77.

———. 1979. *Women as widows.* New York and North Holland: Elsevier.

Lowman, J. 1979. Grief intervention and sudden infant death syndrome. *American Journal of Community Psychology* 7(6):665-77.

Lynn, E. J., and Racy, J. 1969. The resolution of pathological grief after electroconvulsive therapy. *Journal of Nervous and Mental Disease* 148(2):165-69.

Lyons, H. A. 1971. Psychiatric sequelae of the Belfast riots. *British Journal of Psychiatry* 118:265-73.

———. (1972). Depressive illness in Belfast. *British Medical Journal* 1:342-44.

McCourt, W. F.; Barnett, R.; Bremner, J.; and Becker, A. 1976. We help each other: Primary prevention for the widowed. *American Journal of Psychiatry* 133:98-100.

McDermott, N., and Cobb, S. 1939. A psychiatric survey of 50 cases of bronchial asthma. *Psychosomatic Medicine* 1:201-4.

Maddison, D. C., and Raphael, B. 1972. Normal bereavement as an illness requiring care: Psychopharmacological approaches. *Journal of Thanatology* 2:785-93.

Maddison, D. C., and Raphael, B. 1972. The family of the dying patient. Pages 195-200 in *Psychosocial Aspects of Terminal Care*, ed. B. Schoenberg et al. New York: Columbia University Press.

Maddison, D. C., and Viola, A. 1968. The health of widows in the year following bereavement. *Journal of Psychosomatic Research* 12:297-306.

Maddison, D. C.; Viola, A.; and Walker, W. L. 1969. Further studies in conjugal bereavement. *Australian and New Zealand Journal of Psychiatry* 3:63-66.

Maddison, D. C., and Walker, W. L. 1967. Factors affecting the outcome of conjugal bereavement. *British Journal of Psychiatry* 113:1057-67.

Maguire, P. 1976. The psychological, social sequelae of mastectomy. In *Modern perspectives in the psychiatric aspects of surgery*, ed. J. G. Howells. New York: Brunner/Mazel.

Mahler, M.; Pirie, F.; and Bergman, A. 1975. *The psychological birth of the human infant.* London: Hutchison.

# References

Malinak, D.; Hoyt, M.; and Patterson, V. 1979. Reaction to the death of a parent in adult life. *American Journal of Psychiatry* 136:1152–56.

Mandell, F.; McAulty, E.; and Reece, R. 1980. Observations of paternal response to sudden unanticipated infant death. *Paediatrics* 65(2):221–25.

Mandell, F., and Wolte. L. 1975. Sudden infant death syndrome and subsequent pregnancy. *Paediatrics* 56:774–76.

Markusen, E., and Fulton, R. 1971. Childhood bereavement and behaviour disorders: A critical review. *Omega* 2:107–17.

Marris, P. 1958. *Widows and their families.* London: Routledge & Kegan Paul.

Marshall, V. 1975. Age and awareness of finitude in developmental gerontology. *Omega* 6(2):113–29.

Martin, H. L. 1970. Parents' and children's reactions to burns and scalds in children. *British Journal of Medical Psychology* 43:183–91.

Martin, H. L.; Lawries, J. H.; and Wilkinson, A. W. 1968. The family of the fatally burned child. *Lancet* 14 September, 1968, pp. 628–29.

Masterson, J. F. 1967. *The psychiatric dilemma of adolescence.* Boston: Little Brown.

Maurer, A. 1964. Adolescent attitudes towards death. *Journal of Genetic Psychology* 105:75–90.

———. 1966. Maturation of concepts of death. *British Journal of Medical Psychology* 39:35–41.

Mawson, D.; Marks, I. M.; Ramm, L.; and Stern, R. S. 1981. Guided mourning for morbid grief: A controlled study. *British Journal of Psychiatry* 138:185–93.

May, H. J., and Breme, F. J. 1982–83. SIDS family adjustment scale: A method of assessing family adjustment in sudden infant death syndrome. *Omega* 13(1):59–74.

Meares, R. A. 1981. On saying good-bye before death. *Journal of the American Medical Association* 246(11):1227–29.

Melges, F. T., and DeMaso, D. R. 1980. Grief-resolution therapy: Reliving, revising and revisiting. *American Journal of Psychotherapy* 34(1):51–61.

Milne, G. G. 1977a. Cyclone Tracy: I. Some consequences of evacuation for adult victims. *Australian Psychologist* 12:39–54.

———. 1977b. Cyclone Tracy: II. The effects on Darwin children. *Australian Psychologist* 12:55–62.

Montagu, A. 1976. The illusion of immortality and health. *Preventive Medicine* 5:496–507.

Montgomery, R. 1978. A study of stillbirth. Unpublished manuscript.

Morillo, E., and Gardner, L. I. 1980. Activation of latent Grave's disease in children. *Clinical Paediatrics* 19(3):160–63.

Moss, M. S., and Moss, S. Z. 1979. The image of the dead spouse in the remarriage of elderly widow(er)s. Paper read at the Thirty-second Annual Meeting of the Gerontological Society, November 1979, Washington, D.C.

Nagera, H. 1970. Children's reactions to the death of important objects. *Psychoanalytic Study of the Child* 25:360–400.

Nagy, M. 1948. The child's theories concerning death. *Journal of Genetic Psychology* 73:3–27.

Nelson, L. D., and Nelson, C. C. 1975. A factor analytic inquiry into the multidimensionality of death anxiety. *Omega* 6:171–78.

Newman, G., and Denman, S. B. 1971. Felony and paternal deprivation: A sociopsychiatric view. *International Journal of Social Psychiatry* 17(1):65–71.

Nixon, J., and Pearn, J. 1977. Emotional sequelae of parents and sibs following the drowning or near drowning of a child. *Australian & New Zealand Journal of Psychiatry* 11:265–68.

Noyes, R., and Kletti, R. 1977. Panoramic memory: A response to threat of death. *Omega* 8(3):181–95.

Nunn, K. 1982. Personal Communication.

O'Brien, D. 1979. Mental anguish as an occupational hazard. *Emergency* 1:61–64.

Offer, D. 1980. Normal adolescent development. In *Comprehensive textbook of psychiatry,* 3rd ed., ed. H. Kaplan, A. M. Freedman, and B. J. Sadoch, chap. 34.3, pp. 344–47. Baltimore: Williams & Wilkins.

Offer, D., and Offer, J. B. 1975. *From teenage to young manhood: A psychological study.* New York: Basic Books.

Oliver, R. 1977. The empty-nest syndrome as a focus for depression: A cognitive treatment model based on rational emotive therapy. *Psychotherapy, Theory, Research, and Practice* 14(1):87–94.

Orbach, I., and Glaubman, H. 1979. The concept of death and suicidal behavior in young children. *Journal of the American Academy of Child Psychiatry* 18(4):668–78.

Ostrov, E., and Offer, D. 1978. Loneliness and the adolescent. Pages 434–50 in *Developmental and Clinical Studies,* Vol. 6 of *Adolescent Psychiatry,* ed. S. C. Feinstein and P. L. Giovacchini. Chicago: University of Chicago Press.

Parker, G. 1977. Cyclone Tracy and Darwin evacuees: On the restoration of the species. *British Journal of Psychiatry* 130:548–55.

Parker, G.; Tupling, H.; and Brown, L. B. 1979. A parental bonding instrument. *British Journal of Medical Psychology* 52:1–10.

Parkes, C. M. 1964a. Recent bereavement as a cause of mental illness. *British Journal of Psychiatry* 110:198–204.

———. 1964b. The effects of bereavement on physical and mental health: A study of the medical records of widows. *British Medical Journal* 2:274–79.

———. 1965. Bereavement and mental illness. *British Journal of Medical Psychology* 38:1–26.

———. 1970. Seeking and finding a lost object: Evidence from recent studies of reaction to bereavement. *Social Science and Medicine* 4:187–201.

———. 1971. Psychosocial transitions: A field for study. *Social Science and Medicine* 5:101–15.

———. 1972a. The components of reaction to loss of a limb, spouse or home. *Journal of Psychosomatic Research* 16:343–49.

———. 1972b. *Bereavement: Studies of grief in adult life.* London: Tavistock.

———. 1975a. Psychosocial transitions: Comparison between reactions to loss of a limb and loss of a spouse. *British Journal of Psychiatry* 127:204–10.

———. 1975b. Determinants of outcome following bereavement. *Omega* 6(4):303–23.

———. 1979. Evaluation of a bereavement service. Pages 389–402 in *The Dying Human,* ed. A. DeVries and I. Carmi. Ramat Gan, Israel: Turtledove.

———. 1980. Bereavement counseling: Does it work? *British Medical Journal* 281:3–6.

Parkes, C. M.; Benjamin, B.; and Fitzgerald, R. G. 1969. Broken heart: A statistical study of increased mortality among widowers. *British Medical Journal* 1:740–43.

Parkes, C. M., and Brown, R. J. 1972. Health after bereavement. *Psychosomatic Medicine* 34(5):449–61.

Parsons, T. 1963. Death in American society: A brief working paper. *American Behavioral Scientist* 6:61–65.

Paul, N. L. 1967. Empathic excavation of buried grief. Roche Report. *Frontiers of Clinical Psychiatry* 4:1–2.

Paul, N. L., and Grosser, G. H. 1965. Operational mourning and its role in conjoint family therapy. *Community Mental Health Journal* 1:339–45.

Pearn, J., and Nixon, J. 1977a. Attempted drowning as a form of nonaccidental injury. *Australian Paediatric Journal* 13(2):110–13.

———. (1977b). Prevention of childhood drowning accidents. *Medical Journal of Australia* 1:616–18.

Pedder, J. R. 1982. Failure to Mourn and Melancholia. *British Journal of Psychiatry* 141:329–37.

Peppers, L. G., and Knapp, R. J. 1980. *Motherhood and mourning.* New York: Praeger.

Perman, J. 1979. The search for the mother: Narcissistic regression as a pathway of mourning in childhood. *Psychoanalytic Quarterly* 48:448–64.

Piaget, J. 1955. *The Child's Construction of Reality.* London: Routledge & Kegan Paul.

Pihlblad, C. T.; Adams, D. L.; and Rosencranz, H. A. 1972. Socioeconomic adjustment to widowhood. *Omega* 3(4):295–305.

Pincus, L. 1974. *Death in the family.* New York: Random House.

Polak, P. R.; Egan, D.; Lee, J. H.; Vandenbergh, R. J.; Williams, W. V. 1975. Prevention in mental health: A controlled study. *American Journal of Psychiatry* 132:146–49.

# References

Pollock, G. H. 1970. Anniversary reactions, trauma and mourning. *Psychoanalytic Quarterly*, 39:347–71.

———. 1971a. Temporal anniversary manifestations: Hour, day, holiday. *Psychoanalytic Quarterly* 40:435–46.

———. 1971b. On time, death, and immortality. *Psychoanalytic Quarterly* 40:435–46.

———. 1975. On mourning, immortality, and Utopia. *Journal of the American Psychoanalytic Association* 23:334–62.

Popovic, M., and Petrovic, D. 1964. After the earthquake. *Lancet* 28 November 1964, pp. 1169–71.

Portnoi, A. 1981. The natural history of retirement: Mainly good news. *Journal of the American Medical Association* 245:1752–54.

Powell, B. 1977. The empty-nest, employment, and psychiatric symptoms in college-educated women. *Psychology of Women Quarterly* 2(1):35–43.

Poznanski, E. O. 1972. The replacement child: An unresolved saga of parental grief. *Behavioral Pediatrics* 81:1190–93.

Purisman, R., and Maoz, B. 1977. Adjustment and bereavement: Some considerations. *British Journal of Medical Psychology* 50:1–9.

Quinn, M. A. 1980. Endocrine changes in the climacteric and post-menopausal years. In *The Biology of Aging in Man*, pp. 131–41. Report of a workshop on Biomedical Research into Aging, National Health and Medical Research Council, Canberra, Australia.

Rabkin, R., and Krell, L. 1979. The effects of sibling death on the surviving child: A family perspective. *Family Process* 18:471–77.

Ramsay, R., and Happee, J. A. 1977. The stress of bereavement. In *Stress and Anxiety*, ed. C. D. Speilberger and J. G. Sarason. London: Wiley.

———. 1979. Bereavement: A behavioral treatment of pathological grief. Unpublished manuscript.

Raphael, B. 1972a. Psychosocial aspects of induced abortion: Part 1. *Medical Journal of Australia* 2:35–40.

———. 1972b. The crisis of hysterectomy. *Australian & New Zealand Journal of Psychiatry* 6:106–15.

———. 1973. Bereavement: A paradigm for preventive medicine. *Sandoz Therapeutic Quarterly* 2:1–9.

———. 1974a. Parameters of health outcome following hysterectomy. *Bulletin of the Postgraduate Committee in Medicine, University of Sydney* 30:215–19.

———. 1974b. Bereavement and stress. *Bulletin of the Postgraduate Committee in Medicine, University of Sydney* 30:54–59.

———. 1975a. The management of pathological grief. *Australian & New Zealand Journal of Psychiatry* 9:173–80.

———. 1975b. Psychology and management of the menopause. *Bulletin of the Postgraduate Committee in Medicine, University of Sydney* 31:131–37.

———. 1975c. Crisis and loss counselling following a disaster. *Mental Health of Australia*, 1(4):118–22.

———. 1975d. Grief. *Modern Medicine of Australia* [1 September]: 55–57.

———. 1976a. Psychiatric aspects of hysterectomy. In *Modern Perspectives in Psychiatric Aspects of Surgery*, ed. J. G. Howells. New York: Brunner/Mazel.

———. 1976b. The management of bereavement. In *Handbook of Depression*, ed. G. Burrows. Amsterdam: ASP Biological Press.

———. 1976c. Care-eliciting behavior of bereaved children and their families. Paper presented at the Meeting of the Section of Child Psychiatry, Royal Australian and New Zealand College of Psychiatrists, Sydney, Australia.

———. 1977a. The Granville train disaster: Psychosocial needs and their management. *Medical Journal of Australia* 1:303–5.

———. 1977b. Preventive intervention with the recently bereaved. *Archives of General Psychiatry* 34:1450–54.

———. 1978a. Mourning and the prevention of melancholia. *British Journal of Medical Psychology* 51:303–10.

———. 1978b. The mind of the adolescent girl. In *Obstetrics, gynaecology and psychiatry*, ed. G. D. Burrows and L. Dennerstein. Proceedings of the 6th Annual Conference of the

Australian Society for Psychosomatic Obstetrics and Gynaecology. Melbourne: York Press.

———. 1979a. Preventive psychiatry of natural hazard. In *Natural Hazards in Australia,* ed. J. Heathcote.

———. 1979/80. A primary prevention action programme: Psychiatric involvement following a major rail disaster. *Omega* 10(3):211–25.

———. 1980a. A psychiatric model of bereavement counseling. In *Bereavement Counseling: A Multidisciplinary Handbook,* ed. Mark B. Schoenberg. Westport, Connecticut: Greenwood Press.

———. 1980b. Primary prevention: fact or fiction. *Australian and New Zealand Journal of Psychiatry* 14:163–74.

———. 1981. Personal disaster. *Australian and New Zealand Journal of Psychiatry* 15:183–98.

———. 1982. The young child and the death of a parent. In *The Place of Attachment in Human Behavior,* ed. C. M. Parkes and Joan Stevenson-Hinde. New York: Basic Books.

Raphael, B., and Cubis, J. 1982. An investigation of adolescent psychosocial morbidity in girls. Grant Application, New South Wales Institute of Psychiatry, Sydney, Australia.

Raphael, B.; Field, J.; and Kvelde, H. 1980. Childhood Bereavement: A prospective study as a possible prelude to future preventive intervention. In *Preventive Psychiatry in an Age of Transition,* ed. E. J. Anthony and C. Chiland. Yearbook of the International Association for Child and Adolescent Psychiatry and Allied Professions, vol. 6. New York: Wiley.

Raphael, B., and Maddison, D. C. 1976. The care of bereaved adults. In *Modern Trends in Psychosomatic Medicine,* ed. O. W. Hill. London: Butterworth.

Raphael, B., and Maddison, D. C. 1981. Attitudes to dying. In *Gynaecological Oncology,* ed. M. Coopleson, pp. 1055–59. Edinburgh: Churchill Livingston.

Raphael, B.; Singh, B. S.; and Adler, R. G. 1980. Childhood loss and depression. Paper presented at the Meeting of the Section of Child Psychiatry, Royal Australian and New Zealand College of Psychiatrists, April 1980, Sydney, Australia.

Raphael, B.; Singh, B.; and Bradbury, L. 1980. Disaster: The helper's perspective. *Medical Journal of Australia* 2:445–47.

Rees, W. D., and Lutkins, S. G. 1967. Mortality of bereavement. *British Medical Journal* 1:13–16.

Reid, J. 1979. A time to live, a time to grieve: Patterns and processes of mourning among the Yolngu of Australia. *Cultural Medical Psychiatry* 3(4):319–46.

Rennie, D. 1970. After the earthquake. *Lancet* 3: 604–707.

Richards, J. G., and McCallum, J. 1979. Bereavement in the elderly. *New Zealand Medical Journal* 89:201–4.

Richmond, J. B., and Waisman, H. A. 1955. Psychologic aspects of management of children with malignant disease. *American Journal of the Diseases of Children* 89:42–47.

Rickarby, G. A. 1976. The wider uses of conjoint psychotherapy. *British Journal of Medical Psychology* 49:183–87.

Rickarby, G. A.; Single, T.; and Raphael, B. 1982. The development of rebonding therapy. Unpublished manuscript.

———. 1977. Four cases of mania associated with bereavement. *Journal of Nervous and Mental Disease* 165:255–61.

Roberts, C. L., and Lewis, R. H. 1981. The empty-nest syndrome. In *Modern perspectives in the psychiatric aspects of middle age,* ed. J. G. Howells. New York: Brunner/Mazel.

Robertson, J. 1952. *A Two-Year-Old Goes to Hospital* (film). London: Tavistock Child Development Research Unit.

Robertson, J., and Robertson, J. 1971. Young children in brief separation: A fresh look. *Psychoanalytic Study of the Child* 8:288–309.

Rochlin, G. 1967. How younger children view death and themselves. In *Explaining death to children,* ed. E. A. Grollman. Boston: Beacon Press.

Rogers, J. G., and Danks, D. M. 1981. Editorial: Is death the end? *Medical Journal of Australia* 1:272–73.

Rosenblatt, P. C.; Jackson, D. A.; and Walsh, R. P. 1972. Coping with anger and aggression in mourning. *Omega* 3(4):271–83.

# References

Rosenblatt, P. C.; Walsh, R. P.; and Jackson, D. A. 1976. *Grief and Mourning in Cross-Cultural Perspective.* New Haven: HRAF Press.

Rutter, M. 1966 Bereaved children. In *Children of Sick Parents,* pp. 66–75. Maudsley Monographs, vol. 16. London: Oxford University Press.

———. 1979. *Changing Youth in a Changing World.* London: Nuffield Publications.

———. 1981. *Maternal Deprivation Reassessed,* 2nd ed. Sydney, Australia: Penguin.

Rynearson, E. K. 1982. Relinquishment and its maternal complications: A preliminary study. *American Journal of Psychiatry* 139(3):338–40.

Ryser, C., and Sheldon, A. 1969. Retirement and health. *Journal of the American Geriatric Society* 17:180–90.

Sadock, B. J.; Kaplan, H. I.; Freedman, A. M. 1976. Frigidity, dyspareunia, and vaginismus. In *The Sexual Experience,* ed. J. Marmor. Baltimore: Williams & Wilkins.

Sanders, C. M. 1979–80. A comparison of adult bereavement in the death of a spouse, child and parent. *Omega* 10(4):303–21.

Sandler, I. 1980. Social support resources, stress and maladjustment for poor children. *American Journal of Community Psychology* 8(1):41–52.

Sarnoff, C. A. 1980. Normal and pathological development during the latency age period. In *Child Development in Normality and Psychopathology,* ed. J. R. Bemporad. New York: Brunner/Mazel.

Sarwer-Foner, G. J. 1972. Denial of death and the unconscious longing for indestructibility and immortality in the terminal phase of adolescence. *Canadian Psychiatric Association Journal* 17:51–57.

Schafer, R. 1976. Fascination with death as a function of need for novel stimulation. *Omega* 7(1):45–50.

Schlesinger, B. 1971. The widow and widower and remarriage: Selected findings. *Omega* (2):10–18.

Schmale, A. H. 1958. Relationship of separation to depression and disease. *Psychosomatic Medicine* 20:259–77.

Schmale, A. H., and Iker, H. 1971. Hopelessness as a predictor of cervical carcinoma. *Social Science and Medicine* 5:95–100.

Schneiderman, E. S. 1971. On the deromanticization of death. *American Journal of Psychotherapy* 25(1):4–7.

Schoenberg, B. M. 1980. *Bereavement counseling: A multidisciplinary handbook.* Westport, Conn.: Greenwood Press.

Schoenberg, B. M., and Carr, A. 1970. Loss of external organs: Limb amputation, mastectomy and disfiguration. In *Loss and Grief: Psychological Management in Medical Practice.* New York: Columbia University Press.

Schulterbrandt, J. G., and Raskin, A. 1977. *Depression in Childhood: Diagnosis, Treatment, and Conceptual Models.* New York: Raven Press.

Segal, M. M. 1963. Impulsive sexuality: Some clinical and theoretical observations. *International Journal of Psychoanalysis* 44(4):407–18.

Seligman, R.; Gleser, G.; Rank, J.; and Harris, L. 1974. The effects of earlier parental loss in adolescence. *Archives of General Psychiatry* 31:475–79.

Sharp, V. 1980. Adolescence. In *Child Development in Normality and Pathology,* ed. Jules R. Bemporad, New York: Brunner/Mazel.

Shepherd, D. M., and Barraclough, B. M. 1976. The aftermath of parental suicide for children. *British Journal of Psychiatry* 129:267–76.

Sherizen, S., and Paul, L. 1977. Dying in a hospital intensive care unit: The social significance for the family of the patient. *Omega* 8(1):29–40.

Sholnick, V. 1979. The addictions as pathological mourning: An attempt at restitution of early losses. *American Journal of Psychiatry* 33(2):281–90.

Shoor, M., and Speed, M. 1976. Death, delinquency and the mourning process. In *Death and Identity,* revised ed., ed. R. Fulton. Bowie, Md: Charles Press.

Shukla, G. D.; Sahu, S. C.; Tripathi, R. P.; and Gupta, D. K. 1982. A psychiatric study of amputees. *British Journal of Psychiatry* 33(2):281–90.

Shulman, K. 1978. Suicide and parasuicide in old age: A review. *Age and Aging* 7:201–209.

Siggins, L. D. 1966. Mourning: A critical survey of the literature. *International Journal of Psychoanalysis* 52:259–66.

Silverman, P. R. 1967. Services to the widowed: First steps in a program of preventive intervention. *Community Mental Health Journal* 3(1):36–44.

———. 1969. The widow-to-widow program: An experiment in preventive intervention. *Mental Hygiene* 53(3):333–37.

———. 1971. Factors involved in accepting an offer of help. *Archives of the Foundation of Thanatology* 3:161–71.

———. 1972. Widowhood and preventive intervention. *Family Co-ordinator* 21:95–102.

Silverman, S. M., and Silverman, P. R. 1979. Parent-child communication in widowed families. *American Journal of Psychotherapy* 33(3):428–41.

Simon, N. M.; Rothman, D.; and Goff, J. T. 1969. Psychological factors related to spontaneous and therapeutic abortion. *American Journal of Obstetrics and Gynecology,* 104:799–806.

Singh, B. S. 1982. Work and well-being. Paper presented at the Annual Royal Australian and New Zealand College of Psychiatry Section: Social and Cultural Meeting, Salamander Bay, New South Wales, Australia, 1–4 April 1982.

Singh, B. S., and Raphael, B, 1981. Post-disaster morbidity of the bereaved. *Journal of Nervous and Mental Disease* 169(4):208–12.

Singh, B. S.; Raphael, B.: and Bradbury, L. In press. Who helps the helpers? *Omega*

Smith, Carole, R. 1976. Bereavement: The contribution of phenomenological and existential analysis to a greater understanding of the problem. *British Journal of Social Work* 5:75–92.

Smith, J. H. 1971. Identificatory styles in depression and grief. *International Journal of Psychoanalysis* 52(3):259–66.

Snowdon, J.; Solomons, R.; and Druce, H. 1978. Feigned bereavement: Twelve cases. *British Journal of Psychiatry* 133:15–19.

Solnit, A. J., and Stark, M. H. 1961. Mourning and the birth of a defective child. *The Psychoanalytic Study of the Child* 16:523–37.

Spence, D. L., and Lonner, T. D. 1971. The empty nest: A transition within motherhood. *Family Co-ordinator* 20(4):369–75.

Stamm, J., and Drapkin, A. 1966. The successful treatment of a severe case of bronchial asthma: A manifestation of an abnormal mourning reaction and traumatic neurosis. *Journal of Nervous and Mental Disease* 142(2):180–89.

Steele, R. L. 1977. Dying, death and bereavement among the Maya Indians of Mesoamerica. *American Psychologist* 32(12):1060–68.

Stein, M. M. 1967. Fear of death and trauma. *Progress in Neurology and Psychiatry* 22:457–63.

Stein, S. P., and Charles, E. S. 1978. Emotional factors in juvenile diabetes mellitus. *American Journal of Psychiatry* 128:700–704.

Stein, Z., and Susser, M. 1969. Widowhood and mental illness. *British Journal of Social and Preventive Medicine* 23:106–10.

Stern, D. 1977. *The First Relationship: Infant and Mother*. London: Fontana/Open Books.

Stierlin, H. 1973. The adolescent as a delegate of his parents. *Australian & New Zealand Journal of Psychiatry* 7:349–56.

Stone, M. H. 1981. Depression in borderline adolescents. *American Journal of Psychotherapy* 35(3):383–99.

Storolow, R. D. 1973. A note on death anxiety as a developmental achievement. *American Journal of Psychoanalysis* 34:351–53.

Stretton, A. 1976. *The furious days*. Sydney: William Collins.

Sugar, M. 1968. Normal adolescent mourning. *American Journal of Psychotherapy* 22:258–269.

Sunder Das, S. 1971. Grief and the imminent threat of non-being. *British Journal of Psychiatry* 118:545–68.

Taylor, A. J. W., and Frazer, A. G. 1980. Interim report of the stress effects on the recovery teams after the Mt. Erebus disaster, November 1979. *Medical Journal of New Zealand* 91:311–12.

# References

Taylor, P., and Gideon, M.D. 1980. Crisis counselling following the death of a baby. *Journal of Reproductive Medicine* 24(5):201–11.

Templer, D. J. 1970. The construction and validation of a death anxiety scale. *Journal of General Psychology* 82:165–77.

Tennant, C.; Bebbington, P.; and Hurry, J. 1980. Parental death in childhood and risk of adult depressive disorders: A review. *Psychological Medicine* 10:289–99.

Terr, L. C. 1981. Psychic trauma in children: Observations following the Chowchilla school-bus kidnapping. *American Journal of Psychiatry* 138:14–19.

Thauberger, P. C.; Thauberger, E. M.; and Cleland, J. F. 1976. Avoidance of the ontological confrontation of death and physiological measures in a field setting simulating a death atmosphere. *Social Science and Medicine* 10:527–33.

Thompson, W., and Strieb, G. S. 1958. Situational determinants: Health and economic deprivation in retirement. *Journal of Social Issues* 14:18–34.

Tichener, J. L., and Kapp, F. 1976. Disaster at Buffalo Creek: Family and character change. *American Journal of Psychiatry* 133:295–99.

Tichener, J. L., and Lindy, J. D. 1978. Affect, defense and insight: Psychoanalytic observations of bereaved families and clinicians at a major disaster. Mimeographed. Cincinnati, Ohio.

Tobin, D., and Treloar, D. 1979a. A study of high school students' experience of death. Mimeographed. Melbourne, Australia.

———. 1979b. A survey of responses to death in Victorian high school students. Mimeographed. Melbourne, Australia.

Tooley, K. 1975. The choice of a surviving sibling as the "scapegoat" in some cases of maternal bereavement: A case report. *Journal of Child Psychology and Psychiatry* 16:331–39.

Turco, R. 1981. The treatment of unresolved grief following loss of an infant. *American Journal of Obstetrics and Gynecology* 141:503–507.

Turnbull, H. 1980. The concept of death in bereaved and non-bereaved latent and adolescent children, related to attribution and school performance. Master's thesis, University of Newcastle, NSW, Australia.

Tyhurst, J. S.; Salk, L.; and Kennedy, M. 1957. Mortality, morbidity and retirement. *American Journal of Public Health* 47:1434–44.

Uddenberg, N.; Englesson, J.; and Nettelbladt, P. 1979. Experience of father and later relation to men: A systematic study of women's relations to their father, their partner and their son. *Acta Psychiatrica Scandinavica* 59:87–96.

Vachon, M.; Lyall, W.; Rogers, J.; Freedman-Letofsky, K.; and Freeman, S. 1980. A controlled study of self-help intervention for widows. *American Journal of Psychiatry* 137:1380–84.

Vachon, M.; Sheldon, A. R.; Lance, W. J.; Lyall, W. A.; Rogers, J.; and Freeman, S. 1982. Correlates of enduring distress patterns following bereavement: social network, life situation, and personality. *Psychological Medicine* 12:783–88.

Van Eerdewegh, M. M.; Bieri, M. D.; Parilla, R. H.; and Clayton, P. J. 1982. The bereaved child. *British Journal of Psychiatry* 140:23–29.

Videka-Sherman, L. 1982. Coping with the death of a child: A study over time. *American Journal of Orthopsychiatry* 52(4):699–703.

Volkan, V. 1970. Typical findings in pathological grief. *Psychiatric Quarterly* 44:231–50.

———. 1971. A study of patients "re-grief work." *Psychiatric Quarterly* 45:225–73.

———. 1972. The linking objects of pathological mourners. *Archives of General Psychiatry* 27:215–21.

Volkan, V., and Showalter, C. R. 1968. Known object loss, disturbance in reality testing, a "re-grief" work as a method of brief psychotherapy. *Psychiatric Quarterly* 42:358–74.

Vollman, R. R.; Ganzert, A.; Richer, L.; and Williams, W. V. 1971. The reactions of family systems to sudden and unexpected death. *Omega* 2:101–6.

Wahl, C. W. 1976. The differential diagnosis of normal and neurotic grief following bereavement. *Psychosomatics* 11:104–6.

Wainwright, A. L. 1980. Children's perception of and affective responses to death. Master's thesis, School of Education, University of New South Wales, Australia.

Walker, K. N.; McBride, A.; and Vachon, M. L. 1977. Social support networks and the crisis of bereavement. *Social Science and Medicine* 11:35–41.

Wallerstein, J. L., and Kelly, J. 1974. The effects of parental divorce: the adolescent experience. In *The child in his family*, ed. J. Anthony and C. Koupernik, New York: Wiley.

———. 1980. *Surviving the breakup*. New York: Basic Books.

Walrond-Skinner, S. 1977. *Family therapy*. London: Routledge & Kegan Paul.

Warr, P. 1982. Editorial: Psychological aspects of employment and unemployment. *Psychological Medicine* 12:7–11.

Warren, W. G., and Chopra, P. N. 1979. An Australian survey of attitudes to death. *Australian Journal of Social Issues* 14:140–52.

Wasylenki, D., and McBride, A. 1981. Retirement. In *Modern perspectives in the psychiatry of middle age*. ed. John G. Howells. New York: Brunner/Mazel.

Watson, E. 1981. An epidemiological and sociological study of unexpected death in infancy in nine areas of South England. *Medicine, Science and Law* 21(2):99–104.

Watt, N. F., and Nicholi, A. 1979. Early death of a parent as an etiological factor in schizophrenia. *American Journal of Orthopsychiatry* 49(3):465–73.

Weiner, A.; Gerber, I.; Battin, D.; and Arking, A. 1975. The process of phenomenology of bereavement. In *Bereavement: Its psychosocial aspects*, ed. B. Schoenberg, I. Gerber, A. Weiner, A. H. Kutscher, D. Peretz., and A. C. Carr. New York: Columbia University Press.

Weiss, R. S., ed., 1974a. *Loneliness: The experience of emotional and social isolation*. Cambridge: M.I.T. Press.

———. 1974b. "The provisions of social relationships." In *Doing Unto Others*. Englewood Cliffs, N.J.: Prentice-Hall.

Werner, A., and Jones, M. 1979. Parent loss in college students. *Journal of the American College Health Association* 27:253–56.

Western, J. S., and Doube, L. 1979. Stress and Cyclone Tracy. In *Natural hazards management in North Australia*, ed. Pickup, G. Canberra: Australian National University.

Wetmore, R. 1963. The role of grief in psychoanalysis. *International Journal of Psychoanalysis* 44:97–103.

Whitis, P. R. 1968. The legacy of a child's suicide. *Family Process* 7(2):159–68.

Williams, R. M., and Parkes, C. M. 1975. Psychosocial effects of disaster: Birth rate in Aberfan. *British Medical Journal* 2:303–304.

Williams, W. V., and Polak, P. R. 1979. Follow-up research in primary prevention: A model of adjustment in acute grief. *Journal of Clinical Psychology* 35(1):35–45.

Winnicott, D. W. 1949. Mind and its relation to the psychesoma. In *Through Paediatrics to Psychoanalysis*. London: Hogarth Press (1977).

Wolfenstein, M. 1966. How is mourning possible? *Psychoanalytic Study of the Child* 21:93–123.

Wolff, J. R.; Nielson, P. E.; and Schiller, P. 1970. The emotional reaction to a stillbirth. *American Journal of Obstetrics and Gynecology* 108:73–76.

Woodfield, R. L., and Viney, L. L. In Press. Bereavement: A personal construct approach. *Omega*.

Wretmark, G. 1959. A study in grief reactions. *Acta Psychiatrica Scandinavica* 136 (supplement):292–99.

Yamamoto, J.; Okonogi, K.; Jurasaki, T.; and Yoshimura, S. 1969. Mourning in Japan. *American Journal of Psychiatry* 125:1660–65.

# Name Index

Ablon, J., 56, 203
Abraham, K., 67
Abrahams, M. J., 331
Adam, K. S., 133, 134, 136
Adams, D. L., 314
Adler, R. G., 130–131
Alderstein, A. M., 147
Aldrich, E. K., 26, 51, 317
Alexander, J. E., 147
Alexy, W. D., 388
Altschul, S., 385
Anthony, S., 85
Aries, P., 19
Arthur, B., 124, 127, 129
Averill, J., 72

Bahr, H. M., 199
Bak, R. C., 44
Baker, H. W. G., 287
Barglow, P., 290
Barraclough, B. M., 120
Barrett, C. J., 397
Barry, M. J., 386
Bartrop, R. W., 61, 71, 212, 213, 384
Batson, J. W., 129
Baum, J., 129
Bebbington, P., 133
Bedell, J., 128, 129, 223
Bendiksen, R., 132
Benjamin, B., 62, 212, 314
Bennet, G., 331
Bergman, A., 75
Bernstein, S. M., 166
Binger, C. M., 129
Birtchnell, J., 62, 124, 125, 133, 134, 136, 310
Black, D., 129, 390, 395, 399
Blos, P., 169
Bluglass, K., 255, 257, 261, 263, 264

Boman, B., 72, 214, 346, 384
Bornstein, P. E., 134, 216
Bostack, F. T., 335
Bowie, W., 248
Bowlby, J., 6, 33, 41, 42, 59, 60, 64, 65, 67, 68, 69, 75, 77, 83, 86, 89, 94, 102, 103, 121, 125, 126, 134, 135, 136, 145, 150, 182, 202, 206
Bozeman, M., 271, 274
Bradbury, L., 337, 339
Breme, F. J., 255, 257, 263, 264
Breslin, M., 213
Brody, E. M., 307, 318
Brown, C., 254
Brown, G., 97, 132, 134, 136, 199, 226
Brown, R. J., 72, 213, 216
Brown, S., 8
Butler, R., 318
Byrne, D. G., 6, 196, 224

Cain, A. C., 30, 93, 120, 121, 124, 129, 277
Cain, B. S., 262, 277
Calvert, P., 211
Caplan, G., 70, 134, 194, 368
Caplan, M. G., 130
Carlton, I. G., 335
Caroff, P., 391
Carr, A., 292
Charles, E. S., 128
Chodoff, P., 273, 348
Chopra, P. N., 21
Church, J. S., 333
Clayton, P. J., 71, 134, 211, 213, 214, 216, 217, 223, 314

Cleland, J. F., 21
Cleveland, W. P., 312
Clyman, R., 249, 250
Cobb, S., 213, 334
Coddington, R. D., 168
Corney, R. J., 237
Cornwell, J., 257, 259, 260, 261, 262, 263–64
Cottington, E. M., 212
Cramond, 395
Crisp, A. H., 213, 216
Cubis, J., 143
Cumming, E., 307
Cunningham-Dax, E., 211
Curlee, J., 308

Darwin, C., 72–73, 353
Davidson, A. D., 336
Davis, H. K., 385
Defrain, J. D., 261
DeMaso, D. R., 375, 388
Denman, S. B., 124–25
Dennehy, C., 132
Deutsch, H., 59, 94, 143, 146, 205, 237, 290
Dicks, H. V., 5, 10–11, 179
Dillon, H., 335
Dobrof, R., 391
Doube, L., 330–31
Douglas, J. W., 125
Douglas, V. I., 130
Drapkin, A., 384
Druce, H., 72
Duncan-Jones, P., 6, 196, 224

Eliot, T. D., 56
Elizure, E., 130
Emde, R. N., 254

423

Engel, G., 227
Engel, G. L., 17, 71, 76, 212
Englesson, J., 8
Epps, L. S., 331
Erickson, M. E., 93, 113, 129
Erikson, E. H., 83, 141, 179, 318, 319
Erikson, K., 333
Ernst, L., 261

Fast, I., 93, 113, 120, 121, 124, 129
Felner, R. D., 129
Fenichel, O., 67
Field, J., 89, 99, 127, 136, 137, 391
Fisher, S., 26
Fitzgerald, R. G., 62, 212, 314
Fleming, J., 385
France, R. D., 384
Frankel, S., 225
Franklin, R. W., 385
Fraser, M., 345
Frazer, A. G., 336, 337
Freedman, A. M., 287
Freeman, P. J., 308
Freud, A., 141
Freud, S., 20, 33, 44, 45, 59, 64, 66, 187, 217, 222, 373
Freundt, L., 237
Fried, M., 305
Friedman, J. H., 218
Friedman, S. B., 71, 273, 348
Fulton, R., 50, 53, 63, 132, 223
Furman, E., 81, 85, 89, 93, 94, 103, 120, 137, 257, 391
Furman, R. A., 100, 136

Gapes, C., 150–51, 154, 162
Gardener, L. I., 129
Gardner, R. A., 123, 124, 125
Gauthier, Y., 70, 375, 387
George, L. K., 287
Gerber, I., 374
Giantureo, D. T., 312
Gideon, M. D., 251
Gilson, G., 257, 399
Glaubman, H., 121
Gleser, G. C., 333
Glick, I. O., 199, 201
Gorer, G., 20

Gorlitz, P., 290
Gottesman, D. J., 50, 53, 63, 223
Granville–Grossman, K. L., 132
Graves, J. S., 173
Grayson, J., 284
Green, B. L., 333
Greenberg, N. H., 168
Greenblatt, M., 212
Grosser, G. H., 55, 390
Gutmann, D., 290
Gyulay, J., 224

Hagglund, J. B., 52
Halikas, J. A., 71, 211, 213, 214, 216, 217, 314
Halpern, W., 262
Hamburg, D., 71, 273, 348
Hamilton, J. W., 302
Happee, J. A., 375, 386, 387
Harlow, H. F., 130
Harrari, E., 225
Harris, S., 227
Harvey, B., 276
Harvey, C. D., 199
Helmrath, T. A., 249, 250
Henderson, A. S., 162
Henderson, S., 6, 72, 196, 224, 335, 354
Hendrick, C., 8
Henry, W. E., 307
Herioch, M. J., 129
Hilgard, J. R., 114, 132, 134
Hinde, R. A., 4–5, 8, 11–12, 14–15
Hocking, F., 346
Hodgkinson, P. E., 375
Hofer, M., 61
Holinger, D. C., 181
Holland, J., 227
Holmes, J., 227
Hooper, D., 180
Hope, D., 315
Horowitz, M. J., 28, 41, 70, 222, 247, 309
Horton, F. T., 237
Hoyt, M., 310
Hudson, B., 287
Hurry, J., 133

Iker, H., 131
Inhelder, B., 140
Ironside, W., 349
Izen, J. E., 213

Jackson, D. A., 43, 64, 65
Jacobs, S., 62, 212
Jacobsen, G., 134
Jacques, E., 283
Jamison, K. R., 292, 294
Jennings, L. E., 384
Johnson, P., 104
Jones, M., 151
Jung, C. G., 20

Kaffman, M., 130
Kaplan, H. I., 287
Kapp, F., 333
Kellehear, A., 22
Kellner, K. R., 242
Kelly, G. A., 69
Kelly, J., 123, 125, 175, 228
Kemme, M., 124, 127, 129
Kennard, J., 133, 134
Kennedy, M., 306
Kennell, J. H., 249, 250
Kerner, J., 276
Kinston, W., 320, 331
Kirkley–Best, E., 242
Kitson, G., 228
Klaus, M. K., 249, 250
Klein, M., 64, 67–68
Klerman, G. L., 213
Kletti, R., 350
Kliman, G., 94, 137, 395
Klingfield, B., 66
Knapp, R. J., 244, 248, 249, 251, 266
Kreitman, N., 5
Krell, L., 113
Krupp, G. R., 66, 67, 215
Kubler–Ross, E., 26, 27, 50, 51, 52, 317, 395, 398
Kvelde, H., 89, 127, 136, 137, 391

LaGrand, L. E., 154, 175
Lakin, M., 168
Langer, T. S., 131
Larson, R., 296
Lawries, J. H., 268, 276
Leaverton, D. R., 128
Lehrman, R., 31, 223
Leopold, R. L., 335
Levinson, P., 223
Lewis, E., 247
Lewis, R. A., 308

# Name Index

Lewis, S., 257
Lewiston, N., 276
Lidz, R., 213
Lifshitz, M., 125, 137
Lifton, R. J., 22, 347, 348
Limerick, L., 264
Lindemann, E., 33, 59, 64, 152, 212, 334, 375
Lindy, J. S., 334, 348
Loesch, J. C., 168
Loewald, H. W., 67
Lonner, T. D., 308
Lopata, H. Z., 199, 202, 315
Lowman, J., 259, 260, 262, 263, 264, 399
Lutkin, S. G., 223
Lynn, E. J., 218, 385
Lyons, H. A., 344

McAulty, E., 257, 260, 263
McBride, A., 195, 306, 308
McCallum, J., 314
McCourt, W. F., 397
McDermott, N., 213
Maddison, D. C., 26, 48, 52, 70–71, 72, 128, 189, 196, 199, 200, 210, 212, 213, 214, 216, 217, 221, 222, 224, 359, 368, 372, 384
Maguire, P., 292, 294
Mahler, M., 75
Malinak, D., 310
Mandell, F., 257, 260, 263
Maoz, B., 280
Markuson, E., 132
Marris, P., 211
Marshall, V., 317
Marshall, W. L., 70, 375, 387
Martin, H. L., 268, 276
Masterson, J. F., 141
Maurer, A., 85, 147
Maurice, W. L., 71, 211, 213, 214, 216, 217, 314
Mawson, D., 375, 387
May, H. J., 255, 257, 263, 264
Meares, R. A., 27, 52
Melges, F. T., 375, 388
Michael, S. E., 131
Milne, G. G., 330
Montagu, A., 22
Montgomery, R., 243–44
Morillo, E., 129
Moss, M. S., 198, 313, 315
Moss, S. Z., 198, 313, 315

Nagera, H., 94, 100, 136
Nagy, M., 85
Nelson, C. C., 21
Nelson, C. D., 21
Nettelbladt, P., 8
Newman, G., 124–25
Newman, M. F., 134
Nicholi, A., 132
Nielson, P. E., 247
Nixon, J., 268, 277
Northeast, J., 211
Noyes, R., 350
Nunn, K., 390
Nurcomb, B., 257, 259, 260, 261

O'Brien, D., 336
Offer, D., 140, 141, 142, 143
Offer, J. B., 141, 142, 143
Ohrbach, C. E., 271, 274
Oliver, R., 309
Orbach, I., 121
Ostfeld, A., 62, 212
Ostrov, E., 142

Page, A., 247
Parker, G., 16, 330
Parkes, C. M., 31, 33, 41, 42, 56, 59, 62, 69, 71, 72, 128, 199, 201, 211, 212, 213, 214, 216, 221, 222, 223, 224, 285, 290, 291, 314, 334, 374, 397, 399, 400
Parson, T., 20
Pasnau, R. O., 292, 294
Patterson, V., 310
Paul, L., 29
Paul, N. L., 55, 390
Pearn, J., 268, 277
Pedder, J. R., 47, 63
Peppers, L. G., 244, 248, 249, 257, 266
Perkins, M., 72, 214, 384
Perman, J., 104
Petrovic, D., 321
Piaget, J., 75, 83, 140
Pihlblad, C. T., 314
Pincus, L., 56
Pirie, F., 75
Polak, P. R., 373, 390
Pollock, G. H., 22, 134, 190
Popovic, M., 331
Portnoi, A., 305
Powell, B., 309
Poznanski, E. O., 262

Priest, R. G., 213, 216
Purisman, R., 280
Pye, C., 375, 387

Quinn, M. A., 287

Rabkin, R., 113
Racy, J., 218, 385
Ramsay, R., 375, 386, 387
Raphael, B., 14, 26, 31, 45, 52, 60, 64, 71, 72, 88, 90, 127, 128, 130–31, 136, 137, 143, 188, 196, 205, 208, 214, 217, 218, 221, 222, 223, 224, 226, 231, 238, 247, 279, 289, 292, 294, 320, 337, 339, 343, 349, 368, 372, 373, 374, 375, 384, 391, 399, 401, 405
Raskin, A., 131
Reece, R., 257, 260, 263
Rees, W. D., 223
Reid, J., 39, 64–65, 400
Rennie, D., 331
Richards, J. G., 314
Richmond, J. B., 52
Rickarby, G. A., 61, 134, 208, 218, 247, 277
Roberts, C. L., 308
Robertson, J., 79
Rochlin, G., 85
Rosenblatt, P. C., 43, 64, 65, 104
Rosencranz, H. A., 314
Rosser, R., 320, 331
Rutter, M., 129, 130, 135, 137, 141–42, 143, 150, 161, 173
Ryder, R., 134
Rynearson, E. K., 253
Ryser, C., 306

Sadock, B. J., 287
Salk, L., 306
Sanders, C. M., 282
Sandler, I., 137
Sarnoff, C. A., 98, 106
Sarwer–Foner, G. J., 147
Schiller, P., 247
Schlesinger, B., 200
Schmale, A. H., 131, 212
Schneiderman, E. S., 20, 390

425

Schoenberg, B. M., 292, 388–89
Schulterbrandt, J. G., 131
Segal, M. M., 202, 214
Seligman, R., 131, 169
Sharp, V., 142, 143, 144
Sheldon, A., 306
Sheperd, D. M., 120
Sherizen, S., 29
Sholnick, V., 131–32
Shoor, M., 173
Showalter, C. R., 375, 385
Shukla, G. D., 291
Shulman, K., 314
Siggins, L. D., 67
Silverman, P. R., 87, 137, 396, 397, 399
Silverman, S. M., 87, 137
Simon, N. M., 237
Singh, B. S., 64, 130–31, 205, 223, 226, 298, 337, 339, 343, 373, 401
Single, T., 247
Slyter, H., 249, 250
Smith, C., 70
Smith, D., 225
Smith, J. H., 67
Snowdon, J., 72
Solnit, A. J., 254
Solomons, R., 72
Speed, M., 173
Spence, D. L., 308
Spitz, R., 130
Stamm, J., 384
Stark,. M. H., 254
Steele, R. L., 65
Stein, S. P., 128
Stein, Z., 213
Steinitz, E. M., 249, 250
Stern, D., 15
Stevens, L., 257, 259, 260, 261
Stierlin, H., 142
Stone, M. H., 173
Storolow, R. D., 20–21
Streib, G. S., 306

Streimer, J., 72, 214, 384
Stretton, A., 328, 330
Sugar, M., 141
Sunder Das, S., 70
Susser, M., 213
Sutherland, A. M., 271, 274

Taylor, A. J. W., 336, 337
Taylor, P., 251
Templer, D. J., 21
Tennant, C., 133
Terr, L. C., 81, 345
Thauberger, E. M., 21
Thauberger, P. C., 21
Thompson, W., 306
Tichener, J. L., 333, 334, 348
Tobin, D., 145, 148, 153, 176
Tooley, K., 277
Treloar, D., 145, 148, 153, 176
Turnbull, H., 107, 147–48
Tyhurst, J. S., 306

Uddenberg, N., 8
Urbanowitz, M., 395, 399

Vachon, M., 195, 196, 224, 374, 397, 399
Van Eerdewegh, M. M., 88, 105, 127, 128, 129, 130, 161, 173
Videka–Sherman, L., 397
Viney, L. L., 42, 69
Viola, A., 128, 195, 210, 211, 212, 213, 214, 216, 224
Volkan, V., 46, 194, 221, 223, 375, 385
Vollman, R. R., 55, 117, 194, 203

Wahl, C. W., 215
Wainwright, A. L., 107
Waisman, H. A., 52
Walker, K. N., 195
Walker, W. L., 48, 70–71, 189, 196, 199, 200, 221, 224, 225, 359
Wallace, D. K., 292, 294
Wallerstein, J. L., 123, 125, 175, 228
Walrond–Skinner, S., 53
Walsh, R. P., 43, 64, 65
Warr, P., 299
Warren, W. G., 21
Wasylenki, D., 306, 308
Watson, E., 257, 259, 263, 264
Watt, N. F., 132
Weiler, S. J., 287
Weiner, A., 310–11
Weiss, R. S., 4, 198, 199, 201
Werner, A., 151, 310
Western, J. S., 330–31
Wetmore, R., 385
Whitis, P. R., 280
Wilkinson, A. W., 268, 276
Williams, R. M., 334
Williams, W. V., 373, 390
Winget, C. N., 333
Winnicott, D. W., 84
Woodfield, R. L., 42, 69
Wolfe, L., 261
Wolfenstein, M., 94, 169
Wolff, J. R., 247
Wretmark, G., 215

Yamamoto, J., 198, 212

Zaris, D., 218

# Subject Index

Aaron (adolescent bereavement case), 363–64

Aberfan, Wales, avalanche disaster, 333–34

Abortions: in adolescence, 146, 175; bereavement after, 237–42; spontaneous, *see* Miscarriage

Absent grief, 59, 60; in conjugal bereavement, 205–6; focal psychotherapy for, 375–78

Abused children, 266

Acceptance of death, 27, 34, 43; in adolescence, 152–53; of elderly spouse, 313; in parental bereavement, 271; support in, 359–61

Accident proneness, 214

Accidental deaths, 28–30; in adolescence, 146, 167, 278; in childhood, 234, 235, 268–70, 276; in infancy, 266; mourning process after, 48–50; seeing body after, 36; of spouse, 181, 223

Acting-out, 61; in adolescent bereavement, 144, 152, 162–64, 171, 173; bereavement counseling and, 384; in conjugal bereavement, 214; parental divorce and, 123; after personal disaster, 351

Activity theory, 306

Acute disease, 30

Acute grief, syndrome of, 334

Addictions, parental loss and, 131–32

Adjustment disorders in childhood bereavement, 129

Adolescence: childhood bereavement and loss responses in, 169; death in, 278–80; developmental changes in, 140–41; falling in love in, 9; marriage in, 204; parental attachment and, 233–34; pregnancy in, 124, 146, 163, 168; relinquishment of newborn for adoption in, 253

Adolescent bereavement, 139–76; care-eliciting behavior in, 162–64; continuous and intermittent mourning in, 155–57; denial of grief in, 158; depression in, 130; identification in, 158–59; longer-term effects of,

170–71; in losses other than death, 175–76; outcomes of, 172–75; pathological patterns of, 171–72; relationships and, 142–47; sexuality and, 164; support in, 392, 395; and understanding of death, 147–50; withdrawal and depression and, 159–62

Adoption, relinquishment of newborn for, 252–54

Adult children: conjugal bereavement and, 194–95; death of, 280–81, 310; parental attachment to, 234; parental death and, 309–10; parental symbiosis with, 227

Adult pair bonds, 8–13; *see also* Marital relationship

Affects, 5; expression of, in preventive intervention, 370; lack of, focal psychotherapy and, 375–76; in review process, 45; of separation, 42

Afterlife, 31; fantasies of, 52

Age-correspondence phenomena, 134–35

Aggression, 42–43; adolescent, 144–45, 150, 163; in childhood bereavement, 126–28, 130; in early childhood bereavement, 90; as expression of death instinct, 68; externalized, in civilian violence, 344; fantasies of, 23; in latency, 99; mastery of, 83; relationships based on, 221

Aging, 283–319; death and, 317–19; impairment of function in, 285–97; loss of relationships in, 307–12; retirement and, 304–7; *see also* Elderly

Agoraphobia, 384

Air disasters, 335–38

Air New Zealand DC-10 crash, 336–38

Alan J (disaster case), 325–27

Alan K (conjugal bereavement case), 209–10

Alcohol use, 61; bereavement counseling and, 384; childhood bereavement and, 126; conjugal bereavement and, 214; "empty nest" syndrome and, 308; parental loss and, 131; in unemployed, 301

427

Alec S (unemployment case), 302–4
Alice (conjugal bereavement case), 177
Alice (sudden infant death syndrome case), 265
Alliance, reliable, 4
Altered relationship patterns, 62
Ambivalence: about abortion, 238–40; in adolescence, 144, 145; in adolescent bereavement, 155, 171, 172, 174–75; in adult pair bonds, 10, 11, 179, 180; in anticipated deaths, 27; assessment of, 364; bereavement counseling and, 385; and bereavement in infancy, 81; in childhood bereavement, 135–36; of children about remarriage, 200; in conjugal bereavement, 187, 188, 221–22; conversion reactions and, 216; depression and, 218; distorted bereavement and, 209; divorce and, 123, 228; in early childhood, 84; in early childhood bereavement, 95; of early object relations, 47; "empty nest" syndrome and, 308, 309; in father-infant relationship, 16; focal psychotherapy and, 380; toward infant, 232, 233; infant deaths and, 266; in infant-parent relationship, 17; in loss of sexual function, 288; mania and, 218–19; in middle childhood, 101; in mother–infant relationship, 15–16; in neonatal death, 250–51; and outcome of bereavement, 63; in parental bereavement, 269, 273, 278, 280; in parents of defective children, 254; personality factors in, 225; in pregnancy, 230–32, 237; preventive intervention and, 368, 373; psychodynamic explanations of, 66–68; in psychological mourning process, 44–45; in relinquishing newborn for adoption, 252; and response to loss, 18; stillbirth and, 242, 243; sudden death and, 31, 223; sudden infant death syndrome and, 263; about work, 299, 301
Amputation, 290–95
Anaclitic depression, 130
Anencephaly, 242–44
Anger: after abortion, 240; in adolescent bereavement, 150, 152, 172; adolescent death and, 279; in anticipatory bereavement, 51; assessment of, 365; childhood terminal illness and, 272, 274; in conjugal bereavement, 185–86, 222; at death of elderly spouse, 313; at deceased, 42–43; in disasters, 323, 332, 334; in distorted bereavement, 60, 208; at divorcing parents, 123; in early childhood bereavement, 91; focal psychotherapy and, 378–79; over impairment, 286; inhibition of, 206; in later childhood, 108; in loss of body part, 291; during menopause, 290; in mid-life crisis, 284; after miscarriage, 236; in neo-

natal death, 249; preventive intervention and, 368–69; in psychological mourning process, 45; sudden infant death syndrome and, 258, 259; transcultural expressions of, 65, 66; of unemployed, 300, 301; ventilation of, 358
Anglo-Saxon culture, 184; expression of grief in, 38
Anna H (conjugal bereavement case), 392–95
Annie (multiple bereavement case), 3, 6–7, 12–13, 19, 32, 48–50, 58–59
Anniversary phenomena, 61, 62; in childhood bereavement, 134–35; in conjugal bereavement, 190, 210; sibling death and, 114; after stillbirth, 246; transcultural aspects of, 66
Anorexia, *see* Appetite disturbance
Antarctica air crash, 336–38
Anticipated deaths, 24–28; adolescent response to, 150; early childhood response to, 90; effect on infants of, 79; of elderly, 313; older children's response to, 107; and seeing body of dead person, 36; of spouse, 182, 223
Anticipatory grief, 50–53; in death of children, 234–35; infant deaths and, 266; management of, 395–96; in neonatal death, 248; parental, 270–75; physiological stressor effects of, 71; in preparation for death in old age, 317; transcultural aspects of, 64–65
Antidepressants, 216–17, 311
Antisocial behavior, 124
Anxiety: in adolescence, 150; in anticipatory grief, 51; in childhood bereavement, 126; in conjugal bereavement, 214; death, 20–21; disasters and, 321, 333; in middle childhood, 103; about parental death, 92; after parental suicide, 120; separation, 40–42; of unemployed, 300
Anxiety states, 61, 384
Appetite disturbance, 61: in childhood bereavement, 127; in conjugal bereavement, 210, 213, 217
Arthritis: loss of mobility in, 295; parental loss and, 129
Assumptive world, changes in, 69–70
Asthma, 213; bereavement counseling and, 384
Atomic warfare, 346–47
Attachment: abortion and, 239; care-eliciting behavior and, 353; childhood death and, 267; definition of, 6; need for, 4; neonatal death and, 248; parental bereavement and, 230–34; in preventive intervention, 369; stillbirth and, 242; sudden infant death syndrome and, 255; survival of disasters and, 335

Attachment theory, 68–69
Attitudes, complementarity of, 8
Australia, bushfires in, 331–32
Australian National Disaster Organization, 327
Autopsy reports: on neonatal deaths, 249; in sudden infant death syndrome, 256, 259
Avalanches, 333–34
Avoidant relationships, 62, 116–17, 220

Basic trust, phase of, 83
Battered children, 266
Battle stress, 346
Behavioral therapy, 386–87
Beirut, effect of violence in, 345
Belfast, effect of violence in, 344–45
*Belle Star* (ship), 335
Bereavement counseling, 375–89; concurrent with management of other pathological syndromes, 384–85; training in, 400–401
Bernice C (conjugal bereavement case), 182
Beryl P (conjugal bereavement case), 209
Bill (childhood bereavement case), 91
Birth process, emotional experience of, 14
Bladder function, loss of, 296
Blindness, 285–86
Body of dead person, importance of seeing, 35–37
Body image in adolescence, 140
Body language of grief, 353
Body parts, loss of, 290–95
Bonds, 4–19; adult-to-adult pair, 8–13; anticipatory grief and, 51, 52; attachment theory on, 68; father-infant, 16–17; infant-parent, 17; mother-infant, 13–16; primary, models of, 6–7; *see also* Attachment
"Bound" child, 277
Bowel, cancer of, 26
Bowel function, loss of, 296
Brain damage deaths, 25
Brain function, loss of, 297, 317
Breast cancer, 292–93
Brenda (mastectomy case), 283, 292–93
Briquet's syndrome, 294
"Broken heart," death from, 62, 212
Buffalo Creek disaster, 333
Burial, 22, 38, 39; in different cultures, 65
Burn deaths, 268–69
"Burnout" of caring professionals, 405
Bushfires, 322, 331–32

C, Mr. (conjugal bereavement case), 367

Cancer: in adults who suffered childhood bereavement, 131; in childhood, 235; symbolic meaning of, 25–26
Cardiovascular disease, 295; in bereaved, 212
Care-eliciting behavior, 353; in adolescent bereavement, 162–64
Care-giving, compulsive, 102, 110, 126; in conjugal bereavement, 220
Castration anxiety, 20
Cataracts, 285–86
Cathy (childhood bereavement case), 103
Causality, 98; adolescent concepts of, 147
Cerebral function, loss of, 297
Cerebrovascular accident, 297
Cerebrovascular disease, 295
Chaotic families, 117–18
Childhood bereavement, 74–138; adjustment disorders in, 129–30; adolescent loss responses and, 169; in deaths other than parents', 113–14; depression in, 130–31; after divorce, 122–24; in early infancy, 75–77; from eight to twelve, 106–13; family therapy for, 389–90; from five to eight, 97–105; general symptomatology in, 127–28; influence of family on, 114–19; longer-term effects of, 131–35; need for care in, 391–95; outcome of, 126–37; and outcome of conjugal bereavement, 225; pathological, 125–26; preventive programs for, 399; psychosomatic effects in, 128; as risk factor, 367; in suicide of parent, 120–22; from two to five, 83–97
Childhood death, 267–78; anticipated, 271–75; attachment and, 267; causes of, 268–70; in disasters, 333–34; sudden, 30; violent, 29
Children: attachment to, 233; as replacement for lost spouse, 220; trauma of disasters for, 331; unresolved losses of, 63
Chronic death, 27
Chronic grief, 60; in adolescence, 172; in childhood, 126; concurrent crises and, 224; in conjugal bereavement, 205, 209–10; dependence and ambivalence and, 221–22; after disasters, 343; focal psychotherapy for, 383–84; over loss of sexual function, 288; over lost body part, 293; for lost work, 301; parental, 271, 274, 276, 279; after sudden infant death syndrome, 263
Chronic obstructive airways disease, 295
Civilian violence, 320, 344–45
"Clinging" relationships, 222
Clive S (conjugal bereavement case), 182
Cocoanut Grove nightclub fire, 334–35
Cognitive aspects of relationships, 5; in adult pair bonds, 8

Cognitive development in adolescence, 140
Cognitive models of bereavement, 69–70
Cognitive structuring, 388
Colostomy, 294–95
Combat disorders, 346
Comfort, 353–56
Commitment, 9
Communication: adolescent bereavement and, 154–55; about death, 35; distortions of, 87; in family system, 53, 55; in family therapy, 389; hearing loss and, 286; in mother-infant relationship, 14; parental bereavement and, 259, 260; with terminally ill child, 273
Community education programs, 398–99
Compassion, 404
Compassionate Friends, 275, 277–78, 397
Complementarity, 5; anticipated death and, 28; in parent-infant/infant-parent dyad, 18; stage of relationship and, 8
Compulsive care-giving relationships, 62; in conjugal bereavement, 220
Concentration camps, 346; *see also* Nazi concentration camps
Conduct disorders in childhood bereavement, 129
Congenital disorders, 234–35; childhood death from, 268, 270; stillbirth due to, 242, 243
Conjoint family therapy, 390
Conjugal bereavement, 177–228; concurrent life crises with, 224; depression and, 216–19; in disasters, 343; effects on relationship patterns of, 219–21; in elderly, 312–16; factors affecting outcome of, 221–27; general symptomatology in, 210–11; influence of family and social group in, 192–97; longer-term adaptation in, 197–205; mourning process in, 186–92; nature and circumstances of death and, 222–23; and nature and quality of lost relationships, 221–22; pathological patterns of, 205–10; personality variables in, 225–27; preventive intervention in, 372–73; preventive programs for, 399; psychological symptoms and disorders in, 213–16; psychosomatic reactions in, 211–13; relationship and, 178–81; self-help organizations for, 396–97; social-network support and, 224–25; sociodynamic variables in, 225; stress of, 71; and understanding of death, 180–81
Consolation, 356–61; acceptance of loss and, 359–61; to help bereaved bear separation pain, 356–59
Contamination, cancer and sense of, 26
Control, 5
Conversion reactions, 61; bereavement counseling and, 384; conjugal bereave-

ment and, 213, 215
Correspondence phenomena, 62
Corticosteroid effects, 61, 71
Creativity: aging and, 283–84; work and, 298
Cremation, 38–39, 184
Crib death, *see* Sudden infant death syndrome
Crisis theory, 70
Cruse Club, 396
Crying, 46; in conjugal bereavement, 190, 211, 217; in neonatal death, 249
Cultural value systems, 9; expression of grief and, 38
Cyclones, 322, 324–31
Cynthia R (parental bereavement case), 365


Dam, bursting of, 333
Damien (adolescent bereavement case), 158
Danielle (childhood bereavement case), 90
Darwin, Australia, cyclone disaster, 324–31
David (childhood bereavement case), 79
Deafness, 286
Death, 19–32; acceptance of reality of, 35; adolescent understanding of, 147–50; anticipated, 24–28; development of concepts of, 85; medicalization of, 37; notions of causality and, 98; sudden, 28–32
Death instinct, 20, 68
Decompensation: anniversary phenomena and, 134; concurrent crises and, 224
De facto relationships, 227
Defective children, grief at birth of, 254
Defenses: of caring professionals, 405; against death anxiety, 21; disaster and, 321; in early childhood, 84; focal psychotherapy and, 376, 383; in latency, 100; of older children, 107; against pain of loss, 67; parental divorce and, 123; personal disasters and, 350; in preventive intervention, 369–70
Delayed grief, 59, 60; in conjugal bereavement, 206; after miscarriage, 236
Delinquency, 172, 173
Dementia, 297
Denial, 20, 21, 27, 34; abortion and, 238, 239; in adolescent bereavement, 151, 158; in anticipatory bereavement, 50, 51; assessment of, 364; in caring professionals, 405; of childhood bereavement by adults, 82; in conjugal bereavement, 222; of disability in handicapped child, 254; in early childhood, 95; family relationships based on, 117; focal psychotherapy and, 376; of impairment, 286; in latency, 100; in later childhood, 107; in parental bereavement, 271; parental divorce and, 123; in patho-

logical mourning, 60; personal construct theory on, 70; in personal disasters, 350; of potential disaster, 322; in retirement, 305; rituals and, 37; sudden infant death syndrome and, 260; in survivor syndrome, 347, 349

Dependency, 61; in adolescence, 145; in adult pair bonds, 11, 180; anticipated death and, 27–28; assessment of, 364; of bereaved elderly, 314; in childhood bereavement, 130; conjugal bereavement and, 221; conversion reactions and, 216; distorted bereavement and, 60, 208; in early childhood, 84, 94; of infants, 16, 17; outcome of childhood bereavement and, 135–36; in parent-child relationship, 267; personality factors in, 225; and response to loss, 18; and sense of desertion, 42

Depression, 61–62; in adolescence, 142, 145, 150; in adolescent bereavement, 154, 159–62, 173; in adult children with symbiotic parent, 227; anniversary phenomena and, 134; in anticipatory bereavement, 52; bereavement counseling in, 384–85; in bereaved elderly, 314–15; childhood bereavement and, 126, 130–31; conjugal bereavement and, 216–19; dependence and ambivalence and, 222; in elderly, 311–12; "empty nest" syndrome and, 308–9; guilt and, 44–45; guilt over abortion and, 241; after hysterectomy, 294; identification in, 67; over impairment, 286; over loss of sexuality, 288; after mastectomy, 294; during menopause, 290; after miscarriage, 237; in parental bereavement, 276; parental death and, 97, 310; after parental divorce, 124; parental loss in etiology of, 132–34; parental suicide and, 121; after personal disasters, 351; preventive intervention and, 373; sadness distinguished from, 45; after stillbirth, 247; sudden infant death syndrome and, 260, 261; in survivors of disasters, 333; in unemployed, 301; in Vietnam veterans, 346

Deprivation, influence of early maternal experience of, 13–14

Desertion, feelings of, 42; in adolescent bereavement, 152; in distorted bereavement, 60

Despair, 45; existential, 20; in infancy, 79; of unemployed, 301

Destructive fantasies, 28

Diabetes mellitus, 128

*Diagnostic and Statistical Manual of the American Psychiatric Association* (DSM-III), 71–72

Differentiation subphase, 75

Disasters, 29, 320–51; avalanche, 333–34;

air, 335–38; of civilian violence and terrorism, 344–45; of dam bursting, 333; fire, 334–35; man-made, 332–47; maritime, 335; natural, 322–32; personal, 349–51; preventive intervention in, 373; rail, 338–44; survivor syndrome in, 347–49; of war, 345–47

Disbelief, 34–37; in adolescent bereavement, 151; in anticipatory bereavement, 50; in conjugal bereavement, 183; at death of elderly spouse, 313; in neonatal death, 248; unemployment and, 300

Disease models, 71–72

Disengagement, 307–8; in retirement, 306

Displacement, 21

Dissociated reactions, 61

Dissociative conditions, 384

Distorted bereavement, 59, 60; in adolescence, 172; conjugal, 208–9; dependence and ambivalence and, 221; focal psychotherapy for, 378–84

Divorce: adjustment disorders after, 129; adolescent response to, 175; childhood bereavement after, 122–24; "empty nest" syndrome and, 308; family life after, 124–25; grief over loss of spouse in, 228; in mid-life crisis, 284; psychosomatic effects of, 128

Dominance, 5

Donna M (illustration of caring professional), 357–58

Down's syndrome, 254

Dreams: in conjugal bereavement, 185, 189; about deceased, 41; interpretation of, in re-grief therapy, 386; in psychological mourning process, 46

Drowning deaths of children, 268, 276

Drug use, 61; bereavement counseling and, 384; in unemployed, 301

Dying: anticipatory bereavement and, 50–53; fantasies of, 22–23; farewell aspects of, 27; fear of process of, 21; medical technology and, 29

Early childhood bereavement, 83–97

Earthquakes, 322, 331

Eating behavior disorders, *see* Appetite disturbance

Educational methods, 398–99

Ego: in adolescence, 144, 147, 159, 169, 171; conjugal bereavement and, 223; disaster and, 322, 323; in early childhood, 87–88, 94, 95; in latency, 98; in later infancy, 79, 80; mobilization of, 34; object loss and, 66, 67; in response to sudden death, 28; stresses of childhood bereavement and, 137; vulnerability of, 47

"Ego integrity," 318

Elaine P (conjugal bereavement case), 207
Elderly: anticipated deaths of, 24, 25; bereavement in, 310–12; conjugal bereavement in, 312–16; preparation for death by, 317–19
Elizabeth (conjugal bereavement case), 201
Elizabeth S (conjugal bereavement case), 370–72
Empathy, capacity for, 401
"Empty nest" syndrome, 308–9
Endocrine function, 71; in adolescence, 140
Ernie (retirement case), 283
Existential despair, 20
Explanatory models of bereavement, 64–73
Extended family, 3; support from, 56
Extramarital relationships, bereavement in, 227

Facial expressions of grief, 353
Falling in love, 9–10; attachment theory on, 68
Family relationships, 3; in adolescence, 142–46; anticipatory bereavement and, 52–53; assessment of, 366–67; childhood death and, 276–77; childhood terminal illness and, 272; comfort in, 352–53; early childhood bereavement and, 89; conjugal bereavement and, 192–97; effect of bereavement on, 53–56; and identification in adolescence, 159; influence on adult object choice of, 8; influence on childhood bereavement of, 114–19; loss and, 18–19, 124–25; in middle childhood, 98; mourning process and, 47; neonatal death and, 250; outcome of bereavement and, 63; preventive intervention and, 368; sexualized cross-generational, 165; sudden infant death syndrome and, 260–62
Family therapy, 389–91
Famine, 320
Fantasies: in adolescence, 140, 144, 150, 159, 164–65, 172; in adult pair bonds, 8; of amputees, 291; in anticipatory bereavement, 52; attachment theory on, 69; in childhood terminal illness, 272; in conjugal bereavement, 180, 186, 215, 217, 219, 223; of death and dying, 22–23; destructive, 28, 29; disasters and, 320, 329, 336, 341; in early childhood, 84, 86–88, 94; of elderly bereaved, 313; focal psychotherapy and, 381; in latency, 98–100; in mid-life crisis, 284; in mother-infant relationship, 13, 14; in neonatal death, 250; in parent-child attachment, 230; in parental bereavement, 269; parental divorce and, 123; personal disasters and, 350; during pregnancy, 237; of rebirth of

deceased, 58; in relinquishment of newborn for adoption, 252; of state of death, 36; stillbirth and, 243; in sudden infant death syndrome, 256; suicidal, 121; of unemployed, 301
Farewell process, 35–36; funerals and, 37
Father, death of, *see* Parental death
Father-daughter relationship, 8
Father-infant relationship, 16–17
Fears: adolescent, 147; of affect, 375–76; of death, 20–21; death of siblings and, 113; in early childhood, 86; in later childhood, 106–7
Fertility, loss of, 289–90
Fire disasters, 334–35
Floods, 322, 331
Focal psychotherapy: for pathological grief, 375–85; in preventive intervention, 368
Forest fires, 322
Formal operations stage, 140, 147
Friendships: based on similarities, 8; bonds of, 3; need for, 4; *see also* Social relationships
Fulminating disease, 30
Fundamentalism, 20
Funerals, 37–39; children at, 88; conjugal bereavement and, 183–84; for disaster victims, 341; exclusion of adolescents from, 151; exclusion of children from, 115; for infants, 258; for neonates, 250
Future oriented identity reconstruction, 388

Galvanic Skin Response (GSR), 147
Gastrointestinal function, loss of, 295
Gender-identity disturbance, 166
General symptomatology, 61; in childhood bereavement, 127–28, 131; in conjugal bereavement, 210–11; sudden infant death syndrome and, 261
General systems theory, 53
Genetic vulnerability, 63
Genital cancer, 26
Genitourinary disease, 296
Geoffrey (adolescent bereavement case), 176
Gestalt techniques, 388
Glaucoma, 285
"Good-enough" mother, 78, 84
Gordon R (preparation for death case), 283, 319
Grandparents: childhood death and, 274; death of, 113, 114, 145–46; sudden infant death syndrome and, 261
Granville, New South Wales, rail disaster, 338–44, 348
Greek society, 184; expression of grief in, 38; remarriage in, 200

Grief: after abortion, 238; absent, 205–6; in adolescence, 146, 158, 162, 163, 169, 171, 173; in adolescent deaths, 278; of amputees, 290–91, 295; anticipatory, *see* Anticipatory grief; attachment theory on, 68; and changes in assumptive world, 69; chronic, *see* Chronic grief; delayed, *see* Delayed grief; in disasters, 323; after divorce, 228; earliest manifestation of, 76; in early childhood, 88, 89, 95; early differentiation of affects, of, 80; of elderly, 313, 314; ending of, 400; in evolutionary context, 72–73; facial expressions of, 353; in family system, 389; hypochondriasis and, 214; identification in, 67; illness model of, 71; in infant deaths, 266; inhibited, *see* Inhibited grief; in late childhood, 108–9; in later infancy, 77; at menopause, 290; in middle childhood, 102–3; in midlife crisis, 284; after miscarriage, 236; in neonatal death, 249; in parental death, 309; parental divorce and, 123; pathological patterns of, 59–61; personal disaster and, 350, 351; pining and longing of, 42; preventive intervention and, 368; after relinquishing newborn for adoption, 252–53; rituals and, 184; sanctions for expression of, 38; after stillbirth, 244; in sudden infant death syndrome, 256, 258–61; support in expression of, 137; therapeutic assessment and, 362–67; transcultural aspects of, 64; for "young old," 310
Guided imagery, 388
Guided mourning, 387
Guilt, 45; after abortion, 238, 241; in accidental death, 28, 29; in adolescent bereavement, 150, 152, 155, 159, 165, 172; in anticipatory bereavement, 52; assessment of, 365; in conjugal bereavement, 188, 221, 222; and death of same-sex parent, 124; over death of sibling, 113; about destruction, 350; in distorted bereavement, 60, 208, 209; after divorce, 228; family relationships based on, 115–16; focal psychotherapy and, 376, 378, 380–81; in grief syndrome, 71; in latency, 98, 99, 101, 105; during menopause, 290; in midlife crisis, 284; after miscarriage, 236; in neonatal death, 249, 250; in parental bereavement, 235, 268–70, 273; parental divorce and, 123; parental suicide and, 120, 121; in parents of defective children, 254; personal disaster and, 351; preventive intervention and, 368; self-destructive relationships and, 220; after stillbirth, 243, 245; sudden infant death syndrome and, 256, 258–60, 263; suicide and, 42, 280; of survivors of disasters, 44–45, 321, 323, 333, 335, 344, 347–49; of unemployed, 301

Habit disturbance in childhood bereavement, 127
Hallucinatory experiences, 40
Hamish (childhood bereavement case), 121–22
Handicapped children, grief at birth of, 254
Harry K (parental bereavement case), 379–80
"Haunted" child, 277
Health and well-being, loss of, 296–97
Heart disease: symbolic meanings of, 25; *see also* Cardiovascular disease
Helen (adoption relinquishment case), 253–54
Helen (childhood bereavement case), 110–12
Helen (parental bereavement case), 281
Henry (childhood bereavement case), 101
Hiroshima survivors, 347–48
Holocaust, 346–48
Homeostasis, 53
Homosexual relationships, bereavement in, 227
Hostages, 345
Hotel fires, 334
Huli people of New Guinea, 225
Huntington's chorea, 27
Hurricanes, 322
Hypochondriasis: in adolescent bereavement, 162; bereavement counseling and, 384; conjugal bereavement and, 213–15
Hysterectomy, 289–91, 294

Idealization: in adolescent bereavement, 155; in adult pair bond, 179; in childhood bereavement, 94, 100, 121, 124; in chronic grief, 60; in conjugal bereavement, 188, 222; of deceased, 44; falling in love and, 9–10; in fantasy relationship with lost partner, 219; inhibition of mourning through, 207; loss of, after divorce, 122; in parental bereavement, 114, 274; personal construct theory on, 70; of public figures, 147; after sudden infant death syndrome, 263
Identification, psychological: in adolescence, 150; in adolescent bereavement, 158–59; in conjugal bereavement, 215; with dead sibling, 113; with disaster victims, 336; of father with infant, 16; and lack of role models, 124; in late childhood, 106, 109; in latency, 98, 103–5; with lost object, 66, 67; parental death and, 310; parental bereavement and, 267; parental suicide and, 121; of parents with adolescent, 142; sexual, loss of source of, 166; in survivor syndrome, 348
Identification of disaster victims, 341

Identity: in adult pair bond, 12, 180; assumptive world and, 69; of bereaved, 57; and bereavement in infancy, 77; in conjugal bereavement, 203–5; development of, 141; "empty nest" syndrome and, 308; future oriented reconstruction of, 388; in middle childhood, 102; work and, 298
Ileostomy, 294–95
Ill health of bereaved, 61
Illness: anticipated deaths from, 24; social meanings of, 25
Illness models of bereavement, 71–72
Immortality: religious concepts of, 31; symbolic concepts of, 20–22
Immune function, 61, 212; bereavement counseling and, 384; effect of stress on, 71
Impairment of function, 285–97; cerebral, 297; hearing, 286; in menopause, 289–90; sexual, 286–89
Imprint of death, 347–49
Incest taboo, 144
Indian society, remarriage in, 200
Individuation, fear of, 20
Infancy: attachment in, 232–33; death in, 30, 266–67; *and see* Sudden infant death syndrome; bereavement in, 75–82; object loss in, 67; separation in, 402–3
Infant-parent relationship, 17
Inhibited grief, 60; after abortion, 239; in adolescence, 171, 172; in childhood, 125–26; concurrent crises and, 224; in conjugal bereavement, 206–7; dependence and ambivalence in, 221; in early childhood, 95; focal psychotherapy for, 375–78; in middle childhood, 102; after stillbirth, 246; in sudden infant death syndrome, 264
In-laws, conjugal bereavement and, 195
Inner bereaved child, 403
Intellectualization, 21
Intensity of relationships, 18
Intensive care, 29; neonatal, 248; technology of, 22
Interactions, levels of, 5
Internalized objects, 63
Interpretation: in focal psychotherapy, 376; in preventive intervention, 370; in re-grief therapy, 385, 386
Intimacy, 9; in anticipatory bereavement, 27, 52; avoidance of, 220; physical power of, 11–12; sudden death and, 31
Introjection of lost object, 67
Irish wakes, 39
Israeli War of Attrition, 280
Italian society, 184; expression of grief in, 38

J, Mrs. (conjugal bereavement case), 206

Jack (conjugal bereavement case), 207
Jack L (disaster case), 320, 327–28
Jake (conjugal bereavement case), 177
James (adolescent bereavement case), 159
James H (childhood bereavement case), 392–95
Jane S (conjugal bereavement case), 196–97
Japan, conjugal bereavement in, 198
Jason (childhood bereavement case), 86–87, 91
Jennifer (conjugal bereavement case), 177
Jenny (childhood bereavement case), 95–96
Jeremy (childhood bereavement case), 81–82
Jessica (childhood bereavement case), 74, 138
Jewish mourning ceremony, 39
Joan (loss of sexuality case), 288–89
Joan S (conjugal bereavement case), 204
Joanna (childhood bereavement case), 74
Job loss, 299–304
John (childhood bereavement case), 74
Jonestown, Guyana, mass suicide, 345
Joyce B (conjugal bereavement case), 366–67

K, Dr. (illustration of caring professional), 359–61
K, Mrs. (conjugal bereavement case), 216
Karen L (conjugal bereavement case), 226–27
Kate (childhood bereavement case), 95–96
Kay (childhood bereavement case), 102
Kay (conjugal bereavement case), 201
Ken (adolescent bereavement case), 173–74
Kentucky nightclub fire, 348
Kidnapping, 345

L, Mrs. (parental bereavement case), 270
Latency, bereavement during, 97–113
Later childhood, bereavement in, 106–13
Learning theory, 70
Legal processes: and acceptance of reality of death, 35; violent or accidental deaths and, 30
Lena (parental bereavement case), 229, 245–46
Leukemia, 26, 27, 81; childhood deaths from, 269, 270, 275; sibling death from, 129
Libido, withdrawal of, 66
Life-cycle stages, 179
Life review in old age, 317
Limbs, loss of, 290–95
Linking objects, 385–86
Loneliness: in conjugal bereavement, 199–200; of elderly, 307

Longer-term effects of bereavement, 57–59; in adolescence, 170–71; in childhood, 131–35; conjugal, 197–205; in infancy, 77
Lorraine F (conjugal bereavement case), 381–83
Los Angeles, earthquake in, 331
Lung cancer, 26

Magical thinking, 20, 36; in adolescence, 146, 150; in conjugal bereavement, 180; in early childhood, 86; in later childhood, 107
Make Today Count, 398
Malcolm (loss of sexuality case), 283, 288–89
Malignant disease: childhood deaths from, 268–70; infant deaths from, 266; *see also* Cancer
Mania, 61; conjugal bereavement and, 218–19
Man–made disasters, 332–47
Margaret (childhood bereavement case—death of grandfather), 86
Margaret (childhood bereavement case—death of mother), 102
Margaret (conjugal bereavement case), 208
Margaret (parental bereavement case), 229, 251–52
Maria L (conjugal bereavement case), 354
Marital relationships, 178–81; effect of sudden infant death syndrome on, 262; of elderly, 312; menopause and, 290; parental bereavement and, 277; parental loss and, 134; parent-child attachment and, 267; reciprocity and complementarity in, 5; retirement and, 305
Maritime disasters, 335
Mary (adolescent bereavement case), 139, 159–61
Mary (childhood bereavement case), 104–5
Mary (parental bereavement case), 279–80
Mary K (grief of aging case), 283, 296–97
Mass suicide, 345
Massacres, 345
Mastectomy, 292–94
Matthew (childhood bereavement case), 110–12
Maudsley Personality Inventory, 8
Maya culture, 65
Medical technology, 22
Melancholia, 59; mourning distinguished from 66, 67
Menopause, 287, 289–90
Michael (childhood bereavement case), 109
Mick (conjugal bereavement case), 315–16
Middle childhood, bereavement in, 97–105
Mid-life crisis, 283–84
Midtown Manhattan Survey, 131
Miscarriages: in adolescence, 146, 175; be-

reavement after, 235–37; following sudden infant death syndrome, 261; support groups for, 398
Mobility, loss of, 295
Mortality among bereaved, 62
Mother, death of, *see* Parental death
Mother-infant bond, 13–16, 75, 78, 79; attachment behaviors of infant and, 6; falling-in-love bonding in, 9
Mt. Erebus air disaster, 337–38, 348
Mourning: in adolescence, 146, 155–57, 162, 163, 167, 169; of amputees, 291, 295; anticipatory, 50–52; case illustration of, 48–50; for children, 274; in conjugal bereavement, 186–92; definition of, 33; dependency of children and, 135–36; in disasters, 323; after divorce, 228; in early childhood, 88, 89, 93–95; for elderly spouse, 313; facilitated by assessment, 362–67; by fathers after abortion, 240; guided, 387; inhibited, 206–7; in later childhood, 108–9; in later infancy, 77; for loss of function, 286; in middle childhood, 102–3; in midlife crisis, 284; after miscarriage, 236; after neonatal death, 249, 250; "normal adolescent," 141; operational, 390; in parental death, 309; parental divorce and, 123; pattern and duration of, 58; in preparation for death in old age, 317; preventive intervention and, 368; psychodynamic explanations of, 66–68; psychological process of, 39, 44–50; in retirement, 305; rituals of, *see* Rituals; of stillbirth, 243–44; in sudden infant death syndrome, 263; support in, 137; transcultural aspects of, 64
Multiple concurrent bereavements, 224
Munchausen syndrome of bereavement, 72
Murder, 29; equation of abortion with, 238; of spouse, 180
Mutual negative projections, 10–11
Mysterious sudden deaths, 30–31
Myths, 19; of family unit, 53–55; of immortality, 22

Nancy (adolescent bereavement case), 139
Narcissistic supplies, 12; absent grief and, 205–6; impact of childhood bereavement on, 136; work and, 299
Nathan (parental bereavement case), 229, 275–76
Natural disasters, 322–32
Nazi concentration camps, 346–48
Neanderthal man, 22
"Near-death" experiences, 22
Needs, complementarity of, 8
Negative interaction: in mother-infant relationship, 15–16; *see also* Ambivalence
Negative projections, mutual, 10–11

Neglect, childhood death due to, 268–69
Neonatal death, 248–54; early childhood response to, 93; support groups for parents, 398
Neoplastic disease, 212–13
Neuroses: in adolescent bereavement, 173; in childhood bereavement, 129; in conjugal bereavement, 213; traumatic, 350
Nightclub fires, 334
Nightmares: in childhood bereavement, 127; in survivors of disasters, 329
Nuclear family, 3; *see also* Family relationships
Numbness, 34–37; in adolescent bereavement, 151; in anticipatory bereavement, 50; in conjugal bereavement, 183; in neonatal death, 248; and sudden infant death syndrome, 256; unemployment and, 300
Nurturing, 4; conflicts related to, 348

Object choice, influence of family relationships on, 8
Object constancy, 75
Object loss: cognitive theory on, 70; fear of, 20; psychodynamic theories of, 66–68; in stress models, 70
Obsessional neurosis, 173
Oedipal factors, 8, 67, 84; in adolescence, 140, 144, 164–65; after loss, 124; parental divorce and, 123–24; resolution of, 98
One-parent families, 125
Openness, family relationships based on, 119
Operational mourning, 390
Opposite-sex parents: adolescents and, 144; oedipal conflicts and, 84; relationship with, 8
Oropharyngeal cancer, 26
Outcomes of bereavement, 61–64; in adolescence, 172–75; in childhood, 126–37; conjugal, 195–96, 221–27; in disasters, 343–44; in early childhood, 97; factors affecting, 62–64; in middle childhood, 105; preventive intervention and, 370–72; after stillbirth, 247–48; in sudden infant death syndrome, 261–66
Overprotectiveness, 16, 62; after death of sibling, 114; parental bereavement and, 276; after sudden infant death syndrome, 262

P, Dr. (illustration of caring professional), 355–56
Pain, conversion, 215
Pair bonds: in adolescence, 166; adult, 8–13; death of partner in, *see* Conjugal bereavement

Panic states, 384
Panoramic memory, 350
Paralysis, conversion, 215
Paranoid-schizoid splitting, 222
Parasuicide, 314
Parental bereavement, 229–82; abortion and, 237–42; in adolescent death, 278–80; anticipatory grief in, 271–75; attachments and, 230–34, 267; cause of death and, 268–70; in childhood death, 267–78; counseling approaches for, 388; in death of adult child, 280–81, 310; in disasters, 333–34, 343; in miscarriage, 235–37; in neonatal death, 248–54; outcomes of, 276–78; preventive programs for, 399; self-help organizations for, 397–98; in stillbirth, 242–48; in sudden infant death syndrome, 255–66
Parental bonding instrument, 16
Parental death, 124–25; adjustment disorders after, 129, 130; in adolescence, 144–45, 151–53, 156–61, 163–66, 170, 173; adult children and, 309–10; age at, 317; availability of supportive care after, 136–37; circumstances of, 136; depression after, 130, 131; in early childhood, 84, 86–97; in early infancy, 76; effects during later life of, 131–35; general symptomatology following, 127–28; in later childhood, 107–13; in later infancy, 78–82; in middle childhood, 99–105; outcomes and, 126; by suicide, 120–22
Parent-infant/infant-parent dyad, loss in, 17–19
Pat (disaster case), 329–30
Pathological bereavement: in adolescence, 171–72; in adults who suffered childhood bereavement, 134; assessment and, 367; behavioral therapy for, 386–87; in childhood, 125–26; conjugal, 205–10; focal psychotherapy for, 375–85; identification in, 103; illness model and, 71–72; management of, 375–89; after miscarriage, 237; in neonatal death, 250–51; parental, 271; re-grief therapies for, 385–86
Peer-group relationships in adolescence, 146; bereavement and, 154, 170–71
Penny H (childhood bereavement case), 392–95
Permissiveness, 5
Personal construct theory, 69–70
Personal disasters, 349–51
Personality variables, 225–27; work and, 298–99
Peru, earthquake in, 331
Peter (conjugal bereavement case), 177, 190–92
Pets, death of: adolescents and, 146, 175–76; elderly and, 311
Phantom limb, 291
Phobic reactions, 61; in adolescent bereave-

ment, 162, 173; behavioral therapy for, 386, 387; in childhood bereavement, 127; in conjugal bereavement, 213, 214
Physical attractiveness, 8
Physiologic stressor effects, 71
Pintjantjatjana Australian aborigines, 315
Play therapy techniques, 392; assessment through, 91; projection of death in, 85; working though bereavement in, 80–81
Pollution, 320
Pornography of death, 20
Positive thinking, 20
Posttraumatic stress disorders: in Vietnam veterans, 346; *see also* Traumatic stress syndrome
Power relationships, 5, 221; conjugal bereavement and, 194
Practical support, 356
Pregnancy: adolescent, 124, 146, 163, 168; conjugal bereavement and, 214; delayed grief and, 206; interactional effects of, 14; parent-child bond during, 230–32; premarital, 133; after sudden infant death syndrome, 262, 263; termination of, 237–42; *see also* Miscarriage
Premarital pregnancy, 133
Pre-retirement planning programs, 304
Preventive intervention: effectiveness of, 372–74; for families, 390; format for, 368; goals of, 368; outcome in, 370–72; techniques in, 368–70; timing of, 368
Preventive programs, 398–99
Primary affects, 17
Primary attachment figure, 6; in disasters, 323
Primary bonds, models of, 6–7
Principal theme postulate, 388
Projection, 21; in child abuse, 266; in conjugal bereavement, 201; of death, 85; onto infant, 232; in mother-infant relationship, 16; mutual, 179; negative, 10–11; in preventive intervention, 369; sudden infant death syndrome and, 256, 259
Projective techniques, 392
Promiscuity: adolescent, 162–64; after death of spouse, 202
Property, distribution of, 194
Prostatic hypertrophy, 296
Pseudoadult behavior: in adolescence, 158; in later childhood, 109–10
Psychiatric disorders, 61; in adolescent bereavement, 172–73; battle stress and, 346; bereavement counseling and, 384–85; childhood bereavement in etiology of, 131–32; in conjugal bereavement, 213–16; "empty nest" syndrome and, 308–9; after sudden infant death syndrome, 261–62; in unemployed, 299
Psychic numbing, 347–49; in personal disasters, 350

Psychodynamic aspects of bereavement, 66–68
Psychological debriefing of rescuers, 338–40
Psychosocial disorders, 61
Psychosocial transitions, 69
Psychosomatic disorders, 21, 61, 62; adolescent bereavement and, 172; bereavement counseling and, 384; after childhood bereavement, 128–29, 131; in conjugal bereavement, 211–13; after sudden infant death syndrome, 261; in unemployed, 301

Rail disasters, 338–44
Reaction formation in pseudoadult behavior, 158
Reality testing, 40, 43; in childhood bereavement, 136; in conjugal bereavement, 189, 198; consolation and, 358; in early childhood, 94; funerals and, 37
Reassurance of worth, 4
Reciprocity, 5
Recovery process, 47; transcultural aspects of, 66
Regression: in adolescent bereavement, 156; in bereaved infants, 80; in early childhood bereavement, 89; of family of adolescent, 142; after parental divorce, 123
Regret, 45
Re-grief therapies, 385
Relationships: in adolescence, 142–47; assessment questions on, 364–65; in early infancy, 75–76; effects of conjugal bereavement on patterns of, 219–21; influence of possibility of loss on, 402; in later childhood, 106; in later infancy, 77–78; longer-term effects of parental loss on, 134; loss of, aging and, 307–12; mid-life crisis and, 284; in middle childhood, 98–99; of two- to five-year olds, 83–84; work and, 298; *see also* Family relationships; Marital relationships; Social relationships
Reliable alliance, sense of, 4
Religion, 31–32; abortion and, 238; in adolescence, 150; anticipatory bereavement and, 51, 53; family and, 56
Remarriage, 199–200; children and, 125; of elderly, 314, 315; in mid-life crisis, 284
Repetition compulsion, 10; in abortion, 240; after adolescent bereavement, 165; relationships based on, 221
Replacement child syndrome, 246, 277; sudden infant death syndrome and, 262–63
Replacement relationships, 62, 219–20; preventive intervention and, 370
Repression, 21; in adolescent bereavement, 143, 152, 154; of grief, 41; in later childhood, 108; of yearning, 206

Rescue workers, 337–41

Resentment, 45

Resistance in preventive intervention, 369–70

Respiratory disorders: loss of function in, 295; symbolic meaning of, 25

"Resurrected" child, 277

Resuscitative technology, 22, 29

Retinal detachment, 286

Retirement, 304–7; loss of roles after, 203

Review process, 44–45; in adolescent bereavement, 155; in anticipatory bereavement, 52; avoidance of, 60; in conjugal bereavement, 187, 188; inhibition of, 206–7; in neonatal death, 249; preventive intervention and, 369, 370; after stillbirth, 245; support in, 359–61

Rheumatoid arthritis, parental loss and, 129

Richard (sudden infant death syndrome case), 265–66

Riots, 320, 344–45

Risk factors: assessment of, 367; preventive intervention and, 367–74

Rituals, 19, 20; conjugal bereavement and, 183; for disposal of dead, 37–39; and dread of dead body, 36–37; early childhood participation in, 88; exclusion of adolescents from, 175; exclusion of children from, 115; facilitating transitions, 57; of family life, 41; myth of immortality and, 22; religious, 32; and transcultural aspects of bereavement, 64–66

Role models: lack of, 124; in self-help groups, 361

Roles: conjugal bereavement and, 203–5; in family, 54, 55

Romantic love, 9

Romanticization: in adolescence, 150; of death, 20

Ron (adolescent bereavement case), 139, 156–57

Ross (parental bereavement case), 281

Ruth (parental bereavement case), 229, 275–76


S, Mrs. (parental bereavement case), 271

Sadness, 45; after abortion, 239–40; assessment of, 365; in childhood bereavement, 127; childhood terminal illness and, 273; in early childhood bereavement, 92; during menopause, 290; after miscarriage, 236; at neonatal death, 249, 250; physiologic responses to, 71; transcultural expressions of, 65, 66

St. Christopher's Hospice, 374

Same-sex parent: adolescent loss of, 165,

166; death of, 105, 124; oedipal conflicts and, 84

Samoan family systems, 56

Sandra (miscarriage case), 229, 236–37

Sarah B (conjugal bereavement case), 376–78

Scapegoating, 55, 116; of adolescents, 142, 171; conjugal bereavement and, 194; after death of sibling, 114; family therapy and, 390–91; sudden infant death syndrome and, 258, 259, 261

Schizophrenia, parental death in etiology of, 132

Schizophreniform conditions, 61

School refusal, 129; in adolescence, 164

School-bus kidnapping, 345

Sea disasters, 335

Sedation, 213–14; inappropriate, 353; in stillbirth experience, 244, 247

Self: death of, 317–19; redefinition of, 57; sense of, 12, 140

Self-destructive behavior, 101; after parental suicide, 121

Self-destructive relationships, 220; after abortion, 241

Self-disclosure, 11

Self-esteem: abortion and, 239; conjugal bereavement and, 204; depression and, 218; work and, 298, 300

Self-help organizations, 396–98; for parental bereavement, 275, 277–78; preventive intervention through, 374; role models in, 361; for sudden infant death syndrome, 264

Self-reliance, compulsive, 102, 126

Self-reproach in conjugal bereavement, 222

Separation: in adolescence, 145; amputation and, 291; childhood bereavement and, 127; in childhood terminal illness, 271–74; in conjugal bereavement, 184–86; consolation for, 356–59; in disasters, 323, 331; in early infancy, 76; fear of, 20; funeral as symbol of, 37; in infancy, 79–81, 402–3; pain of, 40–43; preventive intervention and, 369; transcultural aspects of, 66

Separation individuation, 75

Sexual acting–out, 61; in adolescence, 162–64, 168–69; in conjugal bereavement, 202, 214

Sexual attraction, 10

Sexual organs, amputation of, 294

Sexuality: adolescent, 140, 144, 145; adolescent bereavement and, 165–69; in adult pair bond, 180; aging and, 286–89; childhood bereavement and, 128; conjugal bereavement and, 201–2; loss of, 317; midlife crisis and, 284

Shadow grief, 266–67

Shared feelings, family relationships based on, 119

Shock, 34–37; in adolescent bereavement, 151; in anticipatory bereavement, 50; in conjugal bereavement, 183; at death of elderly spouse, 313; during disaster, 322; in neonatal death, 248; of unemployment, 299

Shoplifting, 214

Short-term focal psychotherapy, 368

Siblings: adolescent relationships with, 146, 151, 171; age at death of, 317; ambivalent relationships with, 84; birth of, 83; compulsive care-giving toward, 102, 110; death of, 77, 87, 93, 95, 99, 113–14, 126, 129, 136, 173–74, 227, 267; early childhood bereavement and, 92; of latency-age children, 98; parental bereavement and, 274, 276, 277; protective effects of, 136–37; sudden infant death syndrome and, 256, 259, 260, 262; of "young old," 310

Sick role, 211; secondary gain from, 216; of unemployed, 301–2

SIDS Family Adjustment Scale, 264

Sleep disturbance: in childhood bereavement, 127, 128; in conjugal bereavement, 210, 211, 213, 217; neonatal death and, 250

Social development in adolescence, 140–41

Social integration, 4

Social relationships: assessment of, 366–67; conjugal bereavement and, 192–97, 202–3, 224–25; disengagement from, 307; funerals and, 37–38; in later childhood, 106; in middle childhood, 98; mourning process and, 47; outcome of bereavement and, 63; preventive intervention and, 368; after stillbirth, 245; sudden infant death syndrome and, 261; *see also* Friendships

Social value systems, 9

Sociobiological model of bereavement, 72–73

Sociodemographic variables, 225

Somatic distress, 40; in grief syndrome, 71

Spasmodic torticollis, 215

Specific smiling response, 75

Splitting, 94; in adolescence, 150; in conjugal bereavement, 219; paranoid-schizoid, 222; in parental bereavement, 274; personal disaster and, 350–51

Spouse, death of, *see* Conjugal bereavement

Status transitions, 57

Stealing, 164

Sterilization, 289–90

Steve (adolescent bereavement case), 139, 167–68

Stillbirth, 242–48; early childhood response to, 93; support groups for, 398

Stress models, 70–71

Stress-response syndrome, parental death and, 309–10

Stress-specific grief responses, 59

Stroke, symbolic meaning of, 25

Substance abuse, *see* Alcohol use; Drug use

Sudden deaths, 28–32; in adolescence, 278; adolescent response to, 150, 175; anger in response to, 42; childhood bereavement and, 136; of children, 234; early childhood response to, 87, 88, 90, 92; effect on infants of, 79; middle childhood response to, 103; of neonates, 248; older children's response to, 107; outcome of bereavement after, 63; preventive intervention and, 374; seeing body after, 36; shock and numbness in response to, 34; of spouse, 181–82, 222–23

Sudden infant death syndrome (SIDS; crib death), 30–31, 255–66; consolation of bereaved in, 357–58; early childhood response to, 93; outcomes of bereavement in, 261–66; self-help organizations for, 397–98

Suicidal behavior, 61; parental death and, 133–34, 310

Suicides, 30; in adolescence, 146, 150, 167, 280; anger in response to, 42; of bereaved, 62; bereavement counseling and risk of, 385; of elderly, 314; incidence in widowed, 218; mass, 345; of parent, 120–22, 136; after personal disasters, 351; risk of, childhood bereavement and, 126; of spouse, 181, 182

Superego: in adolescence, 150, 165; formation of, 67; in latency, 98, 99, 105

Superego abandonment, 20

Support for bereaved, 352–401; in adolescence, 175; after amputation or mastectomy, 294; in anticipatory grief, 395–96; in childhood, 136–37, 391–95; comfort and, 353–56; consolation and, 356–61; in disasters, 341, 343, 344; elderly, 315; facilitating recovery, 361–74; in family therapy, 389–91; after neonatal death, 250; parental bereavement, 274–75; in preventive intervention, 367–74; in self-help organizations, 396–98; after sudden infant death syndrome, 263–64

Suppressed grief, focal psychotherapy for, 375–78

Surgical emergency, 30

Survivor syndrome, 347–49

Susan J (disaster case), 320, 325–27

Symbiosis: adolescent longing for, 145; between adult child and parent, 227; in adult pair bond, 180; with bereaved mother, 92; conjugal bereavement and, 222; distorted bereavement and, 208; fantasies of, 52; fear of, 20

Symbolization of death, 20

T–cell function, 71, 212
Technology, symbols of immortality and, 22
Termination of preventive intervention, 369
Terrorism, 320, 344
Therapeutic assessment of bereaved, 362–67
Thyrotoxicosis, 129, 213
Tidal surges, 322
Tom (childhood bereavement case), 104–5
Tony (childhood bereavement case), 96–97
Tornados, 322
Train crashes, 338–44
Tranquilizers, 311; conjugal bereavement and use of, 213–14
Transcultural aspects of bereavement, 64–66
Transference: in preventive intervention, 369; in re-grief therapy, 385
Transitional objects, 89–90
Transitions, psychosocial, 69
Traumatic stress syndrome, 28, 222; in children, 345; in natural disasters, 329; preventive intervention and, 368
Trust in adult pair bond, 11
Twin death, 227; as stillbirth, 246

Ulcerative colitis, 212; bereavement counseling and, 384
Unconscious processes: in choice of work, 298; in conceptualization of death, 20; in falling in love, 9; in mother-infant relationship, 13–14
Unemployment, 299–304; loss of roles in, 203
Unrequited love, 10
Untimely deaths: of adult children, 280, 310; childhood bereavement and, 136; from disease, 24, 25; outcome of bereavement after, 63; of spouse, 222
Utopia, concepts of, 22

Vaginal mucosal atrophy, 287
Values: compatibility of, 9; parental, adolescent rebellion against, 143

Vietnam veterans; survival syndrome in, 349
Vietnam war, 346
Violence: civilian, 344–45; of war, 346
Violent deaths, 28–30; adolescent response to, 150, 167; focal psychotherapy and, 378; seeing body after, 36; of spouse, 181–82, 223
Visual loss, 285–86
Volcanic eruptions, 322
Vulnerability to loss, 62; genetic, 63

Wakes, 39
Wal (illustration of caring professional), 355
Walthamton study, 132
War, 320, 345–47; violent deaths in, 29
Washington, D.C., air crash, 336
Weight loss in conjugal bereavement, 210, 211, 213, 217
White, Katherine (multiple bereavement case), 311–12
Widowhood, *see* Conjugal bereavement
Widow-to-widow programs, 396–97
Wish fulfillment, 40; in early childhood, 86
Withdrawal: in adolescent bereavement, 159–62; in childhood bereavement, 127; at death of elderly spouse, 313; in early childhood bereavement, 91; in later childhood, 109; of libido, 66; sudden infant death syndrome and, 260
Words of death, 34
Work, loss of, 298–307; anticipated, 304–7; sudden or unanticipated, 299–304
Worth, reassurance of, 4

Yearning: in adolescent bereavement, 151–52; assessment of, 364; in conjugal bereavement, 184–85; consolation and, 357, 358; in early childhood bereavement, 91–92; in late childhood, 108; for lost body part, 291, 292; in middle childhood, 101; in neonatal death, 248–49; in parental bereavement, 271; pathological, 222; preventive intervention and, 368; repression of, 206; after stillbirth, 244
Yolngu aboriginal tribe, 64
"Young old": conjugal bereavement in, 314; grief for, 310; retirement of, 305; sudden deaths of, 30